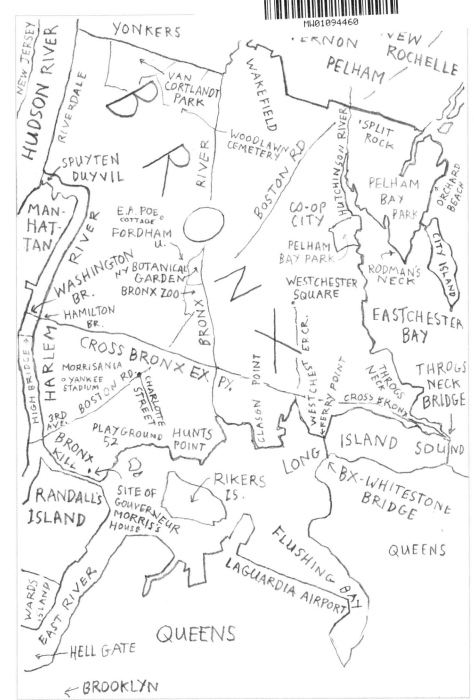

NEW JERSEY

HUDSON RIVER

YONKERS

VERNON

NEW ROCHELLE

PELHAM

WAKEFIELD

RIVERDALE

BRONX

VAN CORTLANDT PARK

WOODLAWN CEMETERY

SPLIT ROCK

HUTCHINSON RIVER

SPUYTEN DUYVIL

RIVER

BOSTON RD

PELHAM BAY PARK

ORCHARD BEACH

MAN-HAT-TAN

E.A. POE COTTAGE

FORDHAM U.

CO-OP CITY

CITY ISLAND

WASHINGTON BR.

NY BOTANICAL GARDEN

BRONX ZOO

PELHAM BAY PARK

RODMAN'S NECK

HAMILTON BR.

BRONX

WESTCHESTER SQUARE

EASTCHESTER BAY

HARLEM

CROSS BRONX EX. PY.

WESTCHEST. CR.

THROGS NECK

THROGS NECK BRIDGE

HIGH BRIDGE

MORRISANIA

YANKEE STADIUM

BOSTON RD.

CHARLOTTE STREET

CLASON POINT

WESTCHEST CR.

FERRY POINT

CROSS BRONX

3RD AVE.

PLAYGROUND 52

HUNTS POINT

LONG ISLAND SOUND

BRONX KILL

RIKERS IS.

BX-WHITESTONE BRIDGE

RANDALL'S ISLAND

SITE OF GOUVERNEUR MORRIS HOUSE

FLUSHING B

QUEENS

WARDS ISLAND

EAST RIVER

LAGUARDIA AIRPORT

HELL GATE

QUEENS

← BROOKLYN

ALSO BY IAN FRAZIER

Cranial Fracking

Hogs Wild

The Cursing Mommy's Book of Days

Travels in Siberia

Lamentations of the Father

Gone to New York

The Fish's Eye

On the Rez

It Happened Like This (translator)

Coyote v. Acme

Family

Great Plains

Nobody Better, Better Than Nobody

Dating Your Mom

PARADISE BRONX

Paradise
BRONX

THE LIFE AND TIMES OF NEW YORK'S
GREATEST BOROUGH

IAN FRAZIER

Farrar, Straus and Giroux
New York

Farrar, Straus and Giroux
120 Broadway, New York 10271

Printed in the United States of America
First edition, 2024

Portions of this book originally appeared, in slightly different form, in *The New Yorker*.

All emojis designed by OpenMoji—the open-source emoji and icon project.
License: CC BY-SA 4.0.

Art on title-page spread and part openers by Milen Mkv / Shutterstock.com.

Library of Congress Cataloging-in-Publication Data
Names: Frazier, Ian, author.
Title: Paradise Bronx: the life and times of New York's greatest borough /
    Ian Frazier.
Other titles: Life and times of New York's greatest borough
Description: First edition. | New York : Farrar, Straus and Giroux, 2024. | Includes
    bibliographical references and index.
Identifiers: LCCN 2023059579 | ISBN 9780374280567 (hardcover)
Subjects: LCSH: Bronx (New York, N.Y.)—Description and travel. | Bronx
    (New York, N.Y.)—History. | Bronx (New York, N.Y.)—Social life and customs. |
    New York (N.Y.)—Description and travel. | New York (N.Y.)—History. | New
    York (N.Y.)—Social life and customs. | Walking—New York (State)—
    New York. | Frazier, Ian.
Classification: LCC F128.68.B8 F74 2024 | DDC 917.47/275—dc23/eng/20240221
LC record available at https://lccn.loc.gov/2023059579

Designed by Patrice Sheridan

Our books may be purchased in bulk for promotional, educational, or business use.
Please contact your local bookseller or the Macmillan Corporate and Premium Sales
Department at 1-800-221-7945, extension 5442, or by email at
MacmillanSpecialMarkets@macmillan.com.

www.fsgbooks.com
Follow us on social media at @fsgbooks

3 5 7 9 10 8 6 4

In memory of Janet Malcolm, with love

CONTENTS

PART I

NOBODY, OR A NATION

1

THE BRONX IS A HAND reaching down to pull the other boroughs of New York City out of the harbor and the sea. Its fellow boroughs are islands or parts of islands; the Bronx hangs on to Manhattan and Queens and Brooklyn, with Staten Island trailing at the end of the long towrope of the Verrazzano-Narrows Bridge, and keeps the whole business from drifting away on a strong outgoing tide. No water comes between the Bronx (if you leave out its own few islands) and the rest of North America. The Bronx is the continent, and once you're on it you can go for thousands of miles without seeing ocean again. The other boroughs, for their part, cling to the Bronx for dear life. The chafing and strife of this connection have made all the difference to the Bronx.

No other borough has "the" in its name. We don't say "the Staten Island" or "the Manhattan"; for some reason, no island is ever called "the." Only certain more or less continuous geographic features merit a "the," such as "the Antarctic" or "the tropical rainforest." Before Europeans had any formal name for what is now the Bronx, they referred to it simply as "the continent," "the mainland," or "the maine," distinguishing it from the ocean they came on and the nearby islands where they'd settled first. Concerning the question of whether to capitalize both words of its modern-day name, the city's daily newspapers are divided. In *The New York Times* and the *Daily News*, "the" is lowercase: "the Bronx." The *Post*, however, gives it two caps: "The Bronx." Perhaps the *Post* has a hidden agenda; the borough is home to the *Post*'s printing plant. In this book I follow the majority and write "the Bronx."

The northernmost part of the Bronx's western border is the Hudson River. Then Manhattan fits up next to the Bronx on its western side for more than half its length, lying approximately north and south. Here, the Harlem River, which is a strait and not a river, and which connects the East River to the Hudson, runs between the two boroughs. Steep hills and bluffs rise above the Harlem River valley. Much of the Bronx is hilly. Stone ridges extend like tendons, knuckles, and fingers from the northern border of the borough southward; these discouraged the construction of east-west roads and make the Bronx difficult to cross from east to west even today. After the Harlem River branches off around one side of Randall's Island, a smaller tidal stream, the Bronx Kill, continues along the borough's southern border. Going along the top of Randall's, the Bronx Kill also flows into the East River, which is part of Long Island Sound, which is part of the Atlantic Ocean. The Bronx's entire eastern border is the East River and the Sound. Thus, the borough has a major river that comes from inland—the Hudson—to its west, and saltwater on its east. Some of the Bronx is rocky and wooded like upstate, and some is oceanfront marsh and beach.

A straight line with a few bureaucratic zigzags marks the Bronx's northern border. That line is also the border of New York City. In general, people in the suburbs to the north of this line are richer than most people in the Bronx. By some measurements, large areas of the Bronx are poorer than anywhere else in the nation. But that assumes a population frozen in time. Everybody has to start somewhere, and the poor parts of the Bronx are often where people start when they have very little. They work, and earn, and in time, with luck, they move upward, and new arrivals take their place. This cycle has tended to wear out some areas of the Bronx.

The Bronx is the part of New York where the city merges into the rest of North America. The process has never gone smoothly.

ITS NAME HONKS, "Bronx!" Ideally, we could ask for a better-sounding name, one that did not suggest a Bronx cheer, but "Bronx!" is what we've got. The name comes from the Bronx River, which begins at a reservoir north of the city and runs south through the middle of the borough until it empties into the East River. The Bronx cuts the Bronx into two sections—east of it and west of it. Surface streets sometimes dead-end at it. If you're at ground level and not on one of the big highways, you can go a mile or more without finding a bridge. From source to mouth the river is twenty-three miles long, with about eight of those miles in the borough. It is the longest river within the borders of New York City, and it used to be beautiful and idyllic, until the usual city factors ruined it. By the 1980s, it was so full of junk—old refrigerators, washing machines, cars—that you could barely see it. Intrepid environmental groups and the Parks Department cleaned it up. It now runs clear, and parts of it are even almost idyllic again. People sometimes canoe on it, but you're still not advised to swim in it.

An eminent old-time historian wrote that the Indians called the river Aquahung. I find that hard to believe, but I can't explain why. Tribes with villages in what's now the Bronx were the Siwanoy, the Munsee, and the Weckquaesgeek, all subgroups of the Lenape. They belonged to the Algonquian language family, an eastern linguistic grouping that did not include the powerful Iroquois, their inland enemies. In December 1639, several local Munsee headmen sold five hundred acres of land adjoining the river to Jonas Bronck, or Bronk, a Swede who had arrived on his own ship, *The Fire of Troy*. (One day, fire and destruction would be what people thought of when they thought of the Bronx.) Jonas Bronck also paid the Dutch West India Company for the land. The Dutch were the European power in the region and had founded New Amsterdam, their outpost on lower Manhattan Island, fifteen years before.

Bronck built a house on what's now 132nd Street, or maybe 138th Street—in either case, it was in what's now a southerly part of the South Bronx—and leased his land out for farming maize and tobacco. Eventually the river at the eastern edge of his holdings became known as Bronk's River, and Bronk's Land was the area in general. A man named Pieter Schorstinaveger (chimney sweep, in Dutch) owned a farm next to Bronck's, which he cultivated using Black slaves. Apparently, "Schorstinaveger's River" was never even in the running as a name, such being the workings of everyday poetics and spoken language.

In 1939, three hundred years after Jonas Bronck, three reporters set out to discover if he still had any descendants in the area. In the magazine article they wrote, they noted that "there are no Broncks in the Bronx." The reporters did find one descendant, William H. Bronk (by then the family had dropped the *c*), who lived in Pelham, just north of the Bronx. He said he commuted on the New Haven Railroad every day past the site of his ancestor's house and never gave it a thought. Another Bronk, a retired lawyer named Leonard Bronk Lampman, who had been living at the Yale Club for twenty-two years, cleared up a question about the Bronx borough flag. It depicts a rising sun with a bowling-pin-shaped bird standing above it. Lampman said that the bird is an auk, a species found in the Faroe Islands, where Jonas Bronck lived before going to Holland and then to America. The bird and the rising sun are on the Bronck family coat of arms, along with the motto *Ne Cede Malis*, "Do Not Yield to Evil," which became the motto of the Bronx. Designers included the Bronck coat of arms—motto, bird, and all—in the borough flag when they created it, in the late nineteenth century.

Jonas Bronck and his wife, Antonia Slagboom, had a son named Pieter. He moved to Coxsackie, New York, near Albany, and built a stone farmhouse that still stands. I meant to visit it—it's now a museum—but it was closed because of the virus. Pieter Bronk had offspring and there are many Bronks in the Coxsackie area. A poet named William Bronk (1918–1999), who claimed descent from Jonas, ran his family's coal and lumber business in Hudson Falls, a town about eighty miles north of Coxsackie. He never got a driver's license and, in his lifetime, published about two dozen books of poetry, one of which won a National Book Award.

THIRTEEN BRIDGES CONNECT Manhattan to the Bronx, and two more cross the East River from Queens. Other links exist underground in tunnels and pipes, which carry subway lines, drinking water, gas mains, power cables, and wastewater. Every which way, the Bronx is sewn and bound and grappled and clamped to the rest of the city. Every kind of transportation passes through it or over it. Walking on Bruckner Boulevard one morning, stunned by the loudness of the trucks (no other borough has truck traffic like the Bronx's, partly because its Hunts Point Market, for produce, meat, and fish, is the largest food distribution depot in the world), I also heard cars, vans, motorcycles, an Amtrak train, airplanes, and, on the lower Bronx River nearby, the horn of a tugboat pushing a barge. Even during the emptiest days of the Covid shutdown the Bronx's pulse of transport kept pounding.

Interstate highways slice and dice the borough. The interstates within the Bronx's borders are these: On the west, running approximately north and south, is I-87, also known (in the city) as the Major Deegan Expressway, or simply the Deegan. I-87 is bound for Albany and Canada. The Bruckner Elevated Expressway, aka I-278, connects to I-87 in the southern part of the borough. From there I-278 veers to the northeast. Across the borough's middle, Interstate 95, aka the Cross Bronx Expressway, that road of infamous history, moves traffic east and west before I-95 merges with the Bruckner, veers north, and then follows the coast up to New England. A spur, I-295, splits off and goes south across the Throgs Neck Bridge to Queens. Another spur, I-678, also goes to Queens, over the Bronx-Whitestone Bridge. At the point where I-678 goes south from I-95, the Hutchinson River Parkway goes north from I-95, crosses the Bronx, and continues into Westchester County.

I am leaving out several other parkways, such as the Mosholu Parkway, the Bronx River Parkway, and the Pelham Bay Parkway. These roads refer to an earlier, more optimistic era of travel, and they sometimes have green spaces along them. Otherwise, the parkways now resemble the interstates in most respects, and aid and abet them. All the major highway corridors and their street approaches are generally filled with traffic. The speed limit on the Cross Bronx Expressway is fifty miles an hour, but the average speed on it during the evening rush hour is fourteen. For a while in the mid-twentieth century, planners thought that building new highways would relieve the already bad congestion, but the new highways became just as busy. Night and day, the wheels roll. Potholes are common. Among the most common signs in the borough are the red letters that announce, on a yellow background, FLAT FIX.

Before the highways, transportation was more Bronx-friendly. In the early 1900s, the subways came, building north from Manhattan. In 1905, the tracks for what are now the number 2 and number 5 trains reached a terminus at the neighborhood called West Farms, on the Bronx River. By 1910, the Broadway Local, also known as the number 1 train, which goes up the West Side, got to Van Cortlandt Park, in the northwest Bronx. By 1920, tracks for today's number 4 and number 6 trains had also been completed in the Bronx (to its near-middle and northeasterly parts, respectively).

All these trains were mostly elevated in the Bronx, and still are. The lines spread out in a generally north-south configuration, causing land booms and frenzied construction along their routes. In the 1920s, the population of the Bronx increased by 72 percent. Another subway line, this one entirely underground, carrying the B and D trains, came in the thirties. In 1900, the borough had 200,507 residents. By 1940, almost 1.4 million people lived in the Bronx. Then, in the 1940s, the city and state started pushing through the big limited-access highways that would become interstates or link up to them.

A history of the Bronx in the twentieth century can be sketched in a sentence: The subways created the modern Bronx and the highways almost destroyed it.

I STARTED WANDERING the Bronx about fifteen years ago. Usually I had a destination, a place I wanted to check out. At first, I was interested in the neighborhood of the Stella D'oro Bakery, at Broadway and 237th Street, in Kingsbridge, in the northwest Bronx. I was writing an article about a strike that took place at the bakery after a hedge fund bought it; previously, a generous and public-minded local family had owned it. People all over the city knew this good Bronx company. It won its reputation with its breadsticks, its anisette toast, and its chocolate-cream-center cookies, all baked with no dairy products, for reasons of keeping kosher. New immigrants got jobs at Stella D'oro, earned good wages and benefits, and put their children through college. Everybody in the neighborhood knew the smell of the bakery, with its emanations of chocolate and almond and licorice. The Major Deegan Expressway's six lanes ran right behind the bakery, and drivers stuck in traffic inhaled its aromas and briefly felt happier and more sane.

My first Bronx walks were to discover how far the smell of cookies extended from the bakery. I went in every direction all around it, seeing the mansion-covered hills of Riverdale, the fields of Van Cortlandt Park, the diners of farthest upper Broadway, and the offices of a small Bronx newspaper that had once been firebombed by Islamic terrorists. The baking cookie smell became undetectable about half a mile from the factory, though if the wind was right, it could spread for a mile. The wealthy owners of the hedge fund, located in Greenwich, Connecticut, in one of the richest counties in America, outfoxed the strikers by selling Stella D'oro to a snack-food giant with headquarters in North Carolina, and the giant moved the bakery to a nonunion factory in the Midwest. One hundred and thirty-four workers, most of them Bronx residents, lost their jobs. The aroma of Stella D'oro cookies now wafts unsmelled through a second-growth forest in semirural Ohio.

From the Stella D'oro smell radius I then went farther. When you cover any distance in this borough, its ridged, up-and-down geography lets you know you're on a hike, and registers in your calves. I walked thoroughfares that traversed the borough north to south, such as Boston Road, which at one time was the post road to Boston; for most of a day I followed it, all the way to the northern border, where the road leaves the Bronx. I also walked Tremont Avenue, which goes from the Harlem River, on the west, to the East River, on the east, and I contemplated how Tremont Avenue's survival has been the survival of the Bronx. I took inventory of the parklands, of which the Bronx has four thousand acres, and went along off-map paths under interstate highway overpasses and plunged through phragmites-reed thickets next to rocky beaches.

On the heights above the Hudson River, in Riverdale, I found the white stucco Moorish-Dutch-style mansion, now empty and in disrepair, which John F. Kennedy moved into with his family in 1927, when he was eleven. I peered through the windows at its huge downstairs rooms and empty parquet floors; John's mother once was obliged to invite the children of his father's mistress, Gloria Swanson, to a Halloween party with the Kennedy siblings here. Now planes flew overhead, perhaps on their way to John F. Kennedy International Airport, in Queens, but the house where the president-to-be spent a part of his boyhood bears no plaque or marker. In that way it resembles most other places of historical significance in the borough. From the former Kennedy mansion, one can walk 4.7 miles to 815 East 179th Street, in the East Tremont neighborhood, where a twelve-year-old Lee Harvey Oswald lived with his mother in 1952. Not only is there no historic marker, but the building that Oswald lived in no longer exists, and the address itself seems to have been abolished.

As I walked in the Bronx I watched the sky—the way it opens out at the ends of streets approaching the water, the way it goes upward to heaven at the tops of "stair streets," which is the name for sections of streets so steep that they morph into stairways. A stair street with 132 steps, which I was accustomed to climbing at the continuation of 167th Street at Shakespeare Avenue, one day suddenly had drawn a crowd of French and Asian tourists all up and down it, recording themselves with cell phones. I inquired and found out that it's the stairway on which the Joker dances in a Batman-related movie. The sky that the stairway frames is towering and cinematic in the extreme.

At the same time as I watched the sky, I kept an eye on the ground. All kinds of things are on the ground in the Bronx:

Q-tips. A pigeon foot. Those Christmas-tree-shaped air fresheners that hang from rearview mirrors. Syringes with pale orange plastic stoppers on their needles. Sunglass lenses. The butts of menthol cigarettes. A bathroom sink. A single pink, almond-shaped artificial fingernail. The white plastic tips of cigarillos. Little bags that once held fortune cookies, with pagodas faintly printed on them in red. Inside-out surgical gloves. Pennies. Scratched-off scratch-off tickets. Green puddles of antifreeze. Hair picks with handles shaped like fists. Pieces of broken mirrors. Flattened pieces of sugarcane. Corona beer bottle tops. Coconut husks. Crumpled paper handouts offering cash for diabetic test strips, with a number to call. Crushed traffic cones. Dashboard dice. Skeins of hair from reweavings. Spiced-whiskey bottles with devil silhouettes on the labels. Covid masks. Black plastic takeout bags that skitter, ankle-high, on the wind. Pavement graffiti: "Lost Virginity at this Spot 11–1–16."

In the middle of the Bronx, a block and a half from the Cross Bronx Expressway, I came across words written in the cement of a sidewalk. They're at the corner of Fairmount Place and Crotona Avenue, in a neighborhood of apartment buildings and Pentecostal churches. I wrote the words down and have returned to the place more than a few times. They are not only graffiti, but an inscription, a historical marker, and a Bronx poem that takes up eighteen or twenty feet:

I RUN
THIS FUCKING
Block
Since
1988
YA KNOW
WHO
THE FUCK
I aM
BEBO
FUCK YOU
FUCK
POLICE
MATTER
FACT
FUCK
THE WORLD
I STAN
ALONE

I have lingered at the inscription and asked passersby if they know who this Bebo is or was, but no one does. It's not an uncommon nickname. Fifty Cent, in his song "Ghetto Qur'an," refers to "crews like Bebo and killers like Pappy Mason." Everywhere I've walked I've looked for this Bebo's writing again, and recently I found another Bebo inscription, about a mile away on Crotona Avenue, across from the main entrance of the Grace Hoadley Dodge Vocational High School. The handwriting is the same. This one says, simply:

2002
East Tremont
BEBO
A-JAY MKE

Near the original Bebo tag there's another that also says "BEBO 2002." I wondered if maybe Bebo had left the neighborhood, returned in 2002, and wanted to let people know he was back.

Most of the places where important things happened in the Bronx in recent times are less than an hour by foot from the Bebo inscription. Many are only a forty-minute walk or closer. I set out to walk a thousand miles in the Bronx. I was looking for hints about what has happened here, and about how we got to the present. In general, the human events from farther back in Bronx history took place along the borough's edges, while the more recent ones were closer to the center. If almost everyone who lives and almost everything that happens will be forgotten, that must be even more true in a zone of connection like the Bronx, where so much energy is zapping back and forth constantly. An emptier place might be kinder to the past but have less of it. One day another crew, not Bebo's, will come along and break up the sidewalk that bears his inscription, and the chunks of concrete will go into a dumpster and vanish forever, and unknown new works will occupy the site. But I've taken photos of the sidewalk with my phone, and what Bebo wrote will also be preserved here.

2

MOST OF NEW YORK CITY used to be covered by forest. Although seven million trees grow in the city today, only a tiny fraction of them are original-growth—part of a section of forest that was never cut down. In the New York Botanical Garden, which occupies 250 acres of city parkland in the central Bronx, you can walk in 50 acres of this original forest. A late-nineteenth, early-twentieth-century botanist who co-founded the garden wanted especially to preserve the ancient hemlock trees. You can see why he loved them. Hemlocks are conifers and evergreens, but they're sketchier and sort of wispier and more romantic-seeming than the other pines. The garden's hemlock grove looks like a gathering of tall, thin, very old ladies in wispy shawls. A mysteriousness that still endures gives you an idea of what it must have been like to come ashore for the first time and enter the forest of this new world.

The chestnut blight, back in the early 1900s, killed fifteen hundred chestnut trees in the garden. More recent scourges have almost wiped out the forest's hemlocks. The woolly adelgid, a type of aphid, gets in the hemlock's bark and sucks out nutrients, while the elongated hemlock scale, another bug, does a similar number on the needles. The draining and defoliation weaken the tree and eventually destroy it. On the bright side, many of the forest's surviving ancient deciduous trees are doing okay. One of the oldest of them is a red oak that began to grow in 1748, or 276 years ago. The base of its trunk encroaches on the trail and has broken part of the wood-rail fence alongside it. This venerable oak was a sapling at the time of the birth of Gouverneur Morris, whose family then owned much of the present-day South Bronx, and who will figure in this story.

Once, a glacier a thousand feet thick sat atop this garden, and on most of present-day New York City, extending south to what is now Hylan Boulevard, on Staten Island, which roughly delineates that part of its terminal moraine. The glacier came and went, melting away for good about fourteen thousand years ago. Before it, there had been between sixty and seventy major glaciations during two million years of the Pleistocene epoch. On Long Island there are hills that were left by a glacier a hundred thousand years ago.

About half a billion years before that, North America was part of a landmass geologists call Laurentia, which joined other landmasses in creating supercontinents that came together, broke apart, and formed new supercontinents as immensities of time rolled by. Offshore from Laurentia lay a smaller landmass in a position like that of Timor off Australia. Through tens of millions of years of drift and folding, the island complex moved toward the supercontinent and crashed into it, while the seafloor was subducted beneath. The collision, called the Taconic orogeny, is the signature geologic event of northeastern North America (although when it happened these landmasses were in the Southern Hemisphere).

A large chunk of rock that was involved in the collision kept going—geologists use the analogy of a battering ram—until it stopped in what is now western Connecticut. Some of the rock that underlies the Bronx was formed by forces acting on shallow-water sediments, and some is the deep-water sedimentary rock that became tucked beneath the shallow-water rock and collided with it. Between the two kinds there are gaps of as much as fifty million years in the times they were formed. Different kinds of rock meet at suture zones that run through the Bronx, among other places. One of the suture zones, called the St. Nicholas Thrust, can be seen in outcroppings along

St. Nicholas Avenue in Manhattan, from which it extends northward. It appears again in two parks in the Bronx, and in the botanical garden.

Another suture zone, known as Cameron's Line, coincides in some places with Webster Avenue and in others with the valley of the Bronx River, and it continues northward to West Torrington, Connecticut. Academic papers about these geologic features include "Annealed Mylonites of the Saint Nicholas Thrust (SNT) from a New Excavation at the New York Botanical Gardens," by Charles Merguerian and John E. Sanders. I read this paper with very low comprehension, but I note that the dictionary defines *mylonite* as "a siliceous schist produced by intense crushing of rocks." The part about intense crushing makes sense to me, as does the whole idea of huge masses of rock, some inshore and some from offshore, crashing into one another and uplifting and eroding, extremely slowly, to create the future Bronx.

The glaciers belonged to a different category of collision— arriving, as they did, much more recently, and from the sky. Long winters of falling snow piled on each other, creating ice, the weight of which caused an increase of heat where the glacier met the ground. Eventually the very bottommost layer of ice began to melt, and the glacier to slide. As it did, the rocks in it scraped the stationary rock it was on. Glaciers grind: it is said that if you listen closely, you can hear them. New York's glaciers left the local landscape a scratched-up place. Not far from the original-growth forest in the botanical garden is an expanse of exposed rock covered with glacial striations, as they're called—gouged-out lines made by the scraping of stones on the bottom of a glacier. As glaciers disappear, they drop whatever they're carrying. When they calve icebergs into the ocean, the icebergs float like bottles with messages in them, and the messages are rocks. Icebergs have held rocks they picked up in the north and not let go of them until they melted in the middle of the Atlantic far to the south. The geologic anomalousness of certain rocks on the ocean bottom puzzled scientists until they thought of icebergs.

Across the landscape, the melting glaciers dropped large boulders, called glacial erratics because they wandered, ice-aided, from elsewhere. In the Bronx, a number of these boulders remain, but people don't notice them as much as they used to. Some are the size of panel trucks standing on end and have acquired names, such as Glover's Rock, Gray Mare, or Split Rock. A glacial erratic called the Rocking Stone even became famous. Visitors used to journey to see it and enjoy the fact that two people positioned just right could give a push and set the great boulder gently rocking. Today the Rocking Stone is a no-longer-famous celebrity. It remains at or near the spot where it has always been, but the Bronx Zoo has been built around it. Looking odd and too big, the Rocking Stone now sits unlabeled and ignored beside a walkway next to the former Hall of Darkness, a zoo exhibit that has been shuttered for years.

When the glacier stopped at Staten Island, 120 miles of tundra stretched beyond it to the east before the land met the ocean. Then, as the glaciers all over the planet melted and retreated, sea levels rose. Native American friends have told me that their people were always on this continent, which they call Turtle Island; they believe that their ancestors emerged onto it from out of a hole in the ground. Anthropologists say that human beings migrated into North America from Asia by way of Beringia, a land bridge that existed between the continents during the low-sea-level period of glaciation. The earliest evidence of human occupation in what's now New York City dates to eleven thousand years ago. By that time, the shoreline was 60 to 90 miles away. Presumably, many early inhabitants of the region would have lived by the sea. The search for the oldest paleo-Indian sites is complicated by the fact that most of them are probably underwater, miles from the current shore.

Like giant bulldozers, glaciers make a mess, and the soil they leave behind consists of sands, clays, pebbles, and an unhelpful rock dust known as glacial flour. At first, only grasses, sedges, and willows grew in the glacier's wake. Their decomposition built up a more fertile soil at the rate of an inch every hundred years. Trees like those in the botanical garden's old-growth forest did not appear until five thousand years after the glacier was gone, or about nine thousand years ago. Sea levels reached approximately their present height about four thousand years ago. Indian villages dating from that period until about 1700 have been discovered and excavated in the Bronx. The first enthusiasts who dug up Native American sites had no formal training as archaeologists. Although disturbing such sites would be prohibited today, they probably would have been destroyed anyway in the Bronx's early-twentieth-century rush to development.

Some of the Native American sites of note in the Bronx are on the shore of the East River/Long Island Sound, or near it. To anyone who knew what to look for, oyster middens were a clue. A midden is a refuse heap, usually seen in an archaeological context. Oyster middens are places where shells have been discarded, sometimes over the hundreds or thousands of years of a site's occupancy. Even with centuries of vegetation on them the mounds stand out.

The Native people who lived in present-day New York ate a lot of oysters. Before this place was New Amsterdam or New York, it could have been called Oyster City. Its waters were a metropolis containing perhaps half of all the oysters in the world. The lower Hudson River and New York Harbor held 350 square miles of oyster beds. For comparison, the five boroughs of New York City cover about 300 square miles today. In size, Oyster City had modern New York City beat. Some of the oysters grew extra-large; the Dutch reported oysters in the Gowanus River "not less than a foot long." Though plentiful, and no doubt delicious, these shellfish would not have provided many calories per piece. Oysters are a low-fat food. To maintain a daily caloric requirement a person would have to eat a Diamond Jim Brady spread of more than twenty dozen oysters every day. Ergo, the villages' large oyster middens.

Alanson Buck Skinner (1886–1925) was a child-prodigy ethnologist and anthropologist who grew up in New York and did his first excavations of Native American sites as a teenager on Staten Island. He attended Columbia and Harvard, traveled to Hudson's Bay to study the Cree tribe, and published dozens of scholarly papers, not to mention thrilling wilderness adventure stories, all before he was thirty. Skinner excavated two Native American sites in the Bronx in 1918. One of them, the site of a Siwanoy village called Snakapins, looks so ordinary that you couldn't guess it ever was anything other than the Bronx intersection it is now. The other, a shoreline site that Skinner referred to as the Schley Avenue Shellheap, still can be imagined as the ideal spot for a village that it was.

Somehow it's weird to stand in the Clason Point neighborhood, at the intersection of Soundview Avenue and Lacombe Avenue, where there's a hair salon on one corner and a deli grocery on another, and people wait for the Bx27 bus, and a jet banks overhead as it comes in to land in Queens, and its engines make that comfortable turbine-whine sound, and a woman is sweeping a front walk—somehow it's weird to stand here and imagine this was once a large Native American village. Soundview Avenue used to be Clason's Point Road, and a trolley ran along it to an amusement park at the end of the point. In Skinner's day, some of the oldest local old-timers remembered being told that Indians used to come back here and hold ceremonies for their dead. Skinner had also noticed oyster shells—a promising clue—in the roadcut for the trolley line.

So, after getting permission from a Mr. A. P. Dientz, of the Sound View Improvement Company, owner of the land, Skinner began to dig. He found fifty-five pits, which held human skeletons, artifacts, and ancient refuse. Among other animal remains, the deepest levels revealed the bones of elk, a species no longer in the area when the Dutch arrived. In shallow burials he found seven human skeletons, some in flexed position with their knees tucked into their chests and their hands in front of their faces. He could identify them as Native because the teeth were worn down; Indians' teeth became stubs from eating stone-ground maize and roots, mixed with pieces of sand from the grinding. The people of Snakapins also ate all kinds of sea and land animals. He unearthed the bones of bear, deer, raccoons, otters, wild turkeys, bluefish, dogfish, turtles, and sturgeons, and the shells of oysters, clams, quahogs, blue crabs, lobsters, cockles, mussels, and conchs. The artifacts included hammerstones, gorgets (stones with holes in them, worn as neck pendants), grinding stones, axe heads, arrowheads, a bone fishhook, a stone drill, clay pipes (both Native-made and commercial), and a piece of red limonite, known as a paint stone, which the Indians scraped to obtain a red powder for face paint.

The hundreds of pottery shards he found followed a progression in design. Older shards were simpler while more recent ones showed the stylistic influence of the Iroquois, the upstate Indians, who were skillful potters. The Iroquois obtained guns from the French in Canada and raided in this vicinity, taking captives. Skinner speculated that the Iroquois influence on pottery-making spread by way of captured Siwanoy women who escaped and returned.

At the other Bronx site he excavated, near the T-intersection where Clarence Avenue meets Schley Avenue, he had observed a large shell heap. Here, permission to dig was obtained from a Mr. Joseph Horowitz, of the Bronx Shore Park Development Co. The name of that company is tantalizing. The Snakapins site is in the middle of Clason Point and it lies squarely athwart the most logical path for a road, but the Schley Avenue site is by the water and not on the way to anywhere. It could have been developed as a park. Throughout the whole city you won't find a prettier cove. A creek called Weir Creek, now buried under houses and pavement, used to enter the cove from the northwest. A little point that curves eastward encloses the cove and shelters it from nor'easter storms. Add a patch of lawn, a walkway, a few benches, maybe a small fishing pier—a park here would have been perfect.

When I first started coming to the cove, you could easily get to the beach, which is mostly rocks and pebbles. Skinner found fishing-net weights—stones with grooves or holes, used to weight down nets—on the beach, and lots of arrowheads. Exploring the beach myself I found only ordinary rocks, plus the pleasure (always a strong one for me) of being in an ancient place. Today development has performed to expectations. The cove is now encircled by waterfront houses and almost completely fenced off. There's still one small fence gap, just across the cove from the village site, where I can squeeze through, and sit on a piece of breakwall among discarded liquor bottles and watch silvery minnows shivering in the clear water.

A few small bumps that I take for shell heaps can still be seen in the side yard of one of the houses on the village site. Skinner's excavations along Schley Avenue turned up six human skeletons and a dog skeleton. This site held more artifacts dating from the colonial period than did the Snakapins site. Here he found "a blue glass trade bead, several gun-flints, and round leaden bullets of small caliber."

(No beads or evidence of firearms turned up in the dig at Snakapins.) Skinner theorized that the Indians had moved to the cove after they sold Snakapins and all of Clason Point to that area's first European landowner, Thomas Cornell. Skinner also believed that the bodies he found here might have been slain by the Dutch during the Indian war of 1642–1643 (more accurately described as the massacres and countermassacres that took place during the Dutch campaign to wipe out the Indians starting in 1640). Later historians disagreed with Skinner's speculation.

Aside from arrowheads—of flint, white quartz, jasper, argillite, chalcedony—the most common objects he found at both sites were awls. Indians seem always to have carried a lot of awls. When the Sioux and Cheyenne women were dismembering the dead of the Seventh Cavalry on the Little Bighorn battlefield, they pierced General Custer's eardrums with an awl, because he had not listened to the Indians' warnings. To sew pieces of hide together with thread made of sinew, you first must make a lot of holes through the skins, and for that you need awls. At the Schley Avenue site Skinner found about a hundred bone awls, including "a worked and polished spine from a sting-ray." This probably was the weapon of a stingray, the pointed spike on the end of its tail. At Snakapins he found another awl that stood out. Made from the sharpened bone of a mammal, it had rows of small notches incised on it. He looked closely at the notches and wondered about them.

Unlike perhaps every archaeologist before him, and most who came after, Skinner worked with a colleague who was Native American. Amos Enos Oneroad, two years older than Skinner, came from the Sisseton Sioux tribe, of South Dakota. The Sisseton are easterly cousins of the western Sioux who fought Custer. They had their own history of warfare. In the Sioux War in Minnesota in 1862, the Sisseton and other tribes, having been sorely provoked, rose up and killed hundreds of settlers before the army defeated them. The warriors whom the army captured were tried, and thirty-eight of them were hanged in the largest mass execution in U.S. history. Amos Oneroad's father had been among those Sisseton who were tried, acquitted, and released.

In his twenties Oneroad left South Dakota for Haskell Indian College, in Lawrence, Kansas, where he received an agriculture degree. Then he entered what's now Union Theological Seminary, in New York City. He was ordained and licensed as a Presbyterian minister in 1917. Interest in writing about Sisseton stories and traditions brought him to the American Museum of Natural History, where he met Skinner, whom he later would accompany on digs not only in the Bronx but out west. Oneroad divided his time between his archaeology and his preaching. He and Skinner wore suits, white shirts, collars, and ties as they worked in the field. In a photo of them, Skinner faces the camera, while Oneroad is behind him, looking away.

When Oneroad examined the awl with the notches on it, he recognized what he was seeing. He told Skinner that the Sioux women made similar marks on the antler-bone handles of the scrapers they used in preparing hides. For each hide they finished, they added a notch to the handle. The notches on Skinner's awl were in four different groupings, which may have stood for four different kinds of garments its owner had made. The awl from this Bronx site showed evidence of a Native American practice that was observed among the Sioux hundreds of years later and twelve hundred miles to the west.

Oneroad adopted Skinner as his Indian brother, an honor no doubt gratifying to Skinner, who admired and sympathized with Native Americans. Skinner even had a half-Indian child. After his first wife and child died, he remarried, and his second wife also died. He then remarried again, to a Wyandotte, and they had a daughter. In 1935, Skinner and Oneroad traveled to the Devil's Lake (now Spirit Lake) Reservation, in North Dakota, on behalf of the Heye Foundation for the American Indian. George Gustav "Slim-Shin" Heye, a rich and avid collector of Indian artifacts, sometimes bought out the possessions of entire Native American villages. (The Heye Foundation acquisitions became part of the collections of the Smithsonian Museum of the American Indian, on the Mall in Washington, D.C.) As Oneroad and Skinner were driving in a Ford touring car on a muddy reservation road near Tokio, North Dakota, the car slipped to one side and rolled down an embankment. Oneroad climbed out of the wreck unhurt, but Skinner, caught underneath, had his head crushed. He was thirty-nine years old.

A tribal historian later told a writer that the Sioux said the spirits had killed Skinner for not respecting the sacred mysteries. In his Bronx excavations, did Skinner take the thirteen human skeletons he exhumed—seven at Snakapins and six at Schley Avenue—and rebury them where he found them? Or were the bones of those early proto-Bronxites removed to drawers at the Museum of Natural History or the warehouses of the Heye Foundation? Skinner's monograph about the two digs, published in 1919 by the foundation, does not say.

Snakapins and the Schley Avenue village may have been, briefly, industry towns—the industry being the hand-manufacture of wampum. From the shells of periwinkles and quahog clams, local Indians made tubular beads, about a quarter of an inch long and less than an eighth of an inch across, called wampum. Unlike, say, arrowheads or hammerstones, wampum beads have a uniformity of tiny size and a simplicity of design that give them a modern look; a wampum bead could easily pass unnoticed amid the wiring of a circuit board. Working with stone and bone tools, a bead maker could produce as many as forty-two beads a day. The expenditure of so much time and skill on such small objects gave the beads a hypnotizing quality; to the Indians, wampum also held medicinal and spiritual powers.

Strung together into six-foot-long belts, each belt containing 288 beads (a measure that white people called a "fathom" of wampum), the beads served widely as money throughout the region in the early 1600s. For example, to cross the Harlem River from "the mainland" over to Manhattan by ferry you could pay the fare in pence or wampum. Skinner found partly finished wampum beads among the artifacts at Snakapins and pointed out that on the shore within sight of the village was "a shellheap almost entirely composed of the debris of wampum making."

For a while, the Iroquois, that dangerous and highly mobile tribe, craved wampum. The shells necessary to make it existed on the coast but not in their forests, where, on the other hand, fur-bearing animals were abundant. Wampum for furs was an exchange that worked for both the Dutch and the Iroquois. The Dutch got wampum easily enough by trading alcohol for it or by imposing taxes on the Indians. In 1640, William Kieft, the governor of New Amsterdam, levied on the Indians a tax payable in "wampum, corn, or furs." The enhanced ability of the Indians to make a profit from their shell heaps motivated them; they called an island just up the coast from the Schley Avenue village Laap-Ha-Wach-King, or "Place of Stringing Beads," because of its plentiful supply of the right kind of shells for wampum. Later the island's name became Hunter Island, and in the 1930s its existence as an island ended when a landfill project connected it to Pelham Bay Park. I have walked all over the former island, where there are still a lot of shells.

Indians who acquired metal tools could make more wampum faster. Then outsourcing hit the business. Dutch and English farmers' wives began using lathes to make wampum out of conch shells imported from the West Indies. Then—even worse—counterfeit wampum from Holland debased the coinage. The Iroquois decided they preferred other trade items and the wampum market collapsed. This is the earliest known rise and fall of a manufacturing enterprise in the Bronx.

Another force that drove out wampum would have been the popularity of imported glass trade beads from places like Italy. For a while, these beads of many colors and sizes were also a medium of exchange. But before long, they, too, became not money anymore, and the hoards of beads that people had been hanging on to were thrown out. To those who know where to look, old trade beads can still be found on the ground in New York City. I have found three myself, in Inwood Hill Park, with the help of my friend Matthew López-Jensen, an artist whose keen eyes light upon all kinds of ancient, overlooked things.

Once when Matt was walking in that park after a windstorm, he saw a downed tree with its root system sticking up in the air. When he peered in among the root tendrils, he saw something red. It was a small red bead, of a type called "seed beads," in a cache of what turned out to be more than sixty other red beads just like it. Maybe the cache had been hidden and forgotten in the 1600s. Another time, in Brooklyn's Green-Wood Cemetery, beside a road that had been an Indigenous trail, he saw a glimmer of white, looked closer, and picked up a wampum bead. He has shown photos of it to me; it bewitches me. I've never encountered such a numinous tiny object in my life.

What has existed in a place, and what has happened there, are hard to cover up. The past bleeds through layers of accumulation like graffiti through whitewash. The truth of a place often is not hidden but can be seen in plain sight. Bulldoze enough dirt, slap down enough paving, and run enough traffic over the past, and you can sometimes eliminate it in one location, only to have it pop to the surface in another. I don't know why this kind of survival fascinates me. I guess it's connected to the idea of eternity—to the way the world might be in the mind of God, or in the nonexistent mind of the-God-who-doesn't-exist.

I like to think about things that have always been the same, from remote human history up to and including now. People's heads have always been about as hard as they are today and have hurt about the same amount when they bumped together. Horses have always shaken flies off themselves, whether waiting to pull Pharaoh's chariots or standing at a kiddie ride at a county fair. Meat cooking on a fire has smelled delicious in exactly the same way forever.

Quiet has always been the same, if it's a peaceful quiet. In the early 1960s, another amateur archaeologist, Edward J. Kaeser, excavated a Native American site in the Bronx where humans lived, probably only in the summers, about three thousand years ago; other occupations probably occurred from about thirteen hundred years ago until the 1600s. The village was next to a cove bigger than the one at Schley Avenue. This cove stretches in a crescent about a mile and a quarter long, from the end of Ferry Point to the foot of East Tremont Avenue. At a few places you can still get down to the water. To your right, the Bronx-Whitestone Bridge, and to your left, the Throgs Neck Bridge, contribute their distant traffic sounds. On peaceful evenings, small waves pet the shore. There are gulls, and quiet.

Kaeser's excavations just above the shoreline turned up relics and artifacts like those Skinner found at Snakapins and Schley Avenue (although no burials). There were awls, arrowheads, paint stones, shells, animal bones, etc. One object Kaeser found that Skinner doesn't mention is "fire-cracked stones." I know what these are. When I was a boy, my family spent weekends in the summers at my grandmother's cottage on Lake Erie, near Cleveland, and we built driftwood fires on the beach. As the fire burned down, and the embers were popping and hissing, sometimes a beach stone that had got into the fire or had been put there to prop up a pan suddenly cracked from the heat and made a sharp report almost like a firecracker. After that minor jolt to everybody's nerves, the night seemed quieter and the stars brighter, with the embers still crackling and hissing.

On calm nights three thousand or one thousand or five hundred years ago, people lay around their fires on the shore of this cove. As they were falling asleep, and the waves were lapping, suddenly a rock in the fire made a bang as it cracked in the heat. Sleepers stirred awake for a moment, then fell back asleep. A few of these fire-cracked stones then lay there for centuries waiting for Edward Kaeser to dig them up. The sound of a stone cracking in a campfire is another of the things that have been the same forever.

Kaeser did his excavation next to property owned by Monsignor Preston High School, a Catholic school. A few years after he finished his work, Preston High expanded its grounds, and built an extension that covered the excavation site. In the late 1980s and early '90s, Jennifer Lopez, the future dancer, singer, and actor, attended the school, where she starred on the girl's track team. Both of her parents had emigrated from Puerto Rico. Today she is one of the Bronx's most famous offspring. In 2012, *Forbes* magazine rated Jennifer Lopez the thirty-eighth most powerful woman in the world. In January 2021, she sang "This Land Is Your Land" and "America the Beautiful" on TV at President Joe Biden's inauguration.

3

IF YOU ARE DRIVING on the Hutchinson River Parkway in the northern Bronx, and you pass under the bridge where Interstate 95 crosses above the parkway and the Hutchinson River, you are near the spot where a woman named Anne Hutchinson died. The river and parkway both take their name from her. In July 1643, Siwanoy Indians killed her and seventeen other members of her family and household and burned their buildings and wiped out her farm. Presumably the bodies went up in the blaze; no last resting places were ever found. By all accounts, the location of the farm would have been near this junction of highways.

She had ended up here, in the religiously tolerant Dutch colony of New Netherland, because of a theological issue. To put it another way, her religious teachings frightened certain high-minded men of the village of Cambridge, in the Massachusetts Bay Colony, so badly that they feared for the very foundations of their society and banished her to the wilderness or whatever community would have her.

Anne Hutchinson can be described as a midwife who bore fifteen children of her own, and as a schoolmaster's daughter who came to Boston from England in 1634 with her husband and most of the children they had at the time—but that only begins to say who she was. Anne Hutchinson was a kind of prophet, who interpreted the Bible, preached charismatic sermons in her home, gathered many followers, and inflamed a theological dispute known as the Antinomian Controversy. The gist of the dispute had to do with whether one needed good works in order to be saved, or whether God's grace—a grace unearned, freely bestowed by God without one's having to deserve it—sufficed for salvation. She came down so persuasively on the side of grace that the leaders of the colony feared a future in which their citizens, confident that they were saved already, might sit around doing nothing.

Abstract as the debate may sound, it was fundamental to the creation of modern America, and even, in a way, to the modern Bronx. The secular version of salvation by grace is the uniquely American invention known as cool. Like grace, cool is something that you simply have or don't have; and if you don't have it, no amount of work, however strenuous or sincere, will get it for you. In fact, striving to be cool will only make you more uncool. America brought the concept of cool into the world, and Anne Hutchinson was one of the early architects of it—of that sense of inner justification which, transposed to secular life, causes people not only to know that they are cool, but to be even cooler because they know they are. I will say more about this complex subject later.

If Anne Hutchinson has no marker for her bones, a benevolent fate—or the grace of God, freely bestowed—gave her something better: an amazing rock. I have mentioned Split Rock as one of the notable glacial erratic boulders of the Bronx. Split Rock sits at the top of a knoll above the valley of the Hutchinson River, hard by Interstate 95. The boulder is granite, the size of a small one-story cottage, and in the shape of an Easter egg lying on its side. Part of it is below the surface of the ground, as if the glacier dropped it from so high up that some of it was buried on impact. Also as if by the force of the landing, the boulder has split in the middle. This clean, straight-edged vertical fissure is about three feet across, slightly wider at the top. The two halves inspire the viewer to fit them together mentally, an exercise that imprints the rock in the brain. Old-time accounts said that if you sighted through the split, you could see the location of Anne Hutchinson's farm on the west side of the river. Other sources said her farm was closer, by a spring that used to be near the rock.

The rock still exists today mainly because of the efforts of two local historians: Dr. Theodore Kazimiroff, who was the Bronx's official historian in the 1960s, and Edgar Brown, historian of the nearby town of Pelham. In 1962, as I-95's route was being laid out—here the shadow of New York City Construction Coordinator Robert Moses crosses the page, to minor-key notes on a bass viol—the historians learned that the rock was to be dynamited out of the highway's path. They made their objections public, gathered support, and finally induced Moses to move the roadway slightly to the north. In this victory, Anne Hutchinson deserves some credit, too. Just as the rock will always commemorate her, her own fame saved the rock from being just another of the local features destroyed by Moses.

An important fact to note about Anne Hutchinson is that she had many young men followers, and Harvard College was founded by her adversaries to defend the colony and its impressionable youth against her. The Puritan elders put her on trial for heresy and for having converse with spirits in 1637, and although she argued successfully on her own behalf, she gave the court such a dressing-down that they banished her anyway. Her statements, transcribed in the records of the trial, represent the first recorded words of a woman in the new land, predating even the poems of her neighbor Anne Bradstreet.

Anne Hutchinson knew that Roger Williams, another Boston dissenter, had recently started a colony in Rhode Island, so she and her husband, William, moved to it. William Hutchinson died during the family's five years in Rhode Island. Ministers from Boston visited her, tried to get her to recant, and said that Massachusetts would be taking over Rhode Island soon anyway. To escape this oncoming theocracy, she asked the leaders of New Netherland for permission to resettle here. They were agreeable, and she found a place west of Bronk's River, in an area then called Vriedelandt (Freeland). She and many of her family and several servants sailed down the Sound and then up the tidal estuary that now bears her name. They built their farmhouse among widely spread-out Dutch-speaking neighbors and Indians who had recently turned hostile because of the Dutch attacking and massacring them.

Split Rock, once it had been saved from Moses, still had to fit in somehow with the new roads surging around it. The result is awkward and demeaning to the landmark—as if the construction coordinator had given it the back of his hand. The northbound lanes of the New England Thruway, aka I-95, its traffic speeding by, are about three paces from the rock. An exit ramp from the Hutchinson Parkway encloses it on the other side; that is, the rock is on a scrap of nowhere land shaped like a fingernail paring in the middle of a complicated highway cloverleaf. If you look north through the split in the rock, you see—not the site of Anne Hutchinson's farm but the cement wall and chain-link fencing of the interstate a few feet away.

Sometimes I visit Split Rock to show it that it hasn't been forgotten. The New York City Parks Department has charge of it now, and has built a hard-to-find, indifferently maintained trail to it. Recently I took a number 5 train to Eastchester–Dyre Avenue, the last stop, walked a couple of blocks to Boston Road, turned left, went over the long bridge that crosses the Hutchinson River, looked down at the riverine industrial zone—heaps of scrapped catalytic converters, muffler pipes, crushed cars, gravel, and asphalt, with conveyor belts shifting the heaps to and from waiting barges. At the far side of the bridge, it's a right on Huguenot Street, right on Hollers Avenue, and left on Eastchester Place.

Past where that road comes to a corner there's a patch of weeds with a barely discernable path in it. The path widens out and becomes a trail that leads under the I-95 bridge, curves to the left, passes a retaining wall covered with shiny, fresh graffiti (KILLA BEES ON A SWARM and WHAT'S YOUR MOTIVE SMURF and COVID SZN and DUST 2 DUST), slopes upward until it's beside the interstate, and goes over the parkway. There, on your right, is Split Rock, in a grove of oak and walnut trees. Up close you can see the bolt holes in the stone where a plaque has been pried up and ripped away. The rock sits in anonymity, unidentified by text or sign.

Anne Hutchinson felt a Christian compassion for Indians. In

Massachusetts, she had discouraged her young men followers from enlisting in the Pequot War, a scorched-earth campaign against that tribe, which the colonists eventually carried to genocidal extremes. She did not allow guns in her house. After she moved to New Netherland, the Siwanoy had made it clear that they did not want her farm where it was and had told one of her party to stop working on it and go away. Her Dutch neighbors had heard from the Indians that an attack was coming. They advised her to leave, as they themselves were doing. She said she did not have anything to fear from the Indians.

She dressed in the Puritan style—plain black dress, white smock, close-fitting white bonnet, and white neckerchief. The Indians arrived one day in July and were surprised to find anyone still there, after the warnings. To judge from Alanson Skinner's excavations, the Indians probably had stubby teeth, and their faces may have been painted with red made from scrapings from a limonite paint stone. They may have had guns; Skinner also found lead shot and gunflints at the Schley Avenue site. A young warrior named Wampage led the Siwanoy. The Indians asked the household to tie up the dogs. Then they killed Anne's sons Zuriel, who was six or seven years old; Francis, twenty-one; and William, eighteen. They killed her daughters Katherine, Mary, and Anne; a son-in-law, William, husband of the younger Anne; and several servants. Wampage killed and scalped the fifty-two-year-old matriarch himself. Later, following Siwanoy custom, he took her name, which he shortened to "An Hoock."

One of Anne's children survived the slaughter. Susan, who was nine, hid in the split in Split Rock, the story says. Wampage took her captive and adopted her. Eight years later, and against her will, Susan was returned to her relatives in Boston, where she married, had eleven children, and lived to be eighty.

The split is easily big enough to hold a nine-year-old child. Six or eight adults, at least, could cram in there. As a hiding place, it seems obvious, and if Susan did take shelter there it's not surprising that she was found. Weeds grow around the rock, and a sprig of Virginia creeper vine has taken root on the top (northern half) where it sits like a topknot. On the ground I found walnuts and an empty wrapper from a Trader Joe's peanut butter granola bar.

The idea that God's grace is freely bestowed, not earned, connects to a powerful belief known as predestination, which holds that certain souls are predestined by God to go to heaven, and nothing they do in their earthly lives can disqualify them. That is, some people are going to heaven no matter what, and (the downside) some people aren't. The predestined were also referred to as the elect. Anne Hutchinson said she could tell if a person belonged to the elect after just half an hour of conversation. She must have believed that she was one of the elect herself. A professor of religion once explained to me that predestination can be compared to a parent's undying and unconditional love for a child. Like beloved children, the elect walk in divine protection, always safe in God's love. And if nothing the elect can do removes them from God's approval, somehow that makes them into people who do God's will instinctively. Predestination sounds like an exhilarating idea. It must make a person feel bulletproof.

Of course, someone as confident as Anne Hutchinson could drive other people crazy. If the Indians say they are going to attack, you might take the warning as a God-given message, and get out, and save yourself and your family. You may be ready to be welcomed into heaven, but your children and servants may not feel the same. Anne Hutchinson knew that she had been chosen by God, and that all was in God's plan. What could go wrong? The Puritan elders could not have been more pleased when they heard of her death. One said, "Thus the Lord heard our groans to heaven, and freed us from this great and sore affliction." The elders had their vindication; but she was cooler than they were, and she still is.

WHEN I SAW Rembrandt's *The Night Watch* a while ago in the Rijks-museum, in Amsterdam, and stood in the darkened gallery letting the power of the huge work course through me, I also reflected on the fact that it was painted in 1642, the year before Anne Hutchinson died. At that point in history the Dutch had come near to the top. They pretty much did as they pleased. In the 1640s, egged on by William Kieft, the colony's terrible governor, many of the settlers in New Netherland agreed that the local Indians had to go. The tax Kieft imposed had rankled the Indians. One of them said that Kieft "must be a very mean fellow to come to this country without being invited by them, and now wish to compel them to give him their corn for nothing." For the Indians, the greed and arrogance of the Dutch colonists went without saying, but the true depth of their hatred came as a surprise.

The war, later known as Kieft's War, which went on from 1640 to 1645, began in disputes over alcohol and the settlers' livestock, as would happen across North America again and again. Kieft sent troops to Staten Island to look for hog thieves, and the troops attacked a group of Munsee. (Hog theft probably did occur sometimes. Skinner found hog bones in the middens at the Schley Avenue site; of course, those animals might also have been acquired by trade.) The Indians, for their part, did not like Dutch cattle getting into their cornfields. They retaliated by raiding Dutch farms. Putting even more pressure on the Indians of New Netherland, the Mohicans, a tribe from farther up the Hudson Valley, were attacking their villages.

In February 1643, hundreds of local Indians fleeing the Mohicans came to New Amsterdam, the fort at the foot of Manhattan, and asked for protection. The Dutch let them camp at Corlears Hook, near where the Manhattan side of the Williamsburg Bridge is now, and at Pavonia, today's Jersey City, across the Hudson River. In a treacherous turnabout, Kieft then sent troops to attack both camps, and the Dutch unleashed ghastly butchery on men, women, and children. Fewer than a thousand Dutch lived on Manhattan in the 1640s. Kieft's War resulted in the deaths of sixteen hundred Indians; scores of Dutch also died in Indian retaliatory raids. This was the volatile situation Anne Hutchinson had moved into when she brought her family to Vriedelandt. The attack on her came not long after the massacres of Indians at Corlears Hook and Pavonia. She was trying to start a religious community in the middle of the bloodiest Indian war that ever happened in what is now New York City.

FROM A HIGHER PART of the Split Rock trail you can see, to the southwest, the waters of the Hutchinson River reflecting the sky, and the wide expanses of salt-marsh grasses and reeds on either side of the river, and then the towers of Co-op City, each almost thirty stories high, standing apart from one another on the horizon in Soviet-style solemnity. Beyond the towers, the clouds are brighter on their undersides, with light reflected from Long Island Sound. It's one of those wide-angle views that reveal the grandeur of the region's larger landscape, so right for city-building. No city in the world has been as blessed by nature and geography as New York. When the Dutch set out to exterminate the Indians in the 1640s, they were doing so in a paradise of nature. Few Europeans had ever seen such bounty as this archipelago offered, with its combination of fresh water and salt, bedrock and fertile soil, coastal land and forest. As for the cornucopia of aquatic life, 350 square miles of oysters were just the start.

Jasper Danckaerts, a forty-year-old Dutch religious sectarian, arrived in New-York harbor on the ship *Charles* on September 23, 1679, having endured a three-month voyage. The city had been renamed New-York in honor of its new proprietor, James, the Duke of York, when the English took New Netherland from the Dutch in 1664. James went on to be King James II of England. Under its new masters the city remained Dutch in its essence. What Danckaerts was able to see of the harbor just from the ship's rail dazzled him. In a journal he kept with his traveling companion, Peter Sluyter, he wrote:

> It is not possible to describe how this bay swarms with fish, both large and small, whales, tunnies, and porpoises, whole schools of innumerable other fish, which the eagles and other birds of prey swiftly seize in their talons when the fish come up to the surface, and hauling them out of the water, fly with them to the nearest woods or beach, as we saw.

Danckaerts and Sluyter lodged at a house on Pearl Street—the street still exists in lower Manhattan, though the house, number 255, is gone—and explored on foot all over. One day they hiked from there all the way up to Spuyten Duyvil, the stream that then divided the tip of Manhattan from what's now the Bronx, and they crossed over in a canoe. They noted the peaches strewn all over the road in such numbers that the hogs had grown tired of eating them. After exploring on the stream's other side and admiring some "very high rocks" in the future South Bronx, they recrossed to Manhattan and hiked back to Pearl Street. This day trip mostly on foot covered about forty miles.

Native Americans, their population reduced by violence and repeated epidemics, still lived in the area, but now were greatly outnumbered. The Indians Danckaerts saw interested him. He observed how the colonists treated them:

> The people in this city, who are almost all traders in small articles, whenever they see an Indian enter the house, who they know has any money, they immediately set about getting hold of him, giving him rum to drink, whereby he is soon caught and becomes half a fool. If he should then buy any thing, he is doubly cheated, in the wares, and in the price . . . always managing it so that the poor creature does not go away before he has given them all they want.

Some Indians spoke Dutch. Danckaerts and Sluyter had a long conversation with an Indian whose name was the same as Danckaerts's—Jasper. From the context, this was in a lodging or tavern in Manhattan. They asked him where he believed he and his father and grandfather and great-grandfather and so on back to the beginning had come from. The Indian thought for a while and then with a coal from the fire drew a tortoise on the floor. He said the tortoise was in water surrounding him all around. Then the tortoise rose up and water ran off him, and that was the earth, and it became dry. Jasper took a straw and stood it upright in the middle of the tortoise. He said the straw was a tree, and from the root of the tree a man sprouted. Then the tree bent over until its top touched the earth, and from the top another root grew, and from that root there sprouted a woman. All his people came from that man and woman, he said.

Danckaerts gave Jasper four fishhooks in thanks, and the Indian told him and Sluyter that if Indians ever threatened them in the forest, they should say they knew him, and the Indians would spare them.

Dr. Ted Kazimiroff, the Bronx historian who co-saved Split Rock, roamed the borough widely and found all kinds of artifacts and ancient sites. While walking along the Bronx River in the New York Botanical Garden in the 1970s, he noticed a rock on the east bank. It was roughly oval, a little smaller than a bathtub, and oriented with its longer dimension parallel to the river, pointing north. On the rock he perceived a faint petroglyph—a figure in outline, carved into the stone—depicting a turtle. The turtle's head faced north and angled toward the river. Archaeologists interpreted the glyph as possibly referring to the Native American creation story. The rock was moved from the riverbank and put in a special niche in a conservatory building in the botanical garden.

Bright overhead lights shined on the rock. I looked and looked at it but could make out just a few faint parts of the turtle by following the full rendering of the glyph on the placard alongside. Perhaps the rock was left out too long after Kazimiroff discovered it, and acid rain ate at it. I remembered my late friend Leonard Thomas Walks Out, also known as Le Warlance, an Oglala Sioux from Oglala, South Dakota, chaffing me sometimes, asking what I and all of us other immigrants thought we were doing on his Turtle Island. America has been many things to many people, but the turtle seems to be its oldest surviving avatar.

Kazimiroff's most remarkable discovery, even more than the petroglyph, was an actual Native American still living in the old way in a remote part of the Bronx. According to Theodore L. Kazimiroff, the historian's son, his father met a man named Joe Two Trees when the elder Kazimiroff was a boy. The son wrote a book retelling the story that his father, by then deceased, had told him about meeting Two Trees when the father was eleven. The father lived in Throgs Neck and used to walk up to Pelham Bay Park and spend days in the far parts of it, rarely seeing another person. Two Trees was watching him, however, and one day introduced himself. He showed the boy secrets of what used to be called Indian lore, and eventually told him his life story, which began in those woods in 1840 and involved many adventures after he left at fifteen following the death of his family. Now Two Trees's life was about to end in the same place he was born. The story is second- and thirdhand, and maybe hard to believe. But given Dr. Kazimiroff's indefatigability as an explorer and historian of the Bronx, it has some meaning, if only as his personal myth of origin.

Jasper Danckaerts, the Dutchman, concludes his description of his cosmogony lesson from the Native, Jasper, by saying that the man went off, and then "at noon he returned with a young Indian, both of them so drunk they could not speak, and having a calabash of liquor with them. We chided him, but to no purpose, for he could neither use his reason nor speak so as to be understood." Soon after, Danckaerts and Sluyten continued their journey, bound for Maryland. They were scouting out a site for a new home for their sect, the Labadists, who were even more taken by the concept of divine grace than Anne Hutchinson had been. The Labadists had made such a ruckus, dancing and singing in the streets in religious ecstasy, that they had got themselves kicked out of Amsterdam (old, not New), no small achievement. On the way southward, the two Dutchmen passed the future site of Philadelphia, which did not yet exist.

Wampage, the self-declared killer of Anne Hutchinson, lived to an old age, and signed hundreds of treaties ceding Indian land to the settlers. In the Bartow-Pell Mansion, a historic building now owned by the city, in Pelham Bay Park, there's a copy of a treaty that gave much of the present-day northeast Bronx to Thomas Pell in 1654 in return for various small hardware. Wampage is among the signatories, under his "An Hoock" moniker. Most Indians had left the New York City area by 1700, though some were still attending the Anglican church in Westchester village as late as 1710, where they were said to have been of good behavior during the services. Many of the Munsee removed to a big Lenape village called Minisink that stretched along the Delaware River on the border between Pennsylvania and New Jersey. Later, other Munsee went farther west. Muncie, Indiana, is named for a tribe of Indians some of whom came originally from what's now the Bronx.

The evil done to the Indians of what's now New York City did not just disappear, nor did the people it was inflicted on. The disease and violent death and alcohol that wasted them moved outward across the continent, entered the lives of other Native people, got even worse, and continue to do horrible damage today. There are still merchants watching Native people closely, getting them drunk, taking every dollar they have. In Whiteclay, Nebraska, and Gallup, New Mexico, and other reservation-border towns at this very moment, there are men and women so drunk as to be unable to speak or reason, while the merchants who sold them the liquor are wide-awake and narrow-eyed, watching. I repeat a truth I learned years ago when I saw Lakota friends in these situations: If the devil exists, he's sober.

I first met Leonard Thomas Walks Out (Le Warlance) on the street in New York. He's the only friend I ever had whom I met on the street. I knew him for almost forty years. Nobody, not even Russians, could drink as much as he could. I wrote about him in my book *Great Plains*, and put a photo of him in the book. After he lost all his IDs, he carried the paperback around in his back pocket for photo identification. He said it worked pretty well. Later I visited him in Oglala, South Dakota, on the Pine Ridge Indian Reservation, over a period of several years, and wrote about him in another book, *On the Rez*. He was a delight to be with—funny, knowledgeable about history and pop culture, encyclopedically well-informed about the people and events of his reservation. Also, he was sometimes so insane that I'm still in recovery today. In 2017, his great-niece called to tell me he had died, of kidney failure. He was seventy-six years old; that he had managed to live so long impressed everybody.

His great-niece was a member of the tribal police on the Fort Berthold Reservation in Montana. He had told her not to read *On the Rez* until after he was dead. On the phone, she said she had just finished reading it. She was laughing. "It's hilarious you believed some of that stuff Uncle Leonard told you," she said. "He told you he jumped off the Space Needle in Seattle attached to it only by a bungee cord and a Band-Aid, as a promotion for Johnson & Johnson, and you *believed* him?" She laughed some more and said her uncle had been right to tell her to wait to read the book, because it brought him back for her.

4

ON THE SUBJECT of aerial stunts: You can walk from the Bronx to Manhattan, or vice versa, across the High Bridge, whose traffic is limited to pedestrians and bicyclists. It's at the end of West 170th Street, in the Bronx, and crosses to Highbridge Park, at approximately 174th Street in Manhattan. The city built this bridge in the 1840s to carry the aqueduct that brought water from an upstate river forty-one miles away. The structure, which was the work of mostly Irish laborers following plans by the civil engineer John B. Jervis, consists of stone-and-steel towers that rise from the floor of the Harlem River valley to graceful Romanesque arches holding the bridge a hundred and forty feet in the air. The High Bridge still projects the glow of a great civic triumph from a former age. Its altitude gave the system enough pressure to lift water all the way up to the higher floors of Manhattan apartment buildings. The system also saved the city from the cholera epidemics that had been the result of people using the same sewage-tainted wells, and provided a water supply for fighting its chronic fires.

Rustic scenery used to be a Bronx attraction, as were its picnic grounds and amusement parks. One of these, Kyle's Park, occupied the Harlem River shoreline below the High Bridge. According to

History in Asphalt: The Origin of Bronx Place and Street Names, by John
McNamara, another distinguished old-time Bronx historian, canoe-
ists and scullers on the river could stop in at Kyle's Park for a cold
beer. McNamara goes on to say that Mr. Kyle once hired a tightrope
walker to cross on a slack rope between the Bronx and Manhattan.
For a capper, the daredevil carried a stove to the middle of the rope,
cooked pancakes, and tossed them to the boaters below. As far as I
know, no one does such stunts in the expanses of sky by the High
Bridge above the Harlem River anymore.

Today that's one of the higher bridges between the Bronx and
Manhattan; the lowest is a bridge (also only for bicyclists and pedestrians) that connects the Mott Haven neighborhood of the South
Bronx to Randall's Island. As mentioned before, part of the Bronx's
southern border is formed by a tidal stream known as the Bronx Kill.
The word *kille*, in the Dutch of old New York, meant "river." It may
seem confusing that the Bronx River, that major geographic feature
separating the borough into eastern and western halves, has essentially the same name as the body of water that divides the Bronx from
Randall's Island, Manhattan. Geography likes to get confusing sometimes, just to mess with you. The Harlem River is navigable by ships
and barges; they can also use the Bronx River for some of its length.
The humble Bronx Kill, on the other hand, flows so shallow in certain
places that you can wade across it shin-deep.

Which, for years, South Bronx residents were obliged to do, if they
wanted to take the most direct route to the playing fields and picnic
tables on Randall's Island, and not go roundabout on the walkway of
the vehicular bridge nearby. They could step from rock to rock across
the Bronx Kill and push through the willows along it. In 2013, José
Serrano, the U.S. congressman for the South Bronx, along with local
community groups, got the city to build the Bronx Connector—a trail
for bicycles and pedestrians leading to this bridge that spans the not-
mighty but nonetheless obstructionary Bronx Kill. From the bridge
down to the water it's about twelve feet. About sixty feet above it is a
major railroad bridge—the Bronx is nothing if not a nexus of overlapping infrastructure—built just before the First World War. The bicycle
and pedestrian path runs through the massive sand-colored concrete

arches that support the railroad bridge, which is part of the Hell Gate Viaduct, the bridge-and-overpass connection that the Amtrak Acela and other trains take on the route between New York and Boston.

I've spent so much attention on this bicycle-and-pedestrian bridge not only because its creation was a useful achievement of José Serrano and his community-group allies. Two hundred and fifty years ago, the site of this bridge was close by the home of one of America's and New York's most influential men, Gouverneur Morris. His manor house, Morrisania, a French-style chateau, lay at the end of a lane of cypress trees leading inland from his dock on the Bronx Kill, which back then was a more substantial waterway.

Gouverneur Morris was born at one thirty in the morning of January 31, 1752, in the manor house, which by then had been in the Morris family for three generations. He died sixty-four years and nine months later, in the same room where he had been born. For much of his life, he looked out every day at this scenery—the Bronx Kill, the confluence where it meets the East River, and the islands beyond. As much as any of America's so-called Founding Fathers, Gouverneur Morris remade his country, and sent ripple effects out into the world. He wrote the Preamble to the U.S. Constitution. It would not begin "We the People of the United States" if not for him. During the pandemic lockdown, I saw a news photo of a demonstrator in camo threatening the governor of Michigan because she had told citizens of that state that they should wear masks. In his right hand the demonstrator held an automatic rifle, and on his forearm was a big, dark blue tattoo that said, in the old-time lettering of the Constitution, "We the People." Gouverneur Morris, who lived on this corner of what would someday be the Bronx, had just the right kind of big-picture temperament to be able to write those words.

Working with George Washington, who became a close friend, Morris helped finance the American Revolution. At the Constitutional Convention of 1787, he contributed more to the proceedings than all but a few other delegates. He served as ambassador to France, proposed the idea for the Erie Canal, and worked for the canal's creation. Of a rational and orderly mind, he led the committee that created the rectangular street grid for New York City. He suggested a

decimal-based system of coinage when the new country was develop-
ing its monetary system, and he invented the word *cent*, for penny.

He did kindnesses for his longtime friend and rival Alexander
Hamilton—sat with him as he died, delivered the oration at his fu-
neral, and raised money for the support of Hamilton's widow—but no
character in the musical *Hamilton* is based on him. Dozens of things
all over the Bronx are named for him or his family. There's Morris
Heights, Morris Avenue, Gouverneur Place, Gouverneur Playground,
Gouverneur Morris Square, and Gouverneur Morris Triangle. The
Bronx's Gouverneur Morris Houses are among the biggest New York
City Housing Authority (NYCHA) projects in the borough. Morris
High School (now Morris Campus), which also commemorates him,
was the Bronx's first major public secondary school.

His name is everywhere, and yet almost nobody knows who he
was. This may have to do with his personality. A strangeness, an
alienness, infused it. That same overarching state of mind that en-
abled him to write the opening, "We the People," kept him from being any one specific public person, as if he were all "the People," and
nobody, simultaneously. He slipped away from intimacy, disappeared
on you. Many of the Founding Fathers disapproved of him on moral
grounds; and in this regard, it must be said that he not only left himself open to criticism but ushered it in at the front door. Also, there's
the issue of his name. How was posterity to pronounce it? Some
sources say it should be "Governor," like the state official. Its spelling
suggests it could be "Goover*niere*." A friend of mine's maiden name is
Gouverneur, and she pronounces it "Gover*neer*." Other sources have
persuaded me that's how contemporaries pronounced his name, too.

The real reason for his lack of lasting fame could be even simpler:
He lived in what would one day be the Bronx. And not just any place
in the future Bronx, but on the southeastern edge of it, just above the
water level, in the precise spot where railroads, once they'd been invented, would want to go. Morrisania, the manor house, survived into
the twentieth century, and there are even photographs of it, but local
preservationists' attempts to make the house and grounds a public
park and museum failed. The New York, New Haven, and Hartford
Railroad acquired the property, and in 1905 the house was torn down

in a railroad yard expansion. Thus, it had vanished before the arrival of the highways, and of the Triborough Bridge (now the Robert F. Kennedy Bridge), whose cement support pillars and entry ramp have shouldered themselves into that same location.

Had Gouverneur Morris left his ancestral seat and reestablished himself somewhere more out-of-the way, his second house might have been preserved like the houses of many of the other Founders, and with that kind of landmark he might have stayed alive in memory. Instead, as would happen to so many of his fellow Bronxites, his home got displaced by the city's reaching, tightly grasping infrastructure fingers.

THE MORRIS FAMILY came to what's now the Bronx in this way:

They were Welsh, and their name derived from *Maur Rys*, or Rys the Great, an ancestral warrior. During the English Civil War, the brothers Richard and Lewis Morris sided with Parliament and served in Cromwell's army. After the Stuart Restoration, when Charles II took back the throne, the brothers moved to Barbados. Lewis converted to the Quaker faith. Richard married a rich woman named Sarah Pole and became a sugar planter. George Fox, the founder of Quakerism, visited the Morrises in Barbados. Possibly because of religion-related disputes with the colonial government, Richard then decided to move to New Netherland.

Jonas Bronck had died in 1643, the same year as Anne Hutchinson (though probably of less violent causes). His widow sold Bronk's Land to someone who sold it to someone, and in 1670 it was purchased by Richard Morris. In 1672, Richard and his wife both died, leaving an infant son, Lewis, who had been named for his uncle. What was done about the orphaned baby, and who took care of him for the next year, are not recorded. In 1673, Lewis Morris, the baby's uncle, arrived to settle his brother's estate, and he ended up staying. He received a patent from the English governor affirming his title to the land, and then added more land to it, so that his holdings totaled 1,920 acres (three square miles). He also bought another 3,500 acres in and around what's now Morristown, New Jersey. He saw to the upbringing of Lewis, his namesake, whom he did not like, and whom he tried to disinherit in favor of his wife.

Unfortunately for him, the wife predeceased him, and when the elder Lewis died in 1691 his approximately twenty-one-year-old nephew became the owner of the estate. In May 1697, the governor of the Province of New-York gave this Lewis a royal charter to the land, making it a manor called Morrisania, and him the lord of it. As a manor, Morrisania was its own jurisdiction, and within its boundaries the Morrises had the power of civil authority. Lewis Morris, first lord of the manor of Morrisania, became the first native-born chief justice of the New York Supreme Court. After making an enemy of William Cosby, the colonial governor, Lewis bankrolled a newspaper that printed attacks on Cosby, which caused the paper's editor, Peter Zenger, to be jailed for criminal libel. Lewis hired Andrew Hamilton (yes, *Andrew* Hamilton; earlier era, different person) to defend him. Zenger's acquittal established that the truth of a published statement is a defense against libel and set a precedent for freedom of the press.

After this Lewis Morris, there followed another, who was also a judge, and who produced a bunch of children, including yet another Lewis. The mother of those children died, and the judge remarried, to Sarah Gouverneur, a woman of French Huguenot ancestry, who happened to be his first wife's cousin. Sarah in turn bore him children—none of them, thankfully, named Lewis. In 1752, Sarah Gouverneur Morris gave birth to Gouverneur Morris.

The boundaries of Morrisania included a sizable but hard-to-define part of the Bronx. Descriptions of the boundary lines vary. Some old sources put the manor's northern line at Oak Tree Place, which is about seven blocks north of the Cross Bronx Expressway. The future Bronx was divided into other manors in the Morrises' time; one source says that near Oak Tree Place "was the celebrated oak tree where met the boundaries of the ancient manors of Morrisania, Fordham, and the Jessup-Richardson Patent." Most accounts agree that the eastern boundary of Morrisania was a creek called Sacrahung by the Indians, and Bungay Creek or Boundary Creek by whites. It originated in present-day Crotona Park, flowed south, and emptied into the East River. Whether it still does either of the first two I can't say from observation, because Bungay Creek was covered over and forgotten long ago. But according to old maps compared with new maps, it does empty into the East River in the same place it used to.

The mouth of the former Bungay Creek is easy to find. You go to East 149th Street and walk east, staying on it as it curves around to the south and then dead-ends at the East River. Not much about this waterfront neighborhood ingratiates itself. A concrete-recycling plant used to grind up big chunks of that material night and day, making a racket and dusting the surroundings with a fine, light grit that crunched between your back teeth. Next to the plant's daunting ten-foot-high steel fence, a row of small trees lined the curb, all of them fantastically bestrewn with plastic litter, as if wearing scary costumes for a play. On one side of the creek mouth, a heating-oil tank farm presents a collection of four-story white storage tanks connected by Vishnu-arm pipes that converge at multiple wheel-handle valves. Sometimes the high-security chain-link fence rattles open, and heating-oil trucks, all green and oily, come out. On the other side, a vast beverage distribution center produces a constant traffic of red Coca-Cola trucks with giant, overwhelming pictures of foaming Cokes on them.

A guardrail, and a sign that announces END in black letters on a yellow background, deter traffic on East 149th from continuing onward into the water. The former Bungay Creek joins the East River below the END sign, behind fencing and signage worthy of a toxic waste site. Innocent-looking, clear water flows out of a brick tunnel and down a narrow, rocky beach to meet the East River waves. On the chain-link fence enclosing this mini confluence, a sign says:

CAUTION
Wet Weather Discharge Point

This outfall may discharge rainwater mixed with untreated sewage during or following rainfall and can contain bacteria that can cause illness. If you see a discharge during DRY weather, please call 311—refer to CSO Outfall #WIB-072.

Also on the sign, schematic black figures doing what mustn't be done here—swimming, boating, fishing—are each in a red circle with a bar across it, to make the point visually. Twenty feet out in the East River a black-crested cormorant pops from the water and looks around brightly, having missed the memo.

As important a boundary marker as this creek mouth was for the Morrises, I imagine they must have visited it now and again. In fact, for many years this boundary was the subject of a dispute with their neighbors, which probably fixed it more firmly in the memory of the family. What would Gouverneur Morris think if he could see the place today? Or if you told him that now the mouth of his Bungay Creek is an "outfall" known as CSO Outfall #WIB-072? He liked to talk, and loved to write, and he probably would have had an opinion about this. But it might not have been as negative as we imagine. Throughout his life, he always made the best of what reality gave him and kept his good cheer. Whenever a walk takes me past this landmark, I remind the outfall/creek that I know its real names.

To return to a founding fact about the Morrises: When Richard Morris bought Bronk's Land in 1670, he had come from Barbados, where he made his fortune as a sugar planter. In that occupation he would have used the labor of enslaved people, as all planters did. Thus, the money that established the Morrises in New Netherland, where they could worship as they pleased, and where they would prosper, came from labor stolen from African and Native American slaves. That kind of theft begins many American stories.

ANTHONY VAN ANGOLA was the name of an enslaved African man in New Netherland in the seventeenth century. It's not common to know the name of a slave from a long time ago, so repeating the name—Anthony Van Angola—is worthwhile. There were thousands of others like him in the colony. The Dutch brought enslaved men and women with them almost as soon as they landed. African slaves were in what's now New York from 1626, the year after New Amsterdam's founding. When the Dutch defeated Indians in battles, they also enslaved the captives and kept or sold them or gave them away as gifts. The Dutch West India Company promised prospective settlers, as an inducement, that they would be provided with slaves. Trading slaves was a part of the company's business. Jonas Bronck's neighbor Pieter Schorstina-veger, after whom the Bronx is not named, farmed with Black slaves. When Richard Morris arrived from Barbados and purchased Bronk's Land, he brought enslaved Black people with him "to help plant the fields," as one historian puts it, understatedly.

Morrisania always had slaves. In the early 1700s, two of them, Hannibal and Samson, regularly sailed in a sloop to take the manor's produce to sell in Manhattan. (The manor and vicinity were like a truck farm, or sloop farm, for the city.) In 1712, about 16 percent of the people residing in what's now the Bronx were enslaved. At Lewis Morris's death in 1762 he bequeathed forty-six slaves to his heirs. Gouverneur Morris received a special bequest from his father. Ten years old at the time, he was given "a Negroe Boy called George."

Farming in New York generally did not use large numbers of slaves, unlike on the South's cotton, rice, or tobacco plantations. Slave-owning families here usually had only two or three slaves, and the owners and the owned lived together in the same house. Slavery in the North is sometimes portrayed as a milder form of it, as if such a thing could be. The gradual phasing out of slavery in New York gave the slave owners time to sell their slaves south instead of having to free them. A Morrisania slave was said to be the last enslaved person freed in the state, when New York finally outlawed the institution completely in 1827.

As the writer Jamaica Kincaid has said, "Black people did not like slavery." When Richard Morris and his wife died in 1672, their slaves rebelled, until local authority put the uprising down. More widely spread slave rebellions occurred in New York City twice in the 1700s; the colonists learned from them that rebellions against the status quo were possible. Later, white New Yorkers would follow the example set by the city's more desperate slaves. The American Revolution was one of the first cover versions done by white people of something that Black people had done originally.

In the late 1980s, excavation for a new office building on Foley

Square, in lower Manhattan, turned up a burial ground that had been covered over by nineteenth-century landfill. The site was near what had once been the city's public commons, where executions took place, and some of the remains belonged to people who had been hanged after a slave rebellion in the city in 1741. Other burials in what was called the African Burial Ground dated from before then, some were from later. Closer examination of hundreds of skeletons dispelled any notion of the mildness of northern slavery. The bases of some of the skulls showed ring fractures, probably caused by carrying heavy objects, such as water jugs, atop the head. On the bones, lesions revealed where muscles had been torn away by hard labor. The bones also had evidence of malnutrition, and of diseases such as yaws, rickets, syphilis, anemia, and meningitis. Some of the teeth had been filed into points or hourglass shapes, in African style.

Nutritional indicators suggested where the subjects might have come from originally. The teeth of children presumably born in America were in worse shape than the teeth of African-born adults. The varied diets in Africa had built better teeth than were found in the skulls of the children, who may have been fed mostly with corn. Some of the bodies had been interred with small objects, such as beads or pipes. Shroud pins that had fastened the burial wrappings remained, though the cloth had rotted away. After archaeological work had been going on for a while, protesters stopped the team of white scientists who were doing it, and Black archaeologists from Howard University took over. Later, the dig and the examination of the remains were ended entirely, leaving some hundreds of bodies undisturbed where they lay, and reinterring the ones that had been exhumed. The African Burial Ground is now a national monument maintained by the U.S. Park Service.

Enslaved people in seventeenth- and eighteenth-century New Amsterdam and New-York lived with other-inflicted pain that still shows up four centuries later in their bones. Their mental pain can hardly be imagined. If unearned suffering is redemptive, as the Reverend Martin Luther King said, what redemption did these sufferers find? The African Burial Ground holds enough unearned suffering for the redemption of souls many times over. Maybe all this cemetery's souls are in heaven, alongside their Puritan contemporaries who turned out to be right when they declared themselves predestined to go to heaven no matter what they did on earth, or whether or not they suffered.

I have said that a belief in the power of unearned grace, at a secular level, equals cool. The idea of cool became one of the country's great discoveries, and a contribution for the ages. It took root in America, as I proposed, by way of religious beliefs held by predestinarians like Anne Hutchinson. The idea of cool is important to the Bronx because one day, young people who lived in the then-wasted borough would come up with something so original and so cool that it amazed the world. Hip-hop music, invented in the Bronx, leaped from its birthplace and spread worldwide. The height of American cool is grace and redemption, refined into art. A lightning strike of that transformation happened in the Bronx.

5

AFTER THE ENGLISH took New Netherland from the Dutch and changed its name to New-York (I'm not sure why they put in the hyphen; back then people just used a lot of hyphens), Bronk's Land became part of Westchester County. This new jurisdiction included all the present-day Bronx, as well as land to the north, in what is still Westchester County today. The original county seat was the village of Westchester, now called Westchester Square; today it is the fourth-from-the-last stop on the number 6 train, in the east Bronx.

A puzzler presented by maps of this area is that there is Westchester Square, and there is the neighborhood of Eastchester, and neither appears to be substantially east or west of the other. If anything, Westchester Square looks to be slightly *east* of Eastchester, which is also a mile or so north of it. More logical is the fact that when the Dutch built an outpost at the limit of navigation on the estuary now known as Westchester Creek, they called it Oostdorp, which means East Village—their reason being that it was well east of Manhattan, where most of the Dutch then lived. At Oostdorp, New Englanders in the 1650s founded a village they called West Chester (or Westchester) because, from their point of view, after they'd sailed here along the coast, it was a long way west of Boston.

Westchester Creek provided the best entryway to this part of the county. The village of Westchester had a wharf where for more than two centuries deep-draft ships came and went carrying passengers and cargo. Dock Street, which led to the wharf, later became Ferris Place. Again by comparing maps, I found that Dock Street/Ferris Place still kind of exists, but is no longer a public thoroughfare, having become the driveway of the Howie Stone Adult Day Center. One day when this facility's gate was open, I walked down the drive to its turnaround, where the driver of a senior citizens' van was having a smoke, holding the cigarette out the open window with one hand and checking his phone with the other. The turnaround is at the place where the wharf used to be. Starting in the early 1700s, ships were sailing from here to Manhattan every day.

In the first years of Westchester village, most of the county was wilderness. The bounty for killing a full-grown wolf was thirty shillings for Christians, ten shillings for Indians; what a Christian Indian got is not revealed. Settlers dug wolf traps and banded together for rattlesnake hunts. Darkness extended to spiritual questions, as well; in 1670, one Katherine Harryson was exiled from the village for dealing in "dark and dubious matters" and suspicion of witchcraft. St. Peter's Episcopal Church, the fourth such structure on the site since the 1690s, and its ancient cemetery where giant trees are slowly swallowing some of the gravestones, mark the center of the original village. Today the elevated tracks for the number 6 train put the church and cemetery into noise-filled shade. It's hard to picture what the place looked like before the neighboring salt marshes had been pushed under by landfills. A causeway made of planks connected the village to Throgs Neck, which used to be an island at high tide. The current in Westchester Creek, which flowed under or over the causeway depending on the tide, powered a gristmill.

Five miles west of this settlement, a landowner named Philipse built the first bridge connecting Manhattan Island to the future Bronx. The bridge spanned Spuyten Duyvil, the stream at the tip of Manhattan that Jasper Danckaerts and his companion crossed in a canoe. The elevated tracks for the number 1 Broadway Local run above the spot now. Known as the King's Bridge, Philipse's bridge carried foot and animal traffic for a toll per person, cart, or beast; troops and government messengers crossed for free. Continuing north from the King's Bridge, two roads—the Albany Post Road, paralleling the Hudson River, and the Boston Post Road, paralleling the coast—continued onward through Westchester County. That is, Interstate 87 (here, the Major Deegan Expressway, heading north) and Interstate 95 (here also known as the Cross Bronx Expressway, heading east) have existed in protean form since the seventeenth century.

The Albany Post Road went past the Van Cortlandt manor house, which still stands, and then to Yonkers and beyond. The Boston Post Road swung around to the east of the King's Bridge and climbed out of the Harlem River valley up an incline known as Break Neck Hill. That hill is now part of West Kingsbridge Road, one of the steepest streets in the city. It winds in a switchback configuration made originally by wagon wheels and feet.

The modern bridge that carries the Broadway Local subway train has a superstructure, painted battleship gray, whose girder-reinforced upper part reaches skyward and catches the sunlight. The sense of moment that the bridge gives to this Bronx crossing is exactly right, whether it's intentional or not. This is the site of the first major bridge in the entire region. During the Revolutionary War, the King's Bridge was the most vital strategic point in all of what's now New York City. And Westchester village, five miles east, with its wharf where you could easily disembark if you came from the sea, offered strategic advantages of its own. The bridge and the wharf were the two main points of entry to the Bronx-continent.

IN 1776, the second year of the Revolution, Westchester County was a semi-settled landscape of woodlands, pastures, and fields. Westchester and Eastchester were the biggest villages in its eastern part, but by then the county seat had been moved to White Plains. Twenty years before, the population of the county had been 13,257. When the war started in earnest around here in '76, the number may have increased by a thousand or more. The place's original natural bounty had been depleted. Along the shore, the oyster beds were almost played out. But the county's many hundreds of farms produced abundant agricultural goods—wheat, rye, corn, oats, flax, honey, fruits, vegetables, beef, lamb, butter, cheese, and wool. Westchester village held its own agricultural fair every fall, and sometimes another in the spring. Most of the local farmers were tenants or small landowners. Men at that level occupied the bottom rung of citizens allowed to vote. Unlike other counties, Westchester extended the franchise to freemen without property, so that tradesmen, teachers, clergymen, sailors, dockworkers, and other laborers also qualified.

About a quarter of the landowners possessed some wealth and turned up regularly as candidates for office and as active members of one political faction or another. The influential local families—the Leggett, Willett, Hunt, Vyse, Rodman, Pell, Van Cortlandt, Underhill, and Valentine families, among others—are remembered in Bronx place names. Sometimes the Morris family sat atop the local hierarchy as judges and other official persons, sometimes the power swung to the DeLanceys, their rivals. The richer landowners could claim the status of aristocrats, as was true throughout the colonies. It may seem unlikely that men of their comfortable standing would want to risk war to establish an independent country, but a lot of them did, including Gouverneur Morris. For most of his life Morris lived with disabilities; maybe that enlarged his sympathies and democratized him. When he was fourteen, a household accident severely scalded his right arm, and he spent more than a year convalescing at home. The accident withered the arm and left him only limited use of it. He couldn't ride, shoot, or dance like his peers. (Later in his life, he would suffer an even worse maiming.)

The young Gouverneur studied with a tutor in New Rochelle, probably because of his mother's Huguenot background. He learned to speak French—although, as he discovered during the years he later spent in Paris, not as fluently as he thought he did. For a while, he attended an academy in Philadelphia founded by Benjamin Franklin. Two of Gouverneur's older half brothers, Lewis Morris and Staats Long Morris, had attended Yale, but Gouverneur chose King's College, in New York. In fact, his father's will had stipulated that under no circumstances was he to go to Yale. (King's College, on Greenwich

Street, later became Columbia University and moved uptown.) He graduated as the valedictorian of his class in May 1768, when he was sixteen. Then he stayed two more years at King's College, read law, and got a master's degree. Three months before he turned twenty, he received his license to practice law, and joined the firm of William Smith, the leading attorney in the city.

As a legal prodigy with a rising career, Gouverneur did not at first approve of the rebellion. He derided those who were shouting against the mother country, disliked what he saw as their lawlessness, and for a while believed that compromise with the British was still possible. In his opinion, the Continental Congress preferred to make a "herd of Mechanicks" the officers in its army, rather than choosing men of good families like himself. He said that James Rivington, a printer who published antipatriot views, must not be harassed for them, and he criticized the crowd of Connecticut men who came to the city and smashed Rivington's presses. Mobs and mob violence always horrified him.

His mother, still living at Morrisania, sided with the British, while his mentor and employer, William Smith, chose to remain neutral. His half brother Staats Long Morris was an officer in the British Army, which had honored Staats's request not to be required to serve in the colonies. And yet despite such influences, the spirit of the time soon moved Gouverneur toward revolution. Following the example of friends such as Alexander Hamilton and Robert Livingston, he began to involve himself in the patriot cause. In 1775, when he was only twenty-three, the anti-British electorate of Westchester County chose him to serve in the Provincial Congress of New York; two years later, he was elected to the Continental Congress. Gouverneur would not cross paths with his half brother Staats again for more than a decade, and he went almost seven years without seeing his mother. Like other rebel leaders, he had endangered his status as a member of the gentry and was now at some risk of being hanged.

GOUVERNEUR MORRIS first met George Washington when the general passed through New York on his way north from Virginia to take command of the army in Boston. After having thwarted the British there with his victory at Bunker Hill, Washington then returned to New York, arriving on April 13, 1776, at the head of eight thousand troops. The British had switched their focus from Boston to New York, and Washington came to defend the city from them. Morris had the job of relaying messages between the Provincial Congress and him. People hero-worshipped the general, with good reason, because, as Theodore Roosevelt wrote, "He was not only the greatest American; he was also one of the greatest men the world has ever known." Morris, twenty years younger than Washington, idolized him and loved him. Eventually he managed to be a friend to Washington in a way that few other people did.

A lot of the war occurred in and around New York City; Washington's ghost still rides through the Bronx. Sometimes when I'm walking, I go to places where I know he passed by. Just east of Westchester Creek, and about sixty feet up in the air, a monster of a highway intersection, one of the most complicated in the country, renders everything on the ground below it moot. When I'm under the elevated intersection, among its forest of columns, the GPS on my phone sometimes stops working, and says it has "map issues." From its point of view, I'm nowhere. Here, Interstates 95, 295, 278, 678, and the Hutchinson River Parkway come together, link up with various on- and off-ramps, and form a nexus that looks like a lopsided six-pointed star from above. In the non-place beneath the highways, the jet-engine-like roar of the traffic and the thumping of tires on the seams of the road above never let up.

There are grassy areas in this understory, and blowing trash, and seldom-used foot and bike trails, some of them paved with crumbling asphalt. During the war, Washington would have ridden over this ground on reconnaissance tours. Probably, the enslaved person who was closest to him, William Lee, known as Bill, rode alongside, carrying the general's telescope and other gear. Back then the whole region was more open than it is today, with vastly longer lines of sight, and telescopes were essential for strategy. Both Bill Lee and Washington rode skillfully, and their horses would have been as good as any in the country.

The highway traffic whooshes and thumps overhead. Here on the ground, I imagine Washington, Bill Lee, and the officers of the general's staff trotting by.

(Once, during the Boston campaign, a regiment from Marblehead, Massachusetts, under the command of Colonel John Glover, got into a dispute with a regiment of Virginians. Some of Glover's men were Black. Glover was also a ship's captain, free Black sailors worked for him and other captains, and he led an integrated regiment. Words between the Virginians and the Marbleheaders escalated to a general brawl. Soon more than a thousand men were mixing it up on the Cambridge Common. Washington saw this melee and, accompanied by Bill Lee, plunged into the midst of it. He jumped from his horse, grabbed some of the combatants, pulled them off each other, spoke loudly and sternly to them, and broke up the brawl. "In a few moments George Washington and William Lee had restored order to the army," wrote the historian David Hackett Fischer.)

A truck horn blares, the tires overhead make their double thumps, back wheels almost instantly after front wheels. Down here, riding by, Washington is dressed impeccably. He wore, said one observer, "a blue coat with buff-colored facings, a rich epaulette on each shoulder, buff under dress . . . an elegant small sword, [and] a black cockade in his hat." Washington had always been very aware of his appearance, especially in uniform. As a young officer in the British colonial army in Virginia, he ordered silver lace and blue and scarlet cloth from London and designed his and his officers' uniforms himself. At Mount Vernon, his Virginia estate, he—*employed* is not the right word, because the man was an indentured servant—benefited from the skills of his personal tailor, an Englishman named Andrew Judge. This tailor slept with a half-white slave named Betty, and she bore a girl child, Ona, known by the name Oney Judge. As the child of a slave, Oney Judge, three-quarters white, was added to the two-hundred-some slaves belonging to Washington and his wife, Martha.

Much later, after Washington had become president, he and his wife moved part of their household to the then-capital, Philadelphia. By Pennsylvania law, slaves held in the state became free after six months of continuous residency. To get around that, the Washingtons regularly rotated their slaves back to Virginia before the six months were up. Oney Judge, however, did not go back to Virginia, but escaped from the Washingtons and fled to New Hampshire, where she lived out her life. Washington tried various means to get her back, including sending his stepson in person to persuade her. He stopped short of the use of force, though he could have used it legally. No doubt Washington feared the optics and publicity. In New Hampshire, she married a free Black sailor, Jack Staines. Today Ona Judge Staines is famous for her courage, and in 2008 the city of Philadelphia celebrated an Oney Judge Day at the site of the Washingtons' house near Independence Hall. Her story connects back to George Washington's love of clothes, and his need for a personal tailor.

Slave-owning hypocrite, traitor, upstart, lucky fool—that was how the British who fought against Washington saw him. As a young soldier he had sworn an oath of loyalty to the king. Some colonists who had taken the same oath stayed true to it during the Revolution. For Washington, who was even more careful about his honor than about his uniform, going back on his oath may have worried him; maybe his awareness of the inconsistency made him strive to be even more honorable to compensate. When the British Army was in Boston, one of its generals, John Burgoyne, wrote a play that portrayed Washington as a buffoon wearing an exaggerated wig and armed with an outsized blunderbuss. The British soldiers applauded and howled with laughter when the play was performed for them at their camp. In everyday communications, their officers refused to give Washington the dignity of any rank or title, referring to him as "Mr. Washington." But in the officers' occasional letters requesting a clemency from him, such as the exchange of captured officers, suddenly he became "General Washington."

In one skirmish between the Americans and the British, the commander of the Queen's Rangers, a troop of Loyalist cavalry from Connecticut and New York, described how close he came to killing or capturing Washington. In his memoir of the war, Lieutenant Colonel John Graves Simcoe wrote, "Mr. Washington's ignorance . . . exposed him to a check, from which his usual good fortune extricated him." Simcoe said that although he could have shot and killed the general, he chose to spare him.

Simcoe also wrote that if the colonial troops in the Queen's Rangers were extra-good, they might be given "the honor of being enrolled with the British army." That is, although they fought and died for the king, soldiers from the colonies had second-class status, well below that of British-born soldiers such as Simcoe himself. Throughout Washington's British Army career, when he scouted the western frontier in Virginia and Pennsylvania (where in 1754 he helped start the French and Indian War), he faced this kind of condescension. Had he stayed in the British Army and followed a predictable path, waiting for "the honor of being enrolled" etc., he probably would have ended up a successful nobody. Staats Long Morris, Gouverneur's older half brother, who was wounded in battle, attained the rank of general, and went on to serve in India, provides an example of that type of commendable, unremarkable career.

Washington needed a revolution in order to become his real self. The topmost military men in the British Empire still had to bend the knee to the king. Washington deferred only to his own sense of honor and the opinion of his countrymen, of whom he said, "A people unused to restraint must be led; they will not be drove." Destiny also lay in his name, which was that of a place: Islington, Ashton, Westhampton, Washington. From the contempt the British officers showed for him he could have imagined the disgrace, mixed with horrid politesse, that awaited him if he failed. The execution by hanging that he could have expected would have been a mercy by comparison. To coincide with his identity, he had to be not only *not* British, but a whole new nationality: He had to be America itself. In the words of another former colonial, the Trinidadian poet Derek Walcott, "Either I'm nobody, or I'm a nation." The reverse was also true for Washington. He had to be a nation or he would be a nobody.

THROUGHOUT THE WAR, the British fought in a smarmy way. In the summer of 1776, their fleet arrived in several installments off Sandy Hook, where ships usually waited before attempting the difficult channel into New York Harbor. The command probably numbered about forty thousand soldiers. Sails filled the horizon; "I thought all London was afloat," said one observer. From the perspective of the British, they were merely sending a lot of troops to a place that already belonged to them. For the Continentals, the arrival of this army constituted an invasion—in fact, it remains the largest military invasion of the Western Hemisphere to date. The purpose of the massive display was to chastise and terrify. As these forces assembled, the Congress in Philadelphia signed the Declaration of Independence. Among the signers was another of Gouverneur Morris's half brothers, Lewis Morris, for whom the act of signing took nerve. Morrisania, part of which belonged to him, and where he also owned a house, lay within easy reach of the warships.

Gouverneur Morris did not sign the Declaration. It is possible that the arrival of the fleet caused him to have second thoughts. Two months later, he disappeared from the Provincial Congress and went to Boonton, a town far inland in New Jersey, on a vague mission having to do with finding horses, as he later lamely explained. In any event, he was AWOL from September to early December 1776, while the war got white-hot in New York City and Westchester County. Afterward, Morris would pull other disappearances on friends and lovers and people who depended on him.

The British first made a feint of landing the troops on Long Island. Then they anchored by Staten Island and off-loaded there. Washington built defenses on Manhattan and along the Harlem River in Westchester County, with heavy fortifications at and around King's Bridge. The British sent a large force ashore in Gravesend Bay, in what's now Brooklyn, and drove the Americans through what's now Prospect Park and clear to Red Hook on the East River. The British Army's frontline shock troops, tall Hessian mercenary grenadiers who wore high pointed hats, didn't so much shoot you as trample over you and stab you with their bayonets like a stabbing machine. Bayonetting men to the trees, they panicked the Americans, who broke and ran. Colonel Glover's men—the same Marbleheaders from the brawl on Cambridge Common—saved Washington's army by transporting it from Red Hook over to Manhattan at night with a small flotilla of local boats in a nor'easter fog.

That happened in late August. Having delivered a dose of corrective chastisement, the British then sent a captured American officer to the Congress in Philadelphia with their offer to negotiate. In early September, Congress dispatched three emissaries: Benjamin Franklin, of Pennsylvania; John Adams, of Massachusetts; and Edward Rutledge, of South Carolina. They made the long trip up to New York, arriving at Amboy, New Jersey, on September 11. Nearby, just across the Arthur Kill, was a stone house that had been turned into the Staten Island headquarters of Admiral Lord Richard Howe, commander of the British fleet. His brother, General Sir William Howe, commanded the army. The admiral, the elder of the two, had been given the authority to negotiate with the Americans.

A word about the Howe brothers: They were related to the king, George III, through his great-grandfather's mistress. Their grandmother was the illegitimate but recognized half sister of George III's grandfather George I. That made them second cousins to the king— or semi-illegitimate half second cousins, technically. Their mother, Charlotte, the Viscountess Howe, was a lady of influence at court, and lobbied for her sons, as did their sister. William Howe was even said to resemble George I. One gets the impression of a family clique. The brothers sometimes kept company with their cousin-king and talked and joked with him. Before this assignment, both had compiled distinguished military careers.

Admiral Howe sent his red-and-gilt barge to ferry the three emissaries across the Arthur Kill. Here the smarminess kicked in. They landed on Staten Island at the foot of a waterfront slope leading to the house, which was more than a hundred years old at the time and still stands today. The slope, too, remains as it was, so we can picture the emissaries' welcome in the place where it happened. The three walked up the slope between two lines of grenadiers, those soldiers who specialized in bayonetting people. As John Adams later recalled: "We walked up to the house between lines of guards of grenadiers, looking as fierce as ten Furies, and making all the grimaces, and gestures, and motions of their muskets, with bayonets fixed, which, I suppose, military etiquette requires, but which we neither understood nor regarded." This reminder that they should be afraid was followed by horrid politesse, as the admiral met them in a large room pleasantly decorated with woodland mosses and greens. He served them, said Adams, "with good claret, good bread, cold ham, tongues, and mutton."

But Howe refused to accept that they were representatives of an independent country, and they refused to participate in any discussion that did not include immediate recognition of the independence of the United States, and the meeting went nowhere. Howe's earlier offer of pardon, which would spare their lives if they swore allegiance to the king, didn't tempt them. Rutledge said maybe they could come up with an agreement, country to country, to aid each other's commercial interests in the Atlantic, but the admiral paid no attention to that. So the emissaries started back to Philadelphia, and on the following day American troops withdrew from New-York City; that is, they left what is today lower Manhattan, where they could be easily cut off, and they moved to defensive positions farther north on the island.

On September 15, the British landed at Kip's Bay—on the East River, approximately at today's East 28th Street—and attacked the Americans there. Washington's troops, by this time thoroughly spooked at the sight of Hessians, soon were in headlong retreat while he tried to stop them, shouting and beating on them with the flat of his sword. He threw his hat on the ground and said, "Are these the men with which I am to defend America?" As the Americans kept fleeing north, the British insultingly played the bugle calls used in a fox chase. Finally, the retreat slowed enough that Washington and his officers could rally the troops and mount a counterattack. Against expectations, it succeeded, and drove the British back with losses. The Americans then took up a position on Harlem Heights. Washington hoped he could get General Howe to attack him there and bring on another victory like the one at Bunker Hill.

But Howe was never going to do that. If any single principle motivated him in the fighting in and around New York, it was to avoid another Bunker Hill. He did not want to lose too many of his men; nor, it seemed, did he want to kill too many Americans. He and his brother resembled patient adults trying to quell tantrum-throwing children, first giving hard slaps to get their attention, then wrapping them in a smothering embrace to subdue them. Seeing the Americans ensconced on the heights, Howe switched to the smothering approach. He decided to reach all the way around the American army and take King's Bridge, the only land exit from Manhattan, thus stoppering-up Washington where he could be smothered or destroyed at leisure. With this in mind, the British general looked east to Westchester County.

6

WHICH BRINGS US BACK to Westchester Square, the fourth-from-last
stop on the number 6 train in the Bronx.

A short walk from the elevated station, in a planting of yew
bushes, you'll find one of those uncommon city objects, a historical
marker. It's a slab of pale stone that bears the words "On October 12,
1776, a critical revolutionary battle was won by keeping the British
from crossing Westchester Creek Bridge and surrounding swamp
lands." This inscription constitutes the barest summary of the facts.
Next to the stone, a feather-flag stuck into the ground advertises
"Breakfast All Day." It refers to the White Castle hamburger restaurant nearby. The marker sits next to the White Castle's drive-through
service lane. I think of the encounter that took place here as the Battle
at the White Castle.

To defeat Washington's army, the British would have to prevail
not only on the islands—Long Island (Brooklyn), Staten Island, and
Manhattan—where they had already established themselves. They
would also have to win on the continent, i.e., Westchester County.
Their main headquarters were on Manhattan. No force there could
be safe if it did not control the King's Bridge. John Adams said that
New York was the key to the whole continent. If that was so, then the

King's Bridge, the spot where the Broadway Local subway train now crosses into the Bronx, could be seen as the key to the whole war. And for General Howe, Westchester village, the other access point to Westchester County, was the way to the King's Bridge.

To slide around to the bridge from the east, Howe put about four thousand men and a number of horses and cannon in flatboats at Turtle Bay—near today's East Fifty-ninth Street—on the morning of October 12. Then this sizable flotilla headed for Throgs Neck. From there the British could march to the causeway, cross it to the mainland at Westchester village, and quickly proceed overland to the King's Bridge, five miles west. Throgs Neck got its name from a party of Quakers, led by a man named Throckmorton, who once began a settlement on it and were run out by the Siwanoy in the same uprising that killed Anne Hutchinson. The two-mile-long peninsula, an island at high tide, was commonly known as Frog's Neck, and both generals (Washington and Howe) called it that. As the flatboats rowed the thirteen miles up the Sound, Admiral Howe sent forty-two of his warships to cover them with their cannon. The flatboats arrived without incident and ran up on the beach in a pleasant cove. Their fronts dropped down and the British troops came ashore at the same place where, about two centuries later, the amateur archaeologist Edward J. Kaeser would dig up fire-cracked rocks, and Jennifer Lopez would go to high school.

General Washington had his telescope trained on this activity from the Morris-Jumel Mansion, atop a prominent hill in upper Manhattan near what's now West 160th Street. Despite the foggy morning, he could see the throng of sails, and he fell into a rare swoon of despair. He realized that Howe was attempting to cut him off at the King's Bridge. His army had few horses and wagons, and it could never move fast enough to cross out of danger before the swiftly marching soldiers beat them to the bridge. Once the British force got off Throgs Neck and across the causeway over Westchester Creek, they could be at the King's Bridge, or even the Hudson River, in a few hours. Other parts of Washington's army, moving north, were strung out along the valleys of Westchester County. They could all be captured or destroyed.

General William Heath, whom Washington had put in command of the troops north of Manhattan, earned a mixed reputation in the war. A farmer from Roxbury, Massachusetts, he seemed to define the word *stolid*. As a field general he would be worse than average, though he proved a good administrator; he seemed to like everything about the army except the fighting part. In this particular field command, however, he acted wisely. When scouting the area nine days before General Howe's troops landed on Throgs Neck, he had assigned a troop of Pennsylvania riflemen under Colonel Edward Hand to guard the Westchester Creek causeway. They were stationed by the tidal gristmill, and behind a woodpile next to it, about where the White Castle drive-through is today.

After Howe's forces landed, they quickly marched up Throgs (or Frog's) Neck. As they approached the causeway crossing to the village, Hand's riflemen began to shoot at them. Making Howe's problem even trickier, the planks had been removed from the causeway. The situation gave the general pause. Up to this point the British Army still had not set foot on the continent. He withdrew a short distance, then sent his cannon up a nearby rise and began to shoot at Westchester village. The residents took shelter in the church, whose steeple Howe dinged, doing little damage.

I'VE WALKED AROUND the place where Howe put his cannon. Today it's a residential neighborhood of row houses along Dudley Avenue, Mayflower Avenue, George Street, and William Place. On a mild late-summer day, the plane trees were shedding strips of bark that curled like wood shavings. Houses blocked the line of sight that Howe had, though you can see the top of the church steeple, about half a mile away. A woman was sweeping trash from the tree pits into a long-handled dustpan. She picked up a large clear-plastic clamshell and put it in her trash bag. On the front window of a brown-shingled house a sign read, CLOSED CIRCUIT TELEVISION AND AUDIO MONITORING ON PREMISES. In a garage whose door was open, a man was saying to somebody, "When I was young, in my twenties . . ." At a crosswalk a young father said to his son, who was maybe four years old, "Here, let me carry you." The boy allowed himself to be picked up, then nestled his head as his father adjusted him in his arms. War spent part of an afternoon at this spot 240-some years ago—

And accomplished nothing, other than giving practice to the artillery. The cannonade did not dislodge Hand's soldiers, whose long rifles, of the type made by skilled Pennsylvania-German gunsmiths, were said to be able to hit a squirrel in the eye at 250 yards. Later in the war, when the British happened to capture a Pennsylvanian armed with one of these long rifles, Howe examined it and admired it. Blocked at the tidal mill, Howe probed farther upstream on Westchester Creek, and found another crossing, with more Americans guarding it. His superior force—four thousand trained veterans against maybe not even hundreds of recent recruits—could have forced its way, but here the general showed the diffidence that he was often criticized for. At the end of the day the British marched back down Throgs Neck and went into encampment near their landing spot. Getting onto the actual continent, that difficult transformation, still eluded them.

The next morning, Washington, no doubt relieved to find that he still had an army, ordered troops to reinforce Heath in and near Westchester village. A contemporary who served under Heath later wrote of him, "As an officer of parade and discipline, he was respectable; but for valorous achievements, we look in vain for his laurels." It's good that there's a historic marker by the White Castle, but it ought to mention Heath, too. His conscientiousness and common sense saved the day. Had Howe's encirclement attempt of October 12 succeeded, the war might have ended right then.

BAD WEATHER FOLLOWED, and the British stayed put in their Throgs Neck camp. Meanwhile, Washington rode all over the future southeast Bronx, trying to decide where the next attack would come, and how to defend against it.

He had in his head that the British would encircle him by way of Morrisania manor. Landing there would be easier for them, with no big marshes to cross, and the distance from it to the King's Bridge is shorter than from Westchester village. Therefore, Washington put most of the defenders in and around Morrisania. The possibility also existed that Howe would decide to go even farther east, ferrying his troops to Pell's Point, the next peninsula over from Throgs Neck. Perhaps Howe would reason that by circling around that far from the main body of the Americans he would meet less resistance. The likelihood of his attempting the maneuver seemed remote, but Washington put a small force to block the exit from Pell's Point anyway. It consisted of four Massachusetts regiments—about eight hundred men, under the command of Colonel John Glover, the Marblehead captain whom we've met before.

When Howe finally moved, on October 18, he chose the Pell's Point option. At one in the morning, he loaded his four thousand men into two hundred flatboats, crossed Eastchester Bay, and landed on the point. The more common name for this place today is Rodman's Neck. The NYPD shooting range is there; it's the only historic site I know of where the sound of gunfire still resounds. Thousands of police officers are required to spend a certain amount of time requalifying with their firearms every year, and from a distance the rattle of gunfire on Rodman's Neck sounds like a small-arms firefight.

On the morning when the British landed there, and finally touched their boots onto the actual continent, the sun came up at 6:32. Every few years, history buffs revisit the site of the Battle of Pell's Point (also called the Battle of Pelham) on October 18, and the sun rises at about the same time. Usually it's a beautiful fall morning, with the trees in full color, but there were very few trees around here in 1776; the British referred to the place as Pelham Moor. From a mile or more away Colonel Glover saw the enemy approaching through the dawn and the fog, and he wished he had a general around to tell him what to do.

MUCH OF THE BATTLE took place on what's now the Split Rock Golf Course. It's a public course, well-maintained and laid out on two topographic levels. Between its upper and lower fairways runs a strip of sloping, rocky land, a jungle of greenbrier brambles salted with lost golf balls winking white, yellow-green, and orange in the underbrush. Golfers of many ethnicities play this course. As I've noted, Black soldiers served in Glover's regiment. But in the heroic twelve-foot-by-forty-five-foot mural of the battle (painted in 1937) that decorates an entire wall of the first-floor reception hall of the Bronx Criminal Court building, on East 161st Street, the soldiers are all white, with not a Black face to be seen.

Descriptions of troop movements can be hard to follow; in this battle, what happened was simplicity itself. Because of the geography, and the coves and inlets intermingling with the land, Howe had only one route off the neck—a road, or lane, that made its way along the higher ground. It passed close by a twelve-foot-high glacial erratic boulder known today as Glover's Rock. If you stand by the rock on a foggy morning, the air carries a strong summer-vacation scent of the sea. A plaque that replaced a previously vandalized plaque on the rock says that Glover was born in November 1732. On the day of this battle, he was almost forty-four. The three regimental commanders under him were Colonels Joseph Read, Loammi Baldwin, and Joseph Shepherd, New Englanders all.

The flag of Read's regiment, the 13th Massachusetts, showed two officers in the uniform of the regiment. One of them, who has blood running from a wound in his chest, is gesturing to a group of children, below the motto "For Posterity I bleed." (There seems to be something essentially New England in the guilt-inducing pathos of the motto.)

As Howe marched inland, stone walls lined the road. Improvising wisely on the moment, Colonel Glover had put Read's, Shepherd's, and Baldwin's regiments in ambush behind the walls, one regiment after the next. His own regiment he held in reserve at the rear. Some histories say that the head of Howe's column and a group of forty of Glover's men exchanged a volley at Glover's Rock at seven a.m. Each side withdrew, then the British moved up again. They approached the place where Read's men waited. When the column was about thirty yards away, the Americans rose from their cover and fired.

This is the kind of encounter that people my age were taught about in classes on the Revolutionary War in grade school. We learned that the British, for reasons best known to themselves, dressed all in red, which made them excellent targets, and they marched into battle in straight lines out in the open, where they were even easier to shoot; we

Americans, on the other hand, not being so foolish, wore less flashy clothes and hid behind trees, rocks, and stone walls. The fifth-grade history books did not add that after you fired from behind the trees, rocks, and stone walls, the uninjured majority of the redcoats were on you in an instant, bayonetting you while you tried to reload. This tactic had terrified and overwhelmed Washington's soldiers in Brooklyn.

After the volley, Read's men listened for the command for the bayonet charge, but it didn't come. Dead and wounded Hessians lay in the grass. Beyond them, other British troops were falling back. For the next hour and a half, nothing happened. Then Howe brought the full weight of his superior force to bear upon the Americans, thundering with his seven pieces of field artillery while musket volley followed volley. Now when Read's men stood and fired, the British did not fall back. The two sides exchanged about seven volleys, a process that lasted twenty minutes, given how long it took to reload. Then Read withdrew, the British advanced, and Shepherd's men, in their turn, rose from ambush and fired. Again, volleys were exchanged. Colonel Shepherd was shot in the throat but survived.

To follow the route of the battle, starting at Glover's Rock—Howe's advance, Glover's successive withdrawals—you go along Orchard Beach Road, continue partway around a rotary, and walk uphill along Shore Road to the golf course. From there the battle went for maybe another mile along what was then known as Split Rock Road. The golf course is generally not available to random hikers. I chose a time early one morning when groundskeepers were doing maintenance, rolling the course with hole-punching cylinders to aerate the grass. In some places the golf cart path is the old Split Rock Road. Some of the stone walls are still there, sunk into the earth, back in the greenbrier patch. Among the British casualties, Captain William Glanville Evelyn fell mortally wounded near one of the stone walls. He came from a notable family; the *Diary* of his relative John Evelyn (d. 1705) is sometimes mentioned alongside the diary of Samuel Pepys as a classic of the seventeenth century.

Like John Evelyn, the young Captain Evelyn wrote well. His family preserved letters he sent from America, and a book of these and other writings pertaining to him appeared after his death. Within the letters, and in his last will and testament, a nonfiction epistolary novel unfolds. Evelyn was thirty-four, an officer with the Fourth Regiment, known as "The King's Own," which was part of the force ordered to America in 1774 to suppress the disturbances in Boston. It fought at the opening hostilities at Lexington and Concord. No one could have detested the Americans more than did Captain Evelyn. To his father and to a favorite cousin, he described the Massachusetts rebels as "a set of rascals and poltroons," "a most execrable set of villains," and "the most absolute cowards on the face of the earth." He hoped people at home "will not tamely suffer such insolence and disobedience," but unleash the army so it could hit the rebels without mercy. He favored a policy of "almost extirpating" them.

At Bunker Hill, he saw an outnumbered force of Yankee irregulars kill or wound more than a thousand trained British soldiers before giving up the high ground with less than half as many casualties of their own. The experience so affected him that he made out his will that same day. It bequeathed "all my Worldly Substance" to one Peggie Wright, identified in a footnote as a former servant in the household of his family.

Captain Evelyn's father, an eminent Anglican vicar, almost never wrote to his son, and the son never mentioned Peggie Wright in any of the extant letters, to his father or anybody else. In the will he states that she followed him to Boston. Very likely, this arrangement would not have been applauded by the family. In a codicil to the will written on Staten Island before he went into battle, he made various other bequests to Peggie Wright, and said she was then in Halifax, where she had gone after he shipped out from Boston. How did she get along, a young woman in Boston and then in Canada, waiting for him? The relative who annotated the book said she probably came to him in New York before he died.

As the two sides exchanged volleys at the stone walls, Captain Evelyn had rushed forward and leaped over a wall at a moment when his men were falling back. While he was thus exposed, a bullet grazed his arm and two more shattered his leg and his thigh. Colonel Glover, in a letter about the battle, described Evelyn's wounding, and said that as he lay there an American ran out from the lines, grabbed his hat and canteen, and ran back, to cheers. The British retrieved Captain Evelyn and took him to Manhattan, where he at first refused to have his leg amputated. When he later agreed to the operation, it did not save him, and he died about three weeks after the battle. His death was "a great calamity to his family," relatives said. The original of his last letter to his mother had been reread so many times it almost fell apart. He is believed to lie in the cemetery of Trinity Church, downtown.

SPLIT ROCK, on its fingernail paring of ground in the highway cloverleaf, is of course no longer a part of the golf course named for it. After the battle, the British used St. Paul's Church, half a mile to the north of the rock, for a field hospital, and six Hessians are buried in that church's cemetery. The old St. Paul's still stands thanks to Franklin Roosevelt's mother, Sara, who took a liking to the building and engineered National Historic Monument status for it in the 1940s. David Osborn, the historian at the site, told me that the Battle of Pelham's fiercest fighting was around Split Rock, and that Captain Evelyn fell there. It's scary to think of how close Robert Moses came to eradicating this great Bronx stone.

Glover's men, having checked Howe's advance, retreated down the hill to the Hutchinson River, forded it, and went into camp three miles away. Howe, once again diffident, did not pursue.

So ended the biggest military engagement ever fought in the Bronx. Had Howe got past the greatly outnumbered Glover, he would have had a straight shot to the Hudson River and the encirclement he sought. In this case, as happened at the White Castle and elsewhere, a determined follow-up could have crushed the colonials, maybe for good. People wondered if Howe really wanted to win. It was almost as if he was testing the Continentals to see if they really, truly desired independence. Local historians later said he lost hundreds of troops in the Battle of Pell's Point, while the American casualties were in the low double digits. In a report to a higher-up in London, Howe said he lost only three dead (including Captain Evelyn, whom he called "a gallant officer") and twenty wounded. A British regimental history describes the battle, which fills the 540-square-foot mural in the Bronx Courthouse, as merely "a sharp skirmish."

Three days after the battle, Washington issued a General Order praising the Massachusetts men:

> The Hurried situation of the Gen'l the last two days having prevented him from paying that attention to Col. Glover and the officers and soldiers who were with him in the skirmish on Friday last their Merit & Good Behavior deserved, he flatters himself that his thanks tho' delayed will nevertheless be acceptable to them as they are offered with great sincerity and cordiality.
>
> At the same time, he hopes that every other part of the Army will do their Duty with equal Bravery and Zeal whenever called upon . . .

Glover and Washington did not always get along. The New Englander, described by a French observer as "a little man, but active and a good soldier," who had eleven children, belonged to the "codfish aristocracy" of Boston, and owned numerous sloops and fishing vessels. He thought that Washington preferred the company of southern gentleman officers to that of Massachusetts men like himself. Some of Glover's soldiers wore seamen's tarred hats and tarred breeches, which seems possibly not *comme il faut*; and beyond that, some were Black.

Later in the war, when Glover asked to be discharged from service, Washington resisted, despite Glover's claims of poor health and financial woes. After the Continental Congress finally did release him, his troubles continued. Glover's wife and oldest son had died, and he had to scramble to support his large family. When he petitioned his friend Henry Knox, the secretary of war, for a position at the port of Marblehead, he was passed over, which seems ungrateful, considering that Glover's amphibious troops had saved the army more than once. After years of effort, he partly recouped his fortunes; worn down by it all, he died of hepatitis in 1797.

Howe moved up the valley of the Hutchinson River, joined by nine thousand troops under General George Cornwallis, and they fought a major but indecisive engagement with Washington on the heights above the village of White Plains. Again, the British did not chase the Americans when they retreated. Washington, outflanked, had to order his troops to move north from around the King's Bridge; the Westchester County night rumbled with the sounds of an army moving, and on the hillsides hundreds of decoy campfires were left burning, to make the British think the Americans were still there. Soon Washington was able to cross the Hudson and escape with his forces into New Jersey, heading south for Pennsylvania. On the way he stopped at Fort Lee, near where the George Washington Bridge is now, and he watched the British take Fort Washington, his last remaining outpost in Manhattan.

He had wanted to evacuate this fort, but Congress insisted he keep a presence on the island. On November 15, 1776, the British, in their businesslike manner, cannonaded the approaches to the fort, which was on high ground in what's now Washington Heights. They had taken over the forts on the cliffs above the Harlem River that the Americans had built to cover the King's Bridge. Now they used these forts against the Americans. After the artillery barrage, troops landed on the Manhattan shore. Telescope in hand, Washington watched the redcoats mount toward the fort. He wanted to send a message to the defenders, so a courageous fellow rowed across the river, ran through British troops, climbed the cliff, delivered the message, ran back down through the enemy, and rowed back across the river while the British were shooting at him. This hero's name has somehow not been preserved.

Soon the Hessian advance soldiers surged over Fort Washington's redoubts, the defenders fell back, and the bayonetting began. Between two thousand and three thousand Americans were captured; many of them would later die in prison. Washington Irving, in his five-volume *Life of George Washington*, reported what he was told by witnesses who were with Washington on the Palisades that day. As Washington watched what was happening to his men, the sight "was said so completely to have overcome him, that he wept, with the tenderness of a child." Irving took that detail out of later editions of the biography, perhaps finding tears incongruous on the face of the hero.

GOUVERNEUR MORRIS, when last seen, had gone off to Boonton, New Jersey, on some alleged business involving horses. Set back in the Watchung Mountains, that town was unlikely to be visited by the British anytime soon. His sister Euphemia lived there with her husband, Samuel Ogden, and presumably Morris stayed with them. The Provincial Congress, to which he was a representative from New York, looked for him but could not find him. Robert Livingston, a representative from New Jersey, wrote to Edward Rutledge (about a month after Rutledge, Adams, and Franklin had met with Admiral Howe):

> Gouverneur thro' what cause God alone knows has deserted in this hour of danger—retired to some obscure corner of the Jerseys where he enjoys his jest and his ease while his friends are struggling with every difficulty and danger & blushing while they make apologies for him which they do not themselves believe.

And Rutledge wrote:

> I am amazed at Gouverneur! Good God what will mankind come to? Is it not possible to awaken him to a sense of duty? Has he not one Virtue left that can plead in favour of an oppressed & bleeding Country?

Gouverneur did not return until December 9, after the American army had been chased from the New York islands and Westchester County, and after it had retreated through New Jersey, across the Delaware River, and into Pennsylvania. Morrisania, his family home, with his mother still in it, now lay behind enemy lines. When he showed up in Fishkill, New York, where the Provincial Congress was then meeting, the other representatives evinced no hard feelings. Later Morris hinted in a letter that a love interest had drawn him to Boonton. This could be believed. Among his set he had a reputation for being immoral, irreligious, witty to the point of offense, and a man for the ladies.

Morris did not fight in the Continental Army, for various reasons, perhaps including his damaged arm. Instead, he served in Congress, and in the New York convention to draft a constitution for the state. His main goal for that document was to put in a clause abolishing slavery in New York. He stood above six feet tall, with blue eyes, light brown hair that he tied back in a queue, a prominent nose, and a square-jawed face that became more filled-out as he got older. Without fighting in the war, he would suffer another cruel injury before it was over.

7

I SET OUT for a walk of about ten miles in the Bronx at ten forty-five on a September morning. When I was halfway across the Third Avenue Bridge, heading into the Bronx, a horn of unknown origin blasted twice. Then double barricades with blinking red lights went down at either end of the bridge. I hurried to get to the Bronx side. A guy in a hard hat and bright green vest with bright orange stripes showed me how I could scoot around the edges of the barricades. He said the workers were testing the bridge. Then the bridge's whole middle span began to move, rotating slowly and smoothly on its central pivot, until it was perpendicular to the roadway. Watching it do that was like seeing the Empire State Building telescope down to the size of a Pizza Hut—a technical surprise, but just another event of the day. Most of the bridges over the Harlem River open by rotating. They're what are called swing bridges, as opposed to lift bridges, which go up and down. For ten or fifteen minutes, traffic sat waiting. Then the bridge pivoted back, the barricades lifted, and the traffic moved.

Apartment buildings under construction next to the bridge were raising a racket of metal hammering on metal. I walked along Third Avenue to East 138th Street and turned left. A woman with a blond afro, who wore a yellow, black, and purple dress, was getting her car washed at 138 Hand Wash & Lube. Nearby a sign said, TAXI DRIVERS WANTED FULL OR PART TIME—DAY OR NIGHT, with a number to call. In a few blocks I came to the Grand Concourse, the Champs Élysées of the Bronx, and turned right. The Grand Concourse runs for about five miles north and south on a ridge through approximately the middle of the Bronx. As I've said, farther-back history in the Bronx mostly happened on the edges, and recent history mostly happened in the middle. I'd been exploring the edges; today I was going to the middle.

The rattle of ratchet guns came from a car repair shop. Another apartment building going up rang with metal-on-metal hammering. Lots of new housing is being built in the Bronx. Whether it's affordable for people who live here will be another question. On the Concourse near East 149th Street, the modern buildings of Hostos Community College (officially, Eugenio Maria de Hostos Community College of the City of New York) rose on both sides, with an enclosed walkway above the Concourse connecting the two. This institution was started in a former tire factory on this site by community groups back in the late sixties. Celina Sotomayor, the mother of Supreme Court Justice Sonia Sotomayor, went to night school here after the death of her husband, and graduated with an advanced nursing degree in 1973.

At East 149th Street, the old Central Post Office, with its heroic socialist-realist murals painted by Ben Shahn and Bernarda Bryson, had been boarded shut. Across the street, broken windows at the 7-Eleven convenience store that was looted during the George Floyd protests had been repaired. At 150th and Grand Concourse, ginkgo fruit on a bench showed evidence of having been gnawed by rodents. I passed the Criminal Courts Building, which contains the mural of the Battle of Pelham, and East 161st Street, which Babe Ruth used to walk down on his way to Yankee Stadium when he stayed at the old Concourse Plaza Hotel, diagonally across from the courthouse. The stadium, empty of all fans except cardboard ones, flew the flags of the major league teams from its topmost tier; the crayon-box colors fluttered against the sky. The Lorelei Fountain, also at East 161st Street, is in the Bronx because the German city of Düsseldorf did not want it because Heinrich Heine, whose poem the statue commemorates, was a satirist and a Jew. A committee of New York Germans brought the statue to this location, where at first it was defaced, and required a guard twenty-four hours a day. Now the fountain flows peacefully, unguarded and ignored.

In another few blocks, on my right, I passed the small but excellent Bronx Museum of the Arts, where I've seen shows of graffiti art of the seventies and Gordon Matta-Clark's chain-saw-cutout sections from floors and ceilings of abandoned Bronx apartment buildings—that crazy turquoise-blue kitchen linoleum! Then, on the left, the Andrew Freedman Home takes up a block behind its iron gates and seldom-mowed grounds. It was built originally as a home for indigent millionaires and offered them amenities that they had been accustomed to before they lost their fortunes. Mr. Freedman, the founder and provider of funds, promised that the home would welcome people of all races, religions, and ethnicities, as long as they had at one time been wealthy. Now the building belongs to a community-based nonprofit. For a while on the second floor there was a display about redlining, with detailed 1930s real estate maps that showed redlined neighborhoods mostly in the South Bronx. In many places they coincided with the holdings of the old Morrisania manor.

At East 174th Street and Grand Concourse, about a mile farther on, all at once the sky gapes open to the east and west, above the route of the Cross Bronx Expressway. Years ago, I lived in a neighborhood in Brooklyn where a plane had crashed three decades before. The crash left an absence at an intersection of brownstone residential streets; this sky reminds me of that, in its evocation of the vanished buildings that had to make room for the highway. The Cross Bronx Expressway runs through a roadcut and a tunnel under the Grand Concourse rather than on a bridge over it, for complicated engineering reasons.

The necessity of digging the roadcut so far down created one of the anomalies of the city's subway system. The B and D trains are the only subways in the Bronx that remain underground for their entire routes and never use elevated tracks—that are actual, full-time subways in the Bronx, in other words. At the 174th–175th Streets station for the B and the D, the subway is under the Grand Concourse. This means that the station, to all appearances an ordinary station when you walk down the stairs into it from the Concourse, is inside a span of rock that is thirty or forty feet above the Cross Bronx Expressway, which runs through the roadcut tunnel below.

At Tremont Avenue, another major thoroughfare, I turned right. Back when the Bronx was about 50 percent Jewish, in the 1930s, Tremont Avenue and the Concourse were like the Jewish Main Streets. A ruined synagogue near that intersection, boarded up and fenced off, maybe survives in the memory of people who now live in Boca Raton. I went downhill on Tremont, pausing to look at the hunting bows and arrows in the window of Frank's Sport Shop, which has a sign over the door advertising GUNS—AMMUNITION. It's the only such advertisement I know of in the city. Beyond Frank's, Tremont Avenue goes over the Metro-North commuter train tracks, with their silver trains whizzing from affluence to affluence. A man in forest-green African robes walked by me and said a loud and cheerful "Hello!" I said hello back, but he was talking into a headset.

On Washington Avenue I took another right, now heading south, through a region of warehouses, and dozens of idling Emergency Medical Services trucks at EMS Station 18, and auto junkyards, whose names probably weren't Beware of Dog, despite the signage. I again crossed the Cross Bronx Expressway, which is an elevated road here; Washington Avenue, which I was on, goes under it. South of East 171st Street I was among the Gouverneur Morris Houses. In the past, I've asked people sitting on benches by the entryways if they knew who Gouverneur Morris was, and the name is always unfamiliar. Residents call these two blocks of twenty-story buildings simply the Morris Houses. At East 168th and Washington I stopped at an oasis—Rev. Lena Irons Unity Park, which has benches, and a drinking fountain, and a shade-giving cottonwood tree that you might find on a town square in western Kansas. Late in summer, some of the cottonwood's leaves were already turning yellow.

At Third Avenue, a block away, I turned north, and stayed on Third up to Claremont Parkway, where I took a right, and followed that road through Crotona Park to Boston Road. Now I was near what used to be one of the most burned-out parts of the Bronx. A short walk north brought me to the corner of Boston Road and Charlotte Street.

In recent Bronx history, this intersection has been in the news more than any other single place in the borough. Where there once was a rubble of burned-out, demolished apartment buildings, one- and two-story ranch-style houses now line Charlotte Street on both sides. The house on the southeast corner of the intersection is melon-orange with darker orange shutters, and has a healthy lawn enlivened by rose-bushes and cheery warning signs (picture of a fierce-looking German shepherd, above the words "I can make it to the gate in three seconds. Can you?"). In the yard there's a small fountain with a sculpture of a girl, a big American flag, and a smaller flag of Belize. If the owner of the house is out in the yard, I talk with him. His name is Willie Hemanns, and he was born in Belize. Once, pointing to the sign, I asked him where the German shepherd was who could get to the fence gate in three seconds. "There is no dog," Hemanns said. He tapped his chest: "The dog is me."

SO, WHAT HAPPENED HERE? The Bronx, or what is now the Bronx, has gone through two terrible times since the arrival of Jonas Bronck in 1639. The more recent terrible time began in the 1960s, continued through the seventies and eighties, and improved, with setbacks, in the nineties. The nadir of this period came in 1977. That's the year people remember. During the New York City Blackout of July 13–14, 1977, looting and fires hit the Bronx. A thousand fires burned just on that one night, in this borough that had already been beset by fires for about nine years. On October 12, 1977, while the Yankees were playing the Los Angeles Dodgers in the second game of the World Series at Yankee Stadium, an overhead shot from a helicopter showed a building on fire nearby, in the borough's Melrose neighborhood. Howard Cosell, the dominant sports voice of that era, who was one of the announcers, supposedly said, "Ladies and gentlemen, the Bronx is burning!" Somehow that sentence entered the language, though he never said that, or exactly that. In any case, it's what people remember.

Cosell, and the rest of the country, had the Bronx's troubles in mind because of something that had happened only a week before. On October 5, 1977, President Jimmy Carter, in New York City to address a meeting at the United Nations, got in his limo and made a visit to the Bronx. No announcement preceded Carter's decision, which seemed to be almost spur-of-the-moment. With Mayor Abraham Beame, Housing and Urban Development Secretary Patricia Roberts Harris, a few aides, and an NYPD and Secret Service detail, the Carter motorcade went up Lexington Avenue, over the Third Avenue Bridge, into the Bronx, up Third Avenue, west on East 138th Street, north on the Grand Concourse, right on East Tremont Avenue, right on Washington Avenue, left on East 168th Street, left on Third Avenue, right on Claremont Parkway, left on Boston Road—the same route I took today, as I had walked it before and have walked it at least half a dozen times since.

The route, just in itself, could be considered a historic site. It was chosen with care to expose President Carter to some of the borough's most destroyed neighborhoods, but today the route amounts to an encouragement, because the destruction he saw is gone. The borough has been rebuilt—that is a lot of what this book is about. But to the president and his staff, the burned-out scenes they passed on October 5, 1977, were stunning.

At the intersection of Boston Road and Charlotte Street, where Willie Hemanns's house is now, the limo pulled over and the president got out. Wearing a business suit and tie, he walked a block or two on Charlotte Street. Almost as far as the eye could see were rubble and trash piles, with here and there a few buildings still standing. He stood looking around, his expression blank and dazed. Photographers in a small group of press who had heard about the event took pictures that came out as minimalist cityscapes with a stark, postapocalyptic feel. For a president to allow himself to be seen when he appears so overwhelmed required self-sacrifice and moral fortitude.

From Charlotte Street, the motorcade went down Boston Road the way it had come, continued on it for a couple of miles, turned left on East 163rd Street, passed the building where Joseph Saddler, aka Grandmaster Flash, one of the founding geniuses of hip-hop, lived with his family, and the building where Sonia Sotomayor had lived as a baby (and what would the president and the mayor and company have said if, by some time-travel miracle, you could have pointed out the buildings and told them who those Bronxites were, and who they would become?). At Southern Boulevard the motorcade turned right, kept going to East 149th Street, turned right, went by St. Mary's Park, and turned left on Brook Avenue (site of the old Mill Brook, which once divided the estate of Morrisania into the part owned by Gouverneur Morris and the part owned by Lewis Morris, his half brother).

From Brook Avenue the president and entourage turned right onto East 137th Street, then left onto Willis Avenue, which led them to the Willis Avenue Bridge over the Harlem River, and so back to Manhattan. On my walk I always follow the exact route. This particular late-summer day had become hot. At the corner of East 137th and Willis Avenue I bought a plastic cup of tepid sugarcane juice from a street vendor, and when he handed it to me, he said, "Here you go, Papi." (For those even less versed in Spanish than I am, "Papi" is like a combination of "Pop" and "Grandpa." I'm always honored when I'm addressed as "Papi.")

Carter's visit produced no immediate visible rebuilding or physical remedy for the desolation he saw. A bill he proposed that would have funded low-income housing for the Charlotte Street area went nowhere. But his unexpected Bronx drive-by got a lot of press and caused people all over the city and the country to notice this place that most had been looking away from. In subsequent years, Teddy Kennedy, Ronald Reagan, Bill Clinton, Carter (again), and other dignitaries would visit the intersection of Charlotte Street and Boston Road. Major lenders took notice, the city eventually decided to get more involved, local community groups found they had new allies, and the rebuilding of the Bronx began. I've wondered whether Carter's later volunteer work, building houses for Habitat for Humanity, might also have been influenced by the shock of that Bronx visit.

I SAID THERE WERE two terrible times in Bronx history. The other terrible time began where the previous chapter left off, after Washington's army retreated from New York. With civil authority gone in Westchester County, violence and chaos took over. During the Revolutionary War, no other single place in the thirteen states saw so much strife. Peace did not return here for seven years. Both terrible times—1776 to

1783, and about 1965 to about 1995—originated in the place's geography. The British held on to Manhattan and the other islands, but they never had much luck here on the continent. They needed to defend the King's Bridge, and its near vicinity, to be safe on Manhattan. But the farther they went into Westchester County, the shakier their hold on it was. As the war continued, the American army kept a force in the area, and its front lines sometimes were along the Croton River, about thirty miles north of the King's Bridge. Throughout the war, the land in between, including most of what is now the Bronx, was called the Neutral Ground.

In the Neutral Ground, Continental Army forces sometimes fought British Army regulars. Here Yankee raiders, called Skinners because they plundered people down to their skins, clashed with bands of Tories, called Cow Boys because they stole cattle to sell to their British allies or keep for themselves. People unlucky enough to live in the Neutral Ground were robbed and terrorized by both sides. In-betweenness has always been a problem here. In the twentieth century, planners pushed highways through Bronx neighborhoods and destroyed them, and the place's accessibility made it more vulnerable to the influx of drugs, disease, and guns. Living in the Bronx has sometimes meant surviving in between.

President Carter looked with incomprehension and sorrow at the scene around Boston Road on his brief stroll during his 1977 visit. Almost exactly two hundred years before, in the fall of 1777, the Reverend Timothy Dwight, a chaplain in the Continental Army, observed a landscape of misery along the same road. Carter saw miles of rubble and heaps of trash. Rev. Dwight reported that the houses along the Boston Road were

scenes of desolation. Their furniture was extensively plundered, or broken to pieces. The walls, floors, and windows were injured, both by violence and decay; and were not repaired, because [the inhabitants] had not the means of repairing them, and because they were exposed to the repetition of the same injuries. Their cattle were gone. Their enclosures were burnt, where they were capable of becoming fuel, and in many cases thrown down, where they were not. Their fields were covered with a rank growth of weeds, and wild grass. Amid all this appearance of desolation, nothing struck my own eye more forcibly than the sight of this great road; the passage from New-York to Boston. Where I had heretofore seen a continual succession of horses and carriages; and life and bustle lent a sprightfulness to all the environing objects; not a single, solitary traveler was visible from week to week, or from month to month. The world was motionless and silent; except when one of these unhappy people [the residents] ventured upon a rare, and lonely, excursion to the house of a neighbour, no less unhappy; or a scouting party, traversing the country in quest of enemies, alarmed the inhabitants with expectations of new injuries and sufferings. The very tracks of the carriages were grown over, and obliterated: and, where they were discernable, resembled the faint impressions of chariot wheels, said to be left on the pavements of Herculaneum. The grass was of full height for the scythe . . .

Rev. Dwight, an optimistic and outgoing churchman, who would later be president of Yale, tried to draw the locals into conversation:

They feared every body whom they saw; and loved nobody. It was a curious fact to a philosopher, and a melancholy one to a moralist, to hear their conversation. To every question they gave such an answer, as would please the enquirer; or, if they despaired of pleasing, such an one, as would not provoke him. Fear was, apparently, the only passion, by which they were animated. The power of volition seemed to have deserted them. They were not civil, but obsequious; not obliging, but subservient . . . Both their countenances, and their motions, had lost every trace of animation and of feeling. Their features were smoothed, not into serenity, but apathy; and instead of being settled in the attitude of quiet thinking, strongly indicated, that all thought, beyond what was merely instinctive, had fled their minds forever.

Westchester County during the Revolutionary War prefigured the Wild West before that concept had entered a dime novelist's mind. The Neutral Ground had cowboys (or Cow Boys), Indians, cavalry attacks and rescues, and secret woodland fastnesses known only to the canniest frontiersman. James Fenimore Cooper, the novelist who invented the western and introduced it to the world, and who lived in nearby Mamaroneck, set his first bestseller here. He wrote it in 1821 and titled it *The Spy: A Tale of the Neutral Ground*. It's about an itinerant cobbler named Harvey Birch who passes back and forth between the lines spying for the British—or so his neighbors believe. Heroically he accepts the hatred and contempt of fellow Americans in order to fool the enemy, because in actuality (spoiler) Harvey Birch is not a British spy, but the personal spy of George Washington! *The Spy* uses stories from the Neutral Ground and turns them into romantic fiction that—to me, anyway—is not as interesting as what really happened here.

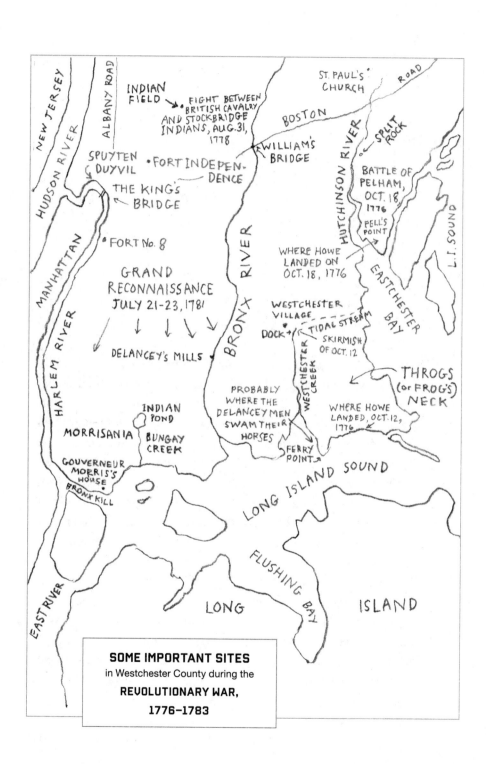

SOME IMPORTANT SITES
in Westchester County during the
REVOLUTIONARY WAR,
1776–1783

8

IF YOU TAKE the number 2 or the number 5 train on your way to the Bronx Zoo, you can get off at the East 180th Street stop and walk a few blocks to the zoo's southern entrance. Near the ticket booth, to the right of it, is a twelve-foot-high dam with a waterfall. It might look like a modern improvement designed to enhance the zoo-going experience. In fact, there has always been a waterfall here. This was, and is, the limit of upstream navigation on the Bronx River—as far as you can go by boat without a portage. George Washington observed that the section of "the Brunx" below the waterfall could not be crossed except with boats; above it, the river usually could be forded. This waterfall has always been a major landmark on the river.

In former times, a convenient drop that produced fast water would be put to work, and this one was. For centuries a gristmill stood beside a dam here. Before and during the Revolutionary War, the mill was owned by members of the DeLancey family, and people called this DeLancey's Mills. It was on the right, or west, bank of the river, with the family's mansion and outbuildings nearby. Mills operated on other Bronx waterways—on Mill Brook, for example, and on Westchester Creek—and they carried implications, because if they weren't working, as freshwater-driven mills sometimes weren't during droughts, the local inhabitants went without flour, i.e., bread. A community had grown around the Bronx River mill. The town was known as West Farms; the neighborhood still has that name. On a rise above the river the Presbyterians built a church, a later version of which still stands. As in the village of Westchester, having a church and mill qualified West Farms as a real town.

Naturally, the DeLanceys ran the place, and in Westchester County at large they held a lot of sway—even dominance. James Fenimore Cooper's wife, Susan, was a DeLancey, so he knew about the family and sympathized with them more than many people did after the war. The DeLanceys had taken the British side. One of the sons, Colonel James DeLancey, who was about thirty years old in 1776, led a group of cavalry known as DeLancey's Refugees because its members were Tories who had fled from the Americans. The Refugees wore red coats, like the British, who gave them provisions but did not enlist them or pay them. What money DeLancey and his men obtained for their service they stole. James DeLancey ran lower Westchester County, and came out of the war a rich man, despite the Americans' confiscation of his property. He plundered household movables, carried off livestock, took captives and exchanged them, had his enemies killed, and hanged subordinates who he believed had betrayed him. In a sense he was the original mob boss of New York.

DeLancey's command numbered about five hundred men. They built a village of huts along the Mill Brook in Morrisania—that is, along present-day Brook Avenue in the South Bronx. Lewis Morris, the signer of the Declaration of Independence who owned the land west of the brook, could not object, being elsewhere. Sarah Gouverneur Morris, Gouverneur Morris's mother, who owned the land east of it, and who was present, presumably went along with quartering these raiders because she was a Tory herself. In any case, neither she nor her son could do anything about it. James DeLancey moved around from place to place between West Farms and Morrisania for fear of being captured by other partisan groups, and he sometimes stayed at Sarah Gouverneur Morris's house at night. Meanwhile, his men and the British were taking advantage of Morrisania's livestock and timber.

Long after the war, people still told stories about James DeLancey. Many old-timers remembered this one:

"Tim Knapp was the handsomest young man I ever saw," said a woman of the extensive Ferris family, who had been a little girl during the war. "Tim Knapp was illegitimate—the only son of his mother, and remarkable for unusual personal beauty," someone else recalled. All accounts agreed that Tim Knapp was good-looking and well-dressed; one remembered him as having freckles, so he may have been almost a kid. He served as an officer in the Refugees under James DeLancey.

In a high-spirited moment, Tim Knapp and other officers—Huggerford, Holmes, Totten, and Kipp—proposed a race of their horses. Knapp left his own horse behind and instead rode one that belonged to the colonel. The horse's name was Goliah. Presumably the colonel did not forbid the borrowing of this prize mount; perhaps he was absent, practicing his usual elusiveness. The five riders took off at a gallop, and when they passed the finish line, Knapp kept going and vanished into the distance. For some time, no more was heard of him, or of the colonel's prized Goliah.

"When DeLancey's horse was taken he offered one hundred guineas to anyone who would bring in the thief," a local woman named Edwards said later. She knew DeLancey to be "very stern and savage" because she had seen him knock down a man who forgot to take off his hat in his presence. Tim Knapp was hiding in Burnt Jacket Swamp, on present day Clason Point, and he had Goliah corralled in an enclosure of hay bales. DeLancey men hoping for the reward went looking for him and found him soon enough. But after catching him they pitied him. As they were riding back to West Farms, one of them told him that he should escape into a nearby woods, because the colonel would surely hang him. Knapp passed up the chance.

DeLancey was waiting on the morning when they brought Knapp to "Head Quarters," as the Refugees called the blockhouse they'd built in West Farms to control the bridge over the Bronx River. Looking black in the face, DeLancey paced the floor, then said, "Tim Knapp, prepare to die! You shall be hung before twelve o'clock by the living God!"

Knapp was taken to Thomas Leggett's barn, on a hill not far from the village. A local farmer, Theophilus Hunt, who had been a schoolmate of DeLancey's, came forward to speak up for the prisoner, but DeLancey drew his sword and said he would cut off the head of the first damned rascal that tried to intercede. A rope was thrown over a beam, and Knapp was stood on a barrel with the noose around his neck. A Black man named Lunnon, who played the fiddle at dances, served as executioner. The condemned man asked DeLancey, with some aptness, "General, if you and your corps were hanged for every horse you have stolen, where would you be?" Then the barrel was kicked out from under him. In payment, the fiddler Lunnon received Knapp's suit of clothes, said to be a fine one.

This story and scores of others were told in the 1840s to a local attorney named John M. McDonald, who went around Westchester County collecting accounts of wartime life in the Neutral Ground from those who were there or knew people who had been. None of the interviewees said what happened to the horse. If DeLancey got Goliah back, the hanging seems excessive; even if he didn't it was going pretty far. His reaction seems to have been more about the disrespect—the diss—than about any property loss. And the fact that so many old-time residents mentioned the handsomeness of Tim Knapp suggests that the colonel might have been jealous of him somehow. Knapp had no luck; and as an illegitimate child, he could count on no powerful male relatives with whom DeLancey might need to reckon. The richness of the McDonald Papers, as they're called, owes something to the old-timers' having saved up their recollections to tell them to Fenimore Cooper, should he ever want to write a sequel to *The Spy*. But he never did, and the novel contains no allusion to the story of Tim Knapp.

DeLANCEY'S REFUGEES WERE just one of many bands of regular troops, partisan forces, and freebooting criminals who roamed the Neutral Ground. The detachments of British soldiers defending the King's Bridge lived in encampments near it. To get their lumber for their barracks and other buildings they tore planks from local farmers' barns and outbuildings. Major Andreas Emmerick, a German, led a troop of irregular cavalry similar to DeLancey's, in the King's Bridge area. Chaotic places produce wild people, and Emmerick was one to match DeLancey. He had a gunpowder-blackened face and he generally inspired dread. In a leather-lined pocket he carried snuff that he frequently administered to himself. He was said to be an excellent shot. Of an uneven disposition, he wept when he ordered that disobedient men be whipped, saying it was only for their own good. He also "made himself agreeable with women," one Neutral Ground person recalled. Emmerick pursued the wife of a Black man named Bull Pete and made her pregnant. Bull Pete said he seduced her by getting her drunk. The boy she gave birth to grew up and was called Loo Pine, after a Mr. Pine, who raised him. As a regular officer of the British Army, Emmerick may have outranked DeLancey, whom he once struck in a quarrel without suffering retaliation.

The Revolutionary War wasn't just a fight between white men in white wigs; many kinds of people, wigged and not, were in it. The British and their Hessian mercenaries traveled with women camp followers who aided in the plundering, pulling dresses off farm wives in the Neutral Ground during foraging expeditions. Native American bands joined up with the Continentals, and Black men served in both armies. One of Washington's French allies estimated that about a quarter of the American army was Black. A man of the Neutral Ground named Palmer owned a slave named Aaron whose enthusiasm for the rebels' cause was so great that he joined a local militia and kept getting into scrapes with the British. As Aaron's fighting reputation grew, it unnerved Palmer, who freed him so the Refugees wouldn't make the connection and take revenge for Aaron's deeds on Aaron's owner.

The British offered freedom to any slaves who came over to their side, an undeniable blow for the rights of humankind; but there was some fine print. The proclamation also said that any Black man captured while fighting for the enemy would be sold, with profits going to his captor. Some of the Blacks in the American army had not been slaves to begin with and, in any case, a policy of selling captured soldiers into slavery would be a violation of accepted practices of war. So the message of freedom was not unmixed.

In *The Spy*, Cooper has a British officer, Colonel Wellmere, challenge a Yankee physician at dinner, "If your cause is freedom, why not set your slaves at liberty?" Editorializing, Cooper then adds that Wellmere's argument "is thought by most of the colonel's countrymen a triumphant answer to a thousand eloquent facts." The physician responds with a restatement of the reasons for the Revolution, pointing out that the British themselves instituted slavery in the colonies and had never objected to it before. He predicts that slavery will pass away with time. Cooper then steps in again to praise the doctor as "prophetic." Slavery had been mostly (but not entirely) phased out in New York State by 1821, when he was writing the book.

Or, as the learned Dr. Samuel Johnson put it, "Why do we hear the loudest *yawps* for liberty from those drivers of negroes?" Neither Cooper nor America ever really came up with an answer, although there must be one.

IN THE NEUTRAL GROUND, the Yankees fielded their own counterparts to DeLancey's Refugees and Emmerick's Chasseurs (light cavalry). Colonel Charles Armand, Marquis de la Rouerie, might be better known today were it not for the Marquis de Lafayette, whom he was similar to but less famous than. Lafayette was nineteen and Armand twenty-six when they entered the war on the American side, and both were noblemen who could self-finance their commands. Armand lived one of those lives of almost unbelievable dash and adventure that seem to be no longer available to human beings. Confining ourselves only to the small fragment of it that occurred in the future Bronx—

Armand led a troop of maybe a hundred cavalry, mostly Frenchmen, that moved around the area. In November 1779, they were quartered in Tarrytown, New York, and on the seventh of that month they set out for the Neutral Ground. They crossed the Bronx River at William's Bridge (today's Gun Hill Road), left a detachment to guard their retreat, and rode down to Oak Point, which is on the East River, just east of Bungay Creek (aka CSO Outfall #WIB-072). In that area, a DeLancey officer, Major Mansfield Bearmore, who had been born on Throgs Neck, led his own group of Refugees. Bearmore stood six feet tall, wore a green uniform trimmed with silver lace, and had a reputation for harsh treatment of Whigs (the political opposite of Tories) in the Neutral Ground.

He was staying at the house of a local Tory when Armand suddenly swept down and captured him and five of his men. Then the bold Frenchman rode back to William's Bridge, recrossed the Bronx River, and returned with his captives to Tarrytown, passing undetected very near a camp of Hessians along the way. The whole army praised this exploit, one of several that Armand pulled off in Westchester County. Because of a skirmish he won against a force of Hessians on Tetard's Hill, in the present-day neighborhood of Kingsbridge Heights, there is now a forty-yard-long dead-end street, Armand Place, named after him. As for what later happened to Armand in the French Revolution (he avoided the guillotine), dozens of books have been written about that.

Another Neutral Ground raider, Colonel Elisha Sheldon, of Connecticut, led a cavalry brigade, the Second Light Dragoons, that had been commissioned by Congress. It was active at times in the Neutral Ground, where it earned a shameful reputation. Locals called a stretch of road along which the British sometimes chased the frantically retreating Sheldon and his men "Sheldon's Race Course." Sheldon's brigade liked to plunder, and the same was said of other Connecticut forces. In the chaos that accompanied Washington's withdrawal, Continental Army soldiers from Connecticut and Massachusetts went on a plundering spree in Westchester County. According to one account, they stole "bags of Feathers and of unmanufactured Wool, the Desks and Tea-tables and Chairs, the Book-cases and Books, the Andirons and brass and copper Kettles, the linen Curtains and Looking-glasses and women's Hats, the Churns and Washtubs, the sets of Sleigh-harness and skips [hives] of Bees . . ." These Yankees did not care which side their victims supported but stole from both alike. One can understand why the locals to whom Rev. Dwight talked along the Boston Road appeared so bleak and traumatized.

In the "Bronx is burning" days of the 1970s, there were borough residents who slept in their clothes so as to be ready to get out fast if their building caught fire. In the Neutral Ground of the 1770s, some citizens did not undress for bed because they feared a raid by Cow Boys or, even worse, Skinners. These pitiless Yankees—Luther Kennicutt was one of the Skinner leaders, Fade Donaldson another—sometimes rousted families out at midnight and strung up the fathers by their necks from tree limbs in the yard to get them to reveal where their money was, or held them down and stripped them and put hot embers from the fireplace on them. During a Skinner raid, a girl named Mary Robbins took her family's gold and silver coins and put them in a mitten and hid it in the turnip pile in the cellar. The raiders ransacked the cellar but did not find the mitten. Sometimes the most rapacious Skinners were close neighbors of their victims. Neutral Ground violence did not spare women, who might suffer "outrages." Several of Emmerick's men robbed a woman named Phoebe Turner, who was able to cut their clothes with scissors during the robbery. When they were identified to their commander, Emmerick had them severely flogged. Three weeks later, Phoebe Turner was found at home hacked to death, and a Black woman in the house was also dead, apparently of fright.

The Bronx has not been rural for more than a century, so it's hard to picture where many of the military clashes, raids, and nighttime alarms took place. A few hints still are out there. When Washington decamped across the Hudson, he left General Heath—he of the Battle at the White Castle—in the Peekskill area with about three thousand men. Early in 1777, Washington ordered Heath to attack Fort Independence, a Harlem River fort that the Americans had built and the British now occupied. Washington had just pulled off the greatest military achievement of his life, crossing the Delaware River overnight from Pennsylvania into New Jersey during a snowstorm on Christmas, surprising a Hessian army quartered at Trenton, and killing or capturing more than eight hundred of the enemy. The victory revived the American cause. Perhaps he was expecting Heath to hit the British with a follow-up haymaker from the north.

But that was never Heath's style. With due circumspection, Heath sent three separate columns of troops down different routes to the vicinity of the fort, where their arrivals coordinated nicely. Then for about a week he looked at the fort and did not much to it. He lacked sufficient cannon, the weather turned nasty, the defenders were stubborn, supplies ran low; therefore, he decided to go back to Peekskill. Washington had told Congress that Heath had taken the fort, and the members were ecstatic. The premature announcement was based on exaggerated reports of a minor first engagement that Heath had won. In Washington's embarrassment and disappointment, he reprimanded Heath, and never gave him a battlefield command again. But what did Washington expect, another Trenton? Leave that kind of masterstroke to visionaries. General Heath, in his own prudent way, had already served well and helped save the army.

Nothing remains of Fort Independence, not even a marker. Its site is also in Kingsbridge Heights, near the Jerome Park Reservoir. There is a Fort Independence Street, but the fort was above it, on what's now Giles Place. A long, sloping street, Cannon Place, is probably the incline up which the cannon were hauled. Near the top, just below the intersection of Giles and Cannon Places, you look down through a chain-link fence onto a dark, rocky cliff too steep to build on. A few spindly maples and ash trees grow from the cliff face. The nearby surroundings are residential, with a nursing home called the Citadel, on Giles Place, flanked by small brick houses. But the cliff itself remains undomesticated. From the bottom of it, on Fort Independence Street, it appears even more formidable. Among the scrubby trees and brush are unretrievable plastic bags of trash that people have managed to toss over the fence. I can imagine General Heath looking up at the fort atop that cliff and saying to himself, in effect, "No way."

RAIDS FOLLOWED RAIDS in retaliation for previous raids. Mounted units ran into each other on dark country lanes and men sometimes died from friendly fire. In a raid below DeLancey's Mills, a troop of American cavalry called Stephenson's Rangers captured James DeLancey himself hiding under a bed. Lieutenant Frederick Stephenson, their leader, said, "Come out, Jimmy!" The Refugee chief, "overcome with vexation, confusion, and shame," rode to his captivity in Connecticut on his own horse. He was quickly given his parole, however, and did not let himself suffer such a mortifying experience again. Release on parole meant he had promised not to return to arms, but he soon did. Many of the later raids from American lines had the specific purpose of catching Colonel DeLancey. Washington himself made it a priority in orders to Continentals who were active in the region. There were close calls. DeLancey was said to have escaped once by hiding in a pigpen, and another time in an outhouse.

For cavalry combatants, the weapon of choice was the broadsword. Muskets with bayonets proved cumbersome on horseback, and tricky to reload, as were pistols. When bands of cavalry fought each other, they drew their broadswords and hacked away. From a distance the clanging of swords against swords sounded like blacksmiths hammering, earwitnesses said. Maybe the metal-on-metal banging and clanging that echo in Bronx buildings under construction today sounds like a cavalry fight.

The weapons caused dreadful wounds. A McDonald interviewee described a man wounded by Refugee broadswords who "wandered about with his head so cut up . . . that his brains could be seen to work." Even more wondrous, the informant continued, a Dr. Belcher dressed this man's injuries and he survived. Dr. James Thacher, a Philadelphia doctor serving with the Continental Army, received permission from the British to travel with another doctor behind their lines in the Neutral Ground to treat a captured American soldier. The prisoner was being held in Westchester village, and after caring for him, the doctors had dinner in a tavern with "the much-famed Col. DeLancey, who commands the refugee corps, & his officers."

Upon crossing back to their own side, Dr. Thacher and his companion learned that DeLancey's men had just caught and killed five Continental soldiers who had stolen cattle from them. The victims had been brought in:

> We saw four dead bodies, mangled in a most inhuman manner by the refugees, and among them one groaning under five wounds on his head, two of them quite through his skull-bone

with a broad sword. This man was able to give an account of the murderer [*sic*] of his four companions. They surrendered, and begged for life; but their entreaties were disregarded, and the swords of their cruel foes were plunged into their bodies so long as signs of life remained.

The quote comes from the memoir entitled *The American Revolution from the Commencement to the Disbanding of the American Army; Given in the Form of a Daily Journal, With the Exact Dates of All the Important Events; Also, a Biographical Sketch of All the Most Important Generals*, by James Thacher, MD. (He is the source of the low opinion of General Heath quoted in chapter 6.) Thacher served throughout the war, marched with the soldiers, wore rags, and went cold and hungry with the men he treated in the winter camps. I read the book with admiration for its clarity, not to mention for what the author had endured. At the end of the book, in an appendix, Thacher tells an irrelevant racist story with great relish and amusement. Nothing about the story would have been unusual for its context or time. It's even kind of a funny story, but not at all in the way that Thacher sees it. The story reminded me of the ongoing past that is also the present.

9

IN MY BRONX EXPLORATIONS I spent some time looking for a place called Indian Field. A fight between British cavalry and Native American troops serving in the Continental Army took place on August 31, 1778, at what's now called Indian Field, and at least eighteen of the Indians were killed. Given the circumstances of the fight, and who was in it, I think of its outcome as more of a massacre. Afterward, the bodies of the Indians were left on the field and later buried there. The field is in Van Cortlandt Park, in the northern Bronx. The reason it's not so easy to find is that highways have cut through the park like broadswords through a skull-bone and made the original landscape more complicated and harder to read.

At first, I tried to get to Indian Field by walking in the park, but the highways defeated me. Finally I reached it by taking a number 4 train to Woodlawn, the last stop, then walking north on Jerome Avenue to 233rd Street and turning right. This is a busy intersection, because exit and entry ramps for the Major Deegan Expressway (Interstate 87) connect directly to it. Traffic sometimes backs up here, honking, which gives me a special feeling, knowing that the construction coordinator himself, Robert Moses (1888–1981), is interred in a columbarium—a wall of mausoleum spaces—just a softball-toss away, in the northwest corner of Woodlawn Cemetery. If he can hear the honking, his wife, Mary A. Moses (1916–1993), can, too, which seems less fair. Indian Field is near that intersection, across 233rd Street from the cemetery. The Parks Department has several signs identifying or referring to it, and there's a stone-and-mortar monument, recently repaired, that was put up in 1906 by the Bronx chapter of the Daughters of the American Revolution.

According to the monument, Chief Nimham and seventeen other Stockbridge Indians died here in the cause of liberty. The inscription does not add that they were Mohican Indians from that Massachusetts town. In the previous century, the Mohicans had lived along the Hudson River and raided in New Netherland; but by 1778 they were not only Christians, but New England Congregationalists. Jonathan Edwards himself had been their minister and missionary. Upbeat as always, he had informed the converts that, having learned about Jesus, they would now suffer more in hell for sins they committed than would the unconverted Indians who still knew nothing about the Christian God.

The Mohicans had bought the whole Congregational New England package. They joined the war at the beginning partly because of their neighbors' enthusiasm for it, and lost two men at Bunker Hill, the victims of friendly fire. In an attempt to get Canadian Indians to support the Americans, a group of the Stockbridge Mohicans had traveled to Montreal, where the authorities locked them up and then decided to hang them for spreading sedition. The Mohicans were spared and released because of the intervention of Canadian Indians of the Caughnawaga tribe, who had been the Mohicans' classmates at Dartmouth.

HERE AT INDIAN FIELD, the Mohican troops came up against two of the cleverest and cruelest cavalry officers in the British Army. One was Lieutenant Colonel Banastre Tarleton, who would nearly capture Thomas Jefferson at Monticello later in the war. The other, Lieutenant Colonel John Graves Simcoe (he of the low opinion of Washington, quoted earlier), wrote a book, *A Journal of the Operations of the Queen's*

Rangers, from the End of the Year 1777, to the Conclusion of the Late American War. It describes this bloody Neutral Ground encounter.

Simcoe was highly ambitious and often lobbied his superiors for better commands. He had big ideas, such as going into the interior, raising regiments of Indian allies, and attacking the Americans from there, thus opening another front in the war. (The higher-ups said no.) Simcoe detested "the rebels" as much as Captain William Evelyn had. His persistence paid off when he was given command of the Queen's Rangers, a prestigious cavalry and infantry unit that he dressed in green; Simcoe was that rare Britisher, apparently, who saw the advantage of not wearing red uniforms in forest combat. In the French and Indian War, about twenty years earlier, this same unit had been commanded by Colonel Robert Rodgers, and some of the Stockbridge Indians had served with it as scouts.

The Queen's Rangers operated in the area for about a year, fighting American troops and partisans and terrorizing the populace. Lieutenant Colonel Simcoe may have been a pyromaniac. He burned houses and farms owned by suspected Whigs in the Neutral Ground. No other commander was as hated by the locals. The best that could be said of the Queen's Rangers was that they burned but did not loot; rather, they sat on their horses and let DeLancey's men do the looting. Once, having raided in and around Bedford, New York, a town where every house except one was burned, Simcoe stopped in the nearby village of Harrison and asked a housewife for a bowl so he could drink from her well. She replied, "Good-for-nothing cruel fellows like you who go about burning people's houses ought to drink like cattle out of the brook on all fours! Away with you!" Seeing her husband nearby, Simcoe ordered him taken prisoner. To the wife, he said, "Now, termagant, I've got your husband!" On the way back to British lines, one of the guides, who knew the captive, persuaded Simcoe to let him go. Before Simcoe agreed, he told him to curb his wife's tongue. (This story is in a local history, not Simcoe's book.)

Setting ambushes in the Neutral Ground and avoiding being ambushed yourself filled the imaginations of cavalrymen on both sides. The game required psychology, because your own eagerness or overconfidence could destroy you, causing you to rush into tight spots without looking. A clever enemy could even establish in your mind the preconditions for your falling into ambush. That's what Simcoe and Tarleton did to the Stockbridge Indians.

The Indians fought differently than regular soldiers. When the Stockbridges first joined the cause, they told the Continental officers they weren't going to do drills or march; instead, they asked, "Only point out to me where your enemies keep, and that is all I shall want to know." They liked to taunt their foes and challenge them. In the fighting in Boston, they shouted insults at the British (like their fellow New Englanders, the Stockbridges spoke English), and turned their buttocks toward them and mooned them (though that word did not yet exist). The sight of cowardice excited their greatest derision.

One day Simcoe and Tarleton were on a reconnaissance with a few of their men when Simcoe pointed out a road through the Devou (or Deveau) farm, just east of the present intersection of 233rd Street and Jerome Avenue. His orderly dismounted and took down the fence rails so they could ride through. Then for some reason the party changed their minds and went a different way. They did not see that about sixty Indians lay in ambush around the farm. Through the British forces' spy network, Simcoe and Tarleton later found this out. They reasoned that the Indians, who were excellent shots, had not opened fire because they were waiting for them to ride farther through the fence, to where they could be surrounded. The prospect of making prisoners of two such important officers had held the Indians back and saved the officers' lives. Simcoe filed away in his mind the closeness of this call. He guessed that the Indians were tantalized by it and hoped for better luck next time.

The other key piece of the psychological ambush fell to Simcoe by chance. Colonel Emmerick's force of Loyalists, while patrolling north of today's Van Cortlandt Park, came upon a group of Indians and, thinking they were part of a larger Continental force (which they weren't), made a quick and headlong retreat with the Indians in pursuit. Again through spies, Simcoe learned that the Indians were elated by the apparent rout. Now the elements necessary for a successful ambush had been planted in the Stockbridges' minds: They had come within an ace of capturing two of the most important British officers, and they had seen for themselves the presumed cowardice of the enemy.

On August 31, Simcoe put his men in ambush near the Devou farm. They brought enough rations to last them all day and prepared to wait. Simcoe doesn't say that he used Emmerick's forces for bait, but that's the effect they had. Marching ahead, Emmerick ran up against a combined unit of forty or fifty patriot militia and about sixty Indians, then withdrew to where the ambush was waiting, while they pressed him. The skirmish got hotter and most of the militia abandoned the Indians and ran away.

Simcoe's forces then moved up, and the Indians were so intent on fighting Emmerick that they didn't see Simcoe and his men until they'd come within ten yards. Daniel Nimham, the Stockbridge chief, turned and fired at Simcoe, wounding him. Suddenly, Tarleton's cavalry, the other hinge of the trap, arrived. The Indians now had enemy horsemen all around. Tarleton swung at an Indian with his broadsword so hard that he (Tarleton) toppled from his horse. The Indian, having already fired his musket, could not shoot him, but easily could have bayonetted him, if only the Indians had used bayonets. Tarleton's orderly rescued him by shooting the Indian. Daniel Nimham told his comrades to run and save themselves. Overwhelmed, he was hacked to death, along with his son Abraham Nimham, as many as forty other Indians, and several militiamen.

In describing the fight Simcoe sets aside his usual tone of contempt. He says the Indians fought hard and bravely to the end; he might as well be praising the stubborn fight put up by a splendid fish he caught. Had the Indians' original ambush gone as planned—had they caught Tarleton and Simcoe—the officers would have been exchanged for Americans of equal rank, or for many regular soldiers. The following year, while fighting in New Jersey, Simcoe fell into an ambush at another place where fence rails had been taken down. He could have been killed, but instead was made a prisoner and exchanged. Apparently, an option like that did not exist for Indian soldiers. Tarleton and Simcoe gave the Indians no quarter and left the hacked-up bodies where they fell.

A few of the survivors of Nimham's men continued to serve with the Continental Army. Some of them guided the expedition of General John Sullivan when he pushed into western New York State and destroyed the cornfields and villages of Iroquois who had sided with the British. Sullivan had to issue a special order forbidding his troops from insulting and ridiculing the Indians who were guiding them. Washington said—rather ungratefully about men who had backed the Americans' cause from the beginning, when it appeared to be far from a sure thing—that Indian troops weren't worth the expense. The surviving Stockbridge Indians returned to their Massachusetts holdings, which had shrunk to almost nothing in the shark tank of land-hungry New Englanders. Even Jonathan Edwards, in his time, had managed to get around provincial laws and acquire parcels of his parishioners' land. The Mohicans of Stockbridge eventually moved west, and today they share a reservation with the Munsee tribe near Green Bay, Wisconsin. If you go by Indian Field in Van Cortlandt Park on a sunny summer day, you will find people sunbathing.

HOW THE MORRISES in exile, Lewis and Gouverneur, felt about having James DeLancey and the rest of the Refugees occupying their land can be imagined. War and its horrors careened through Morrisania, in the future South Bronx, bringing fire and broadsword. Raiders from "above"—the shorthand for northern Westchester County, where the American forces were—sometimes descended on the Refugee huts along the Mill Brook and burned them by the score. Pestilence came in the form of a sickness known as Morrisania fever that carried off many of DeLancey's men. Gouverneur worried about his mother, who was ill with dropsy, which is what edema (swelling caused by excess fluid) used to be called. He asked the British for a pass through their lines so he could visit her. After his fellow patriots criticized him for requesting this favor, he changed his mind and decided not to go. He wrote to her, "I would it were in my power to solace and comfort your declining years. The duty I owe to a tender parent demands this of me; but a higher duty has bound me to the service of my fellow creatures."

New York elected him to the Continental Congress in 1777, even though he did not reside in the family home. For most of the war he lived in Philadelphia. Bills that Washington wanted the Continental Congress to pass found a champion in Morris. To keep up morale in the army, which was too often in danger of quitting and going home, Morris got the pay for all soldiers raised to the higher level previously given only to the soldiers of New England. Washington also wanted all officers to receive a pension of half-pay for life. Morris persuaded Congress to go along, but it limited the term of payment to seven years. He visited the troops under General Philip Schuyler who were opposing General Burgoyne as he moved southward through New York State along the Hudson River trying to cut the thirteen states in half. After Morris's visit, General Horatio Gates replaced Schuyler and defeated General Burgoyne at the Battle of Saratoga, in October 1777. History does not record whether Washington felt satisfaction at the capture of General Burgoyne, the soldier-dramaturge who had written a comedy about him.

In the winter of 1777–1778, Morris was part of a committee of five members of Congress who went to Valley Forge to meet with Washington about reorganizing the army. The condition of the soldiers distressed him, and he succeeded in improving their supplies. New York did not reelect him to Congress in 1779. The criticism of him was that he cared more about the new nation than about New York. Morris ran the army's commissary, quartermaster, and medical departments, and he helped the financier Robert Morris (no relation) manage the money for the army and the Congress. Through their ingenuity they somehow kept the young government funded during lean times. Alexander Hamilton later said that between them, Gouverneur Morris and Robert Morris won the war.

Society in Philadelphia entertained Gouverneur, and vice versa. The city offered the most refined and cosmopolitan company in the thirteen states. Morris usually had friends he could visit of an evening, and women to pay attention to. For some reason, according to Theodore Roosevelt, who wrote a biography of him, Morris did not like his coachman to stand by the heads of his horses when he got into his carriage. On May 14, 1780, he planned to leave the city for a week or ten days in the country. His phaeton, a type of light two-seater, was waiting, harnessed to two spirited grays. The coachman did not have the horses' heads and they weren't tethered. As Morris got in, they shied, his left leg became caught in the spokes of a turning wheel, and it shattered his shin and ankle. While removing his stocking to examine the injury he saw that he had put the stocking on inside out. A superstition said that putting on one stocking inside out brought good luck. For the rest of his life he knew that wasn't true.

His regular doctor had left town, and the one he went to said that the leg would have to be amputated. Later his regular doctor said amputation hadn't been necessary. After the operation, Morris spent months recuperating at the Philadelphia home of George Plater, a congressman from Maryland. Morris had a passion for Plater's wife, Elizabeth, but she discouraged his attentions. After he recovered, he wore a wooden leg that strapped to the stump below the knee. His last wooden leg hangs on the wall of the New-York Historical Society, on Central Park West, and you see it almost first thing when you come into the building. Stephen Jenkins, the dean of Bronx historians, whose indispensable *The Story of the Bronx* came out in 1912, wrote that the floors of the Morrisania manor house still bore the marks of Morris's wooden leg. The house was torn down in 1905, so one can assume that Jenkins must have seen the marks himself.

THE CAPTURE OF Major John André happened in the northern Neutral Ground, near Tarrytown. He had been General Benedict Arnold's contact in the British Army as Arnold negotiated to betray the American fortress at West Point. After the treason was discovered, Arnold escaped by getting local people to row him to a British warship that was waiting in the Hudson River, but André had to make his way back to the British lines by land. He disguised himself in civilian clothes and was riding alone when he met members of a New York militia. In the course of conversation, he mistook them for British, and that was how they caught him. They searched him, found incriminating papers, and took him to their superior officer, whom he nearly persuaded to let him go.

An interesting detail about this story is that the New York militiamen apparently did not give themselves away as Americans by their accents. They must not have talked so differently from André that he could identify them as the enemy by their speech. On other occasions, British and American soldiers, upon meeting in the Neutral Ground, talked amiably before discovering that they were not on the same side. And Washington spelled the name of the river "Brunx," probably writing it as he pronounced it. Simcoe also wrote the name as "Brunx." British people I know still pronounce the name of the borough that way, and not "Brahnx," as Americans do.

I take all this as evidence that antagonists on both sides in the Revolutionary War spoke with what would sound to us today like British accents. At least in this part of the country, no distinct regional accent had evolved among people of British descent. It slightly alters my image of Washington and other founders to think of them as talking like educated Brits or maybe English-speaking Canadians. The American accent must have been changing, though. Abraham Lincoln, I'm sure, did not have a British accent.

Everybody liked Major André, and nobody wanted to hang him, but the Americans had no choice. The British reacted with outrage when they heard of his sentence, and the Americans said they would willingly exchange him for Arnold, which the British wouldn't do. Sympathy for the charming young officer, and a fervent desire to hang Arnold, caused the Americans to come up with a scheme for snatching the traitor. They had a spy in place in Arnold's retinue who might have helped them pull it off, given time. Had they captured Arnold, they would have pardoned and released André. But André admitted his deeds and put up no defense, so his trial ended quickly, and the Americans could only go ahead with the hanging, and the kidnap scheme did not pan out anyway.

FIRE AND BROADSWORD brought pestilence, and more fire: Many of the residents of the Neutral Ground abandoned their homes, and few of those who remained continued to farm. Hay and weeds grew untended in the fields. In the orchards, apples by the bushel lay rotting on the ground. Bridges across creeks were broken down, grass took over the roads and trails. A Westchester County committee assessing damages after the war found that 350,000 fence rails had gone for firewood. Soldiers also dismantled the stone walls in the fields. When enemies were near, they sometimes took stone walls apart and hid in them. A nighttime raid burned the DeLancey blockhouse on the Bronx River near the family's mills. (Aaron Burr, the leader of the raid, would later kill Alexander Hamilton.) Fade Donaldson, the "notorious Skinner," hanged Brom Barrett, a DeLancey man, in retaliation for the hanging of Tim Knapp, and someone hanged Fade Donaldson (presumably at the order of DeLancey) for the hanging of Barrett. From one year to the next, violence and disorder ruled the Neutral Ground.

Colonel Christopher Greene, a native Rhode Islander, commanded an American regiment of Black soldiers from that state. Rhode Island had said it would buy the freedom of any slave who joined the army and served for the duration of the war. The regiment fought with distinction at the Battle of Red Bank, in New Jersey, and took pride in its accomplishments. Stationed near the Croton River, at the Neutral Ground's northern edge, Greene and his Rhode Islanders could strike at Refugee hideouts in the present South Bronx. One winter night he led a group that surprised some DeLancey men in a cabin on a bluff above the Harlem River. Greene sneaked up, burst through a window, and took five men captive, unfortunately not including the main target, DeLancey. Washington wanted Greene to capture DeLancey as a priority. The Refugee leader had plenty of reason to fear Colonel Greene and wish him dead.

Two cousins from the Totten family of North Castle, James Totten and Captain Gilbert Totten, had joined the Refugees. James was said to be worse than Gilbert, but both were bad. In April 1781, Captain Gilbert Totten rode north beyond the Croton River under a white flag of truce. Colonel Greene did not think Totten had any legitimate purpose for being there and ordered him brought in under suspicion of spying. Totten took exception to his treatment, and especially to being placed under a guard of Blacks. After questioning him closely, Greene let him go. When Totten left, he said, "Colonel Greene shall before long repent the treatment I have this day received." He promised that the next flag he arrived under would not be white, but bloody, "and after that *niggers will be scarce!*"

His desire to revenge his supposed honor dovetailed with DeLancey's interest in getting rid of Greene. In May, part of Greene's regiment was camped on the north side of the Croton River at Blenis's Ford, where there was a bridge. Greene and other officers of the regiment had found quarters at the nearby house of a family named Davenport. On the night of May 12, sitting by the fire, Colonel Greene told Richardson Davenport, the father, that next year he hoped to be back in Rhode Island with his family.

That same night, James DeLancey, Gilbert Totten, and about 160 Refugee cavalry rode north from Morrisania and reached the south side of the Croton River before dawn without attracting the attention of American sentries. Through spies, DeLancey knew that the guards posted at the bridge went back to camp at daylight. As soon as they did, on the morning of May 13, the Refugees rode across the bridge, approached the Davenport house, surrounded it, and called for the officers within to surrender. A young lieutenant in the bedroom where the officers slept always kept two loaded pistols close at hand, and he used this opportunity to leap to the window and fire at the attackers, who then yelled, "Kill! Kill! No quarter!" Colonel Greene said to the impetuous junior officer, "You've undone us! We must sell our lives as dearly as we can." Still clad in nothing but underclothes, he and the lieutenant and Major Ebenezer Flagg, the other officer in the room, grabbed their broadswords. Gilbert Totten and other Refugees stormed the house and smashed in the bedroom door with stones.

Greene slashed at Totten with his sword, another DeLancey man parried the blow, and another shot Greene, badly wounding him. He suffered broadsword cuts as well. Major Flagg and the lieutenant were killed. Outside the house, DeLancey men chased down and butchered the Black Rhode Islanders. At the regiment's main camp about two miles away, the Refugees demanded that the Black troops surrender, and their officer told the troops to put down their arms and comply. Some of them chose to go out fighting. They fired at the DeLancey men, hitting Gilbert Totten in the toe. The horsemen then overran the camp and chased down and killed those who fled. A local woman later said, "The negroes were cut up unmercifully."

Colonel DeLancey, who usually sent people out on raids but did not go on them himself, hung back from the action. After Greene had been taken out and put on his horse to ride back as a prisoner to Morrisania—his request of parole having been refused—DeLancey found a letter from Washington in Greene's papers ordering Greene "to take Colonel Delancey at all events." A woman who saw Greene with his captors begged to tend Greene's wounds, but Totten told her that Greene had merely suffered a scratch. Not long after setting out Greene fell off his horse, and he was left by the side of the road.

Washington received the information about the attack and wrote in his diary, referring to the death of Greene and the others, "Several of our soldiers [were] inhumanly murdered." The story of Greene lying hacked-up, shot, and bleeding to death in his underwear among the whortleberry bushes by the Crompond road shocked the residents of Westchester County and stayed in local memory for a long time. The reports of casualties from the raid varied. General Heath, in his memoirs, said the Continentals lost Colonel Greene, Major Flagg, two other officers, and twenty-seven men, with others wounded. He does not add that Major Morrell, an officer of the command, escaped his comrades' fate because he happened to be spending that night at the house of a Mrs. Remsen. The officers, Colonel Greene and Major Flagg, were buried in the cemetery of the Presbyterian church in the town of Crompond. Colonel Greene's widow came to the ceremony. In 1982, 201 years later, Black civic leaders led a successful effort to erect a monument to the Black Rhode Islanders in the cemetery.

THIS SECOND HIGH-CASUALTY FIGHT was the last of its kind in the struggles over the Neutral Ground. At the Indian Field ambush, Native American soldiers took the cruelest hit, and at the raid above the Croton, the enemy's broadsword-chopping frenzy came down hardest on troops who were Black. For white soldiers, the war held more lenient standards of mercy. Officers usually could count on humane treatment if they were captured, and they were eligible to be exchanged. (The masses of regular soldiers, if captured, ended up in disease-ridden prisons, and generally weren't exchanged.) But troops who weren't white had small protection from the war's full brutality. Their situation was binary: win and live, lose and die. By taking command of Black troops Colonel Greene joined their category.

On the Fourth of July one year, I happened to walk by the spot where DeLancey's Mills had stood. A small park now takes up a section of riverbank by the waterfall on the DeLancey side. On the other side of the river, there used to be a 150-foot-tall white pine tree called the DeLancey Pine. Sharpshooters hid in its upper branches during the war. Somebody even wrote a poem about it, part of which goes:

Memorial of the fallen great,
The rich and honored line
Stands high in solitary state
DeLancey's ancient pine.

Near where the pine used to be there's now a tall radio tower that has some connection to a fire department communications network. In the park, Spanish-speaking people, some dressed in stars-and-stripes outfits for the holiday, were setting up barbecues. Families have kid birthday parties here, and as I was standing by a railing and looking at the falls and the radio tower, two men carrying a folding table with a purple plastic tablecloth approached. One of them said, "Hey, Papito, would you mind moving?" I got out of the way, and they positioned the table next to the railing, to which purple "Happy Birthday" cut-out letters had already been masking-taped.

I moved along the path next to the falls. The water came over the dam in sheaves, some of them translucent like thick glass, some a darker, almost olive color, back within the flow and curtained from the sunlight. The falling continued unstoppably, with a white-noise rushing, and it raised a misty spray and a spreading foam of bubbles where it hit the pool below. For centuries that fall of water was made to pull its weight, moving paddle wheels that turned shafts that drove millstones that ground wheat. Now for a century or more the river has been unemployed, and it flows at liberty, its power unneeded and unused. The water once ran the mill that brought prosperity to the DeLancey family. These falls were once the hydraulic origin of James DeLancey's power.

10

ENTER the French.

When the government of France decided to back the American Revolution not only with ships, supplies, and money, but with troops on the ground, the war began a more festive phase. The decision, ultimately on the part of Louis XVI, had more romance and high ideals to it than good sense. The expense of the war, along with the money his treasury loaned to the Americans, which they did not pay back until it was too late to do Louis any good, eventually helped to bring on his own downfall. He might have been better advised to tend to his own country first. But Lafayette, from whom he had originally withheld permission even to go to America, persuaded him that the Americans' cause was not only that of France, but of all humankind. The arrival of French soldiers in 1781 made the war more dashing and fun, in contrast to the British, with their smarminess, treachery, and compulsive bayonetting and broadswording.

The sequence of events that brought the French here had an extra satisfactory element, too, because the defeat of General John Burgoyne, the warrior-playwright, at the Battle of Saratoga helped persuade the French that the Americans could win. The British, seeing that the war had begun to go badly, sent a proposal to Congress aimed at reaching a compromise and ending it. The missive came in a package with triple seals with an image of a loving mother embracing her returning children. Gouverneur Morris told his fellow representatives that the British would never keep faith with men they considered rebels, and that the only way forward was to full independence. He wrote the haughty reply that Congress sent rejecting the proposal. By then the Americans had also received a letter from the French recognizing the "Independent States" as a sovereign country, and that gave them confidence.

Human events are seldom unconfusing, but eventually when they get shaken out you can see the right and wrong of them. In helping the Revolution, the French enjoyed the advantage of being on the right side, and they contributed intrepidity combined with a certain fabulous silliness. To begin with, they sported more interesting facial hair. A French cavalry commander, Armond Louis de Gontaut, Duc de Lauzun, later known as the Duc de Biron, whom the Americans called de Lauzun, told the locals, "The women of this country don't like my whiskers—I can't get along with them—but I can't cut them off." He led Lauzun's Legion, a cavalry and infantry command of some twelve hundred men. After his death, some of his admirers in Paris circulated copies of his handwritten memoirs, which were considered so scandalous that Napoleon ordered them burned and saw to the burning personally. A copy or two escaped the flames and eventually came out in print, and today they also exist in English, in a translation by C. K. Scott Moncrief, better known as a translator of Proust. In just the first few chapters, de Lauzun describes five or six torrid love affairs he had before he departed for America. Marie Antoinette is so crazy about him, in his telling, that she weeps when he goes off to war.

The French liked to dance; American ladies, when they were old and gray, remembered dancing with men who later became heroes of the French Republic, the conquerors of Europe. The French also wore fancy uniforms and weren't afraid of colors that even Washington, the fashion plate, wouldn't try. Some French troops wore white coats with pink collars, crimson lapels, and white buttons. Others had blue uniforms with yellow collars and yellow lapels, while artillerymen's coats were gray with lapels of red velvet. Officers could be picked out by the white, green, and red plumes on their hats. Many American troops marched and fought with no uniforms at all. A French officer later wrote that at a combined review of the forces he got his first look at the American army:

> I was struck, not by its smart appearance, but by its destitution: the men were without uniforms and covered with rags; most of them were barefoot. They were of all sizes, down to children who could not have been over fourteen. There were many negroes, mulattoes, etc. Only their artillerymen were wearing uniforms.

Jean-Baptiste Donatien de Vimeur, Comte de Rochambeau, commanded the French forces. In de Lauzun's memoirs General Rochambeau is described as so in love with military matters that he talked of nothing else and used whatever came to hand—the table, your snuffbox—in explaining one maneuver or another. He disembarked with five thousand troops at Newport, Rhode Island, and marched down to Connecticut, meeting up for a grand strategy session with Washington in Hartford. The American commander wanted to apply their combined armies to retaking New York City, his dream. Rochambeau argued against it. By this time, the British, having given up on trying to cut New England off from the rest of the states, were trying to cut off the South. The main British force under General Cornwallis had moved to Virginia, where it had established itself on the Yorktown Peninsula. Rochambeau convinced Washington that Cornwallis was the easier target. First, however, they would make a large-scale feint against the city to frighten General Sir Henry Clinton, the cautious British commander (by then the Howe brothers had been recalled), so that he would keep his forces in New York and not send reinforcements to Cornwallis.

This decision began a series of moves known as the Grand Reconnaissance, the last large-scale military maneuver to take place in what's now the Bronx. Essentially, it was a sweep of the Neutral Ground from the American lines southward to the Harlem River, the Bronx Kill, and the Sound. The only area from which the Americans and French kept a safe distance was around the King's Bridge, where the British had outposts guarded by the cannon of their Fort Number 8, a major defensive work whose outlines can still be seen in a lawn on the campus of Bronx Community College. In July 1781, American and French forces skirmished with the British near Fort Independence, which the latter had abandoned by then. By July 19, the combined French and American armies arrived in strength. Washington and Rochambeau crossed the Hudson River to New Jersey to see what the Manhattan defenses looked like from there. Then they returned to the New York side, and on the night of the twenty-first they began to march south through the Neutral Ground.

American infantry took the right flank, along the Hudson. French and American forces came down the middle; Washington and Rochambeau proceeded along the ridge that the Grand Concourse is now on. French cavalry under de Lauzun, and Americans commanded by Sheldon and Waterbury, rode the left flank along the Bronx River. The display upset Clinton, the British general, just as intended. "Nothing, certainly, could be more alarming as well as mortifying than my situation at the present crisis," General Clinton wrote in a letter. He noted that the enemy was "parading on the heights on my front," and he could do nothing about it, for lack of troops. Instead of sending reinforcements to Cornwallis, Clinton ended up asking for reinforcements from him.

As Washington, Rochambeau, their aides, and a small escort of cavalry came to the southern part of Morrisania, they surprised about twenty DeLancey men. Louis-Alexandre Berthier, a twenty-eight-year-old officer, and others of the French and Americans chased them to a house where the Tories took cover and began shooting back. The two generals stayed in the rear but close enough to watch. The besiegers called on the men in the house to surrender. They agreed to come out, but when they did, the sight of a larger force across the river (probably the Bronx Kill) ready to support them with cannon inspired them to turn and attack the Americans and French. A DeLancey man pointed his pistols at Berthier and shouted, "Prisoner!" When Berthier did not surrender, he fired one pistol at five paces, grazing Berthier's ear. Then he shouted, "Die, you dog of a Frenchman!" and raised the other. Berthier produced a pistol of his own and shot the

Tory through the chest. Another of Rochambeau's young aides, Baron Ludwig von Closen, lost his hat to a branch when he rode into an orchard in pursuit of a DeLancey man. With bullets flying around him, von Closen dismounted to pick it up.

His fellow officers disappeared, the action having moved elsewhere. Soon the skirmish concluded with two DeLancey men dead, one mortally wounded, and six captured. By the time von Closen rejoined the generals, the other aides and cavalry were back already. Everybody in the generals' escort had been accounted for except him, and all were happy to see von Closen alive. His fellows made a French joke, impossible to understand today, whose punchline was "Oh! He lost his hat there!" Von Closen later wrote:

> When I recounted the incident, I was laughed at for my heedless and excessive pride. The Generals even reproached me for it, and the good-natured Washington, slapping my shoulder, added, *"Dear Baron, this French proverb is not yet known among our army; but your cold behavior during the danger will be it."* [italics *sic*]

The incident deserves notice because whether or not that was a witty remark—without more context we can't tell—it seems out of character. Washington did not often joke, much less slap people on the shoulder. In the aftermath of the skirmish, both generals and men of the escort all must have been miles high on adrenaline and war. They had just killed three of the enemy while suffering no casualties themselves, and the horse of one of the aides had been blasted by a cannonball that left the rider untouched. The generals usually didn't see action that close up. It must have been a rush for everybody, the kind that makes people love war. I figure the skirmish happened near where the Third Avenue and 138th Street subway stop in Mott Haven is now.

Meanwhile, the eastern arm of the advance was pushing other Tory riders south. The women and children of West Farms had fled to Manhattan by ferry, and the DeLancey men were retreating, trying to outrun the enemy, hide in the woods, or turn and fight if given opportunity. Andrew Corsa, a local boy who was only fifteen at the time, told the interviewer John M. McDonald, when Corsa was eighty-nine, about guiding the combined French and American troops. The cavalry he was with scared up some DeLancey men and took off after them. Corsa said, "We had a fine chase in the fields where there were no enclosures, as the fences had all been burnt up."

The DeLancey men kept riding, headed toward land's end—the edge of "the continent." Sometimes I walk the route they might have taken. It goes near Westchester Square, past the site of the White Castle battle, and along where the causeway once led through the marshy parts of Throgs Neck (now, of course, no longer marshy). Then it follows the slightly higher ground occupied by the easternmost part of Tremont Avenue. The neighborhoods here are mostly composed of single-family homes with small front yards and SUVs parked in the driveways. All of Throgs Neck and Ferry Point, just to the west, lies within New York's 14th Congressional District, whose representative is Alexandria Ocasio-Cortez. At the end of Tremont, the DeLancey men might have turned eastward, along a smaller byway now called Pennyfield Avenue, which runs farther out Throgs Neck.

If they took this route, they then had water on two sides, and no way back, because the peninsula here is so narrow that their pursuers could block it off entirely. Once, on this walk, I stopped to talk to a man named Anthony Perretti, who was in front of his house at the corner of Pennyfield Avenue and Alan Place, where the neck is no more than eighty yards wide. Perretti told me that during hurricanes, of which his family had seen a few during the three generations they'd lived there, the water sometimes overtopped the land and flowed in a tidal rip running chest-deep along his street.

Pennyfield Avenue concludes at the entrance to the State University of New York Maritime College, whose campus extends for another three-quarters of a mile to the end of the peninsula. Probably the DeLancey men's horses were lathered, hot, and almost spent by the time they got here. Today the Throgs Neck Bridge stretches above the peninsula's end like the skeleton of a long-necked dinosaur, and its concrete support columns stand like legs among the school's buildings and parking lots. The bridge swoops across, but the peninsula ends abruptly. There is a brief rip-rap shoreline, a low retaining wall, a salt-spray-challenged lawn, a bench or two. I imagine the DeLancey men, here at the end of the continent, waiting as long as they dared and letting their horses blow and cool down. Then, maybe at the very last minute, as the American and French cavalry came galloping into sight, the Tories remounted, turned their horses' heads toward the water, spurred hard, splashed in, and began swimming to Queens.

Or Long Island, as it was called in the old-time accounts of this escape. By my calculation, the distance across is about two thirds of a mile. In July the water would not have been terribly cold, but it's part of the ocean, it sometimes has big waves, and the land the horses were swimming toward appears to be quite far away. Samuel Oakley, the nephew of a famous Neutral Ground guide, told John M. McDonald, "All went over safe, though one or two of the horses came near going down by the head. The troopers were directed to sit back upon the haunches, and the horses then kept their heads more easily above water. Their number was about forty, and they crossed from the Point."

If by "from the Point" Oakley meant they crossed from what's still called Ferry Point, then they didn't swim from the end of Throgs Neck, but from the broader peninsula just to the west, where the ex-Trump golf course at Ferry Point is now. The distance from there to the Queens/Long Island side is about the same as from Throgs Neck. American accounts say not all the Tories got away, but some were captured, along with their horses, and the cattle and sheep they had with them. If the Bronx is a place in between, a junction zone where islands attach to the mainland, then the DeLancey horses win a special mention for crossing the wide expanse of seawater between the continent and Long Island all on their own, tired from a long run, without the help of ferry or bridge, and carrying desperate men on their backs.

WASHINGTON AND ROCHAMBEAU and their troops withdrew to a place north of where the botanical garden is today. Some officers and staff stayed at the farm of the Valentine family, in what one of the French described as "a wretched house." Actually, it was and is a perfectly presentable stone farmhouse, though maybe nothing special inside; it still stands, and today the Valentine-Varian House is the museum of the Bronx Historical Society. For dinner Rochambeau "devoured a fricassee of chicken," he later wrote. Between going over the events of that day and planning for the next, he did not sleep, and Washington probably didn't either.

Early the next morning, July 23, the combined forces again moved south. The previous day's sweep had chased the DeLancey men and had captured, killed, or dispersed most of them. Somehow, James DeLancey had again slipped through the net. De Lauzun and his men made another pass through Morrisania in search of him. Washington and Rochambeau wanted to be seen scouting the shoreline as if planning the best way to strike at Manhattan. With the Throgs Neck peninsula now cleared of the enemy, they rode along it, on the same route that the DeLancey men and their pursuers might have taken the day before. British warships in the Sound saw the party, which probably numbered about a hundred, and fired their cannon at them. Some of the shots hit close enough that the riders were "covered all over with sand." At the end of the peninsula, engineers with the group made measurements to determine how far it was to the opposite shore. While that was going on, Washington and Rochambeau found a place under a hedge to take a nap as the warships kept firing.

Rochambeau awoke first. It will be remembered that to get out onto Throgs Neck you had to cross the causeway by the tidal gristmill near Westchester village, where Hand's Pennsylvania riflemen had stopped General Howe's advance almost five years before. In Rochambeau's memoirs he describes waking from his nap and remembering that they had crossed the causeway at low tide. By now the tide must have come in. If the DeLancey men had been trapped the day before, now the generals could be in a tight spot themselves. Were the British to move fast they could land a force and catch them and their escort between the Sound at one end of the peninsula and the fast-moving tidal stream at the other. Though the chances of this happening were small, a catastrophe of such magnitude—the capture of both the French and the American commanders—might well have cost the war.

Rochambeau roused Washington and reminded him of the tide. The generals then rode back up the neck with their hundred-man entourage. The tide had indeed come in. A boat, or boats, at the tidal stream could ferry the men across, but what of the horses? Again, a feat of aquatic horsemanship saved the day. Baron von Closen recalled:

> I must confess that I was astonished to see the 90 horses of the American dragoons . . . unsaddled and compelled to swim across at once, without a rope or anything. The American officer assured me *"that he had often had his men swim across, and that the horses were accustomed to this from birth."* [italics *sic*; von Closen liked italics]

His amazement at this feat caused von Closen to expatiate on Americans in general:

> I admire the American troops tremendously! It is incredible that soldiers composed of men of every age, even of children of fifteen, of whites and blacks, almost naked, unpaid, and rather poorly fed, can march so far and withstand fire so steadfastly. The calm and calculated measures of General Washington, in whom I discover daily some new and eminent qualities, are already well known, and the entire universe accords him the homage of its highest esteem. He is certainly admirable as the leader of his army, in which everyone regards him as his friend and father.

Part of Washington's mystique no doubt derived from his ability to keep a poker face while extricating himself from situations in which he had erred. General Rochambeau, for his part, took a less awestruck view of his fellow commander. Like von Closen, Rochambeau describes the horses swimming the tidal stream, but adds, pointedly, "This manoeuvre consumed less than an hour, but happily the embarrassment was unnoticed by the enemy."

IT'S ALSO WORTH POINTING OUT, in regard to von Closen's description of the American army, that French observers often make note of its many Black soldiers. In American accounts, I've yet to come across any mention of them.

Having completed the Grand Reconnaissance, the American and French armies then regrouped, crossed the Hudson River, marched to Virginia, and fought a series of engagements with the British under General Cornwallis on the Yorktown Peninsula. The American and French victory there, on October 19, 1781, in effect won the war. From the point of view of cavalry buffs, an engagement between de Lauzun's horsemen and those of Banastre Tarleton, the ruthless tactician who gave no quarter to the Stockbridge Indians, can make one wish de Lauzun had bested the British officer. Instead, de Lauzun only came close to capturing him. After the surrender, the French, American, and British officers exchanged courtesies and had dinner together. General Cornwallis, finding himself short of funds, asked the French if they could lend him the money to pay his troops. And they loaned it to him! Later he returned it and added a present of a hundred bottles of porter in thanks.

AFTER THE BULK of the American and French armies had left the Neutral Ground on their southward march, the lawless region reverted to its previous self. This was when one of the worst atrocities of the war occurred. Several people interviewed by McDonald remembered the story. A French doctor had ridden below American lines in the vicinity of the Croton River, near where the DeLancey men had attacked the Rhode Islanders. Four Neutral Ground badmen—Henry Weeks, James Tillett, James Totten, and another—"ambuscaded" the doctor, took his horse, watch, and money, and kept him captive for a couple of hours. They played cards and talked about what to do with him. Though the doctor spoke no English, he understood what was going on. By signs he begged for his life, holding up fingers to show how many children he had at home. Finally they tied him to a tree and shot him.

James Totten (cousin of Gilbert Totten, the main actor in the deadly events involving Colonel Greene and the Rhode Islanders) went back to the Refugee camp at Morrisania after the murder. He was showing off what he'd stolen from the doctor. James DeLancey said to him, "Totten, you think you have accomplished an honorable and brave exploit in taking the life of a poor French doctor who made no resistance. You are a disgrace to the Refugees, and I want to see you no more." He ordered James Totten to leave the camp (though DeLancey himself was hardly one to talk when it came to unsanctioned killings). James Tillett, another of the murderers, also left the area, but returned after the war and became a Methodist minister. He expressed contrition but was still despised for what he'd done.

After Cornwallis surrendered, General Rochambeau chose de Lauzun to tell King Louis that the Americans had won the war. De Lauzun sailed on the ship *Surveillante* and arrived in France on November 21, after a fast passage of twenty-two days. The king was overjoyed at the news. Rochambeau left America soon after de Lauzun, and all the French army had followed by the middle of the next year. Many French officers who served in what's now the Bronx went on to new adventures, and sometimes death, in the French Revolution.

General Rochambeau commanded the French Republic's Army of the North in 1792, suffered a disastrous defeat in an attack on the Austrian Netherlands, and left the service at his own request. Imprisoned during the Reign of Terror, he barely escaped execution, and eventually returned to his estate, where he died in 1804. The dashing Duc de Lauzun lost his fortune, fell from favor at court, briefly commanded a revolutionary army, and ended up in prison. Along the way he had an affair with a British actress who later became the mistress of Banastre Tarleton, his former enemy. De Lauzun died on the guillotine on the last day of December 1793. Baron Ludwig von Closen, with whom Washington joked after the skirmish in Morrisania, also lost his fortune. He served as an aide to Rochambeau until August 1792, then lived in poverty with his family for ten years because of wartime depredations to his home. He petitioned Napoleon for help, received a minor post, and died in 1830.

Louis-Alexandre Berthier, the aide who killed a DeLancey man at Morrisania, had the most distinguished later career of any of the officers in Rochambeau's American army. Berthier left the service during the Revolution, survived the Terror, and won reinstatement after the fall of Robespierre. Rising in rank during the battles that followed, he eventually became one of Napoleon's most trusted marshals. The emperor rewarded him with principalities—though not born to an aristocratic family, Berthier received the lofty titles of Prince of Neuchâtel, in Prussia, and Prince of Wagram, for his meritorious service in the Battle of Wagram. When Napoleon divorced the Empress Josephine and married Princess Marie-Louise of Austria, he could not attend the wedding in person; Berthier, his deputy, stood in for him at the ceremony. Berthier's own wife was the niece of the king of Bavaria.

Berthier told Napoleon not to invade Russia. After ignoring this advice, and learning a lesson about that country, the emperor departed Moscow ahead of his troops and left Berthier to struggle with them on the winter march back to France. Berthier was made frantic by Napoleon's moods and erratic plans as things got worse for him in 1814. When the emperor abdicated and went into exile, Berthier did not accompany him. Instead, he took over as commander of the army and, on its behalf, welcomed the new king, Louis XVIII. After Napoleon's triumphant return from Elba in 1815, Berthier resigned, and went to join his wife and children in Bavaria. Officials there would not allow him to leave when Napoleon took the field for what turned out to be his last campaign. Berthier said, as the Russian troops marched past, "Poor France, what will become of you and I am here." A remark by a dinner guest that seemed to accuse him of disloyalty caused him to despair. He killed himself by jumping from a high window of his father-in-law's castle. Napoleon's defeat at Waterloo happened three days later.

BETWEEN THE SURRENDER of Cornwallis and the final signing of the peace agreement, the Americans waited almost a year and a half. During much of that time, the army remained encamped near Newburgh, New York, generally in discontent. The soldiers had little to do and often went unpaid. Forestalling mutinies and rebellions within the Revolution kept Washington and Congress busy.

Raids and counterraids continued in the Neutral Ground, and the British Army remained a threat. In September 1782, it made its last large-scale foraging expedition, led by General Sir Guy Carleton, with five thousand or six thousand troops. Accompanying the general was Prince William Henry, later King William IV, the uncle and immediate predecessor of Queen Victoria. That is, among the plunderers who made off with the resources of the future Bronx was a future British king. Most of 1783 went by as the British prepared to evacuate New York City. (It's confusing that Governor George Clinton, the longest-serving governor in the history of New York State, had the same last name as General Sir Henry Clinton, the British commander in the city; fortunately, that source of confusion was removed in 1781 when General Clinton left and General Carleton replaced him.) On November 25, 1783, Carleton and the last remaining British troops evacuated Manhattan, and General Washington, accompanied by Governor Clinton and a detachment of soldiers, rode south to take possession of the city.

The party stopped at the Van Cortlandt mansion on the way. Another mural in the reception hall in the Bronx Criminal Court building, next to the mural of the Battle of Pelham, shows a larger-than-life-size Washington outside the mansion. Behind him, the only Black person in the scene, and in all of the room's four crowded Bronx-history-based murals, is a jockey-like figure half Washington's size who is holding his horse. Is this supposed to be William Lee? Washington and his entourage followed the Albany Post Road to the King's Bridge and continued to what's now lower Manhattan. There, New Yorkers celebrated his arrival and the departure of the British with the largest fireworks display ever seen in the country up until that time. Washington gave a dinner for his officers at Fraunces Tavern, which also still stands. Afterward, November 25 became a holiday, known as Evacuation Day, which was celebrated annually in the city until the early twentieth century.

With the British gone, the property of local Tories was confiscated by the state. The man who owned the house where Admiral Howe had met with Adams, Franklin, and Rutledge on Staten Island sold his property before confiscation could take effect, and he later went to Saint John, New Brunswick, with his wife and children. Gouverneur Morris's mother held on to her mansion and estate, thanks to her son, who also saved from confiscation the property of Isaac Wilkins, a

Westchester County Tory and pamphleteer who had married one of Morris's sisters. The DeLanceys lost their mills, which later went to the Lydig family. DeLancey land became Lydig land, and that family eventually sold it to the city, and now some of it is Bronx Park, site of the zoo and botanical garden. Well before the final evacuation, many Tories had left the country. The British provided ships to take them to England or to settlements in eastern Canada, where allotments for them had been set aside.

During the Neutral Ground days, James DeLancey and the Refugees had seized the farm of Theophilus Hunt, DeLancey's old schoolmate, who had tried to speak up for Tim Knapp at his hanging, and whose head DeLancey had threatened to cut off. By the end of the war, Hunt's houses and outbuildings were ruined, his fences burned, his cattle gone. Before DeLancey departed for Nova Scotia with (people later said) six barrels full of silver dollars, he came to tell Hunt goodbye. Surveying the wreckage, Hunt said, "I don't know how I shall get along." DeLancey replied, "Peace, Hunt! You are better off than I am, for you can stay while I must leave my native country forever!" Then Colonel James DeLancey of the Refugees wept and asked God's blessings on his former friend.

11

GOUVERNEUR MORRIS WENT into the war a man dispossessed of his land, sometimes too strapped for cash to pay the expenses he ran up in serving the country. He emerged from the war an established Philadelphia entrepreneur and lawyer, associated with Robert Morris, one of the country's richest men, and able to charge multi-thousand-dollar fees for legal representation. Gouverneur made his first visit to Morrisania in seven years on May 31, 1783. His mother had not recovered from her illness, and the estate's cattle, horses, sheep, and 470-acre forest were gone. How she reacted to seeing her son, now lacking his left leg below the knee, is not known. Morris celebrated by drinking a bottle of wine that had stood on a shelf in the mansion for at least twenty years. After checking out the losses to her property, he presented the British with a bill for eight thousand pounds. They did not pay it quickly, or maybe ever.

In January 1786, Sarah Gouverneur Morris died, and Staats Long Morris, Gouverneur's half brother, inherited the estate. Staats lived in England, and he agreed to sell the part of Morrisania he'd inherited—the half that lay to the east of the Mill Brook—to Gouverneur for a price he could swing, by borrowing and by arranging to pay the loan over a long term. Gouverneur took over the property without giving up his residence in Philadelphia, which was lucky for the country, because in 1787 Pennsylvania chose him as one of its delegates to the Constitutional Convention. Had he relocated to New York he might not have been selected. Many New Yorkers did not support the idea of changes that could increase federal power and impose national tariffs. As the country's main port, New York preferred setting its own tariffs. Morris's native state had small enthusiasm for the Convention.

The size of the states' delegations varied. Pennsylvania sent eight delegates, Virginia seven, New Jersey five, Connecticut three, etc. In the decisions of the whole, each state had only one vote. Fifty-five delegates in all took part, though at any one time only thirty or forty might be present. Rhode Island declined to send anybody, and two of New York's delegates walked out, leaving only its third, Alexander Hamilton.

Proceedings in Philadelphia's Independence Hall began in mid-May and continued to mid-September. In that assembly, Morris shone. He took the floor 173 times, more than any other delegate. He, his fellow Pennsylvanian James Wilson, and Virginia's James Madison are considered to have been the most influential delegates. George Washington, of the Virginia delegation, was unanimously elected to preside, in the sometimes-sweltering hall where the windows had been nailed shut to preserve the secrecy of the discussions. Delegates whose homes were within a reasonable travel distance took breaks and left the Convention occasionally and returned, but the ones from the far-off southern states couldn't. These men's daily attendance may have given them an extra gravitas, like that of the ever-present Washington.

People knew that the Articles of Confederation, the previous constitution that attempted to create a national alliance from the thirteen states, hadn't worked. Under it, the states became mini-nations: They made independent treaties, set their own customs regulations, and printed their own money, which caused endless trouble in converting one currency to another. Nine of the states had their own navies. Still, the original intent of the Convention, as most Americans understood it, had been only to revise the Articles. Morris quickly put an end to that misconception. He was attending the Convention, he said, as "a

Representative of America . . . in some degree a Representative of the whole human race." In that spirit, on May 30, as the Convention was still at a preliminary stage, Morris proposed that it dispense with the Articles entirely and establish a new supreme national government, to consist of three branches—legislative, executive, and judiciary. (In this he was seconding the delegation of Virginia's proposal, known as the Virginia Plan.) The delegates agreed with this new direction and started to work on a completely new constitution.

Having helped set things on track, Morris then disappeared. Just as he did at the beginning of the war in New York, and at other important points in his life, he suddenly discovered a need to be elsewhere. This time he went to Morrisania, the ancestral manor that now belonged to him, where he busied himself with its restoration. If he traveled to it by boat, he could have seen the manor house from a long way off, because it had a view of the Sound; today the first thing he would catch sight of from a distance would be THE NEW YORK POST, in the black-and-white block letters of the newspaper's logo, on top of its printing plant on the southeastern corner of the Bronx. *The New-York Evening Post* began publishing during Morris's lifetime. Alexander Hamilton, his friend—or "frenemy," that useful modern term—founded it, though after 1787.

If a historical marker existed today at the intersection of Cypress Avenue and East 132nd Street, in the south South Bronx, it might say, "In late May of 1787, Gouverneur Morris, one of the principal authors of the U.S. Constitution, absented himself from the Constitutional Convention, in Philadelphia, to attend to the reconstruction of his house, which had fallen into disrepair during the Revolutionary War, and which stood at or near this spot. About a month later, in early July, Morris returned to the Convention." As I've said, neither the borough nor the city is big on historic markers. However, there is an officially designated New York City Landmark not far from the site of the long-forgotten Morris mansion. In the 1980s, the Landmarks Preservation Commission awarded landmark status to a sewage treatment plant on East 132nd Street, a half block away. It's called the Bronx Grit Chamber; the chairman of the commission praised it as "a real gem of a building." The famous architectural firm McKim, Mead & White designed it, and it was completed in 1937 as part of the Wards Island Sewage Treatment Works.

On a fence by the building are the words "NYC DEP Bronx Grit Facility." The general impression conveyed by the building's high, arched central window with double pilasters on either side is of a Romanesque maw designed to swallow everything. Once when I was passing by, I looked in at a door between the pilasters and asked a guy sitting at a reception window what the place did. He said it screened out large solids from the city's sewage, so they don't clog the system. In every big rain, pieces of roads and parking lots, and boards and plastic tarps and so on, wash into the sewers, and this facility removes them and offloads them to trucks that take them to landfills. After being screened, the remaining sewage travels underground and underwater to a huge treatment plant on Wards Island. So, okay—this is a useful and significant building that arguably deserves to be recognized. But how about also giving a shout-out to the site just down the street where the house of the guy who wrote the Constitution used to be?

Today the intersection of Cypress Avenue and East 132nd Street has been complicated by a ramp for the Robert F. Kennedy Bridge (formerly the Triborough Bridge) that occupies the middle of the avenue and leaves just a narrow lane and sidewalks on either side. There's a T intersection where Cypress meets East 132nd, and a large industrial lot stretches beyond it to the south, with the underside of the bridge shading the place like an awning. This under-bridge area, once Morris's front yard, now rattles and bangs with activity.

According to the sign on the fence, it belongs to the CFS Steel Co., Inc., whose main merchandise appears to be rebars. These steel bars of various lengths, generally about a half inch to an inch in diameter, are used for reinforcing cinder-block walls and poured concrete. Rebars are the twisted pieces of metal that often stick out of blown-up buildings, and the fact that they are ridged or knobbed like spines adds to the anatomical effect. Here in the CFS Steel Co. lot the rebars rest on enormous outdoor shelves while grappler hooks slide back and forth on gantries over them, and workmen fix cables to bundles of them, and the grapplers lift the bundles and stack them lengthwise on flatbed trailer trucks, which then roar out of the main gate with plumes of diesel smoke onto East 132nd Street.

Some days there's a workman who's broad-shouldered and over six feet tall in a sleeveless sweatshirt and a red hard hat standing at a machine not far from the gate. He takes rebars two at a time and sets them on the machine, which makes a single, swift motion, bends them into an L shape, and returns to its original position. The workman then moves the rebars off the machine, stacks them to one side, takes two more rebars, puts them on the machine; it bends them into Ls, he sets those aside, and so on. When he has ten or twelve L-shaped rebars, he bundles them up with pieces of heavy wire that he twists effortlessly, as if tying string. Rebars have been flying out of the lot lately, the supervisor at the gate tells me. He says construction projects in the Bronx are busy these days.

MORRIS RETURNED TO PHILADELPHIA on July 2 and found the Convention at an impasse. The larger states and the smaller states were arguing over representation in the Senate. James Madison later described the situation as "seriously alarming." Benjamin Franklin, the oldest delegate, wrote a statement that another delegate read for him, saying, "We are sent here to *consult* not to *contend*, with each other," and pleading for harmony. Franklin said they should get back to God and call in a pastor to lead them in prayer, but the other delegates thought that unnecessary. Elbridge Gerry, a representative from Massachusetts, said that if the Convention failed "we shall disappoint not only America, but the whole world."

AFTER THE CONVENTION briefly adjourned to celebrate the Fourth of July, Morris was among those who suggested that a smaller committee be appointed to discuss the representation question. According to Madison's notes, Morris "wished gentlemen to extend their views beyond the present moment of time; beyond the narrow limits of place from which they derive their political origin." Morris said the delegates should do more than "truck and bargain for our particular States."

When the committee brought back a proposal giving each state, regardless of size, equal representation in the Senate, the small states were content, the large states acquiesced, and the hump was gotten over. Madison told Morris's first biographer that he doubted Morris's return had made a difference in this outcome, but it does seem as if his taking the Convention's first month off helped him bring in some fresh energy. Also, it may have given him extra stamina later, in the final weeks, when the other delegates were tired and wanted to go home. Morris was that person who hangs on in long meetings—the one who stays to the end, finishes up the details, and incidentally gets his way.

In the discussions he argued for protecting the rights of property, which he said was the purpose of all government. He did not want the many without property to gang up on the wealthy few by imposing excessive taxes on them and forgiving the debts of the unpropertied. At the same time, he did not like the idea of the rich tyrannizing the poor. According to Madison, Morris argued that "The Rich will strive to establish their dominion & enslave the rest. They always did. They always will." Morris believed that if members of the House of Representatives, the more democratic and populous chamber, had no property, the rich would buy their votes. Therefore, all representatives should be property owners, he believed. In the end, the Constitution did not include this requirement, but also did not rule out any state's imposing it.

Morris argued that the executive should be one person, not a triumvirate or other multiperson arrangement, and should serve for life, or be reelectable every four years without limit. To make the executive not dependent on the legislative branch, he should be elected by popular vote. (The compromise preserving this idea helped to create the Electoral College, now much maligned.) To give more unity to the country he wanted the executive to have ample power and be "the great protector of the Mass of the people." In this wish Morris may have had in mind his beloved Washington, who presided over the Convention session after session, through many prolix speeches. Washington made only a single proposal of his own during the Convention's more than four months—that representatives for the House be elected one per every thirty thousand eligible citizens, rather than one for every forty thousand, in the interest of increased democracy. The motion passed by acclamation; as a group, the delegates revered and adored Washington.

On certain evenings the great man invited delegates to receptions at his lodgings. Once, Hamilton remarked to a group including Morris that Washington always maintained his reserve even with his friends and allowed no one to be familiar with him. Morris knew Washington well and had visited him at Mount Vernon; at one point during the Convention the two even took a break to go fishing in the Delaware River. Morris replied to Hamilton that, on the contrary, he could be as familiar with Washington as with any of his other friends. Ever the provocateur, Hamilton challenged him, "If you will, at the next reception evening, gently slap him on the shoulder and say, 'My dear General, how happy I am to see you look so well!'" Hamilton said he would provide a supper with wine for Morris and a dozen of his friends if Morris had the nerve to do that. (We should remember that both men were youths, relatively speaking—Morris twenty years younger than Washington, and Hamilton three years younger than Morris.)

Morris accepted the dare. At the next reception, with a full complement of guests as witnesses, he walked in, bowed to Washington, shook hands, then laid his left hand on Washington's shoulder and said, "My dear General, I am very happy to see you look so well!" Washington withdrew his hand and stepped back. The room fell silent. The lofty and austere Father of his Country stared at Morris with an angry frown, while the upstart shrank away and hid himself among the onlookers. Afterward, Hamilton, true to his word, paid up. At the victory supper, Morris said, "I have won the bet, but paid dearly for it, and nothing could induce me to repeat it."

His fellow delegates said that he had audacity, and that he was a genius. Getting fresh with Washington certainly proved the first, if not the second. Ladies in Philadelphia said Morris was "a very impudent man." Roger Sherman, a delegate from Connecticut, called him "an irreligious and profane man." Not a few other delegates shared Sherman's view. However one judged his character, Morris proposed thirty-nine resolutions at the Convention, more than any other delegate, and had twenty-two of them adopted, also more than any other. In one major agenda he lost out, and that was his opposition to slavery.

During June, the month he was away, the notorious three-fifths compromise had made enough progress in discussion that neither he nor anybody else could stop it. The southern states wanted their slaves counted as citizens in assigning representation, and the northern delegates rejected this as unfair, not to mention illogical. Slaves weren't citizens and couldn't vote in any election; why should they suddenly be the equal of whites when it came to determining how many congressional representatives a state received? The compromise provided that, for representation purposes, a slave would equal three fifths of a white person. This central dispute, and its resolution, caused Morris to make his most-quoted statement of the Convention:

> Upon what principle is it that the slaves shall be computed in the representation? Are they men? Then make them citizens and let them vote. Are they property? Why then is no other property included? . . . The admission of slaves into the Representation when fairly explained comes to this: That the inhabitant of Georgia and S.C. [South Carolina] who goes to the Coast of Africa, and in defiance of the most sacred laws of humanity tears his fellow creatures from their dearest connections and damns them to the most cruel bondages, shall have more votes in a Government instituted for the protection of the rights of mankind, than the Citizen of Pennsylvania or New Jersey who views with a laudable horror, so nefarious a practice.

Note his use of the word *creatures*—Morris, one of the delegates most vehemently opposed to slavery, owned slaves himself and held no high regard for Blacks. The question of their basic humanity had not been settled in his mind. Still, his hatred of the institution was real. He thought slavery such a blight that he said he would "sooner submit himself to a tax for paying for all the Negroes in the [United] States than saddle posterity with such a constitution."

In the many arguments at the Convention on this question, the southern delegates said over and over how much wealth their slaves contributed to the national economy. They believed that their states, which were richer than the northern states, deserved greater power in Congress because they created more taxable income, through the duties on exports produced by slaves. Putting it in the simplest possible terms, Charles Cotesworth Pinckney, a delegate from South Carolina, said that Georgia and South Carolina "cannot do without slaves." The southern delegates insisted they would vote down any constitution that did not allow the continuation of slavery and the slave trade.

We can only regret that their bluff was not called. As it turned out, the Constitution gave more protections to slavery than had existed in the Articles of Confederation. Under the Articles, a slave who escaped to a free state was free and could not be reclaimed. The Constitution enforced federal law throughout the states, so after it went into effect an owner could in theory reclaim an escaped slave anywhere in the country.

Theodore Roosevelt, in his biography of Morris, described the compromise the Constitution made with slavery, and argued that it was essential for the creation of the Union: "If we had at the outset dissolved into a knot of struggling anarchies, it would have entailed an amount of evil both on our race and on all North America, compared to which the endurance of slavery for a century or two would have been as nothing." So wrote a U.S. president, one of the faces on Mount Rushmore. Theodore Roosevelt believed that the greater good required enslaved people to endure "a century or two" of slavery, because their suffering was "as nothing" compared to the general chaos that would have ensued had the Constitutional Convention foundered on that question. By being deprived of their liberty, Black people preserved the liberty of others—indeed, saved the country. The southern delegates' speeches at the Convention, and Roosevelt's realpolitik excuse, make as strong an argument for reparations as anyone could ask for.

BY SEPTEMBER 8, the delegates had a cut-and-paste penultimate draft of the Constitution ready to move into final form. The Committee of Detail, which had assembled the draft, gave it to the Convention, which then passed it on to a group consisting of Morris, Madison, Hamilton, Rufus King, William Johnson, and William Rutledge. These men comprised the Committee of Style and Arrangement, more often referred to simply as the Committee of Style; among its members, Morris was the most active and influential, to such a degree that the others seem to have been more like silent observers of what he did.

If, as the poets tell us, responsibility begins in dreams, then America at its best begins in two dreams, each expressed by a great writer. The first dream is the Declaration of Independence and came from Thomas Jefferson. The second dream, the Preamble to the Constitution, is Gouverneur Morris's, though he never quite admitted he wrote it—as if he personified Everybody, and all "the People" had indeed written it, through him. In a letter he sent from Morrisania twenty-seven years later, Morris said, of the Constitution, "That instrument was written by the fingers which write this letter." The ghostly fingers still moving at the end of his living arm had once belonged to all "the People," rather than to any mere Mr. Morris.

The rough-draft Preamble to the Constitution that the Convention gave to the Committee of Style said:

> We the People of the States of New Hampshire, Massachusetts, Rhode-Island and Providence Plantations, Connecticut, New-York, New-Jersey, Pennsylvania, Delaware, Maryland, Virginia, North-Carolina, South-Carolina and Georgia, do ordain, declare and establish the following Constitution for the Government of ourselves and our Posterity.

Filled with information, functional in a straightforward way, this opening showed the utility and drabness of writing by committee. Morris, who had urged his fellow delegates to look beyond their present moment in time and the states they were from, took a more spacious view, and lifted the draft Preamble to a new level. His revision read (and still reads):

> We the People of the United States, in Order to form a more perfect Union, establish Justice, insure domestic Tranquility, provide for the common defense, promote the general Welfare, and secure the Blessings of Liberty to ourselves and our Posterity, do ordain and establish this Constitution for the United States of America.

He thought of himself as a citizen of the United States, rather than of any one state—appropriately for someone from an in-between place originally. Washington was this country's founding leader, but Morris spoke as its "We," its founding citizenry. He transformed "We the People," a phrase used before in state constitutions, from prose to poetry.

Morris regarded this document as an entity existing in history. He did not say, "in order to form *the most* perfect union," because everybody knew of the failure of the Articles, the preceding constitutional attempt. Instead, he accepted this new version as a work seeking perfection but possibly still not yet very near it, thereby leaving room for later generations to acknowledge imperfections so dire as to be almost disqualifying. The preamble he produced, and especially the words "a more perfect union," set the new American experiment in motion. Now it had legs, it had life. Barack Obama and other leaders have used the words "to form a *more perfect* union," pronounced with that emphasis, often in their speeches 230-odd years later. The point wasn't that the Founders got it right, but that we would all keep trying to get it right.

MORRIS HAD ELEGANT, copperplate handwriting, and the copy of the Constitution that the Committee of Style brought back to the Convention for review probably was written out by him. Anyone who has ever checked a revised and edited manuscript against an earlier version knows what a challenge it can be. All kinds of mistakes can get through, and you must stay alert. In recopying, Morris sneaked in small, hard-to-detect alterations that served his own vision of government. The other delegates lacked the patience to keep up with him; they wanted to apply the rubber stamp and go home. One delegate did notice an unauthorized change that Morris had made by replacing a comma with a semicolon. In what is known as the General Welfare Clause (Article 1, Section 8, in the final version), the draft read:

> The Legislature shall have Power To lay and collect Taxes, Duties, Imposts and Excises, to pay the Debts and provide for the common Defence and general Welfare of the United States.

The revision of this sentence after Morris rewrote it gave Congress the power

> To lay and collect Taxes, Duties, Imposts and Excises; to pay the Debts and provide for the common Defence and general Welfare of the United States.

By changing the comma after "excises" into a semicolon, Morris provided for a potentially major broadening of federal power, in line with his personal wish for an even stronger central government. When the delegates as a body went over the rewrite, Roger Sherman, delegate from Connecticut, caught that semicolon, and the comma was put back in. It is still a comma rather than a semicolon today. Probably Sherman had been paying extra attention because he expected Morris, that "irreligious and profane man," to pull a fast one.

The other changes—more than a dozen in all—Morris got away with. Collectively they showed a surreptitious will to strengthen central government and elevate men of substance and property above the democratic throng. Nor did he forget his failures regarding his opposition to slavery. Perhaps Morris's most significant single-word change appeared in the clause about runaway slaves, which read, in draft:

If any Person bound to service or labor in any of the United States shall escape into another State, He or She shall not be discharged from such service or labor in consequence of any regulations subsisting in the State to which they escape, but shall be delivered up to the person justly claiming their service or labor.

Morris changed this to:

No Person held to Service or Labour in one State, under the Laws thereof, escaping into another, shall, in Consequence of any Law or Regulation therein, be discharged from such Service or Labour, but shall be delivered up on Claim of the Party to whom such Service or Labour may be due.

His version removed the words "justly claiming"—a small victory that went unchallenged by those who might have objected. Later, abolitionists could seize on that removal as proof that the Constitution accepted slavery but did not condone it.

The Committee of Style gave its revision of the Constitution to the Convention in general session on September 12, a turnaround of just three days. Morris must have pulled one or two all-nighters to do that. The delegates deliberated until September 15, when thirty-nine of the fifty-five still present signed the final document, which was then sent to be "engrossed"—copied onto parchment by an inscriber with handwriting even better than Morris's. Preparations were made to submit the new Constitution to the states for ratification, and the Convention adjourned for the last time.

WASHINGTON, GOUVERNEUR MORRIS, and Robert Morris had dinner together afterward at the City Tavern in Philadelphia. (Morris's overly familiar greeting at the reception had not ruined his and Washington's friendship; maybe, counterintuitively, it had strengthened it.) In the evening, Washington wrote in his diary, "[I] retired to meditate on the momentous wk. which has been executed, after not less than five, for a large part of the time six, and sometimes 7 hours of sitting every day . . . for more than four months." From Philadelphia, he returned to Mount Vernon, and Gouverneur Morris to Morrisania. They saw each other again the following year, when Morris spent seven months in Virginia in his capacity as an agent for Robert Morris's tobacco-exporting business. He visited Mount Vernon, and stopped at Tucka-hoe, the plantation of Thomas Mann Randolph, Sr., a major tobacco producer, where he met Randolph's fourteen-year-old daughter, Nancy. Twenty-one years later, Morris would marry her.

A big tobacco deal that Robert Morris was having trouble with in France, plus other business, required Gouverneur Morris's presence in Paris. He sailed from Philadelphia on December 18, 1788, and reached Le Havre on January 27, 1789, after a crossing of forty days. In all of history, he could not have chosen a livelier time to go.

12

AFTER MORRIS'S ARRIVAL on the European continent in early 1789, he did not return to America for almost ten years. During that period, he led a life wilder than that of any other Framer of the Constitution. Helping to win the American Revolution and writing the founding document and its Preamble fill just the opening paragraphs of his résumé. We must follow him to France because he got caught up in the French Revolution; because in Paris he met the woman who was arguably the love of his life; and because he kept a diary of almost graphomaniacal thoroughness that tells what he went through. Its entries reveal an essential lonesomeness, a quality more metaphysical—more American—than ordinary loneliness. Morris was the person arrived from elsewhere and going elsewhere, the everybody who was nobody, the man who disappeared. The place that would be the Bronx—that in-between, in-transit zone—produced this "Representative of the whole human race," and in some ways it would mirror him.

After landing at Le Havre, Morris continued to Paris, where he arrived on February 3, and found rooms at the Hôtel de Richelieu. Though he had never been abroad before, he did speak French. Then he looked up Thomas Jefferson, who was serving his fifth year as the

American ambassador. He also met with Lafayette (Marie-Joseph-Paul-Yves-Roch-Gilbert du Mortier, Marquis de La Fayette), whom he had first known at Valley Forge in 1778. Then, Lafayette had been only twenty-one. Now, at thirty-one, he remained almost a boy. Washington had given Morris letters of recommendation to certain notables, and the specifications of a watch he wanted Morris to buy for him in Paris, like the watch Jefferson had bought for Madison.

Morris began to keep his European diary on March 1, 1789. He already enjoyed some fame among the French nobility who had served in America or knew about its main actors, and he received invitations to social gatherings. An early diary entry says, about these events, "Not being perfectly Master of the Language, most of the Jests escape me." At a dinner he attended, one of the guests, a viscount, retired with the hostess to her "cabinet" in front of everybody and bolted the door. They returned (Morris wrote), "After a convenient Time." The viscount presented the lady to Morris for him to kiss and took his leave. Afterward, she blithely told the guests that her young son did not like her doing *"cette Espèce de Plaisanterie."* Morris was shocked, and probably showed it, despite his own sophistication. Philadelphia was never like this. In letters to his fellow eminences, he said over and over how depraved the French were. But they fascinated and excited him too, though he did not admit it. By a large number, more women took an active, political part in the French Revolution than in the American Revolution. And revolutions can be sexy, as is known.

On March 21, on a visit to Versailles, he met a twenty-eight-year-old countess, Adèle de Flahaut, a minor noblewoman of the court. Her mother had been a mistress of Louis XV, and Adèle's half sister, Julie, was said to be his daughter, and thus a cousin of the king. Mme. de Flahaut's own legal father, a man named Charles-François Filleul, was a provincial commissioner, but her actual father may have been a rich Parisian bureaucrat. Mme. de Flahaut (as I will call her, or sometimes just Adèle) grew up in a nunnery, owing to the death of her mother when she was six. She avoided becoming a nun, and at eighteen married a count, Charles de Flahaut, who was a former military officer in his fifties. An affair that she had with Charles-Maurice de Talleyrand, Bishop d'Autun, a man closer to her own age, produced a son, Charles, who thought her husband was his father. The Count de Flahaut superintended the king's gardens, a job he got through connections. She and Flahaut lived in apartments among those of the court nobility in the Louvre, though they were on different floors.

Elisabeth Vigée Le Brun, one of the leading portrait artists of the day, who painted Mme. de Flahaut, described her: "She had a pretty figure, a charming face with the wittiest eyes in the world, and was so agreeable that one of my pleasures was to spend the evening with her." Admirers praised the ability of those brown eyes to become "*des yeux des velours*." Morris noted in his diary that he had met her: "She speaks English and is a pleasing Woman." Then he added, "If I might judge from Appearances, not a sworn Enemy to Intrigue."

At this point, readers might be misled, as I was when first encountering her in his diary. This charming Frenchwoman of intrigue and seeming faithlessness was a person of substance, and a writer with talents that Morris, the legal genius and debater, could never match. She emerges as a major event in his life; he rates not much more than a footnote in hers. If you look for her under Adélaïde de Souza-Botelho—her literary name, acquired from her second marriage—you will find her as the author of *Adèle de Senange*, a novel published in 1795 that is still in print today. Along with her other novels, it can be ordered in up-to-date paperback editions on Amazon. The meeting between Gouverneur and Adèle took place on equal footing, with the home advantage hers.

American biographers mention his fluent French, but she made fun of it. Fortunately, as he said, she spoke English. They do seem to have conversed also in her language, and doubtless Gouverneur's skill in it improved. About a week after their first meeting, he went for a walk in the Tuileries and happened to run into her. They walked together for a while. She said she would show him the pictures in the Louvre the following day, but when he arrived at her apartment, as planned, she had forgotten and was still in bed. She got up, dressed, and took him to see the paintings, and her husband came along. Afterward, back at the apartment, the husband did not go anywhere, to Gouverneur's disappointment: "In consequence I take my Leave, and thus a Scene which Imagination had painted very well turns out good for Nothing."

As the momentum for revolution kept building, Morris's opinions did not jibe with those of the people he associated with. Mme. de La Fayette, wife of the marquis, disliked him from the start and called him an aristocrat (this from one of the richest and highest-ranking noble ladies in France). Morris believed the French were too morally corrupt and flighty for democracy and desperately needed a king, though he considered Louis "small beer," unequal to the demands of the time. But he also liked Louis and empathized inconveniently with the royals. When he saw Marie Antoinette waving from a carriage to people who weren't applauding for her during a parade, the hurt on her face pained him. Three months after Morris's arrival, hunger caused by a bad harvest the previous year, plus middle-class turmoil and discontent, forced the king to call a meeting of the Estates General for the first time since 1619. Crowds were marching in the streets, agitating for bread and demanding a constitutional monarchy. The Estates General began its sessions on May 5, 1789, sometimes considered the first day of the revolution. Morris attended and watched the king address the opening.

In his spare time, Morris pursued Mme. de Flahaut. She questioned him on the subject of respect. He confided to his diary that he told her, "I never lost my Respect for those who consented to make me happy on the Principles of Affection" (i.e., "Of course, I'll respect you after!"). On July 14 a mob attacked and overwhelmed the Bastille and freed the prisoners. Lafayette commemorated this exciting event by giving the keys of the Bastille to Thomas Paine for him to take to America and deliver in person to freedom's hero, George Washington. At Mme. de Flahaut's apartment, Morris insisted to her that he could never be "only a Friend." He said he knew himself too well for that and felt too strongly. She replied that she could not be unfaithful to Talleyrand (no mention of Flahaut, the husband).

On an outing in the city, Gouverneur and Adèle made a visit to the ruined Bastille. The architect in charge of completing its demolition gave them a tour; one can hardly imagine a more memorable first date. In his diary Morris wrote that the ancient prison "stinks horribly." Scenes of chaos now appeared with nightmare luridness on the Paris streets—Morris was waiting for his carriage at the Palais Royal when a crowd went by, holding the head of a government official on a pike and dragging the rest of the body behind. Morris had recently met and chatted with the man to whom these parts belonged. In the midst of all the excitement, Morris recorded on July 27 that he and Adèle finally became lovers.

What he did next would not have surprised anyone who knew him well (a category that included nobody). His new friend must have been at least bemused when, after five months of bestowing upon her his almost daily attentions, witty poems, and romantic importunities, he disappeared. At the end of July, just a few days after they'd become intimate, Morris went to England and stayed gone for six weeks. He did have real business there. Washington had asked him to be his unofficial emissary, because the British had so far sent no ambassador to the United States, and vice versa. The new government wanted the British to shut down their forts in the frontier backcountry, leave U.S. ships and shipping alone, and stop impressing American seamen into their navy (as stipulated by previous treaty). In England, Morris also hoped to sell lands he had acquired in upstate New York and talk to bankers about buying up some of the war debt the United States owed to France, among other projects.

A question Washington particularly wanted Morris to look into seems unrealistic, even ridiculous today. The British Army had freed tens of thousands of enslaved people during the war, and the American government believed that their former owners deserved reimbursement. The chance that the British government would ever have followed through on these agreed-to payments seems vanishingly small, but Morris made inquiries anyway, without success. Washington himself had returned after the war to find seventeen of Mount Vernon's slaves no longer on the premises. Maybe that was why the question kept troubling him.

Morris's business dealings and backstairs diplomacy, sketchily referred to in the diary, are complicated to understand. Why he decided he had to take care of them just then, no one can tell. If he intended to make Mme. de Flahaut miss him and demonstrate the magic he had (the power to be Everybody and Nobody, the power to be gone), he succeeded. When he returned to Paris, she was out of town. He sent a letter to her, which, when she received it, caused her to fly immediately to him. On the morning of September 22, he got a note from her and went to see her at her Louvre apartment. She had left wherever she'd been and traveled ninety miles by stagecoach, with eighteen changes of horses, and much of the way over bad roads, in fifteen hours. Going to such effort, Morris wrote, "merely to see one's friend is Proof of Sincerity . . . charming Sex [i.e., the female sex], you are capable of every Thing!"

So began for him a giddy period of passion and kibbitzing in somebody else's revolution. He saw Mme. de Flahaut constantly, and his diary is filled with euphemisms: "After Dinner we join in Adoration to the Cyprian Queen, which with Energy repeated conveys to my kind of Votary all of mortal Bliss which can be enjoyed. I leave her reclined in the sweet Tranquility of Nature well satisfied." He found all kinds of ways to say the same thing. "We laugh and chat till the Servants are gone to their Dinner and then perform the usual Rites." On various occasions in her apartment, they "do the whole Duty of Man," they "taste the genial Joy," they "perform the genial Act," and so on. He describes her as very happy, and despite the frequent coldness of his observations it is clear that, in his fashion, he is, too.

She pledges fidelity to him and forswears sleeping with Talleyrand; but the subtle bishop remains present in her life. He is the father of her son, and she has long been his sounding board and collaborator. Talleyrand's ability to survive, often in high positions of power, unguillotined, from the days of Louis XVI through the deadly writhings of the Revolution and the ascent and descent of Napoleon, has amazed history. In some ways he and Morris resembled each other. Both used their brilliance to keep a distance from whatever situation they were in, and both walked unevenly—Morris on his wooden leg, Talleyrand on a club foot. Morris took his rival's measure with his usual clarity; soon after they first met, but before Morris was involved with Mme. de Flahaut, he described the bishop as "a sly, cool, cunning, ambitious, and malicious Man." Napoleon's epithet for Talleyrand—"*merde* in a silk stocking"—remains the gold standard. Though this description owes a lot to the delicacy of a nineteenth-century translator, it somehow captures him better than if all the words were in the one language or the other.

In the headiness of the Revolution during its early stages, Morris remained a skeptic. He predicted that when the government became a constitutional monarchy, Louis would soon lose his crown, violently or otherwise. Jefferson, an ardent booster of the Revolution, thought it would be bloodless after a constitution was in place; Morris saw chaos and mayhem waiting up ahead. At a dinner with the Lafayettes and others at Jefferson's house, he said (according to his diary), "The Current is setting so strong against the Noblesse that I apprehend their Destruction, in which will I fear be involved Consequences most pernicious, tho little attended to in the present Moment." Nobody wanted to hear that. What he foresaw was still a few years over the horizon. For these and similar sentiments, newspaper stories characterized him as a friend of the aristocracy. Later, Jefferson would accuse Morris of poisoning Washington's mind against the Revolution. Jefferson believed the Revolution's real problem was that too many women got involved in it. He blamed it all on Marie Antoinette.

In connection with Jefferson and his Paris household, Morris does not mention Sally Hemings, one of its enslaved people, who was sixteen at the time. Of course, he wouldn't be likely to. The only context in which the lowest class came up might be in an anecdote about the governor of the Leeward Islands, who had his slaves rubbed with butter until they glistened. Sally Hemings had arrived in Paris, accompanying Jefferson's younger daughter, two years before, so presumably she was somewhere nearby the dinner party, maybe elsewhere in the house. This essential and opaque person in American history would bear Jefferson six children and may have become pregnant by him for the first time while in France.

Lafayette, like his wife, argued righteously with Morris. He told him that Morris's opinions were being quoted against "the good Party," i.e., Lafayette and his followers. Morris replied, in so many words, that the mob was leading Lafayette rather than the other way around. He finally got Lafayette to concede that "he is sensible his party are mad . . . but he is not the less determined to die with them."

The young marquis seems to have gone a bit nuts himself. With Jefferson's help, and that of others, he wrote the Declaration of the Rights of Man and the Citizen, which the National Constituent Assembly adopted in August 1789. At one point he said he was tired of power, then told Morris that in two weeks he would be "generalissimo with all authority." Morris went on, "This man's mind is so elated by power, already too great for the measure of his abilities, that he looks into the clouds and grasps at the supreme." Jefferson, though a close friend of his, said that Lafayette had a "canine appetite" for fame.

Gouverneur and Adèle took their affair to the brink of trashiness. They made love when one of her nieces was in the next room with the door open playing the harpsichord, seized quick interludes in Morris's carriage, and seem hardly to have disguised what they were up to, sometimes waiting not a moment after her husband had departed. Morris wrote satirical verses about Flahaut to entertain her that were not only mean but unworthy of Morris. Like thieves without honor the lovers also inflicted some of the hardest blows on each other. She still received Talleyrand in her apartment and worked with him on his projects and schemes as before. The bishop had moved on from her to an affair with Mme. de Staël, the famed diarist and all-around force of nature, but when Morris left Mme. de Flahaut and Talleyrand together of an evening, he wondered if he was being cuckolded himself.

Offhandedly Morris reported in his diary that one day he told her he did not love her, which surprised her, and "wounded [her] to the Soul." With the future looking shakier every day, she was worried about the safety of herself and her son. She asked Gouverneur if he would promise to marry her, if it came to that. He said no. With Flahaut in the picture the idea was not possible anyway, he pointed out. He said they could discuss this again "when we are both free." The refusal hurt her even more grievously and opened her eyes. He described her weeping and pleading: "A Countenance of Anguish, broken Expressions and all other due accompaniments of an agonizing Spirit are well exhibited."

Jefferson and his household left Paris on their way back to America at the end of September 1789. With the Declaration of the Rights of Man and the Citizen safely approved by the Assembly, he could congratulate himself on having birthed another triumph for liberty. Sally Hemings could have stayed in Paris and been free herself—the new French government would abolish slavery in France—but she chose to return with him, on the condition that her children would one day be free. Evidently, the enslaved sixteen-year-old and the forty-four-year-old Founder-enslaver were a de facto couple by this point. Jefferson kept his promise; years later, he did free his children by Sally Hemings.

With Jefferson having resigned the ambassadorship and left, no American of stature able to represent the government remained. Morris filled in unofficially. He offered to counsel Lafayette as Jefferson had done, but the marquis demurred, perhaps finding Morris too realistic and depressing. Shortages of flour had produced a lack of bread, and mobs shouted for it, attacked bakeries, and beheaded bakers. Morris worked on a plan for importing flour, and met with Jacques Necker, the recently reappointed finance minister whose July firing had sparked the riots that destroyed the Bastille. The public kept expecting Necker's brilliance to save the country, and he kept not saving it and being reappointed and refired. Madame de Staël was Necker's daughter. She invited Morris to evenings at which the level of repartee exhausted him, and he wasn't witty, a dispiriting change for a man who usually was. Mme. de Staël let him know she would sleep with him anyway, bestowing upon him a look similar to "what Sir John Falstaff calls the Leer of Invitation," Morris wrote. Apparently, the invitation was declined.

Plans to buy up America's debt, which could have helped stabilize flat-broke, deeply indebted France with an infusion of cash (and make money for Morris and his partners), turned his attention to the bankers of Amsterdam. In March 1790, he set out for that city, from which he would continue to England. Once again, he was disappearing on his friend, and this time he would be gone for more than eight months.

BACK AT MORRISANIA, Gouverneur's half brother Lewis Morris had an inspiration. This year, 1790, was when the United States would choose the site for its permanent capital. Some citizens of Philadelphia wanted it to be on the Delaware River near that city; Gouverneur's associate Robert Morris happened to own a large parcel of land there. Other places were in the running. Southern interests argued for a capital on the Potomac River in Virginia. Jefferson and Madison strongly inclined to this view. When Lewis Morris learned that Congress, then meeting in New York City, had been discussing the question, he wrote the legislators a letter suggesting that the nation build its new capital in what is now the Bronx.

Specifically, in Morrisania, on land he would be willing to part with. He described the place's many attractions. He said it had a good climate free of agues and fevers (this jab aimed at champions of the Potomac site, much of which was swamp). Travelers could get to Morrisania easily by water (true, if one disregarded the shipwrecking rocks of Hell Gate, nearby in the East River). The anchorage remained ice-free all year (possibly also true, though inland waters all around the city had frozen solid in the winter of 1780–1781). A sturdy local population existed in Westchester County and environs to defend the capital (if they all could be persuaded to take the same side, which they certainly had not done during the days of the Neutral Ground). And, finally, he said, Negroes in the area were relatively few, removing the danger of a slave uprising in wartime (a supposed drawback for any capital located in the South).

Lewis Morris knew he lived in a prime location, one of the most strategic in the country. He just did a muddled job of selling it. What was great and indispensable about the future Bronx would be revealed only with time and had little to do with the reasons he gave. In any case, Lewis Morris's proposal would carry no weight in the decision. Bigger forces, and familiar ones, worked it out. Southerners wanted the capital closer to them for reasons of power and convenience. Federalists—Hamilton, especially—were pushing for the new government to assume the individual states' Revolutionary War debts, because if Congress could pay them off that would strengthen federal power.

The two sides compromised: Several southern representatives went along on the issue of the state debts, and the Potomac River site became the capital. (A song based on this compromise is in *Hamilton*, the musical.) Had Gouverneur Morris been home, and not wandering on the other side of the Atlantic, he could not have changed the outcome. It was just as well. Eventually the Bronx, like the rest of New York City, would have too much going on to be merely the capital of a country; now of the *world*, maybe . . .

13

IN ENGLAND, Morris saw his half brother Staats; ate oysters with James Boswell; and made money and mischief. He had become involved in the shipping business, in association with the New York firm of his friend John Constable, who was depositing a share of the proceeds from successful voyages into his account. Soon he would be a wealthy man, and he would remain so for the rest of his life. Morris bought a 550-ton ship in England, the *Goliah*, which set out on a voyage to India. (Goliah, we recall, was also the name of Colonel James DeLancey's horse.) In the mischief department, Morris tried to start a war between Britain and France. A complicated incident between Spain and Britain in the Pacific Northwest of North America showed potential for blowing up into something bigger, and he urged the French foreign minister to dispatch the French navy on the side of Spain. He thought France would unify behind the king if a war started. The foreign minister seems to have decided that his country had enough to worry about; even without Morris's help, war would come to the French soon enough.

Morris returned to Paris in early November 1790, and when he called on Mme. de Flahaut, he met a disagreeable surprise: Now he had competition. He found her with a visitor, Earl Henry Wycombe, son of the Earl of Shelburne, who had been a British prime minister. Just what her relationship with Wycombe was she did not make clear, but she let Morris know that as far as he, Morris, was concerned, she had determined to be *sage*, or chaste. They could continue as friends, she said. Worse news soon followed—on the next day Morris again stopped by, and was denied admittance! That was a first. When he recorded this fact in his diary, he underlined it.

A few days later he went back, and the weather had changed. He found his friend *seule* and no longer *sage*. His pride had been wounded, and he told her this would be the last time. She laughed at him; by now she knew him well. Indeed, their affair continued, even after he understood that she had also been with Talleyrand while he was gone. (To be sure, he had brief affairs himself on his travels, occasionally even in Paris.) In his diary Morris observed that he now had two rivals to contend with, and she held the advantage over him. When her husband, old Flahaut, fell ill, Morris hoped he would die. Perhaps Morris had rethought his refusal to marry her.

The political situation kept changing and the king's position grew more perilous. As the people's anger against Marie Antoinette rose higher, eligible noblewomen feared to be her ladies-in-waiting. But when she asked Mme. de Flahaut to serve in her court, the countess said yes. From this point, Morris communicated with the king and queen regularly, advised them, and even wrote speeches for the king. In July 1791, he took part in arranging an escape attempt that ended with the royals being caught, brought back, and put under house arrest in the Tuileries Palace in Paris. They would remain in increasingly close confinement until their executions. Morris told his partners in America that turmoil in France was good for land sales, because aristocrats were looking for safe places to flee to. Unfortunately, the king's escape attempt was followed by a clampdown on emigration.

All kinds of crowd scenes filled the Paris streets. About a week after the unsuccessful escape, a ceremonial procession honoring Voltaire made its way through the city to the Pantheon. Gouverneur and Adèle went to the house of an acquaintance to watch. The horses drawing the carriage that bore Voltaire's ashes were led by men dressed in classical garb designed by David, the painter. Afterward, the couple went back to the Louvre, and "seize[d] an Opportunity for hasty Enjoyment." At the British ambassador's, Morris met Banastre Tarleton, the British cavalry officer of apparent ubiquity. Tarleton did not know who Morris was and cluelessly told him inflated stories about the American war. Sometimes Thomas Paine, the pamphleteer turned would-be statesman, careened through the city, borrowing money from Morris and making a drunken nuisance of himself.

Early in 1792, the U.S. Senate confirmed Morris as the ambassador to France (technically, the title was "Minister Plenipotentiary"). No one had officially occupied the position since Jefferson left, more than two years before, and Morris was the obvious choice. The Senate vote, 16 for and 11 against, did not represent a strong endorsement. Some senators said highly critical things about the nominee, and Hamilton and Burr got together and spread lies about him from which his reputation never fully recovered. In a letter, Washington informed Morris about some of the negatives. He said that Morris's detractors had accused him:

> of levity, and imprudence of conversation and conduct. It was urged that your habit of expression, indicated a hauteur disgusting to those who happen to differ from you in sentiment . . . That the promptitude with which your brilliant, & lively imagination is displayed, allow too little time for deliberation and correction; and is the primary cause of those sallies which too often offend, and of that ridicule of characters which begets enmity not easy to be forgotten.

Washington himself expressed warm confidence in Morris and said that he supported the appointment "with all my heart." Morris wrote back, promising to show "Circumspection of Conduct which has hitherto I acknowledge form'd no Part of my Character."

Before Morris received this news, he and Mme. de Flahaut had been considering going to America. The unexpected development interrupted their plans—permanently, as it turned out. If they'd married and settled at Morrisania, possibly she would have outlived him, taken over the estate, and had some considerable effect on the future Bronx. She might have been another Bronx author, like Edgar Allan Poe.

EVENTS BEGAN TO ACCELERATE; in Morris's two years in the ambassador post, the French went through five new governments and seven foreign ministers. He would meet each government and each minister. He set up his embassy at 488 Rue de la Planche, in the Faubourg-St. Germain. He was still carrying on his unofficial backstairs consultations with the king and queen. In summer 1792—as in the previous summer—he helped plan another escape for them. The king trusted him and gave him almost a million livres to raise an army of royalist supporters. At the last minute the queen backed out. Theodore Roosevelt ascribed Morris's ill-advised participation to his natural gallantry and desire to be a savior.

The queen was working on her own plans, which included a published threat known as the Brunswick Manifesto, engineered by Axel Fersen, an army officer of Swiss origins who had served as interpreter between Rochambeau and Washington in America. Fersen was believed to be the queen's lover and the father of her son, the two-year-old Louis XVII. The Brunswick Manifesto said that if any harm came to the royals, Prussia and other countries would attack France. By inflaming the anti-monarchists, it hurt rather than helped the royals.

In June, two months after Morris received his credentials, the Jacobin Society, radicals who had power in the National Assembly, had petitioned to suspend the king. This enraged Lafayette, who led the National Guard (or vice versa, as Morris had pointed out). He rushed to Paris, and his letter calling for a coup and the purging of the Jacobins was read before the Assembly. By now the Jacobins had grown stronger than he, and the Assembly ignored him. Morris predicted that the radicals would take over completely in six weeks. He was right almost to the day. On August 9, he and the countess met at her apartment for what would be their last time together there.

On August 10, a mob stormed the Tuileries and butchered the king's Swiss guards, and the royal family were put in the prison of the

Temple. Jean-Paul Marat, the Jacobin leader, called for the slaughter of aristocrats in the streets. Mobs heeded him, murdering people by the hundreds. Mme. de Flahaut sent Charles, her son, now seven years old, to Morris at the American embassy. She followed soon after. Other friends, acquaintances, and men who had fought in the American Revolution asked Morris for refuge, and he took them in.

The hundreds of victims became thousands. Ambassadors from other countries fled, and by the end of August Morris was the only foreign ambassador or diplomat left in Paris. Revolutionary soldiers searched 488 Rue de la Planche twice. Morris stood fast on diplomatic sanctuary, and the foreign minister, Pierre-Henri Lebrun, allowed it, but just barely; the Jacobins wanted to stay on speaking terms with the world's only other revolutionary country. Soon France would be at war with a whole atlas full of nations and principalities, including Britain, Prussia, Austria, Spain, the Netherlands, Sardinia, Naples, and Hanover. On September 30, Mme. de Flahaut and her son escaped to England using passports obtained with bribery money provided by Morris. Talleyrand, always a slippery sort, had made his way there already. When she turned to him, he said he could not help her. The fact that she was with his own son did not persuade him. Fortunately for the farsighted countess, there was still Earl Wycombe.

Many potential victims of what had become the Terror got away because of Morris. Theodore Roosevelt, who never goes easy on him, praises the minister plenipotentiary's courage in staying in France. Morris later explained that he had no orders to leave.

His gift for absence served him well. After being arrested for not possessing the proper documents, and after protesting to Lebrun (who gave him an "insolent" answer but ordered him freed), Morris found a house in Seine-Port, a village some miles from the city. He spent nights there, returning to the embassy in the day. He went through many difficulties trying to obtain the release of American ships seized by the French, and of American sailors impressed into their navy. One day Thomas Paine was helping the French write their new constitution; the next he had landed in jail and was pleading for help from Morris, whom he hated. Lafayette deserted from his army command, fearing his soldiers as well as the guillotine, and ended up in Olmutz prison, in Austria. He petitioned Morris to declare him an American citizen and demand his release. Morris helped him with loans on Morris's own account, but Lafayette had been acting as a citizen of France and an officer in the French army when taken prisoner, and no authority would have accepted that he had suddenly become American.

In Paris, one of the governments of the moment threw Mme. de La Fayette in prison. Morris immediately let it be known that the United States took her safety seriously. She was let go, then rearrested. Morris again interceded for her. While her mother, grandmother, and sister died on the guillotine, Mme. de La Fayette survived. Released in 1795, she went to Austria and joined her husband in Olmutz. Morris also loaned her 100,000 francs of his own money. He kept trying to get the Austrians to let Lafayette go. Had Morris not taken the risk of staying at his post, Mme. de La Fayette almost certainly would have lost her life. She herself later said he saved her. Other supporters, including Washington, wrote letters to various leaders on her husband's behalf. Morris certainly helped keep him alive, too. The Lafayettes deserved all the help that Morris gave them, and more. At considerable risk to himself, he upheld his country's debt of honor to them. But nothing Morris ever did could persuade Mme. de La Fayette to like him.

When France's armies began winning in the field, the king lost his usefulness as a bargaining token. He was guillotined early in 1793. Jefferson applauded the execution, saying it would teach monarchs that they were not above the law. Marie Antoinette suffered the same fate a few months later. As for Flahaut, the husband, Adèle provided him with one of the forged passports she obtained for the family, but he never used it. Having been arrested, he managed to escape and go into hiding. While awaiting passage across the Channel he learned that his attorney and friend was being held hostage because of his escape. Flahaut returned, exchanged himself for his friend, and went to the guillotine.

Morris kept his commercial savvy as the world went sideways and shattered. When confiscated possessions of aristocrats were sold at government auction, he scooped them up. After the king and queen were taken from Versailles to house arrest in the Tuileries, the impedimenta of the royal court went on sale, and Morris found bargains. His friend Washington had given him a list of other items (besides the watch) that he hoped Morris could get for him. Some of the purchases, including a large silver soup tureen embellished with figures from Greek mythology, are now on display at Mount Vernon. Throughout his time in Europe, Morris did not stop selling land. The idea of moving to an America of peace and plenty retained an appeal. At some point he sold Mme. de Staël 23,000 acres he had previously purchased in upstate New York. It seems odd to think that she would ever have gone there to live. In the upshot, she didn't, and her son sold the land after she died. She was a generous woman and Morris doubtless made money on the deal.

In America, the French ambassador, Edmond-Charles Genêt, was causing so much agitation with his attempt to get the United States to declare war on Britain and Spain—equipping privateers, raising troops to fight the Spanish in Florida—that Washington asked the French to recall him. The French government in power at the moment went one better and put out a decree for Genêt's arrest. It also demanded the recall of Morris. At the end of July 1794, James Monroe arrived in France as his ambassadorial replacement. In Paris, the bloodiest part of the Revolution had passed. Between April 17 and June 10, a total of 3,607 people had died on the guillotine. During the eight months that saw the worst excesses, Morris received no communication from his government.

After introducing Monroe around—the blood-drenched government that had just executed Robespierre gave the new ambassador a fulsome embrace—Morris spent two months settling his affairs in France. He seems also to have ended a minor amour, though his romantic adventures during this period went unrecorded. Entries in his diary stop two weeks before the king was killed; Morris feared the diary might be grabbed by some murderous tribune and used against people, including himself. The authorities gave him a passport on the condition that he never return to France. For his travels, he assembled a small caravan: a substantial carriage, accompanied by a baggage wagon, probably with at least two horses for each. Each vehicle had a driver, and Morris also brought his valet. He left Paris for the last time on October 12, 1794. Two days later, after stopping at Seine-Port, he headed for Switzerland.

DURING THE MOST locked-down days of the Covid epidemic, I sometimes drove to the park on Randall's Island just across the Bronx Kill from where Morris's house used to be. I sat at a picnic table on the shore of the confluence where the kill runs into the East River. It's another of New York City's panoramic places. Beyond the wide expanse of water between the Bronx and Long Island (i.e., Brooklyn-Queens), you can faintly make out the towers of LaGuardia Airport on clear mornings. Closer are the tall stacks of a Con Ed power plant, and the troubled prison complex on Rikers Island, and the long, straight caterpillar of a causeway leading to it. When the sun rises, it lights up airplanes against the hazy New York City sky as they take off from the airport or descend to it. During the depths of Covid, long intervals went by between planes.

Humans can change a place a lot, but as for the landscape in its broadest contours, we're pretty much stuck with it. The Bronx Kill still flows into the East River, creating a junction that's accommodating and wide. I think of it as Morris's former driveway. People sailed here to visit him. In his papers is a letter he wrote to Jonathan Dayton, who had been a Constitutional Convention delegate from New Jersey and who lived in Elizabeth, a small city on an inlet just around the corner of Staten Island. Today the inlet is Newark Bay, the port of Newark and Elizabeth, where container ships the size of recumbent skyscrapers come and go. Morris gave Dayton detailed sailing directions—which shore to hug, what tide to choose—so that he could arrive in time for a four o'clock supper. Morris estimated the trip would take him about three hours. In 1952, a history and sailing buff who followed the same route using Morris's directions reported that they still held true, but because of more recent dredging he didn't have to go as indirectly and covered the distance in under an hour.

Among the last details Morris took care of before leaving France was to arrange for the shipping of the luxury items he'd purchased. He dispatched them to Morrisania on a vessel called the *Superb*. As I sat at the picnic table, I imagined the tall ship, guided by a harbor pilot, proceeding slowly up the East River, reducing sail abreast of the Bronx Kill confluence, coming about into the wind, and dropping anchor. Boats row out and attach themselves to the ship by ropes. The ship raises anchor again and the boats tow the *Superb* stern-first to Morrisania's dock just across the way, on the kill's northern bank. The ship's cargo scaffolds swing into place, the hold opens, and Morris's wooden crates of furniture and curtains and silver plate from Versailles are lifted out of the hold and lowered to the dock.

There's a huge recycling warehouse on the bank today, and it resounds with noise that carries across the water. I hear the kettledrum boom of emptied trucks, the beeping of heavy equipment backing up, and a general undefined grinding as the place chews up the city's rinds. A few feet above the water a cormorant arrows past like a flying eyeliner pencil. Farther out, on the East River, barges and ferries glide by. Plastic bags drift overhead on the wind, fall to the surface, and roll a few times before submerging.

Among the government-auction purchases that Morris shipped to Morrisania were liquors and wines from Louis XVI's own cellar. In a letter, Morris instructed his overseer to be especially careful with them. They included several cases of Imperial Tokay whose wax seals bore the Austrian emperor's double-headed eagle. The wine had been a wedding present to Marie Antoinette from her mother, the Empress Maria Theresa. I imagine men lifting the wooden crates from the dock and onto the back of wagons and bringing the empress's repurposed gift up the tree-lined avenue to the Morrisania manor house.

SOON AFTER ARRIVING in Lausanne, Morris experienced symptoms of the syphilis that would recur from time to time throughout his life and contribute, eventually, to his difficult and painful death. In his diary, which he had resumed, he never felt sorry for himself or fell into recriminations when his urethra once again became inflamed. He just forted up in an inn or hostelry and waited in bed for the condition to improve.

For the next four years he wandered about Europe meeting dignitaries, doing business deals, and having rendezvous with women. Why
he decided to delay his return to America is unclear. He said that if he
went back, he would again be called to public service, which he wanted
to avoid—not a very convincing excuse, given how much he seemed to
relish serving his country and his state all his life. The frequency with
which he happened to find himself in places where Mme. de Flahaut
alighted in her own exiled wanderings suggests that she might have
been what held him.

In England, poor smitten Earl Wycombe had provided refuge,
but the countess was not a person to sit around and wait for her luck
to change. In six months of hard work, she finished writing her first
novel, *Adèle de Sénange*, about a French noblewoman who, coincidentally, grows up in a nunnery after the death of her mother, marries an
elderly count, and has a relationship with an English earl. The book
sold well, and she followed it with others. During her wanderings,
Mme. de Flahaut supported herself by writing novels and making
hats. Wycombe seems to have become a victim of her success. He did
not remain in the picture for long. When Morris's own travels brought
him to England, he remet the discarded earl, who complained bitterly
about how she had used him.

She wrote a letter that reached Morris in Germany, and he helped
her get set up in Altona, a village near Hamburg. He kept coming
back to visit her, but although they were now both free, they did
not find each other as agreeable, and she seems to have given up, finally, on their inconclusive romance. She had met a diplomat, Count
de Souza, the Portuguese ambassador to Denmark, a man of consequence who traced his lineage back to a lieutenant of the explorer
Vasco da Gama. Even better, from an author's point of view, the count
had first sought her out because he admired her writing. On one
of Morris's recurrent visits, he learned that Mme. de Flahaut and
de Souza had become engaged.

Before any marriage took place, Talleyrand once again landed on
his feet, this time as the foreign minister in the latest French government, and he was able to get her order of exile set aside. Mme. de Flahaut returned to Paris in September 1797. Morris never mentioned her

in his diary again. The persistent de Souza kept up with her, and they finally married in 1802. Morris's skittishness and callowness aside, he and Adèle probably never would have worked out as a couple, after the way they had treated old Flahaut. Their collusion in her betrayal of him was put to shame by the count's courage when he met death to save his friend. Flahaut showed that the *ancièn régime* had some real nobility to it. Gouverneur and Adèle were not insensitive people, and they must have understood how shabby their own behavior looked next to his.

Overall, Morris made little impact on her life, and none at all on her son's. The old Count de Flahaut, on the other hand, had set an example of sacrifice and dedication that drove the boy to glory. When Charles was fifteen, he wrote a letter to Napoleon offering to serve as his aide-de-camp. He related the story of his father's heroism, and said, "Pray believe, General, that with such an example before me I shall be true both to my honor and to you." Napoleon took notice, and young Flahaut soon became a member of the Hussards Volontaires, Napoleon's bodyguard. Charles went on to a career in which he was wounded many times in battle and rewarded for bravery, with one promotion and title after another. At the end of Napoleon's time in power, when he was forced into exile, the ex-emperor asked Charles to go with him. Adèle told Charles not to. Charles followed his mother's advice, and was never quite the same charming, dashing fellow again. His French biographer says that if Charles had been raised by old Flahaut he would have stuck with Napoleon all the way.

Let us pass over the image of Morris, the man who wrote the words "in order to form a more perfect union," having assignations with the wife of a Prussian diplomat while riding in his carriage in Berlin and Leipzig. He repeated this kind of socializing with various ladies and non-ladies in other European cities, but Morris's candor in his diary should not be given too much attention. He was a loner to the point of eccentricity and had nobody besides himself in whom to confide. Seeing as many places and meeting as many types as he did, he became the first American, after Franklin, whom one could call a citizen of the world. As he traveled Morris witnessed marvels unknown back home, such as a set of locks in Scotland that could lift and lower canal boats through an altitude change of more than a hundred feet. This ingenious piece of engineering made him think again of the wealth of the American interior, and how a canal might connect New York to it.

He pursued justice, where he could, and performed good deeds. He looked up Louis XVI's only surviving child, a daughter, and gave her the money Louis had entrusted to him to arrange the escape and raise an army (though almost none of it remained). For a while, Mme. de Flahaut was traveling with the young Duc d'Orléans, who also could not return to France. His father, a cousin of the king, had voted for his execution, becoming a pariah among his fellow nobles before going to the guillotine himself. The young duc wanted to travel to America, and Morris sent her money to help him. Decades later, the duc would become King Louis Philippe. Nor did Morris forget the La-fayettes. He kept pestering the Austrians about them, and he attended the small ceremony when they were finally released in October 1797 near Hamburg. The couple thanked him rather perfunctorily for his efforts, he thought.

In the summer of 1798, he made plans to return to America. He would sail from Hamburg, a city where he had often spent time. As a favor to a friend, he was accompanying a family with children, one of whom caught smallpox; the group waited several months until the child recovered. On October 4, almost ten years after he'd departed from America, Morris and his charges sailed from that city on the ship *Ocean*. After living in Europe for almost a decade, he would never return to it. The voyage tried everybody's endurance. During the long crossing, the ship almost ran out of food. In November, it came to within eleven miles of Sandy Hook, but bad weather diverted it to Rhode Island. Then for ten days it tried to get out of Narragansett Bay against unfavorable winds. The ship didn't reach New York Harbor until December 23. Parties of Morris's friends fêted him in Manhattan, and on New Year's Eve he attended services at Trinity Church.

On January 5, 1799, at dusk, he returned to Morrisania. Lacking his attention for all these years the house had developed leaks and was falling apart, but still standing.

14

SOMETIMES PEOPLE WHO don't live in the Bronx, don't visit it, and rarely even pass through it tell me what a terrible place it is. The very name struggles with prejudice; in certain parts of the world, "a Bronx" has come to mean a dangerous urban area or slum. The 2020 U.S. census found about 1.4 million Bronx residents. If you ride the subways in the borough during the morning commute, you see people wearing uniform shirts or jackets bearing the logos of companies— Icon Parking Systems, Best Buy, Moishe's Movers, Elite Amenity Management, Best Guy Movers, Bess Electricians, Einstein Electric, FedEx Delivery, Godfather's Pizza, Universal Services ("Everything You Need in a Cleaning Service"), and more.

Men and women in security-guard uniforms carry their police-style hats in plastic bags, construction workers strap their yellow hard hats to their belts or backpacks, and guys in T-shirts printed with the names of messenger services hold their e-bikes pointing toward the ceiling to take up less room. Groups of sinewy men in knee guards and paint-spattered canvas trousers talk together in Spanish; women in beauty-salon smocks and transit employees in their gray-and-blue MTA uniforms check their iPhones. Nurses in loose-fitting V-neck scrubs of light blue, turquoise, light purple, pale green, and other soothing colors get on at seemingly every stop; their ID cards, clipped to shirt hems or pockets, have been turned photo side in, maybe to preserve travel-time privacy. Judging by appearances, health-care worker is the most common profession among the riders.

All these people going to work early in the morning live in the Bronx. How does that square with it being a terrible place?

Terrible things do happen in the Bronx. The same is true in the other boroughs, but when violence occurs here, it sometimes registers as worse—I'm not sure why. I came across few historic markers as I walked in the Bronx, but memorials for recent victims of violence are too common. One day when I was in the West Farms neighborhood checking out the old stomping grounds of James DeLancey and imagining bygone times near the waterfall that once powered DeLancey's Mills, I saw a "Wanted" poster on a light pole. It said that a seventeen-year-old girl, Vlana Roberts, had been shot and killed in front of 966 East 181st Street at 9:05 p.m. on June 2, 2018. The police were offering a $2,500 reward for information leading to an arrest and indictment.

The shooting had occurred just two nights before, about three blocks from the waterfall. Vlana Roberts had lived in a nearby apartment building, at the corner of Boston Road and East 180th Street; now a memorial almost filled the walkway leading to the building's entry. Hundreds of candles, many of them lit, in tall, narrow glass holders with pictures of Jesus on them, clustered together like a mourning crowd. Against a wall, more candles had been lined up to spell "VLONE." People had added mylar balloons, stuffed animals, bouquets of flowers, and small cartons of Tropicana orange juice. One balloon had a picture of a sad-eyed puppy on it, and the words "I'm So Sorry."

Boys in hoodies were standing by the memorial with their arms crossed, stony-faced. One of them said, almost inaudibly, "I loved her. She was like my sister." At the curb by the shooting site, two police vans idled with their flashers going. Police vehicles often park at murder sites for days afterward, just to be a presence. A cop sitting in the passenger seat of one of the vans rolled down his window—a breath of air-conditioned air came out—and told me that the killer had not been caught, but there was video of him on YouTube.

The video showed a boy with a ponytail running around a corner holding something under his shirt against his waist. Later, the sixteen-year-old suspect was arrested and charged with Vlana Roberts's murder. In photos in a video tribute to her online, she appears to be flashing gang symbols, which doesn't make her death any less sad. When I returned to her memorial display two weeks after I first saw it, nothing remained except her name written in colored wax in a couple of places on the pavement. A man sweeping up said this was a New York City Housing Authority building, and NYCHA rules require that all memorials be removed after two weeks.

If a worse killing could be possible, it happened eighteen days after Vlana Roberts's, and about a mile away. In a case of mistaken identity, young men from a Dominican gang called the Trinitarios spotted a fifteen-year-old, Lesandro Feliz-Guzman, known as Junior, on the street in the Belmont neighborhood. They chased him into a bodega at the corner of East 183rd and Bathgate and pulled him out as he begged the employees to help him. Then the attackers swarmed on him and stabbed him repeatedly and cut him with a machete. Security cameras recorded the attack. The boy was able to stagger to the emergency entrance of St. Barnabas Hospital, about a block away, where he bled to death.

I saw the memorial for Junior while walking in that neighborhood on another hot summer day. At the corner of East 183rd and Bathgate, all around the now-shuttered bodega that hadn't helped him, the candles on the sidewalk were lined up—not merely by the hundreds, but by the thousands. Balloons, flowers, stuffed animals, posterboard testimonials, Yankees hats, and other sympathy gifts mounted up almost to the store's awning. Police cars, vans, and a command vehicle like a motor home had their flashers going in the blocked-off intersection. Murals with seven-foot-high portraits of Junior covered several walls. Junior had been a member of an organization for teenagers who want to become police officers. Here the cops weren't sitting in their air-conditioned vehicles but standing silently in the street in their dark uniforms, their faces shiny with sweat.

Whenever I come across memorials, I try to remember the names. On Andrews Avenue in Morris Heights, twenty-three-year-old Joel

Rivera was shot and killed in front of his building. I saw ladies in church clothes and hats carrying casserole dishes covered with aluminum foil into the entry on the day of his funeral. The display, on one side of the doorway, featured a photo of a handsome, smiling young man holding a baby.

Near the corner of Sheridan Avenue and East 167th Street, a gunman who was only a boy shot and killed fourteen-year-old Christopher Duran one morning as he walked to school. As he died, he cried, "Mommy! Mommy!" the *Daily News* said. When I went by, several smaller, two-man police vehicles were monitoring the shooting site, their flashers going. On the sidewalk in front of the victim's building someone had written, "R.I.P. Joppy I love you bro" and "Joppy World." The fact that the boy had posted a picture of a Smith & Wesson automatic handgun on his Facebook page doesn't make his death any less desolating.

On Hall Place, just up the East 165th Street "stair street" from Horseshoe Playground, someone shot Jamarr Vestal, who was thirty-one. He died on a park bench across the street from a children's day care. In the photo of him on the police poster offering a $2,500 reward for information about his killing, he looks mournful. Three men shot and killed Darin Capehart, twenty-five, in the lobby of 730 East 166th Street, in NYCHA's Forest Houses. At the playground next to the building, just two years before, a stray bullet had killed Lloyd Morgan, Jr., who was four years old. The memorials to both had long been removed, but their names were faintly visible, written on the sidewalk. Tyana Johnson, who was nineteen, died after being shot at an outdoor graduation party in Shoelace Park near the intersection of East 226th Street and Bronx Boulevard. Two kids with guns jumped out of a silver BMW and opened fire on the partygoers. Tyana Johnson's memorial, next to a pathway in the park, included small bottles of cocktails, with names like Mango Madness, that she had invented and hoped to sell. She had planned to get a college degree in business.

On Barnes Avenue near Lydig Avenue, not far from the Morris Park subway station, I stopped at a sidewalk memorial for Allan "Ai" Benn, who had been shot and killed at that spot two days before. This memorial was still being set up. A small crowd of people had gathered around it; a woman with a tattoo on the small of her back bent down to put another candle among the growing accumulation. I took off my cap and looked at the posterboard tributes. Allan "Ai" Benn was thirty-six—still young from my point of view. A woman in an orange sweatshirt with pictures of running shoes on it who was standing next to me asked, "Did you know him?" I said I didn't. She said, "He was my son."

"I'm so sorry." After a moment I asked her name.

"Vanessa."

"I will think of you, and pray for you every night," I said.

"Thank you."

A man with a short, scraggly beard was talking. "There was people standing all around, and nobody saw nothin'? How was it that *nobody* saw *nothin'*? This place is over. Ai didn't have no beef with nobody. When Benny fired off a whole clip two weeks ago and nothin' happened, I knew this place was finished. This place is over."

I said "God bless you" and goodbye to Vanessa, and walked on.

THE NAMES AND STORIES of young people who've been murdered in the Bronx could fill too many books. Grief pulses through the borough, more in some years than in others, but unremittingly. Some of the hardworking men and women riding the rush-hour trains in the morning are the relatives or friends or acquaintances of the victims. History in the Bronx collapses into the more immediate and painful past, as the memorials come into existence, disappear, and reappear, with different names on other sidewalks—sometimes even the same sidewalks—while older names fade away.

On and near Beekman Avenue, a two-block-long street on what used to be the grounds of Gouverneur Morris's manor house, ten young men died by violence between 1991 and 1992. Those were some of the worst years of the crack epidemic, when (according to *The New York Times*) a war broke out over discount crack—three dollars a vial versus five dollars a vial. Today no memorials remain on

Beekman Avenue's sidewalks. A bleak peace seems to prevail; but this will never be a happy street.

TO MAKE ANOTHER two-hundred-year jump in time: When Lewis Morris told Congress that Morrisania would be a good site for the national capital because a slave rebellion couldn't happen here, he may also have had the French colony of Saint-Dominique in mind. In the early 1790s, the modern world's only successful revolution by enslaved people began in the place now called Haiti, and it continued through different phases until 1804. The Haitian Revolution produced hundreds of thousands of deaths from violence and yellow fever, and it thoroughly frightened American slave owners.

Gouverneur Morris, Lewis's half brother, had been the most vocal antislavery delegate at the Constitutional Convention. In the case of the Saint-Dominiquins' demands for liberty, however, Gouverneur Morris switched to a brutally pro-slavery view. He believed that the Haitian Revolution posed a serious threat to the United States because it could inspire this nation's hundreds of thousands of enslaved people to rise up. To forestall that possibility, he urged a full-scale military suppression of the revolution in Saint-Dominique. As its violence went on, he exhorted the slave owners of the American South to aid in crushing "the slave insurrection in Ste. Dominique." In a speech to the U.S. Senate in 1803, he said:

> That event [the defeat of the Haitian revolutionaries] will give to your slaves the conviction that it is impossible for them to become free. Men in their unhappy condition must be impelled by fear, and discouraged by despair. Yes—the impulsion of fear must be strengthened by the hand of despair!

If we're wondering why the place that was the home of the man who wrote the Preamble of the Constitution became a killing ground for young people of color, we need look no further than these words. The better angels of our nature require patient exhortation before they appear, but the worst, evilest demons will show up in a blink, if you summon them, and they will be reluctant to leave. They will spread out across the country, and two-hundred-some years later, memorials to young lives cut short will mourn on the sidewalks of the places named after you. People all over will think that the Bronx, where hundreds of thousands of hardworking American families live and raise their children, is a terrible place—which, despite all the efforts of your minions, Fear and Despair, it is not.

15

A MONTH AFTER his return from Europe, Morris tore down the manor house and began to rebuild it from the foundations up. The architect he hired followed the general model of a French chateau. When finished, the house had nine rooms, a balcony over the front porch, and a wide-open vista in its east-facing windows. Theodore Roosevelt, who presumably had seen the house as it appeared in the later 1800s, described it as "not in the least showy, but solid, comfortable, and in perfect taste." He called the house's view of the Sound "superb . . . with its jagged coast and capes and islands." Morris wrote to a correspondent that on his roof terrace he enjoyed taking in the view and "breathing the most salubrious air in the world." He said that here his wanderings would end.

Friends described him as living like a European aristocrat. In his great room hung a tapestry showing Telemachus resisting the wiles of Circe; in bookcases with glass fronts he kept a library said to be one of the finest in America. After the American Revolution, his land lost its status as a manor, and Morris stopped being the lord of it. The change seems to have been mostly semantic. He still owned a wide expanse that included farm fields, pasture, woods, brooks, and shoreline. To keep his chef supplied with game and superintend the foxhunts, he employed a huntsman. As I've said, the estate extended northeast, possibly to an important oak tree mentioned in deeds marking boundaries between family holdings. The geographic marker is remembered today in the name of Oak Tree Place, which is near the entrance to the parking garage for St. Barnabas Hospital. The foreman of Morris's estate was a Scotsman named Bathgate, whose family later had a farm near where Bathgate Avenue is today. Lesandro "Junior" Feliz-Guzman, murdered by the Trinitarios, was attacked on Bathgate Avenue, and he died near Oak Tree Place.

Washington must have missed socializing with Morris while he was in Europe. He wrote to him inviting him not just to visit Virginia, but to move there: "I shall be very happy to see you in this seat of my retirement." On December 9, 1799, hearing that Washington had decided to leave public service, Morris wrote him a letter urging him not to, and saying how important he was to the country. Washington never read the letter. On December 12, he came in from riding, did not change out of his wet clothes, and caught a respiratory illness. Overbled by his doctors, he died two days later. Morris delivered the oration at his memorial service in New York City and afterward expressed his dissatisfaction with it. One attendee noted that the eulogy did not draw a tear, which isn't a surprise, given Morris's lawyerly incisiveness and lack of sentiment. The loss of Washington had major consequences for Morris's later actions on the political scene, when his sense of national purpose deserted him. The older man had been his idol, father figure, and lodestar, and Morris never could replace him.

New York State elected Morris to fill out the term of a U.S. senator who had resigned; Morris served three years but did not win reelection. His popularity in his home state would never be overwhelming. He returned to his dealings in land and traveled all over upstate and as far west as Lake Erie, to the future site of Buffalo. At the moment in that journey when he came around a bend and saw the lake for the first time, a vision superimposed itself: "Hundreds of large ships will, at no distant period, bound on the billows of this inland sea," he wrote. As a boy on my way to my grandmother's lakefront cottage I used to wait for that thrill, leaning over the front seat for the first glimpse of Erie's whitecapped blue between the trees. When we got even nearer, we might see the long, stately ore boats, Morris's vision made real, freighting Wisconsin iron ore to the steel mills of Cleveland and Lorain.

His prediction about being called back to public service proved correct, too. In 1804, the New York City legislature—the equivalent of today's City Council—looked into appointing a commission to provide a street plan for the city. Three years later, the state chose Simeon DeWitt, who was the surveyor general (and cousin of DeWitt Clinton, the mayor); John Rutherford, a New York lawyer; and Gouverneur Morris for the job. From the start this commission was opposed to any system of meandering thoroughfares. The city already had enough of those with its cow-path-based streets downtown. Morris especially did not want a plan resembling what the French architect Pierre L'Enfant had inflicted on the capital city of Washington, D.C. By this time, Morris had become wary of anything he saw as too expressive or too French.

He did not want any D.C.-like stars, triangles, or circles in New York City. Instead of such funny business, he and his fellow commissioners chose a street plan afterward known as the grid. It created a regular pattern of east-west numbered streets that started at First Street, just north of Houston Street (which marked the northern boundary of the original city, with its less orderly arrangement), and continued all the way up to 155th Street, in the village of Harlem. The numbered streets intersected at right angles with twelve numbered avenues that ran north and south. First Avenue went up the east side of Manhattan and Twelfth Avenue went up the west side. Other avenues, Second through Eleventh, ran parallel to them. Aside from allowing for some preexisting streets, most notably Broadway, which went the length of the island and pushed its way diagonally through the commission's rectangles, the grid lay like a metal grating on the then-rural landscape and subdued it to its will.

The numbered streets were spaced about 264 feet apart, so that twenty north-south blocks equaled 5,280 feet, a mile. (Therefore, for example, if you walk sixty blocks, north-south or south-north, and it takes you an hour, you're going three miles an hour.) The avenues were of varying distances from one another—closer together near the edges of the island and farther apart in the middle—with the expectation that development would be denser along the waterfronts. The extra space in mid-island, and a large expanse of open land known as the Parade Ground, which has since been shrunk down to Madison Square, left room for the later insertion of Madison and Lexington Avenues. Critics said the plan destroyed the natural beauty of New York. Edgar Allan Poe, not known as a city planner, complained that the grid ruined "many picturesque sites for villas" uptown.

The commission members reasoned that buildings were rectangular, so therefore the plan of the city should be in rectangles. Commerce depended on street frontage, and the grid would provide a maximum of that. Philosophically, the plan followed the lead of Enlightenment rationalism, as did the decimal-based national monetary system that Morris had helped to devise some years before. Morris believed commerce was the whole purpose of the city. The grid simplified real estate transactions and development and gave a structure for commerce in the same way the Constitution did for national government. Many people disliked the grid, and detractors speak ill of it to this day. Had it not been for Broadway, which already existed, and which the planners had to accept as an unconforming element, the grid would have left us with a less human city. Broadway's disruption of the grid created Times Square, along with Herald Square and Lincoln Square and other vital, nonrectangular city spaces.

The grid plan had two effects on the Bronx: First, many of the east-west streets continue in roughly their same courses on the Bronx side of the Harlem River. West 132nd Street in Manhattan reappears as East 132nd Street in the Bronx, West 133rd as East 133rd, and so on heading north, although the Bronx has numbered streets that don't exist in Manhattan, because the Bronx extends farther in that direction. Two of the avenues are continued, also; Third Avenue in Manhattan lines up (roughly) with Third Avenue in the Bronx, as Manhattan's Park Avenue does with the Bronx's Park Avenue. The imposition of the grid's east-west streets upon certain parts of the Bronx leads to the spectacle of streets meeting hills that are practically cliffs, and trying to go straight up them rather than sidling around, as more sensible streets would do. This grid-based relentlessness created the Bronx's "stair streets," such as the extra-steep one at West 167th Street that the Joker dances down.

Second, dislike of the grid caused a big swing in the other direction. Morris and his fellow commissioners presented the city with their design, and the city approved it, in 1811. One hundred years later, in 1911, the centennial of their achievement was not celebrated, because anti-grid ideas had taken over. If you've ever walked on one of those maddening paths that wind hither and yon in Central Park when all you want to do is cross the park from Fifth Avenue to Central Park West, you can blame the grid. Frederick Law Olmsted objected to the grid so strongly that he laid out the interior of Central Park with hardly a straight line to be found. In the grid, everything goes straight; therefore, in the park, Olmsted made almost everything wind. A later nineteenth-century vision of urban design, called the Garden City movement, promoted green spaces, parkways, and circular plazas like Grand Army Plaza in Brooklyn partly in reaction to the perceived tyranny of the grid.

The Garden City designs, in turn, led to the Garden Suburbs movement, with its assumption that cities were harsh places of mere utility. The grid's relentlessness produced a determination among planners to make it as easy as possible for people to escape to the suburbs' world of greenery, open space, and winding thoroughfares. (It should be added that this suburban utopia was intended for whites only.) The reaction against the grid, and against cities in general, would prove unfortunate for the Bronx.

ANN CARY RANDOLPH, whom Morris first met at her father's tobacco plantation when she was a fourteen-year-old called Nancy, found herself in a serious fix. As a pretty and charming eighteen-year-old, four years after their meeting, she may have become romantically involved with Richard Randolph, the husband of her sister, Judith. Adding to the situation's Southern Gothic *noir*, Richard and the sisters also happened to be not-very-distant cousins. The crucial events of her story occurred while the three were at a plantation called Bizarre, near Farmville, Virginia, west of Richmond. Nancy's screams in the night, some bloody bed linens in the room where she stayed, and a dead baby found in a woodpile by the plantation's enslaved people, added up to a charge of murder against her and Richard. Rumor supposed an affair between the two, perhaps an herbal-induced abortion, and a hasty disposition of the tiny body. Some said Theodorick Randolph, Richard's younger brother, was the actual father. Nancy may have been in love with him, not with Richard. But Theodorick died in February 1792, and the abortion or miscarriage occurred the following September, so—who could say?

Scandal, more gossip, and courtroom drama ensued; in February 1793, only Richard was brought to trial on the charge of killing the baby. Patrick Henry and John Marshall defended him ("Give me liberty or give me death," plus a future chief justice of the U.S. Supreme Court, made for the original legal Dream Team). Richard's high-powered counsel won him an acquittal after the account of a witness who found the dead baby was ruled inadmissible because enslaved people had no standing in court.

For a while afterward, Nancy continued living with her sister and brother-in-law. Then Richard died suddenly. Rumor said that Nancy had poisoned him—another of Richard's brothers, John, strongly inclined to this opinion. Nancy had to leave not only her sister's household, but the high level of Tidewater society that she had occupied hitherto. Her pedigree even predated white settlement, because her family said they were direct lineal descendants of Pocahontas. Also, Nancy's brother, Thomas Mann Randolph, Jr., who served as governor of Virginia, was married to Thomas Jefferson's daughter Martha. All of Nancy's prospects for a suitable marriage having vanished, she left Virginia and supported herself as a schoolteacher in Connecticut and a domestic servant in Rhode Island and New York City.

She remet Morris in Newport or in Greenwich Village in 1808. He said he was looking for a housekeeper of good family to manage his house at Morrisania. No person in the whole country could have been a better match for her. He remained a bachelor at fifty-seven, and when it came to checkered pasts, Morris knew how love and sex could disarrange a life. To people in refined circles, she was someone who had, perhaps, slept with her sister's husband and self-aborted a baby. Or she may have done neither. Theodorick Randolph may have been the father, and the baby's death may have been a miscarriage. (Despite John Randolph's ravings, no one thought she had really poisoned Richard.) Her supposed sins probably seemed considerably less grave to Morris, who had seen it all, and done quite a bit of it himself, in France. Did he mention to her that he suffered from a venereal disease he had picked up probably from having sex with prostitutes in his carriage while driving around the leading cities of Europe? He could not cast stones.

She came to work for him in April 1809. On December 25, after a Christmas dinner with guests at Morrisania, Ann Cary Randolph and Gouverneur Morris were married by the Reverend Isaac Wilkins, Morris's brother-in-law, the former Tory whose property Morris had saved from confiscation. Despite her relatives' continued badmouthing of her, and a vicious letter John Randolph sent to Morris accusing her of various crimes and sexual misbehaviors, she and Morris seem to have had a happy marriage. On February 9, 1813, she gave birth to Gouverneur Morris II. Sardonic relatives who had dreamed of one day inheriting Morris's estate nicknamed the baby "Cut-us-off," playing on the name of General Kutuzov, the Russian military leader who had recently defeated Napoleon at the Battle of Borodino. The younger Gouverneur would live for seventy-five years and become one of the main developers and railroad builders in southern Westchester County, the future Bronx.

GOUVERNEUR MORRIS, SR., specialized in thinking big, and the Erie Canal was one of the biggest and best schemes any civic brain ever spun. He first suggested it in 1777, when he was traveling in upstate New York to inspect the Continental Army as it prepared to fight the incursion of General Burgoyne. A man who was there later recalled:

> [Morris] announced, in language highly poetic, and to which I cannot do justice, that at no very distant day the waters of the great western inland seas would, by the aid of man, break through their barriers and mingle with those of the Hudson. I

recollect asking him how they were to break through these barriers. To which he replied, that numerous streams passed them through natural channels, and that artificial ones might be conducted by the same routes.

Having engaged Morris's talents in the arrangement of the streets of New York City, the state also appointed him chairman of the commission to plan and build the great canal that he (and, by then, others) had proposed. The Canal Commission began its meetings in March 1810, and Morris remained its chairman until his death six years later. Some of the on-site planning and laying out of the waterway's route was done by Morris and Surveyor-General DeWitt. Building such an ambitious example of what was then not called infrastructure took full participation of the city and state. Morris also got the federal government to help. He and his wife made a trip to Washington so he could lobby for the canal, and while there she began a reconciliation with her sister and her sister's in-laws that did not last long and seems only to have made them madder. Morris had better luck—the House came out in favor of the canal bill he wanted, and it passed on June 17, 1812.

The following day Congress declared war on Britain. With the beginning of the War of 1812, Morris entered his angry-old-man phase. Although the canal to which he gave the last big effort of his life would tap into the resources of the interior, he did not like or trust the people who lived there. He blamed them for conflicts with Native Americans that contributed to the war, and he thought they should stop taking Indian lands. Madison's reelection in 1812 seemed a disaster to him, because it reinforced the power of the southern faction in Congress, whose expansionist hunger he also excoriated. The fact that southerners had extra say in the affairs of the country because of the three-fifths compromise frustrated and infuriated him no end. They owned hundreds of thousands of slaves, therefore they could tell the North what to do. They also put New England's shipping at risk of attack from British ships because of their aggressions in the western territories. He thought the three-fifths compromise should be repealed, and slaves should count for nothing in representation.

He concluded that Pennsylvania, New York, and the New England states should secede from the United States, and he gathered like-minded representatives from those places for discussions at Morrisania. In the *New York Herald* he wrote an article arguing for the separation of the northern states from the Union. The secessionists met officially at Hartford in 1814 and established a plan for a new country. Theodore Roosevelt called this late swerve in Morris's career "to the last degree a discreditable and unworthy performance," and went on:

> Morris's opposition to the war led him to the most extravagant lengths. In his hatred of the opposition party he lost all loyalty to the nation. He championed the British view of their right to impress seamen from our ships; he approved of peace on the terms they offered, which included a curtailment of our Western frontier, and the erection along it of independent Indian sovereignties under British protection. He found space in his letters to exult over the defeats of Bonaparte, but could spare no word of praise for our own victories.

Morris's participation in the secession movement probably would not have happened had Washington been alive. We can call Morris a deep-down monarchist because, for all his independence of mind, he needed a fixed point like Washington to navigate from. He would not even have objected if Washington had become king. The Treaty of Ghent, which ended the war, in 1815, removed the seceders' motivation. The first serious secession movement in the United States took place in the North, not the South; and Morris, originally a proponent of a strong federal constitution, contributed to it more than anybody.

His urinary tract problems continued, and he suffered from gout, which sometimes kept him in bed for months. He and his wife received visitors at Morrisania—marrying Morris had somewhat restored her social standing. The Lafayettes asked him if he would let them out of repaying the money he'd lent them, and he suggested they pay only half of it, which they grudgingly did. "Unhappily they will ever bear me a sincere hatred," he wrote. But Lafayette, who outlived his wife, seems not to have hated him. After Morris was dead, the old marquis visited Mrs. Morris and Gouverneur Jr. at Morrisania as part of his triumphal American tour in which towns were named after him and the government gave him $200,000. Another of Morris's French acquaintances also prospered later in life; Louis Philippe, the Duc d'Orléans, whom Morris had helped (via Mme. de Flahaut) with money and lines of credit, later became King Louis Philippe of France. Morris had always said the French needed a king. After the Bourbon Restoration in 1814, Louis Philippe repaid Morris's loans to him, but without adding interest.

A new bridge across the Harlem River made possible the construction of a toll road through Morris's estate. The route connected to the Boston Post Road and provided a shortcut that avoided Breakneck Hill, which you had to climb if you were going to the Post Road by way of the King's Bridge. Morris objected to the taking of his property but lost out to eminent domain. Accepting the inevitable—always one of his strengths—he rode in the inaugural carriage along the new road at its opening. The first steamboats had begun to ply New York's waters, and he must have guessed that the age of steam was approaching. The bridge and the toll road (called the Westchester Turnpike) only hinted at the stampede to come.

Morris died in his bed on November 6, 1816. He had maintained his good humor until the end. As he wrote four months earlier, he still sometimes felt "the Gaiety of Inexperience and the Frolic of Youth." Theodore Roosevelt abbreviates his account of Morris's death, saying merely that it followed "a short illness." In fact, the details are so painful one can see why the future president skipped over them. Morris attempted to ease his urinary tract constriction by forcing a piece of whalebone through it, which caused lacerations, leading to an infection that killed him. He had asked to be buried on a rocky hill overlooking the Mill Brook on his estate. The hill, its graveyard, and his tomb cut into the hillside are all still there. His will provided that his bequest to his wife be increased if she remarried, but she never did. Gouverneur II, who was then three, would inherit everything at adulthood.

Morris had not been in touch with Mme. de Flahaut (later Mme. de Souza, after her remarriage) for almost twenty years. Like

Talleyrand, her sometime lover and the father of her only child, she managed to stay afloat amid the rapids and whirlpools of French politics. Her mothering of Charles, their son, never stopped. She helped to arrange for his marriage to the wealthy daughter of a Scots viscount. Charles had had a son by his mistress, Hortense, the wife of Napoleon's brother, but his Scots wife bore him daughters. Adèle remarked that with no son "they will be condemned to having a new baby every year." She became devoted to her granddaughters, nonetheless. When one of them, Clementine, died of typhoid fever at fifteen, in January 1836, Adèle took to her bed in grief. She never recovered and died several months later. Gouverneur resides in his hillside tomb in a poor part of the Bronx, and Adèle is in Père Lachaise Cemetery, one of the most fashionable afterlife addresses in Paris.

CONSTRUCTION OF THE Erie Canal began in 1817, the year after Morris's death. The work required improvised engineering solutions, black-powder blasting of rock obstacles (dynamite had not yet been invented), and thousands of immigrant laborers from Ireland and Germany, many of them badger-shaped men built low to the ground, just right for digging. Work continued, summer and winter, for eight years. The fact that Lake Erie waited just over the horizon, definitely reachable despite the difficulties, served as inspiration.

Parts of the canal were usable by 1821. On October 26, 1825, the first boat bound for New York City entered the canal from the lake. A cannon fired; farther along the route, people waiting for the sound heard it, and fired another cannon; then, people at the next cannon heard that sound and fired theirs; and so on, in a relay of thousands of cannon all the way down to the city along the waterway. The Echo Cannonade, as this celebratory relay system was called, demonstrated New York State's achievement with a wide-armed, thundering gesture that went from Lake Erie to New York Harbor in eighty minutes, then reversed itself and swept back to the lake in another eighty. When the boat reached the city, it continued to the Narrows, where the governor, George Clinton, dumped a barrel of water from Lake Erie into the ocean to symbolize the uniting of the two geographies.

The Erie Canal, and the dispatch with which New York created it, made New York City's fortune. Boston and Philadelphia, in their attempts to reach westward, had to get over the Appalachian Mountains. New York's Hudson River, which lies west of New England's Appalachians, had given the city a head start. With the opening of the canal, grain from Ohio and other western places began sluicing into the city. In the early 1800s, New York became the first in a long line of great American granary cities, like (later) Chicago, Minneapolis-St. Paul, New Orleans, and Seattle. The city owes its preeminence, in a large part, to the vision of Gouverneur Morris, whose bones and complicated legacy lie at the heart of the Bronx.

PART II

PARADISE

16

SO THE WARS ARE OVER and Morris and the rest of his generation of
Founders are leaving the scene, congratulating themselves on how
well the experiment in self-governance seems to be turning out. As
will happen in the United States after other wars, the country will
become, for a brief while, a kind of paradise. It won't really be one, but
to many people it will look like one. In Westchester County, farming
and its peaceful rhythms will resume. Rich men will buy big sections
of the old Bronk's Land manors and build rustic retreats and travel
back and forth to offices in Manhattan; New York City will develop
commuter suburbs earlier than any other place in the world.

Nobody will know at first what to make of the new city and nation
they're in. For clues, New Yorkers will instead look back to older
times; this will be the stroke of genius hit upon by Washington Irving,
the first American writer to earn his living at writing. Irving will create a local mythology based not on the recently defeated and still-
unpopular English, but on their predecessors, the Dutch. Giving his
New York City everyman the Dutch name and persona of Diedrich
Knickerbocker, he will bring to life a catchy, comical, new-old local
identity that New Yorkers will love and hang on to. (I am indebted for

this idea to the historian Elizabeth L. Bradley, and her book *Knicker-bocker: The Myth Behind New York*.)

Looking backward to the Dutch will be useful in another way. The Dutch produced the greatest landscape paintings in the world, and the reason is that before they painted them, they physically *made* the landscapes by draining their lowlands and marshes and constructing dikes and erecting windmills that pumped the North Sea out the other side. If you've ever mowed a lawn or weeded a garden, and afterward pulled up a folding chair and just sat and looked at the good job you did, you can see why the Dutch painters got to be so skilled. Their countrymen wanted beautiful pictures of what they had made, so they could admire it. Here, likewise, American painters, of a group that will be called the Hudson River School, will paint landscapes that celebrate the country that the Revolution fought for. The nation won the land and created itself, and then the Hudson River painters sat down to their easels and portrayed the fruits. History isn't just written by the winners, it's painted by them.

In this context I keep thinking of the Robert Frost poem "The Gift Outright," and its first line, "The land was ours before we were the land's." Now, this is a debatable statement: How was it ever "ours"? And who is the "we" it supposedly belonged to, and/or vice versa? But if you accept the premise, then the nineteenth-century idea that Westchester County could be a rural paradise might have come from the desire of a people truly to be "the land's"—to connect spiritually and emotionally with the new country. In any case, Westchester County in the nineteenth century will forget its history as the bloody Neutral Ground, and turn into a romantic landscape of woods, streams, hills, and meadows, where city people will go to refresh themselves. The New York Botanical Garden and Woodlawn Cemetery and the parks of the borough preserve some version of this idealized place. Even in the South Bronx, which has been built on and built on, and where traffic and industry and trouble have pummeled the original landscape, you can still find hints of the old arcadian paradise.

WHEN I WALK in the Bronx, or anywhere, I check out the fences. Our whole country seems to become more fenced every year, in the same way that our citizenry becomes increasingly tattooed. No place employs more fences, or more elaborate ones, than the Bronx. It has schoolyards surrounded by ten-foot-high concrete walls with twenty-foot-high chain-link fences topped by strands of barbed wire above that. Apartment building courtyards shelter behind quarter-inch-thick steel gates and pointed steel palings that curve outward over the sidewalk. On playgrounds with tall chain-link fences, guys play basketball during summer afternoons. On the roof of the Vernon C. Bain Center, on the same afternoons, guys also play basketball behind chain-link fences, but these rooftop courts are fenced overhead as well as along the sides; the Bain Center (as it's called) is actually a floating prison docked at the foot of Halleck Street in Hunts Point.

Not far away and in the same neighborhood, one of the most forbidding fences in the city defends a multi-acre installation identified by a sign as the New York City Transit Authority Infrastructure Division. The fence extends along Oak Point Avenue and crushes even the thought that anybody could get through it. Its outer fourteen-foot-high barrier of heavy-gauge chain-link topped by coils of razor wire overawes the sidewalk. But this is only the start. Three or four feet back, a second, inner fence, about three feet shorter than the outer one, rears up with more chain-link and razor wire. And this doubly fenced fence is not done yet. On the few feet of no-man's ground in between fence number one and fence number two, heaps and tangles of yet more razor wire hint at the distress you would fall into if you somehow made it over fence number one and lost your footing while insanely trying to jump to fence number two.

Also on Oak Point Avenue, seven blocks east of the fence, I came upon one of the scraps of nineteenth-century green that survive. It's called Joseph Rodman Drake Park, after a poet who died about two hundred years ago and who rests in the cemetery at the park's center. A fence surrounds the cemetery, and inside it another, fiercer fence protects Drake's grave. This personal fence consists of tall, sharp, outward-curving iron palings in a circle, like a ring of bodyguards, around the marble monument. The personal fence keeps visitors back far enough that it's impossible to read the inscription.

Only once has the gate through the graveyard fence been open when I've passed by. The park may be more accurately described as two and a half acres of lawn, with two old oaks and a few dozen younger trees. The leaves turn colors faithfully each year, and they fall and blanket the grass. There are no benches or swings or slides or other park furniture, just a few paths. People bring their dogs and let them run around. One afternoon when I was leaning on the outer graveyard fence and peering in at Drake's monument, a pit bull almost half my size jumped on my back, followed by a second pit bull. They were playing with each other, smiling toothy pit-bull smiles, tongues out, tails wagging, and they wanted me to join them. At a curb nearby, a man with his car door open and one foot out on the grass was studying his phone and paying no attention to the animals that could only have been his.

You've probably never heard of Joseph Rodman Drake; I hadn't, either. In later reading I learned he was once so beloved that Lafayette stopped at the grave and bowed his head in silent meditation here. The moment of *hommage* occurred on his 1824–1825 trip to the United States, when Lafayette also paid a visit to Morris's widow and son at Morrisania. Probably, he came to Drake's grave right after seeing the Morrises. By then the once-youthful marquis was a serene, tall, austere-looking man of sixty-seven who had outlived his wife and most of his famous American comrades-at-arms and was enjoying the unanimous adulation of this country. Stendhal, the novelist, who met Lafayette at about that time, wrote of him, "He had the same faults as I had. He was chiefly interested in pinching the behind of some pretty girl."

A sign in the park explains about Drake. He was born in New York City, orphaned young, and buried here after he died of consumption, at the age of twenty-five, in 1820. His lack of family may have been why he spent time with the Hunts, whose estate occupied this land and extended to the end of Hunts Point. This was their family graveyard. Others with headstones in the cemetery, such as the Leggett and the Willett families, also have nearby East River points named after them. Drake began to study medicine in his teens and was a doctor when he died. With his friend Fitz-Greene Halleck he published a satire on New York City bigwigs called *The Croaker Papers* that got some attention. His daughter put out a collection of his poetry in 1835 and it made him briefly famous.

Contemporaries praised his poems "The Culprit Fay," "The American Flag," and his locally most relevant composition, "Bronx," which is about the river rather than the borough, which did not then exist. Nonetheless, as an early example of branding, the title helped establish this strong place-name in the public's mind. Drake's work falls into the category of nineteenth-century Nature Poetry, in the style of Romantic poets like Wordsworth. "Bronx" begins:

I sat me down upon a green bank-side,
Skirting the smooth edge of a gentle river,
Whose waters seemed unwillingly to glide,
Like parting friends who linger while they sever;
Enforced to go, yet seeming still unready,
Backward they wind their way in many a wistful eddy.

The next six stanzas talk about "the yellow-vested willow," the rocks draped with ivy, the birds, the "antic squirrel," the "dark cedars with loose mossy tresses," and so on. The last stanza is:

Yet I will look upon thy face again,
My own romantic Bronx, and it will be
A face more pleasant than the face of men.
Thy waves are old companions, I shall see
A well-remembered form in each old tree,
And hear a voice long loved in thy wild minstrelsy.

One of his most popular poems, and his longest, "The Culprit Fay" is about a fairy, or sprite (*fay* is a synonym), who breaks a fairy oath by falling in love with and briefly consorting with a beautiful human maiden. It's unclear exactly what the two did together; since the fay is about an inch long it seems that he did not kiss both her lips but only one of them. This has cost him his wings and his magic power. To regain the first, he must leave the fairy woods and go to the ocean and catch a drop of water tossed into the air by a leaping sturgeon. When he can fly again, he must go far into the sky and catch a spark from a falling star. He does both these tasks, with adventures along the way, and his good standing among the fairies is restored. I thought the poem was unsuccessful, mostly, but I liked the part about the sturgeon. These fish definitely do leap, for no reason anybody has figured out; and a five-foot-long sturgeon, all knobby and prehistoric-looking, suddenly hurtling out of the water is something to see. A fishing guide I know on Staten Island once told me about a fisherman who was knocked out of his boat by a sturgeon.

I did not have much of a reaction to Drake's poems, on the whole, but I thought the fault might be mine for living in a different century. I looked up a review by Edgar Allan Poe that appeared in the *Southern Literary Messenger* of April 1836, the year after Drake's collection came out. The fame of Drake and of Fitz-Greene Halleck evidently had irked Poe, who pointed out in some detail what bad poets they were (though he rated Halleck worse than Drake). He went through "The Culprit Fay" almost line by line, showed how ridiculous it was, and parodied a section of it. He did see some talent in "Bronx," calling it "altogether a lofty and beautiful poem." Only in his twenties himself, Poe perhaps understood that being too hard on a young poet would be unsporting. He thought Drake might have found his true calling not as a poet but as a writer of romantic prose "had the Destroyer only spared him a little longer."

Poe's main quarrel seems to have been with reputations based on patriotic sentiment rather than literary worth. Of "The American Flag," he wrote, "[It] is indebted for its high and most undeserved reputation to our patriotism—not our judgement." Poe did not write flag-waving verse himself, and he had to honor his own vastly superior gift. As if in self-defense, he wrote, "[We] often find ourselves involved in the gross paradox of liking a stupid book the better, because, sure enough, its stupidity is American." Drake's collection included an unfinished poem listed as "Fragment" in which Poe found what he believed to be the book's best passage. It's a description of Niagara Falls:

When o'er the brink the tide is driven,
As if the vast and sheeted sky
In thunder fell from heaven.

Good description! Bravo, Joseph Rodman Drake! In these lines
it all starts to come together—the longing to make sense of the new
country, combined with a Hudson River–style celebration of American landscape, and the romantic ideal of wild nature as the realm of
spirit. But even if Drake had lived longer and succeeded completely in
writing poems about these subjects, only his fellow Americans might
have cared. On the other hand, people all around the world know the
work of Poe, Drake's fellow Bronxite.

Poets gum up the bulldozer treads of progress sometimes, and
in the early 1900s, eighty and ninety years after Drake's death, his
reputation was still enough to keep this cemetery from being built on
or paved over. By then neglect had caught up with it. A walking-tour
guidebook of the time described his grave marker as "a modest shaft,
half hidden by the tangle of bushes and wild flowers that border the
road." In 1903, an effort was made to move his grave next to that of
Fitz-Greene Halleck, who is buried in Guilford, Connecticut, but local Bronx groups objected. Literary enthusiasts saved the cemetery
from road builders, and the Parks Department acquired the property
in 1909. Drake's gravestone was described as "chipped and vandalized" in 1912. A marble shaft replaced it, with the same inscription
that had appeared on the original stone. Taken from Halleck's "Lines
on the Death of Joseph Rodman Drake," it reads:

Green be the turf above thee,
Friend of my better days;
None knew thee but to love thee,
Nor named thee but to praise.

Poe had approved of this poem's "union of tender sentiment and
simplicity," but could not help mentioning the similarity to a stanza
in Wordsworth's "She Dwelt Among Untrodden Ways" ("She dwelt
among untrodden ways / Beside the springs of Dove, / A maid whom

there were none to praise / And very few to love."). In 1961, the second marker was vandalized, and presumably the special additional fence around it went up afterward.

The aura of the poet was not strong enough to reach across the street, to the separate graveyard in which the Hunts and others interred the people they had enslaved. In 1909, that cemetery still existed, but later development graded over and erased it. According to a sign in the park, the bodies of "nanny, coachman, farm laborer, woodcutter, drover, blacksmith, cook, groom, carpenter and seamstress," and others are still there. Various businesses—Kadosh Foods Enterprise, Fratilli's Pizza, New York Truck Refrigeration Corp., Center Sheet Metal—and a widened Hunts Point Avenue hold twenty-first-century tenure on top of them now.

ONLY 2,782 PEOPLE lived in the future Bronx in 1820, and the number had gone up to just 3,023 by 1830. With slavery's official end in New York in 1827, none of those 3,023 were enslaved. The Erie Canal and its flood of cheap grain into the city put the local wheat growers out of business. Agriculture, still the main industry, sent vegetables and other produce to the city by boat or wagon, and beef, pork, and mutton driven to it on the hoof. Over muddy or dusty or tarry roads, the herds walked to the Farmers' Bridge, which had no tolls, just east of the King's Bridge, or to the Harlem Bridge, also toll-free, where the Third Avenue Bridge is now. Then the drovers moved them along similar roads to slaughterhouses on the lower west side of what's now downtown Manhattan.

Two industries—a bleachery and a snuff-grinding mill—began operations and prospered on the faster-flowing section of the Bronx River upstream from the former DeLancey's Mills. A family named Lorillard owned the snuff mill. Roses that they grew for petals to mix with their snuff and give it a pleasant scent were forebears of some of the rose variants in the botanical garden today. The mill that the family built out of stone from a nearby quarry still stands. It's the oldest surviving factory building in New York City; today the Parks

Department uses it for office and event space. The Lorillards eventually got so rich they inspired a New York newspaper to use the new word *millionaire* to describe them. As for the bleachery, which began in 1820, and which rinsed the gray out of newly woven fabric with bleach, one wonders what Drake would have thought of its presence on his beloved river.

The railroads changed everything. In 1837, the New York and Harlem River Railroad completed a single-track line the length of Manhattan Island, from the city at the southern end all the way to the shore of the Harlem River opposite Morrisania. In 1841, it bridged the river and laid track through the middle of the future Bronx, to where Fordham University is now. In its infant form as St. John's College, Fordham had been founded the same year. Traveling by train from the city to the Fordham station took an hour. With the railroad's arrival, important action in Westchester County moved from the edges, and into the harder-to-get-to parts west of the Bronx River. One could say that the New York and Harlem River Railroad opened up "the continent's" interior.

By 1841, Gouverneur Morris II had reached his twenty-eighth year, with the momentum of his powerful ancestors behind him. He had land, money, and ambition, if not his father's literary brilliance or gift for world-shaking. Morris II possessed his own gift, one centered on real estate. Where his father had tended his lands lightly, like a country squire, Morris II saw development possibilities. As a young man he predicted the need for railroads. With other principals he chartered the New York and Albany Railroad, and it had acquired rights-of-way through Westchester County by the time the New York and Harlem River Railroad reached its temporary terminus opposite his land. His railroad, which never built any track, instead merged with, and gave its rights-of-way to, the New York and Harlem River, and Morris II became that company's vice president.

Although he was only three years old when his father died, he later must have heard gossip about his mother. In an attempt to take his inheritance, the relatives who nicknamed him "Cut-us-off" had even gone so far as to contest his paternity in court. It's hard to come up with a more painful insult. Ann Cary Randolph Morris died in 1837. In 1841, the year that the railroad came, Morris II gave the Episcopal Church land for a new brick church on his property next to the family burial ground, above the Mill Brook, the scenic and quickly flowing stream that divided his part of Morrisania from the Lewis Morrises'. He paid for the construction of the church himself and called it St. Ann's in her memory.

Though it's on high ground with dark rocks poking out in places, the old fieldstone church is now overshadowed by the taller apartment buildings around it. Mill Brook, the lively stream, is gone, of course, or maybe moved into pipes underground. In the churchyard a white marble marker facing St. Ann's Avenue tells of the accomplishments of Gouverneur Morris, Sr., and an iron plaque lists some of the prominent members of the Morris family who are also here. According to a history from more than a century ago, Richard, the original Morris, who served in Cromwell's army and came to Bronk's Land in 1670, lies in this churchyard, along with the lineup of confusingly named Lewis Morrises who followed him, plus Morris family members who served in the Seminole, Mexican, and Civil Wars.

Once when I passed by the church, some of its doors stood open—the day was Sunday—and I wandered in a side entry of the church's newer addition. (The original fieldstone building is seldom used today.) An early service had just ended and the next would begin soon. I lingered in the back as a few people prolonged trailing-off conversations. In a few minutes the sanctuary had emptied. A sense of being in the hull of a dependable, much-traveled vessel lulled me. Here was a particular quiet—the quiet of a place of worship after a service has ended and the congregation has just left—which is another of the things that have always been the same. It made me think of Gouverneur Morris II, the founding parishioner, and of how he sometimes used to take out a large bandana handkerchief and blow his nose during services, causing the children in the congregation to fall apart with giggles.

The Reverend Martha Overall, the church's minister, a woman with pale-rimmed glasses and long gray-blond hair, hurried past.

When she gave me a glance, I asked her if she could tell me a bit about the history of the church. She returned the brisk answer my question deserved, saying that she was preaching today and had no time.

A few weeks later, I came back on a weekday hoping to find her with a moment free. A line of people on the street waited for the church's food bank to open. The conversation of those in line was all in Spanish, and the only word I understood was *Trump*. A man in young middle age seemed to be in charge. I introduced myself and explained what I wanted, indicating my notebook. He said he was Joel Spearman, Rev. Overall's adopted son and pastoral assistant. Leading me into the church, he found the minister; again, she was walking someplace briskly. I said I had only one question. I asked whether the graveyard had been moved here after the church was built, or whether the graveyard had been here first, and the church was built next to it. (I now know it was the latter.)

Rev. Overall stopped, gave me a look of exasperation, and waved away my notebook. "I don't concern myself with that kind of thing," she said. "I'm more concerned with keeping this place going." She hurried off.

Her adopted son, perhaps embarrassed by her brusqueness, showed me around the churchyard on my way out. The crypt of Gouverneur Morris (senior) is like a bunker carved into the rock, with fenced-in steps leading down to a small iron door in a frame of white marble. Atop the crypt is the green hillside itself, thickly overgrown with Virginia creeper. Nearby an umbrella elm stretched out its arching branches. A few white feathers and part of a seagull wing lay on the steps. From somewhere came the sound of a basketball bouncing.

"Many, many, many years ago, historians opened this tomb and looked inside," Joel Spearman said. "They found a skeleton that they knew was his because one of the legs was missing below the knee."

He suggested, gently, that if I wanted to know more about the church I should read *Amazing Grace*, by Jonathan Kozol. The book, and two others by Kozol that followed it (*Everyday Resurrections* and *Fire in the Ashes*), center on this neighborhood, the church, the children it serves, and the ministry of Rev. Overall. After reading the books,

I asked a friend of mine who's the priest at an Episcopal church in Manhattan if I was right in considering Martha Overall a saint, and she said, "Yes," without hesitation. Rev. Overall's care for the people of her church's neighborhood, whether they attend St. Ann's or not, approaches the miraculous. One cannot say enough in praise of Martha Overall. Send money to St. Ann's.

17

THE FIRST REAL ESTATE boom in the future Bronx followed the railroad. In this case, real estate meant actual estates—multi-hundred-acre country seats, featuring ornamental gardens and eccentrically designed mansions. Wealth brought by the Erie Canal, having accumulated in Manhattan, figuratively spilled over into this nearby arcadia. The new part- or full-time residents got to and from the railroad stations on horseback and in carriages. Guests arrived for the weekend by train, and stagecoaches carried them the rest of the way. What the Hamptons on Long Island are now, the Bronx once was, minus the cars, buses, helicopters, and jets (but not minus the train).

A list of the rural gentry and commuters to Wall Street offices who owned estates reads like a society column two centuries out of date. H. D. Tiffany, of that famous family, had a mansion on Hunts Point. Edward G. Faile, when traveling from his estate, Woodside, rode the whole distance to the city in his carriage, stopping in Harlem to change horses. John B. Simpson's estate, Ambleside, and William Simpson's, Foxhurst, adjoined each other in what's now the vicinity of Crotona Park. The Vyse family, after whom Vyse Avenue is named, owned a spread called Rocklands. The lawyer William Lewis Morris built a gray fieldstone mansion called Wave Hill in what's now

Riverdale. The investment banker Paul N. Spofford's place was called Elmwood. The railroad executive William B. Ogden situated his estate, Boscobel, on land near the High Bridge; Ogden had been the first mayor of Chicago.

Another new railroad, the New York and Hudson River, laid track along the Hudson's east bank in 1851, opening the region further. Edwin Forrest, the internationally known actor, erected a fancy, castellated mansion, Fonthill, on a high ridge above the river. The house is now part of the administration building of the College of Mount Saint Vincent, in Riverdale. A Brooklyn doctor built a mansion that's now the central structure of the Fordham University administration building; his name was Horatio Shepheard Moat. Collis Potter Huntington, the railroad baron; William E. Dodge, the mining titan and co-founder of the Phelps Dodge Company; William H. Fox, president of the country's first gas company; Richard March Hoe, inventor of a rotary printing press; Frederick C. Havemeyer, owner of the company that became Domino Sugar; the Astors, New York City's leading real estate family; Ynocencio Casanova y Fagundo, the Cuban importer-exporter; Lawrence Waterbury, the trotting-horse breeder, who put headstones on the graves of his favorite horses and dogs; and various other plutocrats summered or lived year-round in this verdant, city-adjacent place.

The Schieffelins, a family that had made money in pharmaceuticals—perhaps they were the Sacklers of their day—owned an estate called Asheburne, near the village of Eastchester. Eugene Schieffelin shook up the natural environment even more than the Sacklers shook up the opioid painkiller scene, but with results less deadly for humans. In 1890, he imported some European starlings to rid his garden of caterpillars. A fiercer, more competitive bird never hit these shores; soon the starlings had departed Schieffelin's garden and spread. Today the European starling has taken over as one of the commonest North American birds, with a coast-to-coast range year-round. Our swarming flocks of European-American starlings had their stateside origins in the Bronx.

ON THE INDUSTRIAL FRONT, the bleachery and the snuff-grinding mill were only the beginning. Kilns that burned Westchester County marble down to lime for concrete, and evaporators producing sea salt, supplied those necessities to the rapidly growing city. In 1841, Jordan L. Mott, an innovator with a healthy self-regard (he named the Mott Haven district after himself), bought land in Morrisania from Gouverneur Morris II and built an iron foundry there. Mott had invented a coal-burning stove, which the Mott Iron Works manufactured. Other foundries came to the area soon after. The Johnson Foundries, on a Harlem River peninsula near what's now the Spuyten Duyvil train station, produced a lot of the ordnance that was shot at the South during the Civil War. Irish laborers filled some of the workforce for the mills and kept the police busy. Although the Irish were only a third of the local population, they accounted for 55 percent of the arrests.

At the eastern end of the Morris property, near the mouth of Bungay Creek, the shoreline depth along the East River shelves off enough that large ships can dock there. Morris II had the nearby swampy land filled in and called the place Port Morris. To create access to his docks he then built a railroad line that was only about six miles long, running from Port Morris to the New York and Harlem River Railroad tracks. In honor of his mother—his life seems to have been devoted to repairing her reputation—he called the line the Pocahontas Railroad. Ann Cary Randolph Morris took seriously her descent from this famous ancestress, and her son did, too. He wanted everyone to call the railroad by its correct name. When people used its common moniker, "the old Pokey," he flew into a rage.

In the late 1850s, the Janes & Kirtland Foundry, another local ironworks, received a federal contract to make the ribs for the dome of the new U.S. Capitol building. More states had entered the union, the House and Senate chambers needed to be enlarged to hold the added members, and the bigger building made the previous dome seem puny. The new dome would be bigger than any in the world at the time. Its ribs, thirty-six in number, curve gracefully on the outside of it as they ascend from the dome's base to its top like the seams on a pointed hat. Janes & Kirtland cast the ribs of high-carbon iron and put them on flatcars on a short spur leading to the Pocahontas

Railroad, which took the ribs to Port Morris, where they were loaded onto barges, which transported them down the coast to the Potomac River and Washington. Janes & Kirtland employees oversaw the lifting of the ribs into place on the dome with ropes, pulleys, and horses. The iron was made, and the Capitol Dome erected, before the existence of gas- or electric-powered tools.

Construction of the new Capitol went on despite the Civil War, at the insistence of President Lincoln. It was not finished completely until 1866, too late for him to see. In 2014, 148 years later, the dome had begun to leak, despite previous renovations. Streaks of rusty water were running down the inside, pieces of ironwork were chipping and falling off. A renovation that would cost almost $100 million began in that year, and it finished, to general applause, one week after the presidential election in 2016. Public attention returned to the Capitol building on January 6, 2021, two weeks before the next president's inauguration. The Bronx-made cast-iron ribs, forged by the Janes & Kirtland Foundry and transported on the Pocahontas Railroad (both now long gone), still support the Capitol Dome.

Another contribution to the Capitol complex would come from Mott Haven. In the 1890s, Giuseppe Piccirilli, patriarch of a family that had been carvers of marble in Pisa since the Renaissance, relocated to East 142nd Street between Brook and Willis Avenues. The family had six sons, all of them carvers. Attilio, the eldest, was regarded as the most accomplished. The Piccirillis made some of America's most famous public statues in their East 142nd Street studio. They did a few of them entirely themselves, but most were taken from sculptors' renditions. The sculptor Daniel Chester French gave them the model of Lincoln seated with his hands on the arms of his chair, for the Lincoln Monument. The Piccirillis scaled up the model in twenty-six blocks of white marble from Georgia. Attilio Piccirilli himself carved the hardest parts—the head and the hands. In New York, the most familiar of the Piccirillis' statues are Patience and Fortitude, the lions (by the sculptor Edward Clark Potter) on the steps of the Public Library.

The Piccirillis' studio closed in 1945, and today there's a Spanish-speaking Jehovah's Witnesses' Kingdom Hall on or very near the site. The illustrious but modest family did not make a lot of noise about themselves, perhaps following the tradition of the great unknown craftsmen of the Renaissance. A few years ago, the city gave East 142nd Street between Brook and Willis Avenues the additional name of Piccirilli Place.

EDGAR ALLAN POE'S career at the *Southern Literary Messenger,* where in 1836 he dispensed justice to the reputations of Joseph Rodman Drake and Fitz-Greene Halleck, lasted less than a year. He had married his cousin Virginia Clemm, a girl of thirteen (he was twenty-six), and they sometimes lived with her mother, his aunt Maria. Poe pursued the life of a freelance writer, a term unknown at the time, and suffered the consequences. Successes and failures, and editing stints at other magazines, and attempts to get government sinecures that would allow him time to write, and episodes of drunken despair—all took their predictable course. His poem "The Raven," published in a New York City newspaper in 1845, began his true fame. In the same way that Washington Irving had struck some wonderful vein of public receptivity with his everyman, Diedrich Knickerbocker, Poe found a national and international hunger for weirdness and gloom with "The Raven." Today the New York Knickerbockers are a professional basketball team, and the Baltimore Ravens (Poe died in Baltimore, and is buried there) are a team in the NFL. To have a professional sports team named after one of your literary creations is an accomplishment practically unheard of.

Virginia Clemm showed symptoms of tuberculosis (then called consumption) early in 1842. Their marriage entered nightmare territory as they listened to her cough and worried that she would die. The New York and Harlem River Railroad opened the lands along its route not only for owners of estates, but for ordinary homeseekers. Between 1840 and 1850, the population of the future Bronx more than doubled, to 8,032. Three of the new arrivals were Poe, Virginia, and Maria. In 1846, Poe rented a cottage a short walk from the Fordham station. Its owner, a man named Valentine, had bought it from a man named Corsa. Both of those families appear in the accounts of events in the Neutral Ground; the Valentines, we recall, owned the "wretched house" that the French officers complained about, and Andrew Corsa was the fifteen-year-old guide who assisted the American forces as they chased the DeLancey men off the continent during the Grand Reconnaissance of 1781.

The Poes hoped that the fresh country air would be a tonic for Virginia. It might seem odd that anybody would think so; now the Bronx has the worst air in the city, along with the highest rate of asthma. On Valentine's Day 1846, Virginia wrote a poem to her husband anticipating the move, with the lines:

> *Ever with thee I wish to roam—*
> *Dearest, my life is thine.*
> *Give me a cottage for my home*
> *And a rich old cypress vine,*
> *Removed from the world with its sin and care*
> *And the tattling of many tongues.*
> *Love alone shall guide us when we are there—*
> *Love shall heal my weakened lungs . . .*

The first letters of the lines spelled his name. But, in the upshot, love did not heal her, nor did the country air. Virginia died in the cottage about a year after the poem was written, and she was buried in the Valentine family crypt. Poe had become friendly with some of the Jesuits at nearby St. John's College, who let him sit in the library staring into space. In his grief he walked all over what's now the Bronx, and he used its picturesque scenery in some of his stories. Sometimes he went out on the High Bridge, which had started carrying water in 1842 but was not yet complete. The view he saw from the bridge stirred him. To get an idea of what this experience was like we would have to go out on, say, a bridge over the upper Deschutes River, in Oregon, and look down its canyon. The canyon of the Harlem River was still a remote and unfrequented place in 1846.

Poe died three years later, in confused circumstances made more so by alcohol. Half a century after his death, literary and civic figures of New York persuaded the state to preserve the cottage and create a park around it. The cottage was moved a few blocks from its original site on Kingsbridge Road and to the other side of the Grand Concourse. The city owns it now, and the Bronx County Historical Society runs it. It's a New York City Landmark and listed in the National Register of Historic Places. Despite its official designations, the cottage at night is still a lonesome and haunted-looking little place.

THE FAILED REVOLUTION of 1848 in Germany caused many Germans to emigrate, and thousands came to what's now the Bronx. Between 1850 and 1860, its population increased almost 300 percent, to 23,593. The Germans settled in the towns of Melrose and Morrisania and opened shops, saloons, and breweries. A gregarious tribe, they formed singing societies, gymnastics teams, and social clubs, one of which was called the Schnorrer Club. New development happened mostly in the corridor established by the New York and Harlem Railroad, along what's now Third Avenue. In 1862, developers built a street railway that paralleled the route of the railroad, from the Harlem River up to Fordham.

Officially, this streetcar line, the first one to be built in what's now the Bronx, had a long and descriptive name—the Harlem River, Morrisania, and Fordham Railway—but it was seldom referred to as that. Its horse-drawn streetcars went so slowly (according to the *New York Herald*) that passengers could get off, pick huckleberries, and return to the same car. People called it the Huckleberry Line. Now and then the cars of the Huckleberry Line would slide off the tracks, and the passengers had to get out and lift them back on. The Huckleberry Line was a predecessor of the Bronx's Third Avenue el, which in a few decades would bring new residents by the tens of thousands.

In Manhattan, rich people had begun to move to fashionable new neighborhoods uptown. Across the Harlem River, plenty of room remained for outdoor venues that required a lot of land. Formerly, many of the wealthy had used the Green-Wood Cemetery, in Brooklyn, for their burials. But getting there from upper Fifth Avenue could be a slog, with the dense traffic, narrow downtown streets, and tie-ups at the busy intersections in the days before traffic lights. And then the casket and mourners had to be ferried across the East River and transferred to another hearse and different carriages. Easier to skip all that and go north, beyond the Harlem River. In 1863, some prominent New Yorkers established Woodlawn Cemetery, a nonsectarian, landscaped graveyard-park on about four hundred acres of woods and farmland three miles north of Fordham station. The New York and Harlem line had continued its tracks in that direction, and it put a new station at Woodlawn. No one took up occupancy in the new cemetery until 1865, when a Mrs. Phoebe Underhill was the first person buried there. Today, if all the dead in Woodlawn were to rise from their graves, the miracle would increase the population of the Bronx by more than 310,000.

The rich of Manhattan owned horses and needed open acreage for racetracks and polo fields. These, too, found ample room across the Harlem River. The great expanse of level ground where the Van Cortlandt family used to grow wheat provided enough for three polo fields. (The land is now the Parade Ground, sixty-six acres of uninterrupted lawn that stretches north from the front door of the Van Cortlandt House, the oldest building in the Bronx.) In Throgs Neck, swells with country estates laid out more polo fields there.

Leonard W. Jerome, a New York financier, disdained the new popularity of sulky racing and wanted to revive the noble sport in which the rider sat right on the horse. He and some like-minded men formed the American Jockey Club, built the Jerome Park Raceway, and in 1867 established an annual race, the Belmont Stakes. With his brother he pushed through a road that went from the Central Bridge (today's Macombs Dam Bridge) for five miles to their racetrack. In the 1860s, the area was still so wide open that a couple of private individuals with money could do that. Local politicians, noting the new road's existence, decided to name it after one of themselves, a certain Murphy. The story goes that Jerome's wife, Katie Hall Jerome, heard about this, got metal street signs made saying "Jerome Avenue," and had the signs bolted to posts along the route. It's Jerome Avenue today. For most of its length it runs in the shadow of the elevated tracks of the number 4 train.

Jerome owned a city mansion on Madison Square in Manhattan, and a country mansion on Kingsbridge Road about half a mile from the Poe cottage. He and his wife and three daughters summered in the Kingsbridge Road mansion. The oldest daughter, Clarita, known as Clara, had met an Englishman named Moreton Frewen, who owned a ranch in Wyoming, and who won her with tales of his adventures in the West. Many eligible young men had sought after Clara, but she chose the eccentric Frewen; he went on to lose two fortunes. The youngest daughter, Leonie, married another wealthy noble. This was the era in which titled Europeans were marrying rich American heiresses and heirs. The middle daughter, Jeannette, known as Jennie, married Lord Randolph Churchill, the younger son of the Duke of Marlborough, and became the mother of Winston Churchill. (Like the starlings, the British wartime leader had origins in the Bronx.) Today the Kingsbridge Armory, a vast brick building often obscured with scaffolding, covers the site of the Jerome house, and the Jerome Park Raceway grounds lie under the waters of the Jerome Park Reservoir.

With all this movement northward, it was clear that New York City would soon take over southern Westchester County. Most of the county's population growth had been in the towns of Kingsbridge, Morrisania, and West Farms, whose expansive boundaries at the time encompassed the entire western half of today's Bronx—that is, all of it west of the Bronx River. In 1873, the state legislature proposed a referendum for voters in those towns and in New York City to decide whether the city should annex the area. The referendum passed, and on January 1, 1874, the towns became the 23rd and 24th wards of New York City, under a bureaucratic name, the Annexed District. As a signifier of undefined in-betweenness, the name evoked the old Neutral Ground. Residents of the Annexed District, following the example of Manhattan's West and East Sides, called the place where they lived the North Side.

The tendency to define the city's geography only in relation to mid-Manhattan reminds me of an unfavorite term, "the outer boroughs." Brooklyn, Queens, and Staten Island, occupying their own landmasses adjoining Manhattan's, fit the phrase. But for Manhattan, which is also an island, to refer to the neighboring and much larger borough on the continent as being somehow "outer" smacks of hubris.

Attaching the Annexed District made the city almost twice as large, in landmass if not in population. (Kings County, Queens County, and Richmond County—Brooklyn, Queens, and Staten Island—had yet to be added to the city.) In the new district, as well as east of the Bronx River, thousands of acres of open land lay waiting for development. At that moment, John Mullaly, a man mostly forgotten today, stepped in. Roads in the Annexed District were dirt, or indifferently improved with tar, while cattle and other livestock still wandered around in certain areas. If you hung your laundry out to dry on a clothesline you might find a goat eating it. Consequently, for the time being, land prices remained low. Mullaly and others started a group called the New York Parks Association and persuaded the city to spend almost three million dollars buying up future parkland.

Born in Belfast, Mullaly had immigrated before the Civil War, full of Hibernian energy for good and ill. His career twined together journalism, rabble-rousing, civic enterprise, and logrolling at Tammany Hall. Though he did a lot for the Bronx, he can boast no public memorials. (A two-block-long park just north of Yankee Stadium that once was named for him has been renamed.) Mullaly wrote for newspapers and edited them, exposed unsanitary conditions in the city's dairy industry, went on voyages that laid the Atlantic telegraph cable, wrote books about that, and made his political reputation by inciting his fellow Irishmen to violence in the Draft Riots of 1863. He thought the Civil War was a swindle perpetrated by abolitionists to give preferment to the Negro race, which he considered inferior. When a hundred or more Blacks died in the riots, his expressions of regret did not rise above the ho-hum. Police arrested him for inciting resistance to the draft, but the charge was soon dismissed.

Pressed by the New York Parks Association, the city bought more than four thousand acres in what everybody now was calling the Bronx. It purchased the land for Bronx Park, where the botanical garden and the zoo are today, from the Lydigs, the Neals, and the Lorillards. Crotona Park, which Mullaly waxed rhapsodic about for its exceptional beauty, had been part of the Bathgate estate. Claremont Park had belonged to the Zborowski estate and farm. Van Cortlandt Park consisted of more than a thousand acres bought from that family, and Pelham Bay Park was acquired from the Pell, Bartow, and Hurst estates, among others. St. Mary's Park had belonged to the Janes family, of the iron foundry. Mullaly thought that Tibbett's Brook, which ran through the western part of the Annexed District, and which is now mostly confined to concrete tunnels, might attract anglers because of its trout. (Trout in the Bronx!)

The fact that a lot of the future parklands lay east of the Bronx River, outside the Annexed District, indicated that the city would soon annex all the eastern section, too. In effect, Mullaly led the way in acquiring the eastern part of the Bronx for New York City. His foresight in providing parks for the ordinary citizen benefited everybody, but his hateful side perhaps has motivated posterity not to go too far out of its way to remember him.

AMERICANS HAD MORE LEISURE in the decades after the Civil War, and more cheap kerosene for their lamps because of the new Pennsylvania oil fields and John D. Rockefeller. They stayed up later and entertained themselves by playing the piano, the new must-have accessory for the middle-class home. Most of the pianos came from the Bronx, the piano-making capital of America. Piano manufacturers lined entire streets of the Melrose and Mott Haven neighborhoods; the sound of piano tuning was everywhere. Row houses began to replace free-standing frame dwellings. Parts of the Bronx were citifying themselves like Manhattan, rather than suburbanizing. More industries—ice-box manufacturers, gasworks, cigar makers, freight services, warehouses—filled in around the original foundries. Jordan Mott dug a canal from the Harlem River to East 144th Street to provide more water frontage for the scores of factories that wanted to move there. The canal later got to be noisome and was filled in; Canal Street West and Canal Place, which together are about ten blocks long, show where it used to be.

More railroad lines crossed the Annexed District, headed upstate or along the coast to New England. The New York and New Haven line established its rail yards on the southeastern edge of old Morrisania. Additional horse-drawn streetcar routes, along Boston Road and Southern Boulevard, supplemented the Huckleberry Line and came together on the other side of the Harlem River, at 129th Street in Manhattan. They were the Annexed District's only local public transportation. In Manhattan, trains pulled by steam engines on elevated tracks thirty-nine feet in the air went along Second Avenue and Third Avenue. On the Third Avenue elevated you could ride the length of the island for a nickel. If you wanted to continue across the Harlem River on a horse-drawn streetcar it cost another nickel. Living near the elevated tracks or walking under them had drawbacks. The trains dropped hot cinders and oil and spewed smoke in people's windows, along with their hellacious noise and shaking.

In 1886, the Third Avenue elevated crossed the Harlem River. In the Annexed District, it continued along the Third Avenue route that the New York and Harlem River line had pioneered forty-five years before. Thanks to the railroad and the Huckleberry Line, by then the corridor was already partly settled. The owner of the el, Jay Gould, charged passengers a double fare—one in the Bronx, and another for the transfer at 129th Street. That double-dip arrangement was done away with in 1894, on a happy day for the city; after that, a nickel could take you all the way from South Ferry, at the southern tip of Manhattan, to beyond Fordham, in the Bronx, and another nickel could bring you back. This made a psychological difference as well as an economic one. Families from the Lower East Side rode the Third Avenue el to the Bronx parks—Crotona Park and the zoo were favorites—for weekend outings, and ordinary citizens could enjoy rural scenery like the plutocrats did, but without having to own any mansions.

ORIGINALLY, IT HAD BEEN the land of the Munsee, Siwanoy, and Weckquaesgeek. Then the Dutch claimed it as part of New Netherland. West of Bronk's River was Bronk's Land and east of it was Vriedelandt. When the English took over in 1664, the entire area became part of Westchester County. During the Revolutionary War, it turned into no-man's-land, the Neutral Ground; afterward, Westchester County reestablished jurisdiction. New York City annexed the part west of the Bronx River in 1874. In 1895, the city also took over the part east of the Bronx River. When Brooklyn, Queens, and Staten Island were incorporated into the city in 1898, each gained the status of a city borough, and the annexations from Westchester County became the Borough of the Bronx.

I am happy to have reached this point, because now I don't need to worry about referring to the place as the Bronx when it had not yet officially become it. After 1898, today's geographic Bronx officially was the Bronx (or The Bronx). For sixteen years, it remained part of New York County—Manhattan's county. Then, in 1914, the Bronx became its own county, Bronx County.

To repeat: In 1850, the population of Westchester County was 8,032. By 1900, the number of people living in the Bronx had climbed to 200,507, a twenty-five-fold increase. A new Bronx paradise waited on the horizon.

18

FLAT FIX

On East 174th Street, up the hill from the Jennie Jerome Playground and the six lanes of the Cross Bronx Expressway crawling through its roadcut farther below, a storefront whose sign says "RD Tire Center FLAT FIX" glitters in the sun. Stacked five feet high on the sidewalk, tires with five-spoke mag-wheel rims polished a bright silver cover almost the entire front. The letters on the awning, which are black and red, stand out against the yellow background. The fancy hubs radiate starburst shapes of light inside their black rubber circles.

FLAT FIX

At Road Runner Auto & FLAT FIX, 1236 Jerome Avenue, "FLAT FIX" is in red, outlined in black, on a yellow-and-white background. Below that it says, "New & Used Tires | Gomas Nuevas y Usadas." Air hoses snake around on the sidewalk. The store's front, half a block long, is open to the street, and tires piled atop one another in seven-foot-high columns recede into an inner gloom where air wrenches are chattering.

FLAT FIX

The sign for Sajoma FLAT FIX, at 4434 Third Avenue, has red and black letters on a yellow background. When I walked by on a rainy spring day, business was slow. Workmen sat on metal folding chairs alongside racks full of tires with numbers written on them in white chalk. A Spanish-language radio station was playing. The men leaned back in the rubber-scented half-light and looked out at the rain.

FLAT FIX

One Sunday while driving in the Bronx with my friend Janet I got a flat. We had just turned onto an entry ramp to the Major Deegan Expressway. I pulled over on the narrow apron and set about changing the tire. It was on the left rear wheel, and the apron adjoined the right lane, so traffic was speeding by just a few feet away. I had the back open and the spare and jack ready when a van pulled up behind me. A man in a suit coat and tie got out, took off his coat, and said he would change the tire for us. In the van, women of varied ages waited with several children. All wore Sunday clothes; evidently, they had just come from church. Tucking his tie into his shirtfront, the Samaritan removed the flat and put on the spare in a few minutes. He told me he worked for a tow truck company and changed flat tires all the time. I'm embarrassed to say we offered to pay him—embarrassed, because he waved off the bills in such a tactful way when he got in his van and disappeared back into traffic.

FLAT FIX

For years I thought the signs said, "Flats Fixed." One day I looked more closely. Unconsciously I had been applying my own language-generating model to a phrase generated by a different model. I do not know what the syntax or grammar of "Flat Fix" is. Maybe it's the more economical way of saying "Tire Repair." If so, it's an improvement. Shorter is better, and "FLAT FIX" punctuates the Bronx streetscape everywhere with its brisk, upbeat promise.

FLAT FIX

One December morning my wife and I drove our son, Thomas, and his girlfriend, Olesya, who is Russian, to JFK Airport for their flight to Moscow. At the time my son had been living in Russia for more than four years. Our route from New Jersey to the airport led through the Bronx—or, more accurately, on highways below and above it. My mind was elsewhere. I used to fly from JFK to Russia as often as three times a year when I was researching a book about Siberia. On a seven-week road trip across Russia from the Baltic Sea to the Pacific Ocean, I carried a satellite phone. At night, which was day in New Jersey, I sometimes walked around under the clear and starry Siberian sky, picked out a satellite I saw passing overhead, and bounced a phone signal off it and around the world to my family. I did not understand the technology, but I had a sense of the relays passing overhead—as the connection got stronger, then faded, then came in again when the next satellite moved into range.

Talking with Thomas on that trans-Siberia trip, I never described anything specific, and he asked me few questions. Mostly we talked about his video games, and his school; he was in the third grade. He seemed to have little interest in where I was or what I was doing, but I think the conversations must have made an impression.

FLAT FIX

I-95 Flat Fix, next to the Cross Bronx Expressway at the intersection of White Plains Avenue, announces itself with at least seven signs that say "FLAT FIX" in red letters on a yellow background. The signs run along the entire top of the store, and the tires stacked in piles on the sidewalk rise almost to the level of the awning. Next to I-95 Flat Fix, there's an easy-access florist, Miguel Flower Shack, whose blooming rows of curbside flowers are lined up in a grandstand display that begins where the fragrant black stacks of tires leave off.

FLAT FIX

The Flat Fix Tire Shop, on East 149th Street in Mott Haven, illuminates the red letters "FLAT FIX" with white lights around each letter, and a rectangle of green lights sets off TIRE SHOP. Next to that sign is a vertical one that says:

F

L

A

T

F

I

X

FLAT FIX

At JFK Airport, my wife and I waited while Thomas and Olesya went through the long back-and-forth line at the Aeroflot Airlines counter. I once loved Russia blindly, then decided it was too damaged. Russia is a country that was abused by the invading Mongols in its childhood and never recovered; it's an abused country. But Thomas saw past his own romantic ideas of Russia and continued to love it anyway. Also, I never really learned Russian, and he speaks it well.

After he and Olesya checked their bags and got seat assignments, we stood with them by the security checkpoint entry. A woman guard made us move to one side, so we didn't block people. There's only so much time you can stand like that, no matter how much you want to stay. Soon Thomas and Olesya joined the packed maze of the security lines and my wife and I went back to the parking lot. On the way home I tried to make sense of exactly where in the Bronx we were when we crossed into it. I took I-678 over the Whitestone Bridge and stayed on that highway heading for I-95, the Cross Bronx. To get to it I had to navigate through the mega-intersection among whose forest of columns I have wandered on foot many times. That nowhere-zone understory, with its blowing trash and constant traffic noise, is where I had imagined George Washington and Bill Lee riding by. Now I was on the intersection's topside, moving along the elevated roadway and its grayish-white pavements with nothing but sky above.

FLAT FIX

At Familia Zapata Flat Fix ("No Credit Needed") cars pull up at the curb. Drivers remove their vinyl rug protectors and give them a few quick blasts with the air hose to clean them while employees in gray coveralls change the tires. Traffic on Westchester Avenue goes by. Passengers wait at a nearby bus shelter that's covered with ads for the movie *Judas and the Black Messiah*. In front of a nearby fruit and vegetable market, on the sidewalk, ears of prickly pear cactus (nopales) are on sale, three for a dollar. A man wearing an apron and heavy gloves is shaving the thorns from the ears with quick swipes of a machete.

FLAT FIX

A garage behind a corrugated-iron fence on East Tremont Avenue has no signs on it; but out in the middle of the street, in traffic, a young man in a sleeveless T-shirt is holding a piece of white cardboard with a red arrow pointing to the garage, and "FLAT FIX" in large red letters. The young man turns back and forth to show the sign to cars going in both directions.

FLAT FIX

It's strange that on almost all the signs that say "FLAT FIX," the letters are the same shade of red, and the background the same yellow. The phrase is not trademarked, and Flat Fix is not a brand or franchise. No Flat Fix corporate offices exist on a landscaped suburban campus somewhere. Flat Fix, LLC, is not traded on the stock exchange, nor does Flat Fix belong to a CEO billionaire. Flat Fix exists on its own, above mere commerce, and beyond the possibility of its ever being co-opted. It's like other roadside-sign shouts—EAT or GAS or DIESEL or MOTEL. But you see those nationwide. As far as I can tell, Flat Fix is found only in New York City, and there mostly in the Bronx.

FLAT FIX

In old-time photos of the Bronx, the variety and the intricacy of the storefronts sometimes crowd the frame. Stores and shops line the business-district streets, and their signs offer everything from pianos to bedsheets to furs to shoes to corsets to pastries to Cadillacs to prescriptions to beer to frappés. The lettering usually is in the same typeface one sees in old newspapers, with modest serifs at the base of the capitals. The most recent of these photos date to the late fifties, just before the beginning of the highway-era Bronx. Nowhere in any of those old photos do you see a single sign that says "FLAT FIX."

FLAT FIX

On my trip across Siberia, my two Russian companions and I finally reached the Pacific after about six weeks of traveling. Outside the cities, Russian roads are generally poor, and we had several flats. In Russian, "flat tire" is *rovno tyre,* which means "level tire." Somehow "level" conveys the discouraging effect of a flat tire better than "flat" does. On the Pacific's Russian shore, I saw large rocks with the logos of the New York Yankees and Los Angeles Dodgers graffitied on them. The day my companions and I arrived at the Pacific happened to be September 11, 2001. I woke up on the morning of the twelfth— which was still the evening of the eleventh on the east coast of the United States—and saw a text message on my satellite phone from my wife that said, "We are OK." Wondering what that could mean, I called her.

I was next to a bay near the village of Olga. My companions, Sergei and Volodya, had set up our camp there. They had met two picnicking widows—the guys' skill at meeting women in remote Siberian regions had been impressing me for eleven thousand kilometers—and one of the widows invited us to her apartment in Olga to watch the coverage. Russian TV news made it look as if all downtown New York had been destroyed. In a shocked, sad, otherworldly frame of mind, I waited out the next week or so until I flew home, via Vladivostok, Seoul, and Anchorage. When I was finally in the parking lot at JFK Airport looking for the car service my wife had sent, the smell of the airport thrilled me. A breeze carried essence of diesel fuel, bus exhaust, fresh asphalt, and the humid sea smell of nearby Jamaica Bay. I crouched down and touched my fingertips to the warm pavement's recently steamrolled pea gravel and black tar that gleamed like sugar glaze.

I loved everything I saw from the window of the unnecessarily large SUV as the car service drove me home. The whole city looked precious and beautiful. The yellow-and-red FLAT FIX signs were like the banner of the Bronx. Going through that borough I took my hat off to it, grateful to be back on the Continent.

UNLUCKY ARE THOSE who love or loved Russia. After the invasion of Ukraine, in February 2022, the U.S. State Department told all U.S. citizens to leave Russia immediately. The company Thomas worked for shut down its Russia operations. He came back to the United States and Olesya joined him here. They then moved to Germany. Their Russian and expat friends from Moscow dispersed all over the world, to northern California or Turkey or Armenia or Berlin or Sri Lanka. Liberal, non-crazy Russia now exists mostly in secret, or outside the country's borders. It's unknown whether we who loved or love Russia will ever go back again.

19

IN THE LATE NINETEENTH CENTURY, events occurred in Russia that would have a big effect on New York City, particularly the Bronx. Failed states radiate shock waves, and during that century Russia disintegrated into one of the most failed states ever. The young emperor, Alexander II, began his reign after the death of his father, Nicholas I, in 1855. At first, his subjects loved him. He had dark, imploring eyes, and he seemed to care. In 1861, acceding to a demand that his country's liberals had been making for more than a hundred years, he freed the serfs. In the United States, the Civil War freed four million slaves: Alexander II freed twenty-three million serfs. But then they weren't given land, or any real start on new lives after serfdom.

Further reforms were too much for him, he retreated into intransigence, and people began to hate him as much as he'd been loved. Every time he turned around, someone else was trying to kill him. Several different would-be assassins took shots at him. A bomb intended to blow up a dinner where he was expected to be present detonated prematurely. Revolutionaries derailed and wrecked his train. Finally, on March 13, 1881, a member of the socialist-terrorist People's Will faction threw a bomb at his carriage as he was riding along a street in St. Petersburg. It killed horses and injured his coachman. Alexander got out to see how the coachman was, and another People's Will assassin threw a second, more accurate bomb. A frenzy of repression, and more terrorism, followed the murder.

In the United States, a parallel disaster occurred in the South. Five years before, during the presidential election of 1876, Samuel Tilden, the Democratic candidate, defeated Rutherford B. Hayes, the Republican, in the popular vote, but the tally of the electoral vote remained in dispute. A bipartisan commission awarded Hayes enough electoral votes to win; in return, to appease the Democrats, the Republicans agreed to remove federal troops from the South, where they had been stationed since the end of the Civil War. Without federal enforcement of the recent constitutional amendments that gave Blacks citizenship, local terror took over. It had predated the departure of the troops, but now white supremacy reestablished itself in full force, with disenfranchisement, lynching, and other violence.

For the rest of the nineteenth century and into the twentieth, terror influenced policy in both countries—either by undoing the advances of Reconstruction and reducing Blacks to near-slavery and Jim Crow segregation, in America; or by crushing dissent and thereby creating more of it, and more terrorism, in Russia. Violence killed almost four thousand public officials in Russia over the two decades following the tsar's assassination: Meanwhile, in the decades after 1880, more than three thousand Blacks are known to have been lynched in the United States. Unrecorded racial violence no doubt claimed thousands more. The effects of repression and terror in both countries led to large population displacements, though the exodus from Russia preceded the flight from the South.

MOST JEWS IN RUSSIA lived in the Pale of Settlement, a district that stretched across the western part of the country from Belarus through northern Ukraine, Poland, and portions of Latvia and Lithuania, up to the border of Prussia. Jews were thought to be fomenters of political radicalism; a woman of Jewish background had been associated with the murderers of Alexander II. Many Russians needed no excuse for hating and attacking Jews, who were blamed for all kinds of economic problems, such as the international fluctuations in the price of grain. After the tsar's assassination, a series of pogroms killed or injured thousands of Jews in cities in the Pale, notably in Kiev, and in hundreds of villages and towns. The riots also destroyed tens of millions of rubles' worth of Jewish property. From 1881, pogroms continued happening at random intervals. The first memory of Israel Baline, born 1888, was of lying by the road and watching his family's house and village burn in a pogrom. In America, he would change his name to Irving Berlin and write the songs "White Christmas" and "Easter Parade."

Alexander III, who came to the throne after his father's assassination, may or may not have encouraged the attacks on Jews. The House of Romanov were not philo-Semites, in any event. The tsar's secret police are believed to have created the notorious anti-Semitic hoax-text, *The Protocols of the Elders of Zion*. Alexander III responded to his father's death with a crackdown that filled the prisons of Siberia. He also enforced previously unenforced laws restricting where Jews could live and travel and study, and what jobs they were allowed to do (such as not making or selling vodka, or styling hair).

In response, the Jews of Russia began to leave en masse. They emigrated to other countries in Europe, and to Great Britain, Palestine, and the United States. Between 1880 and 1910, about 1.4 million Jews came to New York City, and more than a million settled there. More than half a million Jews moved into the tenements of Manhattan's Lower East Side, which took on the character of cities like Minsk and Lvov and other capitals of the Pale. But in those old-world places at least people did not live so much on top of one another. In New York, Jewish and other immigrant families crammed into small apartments with tiny rooms, in buildings where an acceptable air shaft could be twenty-eight inches across. By 1900, the Lower East Side was the most densely populated place on earth. The historian Mike Wallace says (in his book *Greater Gotham*) that the Tenth Ward had a concentration of more than fifteen hundred people per acre, "out-peopling the Koombarwara District of Bombay."

Lower East Side streets and avenues enclosed the newcomers' lives. The fur trade had founded Manhattan; Jewish immigrants got jobs alongside Italian and German furriers already established in the business in the neighborhood from East Twenty-third Street to East Thirty-fourth. Jews who arrived from Russian villages and had no skills learned to operate foot-pedal sewing machines, laboring in sweatshops in the furriers' neighborhood or on piecework in their own apartments. Plenty of jobs were to be had; at the time, New York City manufactured about three fourths of all the clothing in the United States. Going to the Garment District and coming home, the Lower East Side workers took the Third Avenue el. On their days off, they and their families rode the el farther north, to the parklands of the Bronx.

THE SECOND GREAT Bronx real estate boom seemed predictable in retrospect, but in fact, almost no one did predict it, except J. Clarence Davies, the real estate agent who is given credit for laying out much of the twentieth-century urban Bronx. Davies, born in 1867, came from a German Jewish family of some standing. His father owned a rubber factory, and his grandfather was a founder of the West End Synagogue and Mount Sinai Hospital. As a young man, Davies broke his ankle while running to renew an insurance policy. Not only did he suffer the injury, but the policy lapsed. Afterward, Davies walked with a limp that did not slow him down. (I note here the parallel to Gouverneur Morris, Sr., the proto-Bronxite who also broke a leg as a young man.) While Davies healed, his cousin, who owned a surrey, took him driving. They crossed the Harlem River at the Central Bridge and went up Jerome Avenue, which had just been paved. Men of Leonard W. Jerome's set and others used the avenue as a place to ride in light carriages and let their horses run. Davies was impressed by the fashionable spectacle and by the open land on either side. Here is where the vision came in; all over the rural hills, he imagined rows of handsome new apartment buildings.

By then the original owners of local estates had died, and their heirs were ready to move on. After his ankle healed, Davies explored the Bronx. He walked up the driveways of the big estates, knocked on the mansion doors, and discovered that many of the owners did indeed wish to sell. He was thinking in terms of hundreds of acres; so were they. At first, he did not buy the land himself, but put it on the market through the real estate agency he established with his cousin. No purchasers immediately appeared; his cousin quit the business. Davies kept his fingers crossed and persuaded more owners to list with him. He collected old prints of New York City, and one of the selling points he used with new prospects was to show them a print of the rural countryside that had since become the corner of Forty-second Street and Fifth Avenue. The same magnitude of change was coming to the Bronx, he told them—get in now!

He sat back patiently as the infrastructure tendrils grew nearer. A committee of citizens wanted a showpiece avenue built along the central ridge of the three main ridges that run parallel in the borough. The job of designing it went to Louis Risse, New York City's chief topographical engineer. He had grown up and studied in France, and he conceived a longer and bigger version of the Champs Élysées, to be called the Grand Boulevard and Concourse. It would run for four and a half miles in roughly the same north-south direction as Jerome Avenue, a few blocks east of it. Traffic crossing from Manhattan on the Macombs Dam Bridge (also called the Central Bridge) could connect to it easily. The Grand Concourse, as it became known, would be almost two hundred feet wide, with a garden strip down the middle, and four lanes in each direction. Instead of intersections it would have underpasses at the cross streets, so as not to interrupt its sight lines and traffic flow.

Construction of the Grand Concourse began in 1902. While it was still in the planning stage, technical advances made possible the electrically powered train engine. Streetcar and elevated lines in the city electrified, losing the disagreeable steam locomotives. Because the new engines did not belch smoke, putting the trains belowground now became an option. In a referendum that drew the largest turnout in city history, New Yorkers voted three to one for municipal ownership and development of a belowground transit system. A charter was drawn for the Interborough Rapid Transit Corporation, or IRT. Mayor Robert A. Van Wyck dug the first shovelful of earth for the subway on

March 24, 1900. The construction, a cut-and-cover operation, began just south of City Hall, then went up Park Row and over to Broadway, on what is now the line for the numbers 1, 2, and 3 trains.

At West Ninety-sixth Street, an adjunct line branched off, running under the northwest corner of Central Park, and then under Lenox Avenue (now Malcolm X Boulevard). At West 140th Street it veered right, went below the Harlem River at West 145th, continued under East 149th Street in the Bronx, and emerged as an elevated train beyond East 149th and Westchester Avenue. The tracks then proceeded northward along that avenue and Southern Boulevard. On July 10, 1905, subway and elevated IRT service began between City Hall and the station at West Farms, in the Bronx. The terminus was at East 180th Street and West Farms Road.

J. Clarence Davies's ship, in the form of an electrified subway train, had come in. The land rush that accompanied the arrival of the subways in the Bronx outdid any in the history of the city. Land prices went up tenfold, high exuberance took over, buyers changed to sellers and back to buyers overnight. In two months, Davies made $200,000 on commissions. As the boom accelerated, he sold Bronx farmland by hundred-acre parcels and sometimes cleared commissions of $150,000 in an afternoon. Henry Morgenthau, another German Jew, whose family had immigrated in the 1850s, put up investment money, and he and Davies formed their own development company. Davies had streets surveyed, laid out building sites, and invented whole new neighborhoods in former woods and pastures. He and Morgenthau made millions.

Morgenthau later served as U.S. ambassador to Turkey and told the country and the world about the Armenian Genocide of 1914–1915. His son, Henry Morgenthau, Jr., was a banker, and secretary of the Treasury under Franklin Roosevelt. Henry's son, Robert M. Morgenthau, served as district attorney of New York County (Manhattan) for thirty-five years. Robert Morgenthau met a law student, Sonia Sotomayor, when he was participating in a poorly attended panel entitled "Public Service Career Paths" at the Yale Law School, where she was in her second year. Sotomayor happened to stand next to Morgenthau in the line for wine and cheese afterward. They talked, he urged her to come and see him the next morning at the Career Office, and he ended up giving her a job as an assistant district attorney. This set Sotomayor on the path of public service, as opposed to big-money, corporate law, that led her from the Bronx eventually to the Supreme Court.

Apartment buildings went up fast along the route of what are now the numbers 2 and 5 trains. Tenants moved in, the population within walking distance of the subway doubled and redoubled. Riders crammed the trains; sometimes the motormen had to stand on the platforms and shove to get everybody in. The Bronx historian Stephen Jenkins, writing in 1912, deplored the trains' overcrowding, which produced "scenes of brutal indecency that I do not believe would be submitted to by any other people in the world."

A second line arrived in the Bronx in 1910, when the number 1 Broadway Local reached 242nd Street and Van Cortlandt Park. Its crossing out of Manhattan involved two bridges—one over the United States Ship Canal, usually called the Harlem River Ship Canal, which the Army Corps of Engineers had dug in 1895 to continue the Harlem River all the way through to the Hudson River. The canal cut off the tip of Manhattan and unnavigable Spuyten Duyvil Creek, giving ships direct passage between the East River and the Hudson. A second bridge carried the train over Spuyten Duyvil Creek and into the Bronx. Later the city filled in the creek and erased that ancient landmark.

In 1914, a line (today's number 4 train) was built along Jerome Avenue on elevated tracks and onward to Woodlawn Cemetery, which it reached in 1918. In Manhattan, the 4 was (and is) a Lexington Avenue train. Another Lexington train, the number 6, used the same 149th Street tunnel under the Harlem River that the numbers 2 and 5 trains used, but the 6 went northeast on underground tracks and then elevated tracks to its end at Pelham Bay Park. That line began service in 1920. It was the fourth subway to reach the Bronx. Separate building booms accompanied the arrival of each line. Because of the Bronx's north-south ridges, the trains funneled their ridership southward into Manhattan. Building elevated tracks along the valleys was easier than trying to force lines east and west through the ridges. To this day there is no line in the Bronx that runs all the way across it, east-west. A northward extension of the West Farms line was added in 1957, and since then no new subway lines have been built in the Bronx. Going east and west by bus in that borough can be so slow that some riders take the subway into Manhattan from one side of the Bronx and transfer to a subway line going to the other.

Tenants could find great new apartments in the newly built-up borough. Nowhere else in the city offered so much space, so many modern conveniences. Elevators! Telephones! Electricity! Steam heat! Six-story "New Law" apartment buildings, so called because they conformed to the 1901 law concerning tenements, attracted thousands of tenants to the neighborhoods of Longwood, Hunts Point, and Crotona Park East. The Grand Concourse, completed in 1909, became the site of some of the most architecturally ambitious buildings. Soon the greatest concentration of art deco apartment buildings in the world would assemble along that ample thoroughfare. Not even rich people in Europe had such comfortable and up-to-date flats, and the rents were lower than in Manhattan.

Promoters of civic improvement liked to see the residents of the Lower East Side leaving its crowded, unhealthy tenements for the new Valhalla across the Harlem. Many apartment seekers already knew how easy it was to get there, having gone to the Bronx on outings. Now there were the Lexington Avenue lines that could carry them between the Garment District and their new semi-suburban apartments. The Bronx elevated tracks wound among rows of new buildings whose throngs of water-storage tanks on the roofs resembled a gathering of squat church steeples. At certain times of year, the sun rose among the rooftop tanks as the commuters rode to work in the mornings and set among the tanks in the evenings as the commuters came home.

Like an irrigation matrix, the subways watered the Bronx, and an urbanized suburb sprang up. The new residents, most of them first-generation immigrants, had come from Italy, Ireland, Scandinavia, Germany, Britain. But the greatest number—some hundreds of thousands—were Russian and Polish Jews. Small businesses opened in the new buildings' ground floors; houses of worship proliferated. Splendid synagogues, in architectural styles previously never seen in these regions, added Euro-Asiatic embellishments to the skyline. Half a million people were living in the Bronx by 1912. The most famous Yiddish writer in the world, Sholem Aleichem, moved to 968 Kelly Street, in the Longwood neighborhood. He came from Ukraine, and his birth name was Solomon Naumovich Rabinovitch. His humorous tales of Tevye the Milkman and similar works caused some admirers to call him "the Jewish Mark Twain." When told of this, Mark Twain replied that he (Twain) was the American Sholem Aleichem. Twain himself could be included as a sometime Bronx resident, having leased Wave Hill, the former William Lewis Morris mansion, from 1901 to 1903. Aleichem died in the Bronx in 1916, and his funeral procession, from the Bronx to Manhattan to Brooklyn, was one of the largest ever seen in the city.

New York City's first zoning law passed in the same year, and it restricted industrial development in the Bronx to the places where it had begun—Mott Haven, Port Morris, and West Farms. This established the Bronx as a residential area for people whose jobs would be elsewhere, mainly in Manhattan, which had the most manufacturing in the city at the time. Apartment buildings marched across the still-undeveloped areas, one building next to the other, row after row, as in Davies's vision. Through the boom era, as many as five thousand new apartment buildings were being constructed in the Bronx every year. On just the two blocks on either side of Charlotte Street, south of its intersection with Boston Road (where a stunned President Carter would later get out of his limousine in the rubble), developers put up fifty-one buildings, with a thousand apartments that housed a total of three thousand people.

FOR THE NEW ARRIVALS from Russia and the Pale, the prevailing absence of pogroms, just in itself, made for an improvement. Add that to fresh air and new apartments with more room, and life might even be called good. Once again, the Bronx entered a paradise phase. The nineteenth century had imagined it as a rural arcadia, along the lines of Joseph Rodman Drake's paean to the Bronx River. Now, in the early decades of the twentieth century, the Bronx gave paradise a city accent.

This was the beginning of the front-stoop Bronx, where neighbors sat outside in the evenings and kids played games in the street. In the later recollections of those who grew up then, the subject of stickball, and of the Spaldeen ball you played stickball with, would recur frequently. Ditto egg creams, and the corner candy store, dispenser of egg creams, and the phone in the corner candy store, which would be used as a way of getting in touch with residents of nearby apartments: The candy store phone would ring, and whoever answered would dispatch one of the boys hanging around for that purpose, and the boy would run to a nearby building, and shout up the stairwell, and the person who the call was for would come down, and walk with the boy to the candy store, and take the call, and give the boy a nickel for his trouble, and the boy would spend it on an egg cream in the candy store.

Leon Trotsky, the Bolshevik leader, briefly enjoyed the new paradise Bronx when he and his family lived here in 1917. Trotsky, his wife, Natalia Sedova, and their sons, Lev, who was eleven, and Serge, who was nine, arrived in New York City on January 13 of that year. They came on a Spanish ship; Spain had just deported them. The United States had been their default choice because the only European countries who would accept the dangerous revolutionary were ones that wanted to imprison him. A representative of the Hebrew Sheltering and Immigrant Aid Society met the Trotsky family at the pier. They rented a fifth-floor apartment at 1522 Vyse Avenue, just east of Crotona Park and a few blocks from Charlotte Street. The family could not believe how luxurious their place was. When Mr. Trotsky got a call, no small boy had to run from the candy store and yell up the stairs. For a rent of eighteen dollars a month, as he remembered in his autobiography,

> that apartment . . . was equipped with all sorts of conveniences that we Europeans were quite unused to: electric lights, gas cooking-range, bath, telephone, automatic service-elevator, and

even a chute for the garbage. These things completely won the boys over to New York. For a time the telephone was their main interest; we had not had this mysterious instrument either in Vienna or Paris.

In Manhattan, Trotsky gave speeches to socialist organizations and immediately fell into disputes with his American fellow leftists, for whom he had contempt. And in the contempt department, no one could out-contempt Trotsky. He described a prominent rival named Hillquit as "a Babbitt of Babbitts . . . the ideal Socialist leader for successful dentists." Because of all the work Trotsky did, writing articles for *Noviy Mir* ("New World"), a socialist paper with offices on St. Mark's Place, he had no time to take in the city's attractions. Later he said he regretted that. About two months after he arrived, the February Revolution overthrew Tsar Nicholas II, and orders of exile against people like Trotsky were rescinded. The family made immediate plans to return to Russia. On March 26, fellow Communists gave him a farewell party at a casino in Harlem, where he made an "electrifying" farewell speech, according to Emma Goldman.

Just before the family was about to embark for Russia, their nine-year-old son, Serge, could not be found. Three hours went by with no word of him. Then his mother received a phone call from a police precinct downtown—fortunately, the boy had remembered their phone number. Before leaving the city, Serge had wanted to clear up a question that had been puzzling him. They lived on 164th Street (as Trotsky said in his autobiography, perhaps inaccurately; 1522 Vyse Avenue is at the corner of East 172nd Street). Serge wanted to see if there was a First Street. He set out in search of it, crossed into Manhattan, and lost his way. He went to the police, and they helped him get in touch with his family. The Trotskys made it to their ship on time.

Would they had missed it! Better by far if they had stayed in the new paradise Bronx, in their nice apartment with its affordable rent and modern conveniences. When Trotsky arrived in St. Petersburg (its wartime name was Petrograd), Vladimir I. Lenin had already scored his triumphal return to the Finland Station and had recast the

people's uprising of February as an international proletariat revolution, with his Bolshevik Party—i.e., himself—as its head. But then
in July, Lenin overstepped, with an abortive coup attempt against
the Provisional Government of Alexander Kerensky, and he had to
slip secretly back into Finland. While the authorities looked to arrest
Lenin, Trotsky carried on, and kept the Bolshevik Party in the middle
of the fight. John Reed, the American journalist whose *Ten Days That
Shook the World* is the best account of the Bolshevik putsch, observed
Trotsky maneuvering and speechifying during the riotous meetings
in which factions by the dozen vied to create a new Russia. Reed described Trotsky, his "thin, pointed face positively Mephistophelian in
its expression of malicious irony," as the Bolshevik firebrand stayed
on the attack. In October, Lenin rejoined the front that Trotsky had
held for him, and the Bolsheviks hijacked the revolution.

"Mephistophelian," indeed; it was a dark day for the world when
Trotsky and his family left the Bronx. The Bolsheviks' success would
not have been possible without Lenin, and Lenin might not have
had a functioning party to return to in October 1917 were it not for
Trotsky. A million and a half Russian Jews came to New York; one
Russian Jew going in the other direction helped immiserate half the
world. What if Trotsky had stayed, and his kids had grown up happily
in the paradise Bronx? The family could have become Babe Ruth fans,
and Russia avoided seventy-odd years of bloody despotism.

My friend Roger Cohn, who edits the online magazine *Yale Environment 360*, and whom I've known for thirty-five years, told me
this story as we were walking in the Bronx neighborhood where his
grandparents used to live. He had heard it from his grandfather William "Willie" Cohn, who moved to the Bronx from Manhattan with
Roger's grandmother Sadie, soon after they married. Willie Cohn
would go on to be a postal inspector, but as a young man he worked
in a restaurant.

"My grandfather was one of the regular waiters, and sometimes
Trotsky would come in," Roger said. "It was well-known that Trotsky
did not believe in tipping, because he thought it was disrespectful to
the proletariat—he thought that workers should be compensated for
their labor and not have to depend on a customer's mood. Therefore,

he never tipped, and as a result the waiters gave him lousy service. To get back at them Trotsky would linger at his table a long time over his tea, so they couldn't seat another customer. But my grandfather believed that everybody should be treated decently, and he gave Trotsky good service even though he knew he wouldn't get a tip. To show his appreciation, after my grandfather waited on him Trotsky would not hang around and take up space. When he finished, he would pay his check and leave so they could seat somebody else."

Trotsky spoke English, although, by his own admission, not well. A search online reveals that the brief time Trotsky lived in the Bronx is recalled mainly in terms of his adamant refusal to tip. In his clumsy English he also urged diners at nearby tables not to tip, either—old Mr. Trotsky, just another New York City nut.

20

I'M STANDING IN BEDFORD PARK, in the north-central Bronx, at the corner of Bedford Park Boulevard and Jerome Avenue. The number 4 train has a stop here. Workers in the subway yards west of Jerome Avenue use this station, as do students at Herbert H. Lehman College, whose campus is next to the yards. The Bronx High School of Science is a block north of the college. On this weekday morning, crowds exit down the station's foot-smoothed steps. Buses come and go every few minutes on Bedford Park Boulevard, and passengers wait for them in lines that extend along the block.

About 112 years ago, W. E. B. Du Bois, the writer, editor, and activist, lived in this neighborhood. In 1912, his wife, Nina Gomer Du Bois, rented a small house for the family—the two of them, and their young daughter, Yolande. Mrs. Du Bois found the house after some looking, in a city that was at least as segregated as it is today. The address was 3059 Villa Avenue, near the corner of Bedford Park Boulevard, a block uphill from Jerome Avenue. Du Bois stood just under five feet six inches tall, had a small mustache and goatee, dressed in three-piece suits and white collars, sometimes carried a walking stick, and smoked an occasional Benson & Hedges cigarette. I imagine him going up the stairs of the elevated station in the morning as the crowds are coming down.

There's a new eight-story apartment building where the Du Bois house used to be, and (unsurprisingly) no plaque or marker. Out front, a fire hydrant drips, enlarging a hole it has already eroded in the sidewalk. Maple and locust trees shade the street, and residents wait at eight twenty on Tuesday mornings so they can move their cars for the street-cleaning truck. Passersby on their way to the elevated station speak Spanish, Mandarin, Hausa, Twi, Ga, Bengali, and English. The nearby Osvaldo #5 Barber Shop flies a string of pennants that advertise services for sending money to Africa and Bangladesh. All in all, the neighborhood is a pleasant spot in which to contemplate the great man's life.

A walk of half an hour or forty minutes brings you to the Bronx Zoo. It existed in 1912, but the Du Bois family probably did not visit it. The New York Zoological Society, founded in 1895 by Theodore Roosevelt and a group of his friends, persuaded the city to provide it with 265 acres of Bronx parkland for a zoo. It laid out grounds and collected animals, and opened to the public in 1899. A well-connected New York clubman and Zoological Society member named Madison Grant created the zoo, more than did anyone else, and he ran it, sometimes as its director, for forty-one years. Grant despised Black people, and he did not particularly like any other races or ethnicities, either, except for what he considered to be "Nordic" whites like himself; these, he worshipped and fetishized. It is a curiosity of the early-twentieth-century Bronx that Du Bois, Trotsky, and Grant all were in the borough (if only briefly, on Trotsky's part) at the same time. All three would soon be famous: Du Bois as the world's leading Black intellectual, Trotsky as Trotsky, and Grant as an internationally known racist "anthropologist" and advocate of eugenic theories that inspired the Nazis.

Grant belonged to the Knickerbocker, Tuxedo, Union, Turf and Field, Century, and Down Town clubs, in New York City, and to the Shikar Club, in London. He had dark, intense eyes, and a mustache at least ten times the size of Du Bois's. Grant's mustache spread straight out on either side of his face like the arms of an umpire signaling "Safe." A Snidely Whiplash comparison can't be avoided. Fourteen million immigrants came to the United States through New York City between 1886 and 1924, and their numbers and insufficient Nordicness upset Grant and many of his fellow clubman types. Grant devoted all his political energy to stopping the immigrants he hated. With Congress's passage of the Immigration Act of 1924, for which he had lobbied throughout much of his life, he finally succeeded.

Grant may have feared that he, personally, was about to go extinct. The possible extinction of such marvels of nature as himself caused him to worry about (for example) the American bison, known as the buffalo. Just before the turn of the twentieth century, no more than a few hundred buffalo remained in the wild. The zoo acquired a few of the survivors, bred them, and then sent some of its herd to a national wildlife refuge out West, so the species could begin to be restored. Comanche Indians, including the famous chief Quanah Parker, met the animals' train in the town of Cache, in Oklahoma Territory, to welcome the seven bulls and eight cows. Today there are about 200,000 buffalo living on public reserves across the West. The ancestry of many of these animals goes back to the Bronx.

Grant also deserves credit for saving California's redwoods. On an auto trip with a friend, he saw that the ancient trees were being cut down and sawed into railroad ties and grapevine stakes. Using his pull in government, and his friends with power, he helped to get redwood groves made into state or national parks. There might be no redwoods today were it not for him. He and his friends established the American Bison Society and the Save the Redwoods League, and are considered the founders of the conservation movement in the United States. Whatever their motives—they wanted more big-game animals for themselves to hunt, and more wild nature in which to restore themselves, while the possible extinction of the Native American tribes caused them no distress—they did preserve threatened wildlife and lands, and eventually these successes benefited not only themselves. The early conservationists might not have cared what other humans they benefited; they saw certain people as not fully human anyway.

When W. E. B. Du Bois lived in the Bronx, he would have known about an episode that happened at the zoo in 1906. A traveler brought a man from the Congo to New York. The African, named Ota Benga, belonged to a tribe of pygmies whom the Belgians had slaughtered. At first, the traveler left Ota Benga at the American Museum of Natural History, and then he brought him to the zoo, which put him on display in the primate house. By then more than a million people were visiting the zoo every year, and huge crowds wanted to see Ota Benga. When he was let out of the cage, hecklers followed him around, laughing at him, poking him, and tripping him. On just one day, September 16, forty thousand people came to see him.

At the office of the mayor, a group of Black Baptist ministers objected to the zoo displaying a man like an animal; the mayor passed the ministers along to Grant, who brushed them off. Afterward, he said it was important that the zoo not give even the appearance of yielding to their demands. Eventually Ota Benga was moved to the Colored Orphan Asylum, in Brooklyn, and he ended up in Virginia, where he shot himself some years later.

In the summer of 2006, the Wildlife Conservation Society, which now runs the zoo, said it did not think it needed to put up a memorial to Ota Benga, because its efforts to preserve wild places in the Congo were the best way to remember him. In July 2020, the society's director formally apologized for the zoo's treatment of Ota Benga, and for its having waited so long to apologize.

MADISON GRANT'S BEST-KNOWN BOOK, *The Passing of the Great Race,* came out in 1916. A few quotes from it:

> [T]his generation must completely repudiate the proud boast of our fathers that they acknowledged no distinction in "race, creed, or color" . . . it has taken us fifty years to learn that speaking English, wearing good clothes and going to school and to church do not transform a Negro into a white man . . . Americans will have a similar experience with the Polish Jew, whose dwarf stature, peculiar mentality and ruthless concentration on self-interest are being engrafted upon the stock of the nation . . .

Mistaken regard for what are believed to be divine laws and a
sentimental belief in the sanctity of human life tend to prevent
both the elimination of defective infants and the sterilization of
such adults as are themselves of no value to the community . . .

Und so weiter. Grant's *The Passing of the Great Race* became one of the
most widely known racist books ever written. It belongs to a modern
genre that began with Arture de Gobineau's *The Inequality of the Races*,
published in the 1850s. Grant is believed to have coined the term "the
master race." Adolf Hitler read *The Passing of the Great Race* in translation, admired it, and wrote Grant a fan letter, calling the book "my
Bible."

According to Grant, all Western civilization was created by a race
of tall, blond, warlike people with blue or gray eyes who ventured
down from northern Europe every so often to help start great cul-
tures, such as ancient Egypt, Greece, and Rome, before retiring again
into their northern forests. Over time, a lot of these supposed Nordics
became "mongrelized" by mixing with "inferior races" (Grant's books
can't be summarized without the use of many quotation marks), or
else they killed each other off in internecine wars because of their
bravery and love of fighting, as they were doing at that very moment
in the Great War.

Grant believed that the leading men of Western history had been
Nordics. Among the stars he claimed for the team, Leonardo da Vinci,
Michelangelo, and Dante all clearly possessed Nordic blood, as he
had determined by studying the shapes of their heads in portraits and
sculptural busts. A major cause of Nordic "mongrelization" was the
often-uncooperative Nordic women, who had a bad habit of choosing
the wrong men to mate with. This was especially true "among the
women of the better classes, probably because of their wider range
of choice." Strangely for someone so concerned about the oncoming
disappearance of people like himself, Grant never married.

He died in 1937, in time to miss seeing how his Nazi admirers
would put his theories fully into practice. The obituary in *The New
York Times* identified him as a "zoologist" and a "eugenicist of note,"
and described *The Passing of the Great Race* as "a recognized book on

anthropology." The obit's length, running to several columns, and its admiring tone show how Grant's wide circle of friends and acquaintances regarded him. Maybe not all agreed that certain types of humans should be exterminated, but none opposed his ideas enough to make a fuss. The *Times* also noted the creation of the Bronx River Parkway, Grant's other civic effort in the borough. He designed this tree-lined corridor, even to the architecture of its distinctive stone bridges, and oversaw its construction, and won awards for his work. The parkway has served as a model for similar green-space thoroughfares in other cities.

Today Grant's name is remembered nowhere along the parkway, except in a list of names on a small plaque on one of the bridges. A grove of oaks overlooking the river encircles a flagpole at whose base is a plaque honoring—not him, but William White Niles, another member of the parkway commission. The Bronx Zoo, regarded today as one of the world's best, has delighted generations of New Yorkers and brought distinction to the city. There is no public monument to Grant at the zoo. Several roads in the Bronx are called Grant, but none are named for him. Even more than park-builder John Mullaly, who incited murderous Draft Rioters in 1863, Madison Grant has been thrown into history's oubliette. Hate may be an inescapable bequest, but it doesn't make for much of a legacy.

W. E. B. DU BOIS lived or worked within a short walk of Madison Grant in New York City for decades. Had he wished, he could have strolled from 3059 Villa Avenue to Grant's office at the zoo, introduced himself, and counterfactually punched him in the nose. During the years when Du Bois was a director at the NAACP, he could have taken a cab from its headquarters at Fifth Avenue and Thirteenth Street to Grant's office at 1 Wall Street, or to his apartment on the Upper East Side. No evidence exists that the two men ever met. However, Du Bois did cross paths with Grant's fellow white supremacist and chief proselytizer, Lothrop Stoddard, a popular writer of the day. As Huxley was to Darwin, Lothrop Stoddard was to Madison Grant. In fact, W. E. B. Du Bois and Stoddard did have one notable public encounter, which produced a brief but unique entry in the category of Great American Debates.

Both Stoddard and Du Bois held PhDs in anthropology from Harvard. Du Bois was the first Black ever to earn a PhD there, while Stoddard, who described himself as having Puritan ancestry, belonged to a long line of Harvard graduates. Stoddard's father, John L. Stoddard, traveled the world and gave lectures using stereopticon slides, a then-radical innovation. For a while, he was the most popular public speaker on the circuit. Stoddard the son hardly knew Stoddard the father, who left the family when the son was small. A biography of Stoddard the father written by a devotee fails even to mention that he had a son. Adrift and fatherless, Lothrop Stoddard looked for elders to base himself on. He seems to have navigated his own early writings by echolocating off the work of Du Bois.

Du Bois published *The Souls of Black Folk* in 1903. The book begins with perhaps his most enduring sentence, "The problem of the twentieth century is the problem of the color line." Lothrop Stoddard's first book, *The French Revolution in San Domingo*, published in 1914, begins, "The world-wide struggle between the primary races of mankind— the 'conflict of color,' as it has been happily termed—bids fair to be the fundamental problem of the twentieth century." Stoddard then goes on to say that for countries like the United States and South Africa, the conflict is "perhaps the gravest problem of the future."

In explaining the Haitian Revolution, Stoddard warns that not only can a race war happen, but whites can lose. Throughout his career, arousing fear and hatred was his secret for selling books. Not long after the Haiti book appeared, Stoddard came across Madison Grant's *The Passing of the Great Race*, and suddenly everything fit. In Grant, Stoddard found a spiritual father (though Grant was never much warmer to him than his real father had been). Even better, Grant gave him Nordics. Fear that the approaching race war would wipe out generic white people didn't have as much traction as did the more specific and fantastical fear that it would cause the extinction of the noble, civilization-bearing Nordics. Now the story had continental sweep, characters, setting, and plot. Now the tale of race murder had a hero-victim.

Writing one book can determine the rest of an author's life. Stoddard's major opus, *The Rising Tide of Color Against White World-Supremacy*, published early in 1920, did that for him. Madison Grant endorsed it by supplying the introduction. For Stoddard, Japan's victory over Russia in 1905 in the Russo-Japanese War had rung the global warning bell, because never before had a "colored" nation defeated a "white" one. (Apparently, Russia's own historic multi-ethnicity, and the fact that the Mongols had emerged from Asia to conquer large parts of Russia seven hundred years before, did not concern him.) In *The Rising Tide of Color*, Stoddard predicted an imminent worldwide uprising by the emboldened yellow, black, brown, and red nations against the "Nordic race," outnumbered already two to one.

Stoddard's book was an immediate hit. Reviewers across the country gave it serious consideration. The *Times* wrote an approving editorial, saying that Stoddard warns of "an eventual submersion beneath vast waves of yellow men, brown men, black men and red men, whom the Nordics have hitherto dominated." There was a danger of "race extinction through warfare," the *Times* announced, grimly. In 1921, in an outdoor speech before more than a hundred thousand people in Birmingham, Alabama, President Warren G. Harding declared that Blacks must have full economic and political rights, but that segregation was also necessary to prevent "racial amalgamation." Then, perhaps going off script, Harding added: "Whoever will take the time to read and ponder Mr. Lothrop Stoddard's book on 'The Rising Tide of Color' . . . must realize that our race problem here in the United States is only a phase of a race issue that the whole world confronts." This presidential plug must have sold a few books for Stoddard.

Blacks as well as whites read the book, and Black newspapers used epithets like "the prominent Negrophobist," "the high priest of racial baloney," and "the unbearable Lothrop Stoddard" when referring to him. A Black columnist wrote that the white race's impending demise would probably come as news to Negroes in the South. And the statistic, emphasized by Stoddard, that the "colored races" outnumbered the whites did not unduly alarm the Black demographic, which looked on the bright side. "New Book by a White Author Shows Rising Tide of Color Against Oppression; Latest Statistics Show Twice as Many

Colored People in World as White," said a glass-half-full headline in the *Baltimore Afro-American.*

Stoddard wrote articles for *The Saturday Evening Post,* published follow-up book after book, and lectured widely. In 1926, he gave a talk before two thousand students and faculty at Tuskegee University, informing them that the Nordic race was superior to non-whites, and that for the good of all the races the world must continue to be governed by white supremacy. A Black newspaper, *The Philadelphia Tribune,* reported that the students "sat awe-stricken throughout the address, which terminated without any applause."

But W. E. B. Du Bois had Stoddard's number. The debate between the two came about like this:

In 1928, the Chicago Forum Council, a cultural organization that included both Black and white members, asked Stoddard and Alain LeRoy Locke, a founding figure of the Harlem Renaissance, to write on the subject "Shall the Negro Be Encouraged to Seek Cultural Equality?" for its magazine. Each had done so. Then the organization asked the two to read their pieces in an on-air encounter, live, from the American Broadcasting Company's radio studios in New York. But then Locke went to Europe to recover from an unhappy love affair with Langston Hughes, and on the day of the scheduled broadcast he had not returned. Du Bois was asked at the last minute to fill in.

What he said on air, elaborating on what Locke had written, must have been persuasive, because the magazine's editor told Du Bois that the debate was "a corker" and a consensus said that Du Bois had won. The Forum Council organizers in Chicago then proposed holding the debate again, on a larger stage and before a paying crowd. Stoddard had to have known that the audience would be more Black than white and would certainly root for Du Bois. Why did Stoddard agree to take part? Like any author with books to sell, he probably thought he could use the publicity. Du Bois, who always kept his eye on reality, wondered if Stoddard would even show up. Du Bois advised the debate organizers to have an alternate opponent ready. The comic possibilities of fire-breathing racists were not lost on him. He suggested asking a southern senator such as J. Thomas Heflin of Alabama. "He would be a scream and you would clean up if you could get hold of him," Du Bois told the organizers.

Stoddard made positive noises about his plans to be there. He and Du Bois agreed on the topic—"Shall the Negro Be Encouraged to Seek Cultural Equality?"—as before. It was decided that Du Bois would speak first. Tickets went on sale, fifty cents or seventy-five cents each. The advertisement promised it would be "One of the greatest debates ever held." In smaller letters, the ad asked, "Has the Negro the Same Intellectual Possibilities as Other Races?" Beneath a photo of Du Bois was the word "YES!" Beneath a photo of Stoddard it said, "NO!" Stoddard's headshot projected a roguish, matinee-idol aura, with his slicked-down hair, black eyebrows, and dark mustache. The doors of the venue, a large hall on South Wabash Avenue, opened just before 3:00 p.m. on Sunday, March 17, 1929. Estimates of the crowd ranged from three thousand to five thousand. A photo that ran in *The Chicago Defender* showed a packed hall.

Fred Atkins Moore, the director of the Forum Council, kicked off the program by telling the audience that the Forum itself "takes no stand on any questions whatsoever." That is, the question of whether Black people were inferior to whites and therefore not entitled to full equality remained open. Moore himself was white. Then he introduced Du Bois, "one of the ablest speakers for his race not only in America but in the whole wide world," and Stoddard, "whose books and writings and speaking have made his views known to many hundreds of thousands of people." He requested that the audience be polite to both speakers and refrain from applause.

Du Bois steps to the podium. He begins by asking what exactly "Negroes" are, what "cultural equality" is, and how anyone can be "encouraged" to seek it. He asks why Negroes or anybody else should *not* be encouraged to seek cultural equality. He allows that maybe in the past Negroes couldn't have reached it, but since emancipation they have come wonderfully far, an accomplishment that "has few parallels in human history." For this they had expected to be applauded, he says, but instead white America feared them and said their advancement threatened civilization—as if culture were some fixed quantity, and Negroes having more of it would mean less of it for other people.

He points out that such a view imagines culture as if it were material goods, the best of which belong to only the few who have leisure to enjoy them; and then these people begin to see the universe as made specially for them. They think that if the darker races come forward, they "are going to spoil the divine gifts of the Nordics." But there is no scientific proof that modern culture came from the Nordics, or that Nordic brains are better. "In fact," Du Bois says, "the proofs of essential human equality of gift are overwhelming." He says that if Nordics really do believe themselves to be superior, and do not want to mingle their blood with that of other races, who is forcing them? They can keep to themselves if they wish.

He begins to thunder: "But this has never been the Nordic program. Their program is the subjection and rulership of the world for the benefit of the Nordics." He says they have overrun the earth, brought exploitation and slavery along with their technology and civilization, broken down family life, and "spread their bastards over every corner of land and sea." He says they are responsible for more intermixture of races than any people in history, accomplishing it by force—and then they have the impudence to tell the darker races, when they demand fair treatment, "You shall not marry our daughters!" To this he replies, "Who in Hell asked to marry your daughters?"

He says the racism of white America does more damage to its moral authority than Black people could ever do and mocks its claim to be a Christian nation. Finally, he asks the world of white supremacy a practical question: If it really intends to keep other races in subjection—can it? The white nations don't even get along themselves, as was demonstrated by the recent war, which he says was a struggle over dividing the plunder taken from Africa and Asia, "and by it you nearly ruined civilization." He wonders if a purportedly Christian nation has what it takes to crush the world's darker races as ruthlessly as it will need to.

Stoddard goes next. Having been praised by the moderator for his courage in appearing in this venue, he begins, "Nothing is more unfortunate than delusion. The Negro has been the victim of delusion ever since the Civil War." He does not say (as he has written elsewhere) that white Americans would rather see themselves and their children dead than mix with Black people. Instead, he outlines a plan he calls "bi-racialism," essentially a "separate but equal" setup based not on any inherent inferiority, he says, but only on racial "difference." He uses the famous metaphor of the hand, proposed by Booker T. Washington years before—that "in all things purely social [the races] can be as separate as the fingers; yet one as the hand in all things essential to mutual progress."

The turning point of the debate occurs when Stoddard describes how biracialism will provide each race with its own separate public sphere. The Forum Council later printed the debate and bound it in a small book, which records the moment. Stoddard says:

> The more enlightened men of southern white America . . . are doing their best to see that separation shall not mean discrimination; that if the Negroes have separate schools, they shall be good schools; that if they have separate train accommodations, they shall have good accommodations. [laughter]

There is just that one bracketed *[laughter]*. The transcription is being polite. Blacks who had moved to Chicago from the South knew the Jim Crow cars. The absurd notion that Jim Crow cars were anything except horrible—dirty, crowded, inconvenient, degrading—got a huge laugh. As the reporter for the *Baltimore Afro-American* put it:

> A good-natured burst of laughter from all parts of the hall interrupted Mr. Stoddard when, in explaining his bi-racial theory and attempting to show that it did not mean discrimination, said that under such a system there would be the same kind of schools for Negroes, but separate, the same kind of railway coaches, but separate . . . When the laughter had subsided, Mr. Stoddard, in a manner of mixed humility and courage, claimed that he could not see the joke. This brought more gales of laughter.

Du Bois, in his rebuttal, says the reason Stoddard does not understand why the audience laughed is that he has never ridden in a Jim Crow car. Du Bois adds, "We have." Stoddard, when his turn comes again, scolds the audience, saying that real progress is being made in biracialism and they shouldn't laugh about it or be cynical about it. But it is too late, he is fighting a rearguard action. Du Bois ends by wondering whether the real mistake white supremacists make is in believing that civilization is a gift bestowed by an elite, and not derived from "the great masses of men, the masses of ordinary people." The debate tapers off in the moderator's thanks and congratulations, tactfully obscuring the fact that Stoddard has been more or less laughed off the stage.

News of Du Bois's victory spread fast. Soon there were requests that the debate be repeated in Philadelphia, Detroit, Columbus, Baltimore, and Washington. He and Stoddard could have sold out halls across the country. But Du Bois's prediction that Stoddard would never agree to a rematch proved correct; soon he received word from Stoddard's agent that he would not debate him again. For debates to become historic they must happen more than once, as with Lincoln-Douglas or Kennedy-Nixon. Among the epic clashes, Du Bois–Stoddard remains almost unknown. But the Chicago encounter did set a benchmark. It was perhaps the first major event where a crowd laughed at white supremacy in public. The Ku Klux Klan, of which Stoddard was a member, presented all kinds of opportunities for comedy, with its robes and Grand Kleagles and so on. But no contemporaries did parodies of the movie *Birth of a Nation*, no humorists wrote satires of it. At the time, America routinely made fun of caricature Blacks, but not of Klansmen. Decades passed before the perspective changed; in setting Stoddard up for his pratfall, Du Bois saw over the horizon of American humor.

Afterward, Stoddard kept writing books and articles and receiving acclaim. As with Grant, he was widely accepted and approved of in (white) society. The fact that he visited Nazi Germany before the war and wrote puff pieces about the Nazis for *The Boston Globe* and other papers (noting details like Himmler's "searching" blue eyes and genial laugh) did not cause the society columnists to stop mentioning him. One could be a "nice" person and still know someone like Stoddard. Charles Scribner's Sons, the distinguished publishing house, brought out Grant's *The Passing of the Great Race* and Stoddard's *The Rising Tide of Color Against White World-Supremacy*, as well as other books by both authors, and made money on them. Maxwell Perkins, the "editor of genius" who shepherded the careers of Ernest Hemingway and F. Scott Fitzgerald and Thomas Wolfe, also published Grant and Stoddard.

In *The Great Gatsby*, Tom Buchanan, the rich and overbearing husband of Gatsby's beloved Daisy, asks his guests at dinner, "Have you read *The Rise of the Colored Empires* by this man Goddard?" Here Fitzgerald is making fun of his fellow Scribner's author, and perhaps of Perkins, their mutual editor. When Tom fumblingly explains to the party that he and Daisy and all the guests are Nordics, and says how superior the Nordics are, Nick Carraway, the narrator, finds him pathetic. Stoddard, forgotten today, survives in literature only as the last six letters of his name, combined with a *G* that probably came from Grant.

Du Bois gave America the benefit of the doubt as long as he could. After Pearl Harbor, he said that Blacks should enlist, and work for the integration of the military. In the early fifties, he was investigated as a suspected agent of the Soviet Union; at the age of almost eighty-three he was arrested and handcuffed. Nine months later, at his trial, the judge threw out the case. Then Du Bois became an avowed Communist, visited Russia, spent time in China, and met Mao. In the 1960s, he moved to Ghana, renounced his U.S. citizenship, and became a Ghanaian citizen. He died in Accra on August 27, 1963, the day before the March on Washington. He was ninety-five. The country of his birth sent no representative to his funeral, which was a state ceremony arranged and attended by Ghana's president, Kwame Nkrumah. I don't know who else lived in Du Bois's Bronx neighborhood in 1912, but Africans from many countries live there today.

I have devoted space here to Grant and Stoddard partly to emphasize a bigger, if obvious, point. Professing straight-out racial and ethnic hatred did not at all disqualify a person from respectable white society in mid-twentieth-century New York City. There, as in the rest of the country, it went without saying that white supremacy ruled.

Meanwhile, the Bronx flourished and continued to grow in population and accomplishment—but a drastic decline waited just up ahead. Soon the Bronx would be the victim of planned destruction, aided and aggravated by indifference. The social context I have sketched above may help in establishing state of mind, as the attorneys say.

21

ONE MORNING I set out to walk the length of the Cross Bronx Expressway, west to east. Interstate 95 crosses over the Hudson River from New Jersey on the George Washington Bridge, goes through the tip of upper Manhattan, and spans the Harlem River on the Alexander Hamilton Bridge. Then it enters the Bronx and becomes the Cross Bronx Expressway, which begins at the intersection with I-87 (the Major Deegan Expressway) on the east bank of the Harlem River. That part is a tangle of on- and off-ramps, so I skipped it.

The name "Cross Bronx Expy" first appears on maps just east of the tangle, where the highway cuts Plimpton Avenue in two. I started there. Sometimes an access road next to the highway is considered part of it. Street signs on these roads oversell them as "Cross Bronx Expressway," though they're just surface streets. The corner where this street meets Plimpton Avenue slumbered at about seven a.m. No traffic came or went, and a bearded guy was dozing in the driver's seat of an SUV at the curb. But in the roadcut immediately below— the actual six-lane highway, on which I would not walk, nor should anybody—traffic roared and idled and honked and screeched. The winter sun had risen high enough to lie exactly in line with the road. Light glared on the tops of truck trailers and came through the tinted parts of windshields and colored the eastbound drivers' faces green-ish blue.

Fordham gneiss, one of the three main New York City rock types (Inwood marble and Manhattan schist are the others), had been the road builders' big obstacle here. Also, the grade could not be too steep. Like all interstates, this highway had to accommodate heavy trucks. Here they needed to be able to climb gradually onto and off the Bronx's first ridge; the engineers faced the same problem that Break Neck Hill (now part of West Kingsbridge Road, just to the north) had solved centuries before—that of climbing from the valley of the Harlem River. At Break Neck Hill the road had enough room to sidle back and forth up the ridge, switchback-style. The Cross Bronx, conceived in the age of dynamite, blasted straight through.

I followed the road for three or four blocks until it ended at a T intersection. Then I went over to the interestingly named Featherbed Lane, which winds down the ridge past the Jennie Jerome Playground, becoming East 174th Street. The Cross Bronx goes under the inter-section of Featherbed Lane and Jerome Avenue in a tunnel, emerges again in its deep roadcut, and starts up an incline that's called Walton Slope on the map. Now the highway is ascending the ridge that the Grand Concourse is on. The density of infrastructure here is daunting, and complicated to explain. As I've said before, the Cross Bronx Expressway goes under the Grand Concourse in a tunnel through rock that not only supports the Concourse but contains the city's only sub-way stop that is both underground and above a road. Nearby, a small playground called Morris Mesa fits itself into a small nook beside the westbound lanes of the highway.

Morris Mesa is an unexpected name, at least for around here. Outside of the American Southwest, I have never come across any-place else called a mesa. Geographic mesas probably exist in Mexico and Spain; the Spanish word means "table." In Arizona and New Mexico, mesas are what the Zuni and Hopi and other tribes built pueblos on. This mesa playground is a flat, irregularly shaped piece of ground that the highway construction ended up not needing. Near the playground's fenced-in edge, the wall of the roadcut drops steeply, and the Cross Bronx traffic roars directly below. Sometimes I see a family or two using the slides and jungle gym, but mostly I find the playground empty.

The first time I noticed it, four or five years ago, it had a Parks Department historic marker with a couple of paragraphs, mostly about Gouverneur Morris. More recently, that sign has been replaced. The new sign doesn't mention him. Instead, it says:

MORRIS MESA
What was here before?
This site and surrounding area had about 54 apartment buildings that were demolished to make room for the Cross Bronx Expressway (completed in 1963) at the behest of Arterial Coordinator, Robert Moses (1888–1981). Over 1,000 families were displaced, costing millions of dollars in compensation. This also lead [*sic*] to a lot of households leaving on their own accord thus changing the landscape of East Tremont.

The marker goes on to say that the building of the highway created forty-four new parks, and enumerates the rail, sewer, and power lines, and the roads, subways, and highways that the Cross Bronx Expressway cut through. A concluding paragraph notes that the playground was named for "the prominent Morris family of the Bronx."

"What was here before?" A good question, but the words left out of it are "this highway," as in, "What was here before this highway?" The skyline hole through which the Cross Bronx Expressway runs was the landscape elephant in the room, until the marker asked the obvious question. This highway, in its day, was the most expensive road ever built. Robert Caro, in *The Power Broker: Robert Moses and the Fall of New York*, described one of Moses's engineers standing on a vantage point near where the Cross Bronx would begin. The engineer looked east, awestruck, at the rows upon rows of apartment buildings that would have to come down. Sixty-odd years after J. Clarence Davies imagined the Bronx's green hills covered with apartment buildings, other men devoted themselves to stripping some of the same hills bare. The cost of that destruction, and all it entailed, accounted in part for the highway's extreme expensiveness. The massive hole in the Bronx's skyline had been waiting for official on-site recognition, and the marker at Morris Mesa is a good first try.

What *was* here before? One answer: The heart of the new paradise Bronx was here. About 1.4 million people lived in the borough in 1930, when the infant Cross Bronx, then known by other, provisional names, was in its early planning stages. About half the borough's population was Jewish in 1930, and of that number, about 80 percent lived in the neighborhoods south of Tremont Avenue. By that time, most of the Bronx had transitioned from streets made of mud or gravel or Belgian block to modern streets that were smoothly paved. The decades encompassing the new paradise Bronx fell approximately between the arrival of paving in the 1910s and the completion of the Cross Bronx Expressway in 1963.

In previous city neighborhoods, kids had never had so many smooth, hard, open surfaces to play on. The floors in their apartments and houses might be hard and smooth, but you couldn't roller-skate or play stickball there. On the streets of the Bronx (and Brooklyn, and other city places) you now had paved surfaces that went on and on, where wheels rolled true and balls made predictable bounces, where you could draw neat hopscotch squares in chalk and shoot marbles and take bottle caps (called "loadies") with a piece of carrot wedged into them for weight and flip them from the ground into boxes, like tiddlywinks. Matthew López-Jensen, my artist friend who finds old stuff all over New York just by looking on the ground, has picked up twenty-eight marbles of various sizes in the Bronx. Marbles last indefinitely; they are the most common small artifacts that survive of the twentieth-century paradise Bronx, as glass beads are of the fur-trading Dutch.

The Spaldeen ball, cherished in memory, could be employed not only in stickball (with a bat made of a broken-off broom or mop handle, the broken end rubbed smooth on the pavement), but also in fist-ball (no bat required), handball (ditto), stoopball (in which you threw the ball against a stoop and your opponent played the bounce), and jacks (one game in which girls, who generally didn't play ball, might also use a Spaldeen). Manhole covers in the streets were set into the pavement at regular intervals. For a stickball batter to hit a Spaldeen the distance of three manhole covers—"three sewers"—was considered amazing.

Other games might not always need pavement, but did require a decent quorum of players: dodgeball (also called bombardment ball), Red Rover (an ancient and universal game in which all the players eventually team up against one), Johnny on the Pony (basically, everybody jumping on one another in a big pile), Red Light, Green Light (a sneaking-up game), Hot Peas and Butter (sort of like hide-and-seek), Roller Derby (roller skates, kids crashing into one another), and riding around on bikes and scooters. In the street you kept an eye out for cars. Though infrequent, they appeared now and then; when one did, everybody would yell, "Car!" and get up on the curb and wait for it to pass.

In photos of the Bronx from that period, the new pavements gleam, mostly car-free. So much in the borough was new and splendid and gleaming. In 1923, Jacob Ruppert, the brewer, and his partner, Cap Huston, built Yankee Stadium on 161st Street by the Harlem River. No other ballpark in America was called a stadium or rose to its nosebleed altitude of three tiers. About Ruth and Gehrig and DiMaggio, and their fellow Yankees of that heroic era, the poets have already sung. And at the Kingsbridge Armory, then the largest indoor space in the city, you could see car shows or boat shows or rodeos— bucking broncos and steer ropers in the Bronx! Just a five-cent bus or streetcar ride away! Meanwhile, on any day, you had your local movie theater. Everybody, practically without exception, went to the movies.

For those who did not yet get the point about the new paradise Bronx, you could bowl a few frames at the Paradise Lanes, on the Grand Concourse at East 188th, and then cross the street to see a double feature at Loew's Paradise Theater, which seated four thousand dazzled moviegoers. The Paradise showed first-run movies amid heavenly opulence like you'd never seen: statuary of the baroquest taste, lighted stars in the ceiling behind moving clouds, and gilt on all the embellishments, down to the goldfish swimming figure eights in the fountain. After the evening's features ended—perhaps *I'll Never*

Forget You, starring Tyrone Power, followed by *The Girl on the Bridge*, with Beverly Michaels—and the lights came up, a date night could adjourn to Krum's, the chocolate shop also known for its delicious sodas, which also was on the Concourse, just one block north.

The building where Loew's Paradise Theater used to be is still standing, under scaffolding and black mesh safety netting like a lady's veil. The name is still on the front. The ticket booth, its filigree shedding chips of gold paint, still greets the sidewalk. Beyond the booth the ex-theater's row of golden doors is boarded up from inside, except in one place, where it's possible to see into the burgundy-carpeted outer lobby. In the middle of the far wall, is that a statue of St. Francis? For the smell of popcorn to be so totally absent seems sad and wrong.

Along with these aspects of paradise could be added the ones that remained from the old-time rural arcadia going back to the previous century. The botanical garden and the zoo welcomed millions of visitors annually and offered free admission several days a week. The borough's endless parklands had not yet been cut up by highways. You could see the zoo animals over and over until you knew them by heart, swim in the Bronx River or the East River, climb the beech trees in Van Cortlandt Park, spend afternoons in a branch of the New York Public Library, sit on your fire escape and hear your neighbors' different accents and languages coming from nearby apartments, smell five different culinary traditions wafting through your building's stairwell at suppertime: Paradise.

AT MORRIS MESA, another question might have been, Who was here before? Regarding those fifty-four torn-down apartment buildings that the Parks Department marker refers to, the answer is: I don't know. But in the Bronx in general, all kinds of people who would one day be famous lived here during the years of the new paradise Bronx. Russian and Polish Jews had chosen central neighborhoods like East Tremont and Morrisania. Many of the Italians were in Belmont and vicinity, to the north and northeast, in single-family houses with space for gardens. The Irish mostly lived around Norwood, Kingsbridge, Bedford

Park, and in a neighborhood called Woodlawn; many of them worked in the nearby cemetery or for the rich residents of Riverdale. In the twenties, Edward I. Koch, fifty-some years away from being the city's mayor, lived with his Polish immigrant parents on Crotona Park East in Claremont Village. Mr. and Mrs. Kubrick, the parents of Stanley, had an apartment not far from the Koches, though the two families did not know each other. In 1930, the filmmaker-to-be turned two years old at 2160 Clinton Avenue.

Rosalyn Sussman, later Rosalyn Sussman Yalow, lived in Kingsbridge, and was nine that same year. She would grow up to be one of the first women to win a Nobel Prize in science. Cynthia Ozick, the future writer, born in 1928, spent her childhood in the Pelham Bay neighborhood, where her Russian immigrant parents owned a pharmacy. She loved to lie in a hammock in the small garden behind their building and read. Giacobbe (Jake) LaMotta, the boxer, and Mary Higgins Clark, the suspense writer, grew up a block apart, unknown to each other, in the Pelham Parkway neighborhood in the thirties.

As children, Harold Bloom, the critic and university professor; Leon Fleischer, the concert pianist; and Emanuel "Manny" Azenberg, the theatrical and film producer, all lived with their families in apartments on the Grand Concourse. Robert Gottlieb, the writer and editor, spent his early years in an apartment near the Concourse, on Walton Avenue. From the roof of his building, he could look down into Yankee Stadium. Roy Cohn, the awful lawyer, also came from Walton Avenue. Jerry Vale, the singer, born Gennaro Louis Vitaliano in 1930, lived in Wakefield, at the end of the subway. Colin Powell, the future general, whose family lived on Kelly Street, worked in a baby-furniture store as a youth and picked up some Yiddish from the owners.

Charlie "Chazz" Palmieri, considered one of the best salsa pianists and bandleaders ever, was born in the Bronx in 1927; after an international career, he would also die there, sixty-one years later. Bronx-born Joe Franklin, said to have invented the late-night TV talk show, entered the world in 1926 as Joseph Fortgang, the son of Austrian Jewish immigrants. Regis Philbin, another talk show host and TV personality, who was Irish-Albanian-Italian, grew up as Regis

Philbin on Cruger Avenue, near the zoo. Hal Linden, the actor, was born Harold Lipshitz in the Bronx; Ralph Lauren, the designer and entrepreneur, began life there as Ralph Lifshitz.

Garry Marshall, the TV writer-producer; Daniel Schorr, the journalist; Dolph Schayes, the pro basketball player and coach; A. M. "Abe" Rosenthal, the longtime executive editor of *The New York Times*; and Bill Finger, co-creator of the comic-book character Batman, all attended DeWitt Clinton High School, though not all in the same years. Dominic Chianese, who played Johnny Ola in *The Godfather*, and other Mafioso roles, went to the Bronx High School of Science; so did Walden Robert Cassetto, later known as the singer Bobby Darin. E. L. Doctorow (novelist), Mildred Dresselhaus (physicist), Milton Glaser (artist), Jules Feiffer (cartoonist), and Ray Barretto (drummer) all were born between 1929 and 1931, attended Bronx public schools, and like almost all the others, later moved away.

Two world wars and a depression came and went without seriously denting the paradise. The World War I Victory Monument, in Pelham Bay Park, honors the 947 Bronxites who died in that conflict. A veterans' group planted trees along the Grand Concourse to remember individual soldiers, but the trees had to be moved later, when the Concourse was widened, and they're now in a grove next to the Victory Monument. A memorial road, the Grant Highway, was named after "Harvard Eddie" Grant, another casualty of the war, who played for the New York (baseball) Giants. Grant, an outfielder, had a Harvard education and objected to his fellow players yelling, "I got it!" when fielding fly balls. He preferred to shout the more refined "I have it!" Joyce Kilmer Park is named for that poet ("Trees"), another casualty. The park still exists, but Latkin Square, named for David Latkin, the first Jewish soldier from the Bronx to die in France, as far as I know does not.

In the Second World War, almost a million New Yorkers served. Bronx industries retooled for war, and the boatyards on City Island made PT boats for the navy. On the streets, because of gas rationing, you saw even fewer cars, and women outnumbered men. After the war ended, some of the remaining open land that wasn't parkland provided

space for Quonset hut housing for veterans. The grove honoring heroes from the Second World War and Korea is set into a corner of
Van Cortlandt Park. Oak trees planted too close together silently
eulogize PFC Rodman Wanamaker, who died on Guam, and Lieutenant Peter G. Lehman, who died in England and holds the Distinguished Flying Cross, and Sergeant John Basilone, USMC, a winner
of the Congressional Medal of Honor. Sergeant Basilone received that
medal for heroism on Guadalcanal, holding off a regiment of Japanese, resupplying his machine gun emplacement, and returning to his
unit unhit. After this feat, he was given light duty hosting War Bond
rallies stateside, but he tired of it and asked to be sent back to the war.
Sergeant Basilone fought on Iwo Jima in the war's last year and was
killed while leading a tank through a minefield.

The consequences of the Great Depression could have been
worse, because the Bronx enjoyed advantages that gave it resilience.
The building boom of the teens and twenties had produced more
apartments than there were tenants to fill them, which held down
rents. And Bronx businesses tended to be small and locally owned,
such as groceries and bakeries and shoe stores, which kept the money
circulating in the borough and people working. When the unemploy-
ment rate reached 25 percent nationally, it was only 16 percent in the
Bronx. Some residents held essential city jobs, as schoolteachers or
police officers or firemen or sanitation workers. The fact that a lot of
Bronxites were Communists or Socialists helped, too, because they
believed in cooperative enterprise, often took care of poor people they
knew, and gathered in protests when they saw evictions going on. The
greater cohesion of neighborhoods seems to have kept Depression-era
Bronxites from drastic want.

Still, people lost their jobs, and some families couldn't pay their
rent, cheap as it was. In some of the buildings, all the tenants were
Jews from Eastern Europe who were also Communists, and they
staged strikes for lower rents, reasoning that the landlords made
money when there was money to be had and should share the pain
when there wasn't. City and state law enforcement officers arrived
to enforce evictions and sometimes had to retreat, so fierce were the

punching, kicking, scratching, speechifying Communist men and women who obstructed them. In 1932, the edge resided with the strikers, but then the city passed laws making it illegal even to picket for lower rents. Also, federal rent-assistance money became available, relieving some of the pressure. By 1933, the strikes had mostly ended. The episode seems to have given landlords some ideas about finding new kinds of tenants, as we will see.

Even paradise can be too much sometimes, and middle-class life can oppress the spirit, especially if you're young. The ordinariness of it makes you want to upset your parents and smash everything. To be middle class, you must stay between the lines of too cheap and too fancy, too good and not good enough. Maybe your family wants you to be a doctor or a lawyer or an accountant—commendable dreams, but maybe not your own. The relentless middle-class Good never stops being the enemy of its Best, as it also is the enemy of the Bad and the Worst. Vivian Gornick, a writer who grew up in the Bronx during the thirties and forties, wrote, "It was the bleakness of expectation, the stultified vision and resented courage, that dragged us—the children—down, and made us hate the place." Memories of the paradise Bronx usually leave out the fact that middle-class life exists in tension, and human entropy naturally craves to rip it up. Some of the changes that dismantled the paradise came from inside, in a disquiet of the heart.

I HAD BEEN SITTING on a bench at Morris Mesa playground for a while. Stiff in the joints, I stood up and kept walking. In another half mile, the eastbound Cross Bronx traffic left the Grand Concourse ridge behind and topped Walton Slope, and suddenly the sky was bigger up ahead. There are places like this on some roads—places where complications seem to fall aside, and the vista opens, and you get a feeling of being free. On this winter morning the sky shone a bright blue, tinged with brownish orange near the horizon. The trucks made that lonesome "see you later" sound they make when they pick up speed and disappear down the road. It's a dopplering engine cry that I associate with flat, open places like where I grew up in the Midwest. That the Cross

Bronx Expressway can provide room for such a sound in such a densely populated urban place is a remarkable achievement—monstrous, even.

Alongside the traffic, several plastic deli bags, swept up in the slipstream, did handsprings on their handles. Trash congregates all along the highway. Not so much on the six-lane itself—for safety's sake, crews remove it—but on the access roads, and on the bridges carrying the surface streets, and under the elevated sections. In those places, detritus as small as bottle caps and as large as abandoned motor homes clings to the highway's margins like scraps held by static electricity. One exception is across from the 48th Precinct stationhouse, under an elevated part, where the police park their personal vehicles. In that sheltered space there's hardly any trash. If you had paid as much money for something as was spent on this highway, wouldn't you want to keep it nice? If the 48th Precinct cops can do it, to that limited extent, why can't the city and the state clean up the trash along the Cross Bronx?

I walked past the intricate, thronging intersections where the Sheridan Expressway and the Bronx River Parkway draw off some of the highway's flow and contribute their own to it. Then I went under the elevated mega-intersection, on the no-man's-ground among the support columns, where I often visit. Within the mega-intersection's many lanes, Interstate 95 and the Cross Bronx Expressway separate. I-95 merges its identity with that of the Bruckner Expressway and takes that name as it turns northward toward New England. The Cross Bronx remains itself, with the additional designation of Interstate 295, as it heads south for the Throgs Neck Bridge. Nearer the bridge, the Cross Bronx Expressway officially ends, and I-295 becomes the Throgs Neck Expressway. At that point (identifiable by a change of signage on the access highway) I checked my phone. From Plimpton Street, where I began, I had walked nine and a half miles. The length of the Cross Bronx is six and a half miles but following it on foot you must wind back and forth.

Out here, where the sight lines are longer, the view clearly reveals the Bronx's in-betweenness. Just by the difference in the light in the sky you can tell that the ocean is in that direction and the rest of the continent in the other. The highways I had passed all brought the same message: Traffic coming from elsewhere and going elsewhere needed passage through this landscape in between. Before the big highways came, most residents of the borough probably did not realize that they happened to be standing in the metro area's future express lanes. The new paradise Bronx would not know what hit it.

22

THE IDEA WAS HUGE and came from Chicago. In 1909, architects and civic leaders in that city presented something called the Chicago Plan, which imagined the development of the region as a whole. Nobody had done that before—stepped back and looked at an entire metropolitan area, rather than at just the city in the middle of it. The breadth of the vision exhilarated planners' minds. Charles Dyer Norton, a Wall Street banker as well as a Chicagoan, persuaded the Russell Sage Foundation to underwrite the creation of a similar blueprint for greater New York. Like the Chicago Plan, it would think in terms of the region, conceived of as the city and the outlying communities in Connecticut and New Jersey, within a radius of fifteen to twenty miles. A group of public-spirited men got together and formed what they called the Committee of the Regional Plan of New York and its Environs. Norton served as its first chairman. He liked to quote Daniel Burnham, the nationally known architect and principal author of the Chicago Plan:

> Make no little plans; they have no magic to stir men's blood, and probably themselves will not be realized. Make big plans; aim high and hope and work, remembering that a noble, logical

diagram once recorded will never die, but long after we are gone will be a living thing, asserting itself with growing intensity.

The members of the Committee of the Regional Plan joined it on a volunteer basis. They weren't elected or appointed, and they had no obligations to any entity except the committee itself; they claimed no authority but that of interested citizens. The metro region included many governing bodies, agencies, utilities, and corporations spread across three states, and no single entity could plan for the whole. Somebody needed to rise above localities and think metro. The committee decided it would be them. They would suggest ideas to be adopted or not, according to how much sense the ideas made. Although the members received no pay, they hired a large staff of professionals to assist in the research. Starting in 1922, the committee worked on a report that took seven years to produce and cost a million dollars. The super-metropolis that they imagined would cover more than five thousand square miles and contain 20 million people. New York City itself, we recall, covers about three hundred square miles; in 1920 its population was about 5.6 million.

One of the committee's first recommendations, made in 1923 when the project had just begun, did not bode well for the Bronx. The Port of New York Authority (later, the Port Authority of New York and New Jersey) wanted to build a bridge over the Hudson River. No local bridge spanned the river at that time. The authority's plan had sited the provisionally named Hudson River Bridge at West Fifty-seventh Street, in line with a crosstown route that would link to the bridge at Fifty-ninth over the East River to Queens. The committee reviewed the plan, worried about the congestion the bridge traffic would bring to the center of Manhattan (if there was anything the committee disapproved of, it was congestion), and recommended that the Hudson River Bridge, not yet known as the George Washington Bridge, be moved about six miles uptown, to West 178th Street.

Other interested parties had reached the same conclusion. Downtown Manhattan couldn't support a bridge over the Hudson because the land on both sides was too low, and besides, tunnels under the river would soon be built at Thirty-fourth Street and Canal Street (now the Lincoln and Holland Tunnels). Other critics had pointed out the traffic congestion problem with a bridge at Fifty-seventh Street and said that the structure would also impede ships in the Hudson. North of Fifty-ninth, all the way to 110th Street, city traffic to and from the bridge would have to go through Central Park—an insoluble problem, apparently. Between 110th and 135th, a high ridge, Columbia University, St. Luke's Hospital, and the Cathedral of St. John the Divine all stood in the way. But at 178th and 179th Streets, a point of shoreline extended into the river, making the distance shorter, and the cliffs on each side rose high enough to lift the bridge above the water. Eventually, by consensus, the 178th Street location won out.

In 1925, the legislatures of New York and New Jersey voted that the bridge be built there. The traffic that would have tied up midtown, or collided with Central Park, would now cross upper Manhattan and traverse the most densely populated part of the Bronx. To this decision, made about a hundred years ago, can be traced the origin of the Cross Bronx Expressway, and the huge hole in the Bronx skyline.

The committee released the first volume of its *Regional Plan of New York and Its Environs* in 1929. A second volume appeared two years later. Again and again, the plan argued against the density and crowdedness of city living and promoted development that would be suburban and more spread out. Perhaps the committee had in mind, as a negative example, the concentration of humanity in the neighborhoods of the Lower East Side, that place once populated more densely than Bombay. The Regional Plan favored highway transportation systems with better "circulation," a word it often used, and it conceived of a metropolis built around the "motorcar," "motor buses," and "motor-truck transports." In the future, internal combustion would rule.

To move people and goods quickly, the planners imagined highways radiating from a center. They laid out other highways in concentric circles that linked the radii; metro New York would grow outward in stages like rings on a tree. They gave the name Metropolitan Loop Highway to the circle that would run at an average radius of about twelve miles from New York's City Hall. The Hudson River Bridge would be part of the Loop Highway, as would bridges connecting the Bronx, Queens, Brooklyn, Staten Island, and New Jersey. In time, this plan came to pass, though the proto-Metropolitan Loop Highway is hard to recognize in the various interstates and expressways and parkways that today carry out the original design. All the Loop Highway bridges that the Regional Plan envisioned were later built. Today, along with the George Washington Bridge, they are the Whitestone and Throgs Neck Bridges, between the Bronx and Queens; the Verrazzano-Narrows Bridge, between Brooklyn and Staten Island; and the Bayonne and Goethals Bridges, between Staten Island and New Jersey.

The committee dealt in broad strokes more than in details, but something bothered it about all that Hudson River Bridge traffic potentially clogging the Bronx—bothered it enough that the planners got down to how the flow would actually work. They imagined it exiting the bridge, crossing upper Manhattan, going over another bridge above the Harlem River, exiting at University Avenue and West 171st Street in the Bronx, entering a tunnel, emerging on West 170th Street, continuing along that street by way of a viaduct to Wilkins Avenue, and going from there to Jennings Street, to Randall Avenue, to Ferris Street, and then south to Ferry Point and the bridge to Queens. How this scramble would be possible without creating a mess in the middle of the most populated part of the Bronx the committee did not say.

The members of the committee, listed at the beginning of volume one of the report, were:

Charles Dyer Norton
Frederic A. Delano
Robert W. De Forest
Lawson Purdy
Frank L. Polk
John H. Finley
Frederic B. Pratt
George McAneny
Dwight W. Morrow
John M. Glenn
Henry James

All these men except for Frederic A. Delano and John M. Glenn were listed in the *Social Register of New York, 1924*, published late in 1923, the year in which the committee made its decision about the Hudson River Bridge.

Frederic A. Delano was a railroad executive and banker who lived in Chicago. His sister, Sara, was the mother of Franklin Delano Roosevelt. After Charles D. Norton died in 1923, Delano took over as chairman of the committee. Robert W. De Forest lived at 7 Washington Square and belonged to thirteen clubs, including the Jekyll Island Club, a retreat off the coast of Georgia founded by a hundred of America's wealthiest men. He donated generously to cultural and charitable institutions and served as president of the Metropolitan Museum of Art. Like Delano, De Forest made his money in railroads; he also held interests in insurance and banking.

Frank L. Polk lived at 6 East Sixty-eighth Street and belonged to the Knickerbocker and the Turf and Field clubs, among many others. He was the grandson of Leonidas Polk, "the Fighting Bishop," a famous general in the Confederate Army. Frank L. Polk is remembered as name partner at Davis Polk & Wardwell, the New York law firm. John H. Finley, a professor at Princeton and an editor of the *Times*, lived at 1 Lexington Avenue, which is on the north side of Gramercy Park, at East Twenty-first Street. In 1924, his sons, John Jr. and Robert, were both at Harvard, the latter at the law school. John Finley, Jr., became a famous classicist.

George McAneny was married to Marjorie Jacobi. Her father, Dr. Herbert Jacobi, a Jewish immigrant from Germany, is considered the father of pediatric medicine in America. Jacobi Medical Center, in the Bronx, is named after him. McAneny had a management position at the *Times*. He pursued a political career as Manhattan borough president, and (briefly) acting mayor. Fellow New Yorkers revered him for his lifetime of good works in the city. The McAnenys lived at 120 East Seventy-fifth Street. Dwight W. Morrow, a lawyer, banker, U.S. senator, and partner at the powerful J. Pierpont Morgan bank, lived at 4 East Sixty-sixth Street, two blocks from the Frank L. Polks. Morrow served with great success as a peacemaking ambassador to

Mexico. In 1929, his daughter, Anne, married Charles Lindbergh, the pilot, anti-Semite, and future Nazi propagandist.

Henry James, of the committee, is a mystery. He was of course not the author Henry James, who died in England in 1916. The *Register* lists three Henry Jameses. Possibly the committee's Henry James is the one at 735 Park Avenue (at East Seventy-first Street). He belonged to several of the clubs that other members belonged to, and he golfed. The committee strongly believed in preserving golf courses and other open lands.

Also in the front-of-the-book listings, under the title "General Director of Plans and Surveys," appeared the name of Thomas Adams, the city planner who led the "Garden Cities" movement, which brought village-style layouts and green space into urban-suburban settings. Adams led the staff of 150 architects, planners, and engineers who put together the report. Born in Scotland, he was regarded as the leading city planner in the world.

Three of the committeemen (Norton, Polk, and Morrow) had sons at Groton, the Massachusetts prep school. Norton, De Forest, Polk, and James had all attended Yale. De Forest, Finley, Pratt, McAneny, Morrow, and James belonged to the Century Club. Several committeemen had memberships in Long Island golf clubs (Piping Rock, Garden City). Pratt and De Forest both belonged to the Seawanhaka Corinthian Yacht Club, on Oyster Bay, Long Island. Those who belonged to the University Club, at the corner of Fifty-fourth Street and Fifth Avenue, included Polk, Pratt, De Forest, Morrow, and James. All but one of the committeemen lived in Manhattan. None lived in the Bronx.

Service on the committee combined duty and privilege; men like them had constituted the power structure in New York for centuries. One might wonder how much these men really knew about parts of the city that weren't Wall Street, Midtown, or the Upper East Side. How many personal friends did they have whose names were like Rabinowitz, Vitaliano, Philbin, Palmieri, Gottlieb, Bloom, or Chianese? Were the engineers and planners who worked under Thomas Adams able to ask any of the residents of the East Tremont neighborhood what they thought about the idea of traffic to and from the proposed Hudson

River Bridge filling up their streets? The committee members' clubs sheltered behind heavy wooden doors, off busy city sidewalks whose crowds might never have guessed that such quiet, well-upholstered retreats were so close nearby. On hot summer afternoons in the 1920s, some of the clubmen whose business required them to stay in town might be drowsing in wingback chairs over newspapers in the reading rooms while electric fans whirred in the open windows. Meanwhile, kids in the new paradise Bronx were shouting in their street games or playing in gushing hydrants at the curb. Changes that were on the way would have little effect on the clubmen's immediate world—the world of the members of the Committee of the Regional Plan—while wiping out many stickball-playing neighborhoods entirely.

The notion that Robert Moses, the powerful arterial coordinator, tyrannized the city and trampled other figures of authority overlooks the fact that the deeper power still resided with the old-family WASPs. Many of the highways that Moses hammered into place simply made real what the Committee of the Regional Plan had proposed in 1929.

In *The Power Broker*, Robert Caro describes how Moses almost built a long bridge that would have destroyed Battery Park, undermined the value of Wall Street real estate, and ruined the downtown Manhattan skyline. At a public meeting at City Hall, Moses ridiculed McAneny, by then the president of the Regional Plan Association (the successor to the Committee of the Regional Plan), who had been a leader of opposition to Moses's bridge. The arterial coordinator called McAneny, by then an old man, "an exhumed mummy." Horrified, the establishment did what it had to do. Someone spoke to someone who dropped a note to Eleanor Roosevelt, who said a word to her husband. Soon the War Department decided, implausibly, that the proposed bridge would pose a potential obstruction of access to the Brooklyn Navy Yard. Moses's bridge was not built, and instead we got the Brooklyn Battery Tunnel. In revenge, Moses tore down Battery Park's aquarium, a beloved institution of the old-time WASPs.

The 1929–1931 *Regional Plan of New York and Its Environs* combined farsightedness, sci-fi futurism, and the reactionary nativist fears of the time. In Mott Haven, Jordan Mott's industrial district of the previous century, the Regional Plan proposed the creation of a "great sub-terminal" that would be a civic, commercial, and transport center. Tall docking masts would welcome dirigibles arriving from across the ocean, magnificent public plazas would extend their vistas to the vanishing point—all in the area that had not yet begun to be called the South Bronx. Strangely, the Regional Plan got that prediction sort of right. There is a great terminal near Mott Haven today, just to the east of it, in Hunts Point. The Hunts Point Food Distribution Center, also known as the Hunts Point Market, combines the Cooperative Meat Market, the New Fulton Fish Market, and a huge produce market, all in a single mega-complex. It's one of the largest wholesale markets in the world, distributing 4.5 billion pounds of food annually to twenty-three million people in the metro region by means of tens of thousands of trucks that use the farsightedly constructed network of highways. The trucks' exhaust fills the air and helps to make the Bronx the unhealthiest county in the state.

As the Regional Plan was being put together, Congress passed the Immigration Restriction Act of 1924, fulfilling the dream and life-work of Madison Grant. *The Vanishing of the Great Race* had come out in 1916, and Stoddard's *The Rising Tide of Color Against White World-Supremacy* in 1920. The men of the Committee for the Regional Plan would have been aware of these books. Some of them belonged to the same clubs as Grant, and no doubt knew him or knew of him. If you asked the Regional Plan's committeemen if they believed in white supremacy, they might have asked you what other kind there was. Men like them ran a large part of the world. The inferred audience for their Regional Plan, and the most likely beneficiaries of its vision, were American-born white men like themselves.

When the Regional Plan states, ominously, that New York is becoming an "Oriental" town, and when it says, "Those who conceive of New York of the future must think of it as a place that will be dominated more by the ideals and stability of a well-rooted native population," the meaning is clear. This plan is by us, for us, and for those who are like us but not as well-off or smart. ("Imagination is not a strong point in the mind of the average citizen," the planners noted, airily.) The Regional Plan of 1929–1931 showed geographic and engineering vision but had less of an idea of what was going on with millions of the city's human beings. Everybody was not like the committeemen. Perceived density of population didn't worry everybody as much as it did them. And the oncoming highways would be pushed through neighborhoods that in most cases would not be theirs.

The Regional Plan Association (RPA) incorporated itself as a nonprofit organization in 1929, and still exists today. Since the First Regional Plan, it has issued three others—in 1967, 1996, and 2017. Following the Russell Sage Foundation, dozens of other foundations have underwritten its work. RPA's original purpose was to promote the adoption of its plan, and in that it mostly succeeded. The bridges it said should be built were built, and in the places RPA intended; also the highways, if somewhat more approximately. The first plan saw the future Manhattan as an office center, and it wanted the port facilities of downtown moved to New Jersey. That also happened: Newark Bay, from which Gouverneur Morris's friend had sailed to visit him in the early 1800s, took over most of the docking of cargo vessels in greater New York. The new Port of Newark and Elizabeth, across the Hudson from Manhattan, developed the first systems for loading and unloading ship containers, beginning a global change in cargo transport.

A single clause in a single sentence predicts a major international airport: "Important improvements have been carried out by the City of Newark in the development of its port and of an airplane landing field on the Newark meadows."

In the tristate area, only the most powerful parts of New York City kept the 1929 plan from complete adoption. The planners had imagined an east-west highway running across the New Jersey swamp (not yet called the Meadowlands), and then under the river via the Thirty-fourth Street (Lincoln) tunnel, through the middle of Manhattan on an expressway, into a tunnel (today's Queens-Midtown Tunnel) under the East River, and onward to Long Island. However, Manhattan, perennially one of the highest-income places in the United States, did not want an expressway running across it, and thwarted the idea. To drive straight across Manhattan from the Hudson to the East River or vice versa you still must go stoplight by stoplight.

The First Regional Plan proclaimed, in 1931, "We have carried concentration too far! We must begin to think in terms of decentralization. Think it out." It said that preserving open space was "of vital importance for the future welfare of the communities in the Region," and identified the important areas to save. This motivated local governments to buy up land for the purpose. A big part of Moses's all-but-unstoppability derived from his grasp of this principle. Moses found his first real power as the city's parks commissioner. By giving new parks to the public, he banked up the popularity that he could draw on later, when he turned to harsher purposes. As the region developed along the lines laid out by the plan, it doubled the size of its parklands.

If the Regional Plan Association ever did a major follow-up assessment of why the rise of the metropolitan concept coincided with the ruination of much of the Bronx, I never found it in the thousands of pages of the Second, Third, and Fourth regional plans I scanned. Nor did it ever apologize for the unintended consequences there. From a distance, the situation looks like this: The metropolitan concept of greater New York took hold and thrived, while large parts of the city declined, none more drastically than the Bronx. The construction of bridges and highways essential to the larger region had a lot to do with inflicting suffering on that borough. As with any human-abetted disaster, you wonder if things could have gone differently.

23

THE NEW PARADISE BRONX did not end when Blacks and Puerto Ricans started moving in—more the opposite. With their arrival it became even better. One must say this straight out because people generally don't know it. When the Bronx's mix of residents combined Black and brown newcomers from the South, the West Indies, and Puerto Rico with the Jews, Italians, Irish, Germans, and others who were already there, the place took on a new vitality, and especially so in music. It's true that a downturn followed in too-short order, but it derived from sources that were multiple, complicated, and remote from everyday life. Even as trouble came, the borough's musical inventiveness grew.

Blacks began to move to the Bronx in large numbers in the 1920s and '30s. Many of the then-current Bronx residents, or their parents, were the same Jews who had fled Russia several decades before. Southern Blacks were also escaping—from violence, Jim Crow laws, lack of voting rights, and segregation that was even worse than in the rest of the country. Jews had died in pogroms, Blacks were terrorized and killed in the South. Stories of Black war veterans being lynched in their army uniforms were not unknown. There is no overarching term to describe the departure of Jews by the millions from Russia between

1881 and the early 1900s. The flight of millions of Blacks from the rural South to cities in the North and elsewhere is well-known as the Great Migration. A difference between the two demographic movements was that when immigrants from Europe and Russia and the Mediterranean got to America, their new country would eventually accept them as white. But no matter where Blacks moved in America, they would not be white.

Blacks had always lived in what's now the Bronx, if by "always" we mean since the Dutch arrived in the 1620s and brought the first enslaved Africans. Moving the view back further, we can say that there have been non-white people living in this part of North America for thousands of years. In fact, from that perspective, the period when white people were a majority in the Bronx lasted for just an eyeblink—from perhaps about 1650 to about 1975. The borough's population is more than 85 percent Black and brown today.

Like much else, the story of that change starts in Morrisania. The name of the ancient manor of the Morrises, whose holdings took up much of today's South Bronx, later was the name of a village in the northern part of their old property. Then Morrisania became the neighborhood bounded by 161st Street on the south, Webster Avenue on the west, Tremont Avenue on the north, and Prospect Avenue on the east. Mott Haven and Port Morris, the industrial districts in the farther-south Bronx, occupy the southern part of the former Morris holdings—"the edge of the continent." The neighborhoods of Melrose, Claremont Village, Concourse Village, and Longwood surround Morrisania. It's at the South Bronx's center.

As I've noted, many Socialists and Communists lived there. That's why the supporters of Leon Trotsky found an apartment for him and his family there. The Bronx lefties raised some sociopolitical tumult, just as they had on the Lower East Side and elsewhere, supporting and strengthening the International Ladies' Garment Workers and other unions and leading the rent strikes of the early thirties. Large parts of the city were closed to Blacks, by consent and collusion among white real estate agents, homeowners, landlords, tenants, and city government. Blacks other than domestics who ventured to the Grand Concourse would be followed by police and escorted out of the neighborhood. If they accidentally got off the bus in the Italian district in Belmont, along Arthur Avenue, they risked a beating.

Morrisania would be different. The Bronx had overbuilt in its boom days of the 1910s and '20s. Then came the Depression. Apartments were going unrented. Landlords in Morrisania took the first step and considered renting to Blacks. One can see how these landlords' minds worked. The Communist and Socialist tenants, who believed in worker solidarity across all lines, and who were antiracist in principle, would be less likely to object to having Black neighbors than would the residents of, say, East Tremont or Belmont. And in the unlikely event that any Morrisanians did object, a landlord could imagine worse misfortunes than for these difficult potentially rent-striking lefties to move out. A bold move on the surface, renting to Blacks might be a win-win. Apartments would be filled, either way.

The landlords vetted their prospective Black tenants and hung signs inviting "worthy" Blacks to apply. The rumor was that light-skinned Blacks with steady employment were preferred. Avis Hanson, who would be a high school teacher, went with her mother on a search for good schools in the Bronx in 1930, when Avis was six years old. Her mother was from Antigua and her father from Jamaica. They sought out Jewish neighborhoods because, like other ambitious Black parents, they knew that where there were Jews there would be good schools. Her mother liked the look of PS 23, in Morrisania. Then the family searched for an apartment in the school district and found one in a building owned by two sisters named Jacobs, at 815 East 166th Street. After the Hansons had reached an agreement with the sisters and rented the apartment, Avis came outside and noticed a sign on the building. Her mother had taught her to read by holding her on her lap and going over the funny papers with her. The sign said, "We accept select colored tenants." Avis asked her father, "Are we select colored tenants?" Her father said, "My child, we are select people."

Like many Blacks who relocated to the Bronx, the Hansons had previously lived in Harlem. Besides that neighborhood, Manhattan's other Black areas were the Tenderloin, a residential and nightlife district between Fifth and Seventh Avenues and Twenty-third and Forty-second Streets; and San Juan Hill, a community where the

Lincoln Center complex is now. In 1900, a race riot occurred in the Tenderloin—back when the term *race riot* meant white people coming to neighborhoods where Blacks lived and attacking them and burning their buildings. A hundred or more Blacks were injured, and millions of dollars of property destroyed. None of the white rioters or the police who helped them were punished. Another race riot hit San Juan Hill in 1905. The Tenderloin all but disappeared after 1910, when the Pennsylvania Railroad bought up its buildings and evicted the residents and tore down a lot of those blocks to build Penn Station.

Some of the burned-out and evicted tenants moved to Harlem, which already had its stylish reputation. By 1930, there were 200,000 Blacks living in Harlem, often in conditions as crowded as on the Lower East Side. Families doubled up, in apartments subdivided into smaller rooms, and the rents were high. But you could get to the Bronx just by walking over the Madison Avenue Bridge, at 135th Street, or the Macombs Dam Bridge, at 155th. Some Harlem renters began to look for cheaper places across the river.

Among Black would-be tenants, post office employees and Pullman porters had an advantage. Landlords were known to favor family men who held those jobs. Entire buildings in the Bronx took on the character of postal employee enclaves. In parts of Morrisania, the evenings brought crowds of men walking home from the el stations in their blue-gray postal uniforms. News got out about the low rents, good apartments, and unhateful neighbors; the Pullman porters, who traveled nationally, told other Pullman porters. A third category of Black tenants whom landlords wanted was building supers. Families who became their buildings' first Black tenants often took the basement apartment assigned to the super. Sometimes a Black super would also hold down a day job at the post office.

New arrivals kept coming, by way of Harlem or directly from the South. A young woman named Bessie Jackson left a farm near Calera, Alabama, for the North in 1946, when she was nineteen. One morning she found herself in the Bronx, knowing nobody, brought there by a want ad. She was walking on Intervale Avenue when a man asked her if she would come into his house and light his stove. It was Saturday and the man was wearing a tall black hat. Later she explained, "I didn't know anything about Jews, I only knew white and colored." She asked the man why he couldn't light his own stove. He told her that he could, but it was a sin for him to light it on Saturday. He offered to pay her to do it. She asked him, "It is a sin for you but not for me, you're afraid of going to hell, but I can go to hell?" She felt insulted: "You don't ask anybody else to do what you believe to be a sin."

Welvin Goodwin grew up in Timpson, Texas, a town in the eastern part of the state, near Louisiana. The town is small; only about twelve hundred people live there today. He came to the Bronx in 1946 or 1947, when he was in his thirties. Welvin Goodwin said he could pick three hundred pounds of cotton in a day. After traveling the country as a pitcher in the Negro Leagues, he settled in the Bronx rather than stay in Texas, because he didn't like how he was treated in the South. "Anytime you'd whistle at a white woman or looked at her, or her dress blew up and you looking, they could kill you for that," he told an interviewer in 2005. In New York, he supported himself by shining shoes. For someone from Texas to relocate to New York City did not fit the more usual pattern. People of the Great Migration who began in the western part of the South—in Texas, Louisiana, Mississippi, Arkansas—tended to end up in St. Louis or Chicago or Detroit. People from the eastern South were more likely to choose Philadelphia or New York. The Bronx drew a big part of its southern Blacks from the Carolinas.

Migrants came from little places like Moonville, Orangeburg, Rockhill, and Bishopville, in South Carolina; and from Edenton, High Point, Goldsboro, and Delmar, in North Carolina. They also came from Apalachicola, Florida, and Siloam, Georgia; from Farmville, Virginia, or Bowie, Maryland. Some came from cities— Fayetteville, Charleston, Lynchburg, Savannah. The founding parishioners of Thessalonia Baptist Church, today one of the largest Baptist churches in the Bronx, were from Fluvanna County, Virginia—near Charlottesville—and their arrival preceded the Great Migration. The church began in 1893 but did not have enough of a congregation to expand from a storefront until 1942, when it bought a brick-and-stone synagogue whose original membership had dwindled. The church still occupies the same building, whose façade incorporates a Star of David and a menorah.

By the 1940s, the criteria for Black renters had been expanded or dropped, and Morrisania's Black population grew. Thessalonia Baptist was one of three important churches that anchored the area. It had a dynamic and beloved minister, the Reverend James A. Polite— his last name is pronounced like the adjective—who led Thessalonia Baptist from 1939 to 1980. The church members still speak of him in saintlike terms.

At the corner of East 165th Street and Prospect Avenue, St. Augustine's Presbyterian Church, another community pillar, amassed a congregation of a thousand members. Along with a full schedule of services it offered youth activities, from gospel groups to sports teams; the church's pastor, the Reverend Edler G. Hawkins, had been a top-ranked sprinter. He got involved in the civil rights movement, knew the Reverend Martin Luther King, Jr., and brought both King and Malcolm X to speak at St. Augustine's.

Rev. Hawkins is remembered for closing the Bronx "slave markets." Those were places where Black women would stand, or sit on crates they brought, and wait for white housewives to look them over. Then the prospective employers would bargain with the women for what they would be paid and hire them for a day of housework. (Ad hoc hiring venues like that still exist all over, mostly for workers who are male and Spanish-speaking, but I don't know of any in the Bronx.) He could hardly avoid seeing the slave markets on Prospect Avenue and under the elevated tracks, near his church. Through his activism and shaming of city officials he got employment agencies set up where the women could wait out of the weather, and where wages could be negotiated fairly. Rev. Hawkins served St. Augustine's for thirty-three years before leaving for a position as a professor at Princeton Theological Seminary.

Catholics, of which there were some among the Black emigrants, could attend a Catholic church also called (confusingly) St. Augustine's, which has since been subsumed in a church merger. Another prominent Catholic church, St. Anthony of Padua, remains one of the main churches in the neighborhood. It had a school that went from grades one through eight. The nuns of the Maryknoll Mission ran the school, which is now no more, though the convent still exists. Its residents can sometimes be seen in their long gray-and-white habits walking on Rev. James A. Polite Avenue. In the 1950s, one of the Maryknoll nuns, Sister Richard Marie, the director of the St. Anthony's choir, entered pop music history when she coached the choir members Arlene Smith, Jacqueline Landry, Renee Minors, and Melissa Goring with their harmonizing. In high school the girls teamed up and called themselves the Chantels. Their doo-wop hit, "Maybe," was the first song by a female vocal group to sell one million records. (I will have more to say about doo-wop later.)

Thessalonia Baptist Church still thrives. In September 2022, it held a big street celebration of its 130th birthday. St. Augustine's Presbyterian, on the other hand, has faded. The redbrick Gothic church building, with its darker red roof and clerestory windows bordered in Statue of Liberty green, is double-fenced part of the way around. Some of its stained glass is broken. An abandoned lot on one side of the church has been fixed up with plantings and benches, and several feeding stations of cat-food cans. On another side, the house that was the rectory once stood empty, broken-windowed and damaged by fire. Workmen recently tore it down. Today St. Augustine's lacks a regular pastor.

Just up Prospect Avenue from that church, a service at St. Anthony of Padua was letting out on a recent Sunday morning. A young priest with black-rimmed glasses and close-cropped hair gave blessings and said goodbye to the attendees as they came blinking into the sunlight. Everything about St. Anthony of Padua looks solid. Big, new, full-color canvas banners on the front proclaimed various faith-enhancing sentiments. When all the congregants had left, the priest looked up and greeted me. I asked him a few questions, and he told me that Mother Teresa had once lived in the convent. He added, "And did you know that the Chantels used to sing in our choir?"

IN THE BRONX of the thirties, forties, and fifties—a place much whiter than it is now—being Black could be a hazard. Poor white kids sometimes chanted rhymes at you, like, "We might be stinkies, but we're not inkies!" A girl and her little brother had to walk by a white school on the way to and from their own school every day, and the kids would yell at them and chase them. One time a boy came running at them and the girl stopped and said to her brother, "Why are you running? That boy came to school in a stroller." Movie theaters made Blacks sit in roped-off sections, or in the balcony. Some restaurants would not allow Blacks to eat in them; Howard Johnson's and White Castle let Blacks pick up takeout orders but not sit down in the restaurant. It took years, and protests, before the places changed their policy. (Something to bear in mind if you happen to walk by the White Castle at the place where the Americans repulsed the British in the Revolutionary War.)

Most labor unions refused membership to non-whites. Men who had been carpenters or masons before coming north could not get into the carpenters' or masons' unions and had to find lower-wage jobs. The Sears department store at East 149th Street and Third Avenue—the Bronx's biggest shopping district, known as the Hub—would admit Black shoppers but not hire Blacks as salespeople. The same was true of other Hub stores. Between 1938 and 1942, the Metropolitan Life Insurance Company built a twelve-thousand-unit housing complex called Parkchester, near Westchester Square on the number 6 line. The largest planned community in the United States at that time, Parkchester barred Blacks; "Negroes and whites don't mix," said Frederick Ecker, the chairman of Metropolitan Life. Black people also could not go to white swim clubs, or to certain churches. The Fordham Baldies, a white gang, was known for attacking Blacks. Black kids remembered the shock, when they strayed into Italian areas, of seeing not only kids their own age screaming and throwing things at them, but the local adults joining in.

School offered its own small and large affronts—white students not wanting to hold hands in games during class or recess, white teachers telling Blacks they would never go to college. At some point public educators across the country adopted a tracking system for junior high classes and above, by which, for example, the seventh graders judged to be the smartest would be put in the 7–1 class, the second smartest in the 7–2s, the third smartest in the 7–3s, and so on, sometimes all the way to the 7–13s, 7–14s, 7–15s, or above. Sometimes the numbers went from high to low, or they were assigned randomly. The classes with the higher numbers had mostly Blacks. Kids at all testing levels who had been together through the untracked grades of elementary school were separated when they reached junior high. In the slower classes the teachers tended to be demoralized and demoralizing.

AND YET, for a while, it worked. People who were there agree about that. For a few decades, from the mid-thirties to the mid-sixties, the Bronx's multiracial neighborhoods existed peaceably, and the residents mostly got along. Morris High School, at the heart of Morrisania, was said to be the most integrated high school in the country. Blacks and whites who grew up in integrated Bronx places remembered their childhoods with affection, even as the best time of their lives. In many ways, memories of this paradise Bronx are alike: the doors and windows that were open, the neighbors sitting on the steps in the evening, the friends across the hall who would watch your children when you had to go out, the kids playing games in the street. The more mixed areas developed qualities that were specially theirs.

Certain streets had their own foods, characters, and music; their residents wore sharper clothes. On many blocks, people played the numbers—gambled on numbers they thought would come up lucky—and gave their dimes and nickels to the numbers runner. He was said to be a mathematical genius because of his ability to hold everybody's bets in his head. Usually the runner did not write anything down, so as not to be carrying evidence against himself; playing the numbers was illegal. A runner might wear a snap-brim hat, two-tone wing-tip shoes, and a custom-tailored suit, with trousers cut in what was called an English Drape—twenty-three inches at the knee and eighteen inches at the cuff, the style worn by the Prince of Wales. The runner's pockets jingled with coins. He would drive up in his fancy car, double-park, get out, take everybody's bets, memorize them, and drive off. And occasionally somebody's number would hit, the runner would pay up, and the lucky person would take the three or four thousand dollars and buy a Morrisania brownstone.

When the city opened the Patterson Houses, the first New York City Housing Authority (NYCHA) housing project in the Bronx, the locals cheered. Its apartments were spacious and up-to-date, with lawns so green and well-cared-for that you weren't even allowed to walk on them. The NYCHA communities offered rec rooms, laundry rooms, playgrounds; some of the buildings had doormen. As more NYCHA projects opened, people vied to get into the new buildings. Again, the process of choosing residents was selective. A tenant family had to consist of two parents, married to each other, with the father steadily employed. The lobbies of the high-rises shone, and smelled like the pine-scented cleaner used on the floors. Sunlight came in every window and the rooms didn't face air shafts. NYCHA even assembled its own symphony orchestra, in which tenants and building employees performed. Other housing projects followed Patterson's model in the Bronx and won similar raves.

Back then, if you were a kid and did something wrong (or right), and a grown-up saw, word got back to your parents. Regardless of color or ethnicity, people emphasized this fact in their later memories. Glenn Ligon, the artist, who grew up in the Bronx's Forest Houses, recalled, "When we [he and his brother] were going to school, there were people that I didn't know but who knew us. And so when we would come home, my mother said, 'Oh, you know, I heard you did a very nice thing at the bus stop today with Mrs. So and So.' I was like, 'How do you know that?' 'Well, I have spies everywhere' . . . And so there was this . . . old-fashioned sense of community in the projects and I think that started to change by the early '70s."

NYCHA built dozens of other projects in the Bronx. The Patterson Houses and the Forest Houses, among the earliest ones, pioneered the new kind of living. Then came the Claremont Houses—a complex that included the Gouverneur Morris Houses and the Butler Houses—then the Betances Houses and the Castle Hill Houses and the Melrose Projects. Moving into the projects was considered a step up from a regular apartment. In the projects you no longer had a landlord to worry about; NYCHA, the city, was your landlord. Later, when the bad times came, too many of the Bronx's landlords would be undependable, to put it kindly. The projects would be like a fire wall.

24

EVERYBODY WHO LIVES out in the country in America should move to a city and live there, at least for a while. People from towns or smaller cities should try moving to a bigger city—New York, Los Angeles— just to see what it's like. The experience will knock the rust off you and rearrange your mind. Now imagine tens of thousands of migrants from the rural, highly segregated South, and from far-off, tropical Puerto Rico and the West Indies, suddenly finding themselves in the twentieth-century Bronx. No better method for creating instant Modernism could be conceived of. The subway train is going by on the elevated tracks overhead, sending off rattling, scraping, screeching sounds. A jackhammer is racketing here, a tugboat horn on the Bronx River is blasting there, a rooster is crowing somewhere. (Even today, you hear roosters in the Bronx.) Something momentous is going to happen to minds that get shaken up like this, and in certain parts of the city, especially the Bronx, it did.

Sometimes I take the number 2 or 5 to the Prospect Avenue station. Outbound from Manhattan, the train gets to Prospect Avenue two stops after it climbs from underground onto the el tracks. I always enjoy that feeling of lift and opening out. You're up in the trees, pigeons are flying next to the train windows, and it's a descent of forty worn steel steps from the station down to the sidewalk. When I arrive one spring morning, very early, I go down to the street and then look back. The rising sun is on the red metal roof of the station; the decoration on the peak of the roof, like a rococo exclamation point from an unknown language, catches the light. The sky is extremely blue. All over the four-street intersection (Prospect Avenue, East 160th, Westchester Avenue, and Longwood Avenue) beneath the el tracks, trash of various sorts seems to have settled overnight. Much of it is small squares of white paper, possibly coupons or flyers. The white squares are everywhere, as if dropped by the bushel from a propaganda airplane. In front of the McDonald's restaurant at the intersection, a man with a leaf blower is blowing the pieces of paper off his sidewalk and into the street.

A lifetime ago, Club 845, at 845 Prospect Avenue, ranked as one of the top jazz clubs in the city. Its former location is right by the set of stairs leading to the el station. The storefront has been subdivided. Six businesses—a pizza parlor, a deli, a drug and surgical supply store, a Dunkin' Donuts, a franchise sandwich place, and a Chinese takeout—fill this corner now.

Back in the 1940s and '50s, the Bronx incubated jazz. When I look at the unglamorous establishments where Club 845 used to be, I imagine the stars leaving the venue at sunup after all-night sessions, back when. Charlie Parker and Miles Davis and Dizzy Gillespie and Art Blakey and Thelonious Monk and Henry "Red" Allen and Helen Merrill all performed here. Maybe on a morning like this, the musicians came through the door, cigarette-smoky and red-eyed, counting the handful of bills they'd been paid, and carried their instruments up the steps of the el for the ride back to where they lived. (Charlie Parker lived in a lower Manhattan building that—mirabile dictu!—has a plaque on it today saying that the saxophonist rented an apartment there from 1950 to 1954.) Or maybe the stars left Club 845 before the night was over and went to one of the other clubs in the neighborhood. Music venues lit up the late-night Bronx in those years. The Hunts Point Palace, Sylvia's Blue Morocco, the Boston Road Ballroom, Freddy's, the Blue Flame, Zanzibar, the Tropicana, and other clubs kept performers in rent money, whether they happened to be famous or not.

Plenty of jazz musicians and a few singers lived in the neighborhood and could walk to work. People you've heard of, or never heard of, made up a large, multistrand jazz community centered in Longwood-Morrisania. Local kids noticed the comings and goings of Thelonious Monk, the pianist and bebop pioneer. Originally from Rocky Mount, North Carolina, Monk had family who lived on Lyman Place, a snug street only a block long. He stayed with these relatives in 1956 and again in 1961. The father of the family was a Pullman porter. Monk's niece, Jacqueline Smith Bonneau, who also lived in that apartment, also became a jazz pianist. Monk was known for making dramatic entrances. A German Jewish woman called the Baroness often drove him around in a Rolls-Royce. He used to arrive on Lyman Place in his beret and the ankle-length overcoat he wore winter and summer and step from the Rolls into a crowd of admirers.

A block or two away, a section of Prospect Avenue has been renamed for Henry "Red" Allen, one of the innovators of swing. Allen, who lived at Jennings Street and Prospect, is said to have purchased a new Cadillac every year. Maxine Sullivan, the jazz vocalist, lived on Ritter Place, close by. It is now Maxine Sullivan Way. Valerie Capers, the Juilliard-trained pianist and composer who played both classical and jazz, spent some of her childhood in a brick building embellished with gorgeous stonework that still stands on East 168th Street, around the corner. Her father, a stride pianist, worked for the post office, as did others in the Capers family. Fats Waller played at her parents' wedding. When Valerie was a child, she contracted rheumatic fever that almost killed her and made her blind. Her blood type, AB negative, is a kind that not many people have, but the Reverend Edler Hawkins, of St. Augustine's Presbyterian Church, happened to be AB negative. He gave blood for the transfusion that helped save her life.

At any time, you might hear jazz coming from the windows in the neighborhood. The streets had a New Orleans feel. Some of the original row houses are still standing, but the ambient music has changed. In former times, you walked past the music—the sound would grow louder as you approached and then fade as you went on. Today the music goes by *you*, booming from shiny SUVs that trail clouds of marijuana smoke and Axe cologne. Passing blasts of rap scour these streets like flash floods through a canyon.

The block associated with Monk—Lyman Place—has been renamed not for him, but for another bebop and hard-bop pianist, Elmo Hope. In the sixties, Hope lived on Lyman Place with his wife, Bertha Hope (herself a pianist), and their children, until his drug addiction killed him at the age of forty-three. If the city wanted, it could name more streets for local jazz notables. Irene Higginbotham, who cowrote "Good Morning Heartache," the Billie Holliday classic, lived with her cousin's family at Prospect and East 168th. Higginbotham may not be widely known, but few songwriters will produce anything as memorable as that song.

Erroll Garner, also a pianist, also much beloved, lived on Intervale Avenue, the street Bessie Jackson was walking on when she was asked to light the stove. Dexter Gordon, the saxophonist, resided in the Bronx for a while; his widow, Maxine Gordon, is still there. Billy Bang, the jazz violinist, who once lived at 851 Cauldwell Avenue in Morrisania, told an interviewer, "I play music from the plantation brother. I play Black music from the African plantation to the fiddle to the Billy Bang." This reminds me of Lunnon, who served as executioner when James DeLancey hanged Tim Knapp in the days of the Neutral Ground. An oral history account of the hanging described Lunnon as a "fidler." Odds are that he was enslaved. There must have been more music in old-time Westchester County, but that's the only reference to it I've seen.

More jazz names: Barry Altschul, the drummer, attended Taft High School, on East 170th Street. His parents came from Russia. Altschul started playing the drums at eleven, and as a teenager caught the attention of Art Blakey, who took an interest in him and gave him a job with his band. Harold "Tina" Brooks, the hard-bop saxophonist who also played blues and fusion; Jimmy Smith, who played the organ and used a U-Haul or a camper to carry it around; Elombe Brath, one of the founders of the Jazz Arts Society; the bass player

William Parker, who lived in the Melrose Houses; Arthur Jenkins, the keyboard player-composer; Biddy Fleet, a saxophonist who influenced Charlie Parker; and many other men and women maybe known only to people who know a lot about jazz, or not even to them, passed through the Bronx in those days.

PUERTO RICANS STARTED to come to the Bronx in large numbers in the 1940s, often by way of Spanish Harlem, uptown on the far East Side. They had left Puerto Rico because of lack of jobs; unlike in Russia or the American South, terror was not a motivator. This northward move lagged the Great Migration and then overlapped with it. Most Puerto Rican migrants were families driven from the countryside by the conglomeration and mechanization of agriculture. The United States had taken Puerto Rico from Spain in 1898 and made its residents (nonvoting) U.S. citizens; when they came, they were not immigrants any more than Black Americans were. The arriving Puerto Ricans often lacked money and education, suffered the same kinds of discrimination, and ended up in the same neighborhoods as Blacks. Bigger passenger planes and cheaper airfares made it easier to come here; New York and Puerto Rico are about eighteen hundred miles apart, and the journey by ship had taken days. Once the move gained momentum, the city's Puerto Rican population went up quickly—from 61,000 in 1940 to 817,712 thirty years later. By then more than one in every ten New Yorkers was Puerto Rican.

Under the Prospect Avenue el station, across from where Club 845 used to be, a music store listed in the National Register of Historic Places bears witness to this change. The store, whose full name is Casa Amadeo, Antigua Casa Hernandez (House of Amadeo, Formerly House of Hernandez), was often closed during the pandemic. Now it's usually open again. Casa Amadeo has been a Latin music store since 1941 and is the oldest continuously operating Latin music store in the city. A run of that length must be a record for a music store of any kind. Miguel "Mike" Amadeo, a musician and composer, bought the store from the Hernandez family in 1969. He is a slim, courtly man who wears guayabera shirts in summer and sweaters that button in winter. In 1956, he wrote his first hit song, "El Guapo" ("The Handsome Man"), and he has written dozens more since then. Because of Amadeo's fame, coolness, and longevity, the city named the intersection Mike Amadeo Plaza. He was pleased by the gesture but says he would gladly trade the street sign for his own guaranteed personal parking space.

Puerto Ricans brought drums not often used in other kinds of American music, with a higher-pitched, less John Philip Sousa kind of sound. Drums also figured in the melody and were played by hand. The rhythms of stride and swing and bebop could be heard coming from jazz clubs and apartment buildings, while Latin drumbeats echoed far and wide outdoors, in the parks. Those pulse-quickening rhythms are still out there. People go to sleep on summer nights to Latin drumbeats coming from someplace nearby. The Bronx cityscape and Latin drums have found a symbiosis with each other.

Latin music subcategorized itself into salsa, meringue, mambo, cha-cha-cha, Afro-Cuban, and more obscure types like son and bachata. Collectively these met up with jazz and produced Latin jazz. Since the arrival of Latin music, the style hasn't faded. Tito Puente, the drummer and songwriter, was the king. Hundreds of musicians performed with him over his fifty-year career. Puente and other Bronx residents—Celia Cruz, Tito Rodriguez, Machito, and Eddie and Charlie Palmieri—drew crowds at venues such as Hunts Point Palace, which featured "breakfast dances" that began at ten p.m. and continued into the next morning. The club was near the Hunts Point Avenue station on the 6 train. A leading Latin label, Fania Records, signed dozens of musicians to a group called the Fania All Stars. They could play for an audience of forty thousand at Yankee Stadium and not get a mention in the major newspapers.

Jazz musicians, although usually Black, could be of any background, but if you played Latin music there was an expectation that you actually *be* Latin. If you weren't, you might take a bandstand name. When Peter Simms, a jazz drummer, decided to play in a Latin band, he became Pete La Roca, borrowing the name from the Tito Puente song "Mambo La Roca." Al Fordito, who led a Latin band in the fifties, had changed his name from Al Lang. To follow the discography of the jazz trumpeter Joe Wilder you must know that he sometimes played in Latin bands under the name José Valdez. Larry Harlow, the salsa bandleader (born Lawrence Kahn), performed as El Judío Maravilloso, "The Marvelous Jew." Latin music went through periods of expanding popularity, such as when there was an international craze for dancing the mambo in the 1950s. A country did not have to speak Spanish to love Latin music. For years, Celia Cruz, the Cuban-born, Bronx-residing artist known as the Queen of Salsa, was the most popular musical performer in Finland.

DOO-WOP, ANOTHER MUSICAL STYLE that flourished in the Bronx, sprang directly from happiness. Kids in cities in the Northeast created doo-wop, taking inspiration from older vocal groups like the Ink Spots and the Mills Brothers, and from gospel choirs and barbershop quartets. Doo-wop music and its era—that dreamy period soon after the Second World War—reinforced each other. The dreaminess infused the music, which then made the era even dreamier. Life had been renewed, the Baby Boom had begun. Some Bronxites were living in bigger and nicer apartments than they'd ever lived in. The acoustics of the common spaces in the buildings contributed to doo-wop because the singers loved how they sounded in the tiled halls and lobbies. Harmony could be imagined to have replaced discord everywhere. Once the music got to you it stayed forever, as doo-wop fans now long past retirement age will tell you.

Teens and preteens created doo-wop, which can't be said of any previously existing commercial pop music. Bronx school kids cut million-selling records that you could hear on your car radio across America. The sound is so closely associated with the fifties that movie directors use it to establish atmosphere, as in the first *Texas Chainsaw Massacre* (for example), where the song "Sh'boom" plays in ominous innocence at the beginning. A Bronx group called the Chords wrote and recorded "Sh'boom" in 1954. It was the first doo-wop million seller. Fans will recognize the names of other Bronx groups, such as the Harp Tones, the Chimes, the Chiffons, the Clickettes, the Mellows, and Dion and the Belmonts. Dion DiMucci and other members of that group grew up in the Belmont neighborhood. When the Chantels sold a million copies of their biggest hit, "Maybe," they were still in high school.

Kids sang on Bronx street corners, on buses, and in the bathrooms at school. Boys harmonized to impress girls. PS 99, a large and stately brick high school on Stebbins (now James A. Polite) Avenue, has been called the Motown of the Bronx for all the doo-wop groups that came from there. Its music director, Vincent Tibbs, a five-foot, six-inch muscleman, held doo-wop talent contests in the school auditorium. Students went back to the empty building in the evenings after supper and bounded down the echoing, recently polished hallways to the auditorium. Contest winners were judged on volume of applause alone. The winning groups might go on to other contests and performances at schools in the city and in New Jersey. PS 99 has since been renamed Metropolitan High School, and it's rarely open in the evenings. In general, schools in New York City have been open only during regular school hours since the cuts to education funding back in the 1970s.

Doo-wop was basically a style of rhythm and blues, and a route by which early rock 'n' roll entered pop culture. Frankie Lymon and his group, the Teenagers (from Washington Heights, not the Bronx), performed on *The Ed Sullivan Show* in 1957 and created the same kind of frenzy that the Beatles would scale up gigantically when they went on the show seven years later. By that time, doo-wop was already ossifying into nostalgia, and hip-hop, its less sentimental younger sibling, had not been born.

ANOTHER CHANGE: back then you used to hear more basketballs bouncing in the playgrounds. In good weather, the sound was everywhere. New York in the 1950s and '60s was like a lab for basketball, as New York's Black neighborhoods reinvented the game with a wide-open, aerobatic style of play never seen before.

At the Hilton White Playground, just off East 163rd Street near the Forest Houses, no one is around on a spring morning except a guy on the top of the jungle gym who is taking photos with a long-lens camera. The oaks and London plane trees have recently leafed out and their camo-like shadows swap back and forth on the pavement. According to the historic marker on the equipment house, this playground covers about half an acre. When it was called the Cauldwell Park and Playground, in the sixties, a man named Hilton White, its recreation director, coached a youth basketball team here. The city used to hire hundreds of counselors across the five boroughs to supervise rec programs on the playgrounds. Outstanding athletes and coaches—former high school and college stars, even one or two veterans of the Tuskegee Airmen—served as rec directors, sometimes called "parkies." White's team was the Bronx Falcons. If you knew anything about New York City basketball back then, you knew about the Falcons.

White was born in Harlem in 1932 and attended DeWitt Clinton High School in the Bronx. After graduating from Benedict College, in South Carolina, he joined the army, which stationed him at Fort Bliss, in El Paso, Texas. From that experience he learned that El Paso, on the Mexican border, didn't treat Blacks as badly as other places in the South did. Texas Western College, in El Paso, was one of the first southern schools to integrate.

After the army, White came back to the Bronx, and the Parks Department assigned him to Cauldwell Playground. He and his wife, Naomi, lived a few blocks away, on Tinton Avenue. Soon everybody in the neighborhood knew him. Kids had to try out to be on the Falcons and playing for him was an honor. The team won playground tournaments around the city, including the famous Rucker Tournament, named for another beloved parkie, Holcomb Rucker. White insisted his players pay attention to their schoolwork along with their basketball. He said they could get college scholarships and make a big improvement in their lives.

College basketball coaches began to hear about him, and he received recruiting inquiries from the coach of Texas Western College. He told the coach, Don Haskins, that he would send players to El Paso if Haskins promised they would get an education. By 1965, three former Bronx Falcons—Nevil Shed, Willie Worsley, and Willie Cager—

were playing for Texas Western. In his autobiography, Haskins later wrote that the kids all loved Hilton White, whom he described as "a class guy." At first, the Bronx players objected to Haskins's discipline, but when they complained to White, he took the coach's side. White told the kids not to quit but to listen to Haskins and work harder.

The Texas Western Miners had a good season in 1965–1966 and made it to the NCAA championship playoffs—always an achievement for a small school. After defeating a tough team from the University of Kansas in the semifinals, they went up against the University of Kentucky Wildcats for the championship. Kentucky's coach, Adolph "Baron" Rupp, one of the winningest coaches in college basketball history, did not like Blacks, and had none on his team. The cheering section for Kentucky featured a Confederate flag. In the face of that, Haskins started an all-Black five for Texas Western. One of them was the five-foot, six-inch ball-handling whiz, Willie Worsley, a former Bronx Falcon. No college team had ever started five Black players in a championship game before.

The matchup, held at the University of Maryland Field House, changed basketball forever. Texas Western's center, David Lattin, dunked the ball over Kentucky's Pat Riley (the future Knicks coach) to start the first half. The Miners then went ahead early on a foul shot by Nevil Shed, another former Falcon, and held the lead for the rest of the game. When they won, 72–65, Hilton White was watching from the stands, beaming.

After the Miners' victory, dependable American racism swelled like a bubo. Coach Haskins received forty thousand pieces of hate mail. Baron Rupp disparaged the Texas Western players as "crooks" and said he was above recruiting such disreputable types. Not long after the game, the NCAA outlawed dunking, a rule aimed at Black athletes and the New York playground style. (Eventually the NCAA had to lift the ban because of fan pressure.) All the former Falcons on the championship team got educations, as promised, and went on to have solid professional lives. The four years after the Kentucky–Texas Western championship game saw the biggest increase in integration in the history of college sports. Coaches at southern schools, and elsewhere, had no choice but to recruit Black players if they wanted to be competitive. More Blacks at the college level of course led to more Blacks in pro basketball.

Much of that change can be traced to this half acre named for Hilton White. He died in 1990, at the age of fifty-seven, and the city renamed the playground after him in 2009. About thirty members of his extended family attended the ceremony. There are still people in the neighborhood who knew him. Duane Johnson, proprietor and principal cook at Johnson's Barbecue, the family-run takeout place (founded 1954) on East 163rd Street, remembers White attending the all-day, all-week checkers games on the sidewalk outside the restaurant. "Hilton White knew me before I knew him, when I was four and five years old," Johnson says. "I knew him all my life. If you saw him, you had to respect him. If you were doing something wrong, like smoking weed or drinking, you would hide it, like, 'Hi, Mr. White.' He was a mild-tempered man. He was a giver. The whole Bronx knew who he was."

The Hilton White Playground lost its basketball backboards fifteen or more years ago. Across the Bronx, the population has shifted to a Spanish-speaking majority, and Spanish-speaking people tend not to play basketball. Old-timers say you never used to see a basketball court without a game going on a nice day. Kids used to line up and wait. Now the sound of a basketball bouncing on a summer day in the Bronx is rare enough that I generally stop and check it out.

FOR YEARS IT WAS AS IF Black and brown people didn't exist, officially, in the Bronx; they were barely a presence in its politics. As in the rest of the city, Democrats outnumbered Republicans, and men mostly of Irish backgrounds ran the Democratic Party. In the 1950s, political power belonged to Edward J. Flynn, the leader of the Bronx County Democrats, who controlled the borough for thirty years. The candidates Flynn chose won—thus the (supposed) origin of the phrase "In like Flynn." He could always deliver a solid bloc of votes in national elections, an ability that caused Franklin Roosevelt to pay court to him and make him an ally and advisor. Flynn pushed for Harry Truman to

be FDR's running mate in 1944; no local pol in the United States had
more national power than Ed Flynn. In 1933, he nominated the party
regular James J. Lyons to run for Bronx borough president, and Lyons
held that office until he retired in 1960.

Borough President James J. Lyons smiles in photo after photo
from that time, whether he's introducing a fleet of new public buses or
speaking at the opening of Yeshiva University's Albert Einstein School
of Medicine or dedicating a bridge or welcoming Harry Truman to the
Concourse Plaza Hotel. You must look closely, though, to pick Lyons
out, because the people in the photos resemble one another. They're all
white men in fedoras, suits, and ties; sometimes they wear identical
dark topcoats. None of them are Black or Puerto Rican. A photo from
a Bronx County Democratic dinner in the mid-1950s shows Lyons
in a group that includes the governor, Averell Harriman; the mayor,
Robert Wagner, Jr.; and the newish Bronx Democratic Party chairman, Charles Buckley. All the men in the photo are dressed in evening wear. Edward Lynch, a vice president of the Chase Manhattan
Bank, is the only one who has no position with the government or the
Democratic Party, but he belongs in the group, because the banks will
have a lot to say about the borough's survival.

After Lyons's retirement, the Republican Party, many of whose
members were Italians, finally won the Bronx borough presidency,
and James J. Periconi took over. A split had occurred among the Bronx
County Democrats, with the previously overlooked Blacks and Puerto
Ricans gravitating to the Jackson Club, a group of more progressive
Dems. In 1954, Walter H. Gladwin, a candidate backed by the Jackson Club, won his campaign for state assemblyman, thereby becoming
the first Black elected official in the Bronx. In 1965, James Periconi
was ousted as borough president by Herman Badillo, a Puerto Rico–
born attorney. Bronx politics had finally caught up with its new ethnic
population. Of the nine borough presidents of the Bronx since then,
seven have been Black or Latino.

The perpetual smile on Borough President Lyons's face could represent the benevolent mood of power in that era. With an open hand,
the city spent money on its kids. Not only did playgrounds employ rec
directors, some NYCHA buildings did, too. Schools offered extracur-

ricular classes, such as art and dance, and after-school programs in the classroom buildings, which remained open from two to five o'clock in the afternoons and from seven to nine in the evenings, weekends included. One old-time resident remembered that Christmas was the only day on which his school building closed. School music programs provided instruments for the band or the orchestra, and students could take the instruments home to practice. Teachers paid special notice to talented students, and sometimes gave them extra tutoring for performances outside of class. Playgrounds stocked up on bats and balls to loan out.

Adults who grew up in the Bronx in the postwar years remember the familiar elements of a 1950s and '60s American childhood. They wore Davy Crockett raccoon skin caps, argued about whether Hopalong Cassidy was better than Roy Rogers was better than Gene Autry, played Whiffle Ball (which had captured some of the market from the Spaldeen), improved their reading skills by the SRA method (Study, Read, and Answer), asked for Lionel electric trains and Erector Sets for Christmas, built model airplanes, watched Bugs Bunny and Mickey Mouse and Captain Kangaroo on TV, joined the Cub Scouts, collected pennies in little orange cardboard boxes for UNICEF on Halloween, and carried lunchboxes with pictures of planets and spaceships on them.

All the same, things are going to fall apart—soon, and seriously. When they do, the smiling men in their fedoras and ties and tuxedos and topcoats will have moved on. Instead, there will be President Jimmy Carter standing in the middle of devastation on all sides, and not smiling. Ed Flynn and James J. Lyons and their cohort get points for contributing to the happy circumstances of their time. The borough's politicians oversaw a lighter-hearted Bronx; but as signposts for the future, the smiles deceived.

25

EVERY BOROUGH IN NEW YORK CITY has an official historian. (Every county in the state has one, and every borough is a county.) For twenty-seven years, the Bronx County historian was a professor named Lloyd Ultan. He jokes that the official historian receives a six-figure salary, "and every one of those six figures is zero!" Ultan was born in the Bronx in 1938 and has lived there all his life. His last name is also the name of a village in Iran on the border of Azerbaijan. In the late nineteenth century, Jews who lived in what was then Persia moved north, into a part of Russia that is now Belarus. He knows that his Ultan forebears came to New York in 1902 from that part of Russia, and he surmises, though he has no hard evidence, that the family originally came from the Persian/Iranian village of Ultan and later adopted its name.

He seems to have been a historian from the cradle. As a boy, he was always asking his parents and aunts and uncles what happened before he was born. His father sold women's shoes and rose to the job of distributor for A. S. Beck, which is now National Shoes. His mother was a housewife. Ultan had one sibling, a younger brother, who was an architect. The family lived first in a walk-up on East 165th Street at the corner of Walton Avenue, and then moved to a six-story elevator building on the Grand Concourse near East 158th Street. He went to PS 114, Middle School 22, and William Howard Taft High School, one of the biggest high school buildings in the city, on a rise just east of the Concourse. Four thousand students attended Taft when he was there. Afterward, at Hunter College of the Bronx (now Herbert H. Lehman College), he majored in history and minored in political science. The only time he left the borough for his education was when he won a Rockefeller-sponsored fellowship and used it to study history at Columbia for two years. Today he teaches the subject at Fairleigh Dickinson University in Teaneck, New Jersey, just on the other side of the George Washington Bridge.

Ultan is white-haired, cheerful, and an information fount on the Bronx, which he loves to talk about. He sometimes wears a brown glen plaid jacket, a light pink shirt, a brown tie, and a gray V-neck cable sweater. His eyebrows are pure white, and they spring out above his lively dark eyes like spray in front of a speeding boat. He adores puns. When I suggested over the phone that it would be okay for us to talk in person, because we both had been vaccinated, he said, "Well, I guess that means we're both a couple of 'stuck-up' guys!" After he makes a pun, he pulls a droll face, with his lips pressed together and his mouth in a long line. As historian, he was technically a county official. The borough president swore him in at the beginning of his term. ("I was sworn *in*, now I'm sworn *at*," he used to say.) The duties of the job include collecting historical records, encouraging private concerns such as businesses and civic groups to collect their own, making presentations at schools, and giving lectures and tours. Sometimes he appeared in his role as historian in various celebrations and parades; one year he accompanied the dignitaries marching at the head of the Bronx's Dominican Day Parade.

His view of Bronx history is prelapsarian—so much so that, from his point of view, the Bronx never had a real fall to recover from. Local boosters have told him that by staying positive and talking up the borough, he helped save the Bronx. I have no doubt that's true. I believe that historians can heal a place. I once saw a documentary about a shaman-midwife who brought women through difficult child-birth by telling them tales made up on the spot about the journey of the baby. Historians do something similar, birthing the present from the past; ideally, the stories they tell possess the mystery that comes from being true.

By this point, the reader will have understood that the 1970s were a hard time. The fact that, in 1979, Ultan published a book (written in collaboration with the Bronx Historical Society) whose title was *The Beautiful Bronx: 1920–1950* tells a lot about him. It's a book of black-and-white photos with captions by Ultan. A follow-up book of photos, *The Bronx: It Was Only Yesterday, 1935–1965* (co-authored by Gary Herma-lyn) came out in 1995. Ultan's comprehensive historical survey, *The Northern Borough: A History of the Bronx* (published 2005), covers the place's past from its glaciated early origins up to the late 1980s. He has never lost his love for the Bronx or given up on the Bronx.

Ultan doesn't talk much about himself, but his childhood must have been happy, from the way he describes the place he knew. When writing captions in the photo books, he points out details with a care that gives them the luminosity of objects in a child's drawing. I had never appreciated the old Bronx trolley cars until I read his paean to them in *The Beautiful Bronx*. Trolleys followed major thoroughfares like Tremont Avenue, and afforded a good view of the passing scene, especially in the summer, when the cars' sides were removed and replaced with a metal net so the cross-breezes could cool the passengers. At the end of the line, a trolley car didn't need to turn around, because the motorman could drive it from either end. First, he had to adjust the poles that attached the car to the overhead wires:

> The car came to its final stop, and the pole arising from the rear of the car connecting it to the power source of the overhead wire was hauled down by a rope attached at its end. After the pole had been made to lie parallel to the top of the car, the rope was securely tied to prevent it from rising of its own volition. Then the pole in the front of the car, which had been tied in the same position, was released, and the spring at its base would cause it to fly up to the overhead wire, tamed only by the man guiding it with the attached rope.

The motorman then walked through the car flipping the seats to face what was now the front. Ultan writes, "To children's eyes, it seemed that miraculously the trolley car had turned around without changing its position."

He chronicles his subjects unsentimentally, as a historian should; so he adds that the trolley cars were replaced with buses in 1948. The city tore up the steel rails from the streets and paved the streets over—and gone forever were the trolley cars.

That the Bronx enjoyed decades of successful integration is a fact he often mentions. As a fan of diversity and a devout multiculturalist, he can list Bronx ethnicities in detail: Africans of a dozen-plus nationalities, Albanians, Russians who came after the fall of the Soviet Union, Dominicans (now the most numerous Spanish-speakers in the borough), Garifuna (Honduran descendants of runaway enslaved people and Caribbean Native Americans), Serbs, Croats, Pakistanis, Bangladeshis, Afghans, Vietnamese, Cambodians, Koreans, Yemenis, Peruvians, Kurds . . . He says the Bronx has welcomed everybody: "We have residents from every continent, if you include the penguins in the zoo." In apparent contradiction of reality, he maintains that the Bronx never experienced "white flight." The widespread moving-out of white families in the sixties and seventies is a change he ascribes to the usual cycles of upward mobility, in which Bronx residents of all types participated.

He models himself on Dr. Theodore Kazimiroff, the dentist and amateur historian who co-saved Split Rock from Robert Moses, and who co-founded the Bronx County Historical Society. All the Bronx historians are respected by Ultan as peers and colleagues, though he deplores Stephen Jenkins's occasional prejudice against the Irish. Ultan says that it was he, Ultan, who persuaded John McNamara to assemble his list of the origins of Bronx place-names into the invaluable *History in Asphalt*. Without that book, appreciators of the Bronx today would find themselves lost when trying to figure out which streets used to be which, amid all the recent renaming.

He might not agree with my opinion that James Fenimore Cooper qualifies as the Bronx's earliest historian, for want of any other.

Cooper's novel, whose plot I have described, is set in the Neutral Ground, a subject no other writer seems to have wanted to touch during Cooper's lifetime. The neighbor-versus-neighbor cruelties, the ambushes, and the plundering make for an uncomfortable reality. As I've also noted, a lawyer named John M. McDonald traveled around Westchester County in the years 1844 to 1850 recording the stories that the by-then-elderly survivors from the Neutral Ground and other residents remembered from the war. A time that Cooper had transformed and made bearable through fiction reassembled itself into fact by way of McDonald's interviews.

CURRENT HISTORIANS have compiled a collection of oral accounts much like the McDonald Papers, but from the twentieth and twenty-first centuries. Since 2002, the Department of African American Studies at Fordham University has been interviewing longtime Bronx residents, most of them Black. The McDonald Papers focus on a seven-year period of war. The Bronx African American History Project (BAAHP), as Fordham calls this oral history collection, covers a longer span, and includes the years of fires and devastation that made large sections of the place look as if they had been in a war. The McDonald Papers consist of accounts told to McDonald and written down in good cursive handwriting. The photocopy of a copy of that original document, available to scholars who visit the Westchester County Historical Society Library, in Elmsford, New York, runs to about eleven hundred pages. Aided by two assistants, McDonald conducted 407 interviews with 241 people.

Fordham's interviewers, by comparison, have conducted about 300 interviews, some with only one interviewee and some with two or three or more. McDonald and his helpers in the 1840s spent six years collecting histories; the staff and volunteers of the BAAHP have been working on their task for more than twenty years so far. You don't have to travel to Fordham to study the BAAHP archive, because the interviews are online. Some take up more than a hundred pages. The average length is probably about sixty pages. That is, the total for all the 300-some interviews in the BAAHP runs to perhaps eighteen thousand pages. Aside from total length, the two collections are similar, separated as they are by more than a century and a half. Both tell what happened in an eventful, difficult time, and bear witness to it. With these two collections, history and the recording of history repeat themselves.

Both McDonald and the BAAHP worked against a popular fantasy. For McDonald, it was the romanticism of *The Spy*. For the BAHHP, the obstacle was and is the popular misimpressions of the Bronx that thrive in the media. One example: In Tom Wolfe's novel *The Bonfire of the Vanities* (later made into a movie), all the main character needs to do to bring about his downfall is to leave the safe world of the elevated highways and exit by mistake into the street-level Bronx, where the first humans he sees try to do him harm. Other movies have been even more sensationalist. *Fort Apache, the Bronx* showed the place as a kind of behavioral sink redeemed only by the movie's hero police officers, played by Paul Newman and Ed Asner. Not that the Bronx wasn't (or isn't) sometimes dangerous; but the locals who picketed the filming of *Fort Apache* objected to the portrayal of borough residents like themselves and their friends and families as just a bunch of criminals.

The BAAHP came about because Dr. Peter Derrick, the archivist of the Bronx County Historical Society, was getting requests from people looking for firsthand accounts of Black history in the borough. Robert Gumbs, a publisher and graphic designer who grew up in the Bronx, told Dr. Derrick there was a chance that what Black people had contributed would be lost and forgotten, as happens a lot. Derrick and Gumbs passed the question along to Dr. Mark D. Naison, professor of African American history at Fordham, and asked if the university could create a database of local Black history. Naison liked the idea. He knew that this history had been overlooked; he recalled that in a recent book about Blacks in New York City put out by Harlem's Schomburg Library, the Bronx received just three pages. Naison also remembered the interviews that historians employed by the Works Progress Administration did back in the thirties with southern Blacks, many of whom had been enslaved. He knew how valuable those accounts have been to historians.

Bronx musicians threw a benefit concert to provide him with some start-up money, Fordham agreed to pay for the transcriptions and other expenses, and Naison began interviewing. The news got around, and soon so many people wanted to participate that he had to bring on more colleagues and experts to help. He conducted most of the interviews himself, superintended the sessions, handled the scheduling, even ordered the sandwiches; he has stayed with the project for decades as it continues. In 2016, he and Robert Gumbs published a book containing some of the interviews. (I have used both their book and the online BAAHP interviews in my own research, as readers of endnotes will have noticed.)

Now in his late seventies, Naison has taught at Fordham for fifty-three years. He does not look like the college history professor you may have in your mind. He says that his ancestors on one side of his Russian Jewish family were thugs. If he were of a different disposition, Naison could do thug. He is over six feet tall, gray-bearded, white-mustached, broad-shouldered, long-armed, and thick through the torso. When I met him in his top-floor office at Fordham one morning, he was wearing a blue-and-white-striped collar T-shirt, Bermuda shorts, white knee socks, and large white sneakers. On his head he had a gray fedora whose brim slanted downward, like the hats worn by 1960s TV detectives and large, watchful men in the Diamond District. I told him I admired his hat and he said he had been using it ever since he started needing a haircut and the pandemic made it hard to get one.

Naison is a product of Brooklyn, where he went to elementary and high school, fought kids who teased him, and got good grades, further enraging his enemies. As an only child, he carried a freight of expectations. His father taught high school science, his mother taught social studies and history. Naison followed the script for a while; he captained his high school's tennis team, did well on his SATs, and got into Columbia. There he met a Black woman from the Bronx, and they soon moved in together. His closeness to her and to her family, and his parents' refusal to meet her, had the effect of shifting his loyalties Bronxward. The relationship ended eventually but it had redirected his life.

Not many college professors who got arrested at protests back in the sixties are still teaching, but Naison's old-radical credentials go deep. Andrew Goodman, one of the three young men murdered while trying to register voters in Philadelphia, Mississippi, was an acquaintance. Naison belonged to the Students for a Democratic Society (SDS) and knew one of the radicals killed by the explosion of a bomb they were trying to manufacture in a Greenwich Village town house. After that event, Naison himself was under surveillance. He says he has his own FBI file. Some of his students call him "Notorious PhD."

The nickname also refers to his passion for hip-hop. No other seventy-eight-year-old white college professor in the world knows as much about it as he does. His course From Rock 'n' Roll to Hip-Hop is among the most popular at Fordham. He once went on *Chappelle's Show*, where the host asked him hip-hop-related questions, each more obscure than the next; Naison got every one right. He can recite rap lyrics and knows biographical details about rap stars and random hip-hop facts. In trials that involve hip-hop music, lawyers sometimes ask him to provide background and advice. When I mentioned the classic "The Message," by Grandmaster Flash and the Furious Five, he reeled off a stanza and added, "'The Message' is the only rap song whose lyrics are in *The Norton Anthology of African-American Literature*."

"The Message" is an angry song, and rap's anger makes sense to him. He regrets that kids today have fewer public resources than his generation did, and that their lives are harder in general. When his students ask him the difference between then and now, he says that when he was their age, the top 1 percent in New York City owned 9 percent of the wealth, and today the top 1 percent owns 44 percent. For Naison, some of the thrill of putting together the oral history collection is related to his activist past. In his book *White Boy: A Memoir*, he wrote that when he was discovering his vocation, he "came to see writing history and making history as integrally connected."

Lloyd Ultan, though only eight years older, belongs to a different generation. His sunny frame of mind preserves a miracle: People once saw this place as paradise, and from certain angles it was. For Ultan, every detail of that miracle still holds its delight. His view of the Bronx includes a strong element of the Shining City on the Hill. In his *The Northern Borough*, which is 326 pages long, the years of fire and destruction take up only 18 pages. A longer conclusion, titled "Renaissance," follows that chapter. The way a place is seen can change it; both Ultan and Naison see the Bronx with hope.

NAISON'S FAVORITE HANGOUT SPOT, back in his radical youth, was the Liberation Bookstore, on Lexington Avenue and 131st Street in Manhattan, next door to the New York City headquarters of the Black Panther Party. Some of the early political demonstrations he participated in were to protest government actions against the Black Panthers. The group also had an office on Boston Road in the Bronx.

Despite the big impression the Panthers made on the popular imagination, they lasted not long as an actual functioning group. In the BAAHP oral histories they appear rarely, as when a woman describes going to the Manhattan office to ask if she can join the organization; Afeni Shakur, one of the leaders, tells her she can't be a Panther because she doesn't even know how to wrap a gele (a Nigerian head garment, pronounced "gaylay"). Shakur and another Panther then show her how to wrap it. When she does it correctly herself on the first try, they say, "Wow, you're a Panther now!" J. Edgar Hoover, head of the FBI, called the Black Panthers the country's most serious domestic threat, and set about to destroy them, with informers, jail sentences, and police killings. Afeni Shakur was one of fourteen Panthers charged with major crimes in New York, including plotting to blow up the New York Botanical Garden. After a long trial, a jury acquitted her and the others of all charges in May 1971. She gave birth to her son, Tupac, the following month.

The Panthers did the country no favors with their emphasis on guns, and their insistence that everybody—not only Blacks, but everybody—arm themselves. (They did, however, scare the California state legislature into passing stricter anti-carry laws.) But seeing the Panthers marching in dark glasses and berets and black leather, and hearing their speeches, gave a lift to Black pride, and to a mood of defiant self-possession in general. They also left a civic legacy with their free breakfast and lunch programs for schoolchildren in cities across the country. The scientifically proven idea that kids learn better when they're not hungry—a fact the Panthers made much of—caught on. It underlies the school breakfast programs widely in operation in the United States today. The Panthers understood food. They sometimes even brought meals to fellow organizers and protesters at sit-ins. In 1988, long after the organization was defunct, Bobby Seale, one of its founders, published a recipe book called *Barbeque'n with Bobby*. Food brought out the Panthers' gentler side.

The Young Lords, a group of mostly Puerto Rican activists, idolized and modeled themselves on the Panthers. The life span of the Lords as an organization was also short. They emerged in New York in 1969 with a protest against the sanitation services in East Harlem, during which they blocked the streets with bags of uncollected garbage. Then they occupied a Methodist church and refused to leave. They hijacked a mobile X-ray unit and took patients' chest X-rays on their own, making a point about the high rate of TB among Puerto Ricans, and about the inequality of medical care. Most Puerto Ricans did not want Puerto Rico to be independent from the United States, but the Young Lords agitated for the cause, and pelted the governor of Puerto Rico with eggs and tomatoes during a Puerto Rican Day Parade in Manhattan.

Among their several disruptions, the Young Lords performed one great and lasting service for the Bronx. In 1970, they occupied the administrative offices of Lincoln Hospital, which people called "the butcher shop of the Bronx." Lincoln was filthy, overcrowded, falling apart, and next to the roaring Bruckner Expressway. Twenty-some years before, it had been condemned for demolition. Waiting times in the blood-daubed emergency room ranged above thirty-six hours. Early in the morning of July 14, 1970, a hundred and fifty Young Lords, with precision organization and timing, took over the hospital offices. High on the list of their demands was that the city build the new Lincoln Hospital, which had been promised to the community for fifteen years. Mayor John Lindsay's top aide negotiated with the occupiers and agreed that construction would begin immediately. Police surrounded the building to make arrests, but most of the Lords were able to slip out after twelve hours of occupation.

Three weeks later, as promised, the city broke ground for the new hospital at a site about a mile away from the then-existing one. Construction was supposed to take four years, but it took six. The new Lincoln had 1,000 beds, compared with the old Lincoln's 350. Today Lincoln is the main hospital in the South Bronx, and its emergency room is the busiest in the city and the third busiest in the country. Hospital-rating surveys give it a "C," a compliment under the circumstances, and one that nobody would have ever made to the old Lincoln. Considering the city's neglect of the Bronx in the seventies, it's likely that the new Lincoln would not have been built for decades, or maybe ever, were it not for the Young Lords.

The group persisted, raised more hell, staged other occupations, and drove the authorities crazy. When they took over Lincoln Hospital a second time, and kept intruding in medical management, they so upset the director of Einstein Medical College, which ran the hospital, that he was hospitalized for bleeding ulcers. Internal disputes among the Lords, especially between its feminist women leaders and its nonfeminist men, brought the organization down. It had evaporated by 1972. Leaders of the organization later turned up in media jobs and government. Juan Gonzalez, the Lords' former minister of information, wrote a column for the *Daily News* that I never missed, back when that paper was still thriving.

IN THE LONG RUN, the radical politics of the sixties let Naison down. He believes that he and his (mostly white) allies had abundant passion, but not the sense to focus on what was right in front of them. "Our political vision was too apocalyptic and our rhetoric too strident," he says. He remembers riding the Third Avenue el (that venerable conduit into the middle of the Bronx, which was not taken down until the mid-seventies) and seeing buildings burning nearby. Planners on the political right thought that the Bronx ought to burn, that its destruction was a healthy development overall. Meanwhile, leaders on the left were looking else-where in pursuit of revolution.

Less theoretical problems lay closer at hand, and as for those, feeding hungry schoolchildren and getting a new Lincoln Hospital were good starts. Helping people stay in their apartments and pre-serving affordable housing in a disinvestment desert during a panic-driven exodus—these were the bigger tasks that needed to be done right away. Viewing events as a historian, Naison has written that he and other radicals "could only stand helplessly by . . . as the borough faced the greatest catastrophe in its history."

PART III

FALL AND RISE

26

I HAVE TALKED about the human displacement wrought by the Cross Bronx Expressway, but not about how it was built, the chaos of its construction.

The Cross Bronx came as part of the highway-building craze that took over the country after the Second World War. Industry had produced a war surplus of heavy equipment that was sitting idle. Gasoline cost almost nothing. Customers were begging for new cars, and factories were changing from a war footing to make them. As planners had predicted, internal combustion would be the future. The postwar highway-building boom continued for thirty-plus years and created the paved and suicidal world we live in today.

When the highways arrived, the Bronx covered 41.5 square miles (since then, landfill has enlarged it slightly). The 1929 metro blueprint of the Regional Plan Association (RPA) had waited through depression and war. Now it could be made into reality. The plan encompassed 5,528 square miles, an area about 133 times bigger than the Bronx. Major arteries, as the RPA called them, would radiate outward into New York, New Jersey, and Connecticut through the Bronx's small portion of the metro region. Almost the entire system depended upon and funneled through the borough. Nobody arranged that with

malice, exactly; it was more like indifference plus necessity. The RPA's
arteries had no place else to go. In a fairer world, the Bronx would have
been rewarded for its location, rather than having to suffer for it.

In 1945, New York City announced that $300 million would be
spent to build or improve its highways and bridges. Some of that
money was federal, some came from the city and state. This original
enormous commitment eventually produced not only the Cross Bronx
Expressway, but the Van Wyck, the Harlem River Drive, the Belt Parkway, the Henry Hudson Parkway, the West Side Highway, the Grand
Central Parkway, the Jackie Robinson Parkway, and more. And not
long after the announcement, residents of buildings in certain mid-
Bronx neighborhoods, such as Mount Eden, Morris Heights, and East
Tremont, received notice that they would have to move.

Robert Moses, the dread arterial coordinator, pushed out many
thousands who were in the way of his roadbuilding, and newspapers
referred to Moses's "vision" of the city in their headlines. His power
shocked those who could not believe a public official could operate
beyond restraint in a democracy—a less surprising piece of news
now. But Moses was not the single underlying force evicting people,
any more than the men who carry your belongings to the curb are
the landlord himself or the executives at the bank. The "vision" of
the highway system existed outside of Moses; he simply enacted the
Regional Plan Association's blueprint, among other plans (including some of his own). Moses served as point person for a highway-
building juggernaut that was happening nationwide.

The city's subways, when they arrived in the early 1900s, had
approached in an orderly fashion, one after another, from the south;
but the highways descended upon the Bronx from many points of the
compass and almost simultaneously. Each new road built toward itself
from both directions. The Bruckner Expressway, as it swung around
the southern edge of the borough, turned big areas into bulldozed
dirt. That was a common look along the Bronx's edges. We recall
that the borough's landscape descends from rock ridges in the western
part to coastal plain in the east. It was easier to build in the eastern,
flatter part, so the construction of the Cross Bronx Expressway started
there, and made good progress. At first, planners estimated the Cross

Bronx's projected total cost at $38,670,000. When work had been underway for about a year, the estimate went up to $60 million.

To start on the highway at the other end, on the west, construction had to deal with the Harlem River. The relevant bridge at that point was the Washington Bridge—not to be confused with the George Washington Bridge, just two miles west. The latter crosses the Hudson River between New Jersey and Manhattan, the former crosses the Harlem River between Manhattan and the Bronx. (One must proceed slowly here, to keep the brain from tangling.) Logically, the Cross Bronx Expressway had to connect with the Washington Bridge. Here the Cross Bronx Expressway and Interstate 95 are one and the same. Approaching from the west, I-95 would cross the George Washington Bridge, traverse a small part of upper Manhattan, cross the Washington Bridge, and enter the Bronx.

This straight shot looked comparatively easy. But the Major Deegan Expressway, running along the east bank of the Harlem River, goes under the Washington Bridge. The Cross Bronx (I-95) could not ignore the Major Deegan (I-87) running below and perpendicular to it; obviously, the two had to link up. For technical reasons, making that connection using only the Washington Bridge could not be done. Therefore, the engineers decided that the plan required the construction of a whole new bridge, to be called the Alexander Hamilton Bridge, right next to the Washington Bridge. By means of cloverleafs leading to and from the Alexander Hamilton Bridge, the east- and westbound Cross Bronx (I-95) was able to connect to the Major Deegan (I-87). The array of on-ramps and off-ramps was so involved and complicated that the engineers sometimes referred to them as chicken guts. When I walk the length of the Cross Bronx, that's the part I skip.

In panoramic photos from the 1950s, the future Cross Bronx Expressway crosses the scene as a wide slash of bulldozed earth between far-apart, cowering buildings. Construction distributes power shovels and earthmovers and cranes and flatbed trucks amid piles of I beams and gravel. Workmen in the foreground assume the standard pose, leaning back with one fist on hip, looking on. None of them wear hard hats—nor are there very many workmen, period. The job brought an occupying army of machinery, but not throngs of laborers like those that had built the High Bridge and other megaprojects of the more distant past.

Major construction in former times had required more manpower partly because there was no dynamite; but in the creation of this highway, dynamite blasts shook the Bronx all the time. If you watched a crew from a distance, you might see them hurry at some invisible signal to get behind pieces of machinery. Then a deep, window-rattling concussion followed, a protective blast mat lifted and fell like a beaten rug, and dust billowed to the sky. Kids played on the sites after the work had stopped for the day. Once, some boys found a box of seventy-three sticks of dynamite that a contractor had left lying around. The boys tried to set off the dynamite by lighting it, which didn't work, probably to their disappointment. Scrap lumber nested in clusters all over the sites, like drinking straws in storm drains. Kids sometimes took the scraps and made fires in nearby vacant lots. This had been a tradition of the paradise Bronx—making side-lot campfires, sitting around them, sometimes roasting potatoes.

In April 1956, as construction reached Third Avenue, a boy set a fire that burned down an artificial-flower factory at 4065 Third Avenue, next to the highway site. While fire trucks were fighting the fire outside, from the street, a collapse of the roof trapped and killed six firemen inside—Lieutenant John F. Molloy and Firefighters Edward J. Carroll, Frederick J. Hellauer, Arthur G. Hanson, William P. Hoolan, and Charles J. Infosino. The scrap-lumber campfires, and the lives lost in 1956, augured the fires to come.

THE VIOLENCE OF THE CONSTRUCTION sometimes resembled war. Moses's chief engineer—the same man who had looked, awestruck, at the rank upon rank of buildings directly in the highway's route—had worked on building the wartime Burma Road across the mountains into China. He said the Burma Road was easier to build than this one. Dynamite blasts cracked buildings near the site and a power shovel knocked a gas main apart, causing the evacuation of a nearby elementary school. Another blast showered window glass on a family sitting in their apartment. Rock dust settled on everything. Once emptied of tenants, apartment buildings stood empty for years, demonstrating how ephemeral and disposable they could be. The roadbuilding created a barrier zone—foot traffic changed, and people gave up lifetime patterns of shopping and socializing. Friends who lived on opposite sides of the highway site lost touch.

The then-easternmost part of the Cross Bronx, a 3.4-mile section from Bruckner Boulevard to the Bronx River Parkway, opened to traffic in November 1955. The estimated cost of the project had gone up to $120 million, more than triple the original estimate. Demolition had not yet begun in the East Tremont neighborhood. Some of the residents there had continued to fight, rebounding from one defeat to the next. A group of them proposed a route change that would put the highway through the edge of Crotona Park rather than destroy buildings that people lived in. Independent engineers helped them plot a path that would shave a little from the park and make two minor swerves before rejoining the route as already laid out. The residents began their campaign in 1946, and did not lose, permanently and decisively, until 1954. The message seemed to be that Robert Moses could not be stopped.

But he *had* been stopped, during FDR's administration, when a call to Eleanor Roosevelt ended his plan to build a bridge from downtown Manhattan to Brooklyn. Moses also proposed, but never built, a ten-mile-long bridge from Port Chester, New York, across the Sound to Long Island. The wealthy people who lived in the places around both ends of the proposed bridge did not go for that idea. His desire to lay a highway across Manhattan at Thirtieth Street never had a chance, because midtown didn't want it. And his final attempt at a cross-Manhattan expressway, which would have extended along Canal Street to the East River bridges, demolishing buildings by the score, met solid opposition. Greenwich Village activists, led by Carol Greitzer and the young Ed Koch (both former Bronxites), saw what such a highway would mean for downtown. Koch and Greitzer predicted it would be the first of several roads that "could turn Manhattan into a vehicular paradise at the expense of the residents." That described exactly what was happening to the Bronx.

Another section of the Cross Bronx Expressway, from Long-fellow Avenue to Webster Avenue, opened in April 1960. Two work-men died when a retaining wall in this section collapsed on them; in all, the project killed at least four workers. Finishing the highway so you could drive on it from one end to the other required three more years. At Bruckner Boulevard, traffic still had to go over a drawbridge at Westchester Creek, and often waited there while barges or sail-boats with a couple of people on them went by. As a result, planners devised the intricate elevated span that I've so far been calling the mega-intersection. That's the one I walk under seeking the ghost of Washington (the man, before his name also meant bridges). Officially, the mega-intersection is known as the Bruckner Interchange. Building it cost $68 million and did not wrap up until 1972, twenty-six years after the residents of East Tremont in the highway's path first heard they would have to move.

Twenty-six years was about five times as long as builders had needed to finish the Verrazzano-Narrows Bridge. It was about six times as long as it took for the Throgs Neck and Alexander Hamil-ton Bridges; both opened before the entirety of the Cross Bronx. The highway's final cost came to $238 million, about six times the 1946 estimate, or almost $2 billion in today's dollars, for 6.5 miles of high-way. As I've noted, no road that expensive had ever been built. The tab added up to about $58,275 a foot, or $4,856.25 an inch. In the 1950s, while the work continued, the Bronx's population fell, some-thing that hadn't happened since the years of the Neutral Ground. The number ticked up slightly in the 1960s, only to fall again between 1970 and 1980. During the 1970s, the part of the Bronx to the south of the Cross Bronx Expressway lost about 47 percent of its residents.

PLANNERS IN GENERAL did not foresee the mid-twentieth-century sub-urban boom, the biggest demographic movement in American history. They had not expected that so many people would move out of the cities and use their newly acquired automobiles to commute. The Re-gional Plan Association thought commuting would still be by train, and people would use their cars for "leisure," for "excursions." But if you had a car, and new, convenient highways, and all the railroads were going bankrupt anyway, why take the train? Like many of the new roads, the Cross Bronx brought commuters through poor Black and Latino neighborhoods to suburban towns, many of which excluded non-white residents. All over the country, new highways ran through minority neighborhoods and destroyed housing and separated whites from Blacks. In 1968, during the presidential election, stickers promoting George Wallace, the segregationist from Alabama, appeared on overpasses above the Cross Bronx. Nowadays the politics of the far right seem not to exist in this part of the world. In all the walking I've done in the Bronx, I've never once seen a Confederate flag.

When I interviewed Fernando Ferrer, who served as Bronx borough president from 1987 to 2001, I asked him about recent plans to reduce the harm caused by the highway—to add pedestrian pathways and bikeways, even deck it with green spaces on top. Ritchie Torres, the U.S. congressman from the 14th District, which the Cross Bronx bisects, had said the borough should get some of the $20 billion that a recent Biden bill would provide for communities of color injured by past infrastructure. Congressman Torres talked to Transportation Secretary Pete Buttigieg about the idea, but no improvements have come of it so far. Ferrer told me, "Look, the Cross Bronx Expressway is what it is. It's the ugliest roadway in America. There ain't much you can do to fix that place. People are talking about covering it, putting a deck over it. Hey, why not? That may give you an opportunity to do some interesting things. But it's still gonna be a *wound* in the Bronx."

PEOPLE LEFT THE BRONX and so did jobs. The radio and the phonograph had put the piano factories out of business. Consumers stopped buying iceboxes when gas and electric refrigerators took over, so the icebox factories had closed. Moving companies, a manufacturer of canned hams, a large bakery, a soda bottling company, and numerous breweries disappeared. The huge Morrisania plant of the American Bank Note Company, printer of postage stamps, stock notes, and currencies for countries around the world, shut down. Job losses spread throughout the city. The garment industry began to leave, and what had been 354,000 garment center jobs in New York in 1948 declined to 150,000 jobs by 1984. A complex of clothing factories in the South Bronx, where newly arrived Blacks had been able to find work in the 1930s, couldn't compete with foreign manufacturers after the war, and soon was gone.

Moving the main port facilities to New Jersey erased thousands of longshoremen's jobs in New York. Public sector employment also went through an adjustment. Since 1937, the Lyons Residence Law (named for its sponsor, Bronx Borough President James J. Lyons) had required that city employees live in the city. In 1962, the City Council voted for a repeal that allowed them to live outside it. This hurt the poor, who now faced more competition for jobs. On the network of highways, city employees could commute from the suburbs to jobs in the South Bronx and elsewhere, and their salaries were no longer circulating in the city.

Ice-cream-eating changed—a small thing, but real. The refrigerators that families now owned had freezers, grocery stores and supermarkets installed freezer sections, and frozen foods appeared in quantity for the first time. Grocery shoppers bought supermarket ice cream, which caused the Bronx's ice cream parlors to close. Supermarket ice cream was less expensive but not as good as the small-batch, ice-cream-parlor kind. A Bronx company called Senator Frozen Products, whose factory was just south of East 149th Street on Southern Boulevard, got into competition with a bigger company, Beatrice Foods, and saw that Beatrice's cheaper offering was going to put it out of business. Senator was owned by a Russian immigrant, Leah Mattus, and her son, Reuben. He had driven delivery trucks, sold ice cream from a cart, and come up from the street. Reuben Mattus decided to get around the threat from Beatrice Foods by going upscale with a premium ice cream he would charge more for.

Duncan Hines, the brander and distributor of gourmet foods, showed an interest in the idea. Mattus and some of his executives, including Milton Hurwitz (father of my college friend Eliot Hurwitz), thought of a name that would sound Scandinavian and hint at high-class Swedish-Danish gourmet style. In homage to Duncan Hines, their would-be distributor, they first considered calling the ice cream Hunken Danes. Further brainstorming produced the more exotic, poetic, and brilliantly meaningless Häagen-Dazs. Nowhere on the packaging did it say this ice cream came from the Bronx. There was a map of Scandinavia on the carton, which also said the product was manufactured at "Plant # 932," and distributed by the Häagen-Dazs Company of New York.

Duncan Hines was asking more in licensing and distributing fees than Mattus wanted to pay, so he introduced the product on his own—in only three flavors to begin with: chocolate, vanilla, and coffee. It turned out that supermarket shoppers would indeed pay more for premium ice cream. By 1973, the company was selling 350,000 gallons of Häagen-Dazs a year and had branched out into new flavors. The factory on Southern Boulevard approached capacity and needed modernizing, while the neighborhood it was in was getting worse. The city health department inspectors, who Milton Hurwitz said were so corrupt "[they] were practically on our payroll," along with the unions and the high city and state taxes, motivated the company to relocate to a larger plant in Woodbridge, New Jersey. Milton Hurwitz's unpublished memoir, "Frozen Assets," makes no mention of any efforts on the part of New York City to persuade this successful homegrown business to stay. By 1979, while still in the Bronx, it was selling 2 million gallons a year; by 1982, having moved to New Jersey, it had increased its sales to 9.5 million gallons a year.

Pillsbury, in Minneapolis, bought Häagen-Dazs, and then somebody bought Pillsbury, etc. Reuben Mattus's inspiration for an upscale ice cream resulted in the creation of thousands of Häagen-Dazs franchise stores around the country. Later management strategies took the brand into Canada, Mexico, and around the globe. If only Häagen-Dazs could have kept making some of its ice cream on East 149th Street—the Bronx could have used the jobs.

THE REGIONAL PLAN'S RECOMMENDATION that New York City get rid of its factories proved all too achievable. Just in the Bronx, the number of factories went from 2,000 to 1,350 between 1958 and 1974. As plants closed citywide, the resultant loss of tax base—partly the city's own fault for its costly water and sewer and permit fees, its corporate taxes, its many other taxes, such as its Unincorporated Small Business Tax, and its food-industry regulations, all of which make it one of the most taxed and regulated places on the planet—contributed to the city's financial crisis of the early 1970s. In those years, when New York City almost went broke, half of its Black public employees and one third of its Hispanic public employees lost their jobs.

Some of those jobs would come back when the city's finances improved, as they eventually did. But the manufacturing had left permanently—relocated to a suburb, like Häagen-Dazs, or to somewhere even farther away. In a sense, what happened with the loss of manufacturing in the Bronx and other parts of the city foretold the outsourcing that would destroy jobs all over the country. Products would be made in China and return in giant container ships to entry points such as the ports of Newark and Elizabeth, whence trucks would carry the goods to the giant discount stores battened on open spaces across the land, sucking profits out of Main Street businesses and local factories. The story is old by now, but when it happened to the Bronx, it might have seemed—given the apparent hopelessness of the surroundings—that the problem would be confined to only here.

How many jobs left New York City in the 1960s and '70s is hard to say. According to the Bureau of Labor Statistics, New York City lost 660,000 jobs in just seven years in the sixties. Other sources estimate the loss at half a million jobs between the late forties and the mid-seventies. The model proposed by the Regional Plan in 1929 performed as intended. Observers praised it for having saved the region from chaos. Certainly, it worked well in the case of Häagen-Dazs. The company's New Jersey factory, just a mile or so from I-95, could easily ship its ice cream back to the city, always a major market, by way of the newly built bridges and highways. The restructuring of the metropolitan region as provided for in the Regional Plan gave the company room to grow.

Taking the customary long view, the Regional Plan Association published a Second Regional Plan in 1968, and in 1979 it celebrated the fiftieth anniversary of the First Regional Plan. In 1996, it brought out its Third Regional Plan, whose full title was "A Region at Risk:

The Third Regional Plan for the New York–New Jersey–Connecticut Area." Since its previous plans, the data it had accumulated allowed it to assess the long-term effects of its original model. It said, "From 1970 to 1995, core urban counties lost more than 300,000 jobs while the outer suburban ring gained two million."

A long-range metropolitan plan that did good for the region had nonetheless contributed to the immiseration of the Bronx. Between 1970 and 1980, the borough's population went from 1,471,701 to 1,168,972. Fifty years would pass before it returned to approximately what it had been in 1970.

27

SOME BRONXITES SAY they knew their neighborhoods were going downhill when they saw addicts nodding out on the street openly, not caring who saw. Local people who remembered that moment placed it in the mid-1970s.

In fact, large parts of the Bronx had been put at risk several decades earlier. Their shaky status would have been invisible except to select observers who kept a copy of *Principles of Real Estate Practice*, a publication of the National Association of Real Estate Brokers, on their nightstands, perhaps alongside the 1938 edition of the Home Owners' Loan Corporation "Residential Security Map" for the southern half of the Bronx. The government, the real estate industry, and the banks had noticed that landlords in Morrisania and other Bronx neighborhoods were accepting Black tenants. The wielders of power did not approve. *Principles of Real Estate Practice* informed potential Black residents that they should not look for homes in white neighborhoods because of the "economic disturbance" their presence would cause. The security maps showed, street by street, the neighborhoods into which Blacks and other disapproved-of types had already moved.

I was brought up to admire Franklin Roosevelt for saving the country during the Depression, but as often happens with history when it's looked at again, it discloses a big "on the other hand." FDR was, in balance, not good for Blacks. His New Deal legislation needed the support of southern Democrats, who insisted that it exclude domestic workers and farm labor, categories that were largely Black or brown. The New Deal was designed not to help them, on purpose. It established federal bureaucracies like the Home Owners' Loan Corporation (HOLC), the Federal Housing Administration (FHA), and the Veterans' Administration (VA) to assist white buyers and homeowners. Between 1934 and 1962, 98 percent of government-backed homeowners' loans went to borrowers who were white.

For real estate agents who had lost their jobs in the Depression, the federal government found work compiling "Underwriting and Valuation Reports" on almost 350 residential communities across the country. The reports included the security maps, and through these the concept of redlining took hold. What I want to know is whether the creators of the reports had to color in the maps themselves. The ones who did the Bronx would have used a lot of red pencil. On the published versions of the maps, the red is a kind of sooty color. The map of the borough's southern half shows it spreading like a wine stain over Morrisania and its vicinity, tinting much of what used to be the Morris family's manor and coinciding with many neighborhoods where the fires would come.

The maps also used other colors. Green indicated areas considered safe to invest in, which meant those with only white people. Blue indicated less-good neighborhoods; the presence of "foreign" residents could turn an area blue. For an area to be designated red, all it needed was to have a few Blacks or Puerto Ricans. The term for that was "negro or Puerto Rican infiltration." In redlined neighborhoods, the FHA would not insure loans for property, and therefore banks would not lend, either for a new mortgage or to make improvements on a building. The restrictions applied to any owner or prospective owner, regardless of race. Neither a white landlord nor a Black landlord could get a fair loan to fix up a building in a redlined area. The FHA did not base its decisions only on the neighborhood. It would not insure borrowers who were Black regardless of where they wanted to buy. Blacks and Puerto Ricans remained renters partly because nonpredatory loans were not available to them.

While stability still prevailed in the Bronx's integrated neighborhoods, Capital had sized up the situation with its coldest eye and said no. The racism of it would be the puncture through which infection entered, though the fully blown symptoms took a while to emerge. The fact that Black and brown people generally could not accumulate wealth in property produced cascading long-term effects. City zoning laws had already established the Bronx as a mostly residential place. Before other threats grew serious enough to be seen, redlining had predestined whole sections of the Bronx to be rubble.

AT FIRST, the drugs sneaked in almost as invisibly. Lloyd Ultan says they were brought by the Mob, who were looking for new customers after the end of Prohibition. If we want to trace that back even further, another guilty party would be the bigots behind the Volstead Act. Nativists who wanted to hurt beer-and wine-drinking immigrants instead provided an opening for bootlegging gangsters, some of whom later moved into the drug trade, which fueled gang culture—and on to nightmare. The anti-liquor crowd was trying to solve a problem that did not lend itself to legal redress. They preferred it to problems that urgently did need solving, such as the rollback of Reconstruction and the imposition of Jim Crow laws throughout the South. Banning liquor provided a more satisfying goal. Some of Prohibition's supporters— such as my kindly great-aunts Alice, Grace, and Eleanor Hursh, of Tiffin, Ohio—had been children who witnessed what alcohol did to their parents' and grandparents' generations. Whiskey had damaged nineteenth-century rural America in the same way that opioids and methamphetamines (and alcohol) do today. Plenty of reasons exist for fighting alcohol abuse, but overall the Volstead Act only made the problem worse.

Well, people will always get high, some way or another. Heroin had good fortune in its early clientele because so many jazz musicians in the Bronx and elsewhere loved it. Jazz refined the concept of cool to a pure blue flame; heroin enhanced this image, and vice versa. A chemical that could take you to transcendence was like a magic wand of cool. For the jitters of Modernism, it seemed the bespoke cure, and you could always find reliable dope in the Bronx; the place's accessibility guaranteed that. Some musicians preferred not to travel outside the city because of how hard it could be to find drugs on the road.

Army veterans who came back to the Bronx from serving in Korea observed a change just during the time they had been away. In 1953, you rarely saw drugs in the open; by 1956, they were everywhere. In the sixties, they grew into an epidemic. Neighborhoods had always had winos, but they didn't multiply like the drug addicts. A girl you played jump rope with just a few years before might now be a young woman nodding out in the gutter. Neighbors who had always kept their doors and windows open noticed guys standing on the fire escapes for no reason, looking in at the apartments, slipping in and out of buildings. Household appliances went missing. People started locking their doors and installing bars over their windows. In 1965, New York State instituted the lottery as a revenue-raising measure, a change that cut into the business of the numbers runner. Drug dealers replaced the numbers runners as a tolerated illegal presence on the streets, and the change was for the worse. To keep people interested in what amounted to a regressive tax aimed at the poor, the lottery invented new slogans and raised the jackpots, while the drug dealers innovated with new and stronger highs.

Some residents said that the quality of your average neighbor had gone down—that when the managers of NYCHA projects stopped screening tenants, they ruined the buildings. Tenants who had gone through the process when the projects were new, and who had submitted to interviews and provided pay slips and so on, resented that the recent arrivals didn't have to do any of that. NYCHA could have replied that the city gave it little choice. In the fifties, the government began a slum-clearance program called Urban Renewal, which James Baldwin dubbed "Negro Removal." The renewal-removal fell in line with the original Regional Plan of 1929, and its vision of Manhattan as a white-collar business and cultural center. Some of the displaced for whom NYCHA needed to find room had come from the San Juan

Hill neighborhood, around Broadway and Sixty-sixth Street. The city evicted tenants there and in other neighborhoods and tore down the buildings, which were either decrepit slums or still-functional and much-loved housing, depending on whom you asked. (Robert Moses said the former, Jane Jacobs the latter.) What replaced San Juan Hill was Lincoln Center. If you want to see what the old neighborhood looked like, the original movie of *West Side Story* was filmed there before it was torn down.

Every so often I step into an example of the Regional Plan's original vision. To get to the garage underneath Lincoln Center, you go up Amsterdam Avenue and turn onto a ramp in the middle of the block between West Sixty-fourth Street and West Sixty-fifth. You park, you walk through the fluorescently lit garage, you take an elevator, and you're in Lincoln Center. If you're coming from New Jersey, as I am, you have glided through a tunnel or over a bridge and along the West Side straight to this focus point of the city's cultural life, the home of its symphony orchestra, opera, and ballet company—all without (in theory) having to make contact with the noisier, more "congested" parts of the city. Residents who were displaced to create this bridge-and-tunnel-friendly experience may well have ended up in substandard Bronx housing. For tens of thousands of low-income families removed by Urban Renewal, the South Bronx was a part of the city they could still afford.

ANOTHER WATERSHED POINT in the decline (longtime Bronx residents said) was when grown-ups stopped being able to correct kids on the street. Now the kids' parents, when news got back to them, didn't reprimand the kids but got angry at the grown-ups: "Don't you say anything to my child!" And teachers who in the past might have gone to a student's home to report a discipline problem found that, whereas in the past the teacher was always right, now the parent would likely side with the child. This change could have been predicted, after years of the system's undereducating Black and brown students and ignoring their parents.

A citywide teachers' strike in 1968 did not help. The strike arose over a question of community control, when a local school board in a mostly Black district in Brooklyn ordered the transfer of eighteen teachers, most of them white. Ten of the teachers refused to go, the board insisted, and the union struck. The argument broke along racial lines. The city's teachers, also mostly white, did not want the parents interfering with how they taught, and many of the Black or Puerto Rican parents thought the teachers treated them with contempt. Black teachers crossed picket lines and students stayed away. An informal alliance that had existed in the Bronx between upwardly aspiring Blacks and left-leaning Jews took a hit. Friendships broke off and never mended. The United Federation of Teachers, under its president, Albert Shanker, held fast and won in the end. The teachers who had resisted transfer were reinstated. Afterward, some faculty lunchrooms divided into strikers' tables and scab tables, where almost everyone at the scab tables was Black. Teachers who had put in years of service retired and inexperienced teachers replaced them.

In the Woody Allen movie *Sleeper*, about a man who is frozen in 1973 and unfrozen two hundred years later, the scientists who've thawed him out show him photos of the Empire State Building and the Statue of Liberty, which by then are ruins. The recently awakened sleeper asks them how his civilization was destroyed, and they say, "A man named Albert Shanker got ahold of a nuclear warhead." The joke has some truth to it. I once met a retired teacher's union higher-up who had been a friend of Shanker's. When I mentioned the line about the nuclear warhead, the friend said, "Albert *loved* that joke!"

BY THE SIXTIES, many of the once-new Bronx apartment buildings were falling down, after having stood for maybe half a century. Rent-control laws prevented the landlords from raising rents more than a small amount each year. Maintenance costs couldn't be passed along, repairs weren't made. Some of the new, Urban Renewal tenants did not appreciate the apartments they'd ended up in—or so said some of the original tenants. In their opinion, some of these new tenants were slobs who didn't know any better than to throw garbage out the windows. The lobbies and elevators didn't used to smell like urine. Landlords said they couldn't afford to keep cleaning the buildings all the time.

As the public spaces outside people's apartments disintegrated, television appeared from out of nowhere to improve life indoors. Neighbors would gather to watch shows in the apartments of the few families who owned TVs. Then more families got them, and neighbors did not spend as much time with one another, inside or out; socializing on the front stoop dwindled, movie theaters lost customers and shut down. A parishioner at St. Augustine's Presbyterian Church recalled that *The Ed Sullivan Show* killed off the church's Sunday evening service single-handedly.

Between 1960 and 1970, the number of children in the Bronx went from 314,100 to 512,807, an increase of more than 60 percent. These Baby Boom kids, in their multitudes, raised a lot of commotion and beat on the aging buildings. The streets where a previous generation had enjoyed its games now filled with vehicles. Stickball players who shouted "Car!" when one came along needed to shout it so often, they gave up. Rick Meyerowitz, the artist and writer, remembered that once he hit a line drive through the open window of a passing city bus. He thought he had lost the ball forever, but then he saw it bouncing across the street; it had gone through an open window on the bus's other side. The police rode around in cars more, which meant fewer foot patrols and less face-to-face contact with the neighborhood. Crowded off the pavement, kids hung out on street corners. The hanging-out era, which we are still in, came with the highways and the hordes of cars.

Kids hanging out all the time led to more gangs. The Bronx had always had gangs; even the Cow Boys and the Skinners of the Neutral Ground could be described as gangs. In the pre-car era, Jewish gangs fought Irish gangs, and everyone feared the Fordham Baldies. Now, in the early '70s, police estimated there were a hundred fighting gangs in the South Bronx, with a total membership of about eleven thousand. Every gang had its turf (or turfs, if there happened to be more than one chapter). The Forest Over Everything (FOE) gang dominated the Forest Houses. The clubhouse of a gang called the Cypress Bachelors was on Cypress Avenue, whose name came from the rows of cypress trees that Gouverneur Morris planted after coming back from France. The middle of the bridge over the Bronx River on Tremont Avenue marked a boundary. A gang called the Black Spades ruled on the east side of the bridge, which it guarded like the black knight in a fairy tale.

Residents said there was a different gang on every block. In various neighborhoods you had the Slicksters, the Scorpions, the Suicides, the Sportsmen, the Savage Skulls, the Savage Scars, the Savage Nomads, the Sinners, the Shingalings, the Shapes of Black, the Seven Immortals, the Spanish Daggers, the Spanish Skulls, the Smoldering Souls, and the Seven Crowns. The Arthur Avenue Brothers, Golden Guineas, and War Pigs were Italian gangs, from around Belmont. Kids referred to their gangs as cliques or clubs, and sometimes asked nonmembers, "Would you like to join our club?" As a rule, "Yes" was the safer answer. The Turbans, Royal Javelins, Six Four Goons, Roman Kings, Persuaders, Five Percenters, Dirty Dozens, Ball Busters, Reapers, Dragons, Archmen, Glory Stompers, Black Pearls, Black Cats, Dominican Lions, Latin Aces, Young Saigons, Black Falcons, Little People, Bohemian Crowns, Casanovas, and Purple Knights were some other gangs. A few had adjuncts, like minor league teams for younger kids who hadn't yet made the big gang. The Jabbers' subgang was the Lil' Jabbers. The Disciples had the Disciples Tots, and the Diablos had the Diablo Tots. Gangs like the Savage Sisters were for girls, but also tough.

Kids still played outside, just not as much in the streets. They raced their bicycles down hills of dirt piled up by the highway construction and jumped out of abandoned buildings onto piles of mattresses and disappeared into the deep weeds, such as along the banks of the Bronx River where railroad bridges crossed overhead. They climbed up the bridge stanchions and tied ropes to the beams and swung from the ropes and tried to knock each other into the river. Sometimes daredevils scrambled to the tops of subway trains and rode there, ducking down for bridges and tunnels. In 1957, an extension of the number 2 line had been built to Dyer Avenue, which is now the terminus of the 5 train. In the nearby train yards, you could sneak in at night and spray-paint on the cars.

You were careful where you walked. If you went on the wrong block, and the gang that controlled it did not know you, bad things could happen. Gangs wore denim jackets with the gang insignia—"colors"—on the front and all across the back. Always they cut the sleeves off the jacket. By this circumcision, gang members were known to one another, and to the law. If gang members went outside their own turf and onto the turf of another gang, they turned their jackets inside out, as a sign of respect. In the late sixties, the gangs were fighting constantly, with kids injuring and killing one another. Online, a depressingly large amount of news footage exists of teenage gangs beating the hell out of one another on the street. What it looks like is a bunch of skinny arms flailing away, skinny legs kicking and stomping, and kids grappling on the pavement. Kids were getting killed every year. (The same is still true, though victims today mostly get shot or stabbed, rather than beaten with fists, pipes, chains, or car antennas. There are more guns now.)

Near the Prospect Avenue elevated station, a gang called the Ghetto Brothers ruled. Four brothers named Melendez, led by Benjamin Melendez ("Yellow Benji"), started this gang. What made the Melendez brothers unusual was that they came from a secretly Jewish family, who attended Catholic mass but practiced Jewish rituals at home, as they had done for generations, since the family was forced to convert during the Spanish Inquisition. Yellow Benji's oratory and charisma attracted numerous kids to the Ghetto Brothers. At one point he claimed the gang had two thousand members all over the city and the United States. Unlike other gangs, the Ghetto Brothers were not allowed to use swastikas as insignia on their gear or in their graffiti. They knew how to fight, under their "Warlord," a brawler named Karate Charlie, but the top officers concentrated more on performing their music, which was Beatles-influenced and oddly sweet and easy-listening.

Many years later, Yellow Benji told Mark Naison a story about how another gang psychologically crushed him. One evening he went into his clubhouse, a shack under the el tracks. When he turned on the light, he found rivals waiting, and none of his own guys around. The enemies surrounded him, and one pulled out a sawed-off gun and pointed it at his chest; at that moment, Benji saw himself as someone who was about to die. He thought of his girlfriend and of his parents, and of *Sesame Street*, which he had always liked, and his favorite characters, Cookie Monster and Grover. The leader said to the one with the gun, "Shoot him." Benji closed his eyes, the gun went off, and something hit him in the chest—sand. They had sawed-off a BB gun so it looked like a sawed-off shotgun and loaded it with sand. The enemies left the Ghetto Brothers leader unhurt, weeping, and terrorized.

By 1970, the Bronx's gang violence had grown so intense that the city's newspapers and local TV were covering it regularly. The Ghetto Brothers took pride in the fact that they didn't bother members of other gangs who crossed Ghetto Brothers territory. Also, the Ghetto Brothers could wear their own colors in other gangs' territory. When the Black Panthers and the Young Lords tried to persuade the gangs to stop fighting and work together for the community, the Ghetto Brothers listened to them. The Ghetto Brothers provided security around the mobile X-ray unit that was highjacked by the Young Lords.

A recently recovered former heroin addict named Cornell Benjamin joined the gang and came to the attention of Yellow Benji, who admired his empathy and his kindness to younger kids. People called Cornell Benjamin "Benji," too. Because he was West Indian and darker than Yellow Benji, he was called Black Benji. Yellow Benji saw the growing violence all around and got an inspiration. Gangs generally had ministers of war, but he would make this young man, Black Benji, the Ghetto Brothers' minister of peace. No gang had ever had a minister of peace before. Black Benji was interviewed on television in 1970 talking about how he had come to the Ghetto Brothers. He spoke softly about his recovery from addiction and how the gang had changed his life.

Inspired by what the Panthers had said about working together, Yellow Benji dreamed of making peace among the gangs and building them into a force for doing good. (Beware of big dreams.) On December 2, 1971, he sent Black Benji, his minister of peace, to meet with members of the Savage Skulls, the Mongols, and the Seven Immortals. According to some accounts, the Skulls and the Immortals had been at war with each other. The Ghetto Brothers wanted a truce. The meeting was to be at Horseshoe Playground, near Intervale Avenue. A long staircase, of the kind the Bronx specializes in, with a tall column of sky at the top, led down to the sidewalk beside the playground.

Black Benji came down the staircase at the head of a group of Ghetto Brothers. A crowd of Savage Skulls, Mongols, and Seven Immortals were waiting. At the bottom of the stairs, he stepped forward and said to a guy confronting him, "Listen, brother—we're here to talk peace." The guy said, "Peace, shit!" and attacked him. Then the other guys swarmed on Black Benji and beat him to death with lead pipes and fists.

The murder made page one of the *Daily News*, in a big headline at the top. All the gangs prepared for war. Who would be on whose side was not clear, but the Ghetto Brothers could be expected to retaliate for Black Benji's murder. Karate Charlie and Yellow Benji went to give their condolences to Gwendolyn, Black Benji's mother. Karate Charlie promised her that all their forces were ready to avenge him. Gwendolyn said, "But you forget that my son died for peace." At that moment, Yellow Benji decided there would be no more violence. He called for a conference at the Boys and Girls Club on Hoe Avenue. Two hundred representatives, from dozens of gangs, attended, and they agreed to end the fighting. They said that the newspaper and TV reporters waiting outside would like nothing better than for them to kill one another in a borough-wide war. When the meeting was over, Yellow Benji and other leaders announced to the city that they had voted for peace.

Black Benji died for peace, and it's not often you can say that about a person. In doing so, he also died for freedom. After the conference at Hoe Avenue, kids could walk unmolested through formerly enemy neighborhoods. Now the borough at large was more open to all, and—no small consideration—gang guys could talk to girls on the turf of other gangs without being afraid of getting beaten up. Music historians say that the Boys and Girls Club peace agreement made it possible for a new music form, hip-hop, to be invented at the playground jams that took the place of gang fights. The rise of hip-hop owes a debt to Black Benji. Years later, Yellow Benji, having returned to his non-gang identity of Benjamin Melendez, gave interviews, including to the Bronx African American History Project. He said there should be a plaque remembering Cornell Benjamin. The stairs Black Benji descended to meet his death are still there. On the cement wall that flanks the lowest flight of seven steps, I propose that the Parks Department put a plaque:

> At this spot, on December 2, 1971, Cornell Benjamin, known as Black Benji, died by violence while trying to promote peace between warring gangs. He was minister of peace of the Ghetto Brothers, a gang led by Benjamin "Yellow Benji" Melendez. Cornell Benjamin's death led to a borough-wide gang conference at the Boys and Girls Club on Hoe Avenue from which came a peace treaty that held for ten years. During that time, the young people of the South Bronx, partying instead of fighting, invented hip-hop. Cornell Benjamin gave his life for peace, freedom, and art. He is a hero of the Bronx.

People pass up and down the staircase all day. The sky at the top of it is as big as ever, and bright blue on a sunny morning. London plane trees and honey locusts and lindens shade the steps and the sidewalk below. By the curb is a Citi Bike station, and there's a bodega across the street. No better civic site could be found for telling this part of Bronx history. I know I'm always lobbying for plaques, but if I could have only one, this would be it.

28

WHEN WHITE FAMILIES began to leave Morrisania and other parts of the South Bronx, they may have wanted only to move upward and onward, in the tradition of middle-class aspiring. But to their Black neighbors, they appeared to be running away. A longtime resident said, "I mean, every time you turned around, you saw another moving van . . . the white faces were diminishing, and they were moving out of here like somebody was chasing them." Two hundred thousand white people moved from the Bronx in the 1950s. In the 1960s, the number rose to 256,000, and the figures did not include those who relocated to more middle-class sections of the borough. NYCHA buildings experienced a big turnover. The projects had been part of the integrated Bronx, combining different races and ethnicities in a single complex. But in the sixties, Black and brown people began to predominate. The Bronx River Houses, on the river near East 180th, went from mostly white to no whites at all in a decade.

If panic drove some who left, it was not based on nothing. Jewish tenants of long standing, and other elderly people, were afraid of getting mugged, among other dangers. In the Highbridge neighborhood, in the late sixties, the police did a study of 367 muggings that took place over a ten-week period. Three quarters of the victims were white, and four fifths of the muggers were described as Black or Puerto Rican. More than half of the victims were sixty-one or older. Crime grew more violent. During the mid-seventies, at least twenty elderly people were murdered in the Bronx in one year. Police sometimes escorted the elderly on errands; some were afraid to leave their apartments even to visit friends in their own buildings. A man named Morris Leff told the *Times* he had been mugged three times in one week. In 1969, a group of Black and Puerto Rican housewives marched on the 41st Precinct House in Morrisania and demanded gun permits so they could arm themselves against the drug dealers. But not many Black and brown families were able to move, partly because they couldn't get mortgages.

Upward mobility pulled in one direction, drugs in the other. A family with the resources to move, when it left, took a piece of the stability it had contributed to the neighborhood. The unfortunate locals who fell into addiction then had fewer friends and family members around to support them, and a generally poorer environment to live in. Whole blocks turned into addict territory; one news story at the time estimated that twenty thousand addicts resided in the Bronx south of the Cross Bronx Expressway.

A man whose father owned a trucking business in the Bronx, and whose mother had come from Russia in 1928, said that between 1960 and 1963 the pace of change in his neighborhood "increased geometrically." He was a middle school student at the time, and remembered how he felt: "I got angry at my family, and I got angry at my friends' families who left . . . Everybody was bitching and moaning about things, and I just kept saying, but if you didn't leave it would be okay, if you were here, the schools, everything would be fine. You know, everybody lives together."

The United States goes through phases of being divided into fragments, and phases of being combined into one big seemingly homogenous country—phases of *pluribus*, and phases of *unum*. This is true in both politics and culture. It began as thirteen independent states but became one united country under the Constitution. Then it split into two countries over slavery; had the South won, the former U.S. probably would have broken into even more regions or independent states. After the war, it became one country again, sort of. Today it is still technically one, but in a phase of division and cold civil war unlike anything it has ever been through.

The phases don't necessarily coincide in both categories. In the thirties, America's majority got behind Roosevelt and *unum*, but its mass culture went for ethnic entertainment. Radio, the new medium, offered the pseudo-ethnic *Amos 'n' Andy* show, starring white actors in vocal blackface; it was the most popular show in the country. The second most popular was *The Goldbergs*, a comedy-drama about a fictional Jewish family who lived in a tenement apartment at 1038 East Tremont Avenue.

Gertrude Berg, the Manhattan wife and mother who wrote and starred in *The Goldbergs*, had just turned thirty when the show debuted in 1929. From the start it caught on. People who do Jewish-mother imitations today probably don't know that the voice entered mass culture almost a hundred years ago thanks to Molly Goldberg, Gertrude Berg's character. The show went from CBS Radio to CBS TV in 1949, then to NBC TV in 1952. As the Bronx has suffered through negative media portrayals, people may have forgotten that the warm, funny, sensible Goldberg family, and its beloved matriarch, Molly, made the Bronx their home on radio and TV for more than twenty years.

Berg herself did not live in the Bronx. She had a duplex on Park Avenue, and an eleven-acre estate in Bedford, New York. In 1949, her show got caught in one of the deadly shear lines that develop sometimes between America's *pluribus* and its *unum*. After the war, with both the United States and the Soviet Union in possession of the bomb, America retreated into a frightened *unum*. People wanted to eradicate domestic Communists who they thought would betray it. Communists sometimes were seen in an anti-Semitic light, by the false logic that many Communists were Jewish. Philip Loeb, the actor who played Jake, Molly's irascible but lovable husband, leaned decidedly left and had helped found the Actors Equity Union long before he joined the show. He was not a Communist, but someone put him on a circulating list of Reds in the entertainment industry. When that news got out, CBS, General Foods (the sponsor), and even friends and co-workers ganged up on Gertrude Berg and insisted she fire him.

Berg took the principled stand and refused. CBS and General Foods then dropped *The Goldbergs*. But after a year and a half, she accepted an offer from NBC to restart the show without Loeb. Audiences had loved *The Goldbergs*, the actors and advertisers had depended on it. Berg found an actor who looked like Loeb but she never replaced him satisfactorily. The show declined in the ratings and NBC canceled it. Struggling to find other work while looking after a schizophrenic son, Loeb committed suicide.

A company that produced shows for TV syndication picked up *The Goldbergs* in 1955. By then the nationwide demographic shift from city to suburb had taken hold. A longing to be bland and blond and suburban had laid its trance on the country; undisputed *unum* reigned, and ethnic was out. The syndicators wanted the Goldbergs to tone down their Jewishness and leave the Bronx. Such an act of self-erasure made no sense, and Berg knew it, but felt she had no choice. The Goldberg family began a new season transplanted to a made-up suburb called Haverville. As Berg put it in a press release, their new location "might be anywhere in the U.S." Anywhere, that is, not including the Bronx. Before actual Jewish families had begun leaving the Bronx in large numbers, Berg's fictional Goldbergs were gone. In Haverville-Schmaverville, they blanded themselves to nothingness and disappeared from TV.

Gertrude Berg continued to work, and wowed audiences as a stage actress in plays such as *The Matchmaker* and *A Majority of One*. She died of heart failure in 1965, at the age of sixty-six. Episodes of the original *The Goldbergs* TV show may be found online. They begin with Berg, as Molly, leaning out her apartment window to answer a neighbor who has called from another window, "Yoo-hoo, Mrs. Goldberg!" Molly then delivers an opening monologue or soliloquy from the window, in which she welcomes her audience by way of greeting the neighbor and working in a low-key plug for Ovaltine or another sponsor. These speeches are warm and funny; one can see how she would have comforted audiences during the Depression. If only the image of her leaning out the window of an apartment building could have held the paradise Bronx in place and kept the actual buildings from collapse. But in the long run she could no more save Tremont Avenue than the image of Marshall Dillon walking the main street of Dodge City could save small-town western Kansas.

WHEN BRONXITES WANTED to move, but "Haverville" was out of reach financially—what then? Or what if they wanted to move, but not to the suburbs? Soon there would be a utopian community just for them. In 1965, the Amalgamated Clothing Workers Union announced plans to create the largest housing project ever in the world, to be called Co-op City. It would rise in the far northeast Bronx and consist of thirty-some apartment buildings of twenty-four, twenty-six, or thirty-three stories, along with smaller complexes of town houses, containing a total of 15,372 apartments, more than seventy thousand rooms. More than sixty thousand "cooperators," as the residents were known, would occupy this megaproject. (Even today, Co-op City remains the largest housing cooperative in the world.) For the project's site, the developers chose the same wide-open landscape that had appealed to Anne Hutchinson, along the Hutchinson River. A Disneyland-like amusement park called Freedomland was slowly dying there at the moment.

The announcement came as a surprise; the fact that the election of Herman Badillo, the first non-white borough president, occurred closely afterward looked suspicious, too—as if power in the Bronx would be passed to people of color while the white middle class exited stage left. Badillo himself seemed to see it that way. He told the city's mayor, John Lindsay, "Puerto Ricans and Hispanics don't understand co-ops and don't have the money for co-ops, and neither do Blacks . . . If you're building a co-op and you don't have any rental apartments [as Co-op City did not] you are, in effect, creating a white enclave." The move of so many middle-class whites would devastate the borough, Badillo warned. He spoke prophecy. Decades later, when Bronxites assessed what had done the most harm to the borough, some would mention the creation of Co-op City in the same breath as the Cross Bronx Expressway.

Badillo said, "Everybody knows that the word 'co-op' is a synonym for 'Jewish housing.'" In this case, he was right, too. Most of the first five thousand applications for Co-op City apartments came from the mostly Jewish Grand Concourse. The developers said that three fourths of Co-op City's first residents were Jews, but some of those same residents said the developers hadn't wanted to admit that the number was considerably higher. Redirected idealism drove the planners. By the mid-fifties, believers in communism, that locally popular faith, had been forced to reconsider. History had revealed Stalin for what he was; Khrushchev himself had denounced him at the party congress in 1956. Some believers adjusted their expectations downward from "socialism for all." If that wasn't possible, they would build a cooperative community for a large but select group in the Bronx. Whole buildings full of lefties in Morrisania and elsewhere departed for Co-op City.

To lose so many middle-class families from their former neighborhoods created a void. Anchor institutions pulled loose and drifted away, leaving shells behind. In the part of the Bronx south of the Cross Bronx Expressway, more than 270 synagogues closed. A well-known Hebrew school formerly attended by hundreds of students sold out to the highway builders, shut its doors, and vanished. The subtraction of small businesses—bakeries, butcher shops, delicatessens, furniture stores, locksmiths, pharmacies, shoe repairs, groceries—caused a kind of local desertification, in which your grandmother now might have to take a bus to buy groceries or get the laundry done.

A man who owned a laundromat at East 170th Street and Charlotte Street was killed and robbed of the change he was bringing for the machines early one morning. A local character known as Jake the Pickle Man had a pickle stand at the corner of Charlotte and Jennings Street not far from there. In 1961, he quit the business, and in 1963, he was found dead in his nearby apartment with a rag stuffed in his mouth and the gas on, apparently the victim of a robbery. These murders had receded into history by the time President Carter walked in the rubble blanketing that same neighborhood in 1977.

SOME LANDLORDS WANTED to fill their empty or partly empty buildings with tenants on welfare because the city would pay more than market rate to house them. This brought more very poor people into the Bronx. Other buildings began to be abandoned entirely, which made them tempting to explore. They didn't just sit quietly. Windows waited to be broken. Pigeons flapped in and out. Bottles brought in by drunks and addicts rolled down the stairs and shattered. Lonesome sounds—objects falling, wind whistling, doors banging—echoed. Some of the former residents hadn't been able to take their pets with them, and stray-dog packs loped in and out. In derelict walk-ups along Boston Road, Gordon Matta-Clark, the artist, scouted through the abandoned apartments with his chain saw. Then he started it up and cut rectangular sections clear through from floor to ceiling, and removed them as works of art.

He also took pictures of the buildings—some had an entire outer wall missing and stood naked inside. The big holes he left in the ceiling-floors yawned. His sections of ceiling-floor, when I first saw them in the Bronx Museum of the Arts, spooked me. That wild turquoise-and-blue linoleum might have been part of somebody's dream kitchen. Matta-Clark's artworks were like captured trophies in a never-declared war.

WHAT STARTED the Bronx's fires? The general state of combustibility of the place started them. That is, they started in heavily stressed neighborhoods south of the Cross Bronx Expressway. Gouverneur Morris would have known the places where the fires first burned—would have recognized the basic landscape if nothing else. Much of the worst burning occurred on land that had belonged to him.

Up to now I've been hesitant about using the term "South Bronx," because it's vague and has been applied to different areas at different times. Also, it might sound dangerous and notorious, in a way that makes the real people who live there into fictional characters—unreal types who could be imagined as inhabiting a dangerous, notorious place. At some time in the past, the name referred only to the far south of the borough, the "edge of the continent," i.e., the neighborhoods of Mott Haven, Port Morris, and Hunts Point. As deterioration spread from neighborhood to neighborhood, heading northward, the geographic area considered to be the South Bronx spread with it. In fact, there had not been a need to think of the Bronx in terms of south and north since the Neutral Ground days when the American forces were "from above" and the British "from below." The Cross Bronx Expressway cut the borough in two and isolated the part south of the highway—the South Bronx.

In 1966, fires started burning in apartment buildings in Mott Haven and Morrisania. Two years later, thousands of fires were burning, and not only in buildings. Piles of uncollected garbage went up in boils of dark black smoke, and abandoned cars sat for months along the curbs, collecting parking tickets under their windshield wipers until one day, mysteriously, the cars blew up in flames that melted the asphalt below. Over time, the fires moved north until they reached the highway and jumped it like a blaze crowning in a forest fire. By the mid-1970s, the fire-threatened areas were approaching Fordham Road, a mile and a half north of the Cross Bronx Expressway. Observers wondered if soon the burning, and the name South Bronx, would consume the whole borough. For our purposes, the name will mean specifically the southeastern part of the Bronx between the Cross Bronx Expressway and the Harlem River/Bronx Kill. And by 1970, "South Bronx" meant fire.

The numbers were hard to grasp. The Bronx's apartment buildings, during the boom of the early twentieth century, had been constructed in rows, one next to another. Now when a building burned, the one beside it often followed—and so down the entire row. In the late sixties, about a thousand buildings were burning every month. This was in some ways the hardest time because many of them still held tenants. Later, when the fires got worse, fewer of the buildings were occupied. In 1972, Dennis Smith, a fireman in a station on Intervale Avenue, published a book, *Report from Engine Co. 82*, which said that the company responded to 9,111 alarms in 1970. He called it "the busiest firehouse in the city—and probably the world." Having 9,111 alarms in a year is more than one per hour every day. Keeping track over a three-and-a-half-month period, Smith found that he never ate an uninterrupted meal.

In 1974, 33,000 fires of all types burned in the Bronx. That year, 140 residents died in fires, and 1,500 were injured. Three firemen also died. Sirens were going all the time, at all hours of night and day. Mothers kept bags of clothing and essentials by the door, to be grabbed at the last minute, and lined up everybody's shoes at night. In fire-plagued neighborhoods, the smoke smell didn't go away. A survivor of that time described it as a dull smell. Another said it smelled like tar because of the burning roofs. Fires might burn in only one or two apartments in a building, leaving the other units still inhabited. The burned-out apartments could be identified from the street by the black streaks of smoke spread above the windows like too much eye shadow. Remaining tenants lost utilities and hauled water buckets up with ropes and pulleys.

Going to work in the mornings, people might come upon friends sitting on what few belongings they'd been able to salvage, lined up on the curb in puddles in front of their burned-out building. Other families left their apartments to attend church or visit relatives in Harlem and came back to find their building burned and their belongings destroyed. Chrystal Wade, a Bronx activist and educator, never forgot the TV console the family lost, with the stereo that she had loved and played constantly. Water from the fire hoses had ruined all the new furniture that her mother had bought.

A man who was a social worker in the South Bronx remembered some siblings he tutored who started doing poorly in school, having done well before. He learned that the family had just been burned out for the third time. Some parents sent kids to live with relatives to wait out the plague. Kids fell asleep to sirens at night and walked wide-eyed through fire-dazed daytimes. Teachers noticed that the kids in their classes sometimes smelled like burned buildings. Watching fires from a roof provided giddy entertainment, the kids laughing about how they should be roasting marshmallows. Running through the streets, they got a thrill from pulling fire alarms and then hiding around the corner to see the clamorous engines arrive. Dennis Smith said that his unit received two thousand false alarms in 1971—between five and six a day. When the firehouse gave a party at the intersection of East 172nd Street and Southern Boulevard in an attempt to improve community relations, somebody pulled the fire alarm at the intersection while the party was going on.

Survivors of that time still dream about the fires. Not knowing if or when your building will catch fire puts you on constant alert. Buildings with watchful supers or owners tended to survive. Elias Karmon, the proprietor of Hollywood Clothiers, on Prospect Avenue, owned buildings in the neighborhood. He involved himself in the community, cashed local people's paychecks, organized street cleanups, paid regular visits to his properties, and knew his tenants. His buildings didn't burn. This was the result, he said, of "no magic, only hard work and perseverance." Miguel "Mike" Amadeo, owner of Casa Amadeo, Antigua Casa Hernandez, the long-lived Latin music store by the Prospect Avenue el station, remained in his building after every other tenant had left. The water had been cut off, so he got water from the hydrant out front. Con Ed stopped by regularly to make sure he still had electricity and cut the cables of neighbors who were tapping into his connection. When the lady who lived upstairs moved out, never to return, she gave him the key. He went through her apartment and saw that it still had a couch. A homeless man named Peachy often hung around on Prospect, nearby. Amadeo made an extra key for Peachy and let him sleep on the couch. He wanted to keep someone on the premises at night, when Amadeo would be at his apartment in Castle Hill. Peachy moved in and Casa Amadeo's building did not burn.

Hetty Fox, who grew up on Lyman Place (now Elmo Hope Way), loved her neighborhood and the house her family owned. As a girl she played street games, won foul-shot-shooting contests, and attended Catholic high school and Hunter College. In 1962, at the age of twenty-five, she moved to California, where she became an employment counselor and then taught psychology, sociology, and race relations at California State University at Northridge. She also traveled as a performer in an African dance troupe. In 1970, she came back to the Bronx with the idea of living in the family house on Lyman Place and writing a book about her California experiences. She could not believe the destruction that had taken over. To her it looked like a place with an injury that nobody was trying to heal. At the time, a lot of Bronx residents assumed that the city leaders would see what was happening and begin measures to stop it. Hetty Fox thought so too, at first.

Walking in her neighborhood, she didn't recognize anybody, and nobody recognized her. She realized that her education had trained people to acquire the skills to move away; in a sense, that was (and is) the point of places like the Bronx—to nurture you well enough that you can leave. But what does this system leave behind? It occurred to her that she could spend years in the basement writing her book and emerge to find her block gone. Did the city—did anybody in power—intend to reverse the terrible trends she saw playing out? Lyman Place is on ground that slopes downward to the east. Looking in that direction, she saw the plague of fire slowly creeping up from Vyse Avenue, "like the angel of death, with a sword." Recalling that moment thirty-five years later, she said, "I put that great definitive work [her book] down, and I said, 'I better start saving houses.'"

29

IT WAS AS IF the South Bronx sat under a huge, slowly moving burning-glass. The fires had started because of decaying housing stock, wiring that needed to be replaced, neglected maintenance, overcrowded apartments, and greed. Landlords couldn't do much about rent control, or get loans on their buildings, but they could buy low-premium fire insurance. Drug addicts always needed cash. Tenants knew that if they were burned out of their buildings, they could be put at the top of the list for an apartment in a NYCHA building, and maybe receive payments for new furniture and relocation costs. An act of arson could solve problems for a number of stakeholders simultaneously (although city fire inspectors said that most of the building fires were not caused by arson).

Why the fires started can be halfway explained. But why did they keep burning, year after year, for more than a decade? Only the presence of the metaphorical burning-glass over the Bronx can explain that. The burning-glass stands for deliberate policy, made at a level so removed from ordinary people's lives that it might as well have been at whatever rarified altitude an actual burning-glass would need to be in order to focus its rays on the Bronx. The Regional Plan of 1929 said, "We have carried concentration too far! We must begin to think in terms of decentralization. Think it out." That was the big picture. "Think it out": Think of all those buildings from the insufficiently thought-out Bronx boom of the 1920s, when thousands of them were going up right next to each other in rows, year after year. Think it out: the fires, regrettable as they might be, served decentralization. Think it out: Robert Moses, the most powerful planner and builder in the history of any American city, had declared the Bronx to be "beyond tinkering, rebuilding and restoring."

Think it out: The plan for industry to leave the city partly achieved that goal, which contributed to a drop in the city's revenues. Every year, New York was coming closer to bankruptcy. In 1968, Mayor John Lindsay announced that the city had hired the Rand Corporation to help it save money. The Rand Corporation is a nonprofit research group like the Regional Plan Association, but with a background of doing studies for the military. The public knew of the high-efficiency bombing patterns that Rand had devised for the air force in Vietnam. Working with the New York City Fire Department, Rand analysts recommended that many fire stations be closed. Reallocation of men and equipment from other stations would cover the gaps, in theory. The closings went into effect just as the fire plague was getting worse. Response times grew slower. Fire trucks were coming to alarms in the Bronx from as far away as Staten Island. During the delays, small fires blew up into big ones. Between 1972 and 1974, four fire stations in the Bronx, each serving sixty thousand people, closed. Three more would follow. At the same time, wealthier parts of the city used their pull to keep their own stations open.

Think it out: A new theory, expressed in two words, kept the fires burning. The two words were *planned shrinkage*. According to planned shrinkage, the city, having lost revenues, could not support its former population at the level of services to which it had been accustomed. Therefore, it must shrink. The Rand Corporation's blueprint for fire-house closings epitomized planned shrinkage. The main champion of planned shrinkage, a professor of urban studies named Roger Starr, served as head of the city's Housing Development Administration under Abraham Beame, the mayor who followed Lindsay. Starr suggested closing schools, hospitals, subway stations, and other city services in the Bronx and elsewhere and concentrating residents in areas he deemed more "alive"—perhaps in other states. He said the poor could be given financial inducements that might make them "question whether the ties that bind them to a grossly deteriorated neighborhood are as important as they seemed." After they went away, the empty lots where apartment buildings once were could be left to sit until the hidden workings of fate and economics made the land profitable again. At the time Starr offered this solution, almost half a million people were living in the South Bronx.

Then the federal government gave up on cities. In 1973, President Richard Nixon suspended payments to federal programs intended to create urban housing. Lyndon Johnson–era initiatives such as the Model Cities Program had done only limited good, but now construction of a federal affordable-housing project on fire-cleared blocks in the South Bronx stopped and never restarted. People who lived in the South Bronx, and had no desire to leave, were reprimanded. Daniel Patrick Moynihan, a U.S. senator from their own state, seemed to take pleasure in knocking them. He said that building new housing was not the answer, because "people in the South Bronx don't want housing or they wouldn't burn it down. It's fairly clear that housing is not the problem in the South Bronx." (Again: the fire department had said that arson was not the cause of most of the building fires.) To address the city's problems around race and poverty, Moynihan favored a policy of "benign neglect" and "toning down the rhetoric." Meanwhile, the Bronx kept bursting into flames. In 1976, the number of fires of all kinds in the borough reached 33,465.

VIVIAN VÁZQUEZ was born not just in the Bronx, but in "the old Lincoln." This was the previous version of Lincoln Hospital, at East 141st Street and Southern Boulevard—the one the Young Lords occupied in 1970. To say you were born in "the old Lincoln," as Vázquez and similarly credentialed folks do, is to claim Bronx heritage and pride. Vázquez is a handsome, reserved woman in her early sixties with brown eyes and red-highlighted brown hair. Both of her parents came to the Bronx from Puerto Rico, and both moved back to Puerto Rico eventually. She has never lived anywhere but the Bronx. She spent her youth in two buildings: 990 Leggett Avenue, and 986, next door. A now-famous playground called Playground 52 is about a block away.

She had a happy childhood as the middle one of five, with a brother and sister older and a brother and sister younger. Her father worked in a furniture store on Prospect Avenue, a short walk away, and her mother was a housewife who loved all kinds of American things and listened to all kinds of music. The disintegration of the neighborhood stands out, to Vázquez, more in retrospect than it did at the time. Family rules forbade her and her siblings from jumping on mattresses, which were plentiful in abandoned lots (her father said the mattresses would give them fleas). Her parents also forbade going into abandoned buildings (hard to resist, and she sometimes went into them); approaching stray dogs (which she never did, but she was bitten anyway, by a dog on a leash, while she was splashing at a fire hydrant with some other kids); and walking on certain streets (a prohibition her parents emphasized). Her father also told them to be careful where they put their feet, and to watch for nails.

From the age of twelve, she played on the neighborhood girls' softball team. It was part of a league of boys' teams and girls' teams organized mostly by the kids themselves. The teams had uniforms and played on cement or asphalt in playgrounds. When she went to high school at Murray Bergtraum, in downtown Manhattan, and played on grass for the first time, the surface fooled her, because balls bounce faster off grass. Another organization that influenced her life was the Sweet Sixteen parties. The kids and their mothers did all the planning and sewing and social structuring of the parties. Once you'd had your own party, you remained in the pool of participants for the Sweet Sixteen parties of relatives and friends.

In the early seventies, the burning-glass focused its rays on her immediate neighborhood, but neither 990 nor 986 Leggett burned. She says this was because the super of both buildings was the leader of the Dirty Dozens, the gang that ran her street. Her mother knew the guys in the gang because she was the neighborhood's Avon Lady and sold beauty products to their wives and girlfriends. Vázquez knew these girls and women, too. She and her sister delivered the products and collected the payment.

One can hardly imagine a more abandoned and unredeemed place than the Bronx in those years. The whole city seemed to be headed for the trash pile, and the feds said they wouldn't help. In 1975, the famous *Daily News* headline announced that President Gerald Ford had told New York City to drop dead. "Planned shrinkage" and Senator Moynihan's "benign neglect" expressed the same sentiment in more technocratic lingo. In 1976, the Bicentennial of America's founding came and went without much really happening in the city, other than the arrival of the Tall Ships, which looked good but seemed to commemorate, weirdly, the invasion by the British two centuries before. On July 4, 1976, the promise of a Bicentennial fireworks display drew a crowd of two million to the wide expanse of landfill in lower Manhattan where Battery Park City is now. I went with friends and watched from an elevated span of the West Side Highway (now torn down). The expanse of two million humans rippled like a sea and gave off a murmur of expectation, soon to be doused by the show of tiny pyrotechnics across the river. When it ended, nobody could believe that was it. But we had all showed up, at least, and our numbers made a patriotic point of their own.

Then came 1977, that momentous year. The city's restlessness and discontent had been piling up. In July, a heat wave broke records. On the night of July 13–14, a series of thunderstorms moving down the Hudson Valley brought lightning strikes that knocked out power to the city. The Bronx, like the rest of New York, went dark. Vázquez was fourteen. Her parents feared that riots would be taking over outside, so the whole family stayed in the apartment all night with just a flashlight and a few candles.

A thousand fires burned in the Bronx on the night of the '77 Blackout. To drivers on the highways—as pedestrians darted across here and there—fire seemed to be flickering all around. Other parts of the city were blackout dark, but fires lit the Bronx. Looters pried up security gates and took Pampers and bulk foodstuffs. They took appliances, clothes, watches, and jewelry. They tied sneakers together by the laces and draped strings of them around their shoulders like bandoliers, cleaned out all the trophies from a trophy store, teamed up in groups to carry living room sets away. It's said that a Bronx car dealership lost fifty new Pontiacs that night, driven out through the smashed showroom windows. News footage shows the police outnumbered and watching the looters, and not attempting to make arrests; in fact, hundreds were arrested that night. At Bronx Central Booking the line stretched out the door and into the street.

I was having dinner with my friend Jamaica in her apartment on West 22nd Street in Manhattan when the lights went out at a little after nine thirty. We walked around in the festival atmosphere of that hippieish (in that era) neighborhood. People were playing guitars and drinking up their beer supply before it got warm. Then I hiked back to my loft on Canal Street. The loft was sixty feet long and nineteen feet wide, with almost no furniture. My phone sat on the floor. As I came in it started to ring, and I had to stumble around for it in the darkness. When I answered, it was my mother checking on me. The next day, I took a bus to Ohio to help her and my father move into an apartment on the west side of Cleveland. After twenty years, they were leaving the suburbs, taking that demographic shift full circle, back to the city. Their television, unlike mine, worked, and for the first time I saw coverage of the looting in the Bronx and other places. Up until then I had not known that any looting had occurred.

Prospect Avenue, the shopping district near the Vázquezes' apartment, suffered almost total losses. To this day, Prospect has never come back to what it was. Looters stripped the furniture store where Vivian's father had worked for seventeen years, and it closed. The loss of his job caused her father to go downhill in ways she doesn't specify. He and her mother divorced. The '77 Blackout marked the moment when the Vázquezes' life changed. The name of the store where Vivian's father worked for seventeen years was Paradise Furniture.

AND DID THOSE Bronxites who withdrew by the tens of thousands to Co-op City find their separate peace, and avoid the Bronx's destruction? Not exactly. Even while residents were still moving in, the buildings had already begun to have problems. Walls leaked. Bricks used as facing were so porous and poorly pointed that rain came through them when storms hit straight on. Certain top-floor apartment ceilings showed the sky through big cracks. In fact, cracks spread all over as buildings settled on landfill that had not totally eradicated the swampy places. Pipes ruptured, washing machines in the laundry rooms broke and weren't repaired. Elevators went out of service, sometimes leaving residents long climbs to their apartments. Rumors of theft and corruption during the construction further angered the "cooperators" (a name many residents hated). It was said that whole mansions in Westchester County were built with materials stolen from Co-op City.

The abandonment of large parts of the Bronx by fortune, city government, and maybe even God extended to this supposed refuge. It was open season for plunder in the Bronx during the time of Senator Moynihan's "benign neglect." Estimates of the total cost of building Co-op City rose from $293 million to $340 million to $450 million. Nor could the thieves be caught. Two years after the project ended, no company that had worked on the project remained in business.

To pay for the overrun, Co-op City's management told residents that their maintenance fees would have to go up. First would come a 25 percent increase over two years, followed by a 57 percent increase over three years. Many of the residents ("'Cooperators!' Ha!" they cried) were retirees on fixed incomes. Hoping to be modestly and comfortably set for the rest of their lives, they had fallen suddenly into housing insecurity, that chronic illness of American life. Now fear sneaked up and grabbed them by the throat. In response, the residents first formed a committee that sued Co-op City's management for fraud. The fifteen thousand families paid ten dollars apiece to hire Louis Nizer, a short, famous attorney who sat on a raised throne in his office, to represent them. Then they formed another committee, which turned to that old semireliable tactic, the rent strike.

The strike was led by a young Co-op City cooperator named Charlie Rosen. Only thirty-two, he had grown up in a Communist family, and he worked as a typographer on the production floor of the *New York Post*. His mother, who had fled pogroms in her home city of Kamenets-Podolski, in Ukraine, remained a Stalinist even after the

1939 Hitler pact. She was a passementerie worker—a maker of tassels and fringe—and belonged to the passementerie workers' union. Rosen's father, who had immigrated from Warsaw, set up knitting machines in the Garment District and served as president of the Knit Goods Workers' Union. Coming from such a background, the skinny, intense, chain-smoking Rosen leaped to the fight as one to the struggle born.

For complicated reasons, New York State, which held the mortgage, had taken over as Co-op City's management. It set out to crush the strikers, deploying middle-class terrors—freezing the leaders' bank accounts, threatening the thousands of strikers with immediate eviction, taping eviction notices to everybody's door, publishing thousands of copies of a registry containing every striker's name. Eighty-some percent of Co-op City's residents joined the strike. Rosen kept them focused on their goals and told them not to be scared, repeating over and over that they would win.

About 12,500 of the strikers were retirees. Individually, they may have felt spasms of quiet or noisy desperation, but Rosen knew that as a group they were unevictable. No agency or government could put 12,500 elderly people out on the street. He kept saying that, but privately he feared that if the state evicted only a few the rest would panic and cave in. For unknown reasons the state did not use that tactic, and in the end the strikers prevailed. In 1976, with the help of Mario Cuomo, New York's secretary of state at the time, an agreement was reached. The residents took over management of Co-Op City from the state, which agreed to provide a hundred million dollars for repairs. None of the strike leaders had to pay the fines that had been mounting against them every day. A moratorium let the residents go without paying the increased maintenance for six months, but in a good-news, bad-news twist, the new management decided the increases would be necessary, after all.

Many Co-op City residents cheered Rosen as a genius and a hero. He could have gone into politics, but instead he moved with his wife and two children into a better apartment in the complex, quit the *Post*, and eventually took over as the head of the Gloria Wise Boys and Girls Club, a local organization that provides services to hundreds of children and seniors locally and has a multimillion-dollar budget. In 2006, I interviewed him for an article I was writing about Co-op City. By then he had matured into a filled-out, dramatically gesturing man with senatorial white hair. He drove us to lunch (for which I paid) in a brand-new bright red Porsche. A few months later, he pled guilty to embezzling from the Boys and Girls Club. The charges against him specified the Porsche as one of the things he had bought with the stolen money. The judge gave him no jail time, but at a later hearing many of Rosen's angry neighbors showed up to insist that he go to jail. They were unsuccessful; Rosen did not go to jail.

ON LYMAN PLACE, in the path of the fires, Hetty Fox kept an eye on the neighborhood like a one-woman fire-safety inspector combined with a teacher, camp counselor, band leader, and African-dance choreographer. She wanted there to be eyes on the street and beneficial activity for as much of every day as possible. When the city threatened to take over vacant buildings on the block, she made one of them into a recreation center for neighborhood kids where she provided games, arts and crafts materials, and books. She taught the kids African dances (while she continued to perform professionally), had them memorize Swahili words and the names of 186 African tribes, and kept the center open until ten thirty six nights a week. In her many interactions with city officials, she learned that certain streets that don't have parking meters are eligible to be turned into "play streets"—streets temporarily closed off to traffic, for outdoor activities like block parties, double-Dutch jump rope contests, and musical performances. She closed off Lyman Place for a part of almost every good-weather day.

To her the children of the neighborhood were (as she said later) "little geniuses" and "little kings and queens," whom the public schools did not appreciate. She let the kids know how highly she thought of them. Encouraging them to dream of bigger horizons while not automatically linking that to a goal of leaving the Bronx proved a challenge. She tried to instill the idea that they could stay and make things better right here; but she also said that if they left, Lyman Place would be a home they could remember with love and come back to. Every year, she put on a Christmas party for about a hundred kids. The city, it seemed, could not have cared less. When Ed Koch became mayor, he established a system of Neighborhood Preservation Offices to help poor neighborhoods. Fox wanted him to open one near her, but Koch vetoed the idea. He said that her part of the Bronx was already too far gone.

She continued her mission practically all alone. To walk in her former neighborhood today is to see what the old-time housing stock of the South Bronx looked like. In other parts, the new buildings occupying block after block show where the devastation occurred. On the former Lyman Place and around it, brownstones, frame houses, and apartment buildings from the time before the fires still stand. The fiery angel of death that Hetty Fox saw creeping up from Vyse Avenue stopped at Stebbins (today, James A. Polite) Avenue. That her childhood home and scores of other buildings in a wide radius did not burn was thanks mainly to her. Hetty Fox fought for the defense of a Bronx neighborhood before almost anybody.

VIVIAN VÁZQUEZ GRADUATED from high school and went to the State University of New York at Albany (SUNY Albany). By that time— 1980—the plague of fires had abated, but the citizens had not recovered emotionally. She had never been any place like upstate or met people so different from herself. What she had witnessed in her neighborhood— the building across from hers going up in flames, the disappearance of friends overnight after their apartments burned, the sirens screaming— didn't coincide with the experiences of most SUNY students. She felt lost. Her courses were difficult, and she worried that she would have to drop out. Her roommate told her she would not make it. Soon she found a small group of students like herself, all of them from the city, and they spent time together and lifted one another's morale.

She was grieving, ashamed, and confused. Why had such a disaster happened to the place she loved, the place where she grew up? The huge burning-glass in the sky had been invisible, and at that moment the Senator Moynihan explanation prevailed: "People in the South Bronx don't want housing or they wouldn't burn it down." In the absence of other obvious reasons, she half accepted that one. Nobody she knew well had participated in the disaster other than as observers or victims or both, but she feared that somehow, the South Bronx must have deserved its fate; as she said later, the logic went, "This was what you got for being poor." Collectively the residents internalized the criticism and accepted the guilt. The disaster must have been their fault, though they knew that didn't make sense and couldn't be true. Vázquez didn't understand what had happened, but one day she would try to find out.

30

WALKING IN THE BRONX with my friend Alex Melamid on a summer afternoon; we met at Edgar Allan Poe Park, in Kingsbridge, then headed northwest to Fieldston. Alex was originally a Russian artist and is now an American artist. In his youth he belonged to the Soviet Artists Union, but it kicked him out, along with his then-partner, Vitaly Komar, because the two painted a satirical portrait of Laika, the first dog to be sent into space. Alex left the Soviet Union for Israel and burned his Russian suitcases on a pyre in the desert. Then he came to New York, and he has lived there or in New Jersey for forty-six years. The first time I traveled to Siberia, back in 1993, I went with him and his wife, Katya Arnold, who's an artist and a teacher.

In the spirit of the Cold War, the time of our youth, I first led Alex to the house where John F. Kennedy lived as a boy. I stop by it occasionally and see how it is doing. For a few years, there was a Ford sedan with flat tires in the turnaround driveway. On the car's rear dash, beneath the back window, a rolled-up black umbrella lay in the exact same position, year after year. The window had a Brown University decal. The car remained in the Google Earth satellite photo as the view was updated periodically. If you focused in close enough you could even make out the umbrella, although not the Brown decal.

Now Alex and I wandered around the property, looking in the windows. Katya had once showed me Khrushchev's grave, in Novodevichy Cemetery, in Moscow. The Kennedy house has caught the decay that affects certain Cold War relics in both countries—old missile installations and bomb shelters and whatnot. We found that the umbrella and its flat-tire ride were still there. On the house's back patio sat an exercise machine partly covered in moss. A guy appeared out of the side entrance of the house next door and asked us what we were doing. He identified himself as the caretaker. We said we were just looking around, and left.

In the northwest Bronx, the Russian government maintains a weird mission compound. An immense high-rise, by far the tallest structure in the area, towers at its center; maps identify this as the Russian Mission School, but the building is about twenty stories high—a lot of school. One of the most impressive fences in the entire borough surrounds it. Along and above the sidewalk, a barricade of close-set gray steel palings rises ten or twelve feet high, curving outward at the top; and behind that fence, a lesser fence of chain link woven with green strips keeps you from seeing through. Eyeball-shaped security cameras watch from various heights and angles. There are guard booths with windows of one-way glass, and a double-gated entry for vehicles, and no signage of any kind. Alex stood back and looked at the fortifications and said, "Does Italy have a mission like this? Does Switzerland?"

A woman walked through the outer gate as it slid open on its overhead girder, and Alex greeted her in Russian. He asked if there was anyplace nearby where we could get lunch, and she said she would show us. She said she taught in the school. I asked her why a school needed a twenty-story building. She said there are many immigrants from the former Soviet republics—Tajikistan, Kyrgyzstan, Georgia, Uzbekistan—who want to send their children to a Russian-speaking school. (The subject of Ukraine did not come up; this was before the invasion.) She allowed as how a lot of the building was also offices. Her pale, Russian-Russian face had a friendly expression, without guile.

A few blocks from the mission she stopped in front of a barbecue restaurant and said she recommended it. We thanked her for her help.

Before she walked on, she asked Alex where he was from. He said, "Manhattan." She said that she had meant, from where in Russia. Alex said, "From Moscow—I am a Moscow Jew." She stared at him benignly and intently. "Yes," she said, "you look like one."

BILL McCLELLAND, my friend going back to freshman year in high school, lives not far from me in New Jersey. Sometimes we drive over the bridge and have lunch at Liebman's Delicatessen in Riverdale and combine that with a Bronx walk. Bill is a composer and pianist, so we visit the graves of musical greats in Woodlawn Cemetery. King Oliver, Duke Ellington, Lionel Hampton, Ornette Coleman, W. C. Handy, and Billy Bang all rest in Woodlawn, under monuments of varying sizes. King Oliver shares his grave with another person; his wife lacked money to bury him, and a generous family allowed her to put him in their plot. Lionel Hampton, "the king of the vibes," and Duke Ellington are buried across a cemetery lane from each other, and the grave of Miles Davis is across from Ellington's, on the other side. Davis's large, polished white marble stone says, in script, "Sir Miles Davis," although he was seldom called that in life. He received the title, by way of the French Legion of Honor, just before he died. Maybe he or a relative thought he needed a noble prefix in this company.

I think the grave of Celia Cruz, the Salsa Queen, is the most beautiful in this cemetery, or maybe anywhere. It's a simple mausoleum of white marble, for her and Pedro Knight, her husband and manager. Plantings of night-blue butterfly bush, bright red hibiscus, pink hydrangea, and black-eyed Susans grow around the tomb. Fans bring more flowers in big or small bouquets and leave them on the steps or on the two white marble benches.

Not many cemeteries are quiet, with the various lawn-care machineries they generally have going, but Woodlawn often is. You might hear only an airplane passing overhead, and then in the silence afterward imagine the music of each artist you're remembering. After some searching, with the cemetery map we found the graves of Irving Berlin, his wife, Ellin, and their son, Irving Jr., who died in infancy.

Berlin, whose earliest memory was of watching Cossacks burn his village, lived to be 101.

When he was thirty-six, he met Ellin Mackay, a twenty-one-year-old debutante, at a dinner party. Her grandfather, John W. Mackay, had made one of the great strikes of silver and copper in the Comstock Lode, in Virginia City, Nevada. The family maneuvered high society in Manhattan into accepting them because of their social successes in Paris and London, where they were simply very rich Americans, not (as Manhattan had previously rated them) nouveau-riche nobodies from out west. Returning from overseas triumphs—they had hosted the former president U. S. Grant at a grand ball at their Paris mansion, when he was on his world tour—Ellin's grandparents had established themselves on the Upper East Side. Ellin's father, Clarence H. Mackay, son of the Comstock miner, looked like the millionaire in the Monopoly game. He added to the family fortune with a telegraph company that his father founded. More than a thousand guests attended Ellin's coming-out party at the Ritz-Carlton Hotel. When the Prince of Wales visited America in 1924, Clarence Mackay held a ball for him at his estate on Long Island. Ellin danced with the prince and noticed how calloused his hands were from all the polo he had been playing. Unlike the other young women (and their mothers) in attendance, she had no interest in him. The prince found her indifference charming and refreshing.

She sneaked away from the ball to telephone Irving Berlin, with whom she had fallen in love. Berlin had already made his fortune from his shows performed in his own Broadway theater, and from the sheet music of his many hit songs. When she and Berlin eloped in 1926, no member of her family attended the City Hall ceremony, and her father disowned her. Only when the couple's baby son died, in 1928, did the family begin to break the silence they had put up against her. The loneliness of that time still seems to hang over the three graves. I was reminded of the cemetery in Ohio where my parents are buried next to my brother Fritz, who died at fifteen. Ellin's family, including her father, accepted Berlin, and warmed to him eventually.

Some people say that Irving Berlin was the greatest American songwriter of all time. I remarked on that to Bill, and he didn't disagree. But he had just produced a CD of William Appling, the pianist and conductor, playing all the sixty-four rags written by Scott Joplin, and so he added an asterisk. "Joplin thought Irving Berlin stole ragtime, and never gave him any credit," Bill said. It's true that "Alexander's Ragtime Band," Berlin's first big international hit, takes a lot from Joplin. The song introduced the modern world's first brand-new beat. Ragtime's syncopation rewired the global nervous system and kept it several steps ahead of the rhythms of commerce, where it should always be. Joplin and other Black musicians discovered and created the infectious ragtime rhythm; Berlin heard it and came down with it like a cold.

Then we went to look for the marker for Felix Pappalardi, bassist in the pre-heavy-metal group Mountain. (He's also remembered as the producer of other bands, such as Cream.) Much of Woodlawn is long rows of small markers so close to one another that from a distance they resemble curbstones. Pappalardi's marker is in one of those rows. We looked and looked. Finally, Bill found it. Pappalardi was shot and killed by his wife and is buried next to his mother.

The last marker we checked out was Robert Moses's, in its columbarium. I stop by it when I'm in Woodlawn and take note of the traffic at the intersection of Jerome Avenue and East 233rd Street, nearby. A long time ago, in Morocco, I saw the tomb of a king—Hassan I, maybe—over whose coffin a hafiz chants the Qur'an all day and all night. The sounds of traffic at that intersection are Moses's 24/7 Qur'an.

IN HAYDEN LORD PARK, on Andrews Avenue South near 176th Street, I met a young woman named Shakeema Blount, who maintained the garden plots in the park for the nonprofit that oversees it. She was weeding a bed of nasturtiums and had just found a hypodermic needle in them, which angered her. As I watched, she held it up to show. Then she set it on the paving stones beside her; in a locked shed she had a place to dispose of needles. We got to talking. She wore a John Deere–green T-shirt and heavy dark brown work pants, and her hair in short braids. As she worked, she said this park was her baby. It's one of the handsomest small parks in the city, with mosaics on the walls in the style of Antoni Gaudí's famous mosaics in Barcelona. The lipstick-red tulips and the shiny reds in the mosaics played off each other.

A week or two later, I passed by and again found her working there. She took a break from her weeding, and we sat at a bench. More flowers were blooming, and the beds and mosaics looked even better than before. She told me her mother's family was originally from South Carolina, where her grandmother owned some land and taught her about gardening. Blount had grown up in Bedford-Stuyvesant and now she and two of her three children lived in Hunts Point. After a while, I asked if we could meet in Hunts Point and talk again sometime. I told her I was writing a book. She agreed and we exchanged email addresses and phone numbers.

She was in her early thirties, with a quizzical, open expression, and the relaxed bearing of someone who's good at her work. Arranging another meeting took persistence by me. Twice she said we could meet at the Hunts Point Riverside Park but canceled after I got there. One afternoon I called and said I was at the McDonald's on Hunts Point Avenue and 163rd Street, and she showed up in about half an hour. As we sat, she told me some of her history, from when she got pregnant in the eleventh grade at Boys and Girls High School in Brooklyn. She dropped out and had her son, and her mother took care of him. Now he was fifteen and a star on the basketball team at another Brooklyn high school. She also had two daughters, eight years old and four, by a man who served time in prison but turned his life around and now lived with her and the girls. After moving to Hunts Point, she got her GED and then attended a trade school for seventeen weeks. Through the Job Corps she also completed training that certified her to operate forklifts and other heavy equipment. "I like hands-on work," she said. "I'm really not into sitting down at a desk."

She had been a checkout person at Whole Foods, and a security guard at a children's clothing store ("People get nasty when you catch they ass stealing"), and on the maintenance staff of a NYCHA building. Doing renovation of a hospital, she received paychecks every Friday, and off-the-books cash for work on weekends—"I love jobs like that," she said. For the past several years she had worked for a nonprofit called Sustainable South Bronx, on their Cool Roofs and their Green Roofs projects. Green Roofs installs and cultivates rooftop gardens, mostly of ornamental grasses. She described working on roofs in sunshine and cold, forty-five hours a week, for $11.50 an hour. "When it's hot, you have to bring frozen gallon jugs of water with you, carrying that water with the rest of the equipment and paint and bags of mulch and whatnot, sometimes up five or six flights of stairs. I've never drunk that much water in my life. Then on payday you're looking at your damn check, and you're like, 'I was in the sun all that time for *this*?'"

Recently her pay had been cut, then she was laid off. Other jobs she'd found paid not very much. Her kids' feet kept growing and they wanted three-hundred-dollar sneakers. Their father was looking for work as a stagehand but couldn't get into a union. Part-time work cleaning tree pits on the sidewalks offered what she called "Mexican money"—bottom-basement wages. She took the job anyway. Gardening at the park paid decently, but her hours weren't many, and the job would end when the season changed. Sometimes she didn't have twenty dollars left at the end of the month. For dinner sometimes she cooked whatever was left in the refrigerator and made a pitcher of Kool-Aid. She said her daughters were smart and quick, like the Huxtable kids on TV. Her younger daughter was learning the names of the plants from her. The family was waiting for a bus recently and the girl asked her if the tree by the bus shelter was a honey locust, and it was.

In 2020, the Citizens' Committee for Children, a New York City nonprofit, published its Community Risk Rating, which ranks the city's fifty-nine community districts on the overall risk to the health of children who live in them. Hunts Point and Morrisania tied for the most hazardous districts in New York. Of the city's ten worst districts, the Bronx accounted for eight. Of the least hazardous districts, seven were in Manhattan; the safest district for children was the Upper East Side, just across the Harlem River and one district away from Morrisania–Hunts Point.

When I said goodbye to Shakeema Blount at the McDonald's that day, she said we could keep in touch, but afterward she stopped answering my messages. I often think of her bringing up her daughters in that hard place and doing the underpaid, essential work of the city.

IN CLAREMONT PARK on a cold afternoon in December, I saw a Spanish-language sign taped to a streetlight pole. In small writing, it said that runners carrying a torch honoring Our Lady of Guadalupe were on their way from Mexico and would soon be arriving in New York City. The runners were calling attention to the dignity of a people divided by the border. On December 12, St. Augustine–Our Lady of Victory Church, at 1512 Webster Avenue, would welcome the bearers of the Guadalupe torch at 6:30 p.m., and a solemn mass in honor of Our Lady of Guadalupe would follow at 7:00 p.m. The running of the torch was produced by the Asociación Tepeyac de New York.

Looking up these references, I found that Our Lady of Guadalupe is the patron saint of the Americas and incorporates a goddess of the Aztecs. In 1531, a Chichimec man had a vision of the Virgin Mary at the site of the goddess's shrine, on a hill north of Mexico City called Tepeyac. The Catholic Church refused for two centuries to accept the authenticity of the vision, or to acknowledge the existence of this Virgin Mary of the Western Hemisphere, but eventually it had no choice. Today the Virgin's shrine at Tepeyac is one of the most-visited shrines in the world. The Asociación Tepeyac de New York is a nonprofit that helps Mexican immigrants.

On December 12, I checked out the Tepeyac shrine online. Pilgrims had been showing up at it for days. Nine million people were expected. Here, in our part of the hemisphere, the day had turned cold. I dressed warmly and headed for the Bronx. I arrived about an hour before the scheduled welcome of the torch runners. Then I stood around on Webster Avenue in front of the church, which had not opened. Nobody else seemed to be waiting. I wondered if maybe I'd misunderstood the sign. A woman in a white knit cap came up to me and asked if I was waiting for the runners. I said yes, and she said, "You are welcome here." She introduced herself as Maria Peguero, the associate pastor of the church.

She told me that the torch had come from Mexico City carried by relays of runners. The relay that would bring it here, on the final leg, had started in Philadelphia and reached the United Nations today. The runners set out from the UN that afternoon and were now crossing into the Bronx. More people gathered, the church's doors opened, and the priest, an Anglo man taller than his parishioners, stood in the open door talking with the arrivals. Then, not wanting the church to get too cold, he closed the doors again. Many of the members of this church are Garifuna and Mexican; some are of Aztec background. The clothes the parishioners wore appeared to be hand-sewn bursts of strong basic colors in geometric patterns, under heavy down coats. The little girls' hairstyles used a lot of ribbons, and their skirts were of pink and white muslin, very full, almost ballet-style.

Now everybody was leaning over the curb, staring down Webster Avenue, where a road-construction barrier partway blocking the street blinked yellow orange. I expected some big convoy of city vehicles, but what arrived, finally, was a white pickup truck with no blinking lights, and the runners close behind. As they moved four abreast up Webster Avenue, a man in the lead group held the torch high. About two dozen more runners, in six rows, followed. After them came a second pickup, flashing its hazard lights. The people who were watching cheered, and the little kids jumped around. All the runners wore heavy white hoodies and white sweatpants, and they stepped in right-left synch, at a steady pace, their bodies in unanimous, powerful motion. All were young men and women. They jogged in place for a moment in front of the church, breathing steam that mingled with the light-catching, voluminous exhaust from the pickups. The priest came out in robe and miter and sprinkled holy water on them from his aspergillum. They handed him the torch. It was steel, and smoky, with oval vents at the end like an oil field flare, and it smelled of kerosene.

The church members sang hymns to the Virgin Mary, a woman blew blasts on a conch shell, and a man beat a complicated rhythm on a flat, handheld drum. The church doors swung open wide. The congregation stood back, lining the steps, as the runners went in. Up close, their faces radiated purpose and sanctity. The altar, pulpit, balcony, and walls had been hung with images of a famous painting of Our Lady of Guadalupe. When the crowd took off their heavy coats, the embroidered blouses and shirts of the women and men, and the little girls' dresses, brightened the softly lit space. Church members welcomed me in English. Maria Peguero, looking happier than almost anyone I'd ever seen, brought me a pamphlet with the service in both languages.

The priest, Father George R. Stewart, conducted the service in Spanish, but also provided a summary of his sermon in English. He preached about the man, Juan Diego, who had the vision of the Virgin of Guadalupe, and how he later was canonized as St. Iago. When the future St. Iago saw his vision, he happened to be on his way to take care of his dying uncle. Father Stewart said that tonight his own mother was dying, and he was on his way to care for her; he would go to the hospital after the service. He talked about the holiness of going forth into the world as the hands and feet and arms and legs of Jesus Christ, and doing Jesus's work. The runners had done the same themselves, he said, with their long journey, showing that the land was all one, and continuous, and under the blessing of Our Lady of Guadalupe; and that borders do not exist in the Kingdom of God. In their white hoodies the runners sat listening. Not once did I see anybody take out a cell phone.

All of that happened about six weeks before Covid hit New York. After it did, the church suspended in-person services and Father Stewart spent his days visiting sick parishioners in their homes; once they were hospitalized, he couldn't see them, because of the no-visitors rule, which pained him. The Our Lady of Guadalupe ceremony, with its torchlit winter darkness and sacred runners, seemed like a scene from another century.

31

THIS CHAPTER SHOULD BEGIN with the sound of scratching, like on a record. While the disasters of the 1970s were going on—the abandonment, the destruction, the official policy of neglect, "planned shrinkage," and the fires—kids in the Bronx invented hip-hop. Doo-wop, rhythm and blues, jazz, salsa, and Latin jazz had flourished in the borough, but they all came from somewhere else. Hip-hop music and hip-hop culture began in the Bronx.

The origin is attributed to a specific time and place: August 11, 1973, in the recreation room of a NYCHA apartment building at 1520 Sedgwick Avenue, in the Highbridge neighborhood. People who know a lot about hip-hop can recite the address, and fans visit it in the spirit of homage. The pole with street signs at the curb in front of the entry gets so covered with hip-hop groups' stickers that eventually someone removes them. Soon they're replaced by more. The street signs say, "Sedgwick Av" and "Hip Hop Blvd." I am glad the city did not discard the previous name entirely. It commemorates Major General John Sedgwick, one of the highest-ranking Union officers to die in the Civil War, who was shot by a sniper at the Battle of Spotsylvania. His staff had warned him to move farther back, but Sedgwick, of a distinguished New England family, replied, "They couldn't hit an elephant at this distance."

At 1520 Sedgwick, in the summer of 1973, a young woman named Cindy Campbell organized a party. She is a sister of Clive Campbell; he was eighteen years old at the time. People called Clive "Hercules" because of his size, and he deejayed under the name DJ Kool Herc. The Campbells had moved to this building after having been burned out of an apartment in Harlem. Before that, the family lived in the Trenchtown neighborhood of Kingston, Jamaica. (Bob Marley, the reggae star, also had lived in Trenchtown.) Cindy and her sisters planned to charge twenty-five cents admission (fifty cents for guys) and use the money to buy new clothes for school. To advertise the event on August 11, they made hand-lettered nine-by-five cards that they distributed or posted in the neighborhood. Today one of those cards is in the hip-hop archive at Harvard University, where I have seen it. It has bulbous, vaguely psychedelic lettering, in ballpoint pen that has faded to gray.

The Campbells' father, Keith, had been a part-time impresario in Jamaica, and he continued to do that in the Bronx. In Jamaica, the sound systems relied on massive speakers to make up for a scarcity of local musicians, many of whom had emigrated or gone to work in the tourist industry. Bronxites could not comprehend the size of the West Indians' speakers when they first saw them. "You could live inside some of them speakers, that's how big they were," said a Bronx DJ who learned by watching Kool Herc.

From in front of 1520 Sedgwick, you can see, to the south, the Washington Bridge, which the engineers didn't use as the main Harlem River bridge connecting to the Cross Bronx Expressway; a bit of the Alexander Hamilton Bridge, which they built to perform that function; and, farther south, a bit of the High Bridge, the engineering marvel of the 1840s that brought water to the city. Directly in front of 1520 Sedgwick, a fence and a high berm at the edge of the avenue separate it from the six lanes of the Major Deegan Expressway. Beyond the expressway are the tracks of a commuter line between New York City and points north. The Harlem River flows on the far side of the tracks, and the high, stony hills of uptown Manhattan rise above the opposite shore.

In that direction—west—the sky is big, while the cliff behind 1520 Sedgwick cuts off most of the view to the east. This edge of the Bronx is in the canyon of the Harlem River. Early hip-hop bloomed in outdoor spaces, with high-reaching skies above. We may think of it as music made in closed venues like dance clubs or the 1520 Sedgwick rec room; and it was that, too. But at the beginning, hip-hop lived mostly outdoors, in Bronx playgrounds, under vistas recently opened up, in many cases, by the burning and leveling of so many apartment buildings. On the playgrounds, hip-hop grew to its true dimensions as an open-air sound—landscape-filling, world-shaking music, echoing to the skies.

Kool Herc wore Superfly-style high-collar leisure suits and over-size Sly Stone caps, and when he deejayed he worked two turntables. A single turntable had obviously been the rule for playing songs, but Kool Herc played beats. His father owned a large record collection, and Herc found samples on certain records and played only the part with the beat—the break, the dance part—switching from one turntable to the other to keep the beat going. The records were his instruments. His father had taught him to soak the labels off the LPs so nobody could see what he was playing. Without labels, the records had the identities he gave them by playing them in the contexts he set up. He made the beat unlimited, with the melody and the lyrics demoted in importance or edited out entirely. A hundred years earlier, ragtime's new rhythm had been an irresistible syncopation of melody. This brand-new beat—not yet called hip-hop—lived in the beats themselves.

People who came to the Campbells' party on August 11 danced, and the nonstop beats kept them dancing. Word got around. Later gatherings would be too big for the rec room, so Herc moved them outdoors, to Cedar Playground, seven tenths of a mile to the north. The playground includes a couple of basketball courts and some swing sets. Stairs lead up the steep hill above it. It was the original hip-hop outdoor proving ground.

JOSEPH ROBERT SADDLER, born in Barbados on New Year's Day 1957, is two years younger than Kool Herc. Saddler's family moved to the Bronx before he turned three. His uncle and his father both boxed, and his uncle had been a middleweight champion, but Joseph's asthma would keep him out of sports. He lived in the Throgs Neck Houses, in a complex of three-story apartment buildings in a quiet part of the borough near the approach to the Throgs Neck Bridge. Joseph had four sisters and was the next-to-youngest of the siblings.

As he recounts in his memoir, *The Adventures of Grandmaster Flash: My Life, My Beats* (cowritten with David Ritz), his parents threw parties with music so loud that neighbors called the police. When he was a little kid, he used to get out of bed and join in, doing "that crazy little bug-out dance that kids do." His father, who worked for Penn Central Railroad, beat him and held his hand to the radiator for fooling with his stereo and his record collection, but Joseph, nicknamed Butsy, couldn't stop. The turntable intrigued him, and the mystery of how the music went from the record to the needle to the speakers. When his mother saved up S&H Green Stamps and bought him a two-wheel banana-seat bicycle, he turned it upside down and set it on its seat and spun the wheels and watched them. Sometimes he clipped playing cards to the spokes and listened to them click.

When he was eight, his father's violence and his mother's mental collapse broke up the family. Child Welfare put him in foster homes from which he escaped. Then he was sent to an upstate home for children, where he was happy and did well. After five years, he heard Sly and the Family Stone's "Dance to the Music" coming from a car one day when he went to the nearby town, and suddenly he wanted to be back in the Bronx. His mother had recovered and moved to an apartment at East 163rd and Fox Street. He and two of his sisters reunited with her, and he enrolled in Samuel Gompers Technical High School.

The faculty at Gompers taught him about resistors and capacitors and vacuum tubes and the technology of record players. He enjoyed his subjects and got A's. At home he was constantly taking apart appliances to see how they worked. He wanted to build his own sound system, and the fact that abandoned cars littered the streets meant he didn't have to look far for speakers, which scavengers usually left behind when they ripped out the radios and tape players. In tenth grade he had an assignment to build an amplifier. The Bronx's humiliations had reached such a low that trash haulers from all over were using it as a place for dumping, generally in vacant lots. He went through the junk piles with a screwdriver and a pair of wire cutters and sometimes found good circuitry.

Nobody but his teachers praised him for his tech skills. Briefly, he also was a graffiti artist, calling himself Flash 163 because he lived on 163rd Street and liked the sci-fi character Flash Gordon. At night he went to the train yards and wrote his tag on subway cars, but the hard-core guys crossed it out. He wrote "Flash 163" on buildings in his neighborhood, but someone scrawled "DGA" over it, which stood for "Don't Get Around"—and, in fact, he didn't get around, keeping mainly to a few local streets. In short, he failed as a graffiti artist. At sixteen he was a guy of whom his friends said, "Flash ain't comin' out tonight. He gotta date with a busted-up turntable!"

On Saturday, May 25, 1974, Kool Herc played a birthday party in Cedar Playground. Friends told Flash—as I'll now call him—about the party, and he walked the four miles there from his building. (The peace resulting from Black Benji's death had made that not an unsafe thing to do.) Herc and his crew, the Herculoids, had set up Herc's monster speakers, with his turntables on a board laid on top of two overturned trash cans, and they had connected everything to the power from a streetlight pole by removing the pole's faceplate and tapping into the wiring. When the amps cranked up, they drew so much power that the streetlight dimmed, as did other streetlights nearby. Rotary fans plugged into extension outlets blew air to keep the amps from overheating.

The music reached Flash when he was two blocks away. Herc was playing "The Mexican," by Babe Ruth. It was, Flash said, "*THUNDERING*." He said it was not only the loudest music he had ever heard, it was the loudest sound he had ever heard.

EVERY VIOLENCE THAT could be visited on a place, short of carpet bombing, had been visited on the Bronx. It had been burned and razed and bulldozed, and run over by highways, and blasted with dynamite. It had been disrespected and unbenignantly neglected and used for a toxic waste site and street-side dump. It had been drugged and addicted and planned-shrunk. People drove through it from segregated white suburbs on one side to segregated white suburbs on the other. It had been abandoned and left for dead.

Now the Bronx was answering back. Huge machines had assaulted it; now huge speakers blasted a response. What Herc was playing was not only the loudest music Flash had ever heard, it was the loudest sound he had ever heard. The loudest. The loudest. The Loudest S. The Loudest Sound. Loudest Loudest. Sound. Sound. THE LOUDEST Sound.

The LOUDEST SOUND HE HAD EVER HEARD.

When I stop by Cedar Playground, as I do from time to time, there are never a lot of people there: a few women with strollers, some kids playing two-on-two basketball, an apparently homeless man. The traffic on the Major Deegan speeds or crawls. Either way, it provides a constant aural background. When it's jammed up, trucks give double blasts on their horns that seem to be right in your ear. Trains on the tracks beyond the highway make long wailing moans on their whistles, no different from what you might hear at a grade crossing in central Ohio or western Nebraska. The site of Fort Number 8, the Revolutionary War fort that was built by the Americans and taken over by the British, is on a cliff above the valley. What did the fort's cannon sound like, long ago, when the British opened up on the defenses of Fort Washington, in upper Manhattan, during the attack that made George Washington cry? How did those cannon sound, echoing and reechoing in this canyon?

A song whose break Herc played over and over was an instrumental, "Apache," by the Incredible Bongo Band. Everybody knew this song. Later, the "Apache" break would become a standard for hip-hop DJs. Flash described the Cedar Playground scene: "There must have been a thousand people getting down . . . Folks from four to forty, sweating and bouncing, breakin' and popping, doing the pancake and getting buck wild. But every single head was doing the exact same thing—bouncing up and down to this guy's jams." Toward the end of the evening, when Kool Herc played "Apache," it was like the end of a fireworks show, with the crowd going even higher, everybody showing off their moves. Flash said he stood back in the shadows and watched Kool Herc and thought, "*I* can do that."

LIKE CEDAR PLAYGROUND, the outdoor places where hip-hop started are all still there. On a map, most could be enclosed within a seven-mile radius. Cedar Playground was Herc's capital; he also deejayed at the playing fields behind and below the towering eminence of Taft High School, on the wide expanse where the light poles for night games rise fifty or sixty feet in the air and the sight lines go straight up. Herc's parties there would have been visible from space. He dominated the Bronx on the west; on the east, and slightly later, Afrika Bambaataa, a Barbadian-Jamaican whose original name was Lance Taylor, deejayed out of the Bronx River Houses. Bambaataa lived on the first floor next to a courtyard surrounded by trees, and if he chose, he could stay in his apartment and open his windows and play his beats from there. He had a social scene centered on the local Black Spades gang, many of whom he converted to hip-hop, African spirituality, and peaceful pursuits.

Kool Herc, Bambaataa, and Flash are considered the three founders of hip-hop. If anyone can claim that distinction in a movement that sprang from the people, they can. Flash's revelation in Cedar Playground came to him at sixteen, in the last phase of a childhood that had prepared him for a destination he hadn't looked for because it didn't then exist. His disassembling of stereos, staring at spinning wheels, and scavenging of parts for sound equipment now added up to the perfect means for his newfound ends. He saw how he could improve on Herc's technique. In Herc's switching between the first turntable and the second turntable, a hesitation intervened while the record on the second turntable got started. During that pause, the energy in the crowd began to drain out. Flash believed he could go from one record to another seamlessly.

At first, his self-built equipment didn't equal what he was trying to accomplish. He started playing jams in the park at the Mott Haven

Projects at 142nd and Willis every day in the summer of 1974. Because of that presence he won a following among the Casanovas, the local gang, and they gave him a sound system that had been stolen from the Hunts Point Palace, the old Latin music venue of the fifties. This system included two identical top-of-the-line turntables, a twelve-channel mixer, and a big amp and speaker. He felt bad about accepting stolen goods. But now he had "something to make the ground shake . . . to make the beat vibrate in your soul."

Music, poetry, art, dance, fashion, and philosophy all participated in hip-hop, which is more like an artistic movement or way of being. Experts describe it as consisting of various elements. Graffiti, one of the elements, was hip-hop's visual art. It had existed before hip-hop but then became part of it. Kids with spray cans and permanent markers wrote on just about any visible public space. The MTA subway train yard, or "layup," at Jerome Avenue and Bedford Park Boulevard, and the yard at East 180th Street, by the zoo, provided good targets. One graffiti artist climbed to the top of a number 4 train and put his tag there so planes and helicopters could see it; he broke his shoulder getting down. People wrote on walls, billboards, mailboxes, storefronts, delivery vans, discarded washing machines by the side of the street—everywhere. Once or twice the ubiquitous graffitist Stay High 149 sneaked into a New York City airport and wrote his tag on a commercial airliner.

Hip-hop fashion, another element, played off disco fashion. Disco clubs rejected the younger set, whose clothes as well as their age disqualified them. Bouncers enforced a dress code, and you generally could not wear sneakers in discos. The essential schism between disco and hip-hop could be reduced, fashionwise, to shoes versus sneakers. From that came hip-hop's obsession with perfect, spotless sneakers laced with the widest, cleanest laces possible. The first clothes of hip-hop were kids' play clothes—comfortable, unsleek, and cartoon-influenced. Fans copied the styles worn by characters such as Weird Harold and Fat Albert on the *Cosby Kids* TV show—their floppy hats, extra-large baggy Ts, and loose sweats. Bart Simpson's high cartoon flattop was the haircut.

"B-boying" enacted the dance element. B-boys and b-girls did breakdancing, or dancing during the break. They spun on their shoulders, performed flips and splits, made martial arts moves. Back then you could see kids breakdancing all over the city, doing machine-like popping and locking and the Robot on the steps of the public library at Forty-second Street, in front of the Piccirillis' lions. The Moonwalk, a move that had been around for years under different names, came back. I saw Michael Jackson do the Moonwalk during a concert at Radio City Music Hall; at his first few sliding steps, the audience shrieked as if they were on a roller coaster. Leaving the concert, I looked down from the balcony at the crowd in the lobby going out and there must have been a hundred kids Moonwalking. Some ex-b-boys say they had the move long before Michael Jackson. One of them remembered doing it in his school when he was in the fifth grade. The class had lined up to go someplace, and he started doing the Moonwalk on a landing as they went down a flight of stairs, and everything stopped. The entire crowd, including the teachers, just stood in awe and watched him.

A b-boy known as Kokomo, one of the earliest breakdancers, figures in a story of how hip-hop came to be called hip-hop. Kokomo had enlisted in the army and was about to report to boot camp. The night before he left, his friends were kidding him. Flash worked with an MC called Cowboy, because of his bowlegs. This rhyming star (according to the story) started saying "hip-hop-hip-hop-hip-hop" in a marching rhythm to Kokomo, and somehow people took that up, and "hip-hop" became a thing to say. Another explanation is that in the philosophical split between disco and hip-hop, the term began as a put-down. The disco crowd referred to the sneaker wearers as "those hip-hoppers."

Flash briefly wanted to be a b-boy, too, and he practiced his breakdancing; but as with graffiti, he was not good at it. The breakdancing crew he was with even went so far as to vote him out. He returned to his turntables.

At first, hip-hop music meant just DJs and beats; but subtracting the lyrics had left a void, and that led to MCs—performers who rhymed in front of the DJ. From that you got rap, and rappers, although the emergence of "rap" as a term for the music did not happen for a while. On the video of Run-DMC's hit "Rock Box," which came later in the chronology, the comedian Irwin Corey, who specialized in educated-sounding nonsense and doubletalk, does a brief introductory monologue that begins, "Now, what *is* rap music?" Then the professor, with his flyaway hair, string tie, and baggy black suit, pinballs into nonsense that somehow conveys as much information as a nonexpert like me would be able to tell you here. Essentially, not long after you had the beats, you had front men (and later, front women) who rhymed to the beats: thus, rappers and rap music. Hip-hop is the movement as a whole and rap (or hip-hop) is the music.

Revelations like the one that changed Flash's life in Cedar Playground struck other kids. Danny Martinez, a much-admired DJ who isn't widely famous, lived in an apartment so near the Jerome Avenue MTA yards that he could look out his bedroom window and see the graffiti guys writing on the trains. Sometimes he went swimming at Roberto Clemente Park, on the Harlem River, and to get to it he passed by Cedar Playground. He said that coming back in the evening, "we'd hear this thumping sound, 'Boom, ba-boom.' I was like, 'What the hell is going on?' I ran to the park; it was Kool Herc and his crew doing his thing. And I said, 'That's what I want to do.'"

He was eight years old. Martinez pieced together equipment over the next couple of years and spent all the money he could scrape together looking for beats and building his record collection. By then other people his age and older (but not very much older) were doing the same thing. "A lot of people were catching on quick," he said later. A store called Downstairs Records, off a set of stairs leading to the subway in the Times Square area, sold used and new records that it kept by the thousands on shelves after shelves, like the dim, endless record collection of the Afterlife. Hip-hop DJs, and those who wanted to be, went through the records one by one, stopping when they found a new prospect, or a copy of a song with beats that worked beautifully but they somehow didn't already have, such as James Brown's "Hot Pants," or Johnny Pate's soundtrack to the movie *Shaft in Africa*.

I remember Downstairs Records, because in the seventies I worked in a building on West Forty-third Street between Fifth Avenue and Sixth Avenue, and I often passed through Times Square. The store snuck up on you like one of those hole-in-the-wall New York discoveries. Step out of the commuter stream, turn a narrow corner, open a door, and you were in. The LPs were on one side, 45s on the other. A few shelves on the LP side held comedy records—old, new, weird, little-known, niche-market, risqué (Moms Mabley, Gene Tracy), very risqué (Skillet, Leroy, and LaWanda), and more. I was collecting comedy, but I remember the huddles of kids flipping through the crates with the intensity of fact-checkers, whooping occasionally when they made a find. I figured they were just looking for interesting stuff and I never suspected their larger purpose. I had no idea what they were doing.

Danny Martinez, one of the frequenters of Downstairs Records, had found his life calling at the age of eight. He practiced his deejaying technique and kept getting better. When he was eleven, the teenaged-and-above guys who dominated Cedar Playground let him deejay a set. Later he said, "That was my first time in a historical place that they let me do it." Yes, Cedar Playground is a historical place, and it also deserves a plaque.

BY 1975, Flash was deejaying every night. He did jams at the 23 Playground, at East 166th and Tinton Avenue (where he only mystified his audience the first time); at St. Mary's Park, by East 149th, the heart of Gouverneur Morris territory; at the PS 63 schoolyard, on Boston Road near McKinley Square; and at other playgrounds, as well as nightclubs, in the South Bronx and sometimes in Harlem. His electrical training at Samuel Gompers put him in the forefront of people who knew how to tap into light poles. In 1976, Flash enjoyed another busy year. You may remember that 1976 was also the year in which 33,465 fires burned in the Bronx. The police let the DJs turn it all the way up and go all night. Had the South Bronx still contained the same number of people in the mid-seventies as were living there ten years before, it's possible that the authorities would not have been so lax. But given all the bad occurrences of the seventies, a loud hip-hop jam in a playground amounted to no big deal, and by then there were fewer people to object, anyway. Hip-hop in those years was like a party that got better after the guests who weren't enjoying it went home.

One night, as Flash tells it, he was deejaying at a club that held about a hundred people. It was called the Black Door; a shady promoter named Ray had found him the gig. The crowd included a thuggish and gangsterish element, some of whom were Flash's own bodyguards, a dangerous crew who stomped rival DJs for making bootleg tapes of his performances. A "stick-up artist of the first degree" who requested a song for his girlfriend stood and watched as Flash did some complicated mixing and phasing in of guitar licks. The guy then turned to her and said, "Nigga right there is like some kinda grand chess master. Only with records." The guy dubbed him "Grandmaster Flash." Sometimes a name can be a sorcerer's charm. This one, Flash said, "changed the way I saw myself for the rest of my life."

32

ANDY ROONEY, the writer and TV commentator known for his wry end segments on the CBS newsmagazine show *60 Minutes*, worked at the network's offices in midtown Manhattan. He had an apartment in the city, and weekend houses in Connecticut and upstate New York. Going and coming through the Bronx, Rooney noticed that the place seemed to be on fire. Meanwhile, traffic was speeding past on the highways as if nothing were wrong. He thought his network—Rooney had started at CBS in the late forties—should look into this. Nobody else seemed to be reporting on the Bronx fires, or even to be aware that they were happening. He went to higher-ups, and eventually the idea of doing a story reached Howard Stringer, head of the news-documentary show *CBS Reports*.

Stringer had just hired Tom Spain, an independent producer, and he passed the idea along to him. Bill Moyers, who had recently come to CBS from Public Broadcasting, agreed to be the correspondent. Moyers previously served as press secretary for President Lyndon Johnson and often did political stories. He, too, had wondered about the Bronx's ongoing incineration as he drove through while commuting to his house on Long Island. Rooney's suggestion had been to send a dozen camera crews all over the Bronx reporting on the fires that broke out in a single day. Tom Spain wanted to spend a longer time and take a more thoughtful approach. He focused on a single South Bronx firefighting crew, Battalion 19, working out of the busiest fire station in the city at the time. For about seven weeks in 1976, Spain and his cameramen followed the battalion's trucks and interviewed the firefighters, the displaced victims, and the bystanders. Sometimes the TV crew stayed in the firehouse overnight.

One of the fires they filmed burned part of a building at 1995 Davidson Avenue, in Morris Heights. A tenant of the building, an elderly woman with an Irish accent, had remained in her apartment after other tenants had left. The story as Spain assembled it looked at the plight of this Mrs. Sullivan, who had worked at the Plaza Hotel for forty-six years until her retirement. She said kids were breaking into her apartment from the fire escape and stealing her belongings and even threatening her life. When Moyers asked her, in an interview in front of the building, who these thieves were, she indicated some kids standing in the background. Afterward, with CBS's help, Mrs. Sullivan was able to move out. At the last minute, she couldn't find her cat but then she did. That provided the closest thing to a happy ending.

Other interviewees included a Black woman who was living in a building without heat or water, an outspoken Bronx police chief, a group renovating an abandoned five-story walk-up, and John T. O'Hagan, the city's fire commissioner. Plumes of black smoke, sirens, ladders up next to the sides of buildings, families weeping, and general despair painted a picture of a place in dire trouble. In a single take, Moyers added an ending that Spain did not edit out:

> Somehow our failures at home paralyze our will, and we don't approach a disaster like the death of the Bronx with the same urgency and commitment we carry to problems abroad . . . So the vice president travels to Europe and Japan, the secretary of state to the Middle East and Russia, the UN ambassador to Africa. Nobody of comparable stature comes here.

The Fire Next Door aired for the first time on *CBS Reports* on March 22, 1977. It received good reviews and went on to win dozens of national and international journalism awards. Moyers was in touch with President Jimmy Carter, because after the '76 election Moyers had done an interview with Carter that helped explain him to northern audiences. CBS sent a cassette of *The Fire Next Door* to Hamilton Jordan, Carter's advisor for domestic policy. Carter not only watched it, he played it for the members of his cabinet. *The Fire Next Door* marked the first time that the ongoing disaster in the Bronx got major national attention.

IN 1977, that wild year, New Yorkers followed the story of the city's serial killer, David Berkowitz, also known as the .44 Caliber Killer, or Son of Sam. In '76, before the media excitement grew intense, Berkowitz shot four people with a .44-caliber Bulldog Colt, wounding three and killing one. In '77, he shot nine people, killing five and wounding four. All were young. He attacked most of them as they sat in pairs in parked cars at night. Most of his victims were women with long dark hair. The taunting notes he sent to the police scared and thrilled the city when they appeared in the newspapers. He had a gift for an ironical wickedness of tone, and for evocations of evil seeping out of the cracks in the New York City sidewalks.

Four of the victims were in the northeast Bronx—two in Pelham Bay Park and two on an access road of the Bronx River Parkway. The last victim he killed, Stacy Moskowitz, a twenty-year-old secretary, was in Brooklyn. The coverage in the *Post* and the *News* seems now like the high-water moment for tabloids in New York City. In later decades, the papers' circulation has shrunk until the *Post* needs to be propped up by the Murdoch fortune and the *News* is a struggling leaflet that can be read in about ten minutes. Back in the summer of '77, the Son of Sam story was selling copies of those papers by the millions.

Meanwhile, the spread of hip-hop did not slow down. By '77, more new DJs were joining the ranks of Flash, Herc, and Bambaataa. There even were other DJs called Grandmaster. On the evening of July 13, a pair of DJs, Grandmaster Caz and DJ Disco Wiz, were playing a jam at a playground at the corner of East 183rd Street and Valentine

Avenue. The location is part of a classic Bronx landscape—on top of the ridge that the avenue runs along, and not far from the summit of Kingsbridge Avenue (formerly Break Neck Hill). The sky over the playground is both expansive and intimate, ascending upward and outward from just above the basketball hoops. Following the usual practice, Caz and Wiz had plugged into a streetlight. As they were playing at about 9:30 p.m., the streetlight went dark, and the beats stopped. Caz and Wiz looked at the other streetlights nearby; they also were dark. The DJs wondered what they had done; they had blown out a single streetlight before, but never a whole row of them. Then they noticed that every light on the block seemed to be out. In fact, no lights shone anywhere, except for a few stars, and the blinking of an airplane or two crossing the sky. The Blackout of '77 had begun.

In the humid, possibility-filled summer night, looting started almost right away. Near the Valentine Avenue playground was an electronics store called the Sound Room. While Wiz stayed with their equipment, Caz ran to the store, crawled in through a breach, and came out with a Clubman Two sound mixer, a useful addition to their setup. Amid the chaos, similar tech thefts were happening elsewhere in the borough and across the city. On the night of the Blackout, people who wanted to be DJs looted brand-new sound equipment for themselves, or else they acquired stolen mixers, turntables, amps, and speakers for cheap from other looters. Two turntables and a mixer, entry-level necessities, had cost more than most would-be DJs could afford. Now even big systems looted from clubs could be found at low prices.

The Great Blackout of '77 infused new equipment, and many more DJs, into the hip-hop scene, and brought it closer to the level of a popular movement. As one historian of hip-hop wrote, "A formerly exclusive scene was suddenly democratic." Notions of right and wrong, or of sympathy for storeowners who might have lost everything, did not seem to enter the picture. This major transfer of capital and technology downward to poor and young people, and its artistically enlivening effect, received little coverage at the time.

Son of Sam killed Stacy Moskowitz and wounded her companion, Robert Violante, seventeen days after the Blackout. While stalking them he had left his car parked by a hydrant, and the ticket he got led to his arrest eleven days later. Detectives tracked him to his apartment in Yonkers, where they found abundant evidence, including the .44-caliber Bulldog Colt used in the shootings. Berkowitz made a confession, which was itself copy-worthy and deranged. The bushy-haired, chubby-cheeked postal worker, twenty-four years old, said that a satanic dog belonging to his neighbor, Sam Carr, had told him to commit the murders. That reference explained the name Son of Sam. Berkowitz also said that the press was making him out to be "some kind of a no-goodnik," and added, "That dog has ruined my life." The tabloid headlines talked of nothing but Berkowitz for weeks. Police let news photographers into his apartment, the condition of which supposedly showed how crazy he was. In its single-guy disarray it looked like anybody's, like mine.

In 1977, all of New York City and scores of millions across the country knew about the Son of Sam killings. Only a small number knew about hip-hop. (The first articles about hip-hop, in *Billboard* and the *Amsterdam News*, would not come out until 1979.) Reporters digging into Berkowitz's past discovered he had a Bronx connection. His adoptive parents, Pearl and Nathan Berkowitz, had moved to Co-Op City in 1967, and he lived there for four years. The development prized for its low crime rate nonetheless did house this serial killer during his adolescence, and he committed some of his practice crimes (stabbings) near it. Today Son of Sam is a footnote and hip-hop is all over the world.

PRESIDENT JIMMY CARTER'S famous drive-through visit to the South Bronx happened just after that eventful summer. He had been president for less than a year when he came to New York on October 4 to address the General Assembly at the United Nations. Ed Koch, the U.S. congressman for downtown Manhattan, met the president as he landed at a Wall Street heliport, and Koch gave him a letter accusing him of abandoning Israel in the recent negotiations with the Palestinians. This awkward surprise made Carter so angry that his staff disinvited Koch from riding with him in his limousine up to the UN and canceled a later meeting between Carter and Koch and other New York City Democrats. Strange how such distant things impinge—the animus between Koch and Carter would have negative consequences for the Bronx.

At the UN, the president spoke to a full house, with standees along the aisles. For his main point, he announced that the United States was prepared to reduce its nuclear arsenal by as much as 50 percent if the Soviet Union would do the same. He also said that the United States would use nuclear weapons only in self-defense (a statement perhaps more complicated than it seemed, because it didn't rule out using the weapons to defend an ally when the United States itself had not been attacked). Carter also said, perhaps in reference to Koch's letter, "The commitment of the U.S. to Israel's security is unquestioned."

He spent that night in the UN Plaza Hotel and made his visit to the Bronx the next morning. Nothing in the papers on October 4 or 5 had hinted that the trip was in the offing. The president rode in a cream-colored limousine with Patricia Roberts Harris, his secretary of housing and urban development, whose office had laid out the route, and with Abe Beame, the mayor. Beame had recently come in third in the Democratic mayoral primary, and so would be out of office soon. It's a mystery why Ed Koch, who had come in first, was not included in the group. Maybe Carter was still angry about the ambush of the day before. In 1977, Koch was the city's future and his absence looked unpromising for any immediate Bronx solutions or relief.

Motorcycle cops preceded and followed the motorcade, while three helicopters flew overhead. The police had been given only twenty minutes' notice. The sight of the president surprised bystanders. People yelled, "Give me a job, Jimmy!" and "We need money!" Winos waved bottles in paper bags at him. Along parts of the route, the public housing high-rises, such as the Gouverneur Morris Houses, were some of the only unburned buildings still standing. Carter made two stops but talked to local people only at the first one. *The Fire Next Door* had found some hope for the future in an organization called the People's Development Corporation (PDC), consisting of enterprising locals who were fixing up abandoned buildings on their own, investing their sweat equity and having some success. A man named Ramon Rueda led the PDC. The motorcade stopped at 1186 Washington Avenue, an apartment building in Morrisania that Rueda and others were in the process of restoring. Carter's going there suggests that *The Fire Next Door* had actually inspired his whole Bronx trip.

In the TV news coverage, Carter is standing on the street by the building entry, smiling his big, rectangular smile, looking up at Rueda, a thin young man with an afro, who is on the stoop. Rueda thanks him for coming and says, "We need money, Carter!" The president and Secretary Harris, who is wearing a dramatic burgundy hat, walk along the street. Rueda was thrilled that Carter visited him. He told the *Daily News* that Carter was "a beautiful man." Funding that Rueda's group had used so far had come by way of CETA—the Comprehensive Employment and Training Act—a federal program that still provided some assistance for city improvement, despite the anti-urban mood prevailing at the federal level since the Nixon administration. Referring to the devastation, Carter asked Harris, "Most of this occurred in the last five years after Nixon cut off the urban renewal funds?" She said yes.

From 1186 Washington, the motorcade continued its slow zigzag route to its second stop, near the corner of Charlotte Street and Boston Road, where Carter walked in the rubble and looked stunned. The *Times* quoted him as saying to Harris, "See which areas can still be salvaged. Maybe we can create a recreation area and turn it around. Get a map and show me what could be done." That downbeat, post-apocalyptic tone characterized the coverage. There were plenty of reasons for the dark mood; but with this trip, Carter had answered Bill Moyer's challenge: "Nobody of comparable stature comes here." He had also shown he was sensitive to what critics had said about him after the Blackout. Vernon E. Jordan, then the executive director of the Urban League, had said that Carter never visited places like the South Bronx and showed no concern for the cities or the poor. Nobody made a big noise praising Carter for his bold and unrewarding (to himself) move. Over time, it would shape up as one of those good deeds that don't go unpunished.

Jimmy Breslin, the *Daily News* columnist, followed the Carter motorcade that day. Breslin had outdone all other New York City tabloid journalists in '77. Before Berkowitz's arrest, the killer had written a letter to him, and Breslin had offered to be a go-between if he would turn himself in. The *Daily News* editions with press runs of two-million-plus in the summer of that year often featured a Breslin column bannered on the front page. One evening, back then, I happened to see the columnist himself strolling through Times Square with a small entourage. He had the air of a man totally at ease and on top of the city. He wore a long, toga-like raincoat that draped his stocky form to below the knees. As he went by, speaking to his companions and gesturing, he could have been Cicero strolling in the Forum.

Breslin's reportorial technique was to go where the pack did not. Fourteen years earlier, after the Kennedy assassination, while everybody else was clustering in Washington for the funeral, Breslin went to Arlington National Cemetery and found the gravedigger who was digging Kennedy's grave. Now, following after Carter in the Bronx, Breslin waited for the limo to go by—"The motorcade rolled along the stone desert"—and talked to people in its wake. He asked a little boy along the route why he was not in school. The boy said he stayed home because the teacher cursed at the kids. Breslin asked what the teacher said. The boy answered, "She says, 'Get the ____ out of here.'" Other kids he talked to were truant for other reasons. He interviewed "two women in dungaree suits" who made a few comments about the event and walked off. He ended the piece: "and now, at noon of the day that Jimmy Carter came to Fox Street, the charred street . . . was completely empty."

ON A LATE fall day, I walked the Carter route for maybe the eighth time. Approaching on the Third Avenue Bridge, I saw even more new buildings under construction than I'd seen just a few months before. The sound of metal-on-metal hammering came from high-rise frameworks rising all along the Bronx side of the Harlem River. At the intersection of Third Avenue and East 135th Street, a crane held a four-story-high pile driver that was lifting and pounding as it shook the ground for blocks in all directions. One of the workmen told me it was driving in a support column for a new high-rise apartment building.

The Carter motorcade turned left on East 138th Street, then right on the Grand Concourse. As I passed those corners, the hammering and general construction noise, and the beeping of machinery backing up, continued all around. I passed a gray dumpster with "Liberty Ashes" stenciled on its side in black. A young man was vacuuming his car outside a car wash across the street from a building under construction at 322 Grand Concourse. He was bearded and heavyset and he chewed a wad of bright green gum. The sound system in the car, whose doors were open, played a rap song loud and percussive enough to shout down the racket. I asked him which rapper that was. He said it was Ghost Da God, a Brooklyn-born African rapper who raps in English. I introduced myself, and the young man gave his name as Che Che and said he came from Cameroon, works in construction, and hopes to make enough money to return to Cameroon, "the best, most beautiful place in the world."

Under the aerial passageway at Hostos Community College, two hard hats were unloading thin metal beams from a truck. One said to the other, "So what made him change? Did he call somebody?" The other answered, "I don't know. Maybe he wants to be nice to me." The Central Post Office, at Grand Concourse and East 149th Street, appeared to be still empty when I peered through the windows of the locked front doors. The socialist-realist murals in the former lobby dispensed their faded idealism into the shuttered gloom. A woman passing by told me, "That's closed," and led me around to a side door, where a whole new post office, with eight service windows, had been installed farther back in the building. So maybe the great old Central P.O. wasn't going to be demobilized, after all.

The windows of the art deco apartment buildings along the Grand Concourse extended in straight lines, window after window, into the distance. Rows of pigeons sat on the edges of the roofs, and water tanks distributed themselves along the boundaries where buildings' profiles met the sky. Some of the tanks had rectangular white cell phone relays spackled onto them like Cubistic afterthoughts. Here and there among the pigeons, small white satellite disks leaned out and craned their metal necks skyward. A woman walked by shouldering a roll of Christmas wrapping paper like an axe. A cold wind blew,

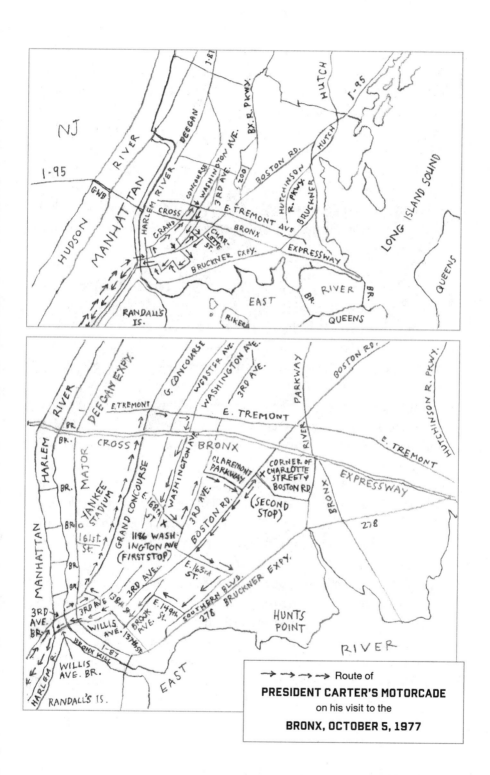

→ → → → Route of
PRESIDENT CARTER'S MOTORCADE
on his visit to the
BRONX, OCTOBER 5, 1977

and I bought a scarf from a street vendor. A larger than usual shrine, with a hundred or more lit candles, sheltered under a clear plastic tarp in front of 1645 Grand Concourse. In color-Xeroxed photos and handwritten testimonials, it remembered somebody named Nene. A hundred and forty-six people were murdered in the Bronx in 2021, 35 percent more than in 2020.

Trash and fallen plane tree leaves covered the ground at the intersection of Tremont and Webster. The sign saying GUNS—AMMUNITION was still over the door at Frank's Sport Shop, at Tremont and Park. I took a right from Tremont onto Washington Avenue, as Carter and company had done. White-and-blue NYPD buses were parked among the pillars holding up the Cross Bronx Expressway where Washington Avenue crossed under it. At East 174th Street and Washington, a former synagogue with Hebrew letters on its front is now the home of Iglesia Christiana El Faro, whose pastor is Reverendo Leopoldo Briscoe. Across from the newish three-story row houses at 1538–1524 Washington, a willow tree rose four stories high in a side lot. On that chilly day, December 10, the willow's bouffant foliage was still luxuriantly green. In front of the Gouverneur Morris Houses, a guy in a Carhartt ski cap was leaning on the fence by the project's sign. I asked him if he knew who Gouverneur Morris was, and he laughed. "Now, don't start me lyin'," he said.

At 1186 Washington, I stood where Carter had stood when he talked to Ramon Rueda on the stoop above him. The building looked to be in good condition. A UPS delivery person came to the door with a package, and a man got out of a car parked at the curb and let her in. The man had on a baseball cap and a jacket, both of which said, "Paper Plane." He told me he lived in the building, and it was a nice place, intended for tenants who have Section 8 housing. (Section 8 is a federal program that pays landlords the difference between market-rate rentals and what low-income tenants who meet certain qualifications can pay; more on it later.) I asked if he knew that Ramon Rueda and the People's Development Corp. had fixed up the building, and that President Carter had visited here. He did not. This onetime lonely outpost of hope from back in 1977 is now just another building on a residential street.

Dreadlocked West Indian workmen in hard hats and green vests smoked reeking marijuana on their lunch break in Rev. Lena Irons Unity Park nearby and talked derisively about scab workers at the building next to the one they were renovating. Farther along on the Carter route, in front of a storefront mosque, forty or fifty men sat on a tarpaulin on the sidewalk and listened to a sermon relayed from inside by a loudspeaker. At the corner of Charlotte Street and Boston Road, where Carter got out for the second time, and where he walked around and seemed to mourn, Willie Hemanns, who owns the ranch-style house that's there now, and whom I sometimes talk to, was not out in his yard.

This corner drew a lot of attention after Carter's visit. The urban planning department of Hunter College led bus tours to see it, tickets eight dollars per person. A city councilman brought a delegation of Russians, including members of the Bolshoi Ballet, and announced that the Bronx was formally requesting foreign aid. Teddy Kennedy came here when he was running against Carter for the Democratic presidential nomination in March 1980. Worse, from a Democratic point of view, Ronald Reagan made a trip to Charlotte Street when he campaigned against Carter for president that summer. Reagan got out of his limo and confronted a group of locals who told him to go home. He gestured at the unchanged rubble all around and said that the Democrats promise to help but do nothing. Over the crowd's jeers he shouted that the government couldn't just wave a magic wand and make things better. His point rang truer than he knew. The city government's reliance on the top-down management theories of the Rand Corporation—and, for that matter, on the mega-plan of the Regional Plan Association superimposed from above—had assisted in the ruination.

If Koch, as mayor, and President Carter had been on better terms, the two might have collaborated on a plan for Charlotte Street. Fixing the place up, after Carter's dramatic visit, was essential for his image, and not doing so left the place wide open for the Republicans and Reagan. A 732-unit housing development had been proposed for the site in the year after Carter came, but the city's Board of Estimate voted it down. Koch did not like Borough President Herman Badillo and did not lobby hard for the project. Carter needed a unified Democratic response between himself and Koch and Badillo, and he did not have it.

The first time I walked this route, six or seven years ago, I didn't know many of the important sites along it. Now, finishing it out, I went by the PS 63 Playground, where Grandmaster Flash played jams in the early days (kids from the school now were lining up in the playground); Morris High School (the teachers' parking lot was full at midday); a bodega at the corner of East 166th Street and Boston Road (a sixteen-year-old boy was shot to death in its doorway in 2020—now the place was closed down); the Kelly Street building where Sonia Sotomayor lived as a baby; Father Gigante Plaza, with its statues of Father Louis Gigante, honored for building thousands of units of housing in the southeast Bronx; the corner of East 149th and Southern Boulevard, where the Häagen-Dazs factory used to be (now replaced by a six-story, many-unit apartment building); the corner of East 142nd and Brook Avenue, near where the Piccirilli Brothers' sculpture studio was; and Brook Park, at the corner of East 141st, where I saw my second enormous, fully green willow tree of the day. And thence to East 137th Street, to Willis Avenue and the Willis Avenue Bridge, which the Carter motorcade took as it exited the borough.

The sun descended behind the skyline of Manhattan. Its glowing aftereffect of mare's-tail clouds spread from the center in a pinwheel configuration across the pale sky. The closer Manhattan buildings were reddish brown, and the silhouettes of those farther in the distance dimmed to blue-gray. The surface of the Harlem River lay dead calm, flat, and shiny. According to my phone, the route I'd just walked covered 9.9 miles. The whole way, I had seen maybe two abandoned houses, no obviously abandoned buildings, and not one vehicle or structure that was burned out. From the viewpoint of anybody who had ridden in the Carter motorcade back in 1977, the transformation would look like a miracle; on the other hand, from the viewpoint of Bronx residents who now feel in danger of being priced out, maybe not.

33

SONIA SOTOMAYOR WATCHED on television as Carter's motorcade passed the building where she once lived with her parents and grandmother on Kelly Street. By October 1977, she had graduated from Princeton, married her high school sweetheart, and entered Yale Law School. The Bronx was not yet far enough in her past that she saw it the way others did; now, looking at it on TV, she realized that the decay had been invisible to her. For the cameras following Carter, the Bronx consisted of ruins; as she had known it, it functioned acceptably, providing jobs for her parents, housing for the family, and educations for her and her brother. As she watched the coverage, she understood that she was from a place where many people did not get justice, and for justice to work it had to be for everybody.

Sotomayor never forgot the Bronx, and she returns to it sometimes, though her parents are no longer living and her brother, a doctor, moved away. In 2016, when I was writing a short article about the Bronx Defenders, a nonprofit that provides legal counsel for defendants who can't afford it themselves, I met her at that organization's headquarters on East 161st Street. As I remember Justice Sotomayor that day, she is wearing her courtroom black robes. Of course, that has to be wrong. More likely, she wore a tailored jacket and skirt, and her gravitas is what makes me supply the robes. Every judge I've ever met possessed an aura, and hers is powerful. It causes people to turn toward her and raise their faces.

An audience mostly of Bronx high school and college students had gathered to hear her give a short speech. In a Bronx Defenders assembly room, she told them about her childhood, and about her mother, Celina, who supported the family after Sotomayor's father died. Celina worked as a nurse in the old Prospect Hospital for thirty-five years. The justice remembered living in buildings with addicts in the stairwells and discarded needles on the stairs, and traveling around the Bronx by herself as a girl to see doctors for her diabetes. She also said it was important that the students look beyond the Bronx, and know that they are part of America, and what a big and amazing country it is. She described her confirmation hearing for the Supreme Court as one of the most eye-opening experiences of her life. As part of the process, she had met individually with senators, some from western states she knew almost nothing about, and they explained their important local issues, such as water rights, a subject she had never given any thought to. In the East, we've got enough water, so that kind of question usually does not come up, she said. She told the students it was wonderful to be from the Bronx, but they were also Americans, and they should learn all they could about their country.

During the questions period, someone asked her if there was any fellow justice she could not stand. A voice yelled, "Scalia!" and people laughed. Justice Sotomayor firmly shut the question down. She said she respects and likes all her fellow justices and is honored to be among them. I admired her seriousness even more a few days later, when Justice Scalia suffered a sudden heart attack and died. Had she used the question to play to the crowd, in retrospect she could have been made to look bad.

After the event, she had dinner in another room with a dozen or so students and asked them about themselves, going around the table. I waited near the door as she was leaving. Through a member of the Bronx Defenders, I asked if I could ask a question, and the justice granted me just one. I asked, "Who was the first Supreme Court justice you ever saw in person?" She stopped, thought, and said, "What an interesting question." Maybe she was only being polite, but that remains one of the best moments in my years as a reporter. She put her left hand on her chin, held her left elbow in her right hand, and pondered. To have caused deliberation in the mind of a justice of the U.S. Supreme Court—I was thrilled. After a few moments, she gave me an answer but said it would have to be off the record.

Walking a Sotomayor route that includes some of the sites she mentions in *My Beloved World*, her memoir, I could see more clearly how things turned out as they did for her family. The building at 940 Kelly Street, where her father's mother lived, and where her parents were living when she was born, is part of a famous block called Banana Kelly because of the way the street curves. The sky overhead curves, too, like the sky above a bend in a tree-lined river. (Sholem Aleichem had lived about a block away on Kelly, forty-some years before; Colin Powell and Clifford Odets, the playwright, also lived on Kelly.)

When I found the building one morning, a woman was coming out of it. I asked if she had time for a question, and eerily reprising the justice, she said I could ask just one because she was on her way to the train. I asked if she knew that Justice Sonia Sotomayor once lived in that building and she said, "Really? I *didn't* know that. That's great!" Then she hurried off. Later, I met the building's landlord, a man named Daniel Madrigal. He also did not know that Sotomayor and her family had lived there. I am always going on about plaques, and Madrigal said he would think about putting one on 940 Kelly Street, but he hasn't done so yet. In the early 1970s, fifteen years after Sotomayor's family had left, many of the buildings on Kelly Street burned. After that low point, Banana Kelly would become one of the most important names in the Bronx's revival, as I will describe.

Leaving the neighborhood for the Bronxdale Houses when Sotomayor was three, the family went from a paradise Bronx situation, with a community of family and friends all around, to what she describes as "exile in a wilderness of concrete and vacant lots." Her mother insisted on the move, but by taking her father, Juan Luis (Juli) Sotomayor, away from where he grew up, it may have shortened his life. The distance between the two places, although less than two miles on the map, is immense. Juli almost never drove, and to walk from one to the other you must cross the Bruckner Expressway–Bronx River Parkway intersection, the Bronx River, and then the Sheridan Expressway. You go along winding pedestrian corridors, and over footbridges, and next to the squashed-pigeon zone of Bruckner Boulevard, traversing another of the parts of the Bronx where the engine noise simply howls. Juli, a good worker who held down jobs in a mannequin factory and a radiator factory, had been a functioning alcoholic before the move, but he drank even more after it, and died when his daughter was nine.

The Bronxdale Houses are now the Sotomayor Houses, and the Justice Sonia Sotomayor Community Center is nearby. It's not a great neighborhood, with trash scattered around, and plastic bags swirling in the courtyards and stuck in the trees, and shootings that destroy young people and replace them with the sad, transient shrines that some parts of the Bronx see too often.

For elementary school, Sotomayor walked from the Bronxdale Houses to Blessed Sacrament, a parochial school a few blocks away. She remembered it afterward with respect but little affection, and willingly put its stern nuns behind her. She then got accepted at Cardinal Spellman High School. During her freshman year, her mother moved the family to Co-op City, giving the lie to Borough President Badillo's assertion that Puerto Ricans didn't know about co-op apartments and wouldn't buy them. (Celina Sotomayor could afford the $5,000 buy-in price because of a bequest from a friend who had been the family's saintly neighborhood doctor when they lived on Kelly Street.) Cardinal Spellman High School is in the northeast Bronx, and to get there from the Bronxdale Houses requires more than an hour by subway and bus; but from Co-op City, Sotomayor could walk to school.

One day I started out from her former building, at 100 Dreiser Loop, and did that walk myself. First you pass through the Co-op City grounds, following winding footpaths among high-rises around whose corners the wind swirls, and you continue past Harry S. Truman High School. Then you cross traffic-filled Baychester Avenue and go up a set of fenced-in steps to a fenced-in walkway above the northbound lanes of I-95. Another fenced-in walkway that borders an exit ramp takes you over the southbound lanes of I-95. The cars and trucks are roaring below you, three lanes in each direction.

Beyond the interstate, you go uphill on Thomas E. Brown Avenue (also called Baychester Avenue) to the massive, multiwindowed high school, which commands the top of the slope. The distance, door to door, is 1.2 miles. I had chosen an afternoon in late February, and the weather was coming from the east, off Long Island Sound. On the walkways above the interstate traffic the chilly ocean wind got under my collar, and as I climbed the avenue the wind wanted to push me back down. For Sotomayor, making that trek was preferable to a long journey by subway and bus, but it must have been a challenge on a dark winter morning. In former times, we used to read about the hikes that various great men had to make in their childhoods to get to school. I propose that Justice Sotomayor's interstate-highway-traversing walk from Co-op City to Cardinal Spellman High School is a modern-day equivalent.

The discovery that she was diabetic came when she was eight. Partly because her father's hands shook, she learned how to administer the shots of insulin to herself. High-quality monitoring and treatment for the disease was available in the Bronx. The Albert Einstein College of Medicine, which did important research into juvenile diabetes, ran a clinic at Jacobi Medical Center, the hospital connected to the college, in the north-central part of the Bronx. Going to and from it also required bus rides. Sotomayor said she acquired more discipline from having diabetes than she ever learned from the nuns. While managing her condition, she also ranked in the top ten in her class at Cardinal Spellman, starred on the forensics team, and participated in student government. She had part-time jobs during the school year, and full-time summer jobs—at the Zaro's Bakery near Co-Op City, a good, still-surviving Bronx company, and at a clothing store called United Bargains, on Southern Boulevard, which paid her a dollar an hour, less than minimum wage.

Her titi (aunt) Carmen also worked at United Bargains, and got her the job, some of which consisted of catching junkies shoplifting and persuading them to give the stuff back. This was in the 41st Precinct, the infamous "Fort Apache," during some of its worst days. After work, Sotomayor stayed at her aunt's house overnight. When she and Titi Carmen had shut the security gates and locked up, policemen would come and walk them home. Sotomayor read *Lord of the Flies* that summer, an apt time and place for it, and the combined experience disturbed her and made her long for the rule of law.

In her senior year, she applied to Harvard, Princeton, Yale, and Columbia, and got into all of them. When she made on-campus visits to decide which to go to, she disliked Harvard (Radcliffe) almost on sight, Columbia seemed too close to home, and the city of New Haven resembled the Bronx. Plus, the Yale campus she saw was exulting and raging with anti–Vietnam War protests, which she understood the point of, but which didn't seem connected to her purpose in going to college. The Princeton campus, by contrast, bloomed, all green and manicured and lovely, as it cannily does every spring to charm prospective students. When she left for Princeton in the fall, her story moves beyond the Bronx.

Her mother was a celebrity at Prospect Hospital after word got around that her daughter was going to Princeton. Orderlies, nurses, doctors, even the owner of the hospital sought her out and congratulated her. Celina's life had taken a big turnaround. The death of her husband had affected her so profoundly that she collapsed in grief and could hardly function, but then she had roused herself and gone on, bringing up her children as a widow with a small income, and enrolling at Hostos Community College to earn an advanced nursing degree. She found the courses hard, and the tests caused her terrible anxiety. But she had a talent for nursing, and gentle hands. She persisted, did well on the tests, and received her certification as a registered nurse during her daughter's first year in college.

Eventually Celina remarried. By then her daughter had been appointed a judge of the U.S. District Court, Southern District of New York, and after six years there, had moved up to the U.S. Court of Appeals of the Second Circuit. Judge Sotomayor's first official act in that job was to perform Celina's wedding ceremony. Nine years after that, Celina held the Bible when Chief Justice John Roberts swore in her daughter as a justice of the Supreme Court. Celina lived to be ninety-four, passing away in 2021.

NOW, TO SWING BACK to Banana Kelly: The name, one of the Bronx's most illustrious, does not appear on any street sign. Its existence has always been folkloric—you just knew that the curved part of Kelly Street was called Banana Kelly, in the same way that one of the un-curved blocks was called Straight Kelly, and another block, where lots of people from the South lived, was called Country Kelly. Following this pattern, Dawson Street, nearby, was the home of tough guys on one block, and of well-behaved middle-class guys on another: hence the well-behaved block's folkloric name, Sissy Dawson. (There was also a block called Sissy Kelly.) That was how the neighborhoods lived, in their variety and connections among their residents; but the South Bronx's distress did not spare many places. As buildings all over began to be abandoned by their landlords, and as the buildings' maintenance, then heat, then electricity, then water, then any evidence of owner-ship at all disappeared, tenants sometimes took over and managed the properties themselves. Ad hoc tenant associations were formed by the dozens throughout the beleaguered parts of the Bronx. This trend had been ongoing by the time of Carter's drive-through. It would provide roots for the Bronx's revival.

Frank Potts, who lived on Banana Kelly, didn't have to worry about an absentee landlord, because he owned his building, as well as five others nearby. He had come up from Mississippi in the Great Migration. Nobody could believe how hard Frank Potts worked—loading trucks at the Hunts Point Market before dawn, then doing maintenance on other people's buildings before coming back to work on his own. He put in fifteen-hour days and sometimes fell asleep on his front steps in the evenings. The fires, as they moved through the neighborhood, destroyed building after building, eventually taking about 70 percent of the housing stock, and not sparing Kelly Street. Frank and his son, Leon, thought about how to keep their own buildings unburned and in one piece. Other longtime residents were moving out; the Potts family did not move or want to move.

Harry DeRienzo grew up on Long Island, where his parents had relocated from Brooklyn during the mostly white postwar shift to the suburbs. After graduating from Manhattan College, in Fieldston, DeRienzo took a job as a tutor and social worker at the Casita Maria Settlement House, on Simpson Street, three blocks from Banana Kelly. The settlement house movement goes back to the nineteenth century, and its purpose was (and is) to get immigrants settled in their new country. Casita Maria staff didn't usually live in the neighborhood, but DeRienzo wanted to experience the area full-time, not just nine to five, so he rented an apartment nearby on Fox Street. Because he was around after work, he got the idea of keeping the gym at Casita Maria open at night so kids and young adults could play basketball and hang out. By doing that he met a lot of people, including Leon and Frank Potts.

After basketball, they would sit around and smoke cigarettes and drink beer and talk about the neighborhood. Near one end of the Banana Kelly block, three abandoned buildings presented the kind of stripped, trash-filled hazards that could catch fire and endanger other buildings. A fire had burned part of one of the three buildings already, and it was already scheduled for demolition; the neighborhood did not want any Banana Kelly buildings to be torn down. The Pottses, DeRienzo, and their neighbors Eric Wingate and Robert Foster decided to act. On their own they set about to gut the three hulks and rebuild their interiors. The group had almost no money. (DeRienzo's salary at Casita Maria was seven thousand dollars a year.)

They knew about Ramon Rueda and his work at 1186 Washington. Although this was 1976, a year before the Carter drive-through, Rueda and the People's Development Corporation already had a reputation in East Harlem and the Bronx. Rueda simply took over the buildings that the PDC intended to rehab and claimed them by squatters' rights. Following his example, the Pottses and DiRienzo and friends took over the three abandoned buildings. Smashing down the cinder blocks that sealed off the front doors gave the group a rebellious thrill, like they were finally taking a stand. Inside, an incredible amount of trash and chaos had accumulated. Frank Potts contributed a dumpster, and with their first funding of nine hundred dollars from a city self-help award program, the group acquired nine dumpsters more.

The buildings in question were 936, 940, and 944 Kelly. The middle building, 940, happened to be the one in which the Sotomayor family had lived. That would have meant little to the rehabilitators then, but might interest them now.

Frances Potts, Leon's sister, said the nonprofit they set up should be called Banana Kelly, and the others agreed. A lawyer working pro bono helped them create a nonprofit, the Banana Kelly Community Improvement Association, Inc., which has now been in existence for almost half a century. Its motto is "Don't Move, Improve."

Most of the group were in their early-to-mid-twenties when they started, and they learned demolition and construction as they went along. In the building at 944 Kelly, a fire that started in the basement wiring had burned upward to the roof. The fire department extinguished it, apparently, but embers in the basement continued to smolder, traveling through the walls until they hollowed out the support structure. One day DeRienzo and Robert Foster were on the third floor when they heard a sound like a gunshot and noticed that the wall in front of them was an inch below the ceiling. Other Banana Kelly people were also working in the building. DeRienzo and Foster got everybody out and went onto the street to see how it looked from the outside. The building seemed okay. They were on the front steps about to go back in when the entire interior—all four floors—collapsed with a roar into the basement. Dust blasted out the front door and from all sides, and spread for blocks around. The rehab team had narrowly escaped what could have been a multifatality event.

In 1979, through a special program that the city created with federal money after Carter's visit, Banana Kelly, Inc., received financing for the rehabs. An actual bank (Chemical Bank, later shorn of its name in a merger) even got involved. Work proceeded, and the buildings were ready for full occupation by 1982. The bureaucracy of making the apartments into co-ops proved too expensive, for complicated reasons, so Banana Kelly, Inc., found a way around that by arranging for residents to belong to a nonprofit membership corporation. The units soon filled up, and the residents themselves operated and managed the buildings.

Before the city's finances got tight and edged toward desperate, landlords could go four or five years without paying their property taxes. The city let them slide, indulging real estate interests, as it is wont to do. Then in 1976, as a fiscal measure, it changed its policy and began confiscating buildings that had been in tax arrears for only one year. In the Bronx (and elsewhere in the city), thousands of landlords simply walked away. They did not have to worry about being sued for back taxes. The city knew how elusive landlords could be, and how expensive it was to sue them, so rather than going after them *in persona*, the city sued *in rem*—that is, it sued the *rem*, the "thing" for which the taxes were owed. By this route, the city ended up taking possession of tens of thousands of what were referred to as *in rem* buildings.

We recall that Roger Starr, the champion of planned shrinkage, hoped the residents of the South Bronx would go away, and he approved of the closing of firehouses and the removal of other city services to induce them to do so. We also recall that in one of those remarkable pieces of counterintuitiveness with which government sometimes outdoes itself, Roger Starr was made head of the Housing Development Administration (HDA) under Mayor Beame. In that capacity Starr ruled over the creation of new public housing. From a certain perspective, the match worked perfectly—the city did not have any money to give him, and Starr did not want to build any public housing. He did, however, have access to $300 million in federal funds left over from before Nixon got the feds out of urban development. But using that money would have gone against his principles, too, so the $300 million remained unspent.

Then Koch replaces Beame, and Starr leaves HDA. Now the city has thousands of *in rem* buildings on its hands and no structure in place for rehabbing or managing them. It also has $300 million in unspent federal money that can be used only for housing. The city is in the middle of trying to avoid bankruptcy, and no longer even controls its own finances, that authority having been yielded to the state of New York, in the shape of the Municipal Assistance Corporation (Big MAC). The solution made sense: connect the *in rem* buildings with a pool of potential managers, in the form of the tenant groups and other organizations that had sprung up among the residents; then give those local entities some of the unspent federal money to fix up and manage some of those buildings.

The Banana Kelly Community Improvement Association, Inc., which started with a name, some willing hands, and a dumpster, now occupied a strategic position. It had proved itself by occupying three abandoned buildings for rehab. In recognition, the city gave Banana Kelly, Inc., ownership of three *in rem* buildings. Later it would give them dozens more. In 1979, Harry DeRienzo became the executive director of Banana Kelly, and by 1990, the nonprofit was managing more than two thousand housing units in the South Bronx and employing 125 people, not including building supers and maintenance workers. A similar transformation, though usually at smaller scale, came to other community-based groups. Across the South Bronx, rental-housing management changed from being mostly an absentee and for-profit business plagued with slumlords, to being partly an on-site, nonprofit business free of them. Many of the old for-profit buildings had burned down after standing for fifty or sixty years. Some of the nonprofit buildings of a later era have now been standing for almost fifty years in their turn; long may they survive.

FIRE REMAINS A CURSE in the Bronx. On January 9, 2022, as I was writing the above, one of the worst fires in the city's history killed seventeen people in a nineteen-story apartment building at 333 East 181st Street, between the Grand Concourse and Webster Avenue. All the victims died of smoke inhalation. They all were immigrants from Gambia or U.S.-born children of immigrants from Gambia (eight were children). The fire happened on a Sunday morning. Fire trucks arrived in three minutes, but residents who ran out into the smoke-filled halls and stairways suffocated almost instantly, before they could be rescued.

The smoke came from a fire that started in the wiring of a space heater. In parts of the Bronx, as in many low-income places, the heating is not good. This is obvious to anyone who sees the tractor-trailer-mounted mobile boiler systems that sit at the curbs outside buildings around the borough. Insulation-wrapped ducts connect these boilers to the buildings as a kind of life support for the buildings' own out-of-service boilers, and though the mobile units are temporary, they seem to persist from one year to the next. When people don't get central heat, they use space heaters, and space heaters sometimes catch on fire. The number of dwelling fires tends to go up in the winter.

An even worse Bronx fire had happened about thirty-two years before, on March 25, 1990, when an arsonist killed eighty-seven people in the Happy Land Disco at 1959 Southern Boulevard. Those victims, too, came from an immigrant community—Garifuans from Honduras. The Happy Land fire was, at that time, the worst mass murder in U.S. history (in 2017, after the Las Vegas shootings, it became the second worst). To have such a record of fire fatalities, and more deaths added to it annually, is a grievous weight for the Bronx. The Happy Land Disco was torn down, and a tax-preparer's office now occupies the site. From there to the apartment building at 333 East 181st Street is less than a mile and a half.

When I passed by 333 East 181st a few days after the fire, the building appeared to be untouched. Only by looking again could you see that plywood had replaced the glass where people had smashed out their windows trying to get air or escape. At folding tables by the entry, donors had left heaps of warm clothes. In a common room on the first floor, a meeting appeared to be in session. A mailman went into the lobby door carrying several packages. At the curb, big letters on a green Servpro van proclaimed that the company cleaned damage from fire and water; Servpro's motto is "Like it never even happened."

On the fence of a school up the street, mourners had posted photos of the victims, along with stuffed animals, flowers, and handwritten messages. Many of the items had been attached to the fence with white plastic zip ties, whose long ends stuck out on the other side of the fence like arrows through the back of a target. Surrounded by a circle of flowers was a quotation from the Qur'an:

Give good tidings to the patient, who, when disaster strikes them, say, "Indeed, we belong to Allah, and indeed to him we are returning."

34

IN 1978, GRANDMASTER FLASH performed a hip-hop concert in the
cafeteria of the Bronx High School of Science. That high school has
produced eight Nobel Prize–winning scientists, more than most countries. Because it hosted Flash, it also gets a mention as a hip-hop early
appreciator. In '78, hip-hop had not yet gone national, or even regional; only recently had it established itself on the Bronx club scene.
A music entrepreneur, Sal Abbatiello, who ran a club at East 167th
Street and Jerome Avenue called The Disco Fever, had begun to book
Flash and his fronting DJs every Tuesday night. When he started at
the club, Flash was Grandmaster Flash and the Furious Three. Later
his three DJs would increase to five.

If hip-hop had penetrated that far in the city, soon it would be
everywhere. For the next four years, its visionary hitmaker was a
woman named Sylvia Robinson. In the fifties, she had recorded some
R&B hits as part of Mickey & Sylvia, a duo whose single "Love Is
Strange" reached number one on the R&B charts. For a while, she presided at a club, Sylvia's Blue Morocco, on Boston Road in the Bronx.
In the late seventies, she founded Sugar Hill Records with her husband, Joey Robinson. Its studio was in Englewood, New Jersey, the
suburb where they lived.

By the late seventies, most well-known hip-hop DJs had fronting MCs. Sylvia Robinson believed the MCs' rhymes could be made into Top 40 hits. Hip-hop music did not have any presence on the radio. The idea that you could somehow reduce a hip-hop jam to the standard few minutes of a pop single seemed unlikely, but the Robinsons did not try to do that. They put together a pick-up group of three unknown rappers they called the Sugar Hill Gang and made a twelve-inch record, "Rapper's Delight," that contained fifteen minutes of rhyming, set to the beat of a remixed hit, "Good Times," by Chic. When "Rapper's Delight" came out in August 1979, radio listeners had never heard anything like it; R&B and rock stations played the full fifteen minutes, and the record sold eight million copies. Rap music—as the name of a musical genre, a shorthand term for the entire hip-hop scene, and a commercially viable product—started with Sugar Hill Records and "Rapper's Delight."

Grandmaster Flash could not rap, occupied as he was at his turntables, and he didn't have a talent for rhyming anyway. Lots of guys showed up who said they could rhyme for him, but he found them unpersuasive, until Cowboy (real name Keith Wiggins; sometimes credited with coining the term *hip-hop*) took over the mic. He was Flash's sole DJ for a while. Two more DJs were added after Cowboy. Then the crew grew to the Furious Five, a number that seems to have approached an upper limit of MCs per individual DJ. The five rappers could spell one another; thinking up rhymes off the top of your head wears a person out. After Cowboy, the other four were the Kidd Creole (Nathan Glover), Melle Mel (Nathan's brother, Melvin Glover), Scorpio (Eddie Morris, aka Mr. Ness), and Rahiem (Guy Todd Williams).

Hip-hop crews had continued to multiply in the Bronx, and Flash faced competition from the Cold Crush Brothers, LuvBug Starski, the Funky Four, the L Brothers, the Rock Steady Crew, Kurtis Blow, Doug E. Fresh, and others. Not only did Mr. Freeze, Baby Freeze, Tiny Freeze, Little Freeze, and Black Freeze all have similar MC names, they all hung out together. Kool Herc was still performing, too, although he would not make a commercial record until later. Hip-hop had developed from party jams that anybody could enjoy outdoors in the playgrounds into indoor entertainment that clubgoers would pay for. The events in playgrounds now served as commercials that brought the paying crowds inside. Flash believed that he and the Furious Five could draw thousands of customers, and proved it by selling out the Audubon Ballroom, in Harlem. (Malcolm X had been murdered there fourteen years before.) The three-thousand-plus fans who bought tickets went crazy for the four-hour show while the throngs who couldn't get in stood outside.

Flash's Tuesday night gig at The Disco Fever put that club close to Manhattan's Studio 54 in terms of 1980s hipness. Fans from the Bronx and beyond came to pack the club every Tuesday. Not long after the success of "Rapper's Delight," Sylvia Robinson of Sugar Hill Records showed up one Tuesday in her cream-colored Rolls, accompanied by an entourage of heavies who situated her up front. She got Flash's attention and, when he had a free minute, told him she wanted to do a record with him and the Furious Five. A few days later, Flash and Rahiem traveled to see her in Englewood, riding on public transportation. Flash hoped that if he ever went back to Englewood, he would have a car. He was twenty-two years old.

The Robinsons persuaded him to sign with Sugar Hill, though he thought "Rapper's Delight" was "cornball," and he already had a contract with a small record company in Harlem. They took care of those obstacles somehow. Sugar Hill then sent him and the Five out on tour, and the group recorded two successful singles, "Freedom" and "Birthday Party." As a perk, Sylvia gave Flash a canary-yellow Lincoln Continental.

He wanted to do a record of just himself that showed his deejaying skills. "The Adventures of Grandmaster Flash on the Wheels of Steel," which Sugar Hill released in 1981, is a seven-minute collage of sounds put together by him switching from one turntable to the other in a single take, solo, as if before a live audience. It's a Modernist one-off, shattered and jangled and ironic, with a driven and erratic beat. My favorite part is when suddenly there's a heartwarming snatch of Hollywood-movie-type dialogue among two little kids and a grown-up. The kids ask the grown-up to tell them a story, and he says he'll tell them the story of his life. He begins, "I was born a long time ago,

see, in Adams, North Dakota . . ." After another avuncular sentence
or two, suddenly Flash jumps in with several short, sharp scratches
of the record followed by a stab of salsa trumpet. The warm, corny
uncle is gone; Adams, North Dakota, is gone; and the music with its
propulsive beat shatters onward.

Grandmaster Flash and the Furious Five's biggest hit happened in
1982. How "The Message" came to be recorded has been told before:
Sylvia Robinson wanted Flash and the Five to do it, they resisted,
and she recorded it anyway with her studio band. When she released
the song, she attributed it to Grandmaster Flash and the Furious Five.
One of her studio musicians, Ed Fletcher, known as Duke Bootee,
had written the song as a shout against ghetto life. Its recurring hook
is "It's like a jungle sometimes / it makes me wonder / how I keep
from going under." Flash didn't like the anger and negativity of it.
The group participated only in the music video of "The Message," and
Melle Mel lip-synched some of the words.

Again, Sylvia Robinson's hitmaking instinct got it right. "Rapper's
Delight" had introduced rap as a promising novelty; "The Message"
established a plot-driven basis for most rap music that followed. It gave
weight and social significance to the form, with words that matched
the power of hip-hop's naked heartbeat, pounding away. *Rolling Stone*
rates "The Message" as the best rap song of all time. Flash never did
warm to it. The group, and his own association with Sugar Hill, disintegrated soon after it came out. He knew things were over when the
canary-yellow Lincoln was repossessed.

As time passed, Flash did not object to having his name on "The
Message." Getting credit for something he didn't do made up for some
of the pioneering that he should have gotten credit for but didn't. Flash
recorded no major hits after leaving Sugar Hill, which went out of
business in 1986. Twenty-five years after "The Message," Grandmaster Flash and the Furious Five were the first hip-hop group inducted
into the Rock and Roll Hall of Fame. Parts of the video of the song
had used run-down locations in the Bronx for background, but the lyrics didn't mention that place, or any other. The song talked about a generic poverty-stricken urban setting, with broken glass and junkies and
rats and roaches and crime. Rhetorically, it addresses a hypothetical

"you" who envies the rich pimps and numbers runners, turns to armed robbery, goes to jail, suffers sexual predation, and hangs himself in his cell. "The Message" uses the same inner-city grimness as does *Fort Apache, the Bronx*, but unlike the movie, the song is real, hard-won, and a work of art.

AT THE INTERSECTION of Kingsbridge Road and Jerome Avenue, in the Kingsbridge Heights neighborhood, a street sign proclaims this part of the avenue to be DJ Scott La Rock Boulevard. Scott La Rock was one of the three members of Boogie Down Productions (BDP), a hip-hop group of the mid-to-late eighties. ("The Boogie Down" is a street synonym for the Bronx.) Although hip-hop started in the Bronx, nobody made any major statement about that in the music until Boogie Down Productions's "South Bronx," a song as foundational, in its way, as "The Message."

The intersection is full of noise and life. Kingsbridge Road buses, some of them double-length, shuttle back and forth, going uphill or down, while the Jerome Avenue number 4 subway trains run perpendicular to them on the elevated tracks above, screeching into the station and dinging their "door closing" noises and screeching away. Crowds get off the trains and come down the stairs from the el and disperse, or line up at the bus stops, and bus passengers go up the stairs in the other direction. At the intersection's northwest corner, the Kingsbridge Armory intrudes its brick, whale-shaped bulk that extends all the way down the block. Once, the Jerome family's summer mansion stood near this junction, and Jennie Jerome, who would marry a lord and give birth to Winston Churchill, spent her summers here. Even earlier, Edgar Allan Poe lived just up the hill with his cousin-wife and aunt-mother-in-law. DJ Scott La Rock, by all accounts a beloved man, deserves to be remembered in this resonant setting.

Scott La Rock was born Scott Monroe Sterling in 1962 in the Bronx. His father did not participate much in his life; he and his younger brother were raised by their grandfather and by their mother, Carolyn Morant, who had a job with the city. In childhood Sterling played basketball in Bronx playground leagues. High school teams heard about him, and the coach at Our Savior Lutheran High School persuaded him to go there. Our Savior is in the north-central Bronx, not far from Jacobi Medical Center. When Sterling was a sophomore, his mother moved the family to Queens. To commute he rode the bus a long way to Our Savior and back, but he kept up his commitment to the sport and got decent grades. He was broad-shouldered, six feet three inches tall, and a hard-to-stop power forward. In his senior year, he won an honorable mention on one of the all-city teams.

Matt Kilcullen, a longtime basketball coach who is now the director of athletics at Mercy College, in Dobbs Ferry, grew up in a mostly Irish neighborhood along East 199th Street. Through a network of coaches and summer basketball camps he kept track of the top area prospects, and he heard about Scott Sterling. A small university in north-central Vermont hired Kilcullen to coach there, starting in the 1979–1980 season. Castleton University (since closed in a merger) was a school of about two thousand students in the town of Castleton. The school wanted to improve its basketball program, and it had a way to go; in Kilcullen's first year it won two games and lost twenty. Reaching out for players, he visited Sterling and his mother in Queens and invited him to visit the school. Kilcullen knew the change of environment would be a shock. At the time, fewer than ten Black students attended Castleton, and Vermont is one of the whitest states in the country.

After a weekend of talking to students and professors and seeing the dorms and the gym and the town—"A pizza parlor, a cafe, two bars, a hardware store, and a bank," as another coach remembered it—Sterling met Kilcullen in the school cafeteria for breakfast. Kilcullen asked the eighteen-year-old what he thought of the place. Sterling pointed to a glass of milk on the table and said he felt like a fly that fell into a glass of milk.

He chose Castleton anyway, and Kilcullen brought other Black players to join him—Bryan DeLoatch, who would set records as a soccer goalie as well as in basketball, and Lee Smith, another basketball star, who was DeLoatch's best friend. Both had gone to Sleepy Hollow High, in Tarrytown. Playing for Kilcullen was a twenty-hour-a-week proposition, sometimes with workout sessions that started early in the morning. One of the biggest changes the Black students had to adjust to was the lack of Black radio stations. Sometimes an R&B station from Montreal might come in, faintly, but only when the weather was right.

Lee Smith now works in IT and lives in Westchester County. I reached him by phone, via Castleton's alumni network. "Scott and I played our music at Castleton for our own survival," he told me. "We brought up crates of his records and they filled his dorm room. Hip-hop was not prominent then and people in Vermont knew nothing about it. We were playing hip-hop and R&B in the dorm, using two belt-drive turntables on cinder blocks, with a small amp and a tape machine—it was like a little factory. Scott and I taught each other how to DJ. People started listening to what we were doing, and the music just evolved." Sometimes the team would play a basketball game in the Castleton gym on a Saturday evening, and Smith and Sterling would show up afterward at one of the town's two bars, Dougan's or the Dog, and deejay for a packed house the rest of the night. Bryan DeLoatch recalled, "At Castleton, Scott and Lee *owned* the weekends."

Matt Kilcullen moved on to a coaching job at a Division I school after three years at Castleton, and Stan Van Gundy, of the famed Van Gundy basketball clan, took over. Van Gundy later went on to coach the Miami Heat and other pro teams. He told me he loved Scott Sterling and considers him one of the most magnetic people he ever met. "Scott was a hell of a player, dominant at power forward—very strong in the upper body, and he loved to go to the basket. He could've played pro, but he was a couple of inches too small." (Sterling had a 62 percent shooting average from the floor, the highest in school history.) "And off the court, everybody wanted to be with Scott, hang out with him, sit with him in the dining hall," Van Gundy continued. "He was definitely a BMOC. Scott made you feel good about yourself, he cared about people." Others who knew Sterling at Castleton said similar things. Olivia Duane Adams, a classmate who went on to found a Silicon Valley software company, remembered how unassuming Sterling was, and what long eyelashes and kind eyes he had.

The Castleton Spartans made it all the way to the District Finals in Division III in his senior year, though they lost heartbreakingly

by two points in the playoffs. The stars of that team are still remembered at the school. Bryan DeLoatch and Scott Sterling are both in
Castleton's Hall of Fame, which calls DeLoatch the best athlete in
the history of the school, and notes that Sterling also did volunteer
work with local kids to help them develop their basketball skills. The
team changed Castleton basketball and made it more Black from then
on. Though briefly on academic suspension, Sterling graduated in
four years with a BA in business. Lee Smith, also a business major,
said that their graduation occurred on Mother's Day, May 13, 1984.
"Graduation was kind of weird and kind of quick—mobs of people all
around, and then suddenly the dorms were empty, just cricket noises,
and we're standing there, like, 'What now?'"

SMITH MOVED BACK to Tarrytown and went to work for NYNEX, the
communications company that later became Verizon. Sterling got a job
as a social worker with the City of New York. He was assigned to the
Franklin Avenue Men's Shelter, near Morris High School, and found
an apartment in the neighborhood.

Lawrence "Kris" Parker was nineteen years old in 1985, younger
than Sterling by three years. He went (and goes) by the name KRS-
One, and sometimes speaks in a self-invented philosophical language.
His name stands for "Knowledge Reigns Supreme Over Nearly Everybody." Known as Kris or KRS to his friends, he had become homeless
after leaving his mother's apartment at sixteen. He has said he went
out on his own because he wanted to prove that God is real. His goals
were to study philosophy and be a hip-hop MC.

Sterling, the recent college grad, wore a coat and tie to his job and
carried a briefcase. The shelter where he worked is another Bronx armory, all castellated and crenellated, built of the usual dark red brick.
Its floor is stone. Skylights in its high, arched roof give an undersea
quality to the light shafting through the cavernous interior. His re-
sponsibilities included handing out subway tokens to shelter residents
when they went to look for jobs. The story goes that Kris Parker/
KRS-One, who had moved to the shelter, began to argue with Sterling
about the subway tokens. The two supposedly got in a fight and had

to be separated by security; but after that they became friends. In a video KRS later said that Sterling was "*not* no social worker!" He had figured out that Sterling cared more about hip-hop. "And I was out on the street *for* hip-hop," KRS said. They had that strong ambition in common.

Some nights, as DJ Scott La Rock, Sterling performed at the Broadway Repertory Theater (BRT), a ballroom party scene in Harlem. One night Sterling/La Rock invited KRS to the ballroom—put him on the guest list, to the latter's astonishment. KRS had never known there was such a thing as a guest list. The experience of seeing La Rock at the turntables impressed KRS. He had his own talent for rhyming, and the two decided to team up. La Rock handled the deejaying and KRS rapped. With another regular at the shelter, Derrick Jones, a sixteen-year-old who went by the name DJ D-Nice, they founded Boogie Down Productions. Sterling, the former basketball star and BMOC of Castleton College, was taking off his coat and tie and learning the street. "Scott gained a freedom hanging out with us," KRS later told a hip-hop magazine.

Sterling/La Rock had not lost touch with his former teammate Lee Smith, whose work schedule of three twelve-hour days followed by four days off left him lots of time to spend in the Bronx, where he helped Boogie Down as their record producer. First, the group did a demo tape and looked for somebody to handle recording and distribution. A company called Rock Candy Records and Film Production offered them their own label. Smith remembers Rock Candy's offices as being under the Triborough Bridge, which squares with descriptions that locate the company at East 132nd and Cypress—the same address, coincidentally, as the long-gone manor house of Gouverneur Morris. The young guys of Boogie Down Productions signed a contract with Rock Candy Records. "But they never paid us our royalties," says Smith. For a while, in lieu of payment, Rock Candy's owners were letting KRS sleep on crates in an abandoned meat freezer on the building's first floor. Gouverneur Morris had once lived among his luxury acquisitions from the French Revolution at that site.

AFTER HIP-HOP'S BRONX BEGINNINGS, the locus of its energy had shifted to Queens. Hip-hop innovators of that borough generally were more middle class than their Bronx counterparts and owned better equipment. (At least for a while, the median income of Black families in Queens was higher than that of white families in Queens.) In 1982, a radio DJ named Mr. Magic Mike hosted the first-ever rap radio show on a commercial station. It was called *Rap Attack,* and it aired on WBLS, an R&B station in Manhattan. Mr. Magic came from Queens himself and promoted Queens hip-hop, which featured the rappers Marley Marl and MC Shan. With Mr. Magic and others, they formed a collective called the Juice Crew, centered on the Queensbridge Houses, the enormous NYCHA housing project just across the 59th Street Bridge from Manhattan.

KRS-One and Scott La Rock brought a demo tape of their early songs to Mr. Magic Mike, hoping he would play it on his show. Mr. Magic Mike not only refused to play it, he told them it was wack, i.e., really not good. Because of this, Boogie Down Productions already harbored bad feelings toward the Juice Crew. Then, in the person of MC Shan, the Queens contingent not only crossed a line but flouted it outrageously and unacceptably. In a song entitled "The Bridge," MC Shan rapped about the origin of hip-hop, and all but declared that hip-hop had been invented in the Queensbridge Houses. For the Bronx-born-and-raised KRS-One, MC Shan's Queens glass jaw came floating into range, and he shattered it into small pieces with his rap answer-song, "South Bronx," in which he warned that if MC Shan ever tried to make such a claim in the Bronx, he "might not live." KRS-One then laid out the actual history, citing Flash and Kool Herc and Bambaataa, and obliquely referencing Black Benji and the peace treaty, all in a percussive, war-chant rhythm whose refrain, "South Bronx, the South South Bronx, South Bronx, the South South Bronx," hammered the message home.

The Bronx hip-hop scene had its own radio champion, DJ Red Alert, who countered Mr. Magic's Queens agitprop. Red Alert was on WRKS, also known as KISS-FM. When hip-hop fans heard "South Bronx" on KISS, they fell silent and listened. Like "The Message,"

"South Bronx" did something rap music had not done before—in this case, brought a geopolitical and turf-oriented approach to rap.

MC Shan then made the mistake of answering "South Bronx" with a song called "Kill That Noise." KRS-One quickly pounced with his response, "The Bridge Is Over," a scorched-earth blast that impugned the masculinity of the Juice Crew's rappers and the reputation of Shante, a female among them, and said again how weak Queens's claim to historic credibility was. That ended the exchange because MC Shan did not respond. The back-and-forth got a lot of attention and sold records for both sides.

Lee Smith says he thought the rivalry amounted to little more than show, on the order of two pro wrestlers fake-savaging each other while making polite conversation in the clinch. The two crews, BDP and Juice, rode to the same battle-rap concerts in the same bus and hung out amiably together en route, Smith says. But the dispute had substance, the truth of the matter lay entirely on the Bronx side, and the Juice Crew came out the losers. In *To the Break of Dawn: A Freestyle on the Hip Hop Aesthetic*, Jelani Cobb wrote, "The verbal manslaughter KRS-One committed on 'South Bronx' and 'The Bridge Is Over' *ended* MC Shan's career," and put all the Queens rappers "on artistic probation."

In hip-hop's early days, no one had needed to assert the "Bronxness" of it, because the fact was self-evident. Once hip-hop had moved outward, and Queens laid claim to its origins, Boogie Down Productions recognized the challenge and slapped it down. With "South Bronx," KRS-One established a new geographic subcategory of American music, to go along with Dixieland Jazz and the Nashville Sound and Texas Swing and the Delta Blues and others. After "South Bronx," rap would develop styles connected to other cities, such as Atlanta or Los Angeles, or even to a single neighborhood, as in *Straight Outta Compton*. In New York, the hip-hop scenes of Brooklyn and Queens and even Staten Island eventually overtook the Bronx in airplay, if not in originality. But nobody else ever tried to steal the Bronx's inheritance by claiming their place invented hip-hop.

Boogie Down Productions also achieved something like what has been done by the oral histories of the Bronx. "South Bronx," the song, lays out a story and a timeline. Hip-hop was music that people could create anywhere, in theory—all you needed was a beat, a voice, and some rhymes—but it had started in this place, and you could never toss away the fact, as the world seemed bent on tossing away the Bronx in general. KRS-One told the rappers of Queens and everywhere else: We invented this and we're still here. By reclaiming hip-hop's origins, Boogie Down Productions planted a flag that contributed to the Bronx's revival.

"SOUTH BRONX" and "The Bridge Is Over" appear on *Criminal Minded*, the first album put out by Boogie Down Productions. The idea behind the title, as KRS-One explained, was that the crew would *look* like criminals, and get the big money, without actually *being* criminals; they were merely "criminal minded." That distinction would be lost on the hip-hop listening public, and *Criminal Minded* is sometimes considered the first gangsta rap album. The cover of the album shows DJ Scott La Rock and his partner KRS-One in a dim interior, sitting at a table lit with a *Godfather*-type palette of somber colors. Both men are holding handguns, and KRS is draped with an ammo belt that appears to contain a dozen or more shotgun shells. These young men look ready for trouble. "People who are criminal minded are the people on top today. Look at the Iran-Contra scandal," KRS noted, in a newspaper story.

On one level, the photo is not to be taken any more seriously than if the two had dressed up as Vito Corleone and Tony "Scarface" Montana for Halloween. Anybody who knew Scott Sterling would understand that he wasn't the imaginary gangster on the album cover. Kim Abbott, Stan Van Gundy's wife, who graduated a year ahead of Sterling at Castleton, told me, "That picture is not Scott. In reality, Scott was *so* not gangsta." To compare the picture to the drawing of him in the Castleton University Hall of Fame is to feel the extreme unlikeness. If "Scott gained a freedom hanging out with us," as KRS said, Sterling may also have experienced a psychological shake-up at the change. Vermont is not the Bronx; rebranding himself as the "criminal minded" DJ Scott La Rock may have involved a mental stretch.

While Boogie Down Productions' fame grew, Sterling continued to work as a social worker at the shelter. Its director later praised his empathy and his skills at group counseling. With his help, homeless men found their own apartments. "He was able to rekindle the hope of those who had lost all hope," the director said later.

His gift for counseling may have gotten him killed.

Derrick Jones, aka DJ D-Nice, the third member of Boogie Down Productions, gave the enterprise the authority of youth. He was sixteen when BDP started, and not yet eighteen in 1987. La Rock/Sterling, in the combined role of D-Nice's hip-hop collaborator and social-worker friend, probably felt protective of him. *Criminal Minded* came out in May '87. One evening in late August, Sterling was at the McDonald's at Broadway and Seventy-first Street in Manhattan. (Sterling loved McDonald's hamburgers. A fellow Castleton alum remembers that once when they were driving back to school after a break, he ran across the Garden State Parkway to get to a McDonald's beside the southbound lanes.) Sitting with him at the Broadway McDonald's were a few of his rap associates: KRS-One; Scotty Morris, BDP's manager; a rapper named Just-Ice; and a bodyguard.

While they were there, Sterling received a call on his cell phone from D-Nice, who said he had just been beaten up and threatened with a gun in Highbridge because of a dispute involving someone else's girlfriend.

The BDP crew left the McDonald's and drove to the Bronx in a ragtop Jeep, intending to stand up for D-Nice and intimidate the opposition. KRS-One did not accompany them but went to see his girlfriend in Brooklyn. According to one account, the BDP crew called Chris Lighty, a producer close to Afrika Bambaataa, and asked him to come with his crew, the Violators, to meet them in Highbridge. Lee Smith says he would have joined them, too, but he couldn't go because he was working a twelve-hour shift. On University Avenue, in front of the Highbridge Gardens Houses, the BDP crew found members of the gang of the guy who had pulled the gun on D-Nice. Apparently, the guy himself was not there. (D-Nice wasn't, either.) Chris Lighty and the Violators arrived and backed up BDP.

Lee Smith says that the BDP bodyguard was a huge person, and kind of unstable. The bodyguard got out of the Jeep and slapped around two of the guys from the Highbridge crew. Sterling then went over and tried to make peace. As he and the bodyguard were walking back to the Jeep, somebody started shooting. The guys with Chris Lighty jumped from their vehicle and shot back. Sterling and the bodyguard got into the Jeep as bullets came through the ragtop. Sterling was hit with two .22-caliber slugs, one in the neck and one behind the ear. His head slammed forward and hit the dash, and at first it seemed his only injury was from that. The driver of the Jeep tried to get out of the tight spot, but cars jammed the street and he had to make several attempts. None of the other passengers in the Jeep were hit. They saw that Sterling had been shot and they sped to Lincoln Hospital.

The shooting occurred on University Avenue between West 165th Street and West 166th Street. The avenue runs along the cliff above the Harlem River and next to high-rise buildings. It and the streets that intersect it have accommodated themselves to the up-and-down terrain, which would favor a defender in a skirmish. I could have sensed that something bad had happened at this spot even if I didn't know about it already. High heaps of heavy-duty black trash bags weigh down the curb, zip ties attach black plastic rat-poison stations to the bottom of nearby chain-link fences, and scraps of plastic flap on the scrawny trees. Sterling was shot in one of the grimmer corners of the borough.

He was talking incoherently as he went into the ER. His mother came, and his girlfriend. She had given birth to his son, Scott Jr., nine months before. KRS arrived from Brooklyn. The hopelessness of Sterling's condition emerged as they waited. Surgery could not save him, and after being taken off life support, he died on the morning of August 27. The incident provided *The New York Times* with a rare occasion to mention the hip-hop scene, which it identified for its readers in a story on August 31, 1987, entitled "Violent Death Halts Rap Musician's Rise": "Hip-hop—a blend of recited street poetry and intricate, rhythmic beats played and mixed by a disk jockey, which was the role played by Mr. Sterling—began 10 years ago in the Bronx and Harlem." Hip-hop had begun in the Bronx fourteen years earlier, not ten, but the *Times* grasped the tragic newsworthiness of the story.

With the success of *Criminal Minded*, Boogie Down Productions joined the most popular groups in hip-hop. The weekend after Sterling died, BDP performed a sold-out concert at Madison Square Garden with Public Enemy and the Beastie Boys. KRS-One led a tribute to Scott La Rock and then rapped over a tape of him deejaying. Warner Brothers had made BDP an offer for an album contract but withdrew it after the murder. Another label replaced them, and BDP's follow-up album, *By All Means Necessary*, came out in 1988.

Police eventually arrested two men for the killing, and the case went to trial in Bronx Criminal Court. Witnesses would not come forward—the familiar problem—and those who did told conflicting stories. Both defendants were found not guilty. No one ever served time for the murder of Scott Sterling. Lee Smith, who attended the trial, is still angry about it. Sterling's friends and admirers from Castleton had been proud when this DJ who honed his art in the green hills of Vermont made a chart-topping hip-hop album. That he would be murdered seemed inconceivable. Stan Van Gundy says his reaction was "Shot? Somebody *shot* Scott Sterling? What enemies could a guy like that have?"

He was the first hip-hop star to be murdered. Other violent deaths—Biggie Smalls, Tupac Shakur—would follow. Some rappers would be shot and survive. Hip-hop feuds and shootings helped bring this formerly obscure music to wider attention. Sterling's death had no connection to the feud between Boogie Down Productions and the Juice Crew, but perhaps the image that BDP projected with *Criminal Minded* caused the Highbridge contingent to be afraid and arm themselves. In any case, they could not have known what kind of man Scott Sterling was. The young Kris Parker—KRS-One—possessed genius, but the essence of Boogie Down Productions came from Sterling's ability to see the spark inside the homeless nineteen-year-old. The original success of BDP began with Sterling's act of imaginative empathy and had nothing to do with anybody being gangsta.

In May 2017, almost thirty years after he died, the city government and local historians of hip-hop combined to rename the street after DJ Scott La Rock. Fernando Cabrera, then the representative of the 14th District, persuaded the City Council to pass a resolution to that effect, at the instigation of Rocky Bucano, founder of the Universal Hip Hop Museum, which is scheduled to open at some future date near Yankee Stadium. Councilman Cabrera made a speech at the renaming ceremony, as did friends and family of Sterling, including Sterling/La Rock's son, Scott Sterling, Jr., who is now a hip-hop promoter. DJ D-Nice was in the crowd. He has remained a presence in the life of Scott Jr. The speakers emphasized Scott La Rock's contribution to the Bronx, while the group's foundational hit, "South Bronx," played loudly in the background.

KRS-One did not attend the ceremony. He is still in the hip-hop world, writing and recording. DJ D-Nice has continued his career as a multitalented prodigy of hip-hop. He deejayed for Barack Obama's farewell party at the White House in 2016. During the Covid pandemic, D-Nice entertained listeners isolating at home with his nine-hour-long "Club Quarantine" online jams, to which hundreds of thousands tuned in. In 2022, he performed at Carnegie Hall and at the Hollywood Bowl, to sold-out crowds. Here on Kingsbridge Road, history still remembers his friend and mentor, DJ Scott La Rock.

35

AFTER THE PLAGUE of fires had died down, it left a landscape that looked like scars. The rubble of the buildings was pinkish and whitish and uninviting to walk on, and it stretched for miles. In videos and photos from the period, the tracks of the elevated trains cross expanses of empty rubble relieved only by the next station. The rubble was widespread because the City of New York tore down abandoned buildings at every opportunity. Its official position was that they constituted a fire hazard and a magnet for lawsuits. Less officially, the city had wanted lower-income Bronx residents to go elsewhere, and leaving them stretches of desert to live in offered another strong hint. "The city would come in and tear down a building in a heartbeat," Harry DeRienzo, of Banana Kelly, told me. "A neighborhood of flattened rubble was easy to manage and it fit with their policy of planned shrinkage." Daniel Madrigal, the Kelly Street landlord, told me that some of the local buildings that are still standing were saved by people lying down in front of the city's bulldozers.

Officials who said grandiose things sometimes expressed the opinion that the now-empty land should be allowed to "go back to grass." It sounded bucolic and natural. Many parts did go back to grass, if not the Kentucky blue or shade-tolerant varieties of the suburbs and golf courses to the north. Timothy grass, cheat grass, turkey-foot, crab-grass, fescue, and other colonizers established a flourishing range in the blank spaces from the Harlem River to Long Island Sound. Of course, the paved streets were still there. Grass didn't grow so much on them, except in the cracks. The street grid now marked off block after block of grasses rampant and triumphant, and other so-called weeds. Ragweed ragged the curbs. Ground vines crawled the rubble. Next to doorsteps that now lacked doors to step into, burdock grew to the size of leaves in a tropical rainforest. Goldenrod evoked its late-summer and early-fall symptoms among hay fever sufferers far down-wind. Pigweed, pokeweed, and joe-pye weed spread, unweeded. The lacy white blossoms of Queen Anne's lace, a plant of the carrot family, nodded at the ends of their thin stalks in the formerly salubrious air.

Not all the vegetation you saw in the Bronx was real. Thousands of empty buildings did not get torn down, for one reason or another. Abandoned hulks along the Bruckner, the Cross Bronx, the Major Deegan, and other highways were thought to be upsetting for motorists, with the broken windows revealing interior glimpses of ruin. The city took on the problem by fitting pieces of new plywood into the windows and trying to make them look like the windows of apartments in which people still lived. Decals that were applied to the wood depicted unbroken glass, window shades, polka-dot curtains, and flowering plants in pots on the sills—all pretend, unlike the weeds below.

In the desert of rubble also were pools of black water, boards, piles of torn-open black trash bags, shopping carts, occasional walls still standing, and extra rubble in heaps that sometimes rose many feet high. The city fenced off some of the empty blocks with chain-link fences. People tossed trash over the fences into the lots, vandals got into the lots and set the trash on fire, and the fire trucks, when they came, had to get through the fences to drive onto the lots to put out the fires.

On the weekend after Fernando Ferrer became Bronx borough president, in 1987, he drove from Riverdale, where he lives, to 588 Fox Street, the address of the building where he had lived as a child. He brought his wife and his daughter, who was about six, because he wanted to show her his old neighborhood. "All she could see, on Fox Street, Beck Street, Kelly Street, was grass," he told me. "Growing to your waist. No buildings, nothing. It was *prairie*, almost."

Look to the west from almost any place in the rubble and you had a view of the Empire State Building and the rest of the Manhattan skyline. The panorama was sweeping, yet up close, as if seen from the rail of an incoming ship. There, across the Harlem River, was the center of the richest city in the world. Meanwhile, this wasteland lay close nearby. The decay of the Bronx—and of parts of Brooklyn and Harlem, but here we're talking about the Bronx—astonished and puzzled the world. Why had the city let this happen? What was to be done?

THE SUBJECT OF housing policy is both complicated and consequential, like the details the contractor is telling you about why you are going to need a new basement. As a subject for public consideration in the United States, housing policy began in New York. In 1842, Charles Dickens came to the city with reformist intent and visited the Five Points slum, situated where the Criminal Courts Building and a part of Chinatown are today. Dickens published *American Notes*, a book of his observations, that same year. Later, Jacob Riis, a Dane, read it and absorbed its descriptions of the Five Points. The book helped to decide Riis on emigrating to New York and working to improve the lives of the poor. After arriving at the age of twenty-one, Riis was homeless for several years, and he traveled around, sleeping in flophouses and graveyards. Eventually he became a journalist and wrote about conditions on the Lower East Side, by then already the most densely populated place on earth. Riis pioneered the taking of pictures with a flash camera, which could illuminate the dark, squalid warrens. His flash used an explosive powder that sometimes started small fires in the scenes he was revealing to the world.

In 1890, Riis published a book featuring his photos and journalism, called *How the Other Half Lives*. It's one of the great reformist books, and a work whose zeal Dickens would have appreciated. Riis's descriptions of ethnic groups in the slums are generally racist and anti-Semitic but you can see he also cares. Theodore Roosevelt, a power in New York City for most of his life, read the book and admired it and looked up to Riis almost like an acolyte. The two became close friends. When Roosevelt was city police commissioner, he had authority over derelict structures; inspired by Riis, he tore down rat-infested tenements and oversaw the construction of new apartment buildings.

The federal government got involved in public housing during the New Deal, with the Public Housing Act of 1937. Robert F. Wagner, U.S. senator from New York, co-sponsored the bill, also called the Wagner-Steagall Act. It provided for federal subsidies for public housing projects nationwide. Senator Wagner's son, Robert F. Wagner, Jr., served as mayor of New York City in the fifties and sixties, overlapping with the tenure of Bronx Borough President James J. Lyons. Mayor Wagner's son Bobby was a friend of my friend George W. S. Trow, and I hung out with them sometimes. We stood together on an elevated span of the West Side Highway watching the puny fireworks display in 1976 during the Bicentennial. I was younger than Bobby and George and always wanted to impress them and others with my individuality. Bobby's unselfish friendliness and warmth came as a revelation. He was the best kind of gent, friendly and open to everybody. Proving his own interestingness was the last thing on his mind; instead, he focused closely on whomever he was talking to. I had never met such a civic-minded person. (Bobby Wagner, who served as deputy mayor and in other posts under Ed Koch, died too young, thirty-some years ago).

But to return to Jacob Riis: He won another fan in Fiorello La Guardia, the city's mayor in the thirties and forties. La Guardia imbibed Riis's compassion for the homeless, and in 1938, during the Depression, he sponsored an amendment to the New York State Constitution that said the city is required by law to provide shelter to every person who asks for it. This signal accomplishment of La Guardia's has been despised and reviled by mayors (Giuliani, Bloomberg) ever since 1979, when a court ruling, *Callahan v. Carey*, affirmed the constitutionally mandated right to shelter. No other city in the nation is legally obliged to provide a person with shelter upon request. (This goes to show where a literary infatuation can take you.) After *Callahan*, the city understood that it would have to build even more public housing, and build it fast. That served as another motivation for the Bronx revival.

I HAVE ALREADY outlined some of the revival's beginnings—how Ramon Rueda founded the People's Development Corporation, and how that group's sweat-equity rehab of 1186 Washington Avenue got national attention because of CBS News and President Carter. I've described the Banana Kelly Neighborhood Improvement Association, founded by the Potts family and Harry DeRienzo, and their gut rehabs of buildings, and their work with *in rem* buildings. Before any of these came on the scene, there was Father Gigante.

Father Louis Gigante served as one of the priests at St. Athanasius Church, on Southern Boulevard, in the South Bronx neighborhood of Longwood. (St. Athanasius was the church of the Sotomayor family during Sonia's childhood.) Gigante rehabbed or built more units of affordable housing in the Bronx than any one person. In 1968, seeing the deteriorating condition of the neighborhood around his church, he founded an organization called SEBCO (the Southeast Bronx Community Organization) and began to take over abandoned residential properties along Southern Boulevard, Bruckner Boulevard, East 163rd Street, and other major streets. When SEBCO started out, crime flourished in the area. Father Gigante sometimes was physically attacked himself; but like the other priests at St. Athanasius, he did not give up in the face of the poverty and terrible circumstances among his parishioners. By 1977, he was working on housing almost full-time. In twenty years, SEBCO created thousands of apartments for low-income residents. Today three larger-than-life-sized statues on the pedestrian mall in front of St. Athanasius portray Father Gigante in different poses: one as if in vigorous mid-sermon, one looking serene and saintly, and one looking wry.

Gigante was a son of Italian immigrants who lived in the West Village. His brother Vincent, known as "Vincent the Chin," was convicted of arranging murders as a boss of the Genovese crime family. Vincent Gigante unsuccessfully attempted to dodge jail by walking around the Village in a bathrobe and pretending to be crazy. He died in 2004. As recently as 2022, the *Daily News* pointed out that one of Father Gigante's nephews (not a son of Vincent's) had a job on the docks of the port of Elizabeth and Newark that required minimal on-site attendance and came with an annual salary of $423,488. I have asked knowledgeable sources if Father Gigante's success owed anything to mob connections and they said they had heard rumors but didn't know. He remained close to Vincent throughout his life and always supported him.

In 2021, Father Gigante was accused of having molested a nine-year-old boy repeatedly over a long period. The priest's death in 2022 forestalled disposition of that charge. By then he had retired and moved upstate. Hoping for an interview with him, I had been in touch with another of his nephews, Salvatore Gigante, the head of SEBCO, but he stopped answering. Father Gigante also turned out to have a son, to whom he left a lot of his estate, along with many complications. Gigante family members are now suing one another, etc.

Here history presents us with another "on the other hand," one in which the negative side of the picture involves serious allegations. These shouldn't take away from Gigante's achievements, nor from the contribution of local Catholic parishes to the rebuilding of the Bronx. The Catholic Church, and its priests and parishioners and others among the faithful and the lapsed, did more than any other single group to lift the Bronx from ruin. When I ask who rebuilt the Bronx, those who know say it was the Catholics, Borough President Fernando Ferrer, Mayor Koch, and the borough's communities themselves.

JIM MITCHELL GREW UP in a churchgoing Catholic family in Winnetka, Illinois. His father was an independent insurance agent and worked in downtown Chicago. For high school Mitchell went to Loyola Academy, in Wilmette, where he met a fellow student, Roger Hayes. The two would be lifetime friends. At Loyola, both felt a vocation to become Jesuit priests, and the order accepted them for training. When they graduated, they entered a novitiate seminary associated with Xavier University, in Milford, Ohio. There they began a program of study and religious instruction scheduled to last thirteen years.

Roger Hayes's family included four other siblings, two older and two younger. Like Mitchell's family, they also lived in the Chicago area. Hayes's father flew planes for Eastern Airlines and his uncle was a Jesuit priest. Both Hayes and Mitchell were born in 1948, so they reached high school and then seminary in the 1960s, when the dreamy country they had grown up in kind of dematerialized. Mitchell and Hayes sympathized with causes on the left but saw the same problems of ineffectuality that bothered Mark Naison. Mainly they wanted to help poor people and actually accomplish something.

Like other Catholics of their generation, they were children of Vatican II, the churchwide convocation held in Rome between 1962 and 1965 that revised the relationship of the church to the world. *Gaudium et spes* (Joy and Hope), the convocation's defining document, called on the church to pay attention to earthly reality, to the poor and the victims of oppression and war. The idea was that, so far in the twentieth century, the church had failed to do this. *Gaudium et spes* also said that every person, not just Catholics, had a responsibility to the world. "Vatican II was a huge influence on my life," Mitchell told me. "It was a spur to action—we are called to go outside the safety zone and accept risks. Everybody is called to make the world better, not just priests and not just Jesuits." From the perspective of the needs of the Bronx, the teachings of *Gaudium et spes* came at the right time.

In the novitiate in Ohio, Mitchell and Hayes met Paul Brant, a man eight years older, who came from Raleigh, North Carolina. Brant planned to move to Fordham in the Bronx and teach philosophy while getting his PhD. Looking to put *Gaudium et spes* into practice, the three got caught up in the radical doctrines of the Chicago labor activist Saul Alinsky. Not only was Alinsky not a Catholic by any stretch, he made fun of Christer do-gooders. Mitchell, Hayes, and Brant read Alinsky's books *Reveille for Radicals* and *Rules for Radicals*. His methods confronted people in power and shook them ("Get close enough to make 'em smell you," he said), and he often won against long odds. In a nonreligious way, Alinsky was doing what Vatican II said that Catholics and everybody else should do.

After their four years of novitiate training, the first two of which were austere, rigorous, and the hardest thing they'd ever been through, Jim Mitchell worked in rehabbing affordable housing in Detroit, and Roger Hayes went to Peru for a year and a half to assist a priest who was building an aqueduct for an indigenous community. Paul Brant moved from Xavier to the Bronx and told his friends they should come and join him. "The Bronx was wide open then, in terms of organizing," Mitchell said. "The housing situation was dire, the fires were moving north, people were losing their homes to abandonment and disinvestment. It seemed like a perfect place for the Alinsky approach." As Fordham's community liaison, Father Brant began by working with a small group called the Morris Heights Neighborhood Improvement Organization, organizing residents and tracking down landlords.

Alinsky had taught that you start small and move up. By way of the Morris Heights group, the organizers got together with a coalition of priests from fourteen parishes called the Northwest Bronx Clergy Coalition (NWBCC), which now teamed up to save at-risk buildings. For that purpose, they added a letter to their acronym and established the Northwest Bronx Community and Clergy Coalition (NWBCCC), the name by which the organization still goes today. From the clergy's point of view, the move had an element of self-preservation. Their churches wanted to continue to exist, which they couldn't do if their congregants kept losing their apartments to fire and decay, and leaving.

The Jesuit authorities allowed Hayes and Mitchell to pursue their training at Fordham. In the seventies, the order had loosened up enough to send its trainees—novices, they're called—to live outside the seminary. With other novices, Hayes, Mitchell, and Brant moved into apartments at 2405 Marion Avenue, in Fordham Heights. As activists of the NWBCCC, they walked the neighborhoods, handed out flyers, and organized tenant meetings. If landlords didn't respond, they tried Alinsky methods. Sometimes they protested outside landlords' homes, and once they made a big noise outside a landlord's daughter's wedding. Their methods displeased some of the Catholic hierarchy—the director of Catholic Charities and the vicar general, among others—but Patrick Ahearn, the bishop of the Bronx, was behind the group and even joined them on picket lines in front of local-capital-exporting banks. The activists took encouragement from the fact that Terrence Cardinal Cooke, the cardinal archbishop of the Catholic Church in New York at the time, raised money for them and once passed along a donation of $10,000.

Roger Hayes's plan had been to go back to Peru and spend his life there serving indigenous people. At 2405 Marion, in the same building with the Jesuits-in-training, lived a family named Loffredo. The father owned an Italian delicatessen on Arthur Avenue known for its homemade mozzarella. Geri, a Loffredo daughter who had recently graduated from college, taught in a Bronx public elementary school. Roger and Geri met in the building. Jesuit instruction includes periods of discernment in which the novice examines his vocation. During a discernment period, Hayes discerned that he did not want to go back to Peru or be a Jesuit. He left the order, married Geri Loffredo, and moved to East 208th Street, in Norwood, while continuing to work for the NWBCCC. The couple has lived in the Bronx ever since. From the NWBCCC he moved to a job at a state housing organization, while Geri taught school and held other city jobs in education. They raised two sons: Luke Hayes, a political strategist who headed Obama campaign organizations in Virginia and Nevada and recently ran Jamaal Bowman's successful campaign for Congress; and Chris Hayes, the MSNBC commentator.

BILL FREY, from Waukesha, Wisconsin, did not go to Notre Dame, as his siblings had done. Instead, he chose Fordham, and he arrived in the city about a year after Mitchell and Hayes. Father Brant saw Frey as another potential organizer for the NWBCCC. Frey liked the idea and joined the team. In the field, he was sometimes asked, "Bill, what *are* you?" The question referred to his apparent lack of any ethnicity at all (it had not been posed to Mitchell and Hayes, whom people correctly took for Irish). Frey is not Irish and did not know what to say: "I'm from Wisconsin?" The actual answer, German Catholic, somehow did not compute.

He enrolled in Father Brant's course on the history of social thought. From people in the community Brant had learned about some Black and Latino homeowners who had paid high prices for houses on Ryer and Valentine Avenues between East 180th Street and East Burnside Avenue. After closing the deals, the buyers found out that the houses were about to be taken by New York City through eminent domain—the city planned to tear the whole block down and build a school there. The price the city was offering for each house, take it or leave it, amounted to about half of what the homeowners had paid. Father Brant thought this looked strange and asked Frey, as a course assignment, to investigate.

Frey checked real estate transaction records downtown and found that just two real estate agents had been involved in all the sales to the current owners. He also discovered that the two agents had purchased the houses themselves for between $12,000 and $18,000 from the previous set of owners. Then he was able to track down some of those owners, who told him that the realtors had told them that the city was going to take their houses and would pay less than the realtors were offering. But the current owners, when the agents had sold to them, had not been told about the city's plans, and had bought the houses for almost twice what the agents paid.

The houses in question are on the west side of Valentine Avenue and the east side of Ryer Avenue, and their small backyards adjoin. Jim Frey, the soft-spoken nonethnic undergrad from Wisconsin, went door to door, told the homeowners what he had discovered, and persuaded them to band together in a residents' group. With his help, they petitioned the city, which heard them out and soon agreed to buy the houses for what they had paid. Then it decided to give up entirely on the taking and moved its plans for the school; none of the homeowners had to sell in the end. This quick and total victory elevated Frey to a more substantial view of his future. For his life's calling, he would work to keep people in good housing, and build more of it.

Twenty-five of the houses he saved still stand. Each expresses a style that varies a bit from that of its neighbors. They are wood frame, brick, or frame and stonework, with decorative iron security grill-work painted white, front patios, dormer windows, awnings, short driveways, and eccentric roofs. They have the dignity of formerly threatened places that were stood up for, and therefore survived.

ONE AFTERNOON JIM MITCHELL drove me around on a tour of some of the buildings that the Northwest Bronx Community and Clergy Coalition had saved in its early years, when he was the executive director. Like Roger Hayes, he had left the Jesuits not long after moving to 2405 Marion. Having led the NWBCCC for eight years, Mitchell then founded another organization, BUILD (Bronx United in Leveraging Dollars), which focuses on buying, rehabbing, and managing buildings. He stayed at BUILD for thirteen years, and now he consults on housing issues and teaches philosophy at Fordham.

As I had discovered when I went to 1186 Washington Avenue, buildings that were preserved when they might have been torn down now look like solid, upright architectural citizens on everyday streets. At the places where we stopped, Mitchell remembered the names of the tenants, landlords, bankers, and local officials involved in each rescue. Many of the details had to do with struggles for the shelter basics: roof, boiler, windows, and a front door that locked. When those elements were in place, you could turn to fixing up the individual apartments. At 681 East 181st Street, a six-story walk-up with fifty apartments, he said, "At one point, this building was down to only one tenant. Her name was Joan Butler. The landlord could not be found, nothing worked, the building lacked heat, electricity, and water, the forty-nine other apartments were empty—and Joan refused to leave. If she hadn't stayed, we would have had a hard time persuading the city not to demolish the building. That was as close as we ever came to giving up. Eventually we found financing, got the building rehabbed, and retenanted it. Now it's a good place to live. At the coalition, and then at BUILD, we never lost a building."

Early on, the coalition moved from concentrating on activism to starting nonprofit housing corporations. Once it got them going, it spun them off. The Fordham Bedford Housing Corp., the most successful of them, now owns and manages 130 buildings and more than 4,000 apartments. The University Neighborhood Housing Corp. and the Inter-Neighborhood Housing Corp. were among the other non-profits founded by the NWBCCC. Today the NWBCCC does not own or manage housing, but its Community Land Trust sometimes buys vacant lots and holds on to them to forestall speculators.

On the community service front, the NWBCCC census outreach team found 20,000 previously uncounted Bronxites to add to the census rolls in 2020. Its staff joined the fight to stop evictions during Covid; after the eviction moratorium ended, in January '22, more than 200,000 people were in danger of losing their homes, and the NWBCCC found lawyers for many of them and has lobbied to make the moratorium permanent. Since the fire in 2022 that killed nineteen Gambian-Americans, the NWBCCC has been pressuring landlords to heat their buildings better. It also offers programs in health justice, asthma reduction, apartment weatherization, and job training and placement. It agitates for universal health care in New York, and it buys and distributes fresh produce.

When Jim Mitchell dropped me off at the number 4 train after the tour, he said, "What we tried to do—Roger and I and the others from the coalition—was to create livable apartments near schools, playgrounds, services, and public transportation, so people could raise families and find jobs that paid enough that they weren't spending most of their income on rent. You want to create housing where folks without much money can get a decent start. For a rich city in a rich country, that shouldn't be so difficult to do."

36

ED KOCH TOOK OVER from Abraham Beame on January 1, 1978. The new mayor had to deal with his own housing glitch at the transfer. Abe and Mary Beame proceeded with due deliberation while vacating Gracie Mansion, and Koch continued to stew, day after day, in his one-bedroom apartment in the Village. He complained to a reporter, "They will never leave!" The Beames finally did, and Koch moved into the mansion while holding on to his apartment.

One of his early mayoral acts was to appoint Felice Michetti, a city planner who grew up in the Bronx, to the Department of Housing Preservation and Development (HPD) in that borough. This would be the beginning of many Felice Michetti successes. Not widely known outside the affordable housing world, she is one of the most highly regarded people in it.

She met me one afternoon some years ago for lunch in a deli-restaurant on Fourteenth Street. A compact, forceful woman with dark hair and humorous dark eyes, she makes you believe that New York City is the greatest place on the planet and creating affordable apartments an activity full of excitement and promise. Like others in the Bronx revival, she obtained her entire education, first grade through college, in Catholic schools. She earned her law degree (Fordham, '83) 'while working for the city during the day and studying at night. The change she wrought in the West Tremont neighborhood of the Bronx, soon after her appointment in 1979, has been retold as a model of how to win housing victories.

Michetti explained the context to me: The fires were approaching the neighborhood in '79, its housing stock had been allowed to run down, buildings were decaying, and her department had only a small amount of money. Nobody was lending in West Tremont; the expectation was that the neighborhood would all but disappear, as others had done. But Michetti passed out leaflets in West Tremont saying there was some city money available for new boilers, plumbing, roofs, wiring, and—most important, from her point of view—windows.

"The city gave us a choice of what kind of windows we could have," she told me. "There were these ordinary, drab, perfectly okay windows, and then there were these other, kind of ugly but good windows with conspicuous white frames. I decided on the ones with the white frames. I wanted people to see those white windows when they looked up, and know that Housing Preservation and Development was here, and we were getting involved. A lot of buildings signed up for the new windows, and soon thirty-some buildings in West Tremont had windows whose white frames you could see from the street. The banks noticed the windows, and loans for other rehabs started to become available. We fixed boilers and wiring and roofs and doors, too, but what reversed the disintegration and disinvestment of West Tremont was those windows. The rebuilding of the neighborhood started with them."

HOW THINGS LOOK makes a difference. Despair manifested itself in the visual element and spread inward from the eyes to the soul. You had to prevent this from happening. Observers made fun of the fake plywood windows, the ones with the decals—as if a picture of a flower in a flowerpot meant the apartment behind it was inhabitable—but Fernando Ferrer, for one, saw the positive side. "Look, the decals were a start," he told me. "It sure beat letting the windows stay open and letting the charred interiors show."

Charlotte Street, the notorious urban desert, remained an open issue for Mayor Koch. There had been meetings and inconclusive plans since '77, but nothing had been built. In 1980, two years into his term, it looked just as desolate as it had three years before, which was why Reagan could visit it and score points during his '80 campaign. Then an urban planner named Ed Logue, who had been involved in the creation of low-income housing in other cities, came up with the idea of turning Charlotte Street and the empty blocks around it into a development of single-family, suburban-style ranch homes.

The idea boggled minds. Logue was proposing to fill mid-city acreage—a place that had once been a densely populated neighborhood, like Chelsea or the Village—with a low-density residential suburb. Nothing against suburbs, I live in one myself; but these homes would be surrounded, each individually, by lawns and even white picket fences. Each was designed to provide housing for maybe five or six people, tops.

The city's infrastructure in the Charlotte Street area, though mostly unused at that moment, had been built to serve thousands. In a place that could support 110 housing units (apartments) per acre, Logue proposed putting 6 units (the ranch houses) per acre. Now all the water and sewer and electric and gas and public transportation infrastructure would benefit just a handful of people. Planners decried the waste and the folly. Felice Michetti called the idea "a farce." But Koch went for it! Pasting a suburban movie set onto these fraught acres might be one of those cliché ideas that are just crazy enough to work. And whatever the city did at Charlotte Street, it could not afford to fail.

Logue needed three years just to get the first two houses built. A community development corporation, Mid-Bronx Desperadoes, led by a Morrisania resident, Genevieve Brooks, built the other eighty-seven houses in the development, which the plan had named Charlotte Gardens. Any resemblance to, say, Maplewood, New Jersey, was intentional. One of the streets laid out in the former desert of rubble was called Suburban Place.

At the dedication ceremony for Charlotte Gardens in 1984, a man at the edge of the crowd shouted, "These houses will be torn down in a week!" Koch screamed back, "The people who have bought them will defend them with their lives!" The houses were not torn down in a week. They still stand. Their lawns (like that of Willie Hemanns, in his melon-colored home at the corner of Charlotte Street and Boston Road) are green and mowed. Japanese cherry trees drop their pink petals in the spring. The original buyers paid in the vicinity of fifty thousand for their houses; today, according to online realty sites, each is worth in the high six figures. Throughout the development, no signs of decay are to be seen. The place is kind of strange and unexpected—this Charlotte Gardens suburb transplanted to a city—but not in a bad way. Nowhere does despair leap to the eyes.

From a certain point of view, Charlotte Gardens did the reverse of the move made previously by *The Goldbergs* television show. The producers of *The Goldbergs* moved a Bronx family to the suburbs; Charlotte Gardens put a suburb in the Bronx.

HOW THINGS LOOK MATTERS. Fernando Ferrer, installed as president of the borough in 1987, took instruction from this truth. Mayor Koch, in office for nine years by then, suddenly had some money to spend, and each borough wanted a piece of it. The question was how to get a whole bunch of the city's housing funds, enough for a major rebuilding of the Bronx, in such a competitive environment. On taking office Ferrer asked experts from outside the Bronx and outside his political circle what they thought he should do. Someone suggested he talk to John Dyson, an advisor from Mario Cuomo's administration when Cuomo was governor. Dyson's tenure as the commissioner of commerce, where he oversaw the Department of Tourism, had produced the world-famous "I ♥ NEW YORK" campaign.

So Ferrer sought Dyson out, and (as Ferrer later recalled) Dyson told him, "The first thing you have to do is fix the gateways into the Bronx. You start fixing that, and you begin to show people who are becoming dispirited, 'Wait a minute—there's some hope.'" By the gateways, Dyson meant the major roads on which motorists by the millions passed through the borough.

Ferrer loved the idea and ran with it. He called the plan "The

Gateway Initiative." And where else to start the Gateway Initiative but along the Cross Bronx Expressway? Ferrer's planning and development director took pictures of every building a driver could see from that highway, "even craning your neck uncomfortably from the car," Ferrer told me. "I wanted pictures of all those buildings. And we did a unit count—how many units are they, how much would it cost us, ballpark, to rehabilitate them, and in my first State of the Borough Report, I had the pictures mounted on easels. About nine or ten easels. And I unveiled them, and I said, 'This is the Gateway Initiative.'"

Leaders all over the Bronx in politics and in housing heard about it. Ferrer got coverage from the press, and then he let the Koch administration come to him. "Koch's housing commissioner was Abe Biderman. A good guy, by the way, a decent guy. He calls me up, 'What the hell is this Gateway Initiative? I never heard of it.' I said, 'I know, you never did. I'm sending the easels, I'm sending the proposal to your office.'

"Look, he was too much of a public servant to respond in a Giuliani-esque kind of way," Ferrer went on. "Biderman read it, he absorbed it, and Gateway became a Koch administration thing. So, I'm okay with that. Gateway was their first big foray into housing. They had done some small, halting moves, but nothing this big, and nothing this focused. We had to show them how this would work, and how it would be to their benefit to do this. I thought it worked brilliantly, actually."

ON THE FOURTH of July 1976, when I stood with George Trow and Bobby Wagner on an elevated span of the old West Side Highway and looked out over the two million people waiting on the empty landfill along the Hudson River for the disappointing fireworks show—I had no idea what I was really seeing. That huge, recently created empty place represented important help for the Bronx. The City of New York had moved the river to one side and inserted that landfill so it could build Battery Park City on it. The mega-development was intended as an enlargement of downtown square footage for the financial business, by then New York's number one industry. Battery Park City would also provide upscale apartments for the industry's well-paid employees. In 1976, the city had just dodged bankruptcy and fallen into receivership, with its finances taken over by the state. Somehow, during those parlous times, Battery Park City got built. In the outcome, the roll of the dice paid off. Battery Park City became a real estate bestseller. The financial community went for it in a big way.

In 1985, Meyer (Sandy) Frucher, president of the Battery Park City Authority, proposed to then-governor Mario Cuomo that the BPCA's excess revenues from rentals be used to renovate vacant buildings in the Bronx. I have already described how the city had taken possession of apartment buildings for unpaid taxes—the so-called *in rem* buildings. Thousands of them still needed to be fixed up. Now the lucrative returns from Battery Park City would provide more capital for the work. That is, one of the richest parts of town would help to revive the poorest. Also at that time, the city regained control of its finances from the state and could once again raise money by issuing bonds.

The federal government provided help, too, if not directly. After 1973, it no longer built public housing, but it did subsidize qualified low-income tenants through the Section 8 program, paying landlords the difference between market rent and 30 percent of the renter's income. Father Gigante filled his buildings with tenants thanks to Section 8; nationwide, it has helped tens of millions of people afford housing. Other federal laws encouraged major investment. These laws are an alphabet box of acronyms, such as the Community Reinvestment Act (CRA), which said that banks must invest in the communities where they do business. The CRA also explicitly outlawed redlining. After Congress passed it in 1977, the CRA made such a difference to advocates of affordable housing in the Bronx that on its fortieth anniversary they got together and celebrated. Another federal program, the Low-Income Housing Tax Credit, or LIHTC (pronounced "Lie-tech"), gave investors and corporations one-for-one tax credits for loans to build low-income housing. It passed during the Reagan administration and has been the most successful program ever created for that purpose.

In April 1986, Koch announced that the city would be spending

$5.1 billion on housing for people who were low-income or homeless. Work on the Ferrer/Koch Gateway Initiative began in 1987; by 1989, the city announced that 16,000 apartments were being rehabbed in the Bronx. Koch called it "the greatest construction program since the pharaohs built the pyramids," and boasted, "Then, there was just one person per pyramid . . . These 15,000 apartments alone will be home for 60,000 people."

DAVID DINKINS, the city comptroller, defeated Koch when he ran for reelection in 1989. When Dinkins took over as mayor in 1990, he appointed Felice Michetti to the post of housing commissioner, and she saw to the continuation of the Koch programs, some of which produced housing even into subsequent administrations because the plans and funding were already in the pipeline. By 2000, the Koch programs had produced 57,361 apartment units and 9,557 units in row houses, just in the Bronx. Koch had earned a reputation as a contentious, sometimes nasty mayor ("I don't get ulcers, I give ulcers"), but after he was out of office, the housing he built would be his legacy. Not long before he died, he had lunch with Robert Hayes, who as a young attorney had brought the *Callahan v. Carey* lawsuit, which established the right to shelter in New York. After leaving office, Koch understood that his housing programs, to which he had been driven partly by the *Callahan* ruling, were the achievement of his life. Robert Hayes later told me that Koch said he was proud of the housing Hayes and others had forced him to build. "Then he did a very un-Koch-like thing," Hayes said. "He thanked me."

Koch's *New York Times* obit, in the issue of February 1, 2013 (bannered, and of course above the fold), said that he was responsible for programs that had built or rehabbed more than 200,000 units of housing for the people of New York.

AND AN AFTERTHOUGHT: What about all the rubble? What became of those tens of thousands of buildings' worth of crushed bricks, and the crumbled mortar and splintered boards and tar paper from the roofs, and the hallway tiles off which doo-wop singing perhaps had once resounded, all of it now shattered to fragments? The copper and other salable metals had been stripped, but what happened to the rubble?

When I asked Fernando Ferrer, he said, "Ah, that's interesting. Obviously, from what we know today, much of it was toxic, from the presence of the asbestos. Before they rebuilt, they would excavate the rubble. Or they would, through a process called 'dynamic compaction'—I'll never forget that, it was an Ed Logue thing—he would pound the rubble and compress it, right on the site. That turned out to be not such a good idea. As all these things settle, there are these air cavities, and buildings crack, so you really have to do it right. 'Dynamic compaction'—Ed Logue called it 'pounding sand.' But anyway, with the vast bulk of the rubble, it wasn't compacted, it was dug up and put in dump trucks and hauled away, and it became landfill somewhere. But I really have no idea where all that rubble ended up."

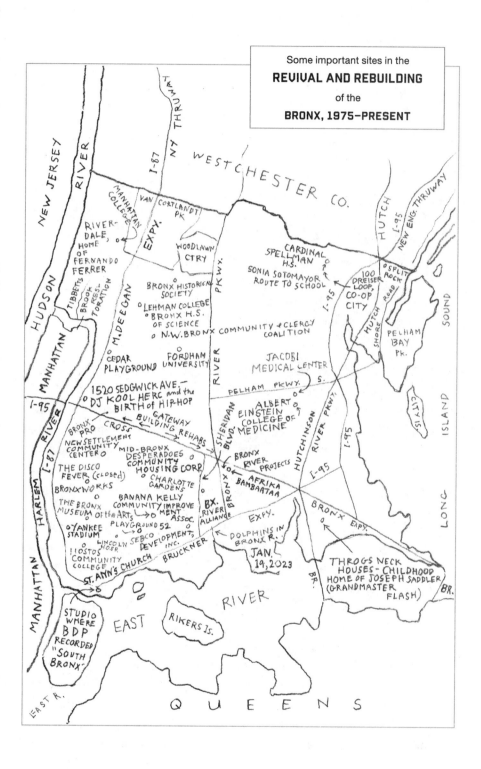

Some important sites in the

REVIVAL AND REBUILDING

of the

BRONX, 1975–PRESENT

37

ONE DAY I went looking for the oldest row houses in the Bronx—a block of four-story-high brick dwellings built between 1863 and 1865, on Alexander Avenue, which used to be called "the Irish Fifth Avenue." They're in the far South Bronx, in Mott Haven just north of the Bruckner Expressway. It's remarkable that these simple, elegant buildings between East 139th and East 140th Streets escaped the twentieth-century destruction. The afternoon sun adds a flat light to their warm-colored bricks, with a frankness that could have been painted by Edward Hopper. This block, when the developer Edward Willis put it up, made a statement. The Bronx then was still mainly a city-adjacent part of Westchester County, a retreat where rich people had estates. These row houses imagined it as a place of city residences like those in Manhattan—as if the well-to-do-family homes then being built on upper Fifth Avenue had sent out rhizomes that established this offshoot across the Harlem River.

The buildings have basement levels, and steps leading down to that level, and more formal doors to the first-floor entrances, with wider steps going up. Iron gates and a fence at about waist height keep passersby from straying off the sidewalk into the entries. I was balancing my notebook on the top rail of the fence and writing in it when a window on the second floor opened, and a woman and a Scottie dog looked down. Both had the same expression on their faces. Before I could say anything, the woman told me that the building was not for sale. The dog seemed to nod in confirmation. I told the woman I was admiring these buildings because they're the oldest row houses in the Bronx. She said, "I know. I've lived here for fifty years." She added that her family had lived across the street for a long time before that.

She wore a green-and-black top and had short dark hair and glasses. The Scottie was whitish gray with intense, coal-black eyes. She said, "I thought you were a realtor. They offer us money for our building, and they come around all the time. *All. The. Time!* I tell 'em I lived through the fires, I lived through crack, and I'm not going anywhere."

No place in the Bronx appears to be gentrifying more than Mott Haven. It's where pianos used to be made, but local anti-gentrifiers objected to developers renaming the area the "Piano District." Considering all that the neighborhood has been through, suddenly deciding it's the "Piano District" whitewashes history and slides the rug out from under the current residents. The renaming of a place always sharpens the gentrifiers' wrecking bar.

Plenty of clues will reveal if a neighborhood is gentrifying. One way to tell is if you see a sign advertising "Karaoke" in the window of a bar. Another is by watching the sidewalk. If you see even one little white plastic spoon of the kind that ice cream shops give out with free tastes, you know the change is far along. After the woman and the Scottie at the window went back inside, I checked in my pocket for the little white plastic spoon I had just found.

LIVING THROUGH THE FIRES and crack conveys some authority. To say you lived through these also means you were here during the epidemic of HIV/AIDS that accompanied crack like a third apocalyptic horseman. The scourges rode together. When the city closed firehouses in the Bronx in the seventies, it also closed all its neighborhood health clinics citywide, cut funds for methadone treatment, stopped maintaining the parks, reduced library hours, ended after-school programs, and basically withdrew from many low-income areas. Then a new drug flooded in. Cocaine had been ruining lives for at least a decade when crack, a crystalized, smokable form of it, showed up in 1985. Crack spread across the city, but it came first to the Bronx. Perhaps following a vogue for acronyms, DOA and TKO were the names of popular "crack stamps," or dealer-invented crack brand names.

The kick from cocaine did not equal the quick bliss from crack, which also cost less. Crack destroyed users by droves, and more cruelly than heroin or regular cocaine. Crack was known as a ladies' drug. Men had been the primary users of heroin and cocaine, but nobody could explain why so many women got addicted to crack. Cocaine had not wasted entire families the way crack did. Women had held families together in the poorest neighborhoods, but if a mother succumbed to crack the whole family might fall apart.

Heroin addicts generally were able to function in their everyday lives, but crackheads usually could not, and crack harmed the body worse and acted faster. Addicts quickly grew thin and spindly, suffered burns on their hands from the pipes, and smelled as if they had been set on fire themselves. At night, at the borders of St. Mary's Park along 149th Street and St. Ann's Avenue, passersby could look into the park and see the flames of crack pipes glowing here and there in the darkness. In October 1776, the Continental Army left campfires burning on the hillsides to fool the British into thinking the Americans were still there, and not in headlong retreat, as in fact they were. The crack pipe brought new visions of fire to the Bronx night.

Prostitution followed addiction, as happens, even more sadly. The street-level Bruckner Boulevard, underneath the elevated Bruckner Expressway, drew prostitutes and truck drivers and suburban motorists and a whole off-ramp world of bad commerce; sex and drugs and money swapped briskly in the easy access. Prostitutes crept in and out of the shadow regions among the expressway's support pillars. Women users got infected with HIV in these danger zones, or— far more often—husbands or boyfriends who caught it from dirty needles or sex passed it on to them. The influx of women into the pool of HIV sufferers increased the plague exponentially. By the late eighties, HIV/AIDS was the leading cause of death among Black women in the city between the ages of fifteen and forty-four.

Bebo, whose sidewalk declaration I noted at the end of chapter 1, wrote that he had run the block since 1988. That would have been in the early-to-mid crack era. Some neighborhoods have never matched the desperation of that time. On Woodycrest Avenue, in Highbridge, a local guy, Larry Davis, robbed crack dealers and sometimes murdered them. At only twenty, Davis was notorious citywide. On November 19, 1986, in his sister's apartment on Fulton Avenue, he shot and wounded six of the twenty-some police officers who had come to arrest him. A woman officer had part of her jaw shot away, a detective took a bullet to the neck, an officer lost the sight in one eye. Escaping through a back window, Davis remained at large for seventeen days. The police set up a special command center in Yankee Stadium to coordinate the hunt for him and raided his relatives' apartments. His mother, Mary Davis, "a lovely churchgoing woman," according to neighbors, was hospitalized for a heart attack after they raided hers. Detectives offered a $25,000 reward for information leading to his capture. Larry Davis was the most sought-after outlaw in the Bronx since James DeLancey.

All the police whom Davis shot survived. Members of the special Larry Davis squad captured him in an apartment on East 183rd Street where he was holding hostages. During the trial, his lawyer, William Kunstler, argued that the police themselves were the drug dealers, and had set up the raid to kill him so he would not reveal their corruption. When the jury acquitted him, police protests followed. Another jury found him guilty in the murder of a dealer, and he got a long term in prison, where a fellow inmate stabbed him to death in 2008.

The terrors of crack and HIV/AIDS provided the backdrop in the early years when the Bronx was rebuilding—as if those two scourges had followed fire to finish the job, and the rescuers arrived almost too late. Mayor Koch's housing victories sat atop his legacy but his failure to take the AIDS crisis seriously and respond to it better was his biggest failure. In the Bronx, nonprofits answered the needs of AIDS sufferers long before the city did, just as local tenant organizations and community development corporations got busy on housing before the official bureaucracy did. In 1988, a nonprofit on the Grand Concourse called the Citizens Advice Bureau (CAB), which is now BronxWorks, started its Positive Living program, offering free services for AIDS sufferers. People would have been worse off, maybe dying on the street, were it not for BronxWorks and nonprofits like them.

And still the dealers kept killing one another. I have mentioned the ten murders on Beekman Place between 1991 and 1992 during a war over three-dollar versus five-dollar crack. Smaller street dealers who smoked up their own supply and then couldn't pay the suppliers were frequent targets. A priest at St. Martin of Tours Catholic Church in Belmont officiated at twenty-five funerals in the space of a single year; all were of boys or young men between the ages of sixteen and twenty-five.

Then, unexpectedly, crack use declined and all but went away. By the mid-nineties, its potential customers seemed to have realized how deadly it was and switched to the gentler highs of marijuana. At the same time, treatments using combinations of drugs began to bring down the numbers of deaths from AIDS.

AFTER FERNANDO FERRER took his daughter to his old address and found nothing but grass and prairie, they walked to his childhood playground, known as Playground 52, because it's across Kelly Street from what was then called Intermediate School 52. Ferrer was pushing his daughter on the swings in the playground when a young man started yelling at him, asking him what he was doing there, calling him a rich guy and saying he should go back to his own neighborhood. Ferrer ignored him but the guy didn't stop. Finally, Ferrer yelled back, "You're a pain in the ass! Who the hell are you, anyway?" The guy said, "I'm Al Quiñones, and *I'm* from around here!" Ferrer thought for a minute and asked, "Is Louis Quiñones your big brother?" The guy said, "Yeah." Ferrer said, "That figures." He had known Louis in elementary school. Not long after meeting Al Quiñones at the playground, Ferrer hired him as a community organizer. "And he was very good at it," Ferrer said.

More than anybody, Al Quiñones rescued Playground 52. At first, the dealers had been all over it, and he called them out and ejected them at physical risk to himself. With the same aggressiveness he showed toward Ferrer, Quiñones kept track of the park's comings and goings. He founded a neighborhood group called 52 People for Progress whose focus was (and is) this playground. When dealers persisted in hanging out on some concrete benches, he took a sledgehammer and demolished the benches. Once he'd started working for Ferrer, he agitated for Parks Department money to fix up the playground. Ferrer's administration funded its first major reconstruction. After that, Quiñones continued to lobby subsequent borough presidents, and persuaded Rubén Díaz (Sr.) to do what Ferrer calls "the mother of all rehabs" on it.

You might already know about Larry Davis. His picture was on front pages, and in magazines, and on TV, and you can find videos about him online. But probably you never heard of Al Quiñones. All over the Bronx, especially the South Bronx, people like him saved their buildings and parks and neighborhoods by community effort, but that's a harder story to describe. In the United States, we have the tradition of the Lone Man. Larry Davis was an antihero Lone Man. Usually our heroes and antiheroes follow their destinies alone. I think that's what caught my eye about the Bebo inscription—"I STAN ALONE"—and what appeals to me about the character of Gouverneur Morris. He was a lonesome person, suddenly going off by himself, or staying in Paris as the only remaining diplomat when chaos ruled. This sort of protagonist fills our national dreams. I like solitude myself, and I was eligible for social security before it occurred to me that a bunch of loners wandering around and doing as they pleased might not make for much of a society.

The cityscape of the Bronx hints at how it was saved. Names of some of the heroes are on murals and street signs and buildings. For example, Evelina Antonetty, a Puerto Rico–born union organizer who became a community activist and parent advocate, led the fight for bilingual education in the Bronx schools. Her movement spread to the other boroughs and even across the United States. She founded the United Bronx Parents, a social services organization that has now been in existence for fifty years. Photos of her show her at demonstrations with her mouth open, yelling. She died in 1985, and there's a playground named for her on the Grand Concourse near 149th Street. In the next generation, Lorraine Montenegro, her daughter, created supportive housing for women with substance abuse problems. She died in Puerto Rico in 2017 while assisting victims of Hurricane Maria. Now on Prospect Avenue there's a residence for women and children that bears Lorraine Montenegro's name.

The mind could grasp the sameness of the ruins when you looked from a distance at the burned-out blocks, but the rebuilding can't be taken in at a glance. It was multicentric and involved thousands of local people. Sometimes Bronx residents improvised their own public services—one woman started her own bus line when the scheduled route to her neighborhood was planned-shrunk. Another, Genevieve Brooks, co-founded Mid-Bronx Desperadoes (MBD), the housing group that completed the Charlotte Gardens project; MDB now owns twenty-nine buildings and oversees twelve hundred units of housing. Juanita "Ma" Carter started an anti-drug and -violence organization called Not In My Neighborhood, You Don't! Dr. Richard Izquierdo founded a health clinic in Soundview that became one of the biggest in the state.

Bronxites by the hundreds got together to clean up the Bronx River, and they had such a good effect on it that in 2013 a daredevil swam its entire eight miles in the Bronx. Six and a half hours in the not-yet-pristine water did him no harm. Volunteers still clean trash from the river and keep watch on it. Several porpoises were seen swimming in it in January 2023.

The city had always dumped stuff in the Bronx. It's used as a trash transfer point and a site for utilities that wealthier neighborhoods don't want nearby, such as incinerators. For years an incinerator that disposed of medical waste issued noxious smoke from its stack at the corner of Locust Avenue and East 141st Street. People said they saw amputated body parts brought there. Joe Perez, born and raised in Mott Haven, co-founded the South Bronx Clean Air Coalition with the goal of getting rid of that noisome incinerator, and after decades of organizing and agitating, the Clean Air Coalition and the neighborhood finally persuaded the city to shut it down. In front of the Bronx Courthouse there should be a stone monument engraved with Joe Perez's name, and the names of the hundreds or thousands of others who participated in the borough's revival, like a town-square monument to residents who fought in a war.

INSPECTOR KEIYON RAMSEY, of the NYPD, grew up in the Castle Hill neighborhood. His grandmother, who raised him, told him that a Black household must never call the police. She also told him over and over how smart he was. At first, he didn't appreciate hearing that, because it meant she expected him to apply himself in school and do well.

Like a lot of people, his grandmother was friends with a woman named Gerri Lamb, who ran the Castle Hill Tenants Association, volunteered with youth groups, led the rebuilding of the community center, and served as president of the local council of NYCHA tenants. Gerri Lamb had seen Keiyon around the neighborhood—she had a daughter his age—and agreed with his grandmother's high opinion of him. His grandmother asked Gerri Lamb if she could get him enrolled in her daughter's class in the honors program at PS 138, which was close enough that he could walk to school. Gerri Lamb did, and Keiyon found that being in an honors program was all right. He did well in English, not so well in math, and got better-than-average grades overall. He began to accept thinking of himself as smart, and he liked having that confidence.

"Gerri Lamb was always a big advocate of me," the inspector told me when I interviewed him at a Bronx precinct house in 2020. She followed his progress through PS 138 and then middle school, which was also within walking distance. Stevenson High School was nearby, too, and she saw that he got enrolled in an advanced program there.

As a teenager in hazardous times, he could have gone wrong with just a misstep. He saw guns and violence and crack. Friends were killed. Once after school, he and some other kids saw the cut-up body of a woman in a suitcase. His two uncles, who also lived at his grandmother's, went through addictions, and did time in prison. In high school Keiyon became a rapper. Once, he got arrested for spray-painting a stencil of his rap group's logo on the sidewalk in front of Truman High School. He was sent to Central Booking, and then to various other holding cells around the Bronx, until a policeman friend of the family he was staying with at the time helped to obtain his release. The judge sentenced him to five weeks of community service, which he fulfilled by picking up trash at the Parkchester Houses.

He continued to do well in high school, and Fordham University awarded him a full scholarship. For the first time in his life, he had to ride a bus to classes, which he hated to do. He felt like an outsider at Fordham and couldn't keep up with the work. Soon he dropped out, thereby giving up a free four-year college education—a decision he later could not believe he had made. Unable to earn enough from his music, he drove a city Access-A-Ride bus, then became a security guard. Then, in a radical swerve, he joined the traffic police. To him this seemed almost like a betrayal of the family's credo. One night he was writing parking tickets with a partner, Eric Murray, who liked to take it easy and enjoy life. Murray bought an ice cream cone from a Mr. Softee truck and was eating it when two white cops in an NYPD cruiser went by. Traffic cops don't carry guns and are sometimes considered to be on a rung below regular cops. Ramsey waved at the cops and the driver gave him the finger.

Ramsey was crushed and furious. He went and sat in the traffic patrol car and said, "Fuck these guys, man." But then Eric Murray surprised him. Murray said they both knew the NYPD could be racist and horrible. But he said, "You can *change* that, man." He said Ramsey could go to the Police Academy, become a cop, and change the culture. He told him he was smart, and a good man, and could do it.

Ramsey took his friend's advice. He applied to the Police Academy, got in, worked hard, and graduated in the top 3 percent of his class. From there Officer Keiyon Ramsey rose quickly in the NYPD and even managed to earn his BA and MA while doing his job. He looks the part of a cop, like a police officer on a poster. He is over six feet tall, broad-shouldered, and easy and level in his manner. He worked in street patrol, then as a transit officer in the subways, then he managed security in schools. All his assignments were in the Bronx. He considered the schools his most productive assignment, because he could remember being like the kids he oversaw. He won promotions to sergeant, lieutenant, and then captain. Captains command precincts. When he was assigned to the 40th Precinct, he had another captain immediately above him. One day, when a community meeting came up, his superior sent him to represent the precinct in the superior's place.

"I'm at this meeting, and the Neighborhood Coordination program is now rolling out," he told me. "They're talking about community stuff, all these local leaders, and who do I see in the crowd? Gerri Lamb! She hadn't seen me in years. They call me up to the podium, I give my presentation, say I'm a CO of the Fortieth Precinct and I'm the community coordination officer, and she gets up, interrupts the whole meeting, and says, 'That's my guy! He's one of us! He's from my community!' Everybody in the crowd clapped. And I was, like, 'Wow.'

"Later we had a conversation, and she was like, 'I'm so happy, so proud of you.' It was a great moment."

Captain Ramsey had a rough 2019–2020. By then he was the head of policing in Police Service Area 8, which consists of twelve housing projects in Throgs Neck with twenty thousand residents. Covid infected more than a quarter of the almost two hundred cops and civilian workers in his command. In January, one of his rookie officers was killed by a drunk driver while on his way home from work. Captain Ramsey went to the hospital and grieved with the family. Not long after, while checking the department reports of recent NYPD deaths from Covid, he saw the name of Eric Murray. He collapsed at his desk and cried. Like him, Murray had quit Traffic and joined the force; Captain Ramsey, always the harder-working and more ambitious of the two, felt bad that he hadn't stayed in better touch, or ever thanked him.

In September 2019, a plainclothes cop on loan to him from another command was shot by a man whom his Street Crime unit was trying to arrest. At the hospital, in front of a small group that included then-mayor Bill DeBlasio and the top NYPD brass, Captain Ramsey gave a report on the shooting and on what was being done to catch the gunman. The plainclothes cop died in the same room where the officer in the car accident had died in January.

Captain Ramsey was promoted to deputy inspector the next year. Of the two thousand graduates in his Police Academy class, he was the first to attain this high rank. Adding to the shocks of this whipsaw period, Gerri Lamb passed away. "I was very messed up by this, too, because I did not realize how influential she was in my life," he said. "This was the lady, you know, that began my whole life. I gave a speech at her wake, and a lot of people in her community were like, 'We want him to be our precinct's commanding officer.'" (In 2023, Keiyon Ramsey was promoted to inspector.)

A street sign that says "Gerri Lamb Way" is at the northwest corner of the intersection of Castle Hill Avenue and Randall Avenue. The immediate surroundings occupy a dominant piece of ground. To the south, Castle Hill Avenue slopes downhill to the shore of Long Island Sound. Trees block the view of the water, but the wide-open sky indicates ocean in that direction. High-rises of the Castle Hill Houses are at each corner of the intersection. Above the buildings, every few minutes, ascending passenger jets go by. On a summer morning, their engine whine and the twitter of sparrows are the main sounds. Gerri Lamb's name, and the other names on street signs and parks around the Bronx and around the city, propose a way of living your life—that its purpose isn't just yourself, its purpose is to serve. If you ask who saved the Bronx and who saves it every day, the answer in the big picture is Gerri Lamb.

38

IN HOT AND STEAMY AUGUST, parts of the city and the suburbs empty out—but not the Bronx, and especially not the South Bronx. On the first Sunday of that month, a big event takes place with its center either at the picnic grounds at the southeast corner of Crotona Park, or about a mile away, at the Basil Behagen Playground, at the corner of East 166th Street and Tinton Avenue. The two centers of this event attract different but overlapping crowds. Collectively, the event is called Old-Timers' Day. Many hundreds of people attend; they are either from the neighborhood or no longer from the neighborhood but from elsewhere in the Bronx, or from farther away. Former residents who have moved back down south sometimes return for this reunion. By my unscientific observation, I would say that the older old-timers prefer the gathering in Crotona Park, and the younger old-timers, down to the teenage old-timers, opt for the one at Basil Behagen Playground.

The first Old-Timers' Day was in 1969, and since then the gathering has missed only one year, 2020 (Covid). I don't know how such a crowded get-together manages to come off with no apparent organization. If people put up handbills announcing the event, I've never seen them. It's hard to find anything about it online. At the Crotona Park

Old-Timers' Day, there are no banners announcing it, no registration, no speakers' table, no schedule—no visible bureaucracy at all. Just a lot of people, and those tents that don't seem to have a name other than "tents," but they're not really tents, because they're just a tent roof supported by poles at the four corners. Shelters? Pavilions? Canopies? I don't know what they're called. When I asked people what they called them, they said, "I don't know—tents?" Red and light blue and pink and yellow tents like these create a sort of enchanted-village effect among the trees, as barbecue smoke rises through the greenery. Every year, families are at the same places in the gathering, which makes it easier for their friends to find them.

Old-Timers' Day is like a Brigadoon that exists in people's minds and reemerges from the mist once every year instead of once every hundred years. At Old-Timers' Day, an ideal version of Paradise Bronx comes back to life.

IN 2021, I stumbled on the Old-Timers' Day in Crotona Park. I had heard rumors of it but didn't know where it was. I wandered around looking for it and found it the way you find other campers in a forest, by the smoke. I could smell the barbecue. From a distance, the sight of the crowd among the trees made me think of what a backwoods camp-meeting revival might have looked like when you were approaching it in a wagon. The sun was coming through the foliage in shafts, and excited flocks of sparrows were flying around. Sometimes in the thick shade you couldn't see them clearly, but when they flew into the light, their many wings shimmered all together. When barbecuers swept the old ashes from the in-place grills and onto the ground, the sparrows swooped in and looked for ancient barbecue scraps and took dust baths.

At a tent that said "Hip Hop Blvd., Inc." I met Al Pizarro, the CEO of that organization, which promotes knowledge of the Bronx as the founding place of hip-hop. Pizarro, a stocky, personable man, is also an ambassador of the United Coalition for Humanity, a charitable organization that works for world peace through a shared love of hip-hop. The UCH was founded by Kurtis Blow, the rapper.

Pizarro had time to talk, because not many people were stopping by to get free promo baseball caps and T-shirts. Hip-hop was not the music of the old-timers, or not of these old-timers. In keeping with the free-style organizational structure, no single sound system played for the whole gathering. Families or groups had brought their own systems, and each seemed to be playing Motown from the 1960s. The Temptations, Diana Ross and the Supremes, Smokey Robinson and the Miracles, the Four Tops, and others of that time competed and combined in a medley effect as you moved around.

At the edge of this corner of Crotona Park, it's possible to see the intersection, just a block away, where Jimmy Carter got out of his limo in 1977 and walked on Charlotte Street. By chance, Jimmy and Rosalynn Carter had celebrated their seventy-fifth wedding anniversary a few days before this Old-Timers' Day, in 2021, and friends of mine had attended the event at the Carter Library, in Plains, Georgia. One of the attendees, Jonathan Alter, had written a biography of Carter that reveals this series of facts: A great-grandfather of Jimmy Carter on his mother's side, James Thomas Gordy, fathered two sets of children. One set was with his (white) wife, and the other was with a woman he enslaved. Both the white and the Black Gordys prospered as Georgia farmers, but only the Black Gordys participated in the Great Migration.

A Black Gordy who ended up in Detroit became the father of Berry Gordy, the founder of Motown Records. Motown produced most of the 1960s hits that the Crotona Park old-timers were listening to today. That is, President Jimmy Carter was the producer Berry Gordy's second cousin—half second cousin, to be exact, because they share a great-grandfather but not a great-grandmother. Both Carter and Gordy lived well into their nineties. (As of this writing, both are still alive.) Why neither made more of their familial link I don't know. Maybe people in general aren't as struck by it as I am. I mean, here's another white U.S. president with Black relatives, and here's a Black artist-businessman who had more influence, culturally, than his presidential second cousin. When I told Al Pizarro about this little-known concurrence, his interest was slight.

The old-timers who did stop by the hip-hop tent were hip-hop veterans themselves. I met the Original Al Capone, who said he deejayed with the Cold Crush Brothers, long ago. His birth name is Ray Carter and he said I should call him Ray. He had a short white beard razor-trimmed along the line of his jaw, and he wore a white jersey top and white Bermudas with a matching design of red-white-and-blue spatter dots on the front. He said, "I'm sixty years old and I started in hip-hop when I was ten. My godfather was *the* Godfather—of Soul, I mean. My father was James Brown's bodyguard for fifteen years, and when I was born, James Brown agreed to be my godfather. So I came to performing naturally. My other love is cooking. I always did both. I became a chef when I was eleven." On his phone he showed me photos of elaborate catering spreads he had prepared, and photos of celebrities whose events he has catered. In one he stood smiling with the former vice president Al Gore.

A Parks Department boss in a white uniform shirt strolled past accompanied by a three-person retinue, then strolled past again. A heron in Indian Pond, next to the gathering, rose in slow, creaky flight and perched overhead in a sweet-gum tree. The night before, police had disarmed a man near the park, and in the struggle, he had shot one of them in the ankle. Police higher-ups had assigned a lot of cops to this event. They stood quietly apart, leaning up against things and checking their cell phones on a street bordering the park.

BY THE FOLLOWING YEAR, I had learned about the other Old-Timers' Day, the one at Basil Behagen Playground. (There may be even more Old-Timers' Days. People say there are some in Harlem on that same Sunday.) The way I learned was by talking with Duane Johnson, of Johnson's Bar-B-Q. I took to stopping by there in the mornings, before he opened for business, to ask him one question or another, such as about Hilton White and the Bronx Falcons basketball team, or about Kool Herc, who Johnson said came to the restaurant sometimes. (I was hoping to meet Kool Herc, but that hasn't worked out yet.) To state it simply, Duane Johnson is a great man. He's someone who was born to feed people, and he does, six days a week (the restaurant is closed Mondays), with barbecue, collards, macaroni and cheese, coconut cake, etc., at reasonable prices. He told me he serves free barbecue at Old-Timers' Day every year at Behagen Playground, and he spoke about that event as if it were the only Old Timer's Day.

On Sunday, August 7, 2022, I arrived at Behagen Playground at 8:45 a.m. The morning was sunny and warm, but at least today the temperatures would not be up in the high nineties, as they had been. The playground consists of an all-purpose open area; a big, grassy baseball field; and a sunken basketball court with concrete bleacher-steps along three sides. Here, Old-Timers' Day would include a basketball tournament. An officials' table had been set up at the no-steps side of the basketball court, and a man on a ladder was putting new white nets on the baskets. From a van at the curb nearby, another man took out boxes of trophies. Then he removed cases of bottled water, set them on the sidewalk, and put the boxes of trophies back in the van. Another man was mowing the baseball outfield with a gas-powered push-mower.

Not much else going on yet, so I walked the almost-mile to Crotona Park. People there had already set up their grills, some resembling small steam engines, with chimneys. Other old-timers were carrying in coolers the size of storage trunks, a man at each handle. A woman was breaking up ice in plastic sacks by hitting them against the side of a picnic table, then pouring the cubes into coolers. A popular brand called the Wheelie Cool cooler had a handle at one end and a set of wheels at the other, so it could be wheeled along like a roll-aboard suitcase. Cops were going by in little bubble-top vehicles, and EMS attendants consulted with one another. The day got hotter. Standing nozzles emitted white misty sprays of water at four or five stations scattered around this corner of the park and the air felt fresher near them. Kids played in the sprays, or bicycled along the paths, or threw rocks in Indian Pond. The splashes made ragged holes in the duckweed that covered the water like pool-table felt.

I was sitting by myself and taking notes at a four-person concrete picnic table in the shade. At a table nearby, in the sun, a young woman with two small boys was setting out the picnic she had brought. She wore a yellow, green, and orange knit dress; her hair, in tightly curled ringlets, had been dyed yellow and pink. On top it was gathered into a pink bun. I asked if she would like to take my table and be in the shade. She thanked me but said she was afraid of bugs falling from the trees into the babies' food. She was brown with light blue eyes. We got to talking. I told her my name, and she said hers was Ruby. She had grown up in the neighborhood and had just moved back to it from Las Vegas. She used to come to Old-Timers' Day every year, but this was her first one in five years.

She said if I needed water or snacks or anything, just to ask her. She asked me what I did. I said I was a writer and was working on a book about the Bronx. She said, "I'm an author, too. I have a book coming out next week from Dorrance Press. It's called *How to Get Your Kids Back from Child Protective Services*, by Ms. Ruby Red. That's my author name." Her little boys, who might have been twins, were playing with identical yellow radio-powered sports cars, running them around on the pavement. After we talked for a while longer, I strolled off, saying I'd be back. Talking to her had made me feel happy, and present in the day.

Some people were dressed up specially for the event. An older guy wore a light gray glen plaid jacket and vest, but with matching shorts instead of trousers, and a knotted gold chain for a tie. Another had on an Indian-pattern dashiki, a black-and-white clerical collar, and a black fez with a wine-red tassel. Hair had been done up. A woman in daffodil-yellow top and slacks had piled her gold braids into a tall, Babylonian-looking tower. A group of little kids followed a young woman who rocked a purplish-red mane of Tina Turner hair. A guy in a black tricornered Revolutionary War hat with a turkey feather dangling from it bicycled around and shouted. A middle-aged man wearing Black Spades gang colors walked a solitary route through the gathering. On the back of his cut-sleeves vest, the insignia was a spade superimposed on two crossed swords, with the words *Black* above and *Spades* below, all in shades of black, gray, and white.

A breeze began to blow, as if to accompany the day's rising heat. Some of the phragmites reeds along the shore of Indian Pond stood twelve feet tall. Their stalks were straight, and their leaves all went off to one side like quick Japanese brushstrokes. The reeds and their leaves bent and thrashed before the wind. White and gray clouds had mounted up high in the blue sky. The tops of tall trees visible to the east tossed like vegetables in boiling soup, and big clusters of leaves showed their lighter undersides.

I spent the day going back and forth between the two gatherings. At Behagen Playground, helpers of Duane Johnson were setting up tents and kiosks next to the chain-link fence along East 166th Street. It looked as if the Johnson's Bar-B-Q presence was preparing to take up almost an entire block. At the basketball tournament, a heavy staccato of sneakers hitting pavement and the ref's whistle interruptions came through despite the stylings of a DJ—this Old-Timers' Day did have an all-prevailing sound system—who played percussive music accompanied by commentary. On the other side of the chain-link fence, a more Spanish-speaking crowd watched a softball game on the adjoining ball field. A similar crowd surrounded a soccer match on the all-purpose play area. Then a sudden downpour moved through the neighborhood. I got under a plane tree next to Tinton Avenue next to the playground. That was what other people were doing, or else putting towels or something over their heads. The storm went by like a short parade and the sun emerged again. The court was wet and puddled and the basketball tournament did not immediately restart.

On one of my circuits between the two Old-Timers' Days, I was walking on a path in Crotona Park when I heard someone shout my name. This surprised me. I looked to see who could be calling for me here. It was Ruby, pushing her boys in a double stroller on a sidewalk on the park's edge. I waved and went over to her. She said she had decided to leave. She wanted to go back to her family's apartment, she said, because she was afraid her babies would get wet in the rain and come down with something. She said it had been a pleasure to meet me and she wished me luck with my book. I wished her luck with hers. She was one of those people you meet only once, and you never forget them because they uplift you in a mysterious way.

On another circuit I detoured slightly to the corner of Charlotte Street and Boston Road, where I found my old acquaintance Willie Hemanns out in his yard. He was talking with Ricky Scott, a tall man in his seventies, who had been one of the original purchasers of a Charlotte Gardens house back in the days of Ed Logue and Mayor

Koch. Ricky Scott still owned his house, which he said was now worth close to three quarters of a million dollars. Willie Hemanns said he had just received and turned down an offer on his own house for eight hundred thousand. They talked about how crime in the area used to be bad, then it went down, and now it was bad again.

The other day, they said, they had been standing and talking just as they were now, when some kids came by on an electric scooter and shot them with an automatic pellet gun. The purpose was to make a video of the shooting, presumably to put on TikTok. There's a TikTok challenge for people to post videos of that kind of attack. One kid shot them, the other videoed the shooting with his phone. The pellets hit them in the shoulder, chest, and neck, and they hurt. Hemanns and Scott thought they'd been shot with BBs, but it must've been gel pellets, which the guns can also shoot. Both men hunted in the grass but didn't find any BBs. Police who responded to their call said they didn't investigate such small incidents.

BY LATE AFTERNOON, the Crotona Park Old-Timers' Day was packed. People greeted one another with embraces and fist bumps and complicated handshakes. I passed many new arrivals coming down paths in the park, trying to locate by cell phone family members or friends who were already there; much joy and long-range waving ensued when they connected. I saw no religious groups or signage, and only one nonsecular T-shirt. In white script on a red background, it said, "Not today, Satan!" Still, I could not shake the impression that this was a camp revival meeting from back when. One overheard remark reinforced that. I heard a young woman say, "Y'all people don't even know who Esau *is*, man!"

At Behagen Playground, the Johnson Bar-B-Que emplacements did indeed take up most of the block of East 166th Street between Tinton and Union Avenues but serving hadn't started yet. The basketball tournament ended and then an awards ceremony wound down. After it, the kids on and around the court dispersed in every direction like a rack of pool balls at the break shot. Near where I sat, on a bench by the plane tree that had not kept off much rain, kids went running past with trophies in each fist. Some even had three trophies and were helping one another stuff them into backpacks. A lanky boy with a cast on his left forearm who carried a big trophy in one hand and a smaller one in the other said to a boy carrying only a smaller one, "I got a Most Valuable Player, with a cast on my arm! The one you got is just a participation trophy."

By five o'clock at Crotona Park, almost everybody was eating. Late joiners brought shoulder carriers that held collapsible folding chairs. The chairs were unlimbered and assembled, and the arrivals appended themselves to various groups. One older man joined in such a way that everybody's backs were to him, but then somebody noticed, and the group rearranged the circle to bring him in. That happened a lot of times—the inclusion of new people. There was happy conversational noise, and the Motown and Barry White and Al Green songs kept coming. The sun declined over the pond, a snowy egret waded in it, and the wind had not quit in the high trees. The planet could almost be heard to turn, click by click. Time went by in its stately summer manner, and there was a sense of everybody being part of its passing.

At Behagen Playground, Johnson's Bar-B-Q had finished serving and its tents and kiosks were already being taken down. I should've come back earlier but the Crotona Park Brigadoon had put an enchantment on me. Duane Johnson was dismantling the barbecue emplacements with his dozen or so helpers. Fit-looking in a T-shirt with the name of his business on it, he shook my hand and greeted me. Accomplishment radiated from him like light. I asked him how many people he had fed, and he said he didn't know. Hundreds? "Oh, yes." A thousand? "I don't know." To feed so many is a princely gesture. I said it was as if he had built a whole community by himself, and he agreed. He looked joyful, justified, and serene.

The playground DJ had not yet run out of steam. He was playing Tom Jones's "She's a Lady" at paint-peeling volume; then, suddenly, came a blessed quiet. In a minute, the microphone reappeared in the hands of a preacher whose name I didn't catch. He stood in the middle of the sunken basketball court with a dozen or more men and a few women and asked them to form a circle, hold hands, and bow their heads in prayer. They all did, and in the silence, a lot of the people in the park also bowed their heads. The minister thanked God for the day and the fellowship, and then said a lot more. The ring of people holding hands and keeping their heads bowed seemed to get restless. Then he prayed for "the people we don't see here today, who we used to see here." That got a quiet and unanimous response from the crowd. It seemed that everybody was thinking of somebody who wasn't there. The minister said that the physically absent people weren't really gone; they were transitioned, but still with us. He prayed that everybody who attended both in body and spirit today would be here for Old-Timers' Day next year. The crowd quietly repeated his "Amen," and the men put their hats back on.

As I walked to the Prospect Avenue subway stop in the mild evening, I thought about the people he mentioned who were physically no longer present. More people died of Covid in the Bronx than in any other borough, proportional to population. That may have taken an extra toll on the old-timers. As for the younger old-timers, the Patterson Houses are a mile from Behagen Playground, and on the high chain-link fence around the project's basketball courts, residents have put up pictures of young men—smiling, candid portraits of the kind that grandparents carry in their wallets, but greatly enlarged and printed on treated canvas with metal grommets at the corners. The portraits hang in rows along the top of the fence and give the young men's names and nicknames, with their dates of birth and dates of death. The latter dates are recent. It pained me to think of the parents and grandparents and other loved ones, and how they had withstood, or maybe not withstood, these blows.

I turned my mind away from that and wondered why I seem to be the only one who's impressed that Berry Gordy and Jimmy Carter are second cousins. Maybe people don't grasp the full implications. Let's say, as a thought experiment, that Aretha Franklin was the eight-greats-granddaughter of Sally Hemings and Thomas Jefferson. That's also a description of a plausible American family tree. I find it hard not to love hypocritical, smooth-talking Mr. Jefferson; and how can you not admire and cherish Sally Hemings? That you love Aretha, Queen of Soul, goes without saying, and you must at least feel sympathy for the hard luck, "no good deed goes unpunished" President

Jimmy Carter. And of course you're grateful for Berry Gordy and Motown. Certain kinds of American grace are so sweet and so undeserved, it's like a textbook demonstration of the mystery of grace. Musing on that, and on all the old-timers, and on the too-quick passing of summers, I walked along Prospect Avenue to the station.

39

PLAYGROUND 52 is on Kelly Street between Leggett Avenue and Avenue St. John, sheltered within its neighborhood just off Southern Boulevard. One summer morning I wandered into it, drawn by a good feeling I got as I passed by. Hetty Fox said she could "tune" her street—she could affect the sound of the kids playing on it by how she set up games and activities, and by how she paid attention to what they said to her and to one another. From the sidewalk, Playground 52 sounded well-tuned.

The man who runs it, José "Reggie" Vasquez, sees all. He came over and introduced himself almost as soon I walked in, and we got to talking. He said he grew up in the neighborhood and Al Quiñones was his hero. He was trying to carry on the park in his spirit. Vasquez is fit-looking and decisive, with quick, dark eyes, and he combs his thinning hair straight back. His yellow T-shirt said "Ecuador" on it, but his family came here from Puerto Rico. For twenty-eight years, he drove a forklift in the fruit market at Hunts Point, and now he was retired. The market had its exciting moments, he said, such as when federal agents searched the fruit shipments for smuggled drugs.

As we talked, some kids came up and asked for a basketball, and he gave them one from a big wire container full of basketballs and soccer balls that was behind a gate to a backyard garden where he has an office. He took the apartment key of one of the kids as a deposit. Then he led me over to show me the basketball courts, making special note of the backboards, which are professional quality and of shatterproof plexiglass. Ralph Salamanca, the local city councilperson, got the Parks Department to install those backboards, he said. Some preschoolers in a group on recess from school were playing just on the other side of a fence nearby. I barely noticed them, but Vasquez stopped and looked more closely at three or four girls and a boy. "Why are you pushing him?" he asked the girls. They looked up guiltily and said the boy had done something or other to them. "If he did something to you, tell the teacher. Don't push him," Vasquez said. How he had even happened to observe this tiny struggle was beyond me.

The fires burned all around this place, back in the seventies, he said. He showed me where piles of junk cars used to be. Now at that spot was an outdoor amphitheater that could seat 350. The theater's bleachers-style seating of bent-iron slatted benches had attracted skateboarders, who liked to skate down the incline and grind on the bench edges. The wax the skaters put on their boards to reduce friction got on the seating, and then the audiences got wax on their clothes. Vasquez and James Melendez, the president of 52 People for Progress, explained the problem to the Parks Department, and to Ralph Salamanca. Eventually the city built a skateboard mini park with steps and ramps in a vacant space next to the theater. The sound of fast-rolling skate wheels now fills that area, and sometimes there's the thud of a kid falling and the clatter of a runaway board.

He showed me a new garden at a corner of the park, with recently planted flowers and vegetables in raised beds, and pots for allium and Japanese pomegranate trees, and walkways made of cement slabs salvaged from the Brooklyn Navy Yard. He said that Iris Rodriguez-Rosa, the Parks Department's first deputy commissioner, had taken an interest in this garden project and had provided the tall black chain-link fence around it. A group called Green Thumb had donated garden hoses with special attachments that hooked to the hydrant at the curb. As we talked, a Parks Department workman went by, and Vasquez reminded him to fix the bolt on the door to the playground's men's room.

Vasquez and I exchanged phone numbers. He said he would keep me up-to-date on events in the park, and I was pleased to get text message greetings from him over the holidays. The next spring, I began stopping by regularly, and sitting in the park in good weather. The drinking fountain worked, and the bathroom was always clean. On hot summer afternoons, kids rode their bikes through the sprinklers or ran through them with their arms in the air. There were salsa performances on the amphitheater stage on Wednesday evenings starting at about seven o'clock. I met James Melendez, who showed me photos of the park's several renovations. He and Vasquez also provided commentaries on the people who came and went. Of a woman panhandler to whom I had given a dollar (against their silent headshaking no), they said who the woman's mother was, and the woman's grandmother, and where the family used to live; they seemed to know her whole biography right up to now.

On some evenings, I took the train into the city from New Jersey to see the salsa performances. One afternoon I got off at the Moynihan Train Hall, where the train had stopped instead of at its usual endpoint in Penn Station. The change disoriented me, and as I crossed Eighth Avenue between the two, I tripped over a traffic divider, fell, and broke my left elbow. I figured it was broken but it didn't hurt much yet, so I kept going, because I had told Vasquez and Melendez I would be there. As usual, Vasquez saw me the minute I arrived. He told me who tonight's bands were and gave me a program. He was glad I came. The sun set during the concert and the stage lights brightened on the performers. Their costumes' spangles, which had been invisible in daylight, glittered in the dark. The lyrics and the musicians' banter between songs were all in Spanish. A wide age range of dancers from the audience salsa-danced in the open space before the stage. One young woman was so energetic she exhausted her partners one after another and new ones kept replacing them.

Just at last light a flight of pigeons made a quick swoop above the park, and Vasquez knew the pigeons, too. They belonged to a local

pigeon fancier like himself. Vasquez had kept pigeons in the neighborhood since he was a boy and his mother would not let him keep them.
When she found out he had them in cages hidden under his bed, she
relented. He raised thousands of pigeons through the years and still
had about two hundred on his building's roof. During the evening,
my elbow got stiff. Later X-rays showed the break. Doctors had me
wear a sling but said I didn't need a cast, and the arm healed slightly
crooked on its own.

ON AN AUGUST weekend afternoon, a group sponsored by the New York
Yankees put on a program in the playground amphitheater featuring
former Yankee batboys. The Bronx has supplied the team with a lot of
batboys—kids of fourteen and older who handle equipment on the field
and off, pick up dropped bats and shin guards and wrist guards and get
them out of the way, bring baseballs to the umpires, supply the dugouts
with chewing gum and sunflower seeds, etc. The former batboys at this
event were now grown men. Before it began, one of them, Ray Negron,
happened to sit next to me, in the last row at the top of the amphitheater where the seating has a back to lean against. Vasquez had already
introduced us. I asked Negron how he had become a batboy.

"When I was a teenager, I got involved in writing graffiti," he said.
"I was kind of a wild graffiti-writing kid. One day some friends and I
were doing graffiti on Yankee Stadium, and we didn't see this limousine roll up beside us. My friends took off, I tripped over my feet, and a
guy jumped out from the limo and grabbed me by the back of the neck.
Then he threw me in the back seat and got in after me, and a couple
guys with him held on to me, and the limo drove through a gate to the
stadium. I took another look at the guy who grabbed me and saw that
it was the owner of the team, George Steinbrenner.

"So the limo goes down into the bowels of the stadium, where
most people never go," Negron continued. "Most people don't know
that there used to be a jail, like a holding pen, down in the stadium
basement. (This was in the old stadium.) Mr. Steinbrenner gets out,
his guys pull me from the limo, and they put me in this jail. The guy
from stadium security who's in charge of the jail, he says, 'One look

at this kid, and I can tell he'll never be anything but the punk he is today.' Mr. Steinbrenner stops, looks at the guy, and says, 'Fuck you. Gimme back the kid.'

"So they take me out of the jail, Mr. Steinbrenner puts me back in the limo, and he asks me my name. I tell him, and he says, 'Ray, you and I are gonna prove that man wrong. You are gonna turn your life around.' He asks me if I play baseball, I said, 'Yeah, of course'—I love baseball, played it all my life—and he says, 'Good. I'm gonna make you a batboy, starting today. You're gonna get a salary, you're gonna do your schoolwork, you're gonna graduate high school, and from now on you're working for *me*.' Then he says, 'Ray, I will be counting on you. And the one thing you have to remember above all—do not *fuck* with me.' So I was a Yankee batboy for six years, and then I got other jobs in the organization, and then I became Mr. Steinbrenner's personal assistant, and I had that job until the day Mr. Steinbrenner died."

This story is the basis of a play called *The Batboy*, which Negron wrote and from which he and other performers planned to do some scenes that afternoon. Negron has also written bestselling children's books and produced movies on baseball themes. His position with the Yankees is community consultant. Today he was doing this event with other former batboys, including Luis Castillo, who grew up nearby, on Kelly Street, and who has known the playground master, Vasquez, for years. Luis Castillo's nickname is Squeegee. He joined us in the last row of bleachers, introduced himself, and said he would tell me the story of his nickname; but at that moment, another former batboy, Raymond Avila, sat down on the other side of Ray Negron, and they started joking around. Avila works for the Hispanic Heritage Baseball Museum Hall of Fame, in San Francisco. He and Negron were batboys during the Yankees' explosive clubhouse years, back in the seventies, when Billy Martin managed the team and Reggie Jackson described himself as "the straw that stirs the drink."

"Thurman Munson never liked you," Negron said to Avila, by way of openers.

The men sat with their arms extended along the bench back—enjoying the summer sunshine, talking just-for-fun. The subject of

Thurman Munson, the starting catcher on that team, returned to present memory. Munson often projected a general sense of disapproval, with his dour, walrus-like mustache, and he had taken exception to the line about the drink and the straw, because he was a star on the team well before Reggie Jackson arrived.

"Munson liked me fine," Avila said. "Munson told *me* he didn't like *you*."

"Bull*shit*," Negron said. "Munson told me that you lost his lucky bat, and that ended his sixteen-game hitting streak. After that, he never liked you."

A pause. Then Avila said, "You know who never liked you? Billy Martin. He told me he never liked you."

"Aw, come on," Negron replied. "Billy Martin. Billy Martin didn't like *anybody*."

Some local volunteers were serving hot dogs, hamburgers, and sodas at tables behind the stage. Luis Castillo, aka Squeegee, got up from the bleachers and went to talk to his friend Ralph Bracco, the actor and Billy Martin impersonator, who was standing by the tables. I followed, and when I got a chance, I reminded Squeegee about the nickname. "Oh yeah, right," he said. "How I got to be called Squeegee—so when I was a kid, I loved the Yankees, and my moms got me tickets for every home game, and I never missed a game. I sat in the bleachers in left field, I was the youngest 'bleacher creature.' The tickets were only six bucks! At one game, I was sitting there with a friend, and he was yelling about something, and he began to use profanity. This woman named Tina Lewis, she is like the head of the bleachers. She heard the profanity, and she kicked us out. She called the ushers and they escorted us out.

"Next game, I was back in the bleachers, as usual, and the first thing I did, I went to Tina Lewis and apologized. She was impressed that I did that. So I got to know her, I saw her at every game, and one day she asked me if I would like to be a batboy. She introduced me to Lou Cucuzza, head of stadium personnel, and he interviewed me, and then he brought me to Brian Cashman, the manager of operations, the guy who hires the players. I guess Mr. Cashman liked me, too, because they hired me. I was fourteen years old, and four feet two inches tall. (I grew a lot since then.) They don't tailor uniforms for batboys, they give you what they got, and all they had for me was this too-big jersey. I wore it, it was baggy on me, and Derek Jeter saw me and said I looked like one of those cloths that the squeegee guys use to wash car windows. So Jeter called me Squeegee, and that became my batboy name."

Castillo/Squeegee got to be friends with Jeter and is still in touch with him. He says Jeter regarded him as a good-luck charm. That was even more the case with the pitcher David Cone, who got a karmic boost from the diminutive batboy during an afternoon game on Sunday, July 18, 1999. The context mattered, because it was Yogi Berra Day at the stadium, a healing event. Berra had been angry at George Steinbrenner ever since the owner fired him as manager some years before. Attempts on the Boss's part to reconcile had been rejected; but now Berra, a kindly and enlightened man, gave up his grudge and agreed to participate in a Stadium Day held in his honor. Don Larsen, the Yankee right-hander who was the only pitcher ever to achieve a perfect game in a World Series, threw out the first ball of this game, and Berra (who had been the catcher for Larsen's perfect game) caught it. Then they joined the crowd of about 42,000 and watched Cone pitch against the Montreal Expos. A rain delay suspended play in the third inning, by which point Cone had not allowed a base runner; but of course it was too early in the game for anybody to draw attention to that.

Cone waited out the thirty-three-minute delay in the dugout, not the bullpen, and when the rain stopped, he didn't have a bullpen catcher to warm up with. He couldn't find Joe Girardi, who was catching that game. Like the other Yankees, Cone was on cordial terms with Squeegee, so he asked the batboy to catch for him on the sidelines. Squeegee got a glove and a mask and caught a dozen or so warm-up pitches until Cone was ready to go back on the mound. There, the right-hander continued to baffle the Expos, setting them down in order through the remaining six innings, and thus recording the sixteenth perfect game in the history of professional baseball (there have been eight more since then). Fittingly, Don Larsen and Yogi Berra, the historic battery, were on hand to congratulate Cone after the triumph.

Luis Castillo/Squeegee is now forty-one, David Cone is sixty, and nothing as historic has happened to either of them since. As Castillo told me this story, he seemed like somebody who had been struck by fate, or maybe lightning. His eyes had a burning quality—like the Ancient Mariner's, only happy. "David Cone and I have remained good friends to this day," Castillo said. "He is active in my Squeegee Children's Literacy Foundation, which promotes reading among city kids, and he participates in benefit events for us, and we talk on the phone all the time. He's my son's godfather. We will never either one of us forget that game."

As I was listening and taking notes, local fans of Squeegee hovered around him. People in the neighborhood admire him and gaze at him with awe. A woman named Cynthia Jackson, who wore her hair in long braids, beamed at him and reached out and took him by the forearm and said, "We all remember Luis when he was a little boy. I used to look after him—he was my knee-baby! And he grew up to be such a fine man. Luis has inspired the whole community."

JOSÉ VASQUEZ TOLD ME that they were having a street-renaming ceremony honoring Al Quiñones in the park on a Friday morning, and I did not miss it. Again, I watched from the top row of the amphitheater. Bronx politicians sat on the stage in folding chairs and stood up one by one and reminisced about Quiñones. The honoree's ornery side was not left out. Rubén Díaz, Jr., then the Bronx borough president, said, "Al Quiñones cursed me out several times—let's not sugarcoat this." Previous borough presidents Rubén Díaz, Sr. (father of Rubén Jr.), and Fernando Ferrer brought their contrasting styles. The former, in a black shirt and black cowboy hat, was loud and haranguing and humorous; the latter, in L.L.Bean-style slacks and sweater, was measured and professorial and humorous. Ferrer said, "This is a good place . . . This is the center of the universe." People were called onstage to be recognized for their contributions to Playground 52. When the playground manager, José Vasquez, went up, he got the most applause.

Then the whole assembly removed to the intersection of Avenue St. John and Kelly Street, by the northwest corner of the playground, where a cousin of Al Quiñones pulled on the cord that slid away the sheath from the new street sign designating that part of the avenue as Albert 'Al' Quinones Way. (Generally, the city does not use diacritical marks on its signage; witness Louis Nine Boulevard, named for the Bronx state assemblyman Louis Niñé. Louis Nine Boulevard sounds like a vanity-plate version of Ninth Avenue.)

This event was where I first met Vivian Vázquez. After the on-stage ceremonies, but before the sign unveiling, I looked down at the attendees mixing and laughing and talking. A woman wearing a narrow-brim straw Panama hat stood amid a crowd of admirers. Some were hugging her, and she was turning her attention to each person, one by one. I have mentioned Vivian Vázquez already, in the context of the burning of the Bronx and the Blackout of '77, and I've described the looting that also destroyed Paradise Furniture, on Prospect Avenue, where her father worked for seventeen years. I've said she went to college upstate, still mystified and grieving because of what had happened to the Bronx of her childhood. The buildings where she grew up are a short walk from Playground 52, and like the rest of the crowd she had come to honor Al Quiñones.

By then I also knew of and admired her because of *Decade of Fire*, the feature-length documentary that she co-produced, narrates, and stars in. The film is about the years when the Bronx burned, and it looks into the reasons for the disaster. I had watched it several times, including once at the Harlem Film Festival, where she and her co-producer Gretchen Hildebran answered questions from the audience after the screening. I asked the playground manager Vasquez if he knew Vivian Vázquez (the two are not related, as their names' spellings indicate). He said he knew her well, she would be at the street renaming, and he would introduce me. From my vantage atop the bleachers, I saw him join the crowd around her and speak to her. Then he looked up at me and waved at me to come down. I did, he introduced me, and I asked her if I could talk to her sometime about how she happened to make *Decade of Fire*.

40

DESPITE HER FRESHMAN roommate's unhelpful prediction that she would fail, Vázquez graduated from SUNY Albany in 1984. She also came back to the Bronx. During her family's hard times, with her parents' divorce and her mother's return to Puerto Rico, she had thought she would leave. But on summer vacations from SUNY, she worked for her city assemblyman in a program to recruit kids from the neighborhood for college, registered people to vote, and did tenant organizing. Marcy, her older sister, had joined Evelina Antonetty and others protesting *Fort Apache, the Bronx*, and Vázquez admired them for speaking out. She later saw the *Fort Apache* demonstrations as the beginning of her own activism. Working with young people gave her the most satisfaction and she decided to make it a career.

The career led her to the Citizens Advice Bureau (CAB), the non-profit on the Grand Concourse that had stepped up during the crises of crack and AIDS. Carolyn McLaughlin, CAB's executive director (now retired), was one of the city's nonprofit dynamos. McLaughlin grew up in western Pennsylvania, where she graduated from Allegheny College and married a Kenyan fellow student. In 1968, she and her husband moved to the Bronx and she found a job as a caseworker with the city's welfare department. They had a son, the couple divorced, and she got her master's at the Columbia University School of Social Work. She remarried and for some years ran programs for the blind in senior citizen centers.

In 1979, the Federation of Protestant Welfare Agencies hired McLaughlin as executive director of the Citizens Advice Bureau office in the Bronx. It had one paid employee beside herself, two interns, and a fifty-thousand-dollar annual budget. As the head of CAB for the next thirty-four years, she built it into a major force for local assistance and improvement. During her tenure, it changed its name to Bronx-Works. Its core mission—to give advice—covers a lot of ground. Its motto is "Whatever your problem, we are here to help."

She and Vázquez have been friends and allies ever since McLaughlin hired her in the late nineties to run CAB's after-school programs for children. McLaughlin credits Vázquez as one of the main creators of CAB's success. Some of the programs taught English and reading to children and their immigrant parents, which also had a community-building function as the parents in the classes got to know one another. Vázquez trained the staff to teach reading by the Whole Language method, which considers words as units, in contrast to the phonics approach of breaking them down into letters and sounding them out. Whole Language presents words not as codes to be cracked but as objects used for a purpose, with a connection to the students' everyday lives. This meant taking account of their surroundings.

At the time, many of the surroundings were ruins. Why the South Bronx had burned had never stopped bothering her. Senator Moynihan talked about social pathologies and said the people of the Bronx must not want housing or they wouldn't burn it down. They destroyed their own neighborhoods because these people had something wrong with them, according to him. Vázquez took offense at the explanation, and did not believe it, but she was afraid that she and others had internalized it somehow. For her teaching to make sense in the holistic way she wanted, the question "Why did the Bronx burn?" had to be part of it.

IN THE 1990S and early 2000s, the New York City Department of Education broke up many of the city's bigger high schools into smaller ones, sometimes starting them from scratch with the help of community nonprofits. In 2002, CAB collaborated with a public high school principal to create the Community School for Social Justice, in Mott Haven. Vázquez helped devise the theme of the new high school, hire the teachers, select the students, and write the curriculum. Julia Steele Allen, a twenty-three-year-old activist and performer raised in Manhattan, who had recently left college in California, joined the CAB staff. Together she and Vázquez planned an introductory course in recent Bronx history.

They had never heard of such a course and put it together as they went along. The two had read *A Plague on Your Houses: How New York Was Burned Down and Public Health Crumbled*, by Deborah Wallace and Rodrick Wallace, which had come out a few years earlier. The Wallaces described how an operations research management philosophy resulted in the decision to shut down firehouses during a fire epidemic. Allen and Vázquez's curriculum looked for that kind of cause and effect in the disaster. They considered the redlining of neighborhoods, the chaos of highway construction, the disinvestment in buildings and infrastructure, the city's financial crisis, the onset of the fires, and the rise of graffiti and hip-hop. The course was intended for ninth graders as an introduction to the school.

Before the school year started, administrators reviewed their curriculum and rejected it. They said that by treating graffiti as a legitimate form of expression it glorified vandalism, and that its overall approach was "too one-sided." The decision presaged a wider falling-out; the relationship between the school's principal and CAB ended two years later. But Allen and Vázquez believed they had been onto something with the course, and they kept thinking about it. Allen told me, "Although the course didn't get taught at that time, it started an ongoing conversation between Vivian and me to get this history to the young people of the Bronx, who get this stigma of being from the Bronx but don't have access to this incredible story. We really wanted to reframe it—like, 'The people of the Bronx didn't burn the Bronx, the people of the Bronx *saved* it, and that's, like, *your history.*'"

Vázquez continued working with after-school programs; Allen moved on to other community organizing jobs, then decided to go back to California and finish her degree. One night, not long after she moved there, she dreamed that she and Vivian turned their Bronx history course into a blockbuster Hollywood movie. (She thinks being in the moviemaking capital influenced her subconsciously.) So much had happened during the period covered in their course; story lines for a movie seemed to be everywhere. Allen called Vázquez in a rapture over the dream and described the blockbuster-to-be. Vázquez liked the idea, and from then on, the two aimed themselves at making a movie. Allen received her BA in Performance Activism at the New College of California, and in 2008 moved back to New York, where she and Vázquez continued to meet and talk. There was a major drawback: Neither of them had ever made a movie or knew anything about making one.

Coincidentally, a person who *had* made movies, and on a big scale, was dreaming along the same lines. Baz Luhrmann, the Australian filmmaker famous for his splashy style, also wanted to do a blockbuster drawn from recent Bronx history. According to his later comments, he started thinking about this movie in the early 2000s. He imagined it as a fast-moving, epic panorama sprawling through events such as the fires and the Blackout and the rise of disco and hip-hop. The abundance of plot would extend beyond the scope of a regular film, so he planned to do it as a series of episodes on Netflix, which was looking for multi-episode content at the time and could afford to spend a lot of money.

Julia Allen had a friend, Gretchen Hildebran, who grew up in a small town in Vermont. Hildebran's family never fit in there, but that was fine with Hildebran, because it gave her the experience of being an outsider—a useful perspective for a documentary filmmaker. She had not yet done a feature-length doc (as the word is abbreviated in doc circles). Now living in the city, she was editing films for the United Nations and making harm-reduction spots for state health agencies and the like. Recently she had completed a short subject about gay couples raising children in Kentucky, and how the state's proposed constitutional amendment banning gay marriage would affect them.

At one of Allen and Vázquez's meetings, the subject of Hildebran came up. Hildebran told me, "Julia was, like, brains on fire with this idea of working with Vivian, and one day she came to me and said, 'You know how to make movies.'"

Allen introduced Hildebran to Vázquez, and now there were three at the discussions of how to proceed—which turned out to be, slowly. As a first step, Hildebran lowered the sights. The siren-song desire for the blockbuster and the epic can throw you. It's exciting to think about, but then you have to step back. A form that's too big can leave you with nothing. Overreaching for the epic has been a recurring artistic problem in America. Hildebran said that rather than wedding themselves to the sweeping fictional blockbuster, they should first try for a nonfiction documentary. If that got attention, then they could think about a bigger, fictional movie. Vázquez and Allen agreed. Now they had the format of their film: It would be a feature documentary. In time, it evolved into a film directed by both Hildebran and Vázquez and produced by all three.

They considered their resources. First was Vázquez herself, who had grown up in the story. She could be a powerful on-camera presence. As a family, the Vázquezes had taken a lot of photos and made home movies. That suggested a biographical element, and maybe a structure. None of the co-producers sat down and wrote a screenplay. They thought they would ask people to talk about their experiences of the fire years, and work from there. Hildebran shot the first footage— scenes of Vázquez talking with family and neighbors—in 2008.

Finishing the film took ten more years; during that time, none of them quit her day job. Vázquez continued to run after-school programs, moving to the New Settlement Community Center and then to other Bronx nonprofits. Allen worked as a community organizer and parents' advocate and toured with a play about solitary confinement. For a while, Hildebran had an assistantship at Big Noise Films, known for its documentary *Dirty Wars*, and she continued freelance film editing and producing. She told Vázquez and Allen they could do the doc on a modest scale for a local audience, or as a full-length feature. The second would be a less-sure thing and require a bigger time commitment. At this in-or-out point all three agreed to go with the full-length feature film. They got serious about looking for support, held an online fundraiser on Kickstarter, raised money from family and friends, and searched for potential big-time funders, many of whom told them that nobody would go to see a film about the Bronx.

A break came when a group that connects film projects with funders put them in touch with Chi-hui Yang, of the Ford Foundation. He liked their idea, and when the foundation provided some backing, it gave them a legitimacy sometimes referred to as the "Ford halo." ITVS (Independent Television Services) then joined the funders—another boost, because ITVS supports programs that appear on Public Broadcasting, which meant that when they finished their film PBS television might air it. Eventually more than a dozen major organizations contributed, including ITVS, PBS, the Ford Foundation, Latino Public Broadcasting, Black Public Media, the New York Council on the Arts, the Bronx Council on the Arts, the Women in Film Finishing Fund, the DCTV Rough Cut Lab, Docs in Progress, and WMM (Women Make Movies).

Meanwhile, Netflix and others plentifully funded Baz Luhrmann. When Allen, who handled research for their documentary, went in search of archival news footage, she often arrived at CBS News or the Associated Press or Getty Images or wherever to find that researchers for the Luhrmann film had been there the day before. She felt she sometimes lost out in getting clips. On the other hand, the Luhrmann crew paid to have some of the old, falling-apart film converted to digital, and the *Decade of Fire* project was able to use some of that rescued footage. Luhrmann's project kept to a demanding and speeded-up schedule. Filming for his series, to be titled *The Get Down*, started in 2015.

People often told Vázquez and company that they should ask Jennifer Lopez to fund their movie and be in it. This happened so often, they referred to it as "getting J-Loed." When offered by a potential funder, the suggestion was a synonym for no. Lopez seemed an unlikely choice anyway, and they never considered her. But potential sources of money wanted a celebrity! The co-producers thought of celebrities who might be interested, but in the end decided that nobody famous should tell this story of Bronx neighborhood people. This brought them back to Vázquez.

Viewed from a distance, the larger plot did not provide enough points where her family's past coincided with it. The Vázquezes' building hadn't burned. The one personal-historic intersection was her father's losing his job at Paradise Furniture because of the Blackout. But if the film concentrated instead on Vivian herself, and on her quest for meaning in the disaster, it could look at her as a part standing for the whole. Hildebran told me, "Vivian is not an actor, she's not a historian, she's just a person. And she really did want to tell this story. She was super committed. She would try anything, and it was lucky we had these years of getting to know each other before we got to that point of intensity because she had to trust that we were going to do justice to her story."

Vázquez is soft-spoken but intense; she's the teacher who lets you know you've done right or wrong with just a look. She told me she learned to hold her emotions in check because she always hated the cliché of the emotional Latina. On-screen her self-possession comes off well. A writer friend of mine who has a problem of weeping at the poignancy of his own writing when he reads in public says that an acting teacher told him, "When you cry, your audience doesn't have to." But the opposite, fortunately, is also true. As the film concentrates on Vivian, her restraint draws the viewer in. But during the filming, she and her co-producers agreed that at some point she also had to let go and reach out with strong feeling, like someone stepping out from behind a door.

Baz Luhrmann's *The Get Down* aired on Netflix between August 2016 and April 2017, with fanfare that included ubiquitous subway ads. The series is mainly about the music business and some of its young aspirants in the Bronx, and how a period of civic breakdown backlit the rise of disco and hip-hop. Lots of city sunsets, streetlights, disco lights, singing, dancing, gang clashes; the flames of burning buildings flicker. Mylene, a girl with a beautiful voice, wants to break into disco, but her father, a repressive Pentecostal preacher, sends her to her room. The boy who loves her, a gifted poet nicknamed "Books," dreams of being with her but is afraid of jeopardizing his rap career. He and his friends learn the deejaying secrets of a character based on Grandmaster Flash.

Drug dealers, a political boss played by Jimmy Smits, a Congressman Koch who hates graffiti, and Eric Bogosian, as a substance-abusing disco songwriter having a breakdown, all figure in the plot. The young actor Justice Smith plays Books, and the newcomer Herizen F. Guardiola is Mylene. There's a sense of historical significance that elevates the action; the young actors are sweet, Bogosian is funny, Smits smolders, but then somehow things seem to scatter and the story gets lost. Although *The Get Down* received mostly good reviews, Netflix canceled it after eleven episodes.

NAS, THE RAP STAR, narrates parts of *The Get Down*. Vázquez narrates her own film, in a voice that's both low-key and passionate. The structure the three producers finally decided on has her telling the story to Antonio, her college-age son, in the kitchen of her sun-filled house in the north Bronx. His presence as listener is presumed throughout. Vázquez knew she needed to demonstrate, emotionally, how the fires crushed her family and her neighbors and herself. "Gretchen and Julia and I were struggling with my not expressing that enough," she told me. One day while looking through records of the response to the upsurge in fires—she's in the quiet setting of the library at the New York Fire Department Academy in Queens—she suddenly understands that the city had not cared in the least about their suffering. For a minute or two her composure breaks, and she starts to cry.

The first time I saw the movie, the scene hit me, and it continues to on rewatching. We all have our lives, our families, our friends we love, our funny stories, our household belongings with their small or large meanings. But to people in power—her more distant neighbors in the city and in the region—none of that mattered. Her siblings, her parents, her friends, her Sweet Sixteen parties: The powers of New York cared about none of it. They let her world be destroyed, and did nothing, and said the disaster was the Bronx's own fault.

Decade of Fire premiered at DOC NYC, a film festival for documentaries, on November 10, 2018. The theater showing it sold out, the audience cheered, the reviewers praised it. But two hundred other films were screened during the festival. *Decade of Fire* got lost in the crush. It traveled to twenty other film festivals and Vázquez often accompanied it. The Metrograph Theater, on the Lower East Side, ran it for a week; audiences kept coming and the run was extended another four weeks. PBS then decided to air *Decade of Fire* nationally, as part of the Independent Lens series. In November 2019, an audience of about two million people across the United States saw or streamed the film.

It established some important facts, for the record: Buildings in the fire-affected areas were old. Redlining made it all but impossible to get loans to repair them. Vázquez's family had planned to leave the neighborhood and move to a house, but her father was turned down for a loan, despite his having been at the same job for many years. Loading modern appliances onto the old wiring in the buildings had put a strain on it; many fires were caused by faulty wiring. Response times to fires became slower after the fire department reduced the number of firehouses. Senator Moynihan claimed, with no apparent hard evidence, that most of the fires were set. The newspapers said a lot about the youths and gangs who supposedly were setting the fires, but little about who might be paying them to set them. John Finucane, a former Bronx firefighter who appears in the film, noted that in the thousands of fires he witnessed, nobody ever went to jail.

The film highlights books by Joe Flood (*The Fires*) and Evelyn Diaz Gonzalez (*The Bronx*), who both appear in it. As historians who had looked closely at this then-little-known story, they described some of the important circumstances. Gonzales talked about urban renewal, and the gentrification of Manhattan that sent at least a hundred thousand poor people into inadequate housing in the Bronx. Flood explained the kickback schemes among insurance appraisers, insurers, and landlords that defrauded the insurance pool established by the state to provide fire insurance in high-risk neighborhoods. In this collusion, he says, "everybody got paid." The film establishes, based on a 1982 federal investigation of arson-for-profit, that the state insurance pool and Lloyd's of London had paid out, between them, $250 million (in 2018 dollars) in fire insurance claims by 1980.

Vázquez wonders, in her narration, how much other insurance companies paid.

No historian or journalist or documentarian has yet found out in any detail where the money for the burned buildings went, or to whom. Before the state passed a law saying that insurance settlements could be used only to rebuild, millions of dollars wound up who-knew-where, as capital did its usual trick of disappearing into privacy and opacity. Today the mystery has slipped into the past, still unsolved.

Decade of Fire does not hesitate to include information that runs counter to its thesis. If the people of the Bronx, as a community, certainly did not burn it, there were some individual Bronxites who did. Vázquez talks to a woman, a former gang member, who says a landlord asked her brothers to burn two buildings, and her brothers arranged for her to burn them. Vázquez asks the woman, "Was there a time that you were involved in torching a building that you regretted?" and the woman says, with tears in her eyes, "Every single one." My only criticism of the movie is that this poignant moment needs a follow-up question.

TO MAKE *The Get Down*, Baz Luhrmann spent $160 million. The combination of his extravagant style, filming problems, and Netflix's deep pockets probably drove the cost. At the time, *The Get Down* was the most expensive Netflix series ever made. You can watch it today if you're a Netflix subscriber. Making *Decade of Fire* cost considerably less—about $1.1 million, which its producers raised almost dollar-by-dollar and week-by-week. Toward the end of filming, they could pay themselves small salaries, but none of them came away with money, and the three were only grateful their film did not end up in debt, as many documentaries do. *Decade of Fire* has the authenticity of a work of art done lovingly and as if by hand, and you can watch it on YouTube anytime for free.

The three producers brought recent Bronx history back closer to What Actually Happened, that elusive demiurge in human affairs. With *Decade of Fire* they joined a corrective tradition: In the 1850s,

John M. McDonald, compiler of the McDonald Papers, uncovered the hard truths of the Neutral Ground that had been hinted at but romanticized in *The Spy*. In the 1970s, when the word *Bronx* was becoming a synonym for *slum*, Lloyd Ultan's histories of the paradise Bronx reminded readers how great the place could be. From 2006 onward, Mark Naison and the participants in Fordham's Bronx African American History Project recorded oral histories that countered the TV-movie cliches. Scott La Rock, KRS-One, and D-Nice set the record straight about the true Bronx origins of hip-hop with their defiant lyrics. And thanks to Vázquez and her co-producers, a Bronx-made feature film spoke up for the history that had been lost in public misinformation and media glare.

Observers would never have guessed how much was going on in the Bronx in the early 2000s, when both *The Get Down* and *Decade of Fire* were gestating. As local communities rebuilt, nonprofits filled in where the city had cut back. At CAB/BronxWorks, Carolyn McLaughlin added dozens of new programs, raised big money, and held events such as an annual Thanksgiving dinner, which she even persuaded Mayor Koch to attend. By the time she retired in 2013, the nonprofit's annual budget had grown from $50,000 to $36 million, and its staff from four to more than six hundred. It was estimated that in McLaughlin's thirty-four years, CAB/BronxWorks helped a hundred thousand people. Today, among its many services, it succeeds in caring for mentally ill people who resist being housed—a hard job that the city desperately needs done.

Screenings of *Decade of Fire* took place in community venues all over the United States, and in Puerto Rico. The co-producers got a grant for a projector and screen and other tech aids so they could show the film in unequipped spaces. At these events, usually in low-income neighborhoods, they always asked the audience, "How many of you cannot afford to live in the home you are in now?" Usually, every hand went up. Vázquez and her colleagues believe that the film foresaw a problem whose bigger dimensions they did not then grasp. As the logic of capital drained value from housing in the Bronx, it's now doing the same all over the country (though, in general, less violently). Complaints of housing insecurity came up constantly in the communities where they showed the film. "Predatory capitalism is sucking the value out of assets," Hildebran told me. "Since about the 1980s, the turning away from public good and the turning toward private profit has been valorized and subsidized. Now, fifteen years after we started to make this film, nobody can afford to live anywhere."

Today a curriculum like the one that Allen and Vázquez proposed twenty-two years ago is being taught in several Bronx high schools, using the movie as an accompaniment. Life goes on for the producers: Julia Allen is still a community activist and organizer. She helps in the promotion of other films, performs in My Gay Banjo, a two-person band, and is self-publishing a sci-fi-fantasy trilogy that she's been writing for years. Vivian Vázquez, who also goes by her married name, Vivian Vázquez Irizarry, retired from New Settlement in 2021. She and her co-producers still travel the country to show *Decade of Fire* when they get requests.

Gretchen Hildebran is at work on a sequel to *Decade of Fire* titled *The People vs. Austerity*. She and Vázquez Irizarry and Allen will again co-produce, along with Neyda Martinez, a veteran producer who helped them with the previous film. *The People vs. Austerity* will be about how governments and money movers use fiscal crises to privatize and take away services, as happened in New York in the fire years, in the city of Detroit in 2013, and as is happening in Puerto Rico today. Hildebran hopes the movie will come out in 2024.

The main thing you learn from *Decade of Fire* is that the city's difficulties do not descend out of the blue. When I first moved to New York, I assumed, as many people did, that the poverty and fires in the Bronx were just the way the Bronx was. As Vázquez said, "It was what you got for being poor." But in fact, everything that you see in the city is the result of a deliberate decision made by somebody. Greed and anger and racism and hate, those addictions deadlier than crack, have motivated too many of those decisions—especially greed. Good and evil battle each other to re-create the city every day. Good may be ahead, but evil is always close behind.

41

AT TEN MINUTES AFTER SIX on a winter morning, workmen get off
the number 6 train at the 138th Street and Third Avenue station in
Mott Haven. They wear Carhartt coats of heavy brown canvas, dark
hoodies, beige or camo or olive-colored cargo pants, and lace-up
leather boots that are pale with Sheetrock dust. Each wears or carries
a backpack. They come out of the subway at Alexander Avenue or
Lincoln Avenue and walk toward the luxury high-rise buildings going
up along the bank of the Harlem River. The night is still fully dark.
Light bulbs in the unfinished framework of apartments ten or twenty
stories up in the sky twinkle like shelved stars. Airplane lights go past.
At the forest-green plywood wall around a worksite, men crowd by a
lighted door where a woman with a clipboard says, "I need to see your
card! If you don't have a card, I'm not letting you in!" A sign on the
wall in English, Spanish, and probably Chinese says that all workers
must have a Site Safety Card showing they've taken forty hours of
safety training.

Flatbed trucks loaded with steel-band-bound packs of Sheetrock
idle at the curbs. A concrete-pumping truck blasts its horn, regardless
of the hour, as it navigates the turn at the intersection of Bruckner
Boulevard and Lincoln Avenue. The truck pulls over, just past the

crowd of workers. Its multisegment pumping boom sits at the ready on its back like a folding ruler.

Bruckner Boulevard is a surface street. The Bruckner Expressway, which is elevated, and generally runs above the boulevard (but here is two blocks away from it), serves as a boundary between the waterfront buildings and the poverty on the inland side. I follow the workmen down Lincoln Avenue. They pass the Mitchel Houses, a NYCHA project, which seem to be surrounded by small foothills of trash. Lincoln Avenue continues under the expressway. On the other side, in the zone of the luxury complexes, there is almost no trash. An empty dumpster is waiting to be employed, and the name on it reads, "Avid Waste Systems." I keep walking, all the way to the riverbank, which is held in place by corrugated steel bulkheads. The sky has just begun to get light. The taillights of cars on the other side of the water unspring their red reflections across the rippled surface to my feet. In active sites like this you always hear the beeping of construction vehicles backing up.

Some of the luxury buildings are already finished and tenanted. The Arches, a twenty-story high-rise now outlined at night in electric-blue neon, sits near an on-ramp for the expressway. Two or three years before, on one of my walks, I saw a support beam for the Arches being driven into the ground.

A brand-new building, called Third at Bankside, whose apartments are either market rate or supposedly affordable for low-income renters, adjoins the Third Avenue Bridge so closely that you could jump from the railing onto the wall. The ground-floor entry to the high-rise is down among the bridge ramps' support columns. You wind among the columns and then you come to a set of concrete steps below a blue-and-white banner that says, "Welcome Home!" The banner hangs from a beam on the ramps' underside. You walk up the steps, and a path takes you to the door of the lobby. Going under the roadways and through the pillars, you feel like a burrowing creature among tree roots. I had told someone who answered the phone that I wanted to see a two-bedroom apartment. Now a young man met me and gave me a tour of the building.

Third at Bankside is a fabulous place. Everything is in suave shades of gray and brushed chrome and taupe. The two-bedroom I looked at on the nineteenth floor offered a view of upper Manhattan from one of the bedrooms, and a panorama of the Bronx from the other. The apartment rents for about four thousand a month, with another four hundred or so for use of the pool, rooftop garden, and exercise room. There are no supermarkets very near, but a large re-frigerator at Reception can hold your takeout orders and other food deliveries if they arrive when you're not home. The building creates a domestic equivalent of cyberspace; to be here is to be nowhere in par-ticular, and everywhere. Almost everybody I saw coming and going in the building was young, professional-looking, and a person of color.

The air pollution problem in the Bronx has been noted already. Because of its heavy truck traffic and high rate of lung illnesses, this part of the South Bronx is sometimes called Asthma Alley. I asked my guide if that was something a potential renter should worry about. He said no one had ever asked him that question before. The building is self-contained, he said, with its own heating, cooling, and ventilat-ing systems, so the quality of the air outside should not cause any problem inside. I said I hadn't seen anybody in the building who was of my generation—I'm seventy-three years old. He smiled and said, "No, we don't have anyone of your young age, sir."

The place reminded me of one of those luxury hotels that are super-comfortable until eight in the morning, when you're still asleep and there's a sharp knock at the door and the cry, "Housekeeping!" Apartment leases at Third at Bankside last for two years, after which your rent can be raised to whatever the market rate is. If you're a young professional, your earnings had better have gone up by then. It's like when the producers of *Decade of Fire*, at showings of their movie, asked who in the audience could not afford to live where they lived, and every hand went up. Third at Bankside is a place designed to move young professionals through a system of paying ever-higher rents or going elsewhere. After two years, your burrow in the sky will writhe beneath you, and if you can't hang on, it will toss you onto the street.

Well, everybody has to live somewhere. More than half of the renters in the Bronx pay more than 30 percent of their income on rent. (To maintain a reasonable budget, the rule is that your rent should be about a quarter of your income.) About 34 percent of Bronx renters pay more than *50* percent of their income on rent. That category is described by housing advocates as "severely rent burdened." Citywide, the figures are also high: About 50 percent of city renters pay more than 30 percent of their income, and about 18 percent pay more than 50 percent. That is, in this rich city, millions of New Yorkers struggle every month to stay in their apartments. New York State has produced five U.S. presidents. The most recent local entry in that category is a real estate tycoon whose company repeatedly broke the law and whose treasurer went to jail. This president fattened on the brutal real estate inequities of New York.

ANOTHER Bronx walk:

Take the number 4 train to the 170th Street station. On one side of the station is East 170th Street, on the other side is West 170th Street. You want West 170th Street. Follow it west as it zigs and zags. You cross Cromwell Avenue, and then the Edward L. Grant Highway, which is a bigger street. Pick up West 170th on the other side of the triangular intersection at Grant, and from there it's a straight shot, uphill and then down, to Highbridge Park. A ramp in the park leads down to the walkway on the High Bridge. No motor vehicle traffic is allowed, but the bicyclists go flying by, and you must watch out.

Looking south—that is, from the left side of the bridge, as you're heading toward Manhattan—you have a wide-angle view. There's the Harlem River itself, always a mocha brown, and usually with no boats on it. (Once, I saw a barge, and once, remarkably, a speedboat pulling a water-skier.) On the Bronx side, the frantic details of traffic on the Major Deegan below you may be observed as if in a petri dish. Between the Deegan and the river there's a blank lot with police cars parked on it, and train tracks next to that, and a Metro-North train yard. The river curves around to the left of the train yard and you can't see the luxury high-rises in that direction. Third at Bankside and the others are more than five miles away.

On the Manhattan side, ahead of you, the Harlem River Drive goes along the base of the cliffs, which appear to be heavily wooded. In the near distance are the Polo Grounds Houses (another NYCHA project), and much farther off, the billionaires' tower, the tallest thing in the city, that has been hammered into Fifty-seventh Street at Fifth Avenue like a stake in the heart. As you stand in the middle of the bridge, looking around, you're on or near the spot where Edgar Allan Poe stood when he came, alone and grieving, after the death of his wife.

On the bridge's upstream side, in the direction of the Hudson River, the Hamilton Bridge and the Washington Bridge block the view. It's like when you're in a plane and there are other planes next to you. All these bridges are jammed close together. At such a height, huge objects should have more room between them. Now turn around, and head back to the Bronx side. People being towed by their large, leashed dogs pass by, and when groups of dog-walkers going in opposite directions meet, they socialize, or not, depending on whether their dogs choose to check one another out. On your right, on the cliff above the shore, a long staircase leads down from the end of the bridge you're on. Stop and look down. Directly below you is Sedgwick Avenue, with a sidewalk next to it, at the bottom of the staircase.

Go down the staircase and turn right onto Sedgwick. This is the tricky part. Sedgwick appears to go uphill to the right. That is actually Undercliff Avenue, and it will lead you astray. What you want to do is keep left, which requires crossing Undercliff to stay on Sedgwick, which you now follow for a while without the benefit of a sidewalk. You are just on a mud path next to Sedgwick. This is a zone that is not designed for pedestrians; after the mud path ends, the sidewalk resumes, and you're still on Sedgwick, under the Hamilton Bridge and the Washington Bridge. Who knows what happens in this region? There's an abandoned motor home with its side door wide open and a chaotic couch visible inside. Traffic noise from above, naturally. A broken bar-type lock for use on motel room doors, with instructions printed on it in French. Oil patches mark the sidewalk, and pigeon droppings in lines that follow the bridge beams overhead. The bridge supports rise around you like the foundations of the Earth itself.

Then, miraculously, you pass under the bridges, you go slightly uphill, and you're standing in front of 1520 Sedgwick Avenue, where Kool Herc and his family lived, and where hip-hop was born. Herc's former building is the second one up from the Washington Bridge–Hamilton Bridge complex. There are the signs that say, "Hip Hop Blvd" and "Sedgwick Av." There are the dozens and dozens of hip-hop groups' stickers on the sign pole. And there's the highway department's tacit acknowledgment of the address's fame, in the blinking yellow "caution" light suspended over Sedgwick Avenue. Evidently, incautious fans sometimes step backward into traffic as they're staring up at the building.

Keep going on Sedgwick. In about half a mile, Cedar Avenue branches off to the left. Take Cedar, and in another few tenths of a mile you come to Cedar Playground, that historic place where Joseph Saddler once heard the loudest sound, and where there should be (but isn't) a historic marker. Sit in Cedar Playground for a while.

Continue on Cedar Avenue to West Fordham Road—about another mile. Turn left on West Fordham Road and go out on the University Heights Bridge. This is another famous place in hip-hop lore. Just across the bridge, on the Manhattan side, are MTA subway train yards where kids used to write on the parked trains (and maybe still do). Graffiti artists called the place the Ghost Yard—I guess because strange, ghostly things used to happen there late at night, such as one group of graffitists getting caught spray-painting over the tags of another group, and the other group beating up the first group and stripping them and spray-painting them.

Along the Bronx shore, south of the bridge, is another blank, half-paved place, and scrub woods next to it. A bunch of small buildings clustered in the middle of the blank space are surrounded by delivery trucks for Farmer's Choice Dairy. A dumpster near the trucks is full to overflowing with white plastic jugs. On the northern side of the bridge, also on the Bronx shore, are more scrub woods, next to rail-road tracks extending into the distance for maybe half a mile. Near the tracks in that direction lies a small mountain of scrap metal, like something on a Malaysian beach where recyclers are gleaning. This unnoticed, no-account, semi-industrial landscape along the shore soon will be gone. A developer called Dynamic Star LLC has bought large parts of it from the CSX railroad to put up high-rise buildings. The development will create thousands of apartments and cost $2 bil-lion. *Crain's New York Business*, which reports on city real estate, says this will be the biggest and costliest development in the city since the Hudson Yards, on the west side of Manhattan.

The development will be called Fordham Landing and will carry on the theme of upscale housing on the banks of the Harlem River. The Manhattan view must be what sells these packages. In fact, no new luxury high-rise buildings are planned for any place in the Bronx except along the Harlem River. Much of the Bronx adjoins other wa-terfronts, such as the Bronx River or the East River/Long Island Sound; but viewed from those places, Manhattan lies remotely on the horizon. Plus, the subway ride to and from it is longer. One must distinguish between Manhattan-facing mostly luxury development and other Bronx development. There has been a greater amount of the second kind, but unlike the high-rises on the shore, the more afford-able buildings in the inland Bronx, whether new or old, do not outline themselves in electric-blue neon.

In photos and films from the bad days, the elevated subway tracks cross huge expanses of rubble. So much development has happened that now those same tracks run through corridors between block after block of new or newish apartment buildings. These structures don't go in for cornices and carved trellises and gargoyles, the decorative stonework of the J. Clarence Davies era; instead, they are plain, in un-derstated colors, with a clean-line simplicity. Along certain elevated tracks the change from the days of rubble (judging from photos) is stunning. A lot of the construction happened between 2009 and 2018, when 70 million square feet of new development was created in the Bronx, at a cost of $13 billion. (For comparison, the Kingsbridge

Armory, thought to be the largest armory in the world, is 355,000 square feet; 70 million square feet equals about two hundred Kingsbridge Armories.)

A LOT OF what is being built is warehouses. One day I took a stroll down East 149th Street, wanting to look again at Bungay Creek, also known as CSO Outfall #WIB-072, by the former corner of Gouverneur Morris's property. Now, on the right-hand side of East 149th, the concrete-grinding plant is gone. In its place is a gray building, still under construction, with a sign on its side: "BLC Bronx Logistics Center . . . 1.32 Million Square Feet Available," and a phone number and email address. I am trying to convey how big this thing is. There's nothing to compare it to. Even Gouverneur Morris would have fallen mute if, via time travel, he could have appeared beside me and taken this in. The building suggests the looming outside of a castle—it's like the endless gray wall, but with no crenellations or other embellishments except for a few tall, narrow windows like giant arrow slits.

I walked past the colossus, to the end of the street, and stood by the outfall where the former Bungay Creek still flows into the East River. This small junction place is unchanged, and the heating-oil depot is still there. A heating-oil truck pulled up next to me. The window rolled down, and the driver asked, conversationally, "What are you doing?"

"Looking at that huge building."

"Yeah. That place is gonna fuck up all the traffic coming over here."

Six miles to the east, at the mega-intersection that I've often explored, another new warehouse looms. That one is slightly smaller, advertising a mere 1.2 million square feet. News stories said Amazon planned to lease this warehouse; but at the site, a traffic officer wearing coppery mascara told me that Amazon was no longer sure it would. Vehicles exiting from the mega-intersection sometimes ricochet around the new traffic patterns created by the construction, and cops are needed to redirect them. The helpful officer, after speaking to me, returned her attention to the lost drivers. The warehouse has its own elevated ramps that connect directly and confusingly to the mega-intersection.

Amazon has acquired many hundreds of thousands of square feet of "last mile" warehouse space in the Bronx—i.e., warehouses in which to store stuff before it's taken the "last mile" to its points of delivery. The last miles may extend farther than a mile, into Manhattan and Brooklyn and elsewhere. As the company has expanded in the Bronx, it has acquired preexisting spaces, such as the former ABC Carpet Warehouse (117,000 square feet), next to the Bronx River, and the old Modell's Sporting Goods warehouse (366,000 square feet) on Bassett Avenue, a few miles north. Thousands of tractor-trailers and panel vans come and go from the warehouses every day. As a housing activist has pointed out, "This just continues the old narrative of the Bronx facilitating the ease of more affluent people."

In the predawn hours as well as later in the morning, I've stood at the corner of Bruckner Boulevard and Lincoln Avenue, in the heart of the luxury high-rise construction, and watched Fresh Direct grocery delivery trucks pull up to that traffic light. All of them have photos of bright red strawberries, blown up to the size of throw pillows, distributed across their sides. Fresh Direct occupies its own vast warehouse nearby, along the Harlem River. Many Mott Haven residents did not want the company to relocate to this area, and they argued and demonstrated against it. Fresh Direct came anyway. The city gave it tax breaks and let it pay less than minimum wage for some jobs. Fresh Direct promised that soon all its trucks would change to electric, so no one needed to worry about air pollution. That conversion turned out not to be possible—something to do with the amount of electricity needed to run the trucks' refrigerators on top of running the engine.

As I watched, a Fresh Direct truck went by about every four minutes. Almost as regular were the twenty-seat shuttle buses with which Fresh Direct ferries its employees to and from the nearest subway stop. None of the vehicles I saw were electric.

Other delivery companies, such as FedEx and UPS, move packages by way of last-mile warehouses in the Bronx. The traffic volume to and from the Hunts Point Market continues heavy as always—twenty thousand trucks a day. The eastbound Cross Bronx Expressway, between the Hamilton Bridge and Interstate 278, remains the busiest and most congested road in the United States. The chances of the Bronx's traffic ever decreasing seem small. If all the vehicles went electric tomorrow, there still would be an awful lot of them—maybe even more of them. As more people shop online, more vehicles are going to pass through the Bronx, the place still inescapably in between.

42

I WENT TO more sites of future upscale apartment buildings between the outer-edge expressways and the river. There's going to be a huge one near Yankee Stadium, at a place called Bronx Point. The Universal Hip Hop Museum will be part of this development. Hammering, pounding, backup-beeping, and engine roaring reverberated all around. Cars and pickup trucks sat tightly parked, hood-to-bumper, legally and illegally, along the dim corridor under the elevated roadway. In every vehicle, a bright orange or other-colored safety vest spread on the dashboard let the traffic cops know these were workers' cars. Not one vehicle had a ticket on the windshield. I became punchy with the noise. It seemed to get faster and louder, like the drumbeat of a war galley at ramming speed.

The word *gentrification*, and the act of gentrifying, are hard to make vivid; as with climate change, you see it best only after it has happened. I was a gentrifier, in my twenties, when I moved into a former candy factory in Soho, in lower Manhattan. Industry was leaving the city, to be replaced in some neighborhoods by people like me, who could pay a higher rent and make use of the loft space. After a dozen years, I was pushed out myself. I could not afford to live in Soho today. The gentry who do the gentrifying are imagined to be young and white. That hasn't been dramatically the case in the Bronx, where the white population went down between 2000 and 2019. Gentrification, as a force, has less to do with visibly changing the character of a resident population than with extracting as much value as possible from a place regardless of who moves out or in.

Real estate runs New York City, and when it comes at you like a ramming trireme, you resist or get run over. Probably it will run you over anyway. About ten years ago, rumors of Bronx gentrification began to appear in the news. The city had proposed rezoning a two-mile section extending north-south along Jerome Avenue. Residents and local businesses began a resistance that went on for years, and finally lost in 2018. The new zoning favors residential development and small business over industry; apartment buildings and bodegas and pharmacies and the like are okay, but industries must leave when their leases expire.

Automotive places are considered industries. The two-mile stretch of Jerome in question, from 167th Street to 184th Street, is almost nothing but auto-repair shops, auto glass replacement shops, auto detailing places, auto-sound-system installers, muffler shops, brake shops, transmission shops, used-car lots, parts places, and garages that do oven-baked paint jobs. This is one of the city's prime areas for FLAT FIX signs. The first eastbound exit on the Cross Bronx Expressway, after the exit for the Major Deegan, is the exit for Jerome Avenue. If you have a problem with your car, you pull off at Jerome Avenue, and help is near. Car places create better middle-class jobs than, say, the food-service industry. An immigrant with little English or education can make a decent living on Jerome Avenue if he can fix cars.

Not a great living, mind you. The average for an auto-repair worker, $44,000 a year, is probably not enough to raise a family in most places. But in 2019 the Bronx's median household income was $43,540. Average pay for a food-service job—a common beginning for new immigrants—is $22,000 a year. Automotive work gives you the better start.

Jerome Avenue rocks, in my opinion. I've always liked to walk on it. The number 4 train overhead has a sheltering effect. Guys from the car places are friendly and yell from the bays, "Hey, Papi, what you looking for? Recaps, twenty dollars!" Since the rezoning, I keep expecting Jerome Avenue to change, but all the FLAT FIX signs that were there five years ago are still there. The only difference seems to be an increase of freelance repair guys and car washers working in the street itself. I saw a disabled vehicle waiting to be worked on in a no-parking zone. On the driver-side window it had a hand-lettered sign that said, "DO NOT TWO." I checked the other side of the vehicle. On that side, also, was a sign that said, "DO NOT TWO." Jerome Avenue is one of the liveliest streets in the city.

A man named Pedro J. Estevez, who came from Santo Domingo forty years ago and started an auto-repair shop in New York, protects the automotive small businesses of the city. Estevez is a tall, athletic-looking man, seventy-two years old, who wears light-colored jeans, well-fitted sweaters with abstract designs on them, and gold-rimmed glasses. Back in the nineties, he founded the United Auto Merchants Association (UAMA)—"The Bridge to a Healthy Automotive Industry"—and today he runs it, with the help of his niece Irene.

In UAMA's headquarters on Woodycrest Avenue, just off Jerome, I have listened to Mr. Estevez talk at length about how the city has screwed the small auto-repair shops. It has absolutely no compunction about this kind of behavior, according to him. Take the dislocation it inflicted on the auto shops of Willets Point, in Queens near the old Shea Stadium. The city forced dozens of shops to move and said it would find a new place for them in the Bronx, but it never did. Instead, the land it had promised them, at 1080 Leggett Avenue, was turned into a warehouse, which is now occupied by (who else?) Amazon. The guys who lost their shops never got back in business, and some even left the country, Estevez says. He will not let that happen to the guys on Jerome Avenue.

"I am the leader of them," he told me, when I stopped by his office one afternoon. "I'm not a politician, I don't owe nothing to nobody. We are mechanics, we come here from other countries, we are legal with the city. One big thing UAMA does is help our members comply with city regulations. So I do not speak for the mechanics in the street, who are working outside the city's regs and not paying taxes. They make life harder for the legal places, take away their business. And we do not represent corporate businesses like Auto Zone, either. They also take business away from the small shops."

Estevez wants the city to compensate the legit businesses fairly. After a struggle, he got it to pay the Willets Point guys nine thousand dollars each—which he dismisses as "nothing, a joke. You can't set up another auto-repair shop for that." The Jerome Avenue shops will need much more in compensation, when and if they move. Estevez also dreams of creating a location that will do what Jerome Avenue does, but in a single, multistory building, to be called the Vertical Auto Merchandise Building, located somewhere near the Cross Bronx Expressway. He wants to start a school to turn mechanics into technicians, so they can learn diagnostics and keep up with the new all-computerized vehicles of the present and future. He has a site for the school already picked out, on Burnside. "Our people don't depend on nobody. They depend on themselves, with help from UAMA. We have two hundred and seventy-five member businesses. We will never let the gentrifying of Jerome Avenue throw these hardworking people into a nowhere abysm!"

My own guess is that Pedro Estevez and the United Auto Merchants Association will prevail against all odds. The future will be more complicated than planners think. Right now, illegal street mechanics and car wash guys can be found not only on Jerome Avenue but all over the Bronx (and no doubt elsewhere in the city). Gentrify the legit, taxpaying auto places out of business, and you create more lawlessness, curbside chaos, and loss of city revenue. The UAMA's Vertical Auto Merchandise Building and the proposed school for auto technicians eventually will make so much sense that the city will beg for the chance to finance these projects. It gave away big parts of the Bronx to cars and trucks long ago. Now it must deal with their dominance if it wants to gentrify. So far, fitting in new luxury high-rises next to the outer-edge expressways and the Harlem River bridges has been an ingenious strategy, but the development of Jerome Avenue will not play out so neatly. Jerome is a natural place for auto businesses. I believe some of the existing businesses will find ways to stay. The city must not count Pedro Estevez and UAMA out.

IN A GENTRIFYING PLACE, businesses start up that appeal to people who have money for more than the essentials. Or maybe the people with the money come first, and then the businesses follow—I don't know. In any case, some of these businesses are restaurants. A food critic discovers one of them, and more people begin to patronize it. When the lease is due, the landlord scythes through the restaurant's profits by raising the rent to a level that almost (but not quite) drives the restaurant under. That's the pattern.

Foodies have known about a restaurant called La Morada for at least ten years. It specializes in the cuisine of Oaxaca, Mexico, which it serves in a storefront café on Willis Avenue near the corner of East 140th Street. At dinner, customers fill every chair. The founders and owners, Antonio Saavedra and Natalia Méndez, do not have citizenship papers. Their grown children, Marco and Yajaira Saavedra, who now help run the restaurant, remember crossing into Texas when they were little. They also are undocumented. La Morada began to draw big crowds after the late Anthony Bourdain featured it on his food show, and more recently when a Netflix restaurant series praised it. Many magazines have written about it. Sometimes the restaurant's success puzzles the family. They fit a gentrification story, but for years they have been a force opposed to gentrification in the neighborhood. When their landlord raised the rent from $1,200 a month to $5,000 a month, not long ago, they hired a lawyer and got it reduced. They intend to stay, and they want their neighbors to be able to stay.

The Saavedra-Méndez family is kind to everybody. That seems to be the essence of their activism, and of their success. I've never had people I was ostensibly interviewing be so nice to me. They think in terms of *all community all the time* (my phrase and italics). They fight the gears of gentrification by acting generously to large numbers of people, and by accepting kind acts from others. Their approach took me a while to understand.

I had never heard of mutual aid. The term *mutual aid* is not capitalized, though it exists as an entity outside of the simple meaning of the words. An unsigned page of type that I found in a church basement says:

> Mutual aid is a movement that encompasses the core values of building and sustaining a community. Mutual aid is feeding each other, but it is not charity. Mutual aid involves challenging current structures that perpetuate harm and injustice and also building up community strength, because the goal is to transform the systems that oppress and divide us . . . Mutual aid is not an organization, it is not an agency; it is a practice. Mutual aid starts with the recognition that our bodies are interconnected, that we depend on one another. This means that we are not some individualized, self-sufficient beings; on the contrary, we are radically interdependent.

Mutual aid underlies a lot of what La Morada does. The restaurant prepares meals all day and into the night. Most of the meals are not for the customers, but for residents of homeless shelters, undocumented immigrants in detention, and people living on the street. Scores of volunteers help with the preparing, cooking, and distribution. People donate food and transportation, all as part of what is referred to as their mutual aid coalition. The family lives out an amazing gift for feeding people, like the gift that Duane Johnson, the barbecue prince of Old-Timers' Day, also possesses. It's a Christlike gift, or a great sense of civic engagement, or wonderfully scaled-up neighborliness—however you want to describe it.

Two minutes after I walked into La Morada, at about nine on a Monday morning, Marco Saavedra was asking if I would like to volunteer, pressing freshly made chicken vegetable soup on me, and telling me about an event for handing out toys at a Bronx church on the upcoming Saturday. All I had said was I was writing a book. His mother, Natalia, brought me a signed copy of her pamphlet about cooking with squash. The pamphlet says that the family believes the U.S. immigration structure should be abolished, as well as the police.

The pages are decorated with paintings of irises done by Marco Saavedra.

To see more of mutual aid in practice, I went to the toy distribution. It was in the basement of the Calvary United Methodist Church, on University Avenue a few blocks from the Burnside Avenue stop of the number 4 train. When I made my way in—it was crowded—and took stock, I estimated the number of gifts awaiting distribution to be in the high three figures. Piles and piles of them, each wrapped in Christmas paper, were stacked high on folding tables along the walls and on the room's small stage. Some teenage boys played with a basketball in the middle of the floor and a lot of younger kids were running around. All were refugees just arrived in the United States, Marco Saavedra had told me. Yajaira Saavedra was dressed like a Christmas tree. At more folding tables (how did churches exist before folding tables?) La Morada volunteers served rice and beans and tortillas. In the children's faces you could see how new this whole experience was. The parents watched with the joy you feel when your kids are happy.

Yajaira Saavedra told me afterward that they had planned to give away a thousand presents, and almost did; at the end of the afternoon, only sixty were left. The families had kept coming. Volunteers took the leftover gifts to kids in homeless shelters. All the presents were mutual aid donations. The ones I looked at had been wrapped in the best style—not perfectly, like in a store, but personally and skillfully. How did La Morada's folks ever wrap them all? Yajaira said a lot of people helped, at different locations. Gift wrappers had been up late in the restaurant the night before. On her phone she showed me a list of the mutual aid people who had pitched in. She scrolled through name after name.

Mutual aid is a revival that began in Covid times. It had always existed, but it became a thing during the pandemic, with neighbors making sure that neighbors had enough to eat. In the Bronx, mutual aid coalitions set up food pantries and distribution centers, sometimes outside community gardens, a few with mutual aid refrigerators available 24/7 on the sidewalks.

La Morada helped hundreds of people register for vaccinations and served as a place to get the shots. Contacts made through mutual aid inspired residents to form tenants' associations. I've heard former housing activists say that the kinds of civic bonds that once helped to bring about the Bronx revival no longer exist. If you're working two jobs to pay rent that takes 60 percent of your income, you don't have time to go to tenants' meetings, or even to get to know your neighbors. But the rise of mutual aid coalitions argues against the inevitability of that.

Rents in the Bronx went up 26 percent between 2010 and 2020. I asked someone who worked in affordable housing whether that meant the renters had somehow upped their incomes by that amount in the decade. He said people were more likely to adjust their home lives— for example, to double up and triple up in an apartment illegally and divide the rent. (*"How many of you cannot afford to live in the home you are in now?"*) Sometimes when he went into buildings, he saw that more people were living in an apartment than were supposed to be there. "I never said anything," he told me.

When I asked Fernando Ferrer, the former borough president, about people carrying heavy rent burdens today, he talked about the affordable housing he built, back when, and how sometimes he was called a gentrifier for building it. He added, "But, look—rent was always a tough thing to scrape up in the Bronx—you know?"

A STORY OF GENTRIFICATION as value extraction:

In the first chapter, I said that I began walking in the Bronx to find out how far the smell of baking cookies drifted from the Stella D'oro bakery at 237th Street and Broadway. At the time, a private equity fund had bought the factory and reduced pay and benefits, and the workers had gone on strike.

Stella D'oro was founded in about 1930 by Joseph and Angela Kresevich, immigrants from Italy. The company made Italian-style breadsticks, biscotti, and cookies that had a subtler, less-sweet taste. In the land of milk-and-cookies, the Kreseviches thought in terms of snacks for coffee or tea. Their recipes did not use any dairy, so the products could be labeled "pareve," i.e., kosher. This made business sense because the Bronx was 50 percent Jewish in 1930.

Angela's son (Joseph's stepson), Felice Zambetti, known as Phil, took over the company when Joseph died in 1965. The years when Phil Zambetti ran Stella D'oro were prosperous. The neighborhood enjoyed the sight of the company's red, green, and white vans coming and going, delivering directly from factory to store. The workers received good wages and benefits and put their children through college. On their birthdays, each employee was given a paid day off. (Later that became a factory-wide celebration of everybody's birthday on the same day.) Thousands of immigrants entered the middle class by way of Stella D'oro.

Phil Zambetti had four children—two boys and two girls. Stella D'oro expanded into other city markets and built factories in Illinois and California. The first child, Marc, moved to San Francisco after college so he could get experience in the factory in San Leandro; the family planned for him and his brother to take over the entire company someday. On October 17, 1989, as he was driving home from work, the major earthquake on that date caused the collapse of the Cypress Street Viaduct in Oakland. He and forty-six other people died in the collapse; the death toll there was the most at any single place during the quake.

A family never completely recovers from a disaster like that. Jonathan, the younger son, did not want to take over the company, nor did his sisters. Three years later, the Zambettis sold Stella D'oro to RJR Nabisco for a reported $105 million. Nabisco was then bought by Philip Morris and subsumed into Kraft Foods, which had no idea what to do with Stella D'oro. The former mom-and-pop company had been bringing in a dependable $65 million a year—excellent money in the Bronx. Nabisco's leading earner, Oreos, the most popular cookie in the United States, makes a billion dollars a year. Stella D'oro got lost at Kraft/Nabisco, which began to use less-expensive ingredients in the products and removed the "pareve" label. This change caused an uproar; consumers complained, rabbis wrote letters. Nabisco restored the pareve recipe, but Stella D'oro had begun an inexorable decline, with sales figures slipping from $65 million a year to $30 million a year.

In 2006, Brynwood Partners, a private equity firm in Greenwich, bought Stella D'oro for $17.5 million. Its value had been reduced by nearly $90 million in fourteen years. Brynwood told the workers it must cut wages and benefits. Hendrik J. Hartong II, known as "Henk," the head of Brynwood, later said that the workers reacted foolishly, objecting to cuts as "draconian" that really weren't, such as losing their annual birthday holiday. The schedule of cuts called for reductions in pay every year. These jobs would no longer be middle-class. To get perspective, the workers took a glance at Brynwood's website; they saw that the private equity fund bragged of providing its investors with returns of 28.8 percent.

The strike began in August 2008 and lasted for eleven months. Mike Filippou, a top mechanic at the factory, led it. In his youth Filippou had come to the Bronx from Kasos, one of the Dodecanese Islands in the Aegean Sea. The strikers picketed at the factory gates by 237th Street under the el tracks of the number 1 Broadway Local, and one could always spot Filippou among the picketers because of his height, sloping shoulders, and large, Zorba-like mustache. I admired his ability to rally his side and engage straight-up with Hartong, the wealthy Harvard MBA. I once asked Filippou if Kasos, his native island, had any connection to classical mythology. In his Bronx accent, he replied, "Oh, yeah—we sent two ships to the Trojan War."

Later I looked it up. Kasos is mentioned in the *Iliad*, in the famous "Catalogue of Ships." Now I understood him better: What's an everyday private equity financier compared to a leader whose home island sent two ships to the Trojan War?

In July 2009, the complaint that the union had filed with the National Labor Relations Board was decided in the strikers' favor, and the NLRB made Brynwood give them back their jobs. It did, and promptly sold the company to Lance, the North Carolina snack-food giant, which announced it would close the Bronx factory—by then the only remaining Stella D'oro factory, the others having already shut down—and move production to a plant that Lance had recently bought in Ohio. This happened to be about a year after the financial collapse of 2008. The Stella D'oro workers learned that Goldman Sachs, the Wall Street investment firm, owned equity in Lance. One afternoon they held a rally downtown to ask Goldman to put pressure on Lance to keep Stella D'oro in the Bronx. The strikers' very reasonable position was that taxpayers like them had saved the bankers' jobs when the government bailed out Goldman Sachs. Now Goldman Sachs should return the favor and save the Stella D'oro workers' jobs.

On the afternoon of the demonstration, the security force that Goldman Sachs massed at the street level of its Manhattan skyscraper— the rent-a-cops, the attack dogs—would have intimidated anybody. Goldman Sachs owns the sidewalk up to the curb, and the police would not let the protesters stand in the street, so Filippou and about three dozen other workers stood precariously crowded together on the curbstone. In his mechanic's coveralls he leaned back and shouted up at the steel and glass, "Goldman Sachs, can you hear us upstairs? Lloyd Blankfein, can you hear us?" Beyond implicitly threatening the workers with violence if they came any closer, neither Goldman Sachs nor Blankfein (its CEO at the time) made any response. I can never forget the sight of the rent-a-cops and dogs on one side, the NYPD on the other, as the protesters with their homemade signs and their reasonable request stood teetering on the curb.

The workers also appealed to Mayor Michael Bloomberg to intervene. On another afternoon, they demonstrated with signs and chanting on the steps of City Hall. I saw men in suits coming down the steps and laughing and making remarks out of the sides of their mouths. Unsurprisingly, Bloomberg did nothing. He has said that the crash of 2008 was caused by the end of redlining, because it brought a lot of borrowers without money into the pool of mortgage holders, thus injuring the lenders—in other words, he could never be a sympathetic audience. At the height of the demonstration, Filippou received a call saying that Lance had decided to close the factory that afternoon. The Stella D'oro workers, all 134 of them, ended the day finally and officially unemployed. None were offered jobs at the new plant in Ohio, which is a nonunion shop. Personal tragedy, big-business stupidity, and suck-it-all-dry greed had destroyed a Bronx enterprise that made cookies and sent good smells into the air.

Not long after the plant's closing, Goldman Sachs announced it was giving its bankers and staff holiday bonuses that amounted to $23 billion. This was the largest bonus total in the history of the company. At the highest salary that Brynwood had offered the Stella D'oro employees—about $780 a week—all of them put together would have had to work forty-hour weeks for about 4,200 years to earn $23 billion.

Gouverneur Morris, the proto-Bronxite, explained a lot when he wrote, two hundred and some years ago, "The Rich will strive to establish their dominion & enslave the rest. They always did. They always will." That is the truth at the heart of gentrification, and of the modern rise of capital. If we emulate the originalists on the Supreme Court, and look again at what Morris declared in the Preamble to the Constitution—especially the line about establishing justice and ensuring the blessings of liberty to ourselves and our posterity—can we say that he imagined a future in which "We the People" spent more than 50 percent of their incomes on rent? Or one in which residents of Greenwich receive a 28.8 percent return on their investments, and pay a tax of 15 percent on that money, while the residents of the Bronx whom they maneuvered out of their jobs pay a higher rate on what they earn by their physical labor? Or that $23 billion should be an amount of money that any small group of human beings receives as a "bonus" for anything? To me it all sounds like the enslavement on the part of the rich that Gouverneur Morris was talking about. Judging by my own originalist interpretation of his intent as revealed by his writings, I believe he would agree.

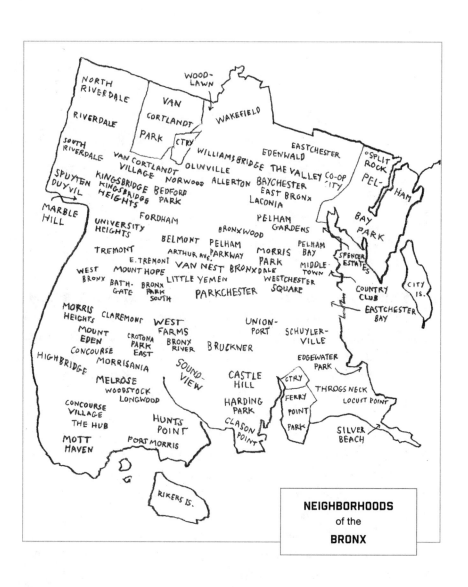

NEIGHBORHOODS
of the
BRONX

43

I DID A LOT of walking in the Bronx with my friend Edwin Velasquez, a person as restless as I am. Mostly I walked by myself, but when I had a companion, most often it was he. I don't ride bicycles—I'm too clumsy—but Velasquez loves them, and a forty-five-mile spin through the Bronx and onward into neighboring regions on a summer afternoon is nothing to him. That's how his own restlessness usually comes out. He is a trim, compact, undemonstrative young man, with dark hair and eyes, and the efficient build of a Tour de France racer. I had a grandfather named Edwin who was an engineer, like he is. That's probably another reason I like him. Velasquez was born in 1991, in Roosevelt Hospital, in Manhattan. My son was born in NYU Hospital, ditto, in 1992.

Velasquez and I met nine years ago when he worked for Bronx Pro, a company that builds and manages affordable housing. I was doing an article about DreamYard, a nonprofit Bronx arts organization for kids from elementary school through high school. He had been a participant in it, then an instructor; then he moved up to a job with Bronx Pro, which is DreamYard's landlord. He also draws and paints, and I had sought him out because of a mural he did. It's part of a large wall installation in the DreamYard parking lot and it takes up the center of a flower that's about seven feet across including the petals.

Within that circular space he combined the Harlem River (eggshell blue), the sky (a darker blue), the Manhattan skyline (silhouette black, with white highlights at the top of the Empire State Building), the Robert F. Kennedy Bridge (blue-gray), and the number 5 subway train (darker gray), riding on elevated tracks in the form of an arrow pointing to the lower left. He stitched the whole composition together with a jagged pink EKG heartbeat line across the center. The painting is a landscape and cityscape combined—to my mind, a true paradise Bronx, without sentiment or flourish. Velasquez signed it "E V" in the lower right. He also superintended the construction and weatherization and installation of this flower and eight others like it—"That was my first big engineering project," he told me. The flower panels are still there, and mostly in good condition.

His father (now retired) worked for the MTA, managing the supply of electricity to the subway trains, which meant he oversaw the third rail. In emergencies he was the one who turned it off. Velasquez's mother ran the Supercuts Hair Salon at East 82nd Street and Lexington; it's now closed, and she works at a hair salon in Scarsdale. He has an older brother, who's in the army, and a younger sister. Until he was nine, the family lived in Soundview, in the South Bronx, and then they moved north, to the Baychester area. When he was eleven, a video game changed his life. While visiting a friend in his neighborhood, he watched the friend play a game Velasquez had never seen called SimCity 2000. The "Sim" stands for simulated. The object of the game is to build a city, from the subway system to the top of the skyscrapers, and all structures and systems in between.

At the annual bookfair put on by Scholastic Books at his school, MS 144, he saw that along with the Harry Potter and Captain Underpants series, Scholastic was offering the latest SimCity iteration—SimCity 3000. Velasquez ordered the CD-ROM, installed it in his computer, and spent hours, entire days playing it. The game starts with a tutorial showing you the tools you need. Then you're given a map that's an open grid and you begin zoning your city for residential, commercial, and industrial. You click on and drag in roads and subway lines, you construct buildings appropriate to the zoning and support-ing infrastructure, and so on. You levy taxes, set a budget, fund civic services such as the schools and police and fire departments, and ev-erything is interconnected. If you defund the fire department your city starts getting fires.

MS 144 had enough kids who played the game that the school was able to enter three teams of three in the Super SimCity Competition, a national contest put on by Brooklyn Polytechnic College. The prize for the winners was scholarships to Brooklyn Polytechnic. If you won, you and your teammates each had a college scholarship waiting up ahead—and you were still only in the sixth grade! Each team also had to build a physical model of the city it designed, and the players were encouraged to use all recycled materials. Velasquez's team worked for months on their city plan and their model. They submitted everything as instructed, and they were disappointed not to win. He thinks the winner was a private school from New Jersey. The end of the com-petition didn't mean he stopped playing SimCity. He continued with the game for another eight years, through high school and after. The makers released a more sophisticated version, SimCity 4 Simtropolis, that allows players to devise new elements that can be added onto the game for other people to play.

After MS 144, he attended Bronx Engineering and Technology Academy (called Engineering and Tech), a smaller high school on the JFK High School Campus in the western Bronx. He describes JFK as a "dysfunctional hotspot of bad activity." Armed NYPD officers patrolled the hallways. Unlike the other kids on the campus, Engi-neering and Tech students had to wear uniforms, which made them conspicuous. Sometimes they got beaten up. One afternoon, as he was waiting for the Bx10 bus on his way home, a guy came walking by with a baseball bat in his hand and a blue Crips flag hanging out of his back pocket. A guy by the stop asked the guy with the bat where he was going. The guy with the bat said he was picking up his little brother. The other guy made a whistling call and suddenly a bunch of Bloods jumped out of nearby storefronts and began to chase the guy with the bat. Velasquez got on his bus—"I'm like, 'Get me out of here!'" The guy with the bat ran in the same direction the bus was going, and the pursuers caught up with him just as it reached the next stop. From the window, Velasquez saw from close up as one of them grabbed the guy's bat and beat him with it. Then the assailant dropped the bat, jumped on the bus, and sat down next to Velasquez.

"He's hyperventilating, he's going, like, 'I can't go back! I can't go back!' and I'm assuming what he means is, like, he can't go back to juvie or prison or whatever. And I'm freakin' out because I'm like, 'I just saw what you did to that guy, and you're sitting right next to me!' So that was very nerve-racking."

The Engineering and Tech principal would not let Velasquez transfer, but finally his father persuaded her—"I think she just got sick of seeing my dad"—and he enrolled at Informational Networking and Technology Academy (called Intech Academy), where he excelled in computer repair. While at Intech, he became involved with the Bronx Arts Council and met Carla Repice, an art teacher, who also was an instructor at DreamYard. Repice would be his good angel for years. After high school, Velasquez went to City College of New York (CCNY), on 137th and Amsterdam, where he majored in civil engineering and then switched to business administration. He graduated in 2013.

I LEARNED THESE and other autobiographical details while we were on our jaunts. Velasquez knows a lot of good places to explore. Once, we met at the Dunkin' Donuts at the end of the number 6 train, by a corner where pigeons were flying around. His parents live nearby, so he often takes the 6. He asked if I had noticed a lot of pigeons on the platform. I hadn't, or no more than usual. He said that the pigeons walk around on the platform and sometimes get on the train while it sits with its doors open waiting to go the other direction. "Sometimes they stay after the doors close, and ride the train for a while," he said. "It seems like they always get off at the Parkchester station, which is six stops away. I don't know why they get off there, or what they're doing in Parkchester. And I've never seen them getting on the train there and coming back. So does that mean they're flying home? Or maybe staying in Parkchester? I don't know."

On that walk, we went all over Pelham Bay Park, and back into

the deep weeds. Some places were cordoned off because of Lyme disease ticks. The park has whitetail deer that carry them. Velasquez
and I scared up a buck with a handsome rack of antlers—one of the
biggest whitetails I've ever seen—while, not far beyond him, traffic
whizzed by on the Hutchinson River Parkway. Looking more annoyed
than anything else, the buck moved off through the underbrush, and
we followed. He stepped leisurely and sometimes stopped to turn his
head in profile, up to his belly in the greenery, which on closer inspec-
tion was a large patch of poison ivy. Like a fairy-tale stag, the whitetail
led us deeper into the weedy nowhere, until we saw, off to our left, an
abandoned railroad station. When we turned to look at the ruin, the
deer disappeared.

Velasquez knew about the ruin already and had been searching
for it. I have no idea what former suburban railroad line it belonged
to. Now the poison ivy, its leaves glistening evilly with urushiol resin,
overlapped the former parking lot as if massing for an assault on
the structure itself. We went in at a doorless entry. Inside, we met
spookiness—plastic crates and other seat-like objects arranged in a
near-circle, as if for a conclave, in one of the waiting rooms. A mannequin, colorfully and cruelly defaced, leaned in a corner by a ticket
window. Graffiti and threats splashed the walls. We were back outside
in the poison garden in about two minutes.

Some walks had a city-planning theme. This was before I had
ever heard about any proposals to mitigate the Cross Bronx Expressway. One afternoon as we followed a part of the Cross Bronx that
runs through a roadcut (in pigeon-magnet Parkchester), Velasquez described how the highway here could be decked over, and green space
and housing put on top. His personal preference would be for making
it part of a corridor to take people quickly east-west and west-east by
public transit. He has spent too much time going in those directions
himself and believes the inconvenience of traveling west or east by bus
or subway remains one of the Bronx's most difficult problems.

Years ago, I knew a powerful and civic-minded man who lived on
an upper floor of a fancy building on the Upper East Side where the
elevator operators wore tuxedos. I was visiting as a friend of his daughter's. The man, a noted economist, had some connection to the Rocke-

fellers. I happened to be among his audience one day when he stood at his apartment window and talked about changes coming to the city. He pointed out buildings that were going to come down and places where buildings would be going up. From his high vantage, he gestured at this building and that, like a public-spirited Jove tossing thunderbolts.

Velasquez gestured like that at the highway as he described what should be done about it. I had never seen a young person make that kind of Jovian, city-creating gesture. Maybe it came from his SimCity frame of mind. Only later did I encounter the topic of Cross Bronx mitigation plans in the news; Velasquez had been studying the mitigation story earlier than any other planners I'd heard of. Now I finally believe that something will be done about the Cross Bronx Expressway. How about putting Pedro J. Estevez's Vertical Auto Merchandise Building on top of it, staffed with technicians trained to work on electric cars as well as regular cars?

Velasquez also showed me a block-long mural he had designed next to Railroad Park, a green space with benches and playground on Courtlandt Avenue between East 161st and East 162nd Streets, in Melrose. There's another abandoned commuter rail station there, in better shape than the poison-ivy one. The northwest edge of the park is a concrete wall by the base of a NYCHA high-rise. The city had asked DreamYard to decorate the eyesore expanse of bare concrete, and Velasquez had designed a Marsden Hartley–like abstract with shapes in basic colors set off from one another by black borders. Nobody had written graffiti on it so far, which he took as a compliment. Meeting such a big work in this frequented place and knowing he had designed it and supervised its creation gave him some satisfaction. Cement had been smeared on it at one end where they'd rehabbed the playground, and a few cracks in the wall had begun to weep a discoloring moisture—oh, well.

As we passed some of the newer buildings, he described their construction—how the prefab panels were fitted together and what kind of loads they could bear. Certain buildings, such as the new apartments along the decommissioned Sheridan Expressway, he disapproved of from a Jane Jacobs point of view, he said, for their blank, sealed-off ground floors and lack of engagement with the street. At 3361 Third Avenue, he stopped to show me a building in which entire prefab apartments had been fitted together like Lego blocks to make the four-story structure. The planning before construction, and the finishing after, had taken two years, but the actual construction was done in two weeks. A crane parked in front of the site and blocked half of Third Avenue, flatbeds showed up with the apartment modules, and the crane picked up the modules one by one and lifted them into place, all the way up to four stories high. Bronx Pro oversaw the construction and the screening of prospective tenants. Today the company runs the building, which provides supportive housing—with counseling and other services—for residents who are mentally ill and/or formerly unhoused.

Velasquez called me one summer morning and said he was painting the roof of an apartment building with reflecting paint to keep the building cool. I found the address, a five-story walk-up on Davidson Avenue. The sun shone intensely up there. He said this roof, and those of neighboring Bronx Pro buildings, once they had been painted, would make a pattern visible from the sky. With a paint pan and a roller at the end of a pole, he laid out white lines indicating geometric shapes that other people would fill in later with different sunlight-reflecting colors. Shiny paint on roofs cuts down on the expense of air-conditioning. It was nice, if dizzying, to be on the roof with the wide sky above, amid the applause-flapping of pigeons. He said he would show me the other Bronx Pro buildings in the plan, and we walked to the edge of the roof and looked up and down the avenue and the cross street. As he pointed them out, he said, "You can always tell our buildings because the fire escapes are Statue of Liberty Green."

Statue of Liberty Green! Everybody knows the color. Peter Magistro, the head of Bronx Pro, had chosen it for Bronx Pro's fire escapes years ago, Velasquez said. Statue of Liberty Green enlightens New York City everywhere, and once the color is in your mind, you can't stop seeing it. Copper oxidizes, of course, as it did on the statue's sheathing. The Norwegian copper shone like a penny when *Liberty Enlightening the World* (the work's name) was erected in the harbor in 1886. After twenty years, the outside had oxidized to a green that was somewhere between sky blue and the aqua greens of the sea. The Department of War, which had charge of the statue at the time, announced in 1906 that it planned to paint over the oxidation, and people objected so much that the higher-ups abandoned the idea. Later suggestions that the statue be buffed to remove the green and restore the original shininess also went nowhere.

When you take the ferry to Liberty Island and see the statue in situ, the guides tell you it's the most recognizable symbol in the world. The color is not applied to the metal, it comes from it, so when you're up close it's as if you're looking into the color—there's a depth and endlessness to it. When the sky is blue, you see another advantage: The color goes perfectly with sea and sky. Seeing the statue itself, in person, with harbor traffic coming and going, makes it clear that the color is caught up with the world-changing thrill of arrival. It's a color in which hope and geography combine.

Lots of other fire escapes in the Bronx are Statue of Liberty Green; it complements the browns and beiges and yellows of apartment-building bricks. Velasquez said that other landlords are now copying Bronx Pro. Paint that is labeled Statue of Liberty Green can be found in paint catalogues and bought in stores. I watched a hardware store employee mix a quart of it; its main components are dark green, yellow, white, and black. The city's infrastructure uses the color widely. The framework of steel beams under some of the Bronx's elevated subway tracks, for example—on a blue-sky morning, the sky cross-hatched with the Statue of Liberty Green girders is gorgeous, if you stand on a sidewalk under the tracks and look straight up.

The color is also found on freeway stanchions, streetlight poles, pipelines, drawbridge houses, fuel tanks, window grates, and the railings of pedestrian bridges; it spatters the coveralls of workmen, and it coats old railroad overpasses, where it ages to an intricate craquelure. You see it on the faces of Statue of Liberty impersonators who hand out flyers for tax preparers at income tax time. There is a Statue of Liberty Green face paint, which goes on thick, dries, and cracks like a mudflat, so that flakes of it start falling off.

Many of the city's exterior moldings and fittings are made of copper and come by the color naturally. It's on rain gutters, and the facings around dormer windows, and the decorative cornices of buildings, and slanted roofs. Stanford White, the architect, considered the statue to be the most beautiful example of metal coloring in the world, and he used copper and brass for the ornamentation on his buildings. The Gimbels Walkway above Thirty-second Street near Penn Station that connects the seventh floors of buildings on opposite sides of the street and provides a magical "Gotham City" effect to the area is Statue of Liberty Green. As if refracted from the statue itself, the color glints in shards throughout New York City.

VELASQUEZ STILL LIVES in the Bronx, on Tiemann Avenue, in Baychester. After he moved into an apartment there, he looked Tiemann up. Daniel F. Tiemann served as mayor of New York from 1858 to 1860. Velasquez admires him for making a useful and much-needed contribution to New York: "Tiemann put the street signs on lampposts so you could see them at night," Velasquez said. "I guess nobody else had thought of doing that before. Also, he looked kind of like the KFC guy—same beard."

Recently Velasquez has been able to forgo the vexing commute from his east Bronx apartment over to the west Bronx, where Bronx Pro is. Now he works in Midtown, a place easier for him to get to. In 2022, he took a job with Endurant Energy, a green-energy company with offices in New York, Chicago, California, and Houston. He made the switch because he wanted to do more with his engineering, and the job pays well. Endurant Energy installs wind- and solar-powered systems and mini grids. When he and I had dinner near his office about nine months after he started, he said he was now site engineer for eight different outdoor battery energy arrays. He had just come from one on Staten Island, and he showed me pictures. These battery arrays are white structures about the size of shipping containers. They have doors in a row like locker room doors, and behind the doors are racks holding hundreds of thousands of batteries that resemble ordinary D batteries. The units sit on cement slabs and are connected to wind or solar energy sources and to the electrical grid. When the sun shines and the wind blows, power flows into the batteries to be stored, and when needed it flows out.

There's overlap between this job and his previous one. He deals with some of the same city agencies for permitting, and with contractors and suppliers. But now he also travels around the United States.

He is following Sonia Sotomayor's advice to the youth of the Bronx and learning about the country. If you're an artist, or anybody, your thirties are the time when you break out and do major work and make your mark. I felt a parent-like pang, thinking he might leave the Bronx, and I asked him if he planned to stay. He said he had no plans to move right now, but he was liking Queens the more he saw of it. Then he said, "Don't get me wrong, I love the Bronx, I grew up there, it's my home. You know who Bad Bunny is? The Puerto Rican rapper? He did a concert last week going down the Grand Concourse on the top of a bus! It was amazing. He had a microphone with him, he was up there singing and dancing and ducking stoplights. He could have done the concert anywhere, but he didn't choose Queens or Brooklyn or Manhattan. He chose to do it on the Grand Concourse in the Bronx."

Velasquez said that in the past sometimes people had showed him off as an example of how well a kid from the Bronx can do if given the opportunity. "Like I'm a poster child, or something," he said. "I did get help, from DreamYard, from Bronx Pro, and from other people, and I'm grateful for it. But I also know in my heart that whatever help I got or didn't get, or even if I never got any help at all, Edwin G. Velasquez was going to be just fine."

HISTORIES LIKE THIS BOOK don't really have endings. Events moved on, for worse and better. Covid seemed to go away, mostly. Putin invaded Ukraine, and the company my son worked for shut down operations in Russia. He and his girlfriend left; they shared a kind of moral panic. Today he says that Russia is the only country he has ever fled. After a stay in Dresden, they had to think about moving on, because the Schengen visa, which lets people from outside the European Union travel and live anywhere in it, expires after ninety days. In the United States, the Uvalde school shooting had happened. They had considered coming back here, but he said, "A country that allows its children to be massacred and then does nothing about it can't say it's the best country in the world." For weeks their deliberations went on. In another conversation, Thomas told me, "The 'Shining City on a Hill' should be a real place that you can go to."

When they finally left Germany, they decided they would continue their search in the United States after all. They flew from Berlin to New York just before Christmas and I drove to JFK Airport one night to pick them up. I took the George Washington Bridge, and as I came into the streams of cars and trucks jockeying from five or six lanes down to three at the entry to the lower level, "She Drives Me Crazy," by the Fine Young Cannibals, came on the radio. I turned it up all the way. The cars and trucks were making small, tense movements, each getting advantage where it could, and the trucks' brake pads were keening as we slowly sorted ourselves from chaos into three lanes, and then we were on the bridge and across it, and onto the Cross Bronx Expressway; and I got a sudden rush of passion for being in this place and driving on this highway. The traffic began to move, and the song blasted, and a thrill of pure acceleration transported me. Feeling this joy on the Cross Bronx, which has done such harm, made me dizzy, too, with guilt that I would somehow be found out and punished. Driving is so much easier than walking. I had often walked along and under and above this highway and now I was flying on it.

After about five miles, I swung into the elevated mega-intersection, aka the Bruckner Interchange, among whose pillars I had wandered. I exited to the right and took I-687 south toward the Bronx-Whitestone Bridge, and the lights of the Bronx were around me and behind me, and I came onto the elevated approach ramp, and I could see the lights of Manhattan and Brooklyn ahead, and bright beams illuminated the towers of the bridge, and then I was in the lights and driving above the place (maybe the exact place) where the DeLancey men rode their horses into the water and swam to Queens, escaping for their lives, in July 1781; and I saw that New York City is the closest thing to a Shining City I've got to offer.

NOTES

Chapter 1

3   *"the continent," "the mainland," or "the maine"*: *The Story of the Bronx: From the Purchase Made by the Dutch from the Indians in 1639 to the Present Day*, by Stephen Jenkins (1912), pp. 5, 6. See also *The Revolutionary Journal of Baron Ludwig von Closen 1780–1783*, tr. and ed. by Evelyn M. Acomb (1958), pp. 92, 99. Also, *The American Campaigns of Rochambeau's Army 1780, 1781, 1782, 1783*, tr. and ed. by Howard C. Rice, Jr., and Anne S. K. Brown (1972), vol. I, p. 36.

4   *The northernmost part of the Bronx's western border is the Hudson River*: Good descriptions of the geography of the Bronx may be found in *South Bronx Rising: The Rise, Fall, and Resurrection of an American City*, by Jill Jonnes (2002), p. 11; also in *The Northern Borough: A History of the Bronx*, by Lloyd Ultan (2005), pp. 1–2.

5   *called the river Aquahung*: Jenkins, p. 16. *the Siwanoy, the Munsee, and the Weckquaesgeek*: Ultan, *Northern Borough*, p. 4. *In December 1639*: See *History in Asphalt: The Origin of Bronx Street and Place Names*, by John McNamara (1978), p. 32.

6   *A man named Pieter Schorstinaveger*: ibid., p. 441. *In 1939, three hundred years after Jonas Bronck, three reporters set out to discover*: "Bronck's Descendants," by Geoffrey T. Hellman, Harold Ross, and Max Elser, in *The New Yorker*, May 6, 1939, p. 15.

6   *A poet named William Bronk*: His *Life Supports: New and Collected Poems* won the National Book Award in 1981.

7   *the largest food distribution depot in the world*: See "Community and Crime Decline: The Causal Effect of Local Nonprofits on Violent Crime," by Patrick Sharkey, *American Sociological Review*, Oct. 25, 2017, p. 186.

7   *the average speed on it during the evening rush hour*: "H'way of Hell: Cross Bronx Rated Most Agonizing Road in U.S.," New York *Daily News*, Feb. 21, 2017, p. 8. *For a while in the mid-twentieth century, planners thought*: See *The Power Broker: Robert Moses and the Fall of New York*, by Robert A. Caro (1974), p. 897.

8   *In 1905, the tracks for what are now the number 2 and number 5*: See Jenkins, p. 245. For more on the coming of the subways, see Ultan, *Northern Borough*, pp. 206, 213 ff., 257; and *Greater Gotham: A History of New York City from 1898 to 1919*, by Mike Wallace (2017), pp. 228 ff. Population figures are in Jenkins, p. 9, and Ultan, *Northern Borough*, p. 257.

8   *I was writing an article*: See "Out of the Bronx," *The New Yorker*, Feb. 6, 2012, p. 52.

9   *On the heights above the Hudson River*: Details about the Kennedys' time in the Bronx
     are in "John F. Kennedy's Life in Bronx," *The Bronx Daily*, Nov. 23, 2011, and in *JFK:
     Reckless Youth*, by Nigel Hamilton (1992), pp. 62, 68–69. The Kennedys lived at
     5040 Independence Avenue. The Oswalds' address during their Bronx residency is in
     "Bronx Tale of a BB Gun and Infamy in the Making," by Dan Barry, *The New York Times*,
     Nov. 20, 2013. See also *Lee Harvey Oswald and the American Dream*, by Paul Sites
     (1967), pp. 69 ff.

10   *A stair street with 132 steps*: The so-called Joker Stairs is now one of the established
     tourist destinations of New York.

Chapter 2

13   *Although seven million trees grow in the city today*: See "A Million More Trees for New
     York City," *The New York Times*, Feb. 12, 2022.

13   *botanist who co-founded the garden wanted especially to preserve the ancient hemlock
     trees*: Hemlock information can be found on a plaque in the Thain Family Forest in the
     New York Botanical Garden. The plaque, titled "Changing Landscape: Old Hemlock
     Grove," is along the trail, beside some of the few remaining hemlocks. (Facts about the
     chestnut blight are on another plaque in the forest.)

14   *One of the oldest of them is a red oak*: The plaque with this information has disappeared,
     but I confirmed the details about the tree in a phone conversation with Eliot Nagele,
     director of the Thain Family Forest. *Once, a glacier a thousand feet thick*: Some of the
     glacier facts are on a plaque by the glacier-scraped rock in the forest. Others I learned
     from a lecture by Eric W. Sanderson, landscape ecologist with the Wildlife Conserva-
     tion Society at the Bronx Zoo. Sanderson is the author of the interesting and informative
     Mannahatta: A Natural History of New York City (2009).

14   *North America was part of a landmass geologists called Laurentia*: Geologic infor-
     mation is from "Annealed Mylonites of the Saint Nicholas Thrust (SNT) from a New
     Excavation at the New York Botanical Gardens, the Bronx, New York," by Charles Mer-
     guerian and John E. Sanders (1998); and from phone conversations and email exchanges
     with Dr. Merguerian. Other relevant papers are: Charles Merguerian, "Tectonic Signifi-
     cance of Cameron's Line in the Vicinity of the Hodges Complex—An Imbricate Thrust
     Model for Western Connecticut," in *American Journal of Science* 283 (1983), pp. 341–
     68; see also Charles Merguerian and Mickey Merguerian, "Geology of Central Park—
     from Rocks to Ice," in G. M. Hanson, "Eleventh Annual Conference on Geology of Long
     Island and Metropolitan New York," April 17, 2004.

15   *Icebergs have held rocks they picked up in the north*: See *The Two-Mile Time Machine:
     Ice Cores, Abrupt Climate Change, and Our Future*, by Richard B. Alley (c. 2000),
     pp. 121 ff.

16   *A glacial erratic called the Rocking Stone*: Description of the Rocking Stone, and a photo
     of it dated c. 1912, may be found in Jenkins, pp. 306–307. *When the glacier stopped at
     Staten Island*: See *Unearthing Gotham: The Archaeology of New York City*, by Anne-
     Marie Cantwell and Diana diZerega Wall (2001), pp. 37 ff. *The earliest evidence of hu-
     man occupation*: ibid.

17   *Its waters were a metropolis containing perhaps half of all the oysters in the world*: See
     Cantwell and diZerega Wall, p. 87. *the Dutch reported oysters in the Gowanus River
     "not less than a foot long"*: See "Journal of Jasper Danchaerts, 1679–1680," ed. Bartlett
     Burleigh James and J. Franklin Jameson (1913), p. 53.

17   *To maintain a daily caloric requirement*: Cantwell and diZerega, p. 56. *Alanson Buck
     Skinner (1886–1925)*: Details of the biographies of Skinner and of Amos Oneroad are
     in *Being Dakota*, by Amos E. Oneroad and Alanson B. Skinner (ed. Laura L. Anderson,
     2003). Description of Skinner's excavations of Snakapins and at the Schley Avenue Shell-
     heap site are in "Explorations of Aboriginal Sites at Throgs Neck and Clasons Point, New
     York City," by Alanson Skinner (1919), in *Contributions from the Museum of the American
     Indian Heye Foundation* V, no. 4.

20 *When the Sioux and Cheyenne women were dismembering the dead*: See *Son of the Morning Star*, by Evan S. Connell (1984), p. 422.

20 *Made from the sharpened bone of a mammal, it had rows of small notches incised on it*: Skinner, p. 92. *Amos Enos Oneroad*: For Oneroad's biography, see Oneroad and Skinner, pp. 18 ff.

21 *George Gustav "Slim-Shin" Heye*: See "Slim-Shin's Monument," by Kevin Wallace, in *The New Yorker*, Nov. 19, 1960, p. 104.

22 *A tribal historian later told a writer*: See Oneroad and Skinner, p. 33. *Snakapins and the Schley Avenue village may have been, briefly, industry towns*: See Skinner, p. 66. Other wampum facts are from "Archery Range Ossuary, Pelham Bay Park, Bronx County, New York," by Edward J. Kaeser, in *Pennsylvania Archaeologist* 40: 9–34. *you could pay the fare in pence or wampum*: See Jenkins, p. 181.

22 *For a while, the Iroquois, that dangerous and highly mobile tribe*: I use "Iroquois" because it was a common name used at the time and afterward; the actual name of that confederacy of tribes is the Haudenosaunee. *In 1640, William Kieft, the governor of New Amsterdam, levied on the Indians a tax payable in "wampum, corn, or furs"*: See Cantwell and diZerega Wall, p. 126. Hunter Island's previous name, Laap-Ha-Wach-King, is mentioned in *History in Asphalt*, by John McNamara, p. 126.

23 *Matthew López-Jensen*: His artwork is represented by the Yancey Richardson Gallery, New York City, and his photographs can be found online.

24 *Edward J. Kaeser*: See his "The Morris Estate Club Site" in *New York State Archaeology Society Bulletin* 27: 38–45 (1963). For details of another dig and more on Native Americans in the Bronx, see Kaeser, "Archery Range Ossuary," in *Pennsylvania Archaeologist* 40 (1970): 9–34. Also see Julius Lopez, "The History and Archaeology of Fort Independence on Tetard's Hill," in *Bulletin, New York State Archaeological Association* 73 (July): 1–23.

25 *Jennifer Lopez*: Details about Lopez are in her memoir, *True Love* (2014), and passim online.

Chapter 3

26 *Anne Hutchinson*: See *American Jezebel: The Uncommon Life of Anne Hutchinson, the Woman Who Defied the Puritans*, by Eve LaPlante (2004).

27 *Old-time accounts said that if you sighted through the split*: See McNamara, p. 216.

28 *The rock still exists today mainly because of the efforts of two local historians*: ibid.

30 *The Indians arrived one day in July*: For a description of the Siwanoy attack on the Hutchinson farm, see LaPlante, p. 236.

31 *"Thus the Lord heard our groans to heaven"*: LaPlante, p. 244. *In the 1640s, egged on by William Kieft*: Cantwell and diZerega Wall, p. 126.

32 *"must be a very mean fellow"*: ibid.

33 *Jasper Danckaerts*: See "Journal of Jasper Danckaerts, 1679–1680," in *Original Narratives of Early American History*, ed. Bartlett Burleigh James and J. Franklin Jameson, reproduced under the auspices of the American Historical Association (1913), pp. 36 ff. *when the English took New Netherland from the Dutch in 1664*: The Dutch briefly took back the colony in 1673, in the third Anglo-Dutch War; it reverted to England by treaty in 1674.

34 *"The people in this city"*: ibid., p. 79. *Dr. Ted Kazimiroff, the Bronx historian who co-saved Split Rock*: The pictograph on the rock that was in the New York Botanical Garden has since been declared of recent origin, and the rock is no longer on display.

35 *Kazimiroff's most remarkable discovery*: His son's book on the subject is *The Last Algonquin*, by Theodore L. Kazimiroff (1982).

36 *Jasper Danckaerts, the Dutchman, concludes his description of his cosmogony lesson*: Danckaerts, p. 79.

36 *the future site of Philadelphia, which did not yet exist*: Danckaerts, p. 100; he made his journey in 1679–1680, and William Penn founded Philadelphia in 1682.

36 *Wampage, the self-declared killer of Anne Hutchinson*: See Skinner, p. 78. Wampage
    put his name to a treaty in 1692, almost fifty years after she was killed. *some were still
    attending the Anglican church in Westchester village as late as 1710*: Skinner, p. 78.
    Many of the Munsee removed to a big Lenape village called Minisink: See Cantwell and
    diZerega Wall, p. 145.

Chapter 4

38 *High Bridge*: Facts about the High Bridge, the Croton Aqueduct, and their construction
    may be found on the NYC Parks Department historic marker titled "Croton Aqueduct
    Triangle Highlights" at the triangle between Reservoir Avenue and Goulden Avenue, in
    Kingsbridge Heights. (The text of the marker is also on the website of the NYC Department
    of Parks and Recreation.) *According to* History in Asphalt: See McNamara, pp. 245, 394.

39 *José Serrano*: See *South Bronx Battles: Stories of Resistance, Resilience, and Renewal*,
    by Carolyn McLaughlin (2019), p. 196. *About sixty feet above it is a major railroad
    bridge*: See "Randall's Island Park: The Hell Gate Pathway," also on the Department of
    Parks and Recreation website.

40 *Gouverneur Morris was born at one thirty in the morning of January 31, 1752*: See *Gou-
    verneur Morris and the American Revolution*, by Max M. Mintz (1970), p. 6. Mintz says
    Morris was born on January 30; other biographers, including Theodore Roosevelt, say he
    was born on January 31. I have taken the word of the majority and accepted January 31.
    (For sources on other biographical details on Morris, see below.)

41 *the issue of his name. How was posterity to pronounce it?*: For evidence supporting the
    pronunciation "Governor," see *Gouverneur Morris, an Independent Life*, by William
    Howard Adams (2003), p. 298. For evidence favoring the pronunciation "Gover*neer*," see
    "The Forgotten Founding Father," by Richard Brookhiser, in *City Journal*, Manhattan
    Institute for Policy Research (Spring 2002): "Abigail Adams, who spelled phonetically,
    wrote him down as 'Governeer.' That will have to do for an answer—it is the best clue
    we are likely to find." Brookhiser's biography of Morris is *Gentleman Revolutionary:
    Gouverneur Morris—The Rake Who Wrote the Constitution* (2003).

41 *The New York, New Haven, and Hartford Railroad acquired the property*: See Jenkins,
    pp. 360, 364.

42 *They were Welsh, and their name derived from* Maur Rys: See ibid., p. 62.

43 *Unfortunately for him, the wife predeceased him*: ibid., p. 73. *the elder Lewis died in
    1691*: Adams, p. 8. *In May 1697, the governor of the Province of New-York gave this
    Lewis a royal charter*: Ultan, *Northern Borough*, pp. 30, 34. *the first native-born chief
    justice of the New York Supreme Court*: Jenkins, p. 268. *After making an enemy of Wil-
    liam Cosby*: For the Zenger trial, see Brookhiser, p. 4, and Ultan, *Northern Borough*,
    p. 57. *who happened to be his first wife's cousin*: Mintz, p. 5.

43 *The boundaries of Morrisania*: Sources give various boundary lines for the Mor-
    rises' manor. In Adams, p. 298, its southern border is described as the East River (and
    presumably the Bronx Kill). He says the property stretched as far north as today's 180th
    Street, with the Mill Brook (today's Brook Avenue) running through its middle. A Parks
    Department plaque at Padre Plaza, at the corner of East 139th Street and St. Ann's Av-
    enue, says that the Mill Brook was the western boundary of Morrisania (see the "Padre
    Plaza" entry on the NYC Parks Dept. website). If Mill Brook ran through the middle of
    Morrisania, the plaque must be referring to Mill Brook as the boundary of only Gouver-
    neur Morris's portion of Morrisania, which was its eastern half. His half brother Lewis
    owned the western half, and the brook divided their holdings. Mintz (p. 6) gives Inter-
    vale Avenue and Bungay Creek as Morrisania's eastern boundary. A map in Jenkins
    (p. 2) backs that up and shows the eastern boundary coinciding with today's East 149th
    Street. Jenkins also says (p. 318), "Bungay Creek, the boundary between the manor of
    Morrisania and the West Farms patent, had its origins within" present-day Crotona Park.
    According to *Historical Guide to the City of New York*, compiled by Frank Bergen Kelly
    (1909), p. 199, the manor's northern boundary was near East 182nd Street: "Just below

[East 182nd], at Oak Tree Place, was the celebrated oak tree where met the boundaries of the ancient manors of Morrisania, Fordham, and the Jessup-Richardson Patent." But the reliable John McNamara says (in the 1978 edition of *History in Asphalt*, p. 16) that Avenue St. John "marks the extreme edge of the Manorlands of the Morris family." From Avenue St. John to Oak Tree Place is about three miles—a wide distance between these supposed former boundaries (Oak Tree Place is north of the Cross Bronx Expressway). Whatever the boundaries of Morrisania were, it is safe to say that the Morris family once owned a large part of today's South Bronx.

45 *Anthony Van Angola*: See Cantwell and diZerega Wall, p. 168.

46 *"to help plant the fields"*: Ultan, *Northern Borough*, p. 19.

46 *Hannibal and Samson*: ibid., p. 41.

46 *In 1712, about 16 percent of the people residing in what's now the Bronx were enslaved*: ibid., p. 44. *"a Negroe Boy called George"*: Mintz, p. 15. *the last enslaved person freed in the state*: See Jenkins, pp. 93 ff. *In the late 1980s, excavation for a new office building on Foley Square*: The story of the African Burial Ground discovered on Foley Square is in Cantwell and diZerega Wall, pp. 277 ff.

Chapter 5

49 *they called it Oostdorp*: See historic marker at Westchester Square (listed under "Owen S. Dolen Park" in NYC Parks Dept. website).

50 *Dock Street, which led to the wharf*: See McNamara, pp. 63, 90. He also says, "[Dock Street] is possibly one of the earliest streets in all the Bronx as it was the landing place for the Dutch outpost of Oostdorp (now Westchester Square)."

50 *The bounty for killing a full-grown wolf was thirty shillings for Christians, ten shillings for Indians*: Jenkins, p. 53. *Katherine Harryson*: ibid., p. 58.

50 *Known as the King's Bridge, Philipse's bridge carried foot and animal traffic*: A Dutchman, Vredryck Flypsen (in English, Frederick Philipse), built the King's Bridge in 1693, to cross Spuyten Duyvil Creek and connect Manhattan with his land on the continent; see Ultan, *Northern Borough*, pp. 29, 36; see also Jenkins, p. 391. (In 1759, a second bridge, called the Farmers' Free Bridge, was built just east of the King's Bridge—Jenkins, p. 191).

51 *Twenty years before, the population of the county had been 13,257*: Ultan, *Northern Borough*, p. 81.

52 *Westchester village held its own agricultural fair every fall*: ibid., p. 85. *When he was fourteen, a household accident severely scalded his right arm*: See *Envoy to the Terror: Gouverneur Morris and the French Revolution*, by Melanie Randolph Miller (2005), p. 2. In *Gouverneur Morris and the American Revolution*, Mintz says (p. 23) that the accident happened in August 1766. (Morris turned fourteen in January of that year.) An overturned kettle of water scalded him on his arm and side. He convalesced at home for more than a year and was left with scar tissue.

52 *The young Gouverneur studied with a tutor in New Rochelle*: See Jared Sparks, *The Life of Gouverneur Morris, with selections from his correspondence, and miscellaneous papers* (1832), vol. I, p. 4. Sparks was Morris's first biographer and interviewed contemporaries who had known him. Sparks says that from this tutor, a M. Tetar, Morris "acquired the basis of the French language, which in after life he wrote and spoke with nearly as much fluency and correctness as his native tongue." Had Sparks been able to interview Adélaïde Filleul, Marquise de Souza-Botelho, Morris's former mistress, who was alive in 1832 and living in Paris, and who survived until 1836, she might have told the biographer that she used to make fun of Morris's bad French.

52 *In fact, his father's will had stipulated that under no circumstances was he to go to Yale*: Mintz, p. 15; Gouverneur's father did not want him to study in Connecticut because of the "low craft and cunning" of the people there. Gouverneur Morris's snobbery and dismissal of the patriot officers as "a herd of Mechanicks" is in Sparks, vol. I, p. 3.

53 *His mother, still living at Morrisania, sided with the British*: Brookhiser, p. 23; Ultan, *Northern Borough*, p. 94. *while his mentor and employer, William Smith, chose to remain*

neutral: Mintz, p. 65. *His half brother Staats Long Morris was an officer in the British Army*: Ultan, *Northern Borough*, p. 94. *In 1775, when he was only twenty-three*: See *The Extraordinary Mr. Morris*, by Howard Swiggett (1952), p. 25; see also Mintz, p. 48. *he went almost seven years without seeing his mother*: Sparks, vol. I, p. 264.

53   *Gouverneur Morris first met George Washington*: See Adams, p. 52.

54   *Morris had the job of relaying messages*: Mintz, p. 60. *as Theodore Roosevelt wrote*: See *Gouverneur Morris*, by Theodore Roosevelt (1975 reprint of 1888 edition), p. 33.

55   *(Once, during the Boston campaign . . .)*: See *Washington's Crossing*, by David Hackett Fischer (2004), p. 25.

55   *He wore, said one observer*: This description of Washington's sartorial elegance is by an eyewitness, Dr. James Thacher, in *The American Revolution from the Commencement to the Disbanding of the American Army; Given in the Form of a Daily Journal, with the Exact Dates of All the Important Events; also, A Biographical Sketch of All the Most Prominent Generals*, by James Thacher, MD, Surgeon in the American Revolutionary Army (1860), p. 30. *he ordered silver lace and blue and scarlet cloth*: See *Young Washington: How Wilderness and War Forged America's Founding Father*, by Peter Stark (2018), p. 287. *a girl child, Ona, known by the name Oney Judge*: See "George Washington, Slave Catcher," by Erica Armstrong Dunbar, in *The New York Times*, Feb. 16, 2015, p. 17.

56   *When the British Army was in Boston, one of its generals, John Burgoyne, wrote a play that portrayed Washington as a buffoon*: See *Traits of the Tea Party*, by George R. T. Hewes (1835), p. 211; see also *Memoir and Letters of Captain W. Glanville Evelyn of the 4th Regiment ("King's Own") from North America, 1774–1776*, ed. and annotated by G. D. Scull (1879), pp. 79–80. Captain Evelyn wrote that the Yankees "cannot stand ridicule." Re: the British officers' contempt for Washington, see *A Journal of the Operations of the Queen's Rangers, from the End of the Year 1777, to the Conclusion of the Late American War*, by Lieutenant-Colonel John Graves Simcoe (1787), p. 34 and passim.

57   *"they will not be drove"*: Fischer, p. 6. *The command probably numbered about 40,000 soldiers*: See *Westchester-County, New York, during The American Revolution*, by Henry B. Dawson (1886), p. 224. *"I thought all London was afloat"*: Fischer, p. 31.

58   *Two months later, he disappeared from the Provincial Congress and went to Boonton*: See Mintz, pp. 69–70; also Miller, p. 3; also Adams, pp. 76–77.

58   *Bayonetting men to the trees, they panicked the Americans*: See Fischer, p. 97.

59   *Nearby, just across the Arthur Kill, was a stone house*: This still-standing house, now called the Conference House, is part of a New York City park. Information about the meeting between the Americans and the British that took place on September 11, 1776, may be found in a booklet, "The Conference House Revisited: A History of the Billopp Manor House," by Field Horne (1990), available at the site. See also "John Adams Autobiography, part I, 'John Adams,' through 1776; sheet 44 of 53, 9–17 September 1776," in the online archives of the Massachusetts Historical Society.

59   *A word about the Howe brothers*: For more on the Howes, see *Complete Peerage of England, Scotland, Ireland, Great Britain and the United Kingdom, Extant, Extinct, or Dormant, Alphabetically Arranged and Edited by George Edward Cockayne* (1892), vol. IV, pp. 269 ff. See also Fischer, pp. 67 ff. (although he gets wrong the degree of blood relationship between the Howes and George III).

60   *On September 15, the British landed at Kip's Bay*: See *Memoirs of Major-General [William] Heath, containing Anecdotes, Details of Skirmishes, Battles, and other Military Events during the American War, written by himself* (1798), pp. 60 ff. See also Fischer, pp. 102 ff. *the British insultingly played the bugle calls used in a fox chase*: ibid., p. 107.

Chapter 6

62   *John Adams said that New York was the key to the whole continent*: Fischer, p. 80.

63   *To slide around to the bridge from the east*: See Ultan, *Northern Borough*, pp. 90–92.

For more on the Battle of Pelham, see also "The Battle of Pell's Point: October 18, 1776. Being the Story of a Stubborn Fight. With a map, and illustrations from original photographs and family portraits," by William Abbatt (1901). Also *Between the Lines: Stories of Westchester County, New York, During the American Revolution*, by Susan Cochran Swanson (1975), pp. 14 ff., and *Westchester-County, New York, during The American Revolution*, by Henry B. Dawson (1886), pp. 241 ff. See also *Westchester County During the American Revolution 1775–1783*, by Otto Hufeland (1926), pp. 117 ff.

63   *Throgs Neck got its name from a party of Quakers, led by a man named Throckmorton*: See Ultan, *Northern Borough*, p. 10; Jenkins, p. 30; and Skinner, p. 52.

63   *a rare swoon of despair*: See Dawson, p. 232; also Jenkins, p. 139.

64   *General William Heath, whom Washington had put in command of the troops north of Manhattan*: For Heath's account of the action on October 12, see his memoirs, pp. 67 ff.

65   *Later in the war, when the British happened to capture a Pennsylvanian armed with one of these long rifles*: Fischer, p. 23. *At the end of the day, the British marched back down Throgs Neck*: ibid., p. 109. *"As an officer of parade and discipline"*: Thacher, p. 413.

65   *Bad weather followed, and the British stayed put in their Throgs Neck camp*: Adverse winds made the passage through Hell Gate difficult, and the troops on Throgs Neck could not be resupplied—see Dawson, p. 240.

66   *When Howe finally moved, on October 18, he chose the Pell's Point option*: ibid, p. 241; see also Jenkins, p. 143, and Hufeland, p. 117.

66   *Black soldiers served in Glover's regiment*: The historian David Osborn says that Glover's regiment was held in reserve during the battle and did not see action, and the regiments that did may not have had Black soldiers. Nonetheless, including Blacks in the mural would have been accurate for representational purposes.

67   *"For Posterity I bleed"*: Abbatt, p. 12.

68   *Then Howe brought the full weight of his superior force to bear*: ibid., pp. 15 ff. See also Dawson, pp. 241 ff.

69   *No one could have detested the Americans more than did Captain Evelyn*: See Evelyn, pp. 27, 29, 53, and passim.

70   *His death was "a great calamity to his family"*: ibid., p. 12. Had the young Evelyn lived, "he would have been the head of the family of Evelyn" (ibid.). The eminence of that family can also be judged by the fact that in 1698, thirty-four years before Evelyn's birth, an ancestor rented the family's house, Say's Court, to Peter the Great, tsar of Russia, when he was in England for three months to learn the art of shipbuilding (ibid., p. 1).

70   *Local historians later said he lost hundreds of troops*: According to Jenkins (p. 147) Howe lost 800–1,000 killed, wounded, and missing, as against the Americans' 6 killed and 13 wounded. Jenkins rates Pell's Point as a disaster for the British on the scale of Bunker Hill. Hufeland (p. 124) says the British (mainly the Hessians) lost between 150 and 800. *In a report to a higher-up in London, Howe said he lost only three dead*: See Evelyn, p. 10. *A British regimental history describes the battle . . . as merely "a sharp skirmish"*: ibid., p. 13. Washington's message, "The hurried situation of the Gen'l the last two days" etc., is quoted in Abbatt, pp. 21–22.

71   *Glover and Washington did not always get along*: Details of the relationship between the two are from the historian David Osborn, and from *General John Glover and His Marblehead Mariners*, by George Athan Billias (1960). *The New Englander, described by a French observer as "a little man, but active and a good soldier"*: See *Travels in North America in the Years 1780, 1781 and 1782*, by the Marquis de Chastellux (rev. tr. with introduction and notes by Howard C. Rice, Jr.; 1963), p. 111. The marquis described people as he saw them, without concern for feelings. In an early edition of this book, he said Martha Washington was fat; he modified that to "rather plump" in a later edition.

72   *He had wanted to evacuate this fort, but Congress insisted he keep a presence on the island*: Jenkins, p. 142.

72   *He wanted to send a message to the defenders*: The story of the courageous messenger is in Heath, p. 86. *Washington Irving, in his five-volume* Life of George Washington: The

story of Washington weeping to see the bayonetting of his men is quoted in Fischer, p. 114. The footnote, p. 502, cites the 1855–59 edition of Irving's *The Life of George Washington* (vol. 2, p. 424).

73   *Robert Livingston, a representative from New Jersey, wrote to Edward Rutledge*: Mintz, p. 69.

73   *"I am amazed at Gouverneur!"*: Adams, p. 76. *Gouverneur did not return until December 9*: Mintz, p. 70. *Among his set he had a reputation for being immoral*: Miller, p. 3. *His main goal for that document was to put in a clause abolishing slavery in New York*: See Roosevelt, p. 43. His effort failed, but Roosevelt says that Morris and the other antislavery delegates "had much hearty support, and by the bold stand they took and by the high ground they occupied they undoubtedly brought nearer the period when the abolition of slavery in New York became practicable" (ibid.). See also Adams, p. 84, and Mintz, p. 76. *He stood above six feet tall*: ibid., p. 36.

Chapter 7

76   *Celina Sotomayor, the mother of Supreme Court Justice Sonia Sotomayor, went to night school here*: McLaughlin, p. 87. *The Lorelei Fountain, also at East 161st Street*: Jenkins, p. 373.

77   *Then, on the left, the Andrew Freedman Home*: Ultan, *Northern Borough*, p. 243; see also "Dedicate a Refuge for Cultural Poor; Andrew Freedman Home, Which Cost $1,000,000, a New Idea in Philanthropy; Aged Couples Not Divided; Are Maintained in Luxurious Surroundings—Open to All Creeds," *The New York Times*, May 26, 1924.

78   *Back when the Bronx was about 50 percent Jewish*: Ultan, *Northern Borough*, p. 238.

79   *Somehow that sentence entered the language*: See *Ladies and Gentlemen, the Bronx Is Burning*, by Jonathan Mahler (2005).

80   *the Carter motorcade went up Lexington Avenue, over the Third Avenue Bridge*: A map of the route President Carter took accompanies the *New York Times* story about the trip— "Carter Takes 'Sobering' Trip to South Bronx," Oct. 6, 1977, p. 1. The map is next to the continuation of the story on p. B18.

81   *I've wondered whether Carter's later volunteer work, building houses for Habitat for Humanity, might also have been influenced by the shock of that Bronx visit*: Carter knew about Habitat for Humanity because it was founded in 1976 in Americus, Georgia, eleven miles from his home in Plains. After his presidency, he served on the board of the organization, and he and his wife led thirty-seven Habitat home-building projects in fourteen countries. See *His Very Best: Jimmy Carter, a Life*, by Jonathan Alter (2020), p. 615.

82   *Almost exactly two hundred years before, in the fall of 1777, the Reverend Timothy Dwight, a chaplain in the Continental Army, observed a landscape of misery along the same road*: See *Travels in New-England and New-York*, by Timothy Dwight (1821–22), vol. 3, pp. 491–92.

Chapter 8

86   *George Washington observed that the section of "the Brunx" below the waterfall could not be crossed except with boats*: See *The Diaries of George Washington*, vol. III (1771–75, 1780–81), ed. Donald Jackson (1978), p. 400.

87   *One of the sons, Colonel James DeLancey, who was about thirty years old in 1776, led a group of cavalry known as DeLancey's Refugees*: DeLancey, sometimes called a lieutenant-colonel, is ubiquitous in accounts of the Neutral Ground, but disappears from local history after his banishment. For his background and historical context, see Ultan, *Northern Borough*, pp. 93 ff., and Jenkins, p. 83 and passim.

88   *"Tim Knapp was the handsomest young man I ever saw"*: The McDonald Papers at the Westchester County Historical Society (hereinafter, TMP), interview with Mrs. Thomas Ferris, p. 208. *"Tim Knapp was illegitimate"*: TMP, interview with Abraham Davis, p. 262. *In a high-spirited moment*: TMP, interview with Samuel Oakley, p. 19. (Samuel

Oakley, in his eighties at the time of the interview, was the nephew of James Oakley, one of the Neutral Ground guides during the Revolution.)

89 *the barrel was kicked out from under him*: The story of Tim Knapp's hanging is from TMP interviews with Mr. and Mrs. Daniel Edwards (pp. 109 ff.), Samuel Oakley, Mrs. Nancy Sarles (p. 437), and a Dr. Lyman (p. 768).

90 *Major Andreas Emmerick, a German, led a troop of irregular cavalry*: Swanson, p. 3. Details re: Emmerick are mentioned throughout TMP. Samuel Oakley told the story of Emmerick and Bull Pete's wife (TMP, 24). Rebecca Odell, ten years old during the war, said his appearance "inspired dread" (TMP, p. 447). *The British and their Hessian mercenaries traveled with women camp followers who aided in the plundering*: Dawson, p. 278. *One of Washington's French allies estimated that about a quarter of the American army was Black*: See von Closen, p. 89. *As Aaron's fighting reputation grew*: See TMP, pp. 743, 827. *The British offered freedom to any slaves who came over to their side*: See Hufeland, pp. 296–97.

91 *In* The Spy, *Cooper has a British officer, Colonel Wellmere, challenge a Yankee physician at dinner*: Cooper, *The Spy*, pp. 134–35.

91 *Neither Cooper nor America ever really came up with an answer*: For more on Cooper and *The Spy*, see the introduction by Curtis Dahl to *The Spy: A Tale of the Neutral Ground* (1821; 1946). *Colonel Charles Armand, Marquis de la Rouerie*: The story of Armand's capture of Major Bearmore is in Hufeland, pp. 310 ff.

92 *Another Neutral Ground raider, Colonel Elisha Sheldon*: In TMP, p. 439, Mrs. Nancy Sarles said, "Sheldon's reputation was not high as a soldier. They called the road where Tarleton pursued him 'Sheldon's Race Course.'" Mrs. Martha Griffin said, "Sheldon's [men] were great plunderers" (TMP, p. 641). *According to one account, they stole*: The list of plundered objects is in Dawson, p. 279.

93 *During a Skinner raid, a girl named Mary Robbins took her family's gold and silver coins*: TMP, interview with Enos Hobby, p. 931. *Several of Emmerick's men robbed a woman named Phoebe Turner*: TMP, p. 512. *Early in 1777, Washington ordered Heath to attack Fort Independence*: Jenkins, p. 156; see also Hufeland, p. 188 ff.; and Heath's *Memoirs*, pp. 106–14.

94 *In a raid below DeLancey's Mills, a troop of American cavalry called Stephenson's Rangers captured James DeLancey*: TMP, interview with Nehemiah Brown, p. 53.

95 *From a distance the clanging of swords against swords sounded like blacksmiths hammering*: TMP, interview with Garret Garretson, p. 452.

95 *A McDonald interviewee described a man wounded by Refugee broadswords*: TMP, interview with Nathaniel Montross, p. 745. *"We saw four dead bodies, mangled in a most inhuman manner"*: See Thacher, p. 256.

96 *At the end of the book, in an appendix*: Thacher, pp. 355–56.

Chapter 9

98 *According to the monument, Chief Nimham and seventeen other Stockbridge Indians died here in the cause of liberty*: See Jenkins, p. 303. (Jenkins also says that he was the one who suggested the monument be built.) *Jonathan Edwards himself had been their minister and missionary*: See *The Mohicans of Stockbridge*, by Patrick Frazier (1992), p. 91.

98 *In an attempt to get Canadian Indians to support the Americans*: ibid., pp. 201–202.

99 *The best that could be said of the Queen's Rangers was that they burned but did not loot*: TMP, interview with Mrs. Nancy Sarles, p. 437.

99 *"Good-for-nothing cruel fellows like you who go about burning people's houses"*: See Swanson, pp. 45–46.

100 *"Only point out to me where your enemies keep"*: Frazier, *Mohicans of Stockbridge*, p. 198. *One day Simcoe and Tarleton were on a reconnaissance*: Lieutenant-Colonel Simcoe tells the story of the Stockbridges' attempted ambush and the successful ambush he devised in his *Journal of the Operations of the Queen's Rangers*, pp. 50 ff.

101 *In describing the fight*: In TMP (p. 430), Susanna Vredenburgh said, "Cavalry pursued

the Stockbridge Indians west and south of Deveau's. They were almost cut to pieces by the British dragoons. Those who escaped were cut about the head and shoulders. Olde Nimham and young Nimham were both killed."

101 *A few of the survivors of Nimham's men continued to serve with the Continental Army*: Frazier, *Mohicans of Stockbridge*, pp. 227–28.

102 *Even Jonathan Edwards, in his time, had managed to get around provincial laws*: ibid., p. 92. *"I would it were in my power to solace and comfort your declining years"*: See *The Diary and Letters of Gouverneur Morris*, ed. Anne Cary Morris (1888), vol. I, p. 9.

103 *Morris got the pay for all soldiers raised to the higher level previously given only to the soldiers of New England*: See Roosevelt, p. 38; also Adams, p. 102. *He visited the troops under General Philip Schuyler*: Mintz, p. 83. *In the winter of 1777–1778, Morris was part of a committee of five members of Congress who went to Valley Forge to meet with Washington*: Adams, p. 97; also Swiggett, pp. 46, 49 (it was during this trip that Morris first met Lafayette). *Alexander Hamilton later said that between them, Gouverneur Morris and Robert Morris won the war*: Adams, p. xii. Hamilton also said Gouverneur Morris was "an exotic genius" (ibid., p. xiii). *Morris did not like his coachman to stand by the heads of his horses*: Roosevelt, p. 71. For more on the accident that deprived Morris of his lower leg, see Mintz, pp. 139 ff.

104 *the Morrisania manor house still bore the marks of Morris's wooden leg*: Jenkins, p. 364. The story of the capture and hanging of Major André has been told many times; see Hufeland, pp. 350 ff.

105 *Simcoe also wrote the name as "Brunx"*: See Simcoe, p. 45.

105 *A Westchester County commission assessing damages after the war found that 350,000 fence rails had gone for firewood*: Hufeland, pp. 444–45. This Commission of Sequestration confiscated Tory property, sold it at auction, and used the proceeds to (for example) pay £70,000 to those who had lost fence rails and other firewood.

106 *When enemies were near, they sometimes took stone walls apart and hid in them*: See TMP, pp. 210, 811. For the hangings of Brom Barrett and Fade Donaldson, see ibid., pp. 440, 577, and 877.

106 *One winter night he led a group that surprised some DeLancey men*: Swanson, pp. 47; the site of the house, called the Archer house, is on the bluff above Cedar Playground (see chapter 31). *James was said to be worse than Gilbert, but both were bad*: see TMP, interview with Zabud June, p. 559. *Colonel Greene did not think Totten had any legitimate purpose for being there*: The story of Gilbert Totten's vow of revenge, and of the DeLancey attack on Greene and his troops, is in Hufeland, pp. 378 ff. See also TMP interviews with Samuel Chadeanye (pp. 240 ff.), Abraham Weeks (p. 721), and Lydia Vail (p. 722 ff.). Vail was the granddaughter of Richardson Davenport, in whose house Colonel Greene and the other officers were staying.

107 *A local woman later said, "The negroes were cut up unmercifully"*: TMP, interview with Mrs. Martha Griffin, p. 643.

108 *A woman who saw Greene with his captors begged to tend Greene's wounds*: TMP, interview with Hannah Miller, p. 296. *Washington received the information about the attack and wrote in his diary*: See Donald Jackson, ed., vol. III, p., 364. *spending that night at the house of a Mrs. Remsen*: TMP, interview with James Wood, p. 654.

109 *"Memorial of the fallen great, / The rich and honored line"*: See *Historical Guide to the City of New York*, compiled by Frank Bergen Kelly (1909, 1913), p. 213. Apparently, the tree was still standing at the time Kelly's book came out. The entry for the tree says "Delancey Pine, 150 feet high, in the thick branches of which the American sharpshooters used to hide . . ."

Chapter 10

110 *But Lafayette, from whom he had originally withheld permission even to go to America*: See *A Diary of the French Revolution, by Gouverneur Morris 1752–1816*, ed. Beatrix Cary Davenport (1939), p. xxxix.

111 *The missive came in a package with triple seals*: Mintz, p. 104. *"The women of this country don't like my whiskers"*: De Lauzun is quoted in TMP, p. 403.

111 *After his death, some of his admirers in Paris circulated copies of his handwritten memoirs*: See *Memoirs of the Duc de Lauzun*, tr., with an Appendix, by C. K. Scott Moncrieff; introduction by Richard Aldington; notes by G. Rutherford (1928), p. x. *Some French troops wore white coats with pink collars, crimson lapels*: Hufeland, p. 388.

112 *"I was struck, not by its smart appearance, but by its destitution"*: This observation, by Jean François Louis, Comte de Clermont Crèvecoeur, is quoted in *The American Campaigns of Rochambeau's Army*, ed. Rice, vol. I, p. 33.

112 *In de Lauzun's memoirs General Rochambeau is described as so in love with military matters that he talked of nothing else*: de Lauzun writes (p. 187), "M. de Rochambeau, Brigadier-General commanding the vanguard, spoke of nothing but deeds of military prowess, maneüvered and took up military positions in the open, indoors, on the table, on your snuffbox if you took it out of your pocket; entirely absorbed in his profession, he had marvellous knowledge of it."

112 *He disembarked with five thousand troops at Newport*: Hufeland, p. 384.

112 *This decision began a series of moves known as the Grand Reconnaissance*: For a summary of this action, see Ultan, *Northern Borough*, pp. 97 ff.

113 *"Nothing, certainly, could be more alarming as well as mortifying than my situation at the present crisis"*: See Rice, ed., vol. I, p. 36. *Instead of sending reinforcements to Cornwallis, Clinton ended up asking for reinforcements from him*: Hufeland, p. 401.

113 *"Die, you dog of a Frenchman!"*: Rice, ibid., pp. 252–53.

114 *"When I recounted the incident, I was laughed at"*: See von Closen, p. 100. *The women and children of West Farms had fled to Manhattan*: Ultan, *Northern Borough*, p. 97.

115 *"We had a fine chase in the fields"*: TMP, Andrew Corsa interview, p. 915.

116 *"All went over safe"*: TMP, Samuel Oakley interview, p. 31. *Some officers and staff stayed at the farm of the Valentine family*: It was von Closen who called it a "wretched house"; see von Closen, p. 100; see also Ultan, *Northern Borough*, p. 100.

117 *Some of the shots hit close enough that the riders were "covered all over with sand"*: TMP, Samuel Oakley interview, p. 36. *While that was going on, Washington and Rochambeau found a place under a hedge to take a nap*: See *Memoirs of the Marshal Count de Rochambeau, relative to the War of Independence of the United States; extracted and translated from the French by M. W. E. Wright, Esq.* (1838), pp. 57–59.

118 *"I must confess that I was astonished"*: von Closen, p. 101.

118 *"I admire the American troops tremendously!"*: ibid., p. 102. *"This manoeuvre consumed less than an hour"*: Hufeland, p. 400; Rochambeau, p. 59.

119 *Instead, de Lauzun only came close to capturing him*: de Lauzun, pp. 208, 249 (in a footnote, Moncrief describes Tarleton as "a magnificent cavalry officer, but less estimable in private life").

119 *And they loaned it to him!*: See *The American Campaigns of Rochambeau's Army*, ed. Rice, vol. I, p. 64: "Lord Cornwallis needed 100,000 écus to pay his troops. The French generals and colonels lent him this sum. When he arrived in New York, the General returned this money together with 100 bottles of porter to express his appreciation to those who had rendered him this service."

119 *This was when one of the worst atrocities of the war occurred*: Accounts of this murder, or mention of it, are in TMP interviews with Samuel Chadeayne (p. 244), Zabud June (p. 559), Nathaniel Montross (pp. 772–73), and Mrs. Cynthia Hobby (p. 968). McDonald, the interviewer, adds that relatives of James Totten are threatening to sue (c. 1845) a man who spread this story.

120 *After Cornwallis surrendered, General Rochambeau chose de Lauzun to tell King Louis that the Americans had won the war*: See de Lauzun, p. 209.

120 *Louis-Alexandre Berthier, the aide who killed a DeLancey man at Morrisania*: The later career of this officer is described in Rice, ed., vol. I, pp. 196 ff.

121 *Raids and counterraids continued in the Neutral Ground, and the British Army remained a threat*: See Jenkins, pp. 174 ff.; also Heath, p. 353.

122 *the largest fireworks display ever seen in the country*: Heath, p. 387. *Afterward, November 25 became a holiday, known as Evacuation Day*: See *The Encyclopedia of New York City*, ed. Kenneth T. Jackson (1991), p. 385: "For more than a century Evacuation Day was marked by martial parades, patriotic oratory, and banquets; its one hundredth anniversary was one of the great civic events of the nineteenth century in New York City. The holiday ceased to be observed after the First World War because of its proximity to Thanksgiving and the decline of anti-English sentiment, except for a brief revival on the occasion of its bicentenary in 1983."

122 *With the British gone, the property of local Tories was confiscated*: See Horne, pp. 26 ff. *Gouverneur Morris's mother held on to her mansion and estate, thanks to her son*: Ultan, *Northern Borough*, p. 104. *saved from confiscation the property of Isaac Wilkins*: Hufeland, p. 46.

123 *The DeLanceys lost their mills*: See McNamara, p. 32. *six barrels full of silver dollars*: TMP, interview with Mrs. Daniel Edwards, p. 105. *"Peace, Hunt! You are better off than I am"*: TMP, ibid., p. 111.

Chapter 11

124 *Gouverneur made his first visit to Morrisania in seven years on May 31, 1783*: Mintz, p. 162. *Morris celebrated by drinking a bottle of wine*: Sparks, vol. I, p. 164. *Staats lived in England, and he agreed to sell the part of Morrisania he'd inherited*: Details of Staats Long Morris's sale of Morrisania to Gouverneur Morris are in Mintz, pp. 172–75; and in Sparks, vol. I, p. 281.

125 *He took the floor 173 times*: Mintz, p. 181.

125 *Nine of the states had their own navies*: Swiggett, p. 113. *He was attending the Convention, he said, as "a Representative of America"*: See *The Records of the Federal Convention of 1787*, ed. Max Farrand (1911), vol. I, p. 529. Morris also said, "We had better take a supreme government now, than a despot twenty years hence—for come he must," ibid., p. 43.

126 *Having helped set things on track, Morris then disappeared*: On May 31, the day after he said that about the "despot twenty years hence," he left for Morrisania, and did not return to the Convention until July 2.

126 *In the 1980s, the Landmarks Preservation Commission awarded landmark status to a sewage treatment plant*: See "Panel Declares Treatment Plant City Landmark," *The New York Times*, June 9, 1982, p. B6. Interesting as this building may be, the fact remains that the city has always put far too much waste-related infrastructure—incinerators, waste transfer stations, etc.—in the South Bronx.

128 *Morris returned to Philadelphia on July 2 and found the Convention at an impasse*: See *The Records of the Federal Convention of 1787*, vol. III, pp. 499–500. *"We are sent here to consult not to contend, with each other"*: *Records of the Federal Convention*, vol. I, p. 197. *"we shall disappoint not only America, but the whole world"*: ibid., p. 515.

129 *Morris said the delegates should do more than "truck and bargain"*: ibid., p. 529. *Madison told Morris's first biographer that he doubted Morris's return had made a difference*: Madison qualified that by saying Morris himself was an example of flexibility, persuadable to "a candid surrender of his opinions" when he decided they were wrong—see *Records of the Federal Convention*, vol. III, p. 499. *"The Rich will strive to establish their dominion"*: Morris's statement about the danger of the tyranny of the rich is one of his two most famous quotations from the Convention (the other is his speech against slavery; see below). It is in *Records of the Federal Convention*, vol. I, p. 512.

130 *Washington made only a single proposal of his own*: ibid., vol. II, p. 644.

130 *On certain evenings the great man invited delegates to receptions at his lodgings*: This anecdote is in *Records of the Federal Convention*, vol. III, p. 85. *the two even took a break to go fishing in the Delaware River*: Swiggett, p. 124.

131 *"an irreligious and profane man"*: Miller, p. 94. *However one judged his character, Morris proposed thirty-nine resolutions at the Convention*: See "The Case of the Dishonest Scrivener: Gouverneur Morris and the Creation of the Federalist Constitution," by William M. Treanor (a paper at Georgetown University Law Center, 2019), p. 9.

131 *"Upon what principle is it that the slaves shall be computed in the representation?"*: See *Records of the Federal Convention*, vol. II, p. 222.

132 *Theodore Roosevelt, in his biography of Morris, described the compromise the Constitution made with slavery*: Roosevelt, p. 105.

133 *"That instrument was written by the fingers which write this letter"*: See *Records of the Federal Convention*, vol. III, p. 420. *"We the people of the States of New Hampshire"*: ibid., vol. II, p. 163.

135 *One delegate did notice an unauthorized change*: The observations of Morris's sneaky changes are from Treanor's excellent paper, "The Case of the Dishonest Scrivener" (see note for p. 131, above).

135 *Collectively they showed a surreptitious will to strengthen central government and elevate men of substance and property above the democratic throng*: See ibid., pp. 2 ff. *Perhaps Morris's most significant single-word change appeared in the cause about runaway slaves*: ibid., p. 83.

136 *Washington, Gouverneur Morris, and Robert Morris had dinner together afterward at the City Tavern in Philadelphia*: Mintz, p. 203; also, *Records of the Federal Convention*, vol. III, p. 84. *In the evening, Washington wrote in his diary*: ibid.

137 *They saw each other again the following year*: Miller, p. 6. *where he met Randolph's fourteen-year-old daughter, Nancy*: Adams, pp. 166 ff.

Chapter 12

139 *like the watch Jefferson had bought for Madison*: Miller, p. 10. (On April 29, 1779, Morris wrote to Washington, "I am almost at the bottom of my paper, without mentioning what I had first intended. Six days ago I got from the maker your watch, with two copper keys, and one golden one, and a box containing a spare spring and glasses, all which I have delivered to Mr. Jefferson, who takes charge of them for you."—see Sparks, vol. II, p. 69.)

139 *Morris began to keep his European diary on March 1, 1789*: See Morris, *A Diary of the French Revolution* (Davenport, ed.), p. 1. *"cette Espèce de Plaisanterie"*: ibid., p. 23. (hereinafter, *Diary*), p. 17.

139 *On March 21, on a visit to Versailles, he met a twenty-eight-year-old countess*: ibid. (hereinafter, *Diary*), p. 17.

140 *The Count de Flahaut superintended the king's gardens*: In this job he succeeded Buffon, the famous naturalist (*Diary*, p. 24).

140 *American biographers mention his fluent French, but she made fun of it*: See *Diary*, where he says she "plays the Mocqueuse upon my bad French" (p. 268).

141 *Mme. de La Fayette, wife of the marquis, disliked him from the start*: Miller, p. 18. *though he considered Louis "small beer"*: ibid., p. 19. *the hurt on her face pained him*: Sparks, p. 303. *"I never lost my Respect for those who consented to make me happy"*: *Diary*, p. 119. *he could never be "only a Friend"*: *Diary*, p. 157.

141 *On an outing in the city, Gouverneur and Adèle made a visit to the ruined Bastille*: *Diary*, p. 158.

142 *A question Washington particularly wanted Morris to look into*: Roosevelt, 145; also Swiggett, p. 203, and Miller, pp. 48–50.

143 *"charming Sex [i.e., the female sex], you are capable of every Thing!"*: *Diary*, p. 225. *"a sly, cool, cunning, ambitious, and malicious Man"*: Sparks, p. 312. *"merde in a silk stocking"*: Swiggett, p. 394.

144 *Jefferson, an ardent booster of the Revolution, thought it would be bloodless*: Adams, p. 176. *"The Current is setting so strong against the Noblesse"*: Sparks, p. 315. *Later, Jefferson would accuse Morris of poisoning Washington's mind against the Revolution*: Swiggett, p. 227. *He blamed it all on Marie Antoinette*: See Adams, pp. 180, 245. *rubbed with butter*: *Diary*, p. 205. *"he is sensible his party are mad"*: Roosevelt, p. 115.

145 *"This man's mind is so elated by power"*: Swiggett, pp. 193–94. *a "canine appetite" for fame*: Miller, p. 19.

145 *one day he told her he did not love her, which surprised her, and "wounded [her] to the Soul"*: Diary, p. 251. *She asked Gouverneur if he would promise to marry her*: ibid., p. 244.

146 *He offered to counsel Lafayette as Jefferson had done, but the marquis demurred*: Miller, p. 39.

146 *a look similar to "what Sir John Falstaff calls the Leer of Invitation"*: Sparks, p. 327. *Back at Morrisania, Gouverneur's half brother Lewis Morris had an inspiration*: Jenkins, pp. 3–4. Ultan (*Northern Borough*, p. 104) says that Lewis Morris first made this proposal in 1783, in the hope that selling the government the land on which to build the new capital would not only make him some money but get his war damages repaired for free.

Chapter 13

149 *Morris bought a 550-ton ship in England, the* Goliah: See *Diary*, p. 543. *Morris tried to start a war between Britain and France*: Miller, pp. 50, 64. *he met a disagreeable surprise*: Adams, p. 123.

150 *she had determined to be* sage: Miller, p. 74.

150 *Morris communicated with the king and queen regularly*: Adams, p. 230; see also Roosevelt, p. 159. *About a week after the unsuccessful escape, a ceremonial procession honoring Voltaire made its way through the city*: Diary, p. 215.

151 *At the British ambassador's, Morris met Banastre Tarleton*: Roosevelt, p. 157. In addition to his exploits, some of them murderous, in the American war, Banastre Tarleton was afterward rumored to be the person on whom Baroness Orczy based Sir Percival Blakeney, the Scarlet Pimpernel, in her play and novel of that name (*Diary*, p. 223). Tarleton came from a slave-trading family and remained a strong pro-slavery advocate during his later career in Parliament. *Washington informed Morris about some of the negatives*: Miller, p. 71.

151 *Morris wrote back, promising to show "Circumspection of Conduct"*: Mintz, p. 223. *Before Morris received this news, he and Mme. de Flahaut had been considering going to America*: Swiggett, p. 228.

152 *He set up his embassy at 488 Rue de la Planche*: Sparks, vol. II, p. 195. *Theodore Roosevelt ascribed Morris's ill-advised participation to his natural gallantry*: Miller, *Envoy to the Terror*, p. 132.

152 *Morris predicted that the radicals would take over completely in six weeks*: Miller, p. 146.

153 *She followed soon after*: ibid., p. 161. *When she turned to him, he said he could not help her*: See *Son of Talleyrand: The Life of Comte Charles de Flahaut 1785–1870,* by Françoise de Bernardy (Lucy Norton, tr., 1965), p. 25. *Morris later explained that he had no orders to leave*: Sparks, p. 414.

153 *Morris found a house in Seine-Port*: Miller, p. 182. *One day Thomas Paine was helping the French write their new constitution; the next he had landed in jail*: Swiggett, pp. 255, 269.

154 *He petitioned Morris to declare him an American citizen*: Miller, p. 117. *In Paris, one of the governments of the moment threw Mme. de La Fayette in prison*: Morris's efforts on behalf of the Lafayettes are a theme that runs throughout his time in France (and after). See Roosevelt, p. 175 (a letter to Morris in which Mme. de La Fayette thanks him for lending her 100,000 livres, and for saving her from the guillotine); see also Adams, p. 261; and *The Diaries of Gouverneur Morris: European Travels 1794–1798*, ed. Melanie Randolph Miller (2011), p. xxx, which mentions that Mme. de La Fayette's grandmother, mother, and sister were executed.

154 *Flahaut returned, exchanged himself for his friend, and went to the guillotine*: This story is found in several sources. See Swiggett, pp. 261–62; Miller, p. 236; and Bernardy, pp. 25, 33 ff.

155 *Morris found bargains*: He bought "paintings, furniture, art objects, telescopes, wine"—see Miller, *Envoy to the Terror*, p. 234. He also bought silver from Versailles (Adams, p. 244). His descendants drank the last of Marie Antoinette's wine at a reunion in 1848. *At some point he sold Mme. de Staël 23,000 acres*: Sparks, pp. 489–93. *At the end of July 1794, James Monroe arrived in France as his ambassadorial replacement*: Adams, p. 249; Roosevelt, pp. 191, 193. *Between April 17 and June 10, a total of 3,607 people had died*: Swiggett, p. 284. *The authorities gave him a passport on the condition that he never return to France*: Miller, p. 235.

156 *In his papers is a letter he wrote to Jonathan Dayton*: Swiggett, pp. 377–78. (The footnote cites "Misc Mss. (Morris) New York Historical Society.")

157 *He dispatched them to Morrisania on a vessel called the* Superb: Adams, p. 244.

157 *They included several cases of Imperial Tokay*: See Adams, pp. 244–45; see also Miller, p. 234. *Soon after arriving in Lausanne, Morris experienced symptoms*: Diaries of Gouverneur Morris, Miller, ed., p. 25; see also Mintz, p. 240.

158 *He said that if he went back, he would again be called to public service*: Sparks, vol. II, p. 75.

158 *Wycombe seems to have become a victim of her success*: See Miller, ed., *Diaries of Gouverneur Morris*, p. 480. *the count had first sought her out because he admired her writing*: ibid., p. 274.

159 *When Charles was fifteen, he wrote a letter to Napoleon offering to serve as his aide-de-camp*: See de Bernardy, *Son of Talleyrand*, pp. 32–33.

159 *if Charles had been raised by old Flahaut he would have stuck with Napoleon all the way*: ibid., pp. 112–15.

160 *This ingenious piece of engineering made him think again of the wealth of the American interior*: See *Diaries of Gouverneur Morris*, Miller, ed., p. 184. *he attended the small ceremony when they were finally released*: ibid., pp. 497 ff.; see also Sparks, pp. 457–58. *In the summer of 1798, he made plans to return to America*: For details of Morris's return, see *Diaries of Gouverneur Morris*, pp. xxxi–xxxiii, 654–64.

Chapter 14

161 *The very name struggles with prejudice*: In Italy, the bad part of a city is sometimes called "la Bronx." See also *The New York Times*, "C'est le Bronx? Ou Sont les Maisons Abandonnes?" Nov. 16, 1990, p. B3; see also *The Bronx*, by Evelyn Diaz Gonzalez (2004), p. 129: "English tabloids dubbed a drug-torn neighborhood in Manchester, England, 'the Bronx.'"

164 *Near the corner of Sheridan Avenue and East 167th Street, a gunman who was only a boy shot and killed fourteen-year-old Christopher Duran*: See "'He Died in My Hands': Bronx Teen Tried to Save Brother, 14, Who Was Shot 16 Times in Suspected Gang Feud," New York *Daily News*, May 24, 2015, p. 4.

165 *ten young men died by violence between 1991 and 1992*: See "Bronx Street of Violence: 10 Killings Sap Hope on Beekman Ave.," *The New York Times*, Oct. 13, 1992, p. B1. The excerpt from Morris's speech to the senate is quoted in Mintz, pp. 232–33.

Chapter 15

168 *Theodore Roosevelt, who presumably had seen the house as it appeared in the later 1800s, described it*: Roosevelt, p. 204. *Morris wrote to a correspondent that on his roof terrace he enjoyed taking in the view*: Sparks, vol. II, p. 161. For descriptions of the furnishings of the manor house, see Swiggett, pp. 338, 378.

169 *The foreman of Morris's estate was a Scotsman named Bathgate*: See Jenkins, p. 319; also McNamara, p. 20. *"I shall be very happy to see you in this seat of my retirement"*: Swiggett, p. 340. *Washington never read the letter*: Sparks, vol. II, pp. 123–25.

169 *"Hundreds of large ships will, at no distant period, bound on the billows of this inland sea"*: Adams, p. 289.

170 *He did not want any D.C.-like stars*: ibid., pp. 281–83. For more on the grid, see "The

Greatest Grid: The New York Plan of 1811," by Edward K. Spann, in *Two Centuries of American Planning*, ed. Daniel K. Shaeffer (1988).

171　*Edgar Allan Poe, not known as a city planner*: ibid., p. 25.

172　*The Garden City designs, in turn, led to the Garden Suburbs movement*: See *Thomas Adams and the Modern Planning Movement: Britain, Canada, and the United States, 1900–1940*, by Michael Simpson (1985). *Ann Cary Randolph, whom Morris first met at her father's tobacco plantation*: Sparks, the earliest of Morris's biographers, mentions Ann Cary Randolph but says nothing about any scandal; she was still alive in 1832, when his book came out. (See Sparks, p. 494; he says only that she is "a lady, accomplished in mind and person, and belonging to one of the ancient and most respectable families in Virginia.") Theodore Roosevelt was similarly unforthcoming. Later biographers gave the scandal's details—see Swiggett, pp. 270 ff., 392 ff., and Mintz, pp. 234 ff.

174　*"[Morris] announced, in language highly poetic"*: Sparks, pp. 497–98.

176　*He concluded that Pennsylvania, New York, and the New England states should secede from the United States*: for the scathing opinion of Morris's secessionist episode, see Roosevelt, pp. 221 ff.

176　*"Unhappily they will ever bear me a sincere hatred"*: Swiggett, p. 371.

177　*After the Bourbon Restoration, in 1814, Louis Philippe repaid Morris's loans to him, but without adding interest*: Roosevelt, p. 202. Louis Philippe did not pay the interest even though Morris's lawyer requested it. The lawyer persisted, however, and the interest was finally paid, though not until after Morris's death. *A new bridge across the Harlem River made possible the construction of a toll road through Morris's estate*: This bridge, built in 1797, was where the Third Avenue Bridge is now. Ultan, *Northern Borough*, describes these first infrastructure incursions into Morris's land (pp. 112, 115).

177　*the details are so painful*: In *The Diaries of Gouverneur Morris*, ed. Miller, a footnote says that the diaries first mention constriction of the urethra in connection with venereal disease when Morris was in Paris (p. 25). Details of his death are in Mintz, p. 240.

178　*"they will be condemned to having a new baby every year"*: de Bernardy, *Son of Talleyrand*, p. 177. *Adèle is in Père Lachaise Cemetery*: Swiggett, p. 448.

178　*On October 26, 1825, the first boat bound for New York City entered the canal from the lake*: See *Wedding of the Waters: The Erie Canal and the Making of a Great Nation*, by Peter L. Bernstein (2005), p. 184.

Chapter 16

183　*New York City will develop commuter suburbs earlier than any other place in the world*: Cantwell and diZerega Wall, p. 272.

186　*Lafayette stopped at the grave and bowed his head in silent meditation here*: See Kelly, *Historical Guide to the City of New York*, p. 196. *Stendhal, the novelist, who met Lafayette at about that time, wrote*: Swiggett, p. 46.

187　*His daughter put out a collection of his poetry in 1835*: See *The Culprit Fay and Other Poems*, by Joseph Rodman Drake (1835). In Edith Wharton's novel *The Age of Innocence*, which takes place mostly in New York City in the 1870s, and which Wharton wrote in the 1920s, she refers to Drake and other writers of his era by way of establishing how old-fashioned one of the characters is: "Mrs. Archer was always at pains to tell her children how much more agreeable and cultivated society had been when it included such figures as Washington Irving, Fitz-Greene Halleck and the poet of 'The Culprit Fay'" (p. 102). Wharton does not mention Drake by name, perhaps to indicate that Mrs. Archer herself has forgotten it. Were it not for my wanderings in the Bronx, I would never have known what Mrs. Archer (and Wharton) were talking about. Also, we may note that a New York society person of Mrs. Archer's stamp is portrayed as having heard of "The Culprit Fay" but not of Drake's more historically significant poem, "Bronx." Had she written, ". . . the poet of 'The Culprit Fay' and 'Bronx,'" the reference would have changed the whole novel, in my opinion, and made it even greater than it is already.

188　*I looked up a review by Edgar Allan Poe that appeared in the* Southern Literary Messenger: This is one of the most famous of Poe's reviews. Scholars refer to it as the Drake-Halleck review. It can be found online.

189 *"When o'er the brink the tide is driven"*: See "Fragment" in *The Culprit Fay, and Other Poems*, p. 67. *A walking-tour guidebook of the time described his grave marker*: See Kelly, *Historical Guide to the City of New York*, pp. 196–97. For more on the cemetery and its survival, see McNamara, p. 112, and Jenkins, p. 382.

190 *Only 2,782 people lived in the future Bronx in 1820*: Ultan, *Northern Borough*, pp. 118–19. *It's the oldest surviving factory building in New York City*: ibid., p. 126.

191 *The Lorillards eventually got so rich*: McNamara says (p. 147) that the word *millionaire* was coined in 1843 to describe Pierre Lorillard in his obituary. The *Oxford Universal Dictionary on Historical Principles* (1933) dates the word's first use to 1826. *In 1837, the New York and Harlem River Railroad completed a single-track line the length of Manhattan*: Gonzalez, pp. 11, 157.

191 *By 1841, Gouverneur Morris II had reached his twenty-eighth year*: Ultan, *Northern Borough*, pp. 124 ff. For more on the development of railroads, see Jackson, ed., *Encyclopedia of New York City*, pp. 977 ff. *had even gone so far as to contest his paternity*: Mintz, p. 235.

192 *plus Morris family members who served in the Seminole, Mexican, and Civil Wars*: Jenkins, p. 267. *blow his nose during services*: ibid., p. 366.

193 *(I now know it was the latter.)*: Jenkins clears up this question. Quoting Robert Bolton's *History of Westchester County* (published 1848), he says the church "was erected by the present Gouverneur Morris, Esq., in a field on his own estate, which for some time had been hallowed as containing the sepulchre of his parents. A vault was constructed to receive his remains" (p. 267).

193 *Jonathan Kozol*: Kozol's *Amazing Grace* came out in 1995, *Fire in the Ashes* in 2000, and *Ordinary Resurrections* in 2012. All three are available in paperback.

Chapter 17

195 *A list of the rural gentry*: See Ultan, *Northern Borough*, pp. 119 and 132 ff. for more details of the country estates and their owners.

196 *In 1890, he imported some European starlings to rid his garden of caterpillars*: McNamara, p. 205.

197 *Mott had invented a coal-burning stove*: Jenkins, p. 370; Ultan, *Northern Borough*, pp. 130–31. *The Johnson Foundries, on a Harlem River peninsula*: Ibid., pp. 135, 140; McNamara, p. 133. *Although the Irish were only a third of the local population*: Jonnes, p. 18.

197 *Ann Cary Randolph Morris took seriously her descent from this famous ancestress*: Many sources say she claimed descent from Pocahontas; see Kelly, *Historical Guide to the City of New York*, p. 195. *he flew into a rage*: McNamara, p. 430. *In the late 1850s, the Janes & Kirtland Foundry, another local ironworks, received a federal contract*: Ultan, *Northern Borough*, p. 135.

198 *The Piccirillis made some of America's most famous public statues*: ibid., pp. 199, 220, and 258. See also *Encyclopedia of New York City*, p. 144.

199 *Three of the new arrivals were Poe, Virginia, and Maria*: For Poe's time in the Bronx, see Ultan, *Northern Borough*, p. 128, and Jenkins, p. 351.

200 *Virginia wrote a poem to her husband anticipating the move*: The text of Virginia Clemm's poem is from a photocopy of her handwritten version that was displayed in the Bronx Historical Society in 2016. His walks on the High Bridge, and how entranced he was by the view, are mentioned in McNamara, p. 268.

201 *The Germans settled in the towns of Melrose and Morrisania*: Jenkins, p. 4; see also *Encyclopedia of New York City*, p. 140. *Now and then the cars of the Huckleberry Line would slide off the tracks*: For details of the Huckleberry Line (also called the Huckleberry Road), see Gonzalez, p. 54; Ultan, *Northern Borough*, p. 150; Jenkins, pp. 238–40; and Wallace, p. 278.

202 *In 1863, some prominent New Yorkers established Woodlawn Cemetery*: See McNamara, p. 259; Jenkins, pp. 321–22; and Ultan, *Northern Borough*, p. 152. *Jerome owned a city mansion on Madison Square*: For more on the Leonard Jerome family, see *The Remarkable Mr. Jerome*, by Anita Leslie (1954). His grandson, Winston Leonard Spencer Churchill, was partly named for him (p. 8).

203 *the Annexed District*: The sequence of the annexations, leading to the Bronx's becoming a borough of New York City, is laid out in Gonzalez, p. 4; Kelly, *Historical Guide to the City of New York*, pp. 176 ff.; and Ultan, *Northern Borough*, pp. 173–75.

204 *John Mullaly, a man mostly forgotten today*: See *Encyclopedia of New York City*, p. 144; see also Ultan, *Northern Borough*, pp. 175–76; and Gonzalez, p. 49. For Mullaly's important instigating role in the Draft Riots, see "The Church and the New York Draft Riots of 1863," by Albon P. Man, Jr., in *Records of the American Catholic Historical Society of Philadelphia* 62, no. 1 (March 1951), p. 33.

205 *his hateful side perhaps has motivated posterity not to go too far out of its way to remember him*: In recent years, there have been calls to change the name of Mullaly Park; see "Critics Want Mullaly Park in the Bronx Renamed, Citing Namesake's Racist Rhetoric," *Gothamist*, July 1, 2020. (In 2022, the name was changed to Rev. T. Wendell Foster Park, in honor of a local pastor and champion of affordable housing.)

205 *Piano manufacturers lined entire streets*: Gonzalez, p. 29; Ultan, *Northern Borough*, p. 185. *Jordan Mott dug a canal from the Harlem River to East 144th Street*: Ibid., p. 134; Jenkins, p. 370.

206 *That double-dip arrangement was done away with in 1894*: Ultan, *Northern Borough*, p. 182.

207 *By 1900, the number of people living in the Bronx had climbed to 200,507*: Jenkins, p. 9.

Chapter 18
210 *I used to fly from JFK to Russia as often as three times a year*: That was in the early 2000s. My book *Travels in Siberia* came out in 2010.

Chapter 19
217 *The first memory of Israel Baline, born 1888, was of lying by the road*: See *Irving Berlin: A Life in Song*, by Philip Furia (1998), p. 6. For a moving account of the Berlins' romance, marriage, and long life together, see *Irving Berlin: A Daughter's Memoir*, by Mary Ellin Barrett (1994).

217 *Between 1880 and 1910, about 1.4 million Jews came to New York City*: See *Encyclopedia of New York City*, p. 620. *By 1900, the Lower East Side was the most densely populated place on earth*: Wallace, p. 254.

218 *New York City manufactured about three fourths of all the clothing in the United States*: ibid., p. 317. *Davies, born in 1867*: See "King of the Bronx: J. Clarence Davies," by Robert M. Coates, *The New Yorker*, Dec. 7, 1939, p. 33.

219 *He collected old prints of New York City*: Wallace, p. 361. Davies lived on the Upper East Side, at 15 East Fifty-eighth Street, and his vision of the Bronx was urban rather than suburban; see also Gonzalez, pp. 46–47. *The job of designing it went to Louis Risse*: See *The True History of the Conception and Planning of the Grand Boulevard and Concourse in the Bronx*, by Louis A. Risse (1902); see also *Encyclopedia of New York City*, p. 499. *In a referendum that drew the largest turnout in city history*: Wallace, p. 228.

220 *On July 10, 1905, subway and elevated IRT service began between City Hall and the station at West Farms, in the Bronx*: Jenkins, p. 245. *Robert Morgenthau met a law student, Sonia Sotomayor, when he was participating in a poorly attended panel*: See *My Beloved World*, by Sonia Sotomayor (2013), pp. 193–94.

221 *"scenes of brutal indecency"*: Jenkins, p. 245. *Later the city filled in the creek and erased that ancient landmark*: Although the creek is filled in, the boundary that it delineated still exists. The neighborhood just to the south of it, Marble Hill, is still considered part of Manhattan. Marble Hill has a Manhattan zip code and area code, even though it is

north of the Harlem River Ship Canal, and thus physically part of the continent-Bronx, and no longer part of Manhattan Island. (This information may be found in a Parks Department plaque in Marble Hill Playground.)

223 *Half a million people were living in the Bronx by 1912*: See Kelly, *Historical Guide to the City of New York*, p. 176. *moved to 968 Kelly Street, in the Longwood neighborhood*: Wallace, p. 444 fn. Other information about Sholem Aleichem comes from a plaque on the entry to the Shalom [*sic*] Aleichem Houses, in Kingsbridge Heights.

223 *New York City's first zoning law passed in the same year*: Ultan, *Northern Borough*, p. 229. *had the most manufacturing in the city at the time*: 70 percent of the city's factories and 68 percent of its industrial workers were in Manhattan in 1912—see Wallace, p. 315. *On just the two blocks on either side of Charlotte Street*: See "After 70 Years, South Bronx Street Is at a Dead End," *The New York Times*, Oct. 21, 1977, p. 29.

223 *the prevailing absence of pogroms*: It's important to note that pogrom-like violence did happen in New York City. On the Lower East Side in 1902, Irish workers' harassment of a funeral parade for a noted rabbi blew up into a police-abetted riot that is sometimes called the Hoe Riot, because many of the harassers worked for the Hoe Printing Company. Jewish leaders who protested to the authorities called the riot "a police pogrom." See *Street Justice: A History of Police Violence in New York City*, by Marilynn S. Johnson (2003), pp. 62 ff.

224 *A representative of the Hebrew Sheltering and Immigrant Aid Society met the Trotsky family at the pier*: See "Expelled from Four Lands: Pacifist Editor Here from Russia, Germany, France and Spain," in *The New York Times*, Jan. 15, 1917, p. 2. Trotsky was a pacifist in that he opposed the war. Later, when the Bolsheviks fought to take over the October Revolution, and after they won, all mentions of pacifism disappeared. *They rented a fifth-floor apartment at 1522 Vyse Avenue*: Most sources agree that this was the Trotskys' address. See McNamara, p. 238, who says they lived there, in apartment 5-D. McNamara adds, "However, some historians believe he lived on nearby Stebbins Avenue." Trotsky's description of the apartment is in his *My Life: An Attempt at an Autobiography* (1970 edition), p. 328. His put-down of Hillquit is in ibid., p. 331.

226 *While the authorities looked to arrest Lenin, Trotsky carried on*: For a summary of the immediate maneuverings that led to the October Revolution, see an article I wrote on the occasion of its centennial, "What Ever Happened to the Russian Revolution?" in *Smithsonian*, Oct. 2017, p. 48.

Chapter 20

228 *The address was 3059 Villa Avenue*: See *W. E. B. Du Bois: A Biography*, by David Levering Lewis (2009), p. 290. *and smoked an occasional Benson & Hedges cigarette*: ibid., p. 461.

229 *Grant belonged to the Knickerbocker, Tuxedo, Union, Turf and Field, Century, and Down Town clubs*: Grant's *New York Times* obituary listed his clubs—see "Madison Grant, 71, Zoologist, Is Dead," May 13, 1937, p. 15.

230 *Fourteen million immigrants came to the United States through New York City between 1886 and 1924*: This fact is mentioned in a display in the museum at the base of the Statue of Liberty. *then sent some of its herd to a national wildlife refuge out West*: The Visitor Center at the Wichita Mountains National Wildlife Refuge, in southwestern Oklahoma, has information about how the buffalo came there from the Bronx. For more about Grant, see *Defending the Master Race: Conservation, Eugenics, and the Legacy of Madison Grant*, by Jonathan Peter Spiro (2009).

231 *A traveler brought a man from the Congo to New York*: Many sources tell the story of Ota Benga and his fate; see Wallace, p. 356. Newspapers covered his confinement at the zoo; see "The Mayor Won't Help Free Caged Pygmy," *The New York Times*, Sept. 12, 1906, p. 9.

231 *"[T]his generation must completely repudiate the proud boast of our fathers"*: See Grant, *The Passing of the Great Race; or, The Racial Basis of European History*,

pp. xxxiii, 16, 49. This book is still in print, in a special "Centenary Edition" (2016), among other reissues. More on Grant, Stoddard, Du Bois, and the debate can be found in my article "Old Hatreds," in *The New Yorker*, Aug. 26, 2019, p. 36. For more on Grant's popularity among the Nazis, see *The Nazi Connection: Eugenics, American Racism, and German National Socialism*, by Stephan Kühl (1994).

232 *The obituary in* The New York Times: See note for p. 229.

234 *A biography of Stoddard the father written by a devotee fails even to mention that he had a son*: See John L. Stoddard: Traveller, Lecturer, Litterateur, by D. Crane Taylor (1935). *"bids fair to be the fundamental problem of the twentieth century"*: See *The French Revolution in San Domingo*, by T. Lothrop Stoddard (1914), p. vii.

235 *Writing one book can determine the rest of an author's life*: Stoddard's *The Rising Tide of Color Against White World-Supremacy* (1920) is exhibit A.

235 *"Whoever will take the time to read and ponder Mr. Lothrop Stoddard's book"*: The *New York Times*, Oct. 27, 1921, p. 1. *"the prominent Negrophobist"*: Negro Star, Wichita, Kansas, Jan. 27, 1928. *"the high priest of racial baloney"*: Philadelphia Tribune, Oct. 13, 1938, p. 4. *"the unbearable Lothrop Stoddard"*: Pittsburgh *Courier*, June 1, 1929, p. 12. *A Black columnist wrote that the white race's impending demise would probably come as news to Negroes in the South*: New York Age, July 9, 1921, p. 4.

236 *said a glass-half-full headline in the* Baltimore Afro-American: May 21, 1920, p. 1. *In 1926, he gave a talk before two thousand students and faculty at Tuskegee University*: Philadelphia *Tribune*, April 17, 1926: "Stoddard at Tuskegee Urges White Leaders; Writer Tells Faculty and Students 'White Control' Is for the Best Interest of All; Terminates Address Without Any Applause."

236 *"He would be a scream"*: Correspondence giving the background of the debate, and of its aftermath, can be found in the W. E. B. Du Bois Papers at the University of Massachusetts at Amherst, available online. Du Bois's remark about Senator Heflin is in his letter to the Chicago Forum Council of February 6, 1929.

238 *"He does not say (as he has written elsewhere) that white Americans would rather see themselves and their children dead"*: See *Re-Forging America: The Story of Our Nationhood*, by Lothrop Stoddard, A.M., Ph.D. (Harvard) (1927), p. 282.

239 *The Forum Council later printed the debate and bound it in a small book*: A copy of this rare and extremely useful bound volume, *Report of the Debate Conducted by the Chicago Forum: "Shall the Negro Be Encouraged to Seek Cultural Equality?"* (March 17, 1929) may be found in the Schomburg Center for Research in Black Culture, a branch of the New York Public Library.

239 *"A good-natured burst of laughter"*: See "5,000 Cheer W. E. B. DuBois, Laugh At Lothrop Stoddard," *Baltimore Afro-American*, March 23, 1929, p. 11.

240 *details like Himmler's "searching" blue eyes and genial laugh*: See Stoddard, "How 'Gestapo' Works Is Told by Himmler," *Boston Globe*, Jan. 23, 1940, p. 1.

241 *In the early fifties, he was investigated as a suspected agent of the Soviet Union*: Lewis, pp. 691 ff.

Chapter 21

244 *Fordham gneiss, one of the three main New York City rock types (Inwood marble and Manhattan schist are the others)*: See Ultan, *Northern Borough*, p. 3. *the road builders' big obstacle here*: This fact is from a Parks Department historic marker, since replaced, at Morris Mesa Playground (see below). *the interestingly named Featherbed Lane*: McNamara (p. 187) says, "Featherbed Lane, so called because it was extremely rough and stony or from the story that the Americans, surprised by the British, were rescued by the ingenuity of the farmers' wives, who spread feather beds on the lane, thus enabling them to escape without being heard."

245 *The new sign doesn't mention him*: The text of the current marker may be found on the website of the NYC Parks Department.

245 *the most expensive road ever built*: See *The Power Broker: Robert Moses and the Fall*

of New York, by Robert A. Caro (1974), p. 886; Caro calls it "the most expensive road constructed in all history." *The engineer looked east, awestruck*: ibid., p. 839.

246 *About half the borough's population was Jewish in 1930*: Gonzalez, p. 93. *about 80 percent lived in the neighborhoods south of Tremont Avenue*: Ultan, *Northern Borough*, p. 238.

246 *The Spaldeen ball, cherished in memory*: Its name came from Spaulding, the ball's manufacturer. Details about street games are in *The Bronx: It Was Only Yesterday 1935–1965*, by Lloyd Ultan and Gary Hermalyn (1992), p. 7 and passim. Another good source for Bronx games of the period is *Just Kids from the Bronx: An Oral History*, compiled by Arlene Alda (2015).

248 *all kinds of people who would one day be famous lived here during the years of the new paradise Bronx*: Information about famous and/or accomplished people from the Bronx may be found in Ultan, Alda, McNamara, various biographies and autobiographies, and in the online listing of honorees on the Bronx Walk of Fame, a twenty-three-block-long section of the Grand Concourse where the honorees' names are displayed on street signs.

250 *David Latkin, the first Jewish soldier from the Bronx to die in France*: See McNamara, p. 141. *the boatyards on City Island made PT boats for the navy*: See *The Beautiful Bronx, 1920–1950*, by Lloyd Ultan (1979), p. 45.

251 *Sergeant Basilone received that medal for heroism on Guadalcanal*: Basilone, one of the country's most famous warriors ever, was from Raritan, New Jersey.

251 *they staged strikes for lower rents*: Gonzalez, p. 102.

252 *"It was the bleakness of expectation"*: See "My Neighborhood, Its Fall and Rise," by Vivian Gornick, *The New York Times*, June 24, 2001, Sec. 14, p. 1. See also Gornick's excellent memoir, *Fierce Attachments* (1987).

Chapter 22

255 *"Make no little plans"*: See *New York Times* obituary for Charles D. Norton, March 7, 1923, p. 14.

256 *One of the committee's first recommendations*: See vol. II of the *First Regional Plan* (1931), p. 6. The caption of a photo of the bridge says, "One of the first acts of the Regional Plan Committee, in 1923, was to recommend to the Port of New York Authority that the bridge over the Hudson be erected at 178th Street instead of at 57th Street, as then proposed."

258 *something bothered it about all that Hudson River Bridge traffic potentially clogging the Bronx*: See *Regional Plan of New York and Its Environs* (1929), vol. I, p. 224.

261 *In* The Power Broker, *Robert Caro describes how Moses almost built a long bridge that would have destroyed Battery Park*: See Caro, pp. 641 ff.

261 *the Regional Plan proposed the creation of a "great sub-terminal"*: See *Regional Plan of New York* (1929), p. 254.

262 *New York is becoming an "Oriental" town*: See *Regional Plan of New York*, vol. 2 (1931), p. 94. *"a well-rooted native population"*: ibid. *"Imagination is not a strong point in the mind of the average citizen"*: ibid., p. 102.

263 *still exists today*: The Regional Plan Association reports are available online. Here I referred to RPA's first report, *Regional Plan of New York and Its Environs: Volume One, The Graphic Regional Plan*, Prepared by the Staff of the Regional Plan (1929). *"an airplane landing field on the Newark meadows"*: *Regional Plan of New York*, vol. 1 (1929), p. 327. *The planners had imagined an east-west highway*: ibid., p. 266.

263 *"We have carried concentration too far!"*: See *Regional Plan of New York*, vol. 2 (1931), p. 347.

264 *it doubled the size of its parklands*: See the "Executive Summary" section of the Fourth Regional Plan (2017).

Chapter 23

265 *Blacks began to move to the Bronx in large numbers in the 1920s and '30s*: In 1920, 4,803 Blacks lived in the Bronx. Twenty years later the number was 25,529; see Gonzalez, p. 99.

267 *Morrisania would be different*: See *Before the Fires: An Oral History of African-American Life in the Bronx from the 1930s to the 1960s*, by Mark Naison and Bob Gumbs (2016), p. 163.

267 *Her father said, "My child, we are select people"*: ibid., p. 2.

268 *In 1900, a race riot occurred in the Tenderloin*: The riot began with an altercation between a Black man and an undercover policeman in which the policeman died—see Johnson, *Street Justice*, pp. 57–58. *post office employees and Pullman porters had an advantage*: See Naison and Gumbs, pp. 77, 115, 163.

268 *A young woman named Bessie Jackson left a farm near Calera, Alabama*: Some of the details in this chapter come from interviews in the Bronx African American History Project (BAAHP), a compilation of oral histories of Bronx residents done by Fordham University. In chapter 25 of this book, I describe the BAAHP project and the contribution it has made to the history of the Bronx. The BAAHP interviews are available online, listed by the name of the interviewee.

269 *Welvin Goodwin grew up in Timpson, Texas*: See ibid.

270 *Rev. Hawkins is remembered for closing the Bronx "slave markets"*: See Hawkins's *New York Times* obituary, "E. G. Hawkins, Presbyterian Leader," Dec. 19, 1977, p. 33. Housework obtained in those street settings paid $.25 an hour (BAHHP, Rev. Marie Thomas interview, p. 4). Mentions of Hawkins and his good works appear several times in the BAAHP oral histories.

271 *the girls teamed up and called themselves the Chantels*: The Chantels took their name from St. Jane Frances de Chantal, a Catholic saint.

272 *"Why are you running? That boy came to school in a stroller"*: Naison and Gumbs, p. 59 (interview with Beatrice Bergland).

272 *It took years, and protests, before the places changed their policy*: Taur Orange, an administrator at Fashion Institute of Technology, remembered seeing "hundreds if not thousands of white teenagers throwing rocks at demonstrators at the White Castle on Allerton Avenue": BAAHP, interview with Taur Orange, p. 28. (That same White Castle restaurant, which of course desegregated long ago, is still there.) *Parkchester barred Blacks*: See *The Color of Law: A Forgotten History of How Our Government Segregated America*, by Richard Rothstein (2017), p. 106. See also Gonzalez, p. 111. *the local adults joining in*: See BAAHP, interview with Annie Calhoun, p. 25.

273 *A runner might wear a snap-brim hat*: Several BAAHP interviewees talk about the numbers runners. See interview with Nathan "Bubba" Dukes, pp. 8–9.

274 *the locals cheered*: Gene Norman, onetime chairman of the New York City Landmarks Preservation Commission, remembered how he enjoyed moving into the Monroe Houses in 1961, when he was a young man, and how he saw it as a step up—see BAAHP, interview with Gene Norman, p. 54. James Fleet, a musician who grew up in the Patterson Houses, said, "What a lot of people today don't know about public housing during the fifties and sixties is that it was a great place to live"—BAAHP, interview with James Fleet, p. 23. *NYCHA even assembled its own symphony orchestra*: See BAAHP, interview with the jazz bassist William Parker, p. 14.

274 *word got back to your parents*: See BAAHP, interview with Glenn Ligon, p. 8.

Chapter 24

276 *A lifetime ago, Club 845, at 845 Prospect Avenue, ranked as one of the top jazz clubs in the city*: Naison and Gumbs, p. ix.

277 *Local kids noticed the comings and goings of Thelonious Monk*: See BAAHP, interview 1 with Robert Gumbs, p. 28. (Gumbs grew up on Lyman Place, which is now Elmo Hope Way.) See also Naison and Gumbs, interview with Jacqueline Smith Bonneau, p. 65.

277 *He gave blood for the transfusion that helped save her life*: BAAHP, interview with Valerie Capers, p. 17.

278 *Irene Higginbotham, who co-wrote "Good Morning Heartache"*: Naison and Gumbs,

p. 101 (interview with Joseph Orange). *Erroll Garner . . . lived on Intervale Avenue*: ibid., p. 113. *Billy Bang, the jazz violinist*: BAAHP, interview with William Walker, aka Billy Bang, p. 38.

279　*Puerto Ricans started to come to the Bronx*: See *Encyclopedia of New York*, pp. 962–63.

280　*A leading Latin label, Fania Records*: See McLaughlin, p. 112.

281　*the most popular musical performer in Finland*: BAAHP, interview with Joe Conzo, p. 14. *The acoustics of the common spaces in the buildings contributed to doo-wop*: Anthony Carter, who grew up in the Bronx and went on to be president of Johnson & Johnson, said, "the sound was *unbelievable* in the hallway and the vestibule"—BAAHP interview, pp. 10, 15.

283　*White was born in Harlem in 1932 and attended DeWitt Clinton High School*: Biographical details are from the NYC Parks Department plaque, "Hilton White Playground." See also BAAHP, interview with Nathan "Bubba" Dukes, pp. 16, 32, 38.

283　*He told the coach, Don Haskins, that he would send players to El Paso*: Haskins's book about the 1966 NCAA championship has much to say in praise of Hilton White. See *Glory Road: My Story of the 1966 NCAA Basketball Championship and How One Team Triumphed Against the Odds and Changed America Forever*, by Don Haskins with Dan Wetzel (2006), pp. 131–33. See also *And the Walls Came Tumbling Down: Kentucky, Texas Western, and the Game That Changed American Sports*, by Frank Fitzpatrick (1999), pp. 25, 39, 105, 165.

285　*About thirty members of his extended family attended the ceremony*: See "More Than Playing Ball on a South Bronx Playground," *The New York Times*, Aug. 3, 2009.

285　*"In like Flynn"*: See, for example, Jonnes, p. 115. For photos of James J. Lyons, see Ultan and Hermalyn, pp. 64, 108, 123, 127.

Chapter 25

288　*the Bronx County historian was a professor named Lloyd Ultan*: In May 2023, Lloyd Ultan stepped down as Bronx County historian. His replacement, Angel Hernandez, the former director of programs and external relations for the Bronx Historical Society, started the Bronx Latino History Project.

290　*"The car came to its final stop"*: Ultan, *Beautiful Bronx*, p. 20.

292　*The Bronx African American History Project (BAAHP), as Fordham calls this oral history collection, covers a longer span*: Since Fordham began the Bronx African American History Project, it has expanded its oral histories to include the Bronx Covid-19 History Project and the Bronx Italian-American History Initiative.

292　*Aided by two assistants, McDonald conducted 407 interviews with 241 people*: See *The McDonald Papers, Part I*, ed. William S. Hardaway (1926), p. x. This book, as well as a companion volume (*Part II*), has information about John M. McDonald and the McDonald Papers, and some information about the history of the period, but no transcriptions of the interviews themselves. As far as I know, the Westchester County Historical Society remains the only repository of those.

295　*In his book* White Boy: A Memoir: Mark D. Naison (2002). *he "came to see writing history and making history as integrally connected"*: p. 44.

296　*"Wow, you're a Panther now!"*: BAAHP, interview 2 with Cleo Silvers, p. 12.

297　*The Young Lords, a group of mostly Puerto Rican activists*: See *The Young Lords: A Radical History*, by Johanna Fernandez (2000).

297　*pelted the governor of Puerto Rico with eggs and tomatoes*: See "Badillo Scores Young Lords for Attack on Puerto Rican," *The New York Times*, June 18, 1970, p. 83. *In 1970, they occupied the administrative offices of Lincoln Hospital*: See "Young Lords Seize Lincoln Hospital Building; Offices Are Held for 12 Hours—Officials Call Points Valid," *The New York Times*, July 15, 1970, p. 34.

298　*he was hospitalized for bleeding ulcers*: See "Lincoln Hospital: Behind the Conflict," *The New York Times*, Nov. 29, 1970, p. 8.

299　*he and other radicals "could only stand helplessly by"*: Naison, p. 138.

Chapter 26

303 *The plan encompassed 5,528 square miles*: See "29 Region Plan Is Short of Goals," *The New York Times*, Jan. 1, 1965, p. 13.

304 *In 1945, New York City announced that $300 million would be spent to build or improve its highways and bridges*: See "City Reveals $300,000,000 Highway Plan," *New York Herald Tribune*, November 26, 1945, p. 1.

304 *The Bruckner Expressway, as it swung around the southern edges of the borough, turned big areas into bulldozed dirt*: See BAAHP, interview with Bernard Keller, who remembered it when it was all dirt.

305 *In panoramic photos from the 1950s*: See Ultan and Hermalyn, pp. 26–27.

306 *Once, some boys found a box of seventy-three sticks of dynamite*: See "Dynamite Terror Spread by 8 Boys," *The New York Times*, Nov. 12, 1956, p. 32. *a collapse of the roof trapped and killed six firemen*: The names of the firemen may be found on the non-descript graffiti-covered warehouse that occupies the site today.

306 *had worked on building the wartime Burma Road*: See Caro, p. 839. (Other facts on the building of the Cross Bronx come from that invaluable book, and from newspaper coverage of the time.)

307 *"a vehicular paradise at the expense of the residents"*: See "Wagner Orders Building of Manhattan Expressway," *The New York Times*, May 26, 1965, p. 1.

308 *the part of the Bronx to the south of the Cross Bronx Expressway lost about 47 percent of its residents*: Ultan, *Northern Borough*, p. 302.

309 *The garment industry began to leave*: See Jonnes (2002 edition), p. 93.

310 *the Lyons Residence Law*: See *Encyclopedia of New York City*, p. 702; see also Mahler, p. 197.

312 *In those years, when New York City almost went broke, half of its Black public employees . . . lost their jobs*: McLaughlin, p. 102.

312 *New York City lost 660,000 jobs in just seven years*: See "Making New York City Smaller," *The New York Times Magazine*, Nov. 4, 1976. *Other sources estimate the loss at half a million jobs*: Gonzalez, p. 118. *In 1996, it brought out its Third Regional Plan*: See *A Region at Risk: The Third Regional Plan for the New York–New Jersey–Connecticut Metropolitan Area*, by Robert D. Yaro and Tony Hiss (1996), p. 7.

313 *Fifty years would pass before it returned to approximately what it had been in 1970*: According to the 2020 census, the population of the Bronx is 1,472,654. This is probably an undercount.

Chapter 27

314 *large parts of the Bronx had been put at risk several decades earlier*: Information on redlining and real estate practices in the Bronx comes from an exhibit, "Undesign the Red Line," which I saw at the Freedman Center on the Grand Concourse, as well as from conversations with Professor Gregory Jost, of Fordham University, who put together the exhibit.

315 *In redlined neighborhoods, the FHA would not insure loans for property, and therefore banks would not lend*: See the BAAHP interview with Elias Karmon, who owned a clothing store on Prospect Avenue and several local residential buildings, and who served as a civic booster and philanthropist. Karmon said, "If you lived in the South Bronx, lived in the redlined areas, you would never get a mortgage on anything." He added that the banks "saw trends and they did not give loans." Karmon was ninety-four when interviewed, and by then had been doing business in the Bronx for seventy years.

317 *In 1953, you rarely saw drugs in the open*: BAAHP, interview with Gloria and Ronald Marshall, p. 41. See also Naison and Gumbs, p. 52 (interview with Gene Norman). *Some residents said that the quality of your average neighbor had gone down*: Gloria Marshall, in BAAHP interview (ibid., p. 44), said, "I don't mean to say it like this, but they were not of our caliber."

318 *stopped being able to correct kids on the street*: BAAHP, interview with Bernard Keller, p. 9. *"Don't you say anything to my child!"*: BAAHP, interview with Rosalind Lawrence, p. 32.

319 *Afterward, some faculty lunchrooms divided*: For perspective on the 1968 teachers' strike, see BAAHP interviews with Valerie Washington (p. 34), Dana Driskell (p. 25), and Frank Belton (interview 1, p. 41).

320 The Ed Sullivan Show *killed off the church's Sunday evening service single-handedly*: See Naison and Gumbs (interview with Avis Hansen), p. 5. *Rick Meyerowitz, the artist and writer*: Alda, p. 139.

323 *The enemies left the Ghetto Brothers leader unhurt, weeping, and terrorized*: BAAHP, interview with Benjamin Melendez, p. 38. (BAAHP interviewed Melendez in 2006, and he died in 2017.) *By 1970, the Bronx's gang violence had grown so intense*: The documentary *Flyin' Cut Sleeves*, by Henry Chalfant and Rita Fecher (Sleeping Dog Films, 1993), tells about the 1960s–1970s world of Bronx gangs.

324 *The murder made page one of the* Daily News: The banner headline, all in caps, read: "TEEN GANGS KILL PEACEMAKER" (Dec. 3, 1971).

Chapter 28

326 *"they were moving out of here like somebody was chasing them"*: Eric Petersen, in BAAHP interview with Basil, Eric, and Ishma Petersen, p. 75. *If panic drove some who left, it was not based on nothing*: Details in this paragraph come from stories in *The New York Times*, including "Fatal Mugging Stirs Fears in Bronx Neighborhood" (Feb. 15, 1967, p. 28); "Two Communities Seek More Police" (March 10, 1967, p. 35); "Bronx Police Aim at Indoor Crime; Robbery Study Prompts New Patrols Inside of Buildings" (Dec. 24, 1969, p. 1); and "40 in Bronx Seek Gun Permits for Protection Against Addicts" (Sept. 26, 1969, p. 31).

327 *"I got angry at my family, and I got angry at my friends' families who left"*: BAAHP, interview with David Greene, p. 25.

328 *Gertrude Berg, the Manhattan wife and mother who wrote and starred in* The Goldbergs: See *Something on My Own: Gertrude Berg and American Broadcasting, 1929–1956*, by Glenn D. Smith, Jr. (2015).

330 *the largest housing project ever in the world, to be called Co-op City*: A summary of Co-op City's origins is in my article "Utopia, the Bronx," *The New Yorker*, June 26, 2006, p. 54.

330 *Decades later, when Bronxites assessed what had done the most harm to the borough*: See McLaughlin, p. 74; see also Mahler, p. 7.

331 *more than 270 synagogues closed*: McLaughlin, p. 27. *A man who owned a laundromat at East 170th Street and Charlotte Street was killed and robbed*: See Smith (1972), p. 210. *A local character known as Jake the Pickle Man*: See "The Glory That Was Charlotte," *The New York Times*, Oct. 7, 1979, SM, p. 11.

331 *Some landlords wanted to fill their empty or partly empty buildings with tenants on welfare*: McLaughlin, p. 64.

333 *By the mid-1970s, the fire-threatened areas were approaching Fordham Road*: See Jonnes, p. 8: "By 1980, the city of New York and the media had redefined the boundaries of the infamous South Bronx to include everything south of Fordham Road, or twenty square miles."

333 *He called it "the busiest firehouse in the city—and probably the world"*: See *Report from Engine Co. 82*, by Dennis Smith (1972), p. 11.

334 *Chrystal Wade, a Bronx activist and educator, never forgot the TV console the family lost*: BAAHP, interview with Chrystal Wade, p. 6. *somebody pulled the fire alarm at the intersection while the party was going on*: Smith, p. 170.

335 *Hetty Fox, who grew up on Lyman Place*: See interviews with Hetty Fox in Naison and Gumbs (p. 68), and BAAHP. (Hetty Fox died in 2016.)

Chapter 29

337 *although city fire inspectors said that most of the building fires were not caused by arson*: See *The Fires: How a Computer Formula, Big Ideas, and the Best of Intentions Burned Down New York City—and Determined the Future of Cities*, by Joe Flood (2010), p. 19.

338 *Robert Moses . . . had declared the Bronx to be "beyond tinkering, rebuilding and restoring"*: See "Guess Who Saved the South Bronx? Big Government," by Robert Worth, *Washington Monthly*, April 1999.

338 *Between 1972 and 1974, four fire stations in the Bronx, each serving sixty thousand people, closed*: See *Break Beats in the Bronx: Rediscovering Hip-Hop's Early Years*, by Joseph C. Ewoodzie, Jr. (2017), p. 25. *a new theory, expressed in two words, kept the fires burning*: Descriptions of the "planned shrinkage" strategy may be found in many sources—see McLaughlin, p. 77, and Jonnes (2022 ed.), pp. 298–99. Roger Starr himself explained the concept in *The New York Times Sunday Magazine*, Nov. 4, 1976: "Making New York Smaller." He wrote, "Planned shrinkage is not a popular idea—for simply suggesting that the Department of City Planning should study it, I was denounced as a genocidal lunatic and enemy of man."

339 *In 1976, the number of fires of all kinds in the borough reached 33,465*: Jonnes (2002 ed.), p. 363.

342 *It's said that a Bronx car dealership lost fifty new Pontiacs that night*: See Ewoodzie (2017), p. 127. *And did those Bronxites who withdrew by the tens of thousands to Co-op City find their separate peace*: See my article "Utopia, the Bronx," cited above.

345 *A few months later, he pled guilty to embezzling from the Boys and Girls Club*: See "Bronx Odyssey: From Rebel to Executive to Felon," *The New York Times*, Oct. 10, 2006, p. B1.

345 *On Lyman Place, in the path of the fires, Hetty Fox kept an eye on the neighborhood*: See Naison and Gumbs, pp. 68–74. See also Hetty Fox interview in BAAHP.

346 *Vivian Vázquez graduated from high school and went to the State University of New York at Albany*: Details of her autobiography are in the documentary film *Decade of Fire* (see below), and from my conversations with Vázquez.

Chapter 30

348 *Alex was originally a Russian artist and is now an American artist*: For the earlier and mid-part of Alexander Melamid's career, see *Komar and Melamid*, by Carter Ratcliff (1988).

351 *She sneaked away from the ball to telephone Irving Berlin*: The Berlin-Mackay romance and marriage are chronicled in Barrett (1995), and in the abundant news coverage of the couple during the 1920s. See also Furia (1998).

Chapter 31

358 *The origin is attributed to a specific time and place*: The story of the Kool Herc party of August 11, 1973, may be found in many books. See Ewoodzie, pp. 17–19; also *The Big Payback: The History of the Business of Hip-Hop*, by Dan Charnas (2010), p. 16; see also Ultan, *Northern Borough*, p. 321.

359 *where I have seen it*: Thank you to Professor Marcyliena Morgan, founding director of the Hiphop Archive and Research Institute at the Hutchins Center for African and African American Research, Harvard University, for showing me this interesting document.

359 *"You could live inside some of them speakers"*: BAAHP, interview 1 with Danny Martinez, p. 24.

361 *As he recounts in his memoir*: See *The Adventures of Grandmaster Flash: My Life, My Beats*, by Grandmaster Flash with David Ritz (2008). (Along with the more than two dozen books that David Ritz has written or cowritten, he is also listed as one of three cowriters of Marvin Gaye's 1982 hit song, "Sexual Healing.")

363 *"There must have been a thousand people getting down"*: See *Adventures of Grandmaster Flash*, p. 47.

364   *Afrika Bambaataa, a Barbadian-Jamaican whose original name was Lance Taylor*:
      See Ewoodzie, pp. 52 ff.; see also Charnas, p. 19.

365   *"something to make the ground shake"*: *Adventures of Grandmaster Flash*, p. 61. *One
      graffiti artist climbed to the top of a number 4 train*: Mike Callender, in BAAHP inter-
      view with him, Robert Caines, Robert Caines, Jr., Melvin Howell, and Keith Johnson,
      p. 36. *shoes versus sneakers*: Kurtis Blow, in BAAHP interview with him and Pete DJ
      Jones, p. 12; see also BAAHP, interview with Troy Smith, p. 15.

366   *One of them remembered doing it in his school when he was in the fifth grade*: BAAHP,
      interview with Matthew Swain, p. 25. *and "hip-hop" became a thing to say*: Ewoodzie,
      p. 129.

367   *"we'd hear this thumping sound"*: BAAHP, interview 1 with Danny Martinez, p. 21.
      A store called Downstairs Records: ibid., p. 25; Grandmaster Flash also loved going
      to Downstairs Records and said it had "a million records in a million different places"
      (*Adventures of . . .* , p. 66).

368   *"That was my first time in a historical place that they let me do it"*: BAAHP, interview
      2 with Danny Martinez, p. 13. *The police let the DJs turn it all the way up and go all
      night*: BAAHP, interview with Troy Smith, p. 24.

369   *This one, Flash said, "changed the way I saw myself"*: See *Adventures of . . .* , p. 98.

Chapter 32

372   The Fire Next Door *marked the first time that the ongoing disaster in the Bronx got
      major national attention*: I learned how CBS happened to become interested in the
      fires and how it produced *The Fire Next Door* in interviews with Tom Spain and Bill
      Moyers.

373   *Then they noticed that every light on the block seemed to be out*: The story of Grand-
      master Caz and DJ Disco Wiz on the night of the '77 Blackout is in Ewoodzie, pp. 125–27.
      "A formerly exclusive scene was suddenly democratic": Charnas, p. 24. Many observers
      noted the democratizing and vivifying effect that the Blackout had on hip-hop music; for
      example, see BAAHP, interview with Todd and Stephanie McKinney, p. 34: "TM: Who
      did not get a new mixer? That [the Blackout] helped DJs out tremendously."

374   *(The first articles about hip-hop, in* Billboard *and the* Amsterdam News, *would not come
      out until 1979)*: Charnas, p. 46. *President Jimmy Carter's famous drive-through visit
      to the South Bronx*: Every contemporary historian of the borough mentions this event;
      see Ultan, *Northern Borough*, p. 300, and Jonnes, pp. 311 ff.; Gonzalez writes (p. 135),
      "President Carter's visit to Charlotte Street eventually led to a major improvement in the
      South Bronx." All the major New York papers covered the president's visit; see "Carter
      Takes 'Sobering' Trip to South Bronx; Finds Hope Amid Blight," *The New York Times*,
      Oct. 6, 1977, p. 1.

376   *Jimmy Breslin, the* Daily News *columnist, followed the Carter motorcade that day*: See
      "Carter Has Little Impact on One Mean Street," by Jimmy Breslin, New York *Daily
      News*, Oct. 6, 1977, p. 4C.

380   *A hundred and forty-six people were murdered in the Bronx in 2021*: See "Insult to
      Injury: Crime Surge amid Pandemic," New York *Daily News*, Jan. 2, 2022, p. 11.

381   *The urban planning department of Hunter College led bus tours*: See "The Glory That
      Was Charlotte," by Ira Rosen, *The New York Times Sunday Magazine*, Oct. 7, 1979,
      p. 11. *A city councilman brought a delegation of Russians*: Jonnes, p. 341.

381   *A 732-unit housing development had been proposed for the site*: See "The Politics
      of Charlotte Street," by Anna Quindlen, in *The New York Times Sunday Magazine*,
      Oct. 7, 1979, p. 27. When I interviewed the former borough president Fernando Ferrer,
      he said the project was not well designed for the site, and the Board of Estimate had
      acted wisely in turning it down. Not only were Carter and the other Democrats divided
      among themselves, they needed a better idea. The housing plan that transformed the
      Charlotte Street neighborhood would be quite a different one (see chapter 36).

382   *(a sixteen-year-old-boy was shot to death)*: See New York *Daily News*, Dec. 24, 2020,

"Teen, 16, Fatally Shot in Head Inside Bronx Deli." The victim's name was James Solano. The man arrested for his murder, Marquis Beckford, was twenty-two. More recently, the King Deli reopened. The bloodstains on the cash machine against which the boy fell have been removed.

Chapter 33

383   *Sonia Sotomayor watched on television as Carter's motorcade passed the building where she once lived*: Much of the information in this chapter comes from Sonia Sotomayor's autobiography, *My Beloved World*, cited above. Through a friend's friend who knows her, I sent the justice an interview request. Through an assistant, she replied that she would consider it; eventually she turned it down, citing the possible impropriety of appearing to endorse the contents of my book.

383   *More likely, she wore a tailored jacket and skirt*: I looked up the article I wrote ("Sonia from the Bronx," *The New Yorker*, Feb. 8 and 15, 2016) in which I described her as wearing almost all black—an unbuttoned black coat like a cape, a black dress, and a knee-length black sweater. I said that the dark ensemble made her face and hands stand out, as in an old portrait painting. That must be why I picture her in judge's robes.

390   *Harry DeRienzo grew up on Long Island*: The pitiless workings of New York City real estate, and the challenges of building low-income housing in an atmosphere of asset stripping and predatory equity, provide the plot lines for *Building Homes, Building Communities: The Ongoing Story of Banana Kelly and Community Development in the South Bronx*, by Harold DeRienzo (2020). I also benefited from many conversations with Harry DeRienzo by phone and by Zoom.

393   *Fire remains a curse in the Bronx*: For details of what is sometimes called the Twin Parks fire (after the official name of the apartment building where it happened), see "19 Killed in New York's Deadliest Fire in Decades," *The New York Times*, Jan. 10, 2022, p. 1.

394   *"Give good tidings to the patient"*: The verses are in Qur'an 2: 155–56, as the attribution on the sign said.

Chapter 34

395   *In 1978, Grandmaster Flash performed a hip-hop concert in the cafeteria of the Bronx High School of Science*: BAAHP, interview with Tony Martinez, p. 16. *A music entrepreneur, Sal Abbatiello, who ran a club at East 167th Street and Jerome Avenue called The Disco Fever*: The story of Abbatiello and The Disco Fever runs throughout *The Big Payback*, by Charnas; see pp. 21–24 and passim.

396   *the Kidd Creole (Nathan Glover)*: In 2022, Nathan Glover was convicted of manslaughter in the stabbing of a man in Manhattan, and he received a sixteen-year prison sentence. *Mr. Freeze, Baby Freeze, Tiny Freeze, Little Freeze, and Black Freeze*: BAAHP, interview with Darney "K-Born" Rivers, p. 22.

397   *Flash believed that he and the Furious Five could draw thousands of customers, and proved it*: See *The Adventures of . . .* , pp. 120–27.

398   *"Adams, North Dakota"*: The sample fragment that mentions this place apparently comes from an album by a Seattle grunge band called the Hellers. Where they got the fragment from—an old movie or radio show?—I don't know. I am one of the (probably) very few people who have both listened to Flash's "Wheels of Steel" and visited Adams, North Dakota. It's a nice town, settled by Norwegians in the late nineteenth century. In 2010 its population was 127, and in 2020 its population was 127.

399   *Scott La Rock was one of the three members of Boogie Down Productions (BDP)*: The story of DJ Scott La Rock, KRS-One, and Boogie Down Productions may be found in Charnas (pp. 177 ff.) and in *Can't Stop Won't Stop: A History of the Hip-Hop Generation*, by Jeff Chang (2005), pp. 248 ff.

399   *he and his younger brother were raised by their grandfather*: Scott Sterling's younger brother, Chris Sterling, also was a basketball standout, and played with Kenny Smith at Archbishop Molloy High School in Queens.

400 *Matt Kilcullen, a longtime basketball coach*: I learned about Sterling/La Rock's time at Castleton State College in interviews with Kilcullen, Lee Smith, Stan Van Gundy, Brian DeLoatch, Olivia Duane Adams, and Kim Abbott Van Gundy.

402 *he wanted to prove that God is real*: This statement and others like it by KRS-One may be found in interviews with him online; for example, see YouTube, "KRS-One Talks About Being Homeless and Meeting Scott La Rock."

403 *"Scott gained a freedom hanging out with us"*: See "R.I.P. Scott La Rock—Remembering the BDP Legend 23 Years Later," *XXL*, Aug. 27, 2010.

405 *But the dispute had substance, the truth of the matter lay entirely on the Bronx side*: See *To the Break of Dawn: A Freestyle on the Hip Hop Aesthetic*, by William Jelani Cobb (2007), p. 81. (Today Marley Marl is a radio DJ on the New York station WBLS.)

406 *The idea behind the title, as KRS-One explained, was that the crew would* look *like criminals*: As KRS-One told *XXL*, the title *Criminal Minded* meant BDP would "get the money, but not become criminals ourselves."

407 *"He was able to rekindle the hope of those who had lost all hope"*: See "Violent Death Halts Rap Musician's Rise," *The New York Times*, Aug. 31, 1987, p. B1.

408 *"began 10 years ago in the Bronx and Harlem"*: See previous note.

Chapter 35

411 *In videos and photos from the period, the tracks of the elevated trains cross expanses of empty rubble*: As, for example, in the movie *Wild Style* (1982). *the now-empty land should be allowed to "go back to grass"*: Roger Starr, the city's housing and development administrator, said that after the buildings and people were removed, the land should lie fallow. Herman Badillo, U.S. congressman from the Bronx's 23rd District, suggested planting "crops and flowers." See "City's Housing Administrator Proposes 'Planned Shrinkage' of Some Slums," *The New York Times*, Feb. 3, 1976, p. 35.

412 *People tossed trash over the fences into the lots*: See Smith (1972), p. 174. *On the weekend after Fernando Ferrer became Bronx borough president, in 1987*: Ferrer, a city councilman from the Bronx, took over the BP's office after Stanley Simon resigned because of his involvement in a scandal involving Wedtech, a Bronx company that swarmed with corruption. After serving as BP for two years, Ferrer was elected to the BP's office on his own in 1989 and remained in office until 2001. The story of his visit to 588 Fox Street with his daughter, and other details in this chapter, are from my interview with him (April 13, 2022).

413 *Later, Jacob Riis, a Dane, read it*: See *The Other Half: The Life of Jacob Riis and the World of Immigrant America*, by Tom Buk-Swienty (2008), pp. 30, 65.

415 *Father Louis Gigante served as one of the priests at St. Athanasius Church, on Southern Boulevard*: For a good overview of Gigante's contributions, and those of St. Athanasius and the larger Catholic Church, see *The Kingdom Began in Puerto Rico: Neil Connelly's Priesthood in the South Bronx*, by Angel Garcia (2021). Connelly was a colleague of Gigante's at St. Athanasius, and Garcia co-founded a community development corporation (CDC) called South Bronx People for Change.

416 *As recently as 2022, the* Daily News *pointed out*: See "It's a Border War in Dock Fight: N.Y. Suing N.J. in Supreme Court to Stop It from Ditching Anti-crime Waterfront Panel," New York *Daily News*, March 15, 2022, p. 2. *Jim Mitchell grew up in a churchgoing Catholic family in Winnetka, Illinois*: from my interviews with Jim Mitchell.

417 *Roger Hayes's family included four other siblings*: from my interviews with Roger Hayes.

419 *Bill Frey, from Waukesha, Wisconsin, did not go to Notre Dame*: from my interviews with Bill Frey.

Chapter 36

423 *One of his early mayoral acts was to appoint Felice Michetti*: Some of the information in this chapter is from my interview with Felice Michetti. She is now president

of Grenadier Realty Corporation, of Brooklyn and the Bronx, which focuses on low-income housing. The story of her success with the white-framed windows is also told in *Neighborhood Success Stories: Creating and Sustaining Affordable Housing in New York*, by Carol Lamberg (2018), p. 238.

425 *In a place that could support 110 housing units (apartments) per acre*: DeRienzo, *Building Homes, Building Communities*, p. 15.

426 *Koch screamed back, "The people who have bought them will defend them with their lives!"*: Jonnes, p. 376.

428 *In 1985, Meyer (Sandy) Frucher, president of the Battery Park City Authority, proposed*: Lamberg, pp. 26–27.

429 *"the greatest construction program since the pharaohs built the pyramids"*: "$5 Billion Plan for Apartments Pushed in Bronx," *The New York Times*, Feb. 28, 1989, p. B4.

Chapter 37

432 *the oldest row houses in the Bronx*: Gonzalez, p. 163. *"the Irish Fifth Avenue"*: Ultan, *Northern Borough*, p. 219.

434 *Crack was known as a ladies' drug*: McLaughlin says, "For the first time, significant numbers of women as well as men became addicted . . . Crack was a female drug" (pp. 49–50). *passersby could look into the park and see the flames of crack pipes glowing here and there in the darkness*: BAAHP, interview with Robert Gaines, Jr. (aka DJ Flawless), p. 8. *In October 1776, the Continental Army left campfires burning on the hillsides*: From the historical marker at Van Cortlandt House Museum in Van Cortlandt Park: "General George Washington kept campfires burning in the area surrounding the house while he gained time for a safe withdrawal of his troops across the Hudson River."

434 *By the late eighties, HIV/AIDS was the leading cause of death among Black women*: *Encyclopedia of the City of New York*, p. 11.

436 *A priest at St. Martin of Tours Catholic Church in Belmont officiated at twenty-five funerals*: BAAHP, interview with Martin Sanchez, p. 74.

437 *More than anybody, Al Quiñones rescued Playground 52*: Information about Quiñones comes from interviews with Ferrer; with James Melendez, president of 52 People for Progress, which oversees the playground; and with José Vasquez, the playground's supervisor. *For example, Evelina Antonetty, a Puerto Rico–born union organizer*: I learned about Antonetty from the 2022 celebration of the centennial of her birth sponsored by Hostos Community College and other organizations. People in various neighborhoods filled me in on other local heroes. Names that are on streets and parks can often be found online, even if they're not in history books.

438 *Six and a half hours in the not-yet-pristine water did him no harm*: See "River of Dreams: He Does It! Host Swims Length of Bronx Waterway," New York *Daily News*, July 30, 2013, p. 27. The swimmer, a man going by the name of Baron Ambrosia, hosted a "culinary adventure" show on cable called *Bronx Flavor*. For stories about dolphins in the river, see CBS News, "Dolphins Spotted in Bronx River for First Time in Years," Jan. 24, 2023.

442 *Captain Ramsey was promoted to deputy inspector the next year*: Since then, he has been promoted to Inspector, and he is now fourth in command at the NYPD Transit Bureau. I predict that someday Keiyon Ramsey will be head of the entire NYPD. You read it here!

Chapter 38

445 *A great-grandfather of Jimmy Carter on his mother's side, James Thomas Gordy, fathered two sets of children*: See Alter, pp. 25–26.

Chapter 39

454 *Hetty Fox said she could "tune" her street*: She describes this in the documentary *Decade of Fire* (2018). Details about the rehabs and the maintenance of Playground 52 are from interviews with José Vasquez and James Melendez.

Chapter 40

463   *Carolyn McLaughlin, CAB's executive director*: Biographical information about Carolyn McLaughlin comes from an interview I did with her, and from her book, *South
Bronx Battles*.

465   *Vázquez helped devise the theme of the new high school*: The account of the making of
Decade of Fire comes from my interviews with Vivian Vázquez, Julia Steele Allen, and
Gretchen Hildebran.

Chapter 41

478   *More than half of the renters in the Bronx pay more than 30 percent of their income
on rent*: Statistics in this paragraph may be found in the 2020 report from the Furman
Center for Real Estate and Public Policy at the Wagner School of Public Service, New
York University. *New York State has produced five U.S. presidents*: The other four are
Martin Van Buren, Millard Fillmore, Theodore Roosevelt, and Franklin D. Roosevelt.

479   *you're on or near the spot where Edgar Allan Poe stood*: See note, p. 200.

480   *Graffiti artists called the place the Ghost Yard*: See BAAHP, interview with the graffiti
artist Albert Mercado, p. 12.

481   *A developer called Dynamic Star LLC has bought large parts of it from the CSX railroad*: See "Developer Plows Ahead with Plans for $3.5b Bronx Megaproject," *Crain's
New York Business*, Jan. 4, 2021.

481   *The development will be called Fordham Landing*: See "Fordham Landing Developer Discusses $2 Billion Mega-Development in University Heights," *Norwood News*,
Nov. 24, 2021. *A lot of the construction happened between 2009 and 2018, when 70 million square feet of new development was created*: See Lamberg, *Neighborhood Success
Stories*, in the foreword written by the then–borough president, Rubén Díaz, Jr., p. xii.

483   *"This just continues the old narrative of the Bronx facilitating the ease of more affluent
people"*: the activist Paul Lipson, quoted in Jonnes (2022 ed.), p. 536.

Chapter 42

486   *the white population went down between 2000 and 2019*: The Bronx was 14.5 percent
white in 2000 and 8.8 percent white in 2019. See "Neighborhood Profiles: The Bronx,"
in the 2021 report from the Furman Center for Real Estate and Public Policy at the
Wagner School of Public Service, New York University.

489   *Foodies have known about a restaurant called La Morada for at least ten years*: One of
the early articles about La Morada was by Nicolas Niarchos, the journalist and shipping
heir; see "La Morada" *The New Yorker*, Oct. 2, 2017, p. 15. (Online title: "La Morada, a
Crucible of Resistance.")

492   *Stella D'oro was founded in about 1930*: My piece on the Stella D'oro bakery, the strike,
and the aftermath of the strike appeared in *The New Yorker* of Feb. 6, 2012, p. 52.

495   *Unsurprisingly, Bloomberg did nothing. He has said that the crash of 2008 was caused
by the end of redlining*: The then-mayor explained to an audience at Georgetown University in 2008 that redlining had been a prudent practice of not lending to poor people
who couldn't pay you back, and when it ended, the more lenient policy that followed
spread a lack of caution throughout the banking system. Ergo, the crash was caused
by indulging the former victims of redlining and others like them. See *The Sum of Us:
What Racism Costs Everyone and How We Can Prosper Together*, by Heather McGhee
(2022), pp. 90–91.

Chapter 43

499   *When he was eleven, a video game changed his life*: The SimCity series of games follows closely the goals, methodology, and experiences of high-tech planning organizations like the Rand Corp.

505   *Stanford White, the architect, considered the statue to be the most beautiful example
of metal coloring in the world*: See *The New York Times Sunday Magazine*, July 29,

1906, p. 2: "How Shall 'Miss Liberty's' Toilet Be Made? Suggestions That the Statue Be Painted Shocks the Artists—What a Visit to Her Last Week Revealed." The general manager of a bronze and copper manufacturing company in Manhattan told the reporter that the statue was in perfect shape and had no need of paint to protect it. The manager went on, "I remember once asking the late Stanford White how he wished us to finish the decorative metal work on a noted building that he was putting up. 'Go down to Bedloe's Island,' he said, 'and study the Statue of Liberty. You will find it the most beautiful example of metal coloring in existence in the world today.'"

BIBLIOGRAPHY

Abbatt, William. *The Battle of Pell's Point: October 18, 1776. Being the Story of a Stubborn Fight . . .* (1901).

Adams, William Howard. *Gouverneur Morris, an Independent Life* (2003).

Alda, Arlene, ed. *Just Kids from the Bronx: An Oral History* (2015).

Alley, Richard B. *The Two-Mile Time Machine: Ice Cores, Abrupt Climate Change, and Our Future* (c. 2000).

Alter, Jonathan. *His Very Best: Jimmy Carter, a Life* (2020).

Barrett, Mary Ellin. *Irving Berlin: A Daughter's Memoir* (1994).

Bernardy, Françoise de. *Son of Talleyrand: The Life of Comte Charles de Flahaut 1785–1870* (Lucy Norton, tr., 1965).

Bernstein, Peter L. *Wedding of the Waters: The Erie Canal and the Making of a Great Nation* (2005).

Billias, George Athan. *General John Glover and his Marblehead Mariners* (1960).

Bronk, William. *Life Supports: New and Collected Poems* (1980).

Brookhiser, Richard. *Gentleman Revolutionary: Gouverneur Morris—The Rake Who Wrote the Constitution* (2003).

Buk-Swienty, Tom. *The Other Half: The Life of Jacob Riis and the World of Immigrant America* (2008).

Cantwell, Anne-Marie, and Diana diZerega Wall. *Unearthing Gotham: The Archaeology of New York City* (2001).

Caro, Robert A. *The Power Broker: Robert Moses and the Fall of New York* (1974).

Chang, Jeff. *Can't Stop Won't Stop: A History of the Hip-Hop Generation* (2005).

Charnas, Dan. *The Big Payback: The History of the Business of Hip-Hop* (2010).

Chastellux, the Marquis de. *Travels in North America in the Years 1780, 1781, and 1782* (Howard C. Rice, Jr., tr. and ed., 1963).

Chicago Forum. *Shall the Negro Be Encouraged to Seek Cultural Equality? Report of the Debate Conducted by the Chicago Forum* (1929).

Closen, Baron Ludwig von. *The Revolutionary Journal of Baron Ludwig von Closen, 1780–1783* (Evelyn M. Acomb, tr. and ed., 1958).

Cobb, Jelani. *To the Break of Dawn: A Freestyle on the Hip Hop Aesthetic* (2007).

Connell, Evan S. *Son of the Morning Star* (1984).

Cooper, James Fenimore. *The Spy: A Tale of the Neutral Ground* (1821; reissued, with introduction by Curtis Dahl, 1946).

Danckaerts, Jasper. "Journal of Jasper Danchaerts, 1679–1680," in *Original Narratives of Early American History*, Bartlett Burleigh James and J. Franklin Jameson, eds. (1913).

Davenport, Beatrix Cary (ed.). *A Diary of the French Revolution, by Gouverneur Morris 1752–1816* (1939).

Dawson, Henry B. *Westchester-County, New York, during the American Revolution* (1886).

DeRienzo, Harold. *Concepts of Community: Lessons from the Bronx* (2008).

———. *Building Homes, Building Communities: The Ongoing Story of Banana Kelly and Community Development in the South Bronx* (2020).

Drake, Joseph Rodman. *The Culprit Fay, and Other Poems* (1835).

Dwight, Rev. Timothy. *Travels in New-England and New-York* (3 vols., 1821–1822).

Evelyn, Capt. W. Glanville. *Memoir and Letters of Captain W. Glanville Evelyn of the 4th Regiment ("King's Own") from North America, 1774–1776* (G. D. Scull, ed., 1879).

Ewoodzie, Joseph C., Jr. *Break Beats in the Bronx: Rediscovering Hip-Hop's Early Years* (2017).

Farrand, Max (ed.). *The Records of the Federal Convention of 1787* (4 vols., 1911).

Fischer, David Hackett. *Washington's Crossing* (2004).

Fitzpatrick, Frank. *And the Walls Came Tumbling Down: Kentucky, Texas Western, and the Game That Changed American Sports* (1999).

Flood, Joe. *The Fires: How a Computer Formula, Big Ideas, and the Best of Intentions Burned Down New York City—and Determined the Future of Cities* (2010).

Frazier, Patrick. *The Mohicans of Stockbridge* (1992).

Furia, Philip. *Irving Berlin: A Life in Song* (1998).

Garcia, Angel. *The Kingdom Began in Puerto Rico: Neil Connelly's Priesthood in the South Bronx* (2021).

Gonzalez, Evelyn Diaz. *The Bronx* (2004).

Gornick, Vivian. *Fierce Attachments* (1987).

Grandmaster Flash (Joseph Saddler), and David Ritz. *The Adventures of Grandmaster Flash: My Life, My Beats* (2008).

Grant, Madison. *The Passing of the Great Race; or, The Racial Basis of European History* (1916).

Hamilton, Nigel. *JFK: Reckless Youth* (1992).

Haskins, Don, with Dan Wetzel. *Glory Road: My Story of the 1966 NCAA Basketball Championship and How One Team Triumphed Against the Odds and Changed America Forever* (2006).

Heath, Major-General William. "Memoirs . . . containing Anecdotes, Details of Skirmishes, Battles, and other Military Events during the American War, written by himself" (1798).

Hewes, George R. T. *Traits of the Tea Party* (1835).

Horne, Field. "The Conference House Revisited: A History of the Billopp Manor House" (pamphlet, 1990).

Hufeland, Otto. *Westchester County During the American Revolution, 1775–1783* (1926).

Jackson, Kenneth T. (ed.). *The Encyclopedia of New York City* (1991).

Jenkins, Stephen. *The Story of the Bronx: From the Purchase Made by the Dutch from the Indians to the Present Day* (1912).

Johnson, Marilynn S. *Street Justice: A History of Police Violence in New York City* (2003).

Jonnes, Jill. *South Bronx Rising: The Rise, Fall, and Resurrection of an American City* (2002).

Kazimiroff, Theodore L. *The Last Algonquin* (1982).

Kelly, Frank Bergen. *Historical Guide to the City of New York* (1909, 1913).

Kozol, Jonathan. *Amazing Grace: The Lives of Children and the Conscience of a Nation* (1995).

———. *Ordinary Resurrections: Children in the Years of Hope* (2000).

———. *Fire in the Ashes: Twenty-Five Years Among the Poorest Children in America* (2012).

Kühl, Stephan. *The Nazi Connection: Eugenics, American Racism, and German National Socialism* (1994).

Lamberg, Carol. *Neighborhood Success Stories: Creating and Sustaining Affordable Housing in New York* (2018).

LaPlante, Eve. *American Jezebel: The Uncommon Life of Anne Hutchinson, the Woman Who Defied the Puritans* (2004).

Lauzun, Duc de. *Memoirs of the Duc de Lauzun* (C. K. Scott Moncrieff, tr., 1928).

Leslie, Anita. *The Remarkable Mr. Jerome* (1954).

Lewis, David Levering. *W. E. B. Du Bois: A Biography* (2009).

Lopez, Jennifer. *True Love* (2014).

Mahler, Jonathan. *Ladies and Gentlemen, the Bronx Is Burning* (2005).

McLaughlin, Carolyn. *South Bronx Battles: Stories of Resistance, Resilience, and Renewal* (2019).

McNamara, John. *History in Asphalt: The Origin of Bronx Street and Place Names* (1978).

Miller, Melanie Randolph. *Envoy to the Terror: Gouverneur Morris and the French Revolution* (2005).

———(ed). *The Diaries of Gouverneur Morris: European Travels 1794–1798* (2011).

Mintz, Max M. *Gouverneur Morris and the American Revolution* (1970).

Morris, Anne Cary (ed.). *The Diary and Letters of Gouverneur Morris* (2 vols., 1888); referred to in the notes as *Diary*.

Naison, Mark, and Bob Gumbs. *Before the Fires: An Oral History of African-American Life in the Bronx from the 1930s to the 1960s* (2016).

Oneroad, Amos E., and Alanson B. Skinner. *Being Dakota* (Laura L. Anderson, ed., 2003).

Regional Plan Committee. *Regional Plan of New York of New York and its Environs* (2 vols., 1929 and 1931).

Rice, Howard K., Jr. (tr. and ed.), and Anne S. K. Brown. *The American Campaigns of Rochambeau's Army* (2 vols., 1972).

Risse, Louis A. *The True History of the Conception and Planning of the Grand Boulevard and Concourse in the Bronx* (c. 1902)

Rochambeau, Count de. *Memoirs of the Marshal Count de Rochambeau, relative to the War of Independence of the United States* (M. W. E. Wright, tr.and ed., 1838).

Roosevelt, Theodore. *Gouverneur Morris* (1975 reprint of 1888 ed.).

Rothstein, Richard. *The Color of Law: A Forgotten History of How Our Government Segregated America* (2017).

Sanderson, Eric W. *Mannahatta: A Natural History of New York City* (2009).

Simcoe, Lieut.-Col. John Graves. *A Journal of the Operations of the Queen's Rangers, from the End of the Year 1777, to the Conclusion of the Late American War* (1787).

Simpson, Michael. *Thomas Adams and the Modern Planning Movement: Britain, Canada, and the United States, 1900–1940* (1985).

Sites, Paul. *Lee Harvey Oswald and the American Dream* (1967).

Smith, Dennis. *Report from Engine Co. 82* (1972).

Smith, Glenn D., Jr. *Something on My Own: Gertrude Berg and American Broadcasting, 1929–1956* (2015).

Sotomayor, Sonia. *My Beloved World* (2013).

Spann, Edward K. "The Greatest Grid: The New York Plan of 1811," in *Two Centuries of American Planning* (Daniel K. Shaeffer, ed., 1988).

Sparks, Jared. *The Life of Gouverneur Morris* (2 vols., 1832).

Spiro, Jonathan Peter. *Defending the Master Race: Conservation, Eugenics, and the Legacy of Madison Grant* (2009).

Stark, Peter. *Young Washington: How Wilderness and War Forged America's Founding Father* (2018).

Stoddard, T. Lothrop. *The French Revolution in San Domingo* (1914).

————. *The Rising Tide of Color Against White World-Supremacy* (1920).

————. *Re-Forging America: The Story of Our Nationhood* (1927).

Swanson, Susan Cochran. *Between the Lines: Stories of Westchester County, New York, During the American Revolution* (1975).

Swigget, Howard. *The Extraordinary Mr. Morris* (1952).

Taylor, D. Crane. *John L. Stoddard: Traveller, Lecturer, Litterateur* (1935).

Thacher, Dr. James. *The American Revolution from the Commencement to the Disbanding of the American Army; Given in the Form of a Daily Journal* (1860).

Trotsky, Leon. *My Life: An Attempt at an Autobiography* (1970 reprint of 1930 ed.).

Ultan, Lloyd. *The Beautiful Bronx, 1920–1950* (1979)

————, and Gary Hermalyn. *The Bronx: It Was Only Yesterday 1935–1965* (1992).

————. *The Northern Borough: A History of the Bronx* (2005).

Wallace, Deborah, and Rodrick Wallace. *A Plague on Your Houses: How New York Was Burned Down and National Public Health Crumbled* (1998).

Wallace, Mike. *Greater Gotham: A History of New York City from 1898 to 1919* (2017).

Yaro, Robert D., and Tony Hiss. *A Region at Risk: The Third Regional Plan for the New York–New Jersey–Connecticut Metropolitan Area* (1996).

Articles in Journals and Magazines

Brookhiser, Richard. "The Forgotten Founding Father." *City Journal*, Manhattan Institute for Policy Research (Spring 2002).

Coates, Robert M. "King of the Bronx: J. Clarence Davies." *The New Yorker*, Dec. 7, 1939, p. 33.

Frazier, Ian. "Utopia, the Bronx." *The New Yorker*, June 26, 2006, p. 54.

————. "Out of the Bronx." *The New Yorker*, Feb. 6, 2012, p. 52.

————. "What Ever Happened to the Russian Revolution?" *Smithsonian*, Oct. 2017, p. 48.

————. "Old Hatreds." *The New Yorker*, Aug. 26, 2019, p. 36.

Hellman, Geoffrey T., and Harold Ross and Max Elser. "Bronck's Descendants." *The New Yorker*, May 6, 1939, p. 15.

Kaeser, Edward. "The Morris Estate Club Site." *New York State Archaeological Society Bulletin* 27: 38–45 (1963).

————. "Archery Range Ossuary, Pelham Bay Park, Bronx County, New York." *Pennsylvania Archaeologist* 40: 9–34 (1970).

Mann, Albon P., Jr. "The Church and the New York Draft Riots of 1863." *Records of the American Catholic Historical Society of Philadelphia* 62, no. 1 (March 1951).

Niarchos, Nicolas. "La Morada, a Crucible of Resistance." *The New Yorker*, Oct. 2, 2017, p. 15.

Quindlen, Anna. "The Politics of Charlotte Street." *The New York Times Sunday Magazine*, Oct. 7, 1979, p. 27.

Rosen, Ira. "The Glory That Was Charlotte Street." *The New York Times Sunday Magazine*, Oct. 7, 1979, p. 11.

Sharkey, Patrick. "Community and Crime Decline: The Causal Effect of Local Nonprofits on Violent Crime." *American Sociological Review*, Oct. 25, 2017.

Skinner, Alanson B. "Explorations of Aboriginal Sites at Throgs Neck and Clasons Point, New York City." *Contributions from the Museum of American Indian Heye Foundation* 5, no. 4.

Starr, Roger. "Making New York City Smaller." *The New York Times Sunday Magazine*, Nov. 4, 1976.

Treanor, William M. "The Case of the Dishonest Scrivener: Gouverneur Morris and the Creation of the Federalist Constitution." Georgetown University Law Center, 2019.

Wallace, Kevin. "Slim-Shin's Monument." *The New Yorker*, Nov. 19, 1960, p. 104.

Worth, Robert. "Guess Who Saved the South Bronx? Big Government." *Washington Monthly*, April 1999.

Newspapers

The *Baltimore Afro-American*
The Chicago Defender
Gothamist
The New York Age
New York *Daily News*
The *New York Herald Tribune*
The New York Times
The Philadelphia Tribune
The *Pittsburgh Courier*

Archives

The Bronx African-American History Project, Fordham University (searchable online). References in my notes are listed by the abbreviation BAAHP, and name of interview subject.

The McDonald Papers, available at the Westchester County Historical Society Library, in Elmsford, New York. References in my notes are listed by the abbreviation TMP, and name of interview subject. Note that the name of the compiler of these papers was actually John M. Macdonald (see *The McDonald Papers, Part II,* ed. William S. Hardaway (1926), p. 79.) To avoid confusion I have used the spelling "McDonald" throughout, as other sources do.

Films and Documentaries

Decade of Fire, directed by Vivian Vázquez and Gretchen Hildebran, produced by Vivian Vázquez, Gretchen Hildebran, Julia Steele Allen, and Neyda Martinez (2018).

The Fire Next Door, directed by Tom Spain, produced by CBS News (first aired on *CBS Reports*, March 1977).

Flyin' Cut Sleeves, directed and produced by Henry Chalfant and Rita Fecher (Sleeping Dog Films, 1993).

Wild Style, directed and produced by Charlie Ahearn (1983).

ACKNOWLEDGMENTS

In the Bronx: Many thanks to Lloyd Ultan, Mark Naison, José Vasquez, Edwin Velasquez, Inspector Keiyon Ramsey, the Saavedra-Méndez family (Antonio, Natalia, Marco, and Yajaira), Matthew López-Jensen, Shakeema Blount, Father George R. Stewart, Gregory Jost, Duane Johnson, and Vivian Vázquez Irizarry. For my description of the making of Ms. Vázquez Irizarry's documentary, *Decade of Fire*, I am grateful for the time she spent with me, and for the generous help of her co-producers, Gretchen Hildebran and Julia Steele Allen.

Fernando Ferrer, past Bronx borough president, hero of the rebuilding, instructed me in the events and chronology of that important era. My interview with him greatly enlightened me, and I thank him.

David Osborn, site manager at St. Paul's Church National Historic Site, Mount Vernon, New York, took time to fill me in on Revolutionary War history in the area. Thanks, also, to Eliot Hurwitz for sharing his father's unpublished memoir about the early days at Häagen-Dazs.

Harold DeRienzo helped enormously with information about housing policy and the reconstruction of the Bronx—thank you, Mr. DeRienzo. Jim Mitchell, Roger Hayes, Bill Frey, and Felice Michetti, all longtime experts in housing, also took time to explain this complicated subject. Many thanks to each of them, and to my friend Elizabeth

Zeldin, whom I've known since she was in elementary school, and who generously shared her grown-up experience in creating affordable housing.

For biographical details about Scott Sterling (DJ Scott LaRock), I am grateful to Carrie Savage, Director of Development and Alumni Affairs at Castleton University; also to Lee Smith, Matt Kilcullen, Stan Van Gundy, Kim Abbott Van Gundy, Brian DeLoatch, and Olivia Duane Adams, all of whom expressed affection and admiration for this man. I got a lot from their knowledge and insights. Special thanks to Lee Smith for his kind and careful help, in affectionate memory of Mr. Sterling, and for Mr. Smith's expertise on the genesis of Boogie Down Productions and the group's mega hits, "South Bronx" and "The Bridge Is Over."

Tom Spain and Bill Moyers told me about the making of the *CBS Reports* documentary *Decade of Fire*. Warm regards and many thanks to them both.

Big thanks to friends who joined in my Bronx explorations on foot: Alex Melamid, Bill McClelland, Tim McClelland, Roger Cohn, and Edwin Velasquez (again). Janet Malcolm, who loved to explore, came with me on one Bronx trip by car—I wish there could have been more.

The Guggenheim Foundation gave me a grant that made a huge difference. Thanks to Edward Hirsch, Andre Bernard, and Stacy Schiff; also to Strauss Zelnick and Wendy Belzberg, whose generous support made the grant possible.

Many thanks also to Rebecca Federman, of the Forty-second Street branch of the New York Public Library, who can solve the most complicated research problems. The NYPL remains one of the greatest institutions and treasures of New York City and I couldn't live without it.

I first published my work in *The New Yorker* more than fifty years ago, and I still publish there, thanks to the kindness of the editors David Remnick, Susan Morrison, and Ann Goldstein (lately retired). I also remember editors of the past: Martin Baron, Pat Crow, Veronica Geng, and the great William Shawn. No one helped me more or gave me more encouragement than William Whitworth, first at *The New Yorker* and later at *The Atlantic*. Bill, I can never thank you enough.

Love and thanks also to Jonathan Galassi, who has edited my books at Farrar, Straus and Giroux for thirty-five years; to Pat Strachan, my first editor there; to my agents, Andrew Wylie and Jin Auh; and to my dear friend forever, Jamaica Kincaid, and her son, Harold Shawn.

Affectionate gratitude also to the Reverend Elizabeth Maxwell, Katya Arnold, Garrison Keillor, Lee Clark, and Boris Zeldin; hugs to John McPhee; and many, many kisses to Mark Singer.

Finally, thanks to my family: to my daughter, Cora; my son, Thomas (who has saved me from every computer problem); and to my beloved wife, Jacqueline Carey, who also writes under the name Jay Carey.

INDEX

Page numbers in *italics* refer to maps.

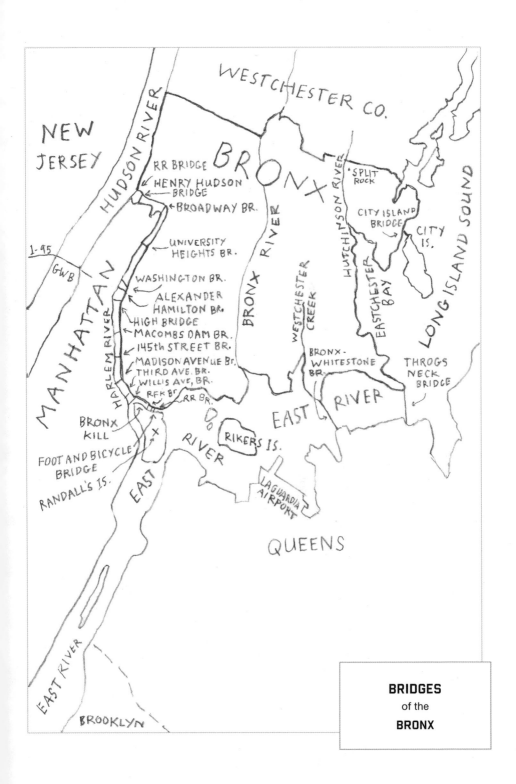

NEW JERSEY

WESTCHESTER CO.

HUDSON RIVER

BRONX

RR BRIDGE
HENRY HUDSON BRIDGE
BROADWAY BR.

UNIVERSITY HEIGHTS BR.

WASHINGTON BR.
ALEXANDER HAMILTON BR.
HIGH BRIDGE
MACOMBS DAM BR.
145th STREET BR.
MADISON AVENUE Br.
THIRD AVE. BR.
WILLIS AVE. BR.
RFK Br.
RR BR.

BRONX KILL

FOOT AND BICYCLE BRIDGE

RANDALL'S IS.

MANHATTAN

HARLEM RIVER

I-95

GWB

BRONX RIVER

WESTCHESTER CREEK

HUTCHINSON RIVER

SPLIT ROCK

CITY ISLAND BRIDGE

CITY IS.

EASTCHESTER BAY

LONG ISLAND SOUND

BRONX-WHITESTONE BR.

THROGS NECK BRIDGE

EAST RIVER

RIKERS IS.

EAST RIVER

LAGUARDIA AIRPORT

QUEENS

EAST RIVER

BROOKLYN

BRIDGES
of the
BRONX